THE GREEK WORLD AFTER ALEXANDER

In this comprehensive and well-documented book, Graham Shipley integrates the diverse aspects of politics, society and culture to create a coherent and thorough survey of the Hellenistic world.

The Greek World after Alexander examines social changes in the cities of the Greek world and in the kingdoms which succeeded Alexander's empire. The investigation is set in the context of an up-to-date appraisal of the momentous military and political changes that took place after Alexander's reign. Graham Shipley's ground-breaking study also considers developments in literature, religion, philosophy, and science, establishing whether they departed radically from Classical Greek culture or developed continuously from it. In addition, he explores the divisions in Hellenistic culture separating an educated élite from the general population which was more mobile than before but perhaps less involved in city politics.

The Greek World after Alexander offers an indispensable introduction to the Hellenistic world, and provides the reader with extensive translated source material and references for further study. It will be invaluable to students, teachers, and researchers alike.

Graham Shipley is Reader in Ancient History at the School of Archaeological Studies at the University of Leicester, and a Fellow of the Society of Antiquaries. He is the author of *A History of Samos 800–188 BC* (1987) and the co-editor of several volumes of papers on Greek and Roman history. A long-standing member of the British School at Athens, he was editor of the School's *Annual* for five years and is a co-author of the *Laconia Survey*.

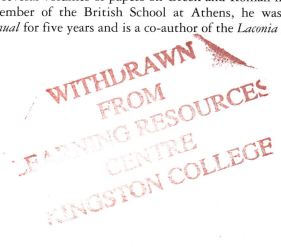

ROUTLEDGE HISTORY OF THE ANCIENT WORLD

General Editor: Fergus Millar

THE ANCIENT NEAR EAST *c.* 3000–330 BC
Amélie Kuhrt

THE GREEK WORLD 479–323 BC
Simon Hornblower

THE BEGINNINGS OF ROME *c.* 1000–264 BC
T. J. Cornell

THE MEDITERRANEAN WORLD IN LATE ANTIQUITY
AD 395–600
Averil Cameron

GREECE IN THE MAKING 1200–479 BC
Robin Osborne

THE ROMAN WORLD
44 BC–AD 180
Martin Goodman

THE GREEK WORLD
AFTER ALEXANDER

323 – 30 BC

Graham Shipley

London and New York

First published 2000
by Routledge
11 New Fetter Lane, London EC4P 4EE

Simultaneously published in the USA and Canada
by Routledge
29 West 35th Street, New York, NY 10001

Routledge is an imprint of the Taylor & Francis Group

Typeset in Garamond by Taylor & Francis Books Ltd
Printed and bound in Great Britain by Biddles Ltd, Guildford and King's Lynn

British Library Cataloguing in Publication Data
A catalogue record for this book is available from the British Library

Library of Congress Cataloging in Publication Data
A catalog record for this book has been requested

ISBN 0–415–04617–3 (hbk)
ISBN 0–415–04618–1 (pbk)

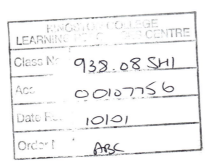

To my students and colleagues
at Leicester, past and present

CONTENTS

List of figures   x
Preface   xiii
Acknowledgements   xv
Note on Greek names and dates   xvii
Note on extracts   xvii
List of abbreviations   xviii
List of dates   xxv

1 **Approaches and sources**   1
   The period and its problems 1
   The literary sources 5
   Non-literary sources 20
   Conclusion 31

2 **Alexander and his successors to 276 BC**   33
   The fourth century and after 33
   The Successors 40
   The Gauls 52
   Armies and emigration 54

3 **Kings and cities**   59
   Representations of kingship 60
   The negotiation of power 73
   Civic society and socio-economic change 86
   Beyond the polis? 106

4 **Macedonia and Greece**   108
   Macedonia to 276 BC 109

Greece under Macedonian domination 120
The Spartan 'revolutions' and their aftermath 140
Athens and Macedonia after 239 BC 148
The limits of Macedonian power 152

5 **Religion and philosophy**   153
Religious change 153
Rival philosophies and common ground 176
World-views and society 190

6 **Ptolemaic Egypt**   192
Land and people 192
Evidence 196
The Ptolemaic dynasty 201
Greeks and Macedonians in Egypt 213
Economic administration 224
The results of Ptolemaic rule 230

7 **Literature and social identity**   235
Writers in society 235
Sites of production 237
Tradition and innovation 243
Different audiences? 247
The public and the personal 253
The 'Other' 259
Historiography and the community 262
Conclusion 269

8 **The Seleukid kingdom and Pergamon**   271
Land and resources 272
Crises and continuities in Seleukid power, 312–164 BC 286
Methods of control 293
The Attalid dynasty (283–133 BC) 312
Seleukid decline 320

9 **Understanding the cosmos: Greek 'science' after Aristotle**   326
Greek thinkers in their society 326
Engineering, mechanics, and physics 330
Understanding life-forms 341
Mathematical speculation 350

Exploration, empires, and economies 359
Conclusion 363

10 Rome and Greece   **368**
Rome in the third century 370
Rome's wars against Macedonia and Syria 371
Mithradates 386
The culmination of Roman hegemony 397

Appendix I: Dynastic chronologies   400
Appendix II: Genealogical tables   404
Further reading   407
Notes   422
Bibliography   475
Index of sources   537
General index   547

FIGURES

1.1	Decree of Athenian military corps for Demetrios Poliorketes	22
1.2	Samian decree for Metrodoros of Sidon	23
1.3	Dedication to Ptolemy IV from Itanos	24
1.4	Manumission document from Sousa in Media	24
1.5	Gold stater in the name of Alexander	25
1.6	Silver tetradrachm in the name of Alexander	25
1.7	Silver didrachm of Samos	25
1.8	Silver hemidrachm of Samos	25
1.9	Silver hemidrachm of Aitolian League	26
1.10	Bronze coin of Antiochos IV	26
2.1	Significant dates in the age of Alexander, 338–322 BC	37
2.2	Significant dates in the age of Antigonos, 323–301 BC	41
2.3	Family tree of Antipater	42
2.4	Significant dates in the age of Demetrios, 301–276 BC	45
2.5	Family tree of Lysimachos	48
2.6	Silver tetradrachm of Lysimachos	49
3.1	Silver tetradrachm in the name of Alexander, issued under Ptolemy I	64
3.2	Portrait of Demetrios Poliorketes from the Villa of the Papyri, Herculaneum	66
3.3	Portrait of Alexander from the Athenian Acropolis	70
3.4	Gold octadrachm of Ptolemy II and Arsinoë II	72
3.5	The Athenian Agora	88
3.6	Plan of Priene	90
3.7	A street in Priene	91
3.8	Plan of Kassope	93
3.9	Plan of Gorítsa	94
3.10	Plan of Demetrias	94

3.11	Plan of New Halos	95
3.12	Plan of Pergamon	97
3.13	The altar of Zeus (or Telephos) at Pergamon	99
4.1	Map of northern Greece	110
4.2	Map of the Aegean	117
4.3	Silver tetradrachm of Antigonos Gonatas	125
4.4	Map of central and southern Greece	135
5.1	Military order of Peukestas, on papyrus	167
5.2	Statue-base of Lysimachos from the Amphiareion	172
5.3	Monument of Agrippa on the Athenian Acropolis	173
5.4	Leading members of philosophical 'schools'	178–9
6.1	Map of Egypt	193
6.2	A Greek papyrus	198
6.3	Ostrakon of Hor	200
6.4	Dates of the 'Syrian' wars	202
6.5	Portrait coin of Ptolemy III Euergetes	203
6.6	Dates of the principal revolts in Ptolemaic Egypt	204
6.7	Plan of Alexandria	216
8.1	Map of the Seleukid empire	273
8.2	Map of western Asia Minor	274
8.3	Map of eastern Asia Minor and Syria	276
8.4	Map of the central and eastern Seleukid empire	280
8.5	Plan of Ai Khanum	306
8.6	The 'Dying Celtic trumpeter' from Pergamon	313
8.7	Silver cistophoric tetradrachm of Eumenes II	316
8.8	The Stoa of Attalos, Athens	318
9.1	The Tower of the Winds and Roman Agora, Athens	334
9.2	Rear wall of the Stoa of Eumenes, Athens	335
9.3	Ktesibios's bronze-spring catapult	337
9.4	The fortifications of Eleutherai, Attica	338
9.5	The south-east tower at Aigosthena, Megarid	339
9.6	Euclid's proof by the method of exhaustion	358
9.7	The Antikythera Mechanism	360
10.1	New Style silver tetradrachm of Athens	383
10.2	Map of the Black Sea	388

Appendix 1: Dynastic chronologies

1	Rulers of Macedonia	400
2	The Ptolemaic dynasty	401
3	The Seleukid dynasty	401–2
4	The Attalids	402
5	Rulers of Baktria	403

Appendix 2: Genealogical tables

1	The Antigonids	404
2	The early Ptolemies	405
3	The early Seleukids	406

PREFACE

This survey of hellenistic society and culture took its initial inspiration from earlier works by Claire Préaux and Frank Walbank, to whom I must acknowledge a substantial debt. Since the time when the book was planned in the early 1990s, however, there has been an upsurge of accessible writings, particularly in English, many of which are highlighted in the Further Reading section; these have made the task of assimilating a wide range of sources and historical events far simpler than it might have been.

Given its limited size, the work cannot pretend to complete coverage, particularly in areas where the author is not an expert. For particular topics and regions it will be obvious that I have relied heavily on earlier investigators; this is particularly the case with Egypt and the Seleukid empire, for I have no knowledge of the non-Greek languages. The book is designed to interlink two aspects often left disconnected in earlier studies: on the one hand, the political, economic, and administrative changes that took place after Alexander the Great, which are explored through examinations of distinct geographical areas (Macedonia, Greece, Seleukid Asia, and Egypt); on the other hand, the cultural and intellectual output of the period (religion, philosophy, and particularly literature and science). The latter, I believe, cannot be understood without the former. I am not the first to have suggested that the element of continuity from classical times may be at least as significant as the element of change. I would also submit that many of the new formations are evidence, not of changes in popular mentality, but of innovations in discourses conducted at an élite level of society; they were not without influence at the grass roots, but the degree of continuity in popular culture was surely far greater.

For making it possible for me to write the book I am grateful, first and foremost, to the University of Leicester for granting me study leave in 1993 and 1998 and additional research leave in 1999. The head of the School of Archaeological Studies, Graeme Barker, and my colleagues in the Ancient History and Archaeology Divisions deserve my appreciation for undertaking extra duties during my absences. I must also thank the Director of the

British School at Athens, David Blackman, and his staff, particularly in the Library, for providing congenial surroundings in which to concentrate on research during 1998 and 1999. I am grateful to the Warden and Fellows of Wadham College, Oxford, for research facilities and accommodation during summer 1998. Final revision was carried out during the tenure of the Visiting Fellowship at the BSA and an award from the Research Leave Scheme of the UK Arts and Humanities Research Board.

Richard Stoneman and his colleagues at Routledge, particularly Coco Stevenson, have been sources of wisdom and practical advice whose value cannot be overstated. For practical help in selecting and obtaining illustrations I must thank Revel Coles, Charles Crowther, Heinrich Hall, Chris Howgego, Andy Meadows, and Marcella Pisani. The School of Archaeological Studies of the University of Leicester assisted with the cost of photographs. Others have been thanked privately or in the Acknowledgements; my apologies to anyone I have inadvertently omitted. The volume has benefited greatly from the intelligent copy-editing of Susan Dunsmore and the proof-reading of Laetitia Grant.

The teaching and supervision I received from Peter Derow and from the late George Forrest remain a source of inspiration in more ways than I can spell out. Colleagues and pupils who helped in more recent years by discussing the specific details or overall shape of the work, by making their own works available, or by reading particular sections include Jamie Bell, Dorothy Buchan, Lin Foxhall, Mogens Herman Hansen, Ioanna Kralli, Brian McGing, Céline Marquaille, Henrik Mouritsen, Graham Oliver, Katerina Panagopoulou, Martyn Richards, Athanasios Rizakis, Sarah Scott, Tyler Jo Smith, and Mark Steinhardt. Others are thanked in the Notes. My father, Donald Shipley, read several versions of the text and made many valuable suggestions and criticisms. I am especially grateful to Dorothy Thompson for helping me improve and revise Chapter 6, to John Davies for reading the entire draft text and making many perceptive and informative suggestions, and most of all to Fergus Millar for his invitation to write this book and for showing, by turns, patience, generosity, and critical acumen as a series editor.

The unstinting support and encouragement of my parents and of many friends, though they can scarcely be repaid, have, I hope, been suitably acknowledged in other ways. The volume is dedicated to my colleagues and pupils at Leicester, particularly those students who attended my course in hellenistic history in its early years and helped to shape this book.

D.G.J.S.
Leicester, August 1999

ACKNOWLEDGEMENTS

Thanks are due to Michel Austin and to Cambridge University Press for permission to reproduce numerous extracts from M. M. Austin, *The Hellenistic World*, and to Cambridge University Press for permission to reproduce an extract from S. M. Burstein, *The Hellenistic Age* (on p. 285).

Quotations from the following translations in the Loeb Classical Library, published by Harvard University Press and © The President and Fellows of Harvard College, are reproduced by permission of the publisher (in some cases with omissions and slight modifications by the present author):

> Athenaeus, *The Deipnosophists*, vol. ii, trans. C. B. Gulick (1928); Diodorus of Sicily, vol. i, trans. C. H. Oldfather (1933); vol. viii, trans. C. B. Welles (1963); vols ix–x, trans. R. M. Geer (1947, 1954); vol. xi, trans. F. R. Walton (1957); *Greek Mathematical Works (Selections Illustrating the History of Greek Mathematics)*, vols i–ii, trans. I. Thomas (1939–41); Livy, vol. x, trans. E. T. Sage (1935); Polybius, *The Histories*, vols iv–v, trans. W. R. Paton (1925, 1926); Ptolemy, *Tetrabiblos*, ed. and trans. F. E. Robbins (1940); Seneca, *Tragedies*, vol. i, trans. F. J. Miller (1917); *The Geography of Strabo*, vol. viii, trans. H. L. Jones (1932); *Theophrastus: Characters, Herodas: Mimes, Cercidas and the Choliambic Poets*, ed. and trans. J. Rusten, I. C. Cunningham, and A. D. Knox (1993); Theophrastus, *Enquiry into Plants and Minor Works on Odours and Weather Signs*, vols i–ii, trans. A. Hort (1916); Theophrastus, *De Causis Plantarum*, vol. ii, ed. and trans. B. Einarson and G. K. K. Link (1990); Xenophon, *Memorabilia and Oeconomicus*, trans. E. C. Marchant (1923).

The diagram of the Antikythera Mechanism (Fig. 9.7) is reproduced from D. J. de S. Price, *Gears from the Greeks*, 37, fig. 29 (artist B. Pope), by permission of the American Philosophical Society. The diagram of Ktesibios's catapult (Fig. 9.3) is taken from Marsden, E.W., *Greek and Roman Artillery: Technical Treatises* (1971), 174, diagram 8, by permission of Oxford University Press.

Other short extracts are based on or quoted from the following sources, sometimes with slight modifications (page numbers refer to this volume): R. J. A. Talbert, *Plutarch on Sparta* (145), I. Scott-Kilvert, *Polybios*, (145, 204–5, 373), R. Wells, *Theocritus: The Idylls* (202, 238, 239, 256–7), and R. Stoneman, *The Greek Alexander Romance* (251), all published by Penguin Books; M. R. Lefkowitz and M. B. Fant, *Women's Life in Greece and Rome* (103, 104), A. A. Long, *Hellenistic Philosophy* (180), and A. Kuhrt and S. Sherwin-White (eds), *Hellenism in the East* (295), all published by Duckworth; N. Lewis, *Greeks in Ptolemaic Egypt* (218, 223), and E. W. Marsden, *Greek and Roman Artillery: Technical Treatises* (336), both published by Oxford University Press; P. E. Easterling and B. M. W. Knox (eds), *Cambridge History of Classical Literature* (244–5, 253, and 256 by A. W. Bulloch, 258 by E. Handley), and *The New English Bible* (266–7, 311), both published by Cambridge University Press; S. M. Burstein, *The Babyloniaca of Berossus*, Undena (11); M. Lichtheim, *Ancient Egyptian Literature*, iii, University of California Press (223); G. E. R. Lloyd, *Greek Science after Aristotle*, Chatto & Windus (364); M. H. Morgan, *Vitruvius: The Ten Books on Architecture*, Harvard University Press and Dover Books (358); J. D. Ray, *The Archive of Ḥor*, Egypt Exploration Society (209); K. J. Rigsby, *Asylia*, University of California Press (81, part); E. S. Shuckburgh, *The Histories of Polybius*, Macmillan (67, 149); F. W. Walbank, *The Hellenistic World*, HarperCollins (37, 363); and C. B. Welles, *Royal Correspondence in the Hellenistic Period*, Yale University Press and Ares (158).

Every effort has been made to credit or contact copyright holders and we apologise for any inadvertent omissions. If any acknowledgement is missing it would be appreciated if contact could be made, care of the publishers, so that this can be rectified in any future edition.

For permission to reproduce photographs, I am grateful to the following: Ashmolean Museum, University of Oxford: Figs 1.5–1.10, 2.6, 3.1, 4.3, 8.7, and 10.1; British Museum, London: Figs 3.4, 6.5; Deutsches Archäologisches Institut, Athens: Fig. 3.3 (DAI Athen, negative no. Akr. 2368); Deutsches Archäologisches Institut, Rome: Figs 3.2 (DAI Rome, negative no. 83.1776, photograph by Schwanke), 8.6 (DAI Rome, negative no. 70.2117, photograph by Singer); Egypt Exploration Society: Figs 5.1 (re-photographed from *Journal of Egyptian Archaeology*, 60 (1974), 239–42, pl. opp. p. 240), 6.2 (*P. Oxy.* 3777), and 6.3 (re-photographed from J. D. Ray, *Archive of Ḥor*, pl. 3); Staatliche Museen zu Berlin, Antikensammlung: Fig. 3.13 (BPK Inv.-Nr. OM 6921, © Bildarchiv Preussische Kulturbesitz 1999). The cover photograph of Agora P 28543 (Rotroff no. 59) (negative no. 99-39-33, photographer Craig A. Mauzy) is reproduced by permission of the American School of Classical Studies at Athens: Agora Excavations.

The digital images of inscriptions in Figs. 1.1–1.4 are reproduced by permission of Dr C. Crowther on behalf of the Centre for the Study of Ancient Documents, University of Oxford. The photographs in Figs 3.7, 5.2, 5.3, 8.8, 9.1, 9.2, 9.4, and 9.5 are by the author.

NOTE ON GREEK
NAMES AND DATES

Everyday forms of Greek names like Athens, Corinth, Rhodes, Aristotle, Philip, Alexander, Menander, and Ptolemy are used, but namesakes of famous individuals may have their names spelled out to distinguish them (e.g. Alexandros, Menandros, Ptolemaios). Other names are generally rendered in Greek-like rather than latinate forms, particularly where there is little difference in pronunciation: thus Achaios, Histiaia, Kleopatra, Kos, Seleukos, and Seleukid rather than Achaeus, Histiaea, Cleopatra, Cos, Seleucus, and Seleucid. Conversely, I retain such anglicizations as Achaea (except for the Roman province of Achaia), Achaean, Antipater (rather than Antipatros), Attica, Cassander (rather than Kassandros), Cappadocia, and Cyrene since these are familiar spoken forms.

Where no era is specified, dates are BC. Contracted dates of the form 318/7 are administrative years, usually Athenian archon-years running from July to June.

NOTE ON EXTRACTS

In quoted extracts, simple points of omission, as here . . . , indicate words omitted by me, whereas [. . .] indicates letters or words missing in the original text. Restorations to fill such gaps are enclosed in square brackets. My comments are normally in italic type, with explanatory information such as regional numbers in round parentheses.

ABBREVIATIONS

Abbreviations of classical authors and their works follow OCD^3, with two exceptions: Varro, *RR*, and Columella, *RR* (*De re rustica* in each case). Full details of the abbreviated modern works can be found in the Bibliography.

AJP	*American Journal of Philology*
Alessandria	*Alessandria e il mondo ellenistico-romano: I centenario del Museo Greco-Romano (Alessandria, 23–27 novembre 1992). Atti del II Congresso Internazionale Italo-Egiziano.* Rome: 'L'Erma' di Bretschneider, 1995
ASAA	*Annuario della Scuola Archeologica di Atene*
Ath. Mitt.	*Mitteilungen des Deutschen Archäologischen Instituts, Athenische Abteilung*
Austin	M. M. Austin, *The Hellenistic World from Alexander to the Roman Conquest: A Selection of Ancient Sources in Translation.* Cambridge: CUP, 1981 (numbers refer to documents)
BAR	British Archaeological Reports
BCH	*Bulletin de correspondance hellénique*
BD	R. S. Bagnall and P. Derow, *Greek Historical Documents: The Hellenistic Period.* Chico, CA: Scholars Press, 1981
BGU	*Ägyptische Urkunden aus den königlichen Museen in Berlin: Griechische Urkunden.* Berlin: Weidmann, 1892–1937
BICS	*Bulletin of the Institute of Classical Studies*
Bilde, *Centre and Periphery*	P. Bilde, T. Engberg-Pedersen, L. Hannestad, J. Zahle, and K. Randsborg (eds), *Centre and Periphery in the Hellenistic World.* Aarhus: Aarhus UP, ¹1993, ²1996
Bilde, *Ethnicity*	P. Bilde, T. Engberg-Pedersen, L. Hannestad, and J. Zahle (eds), *Ethnicity in Hellenistic Egypt.* Aarhus: Aarhus UP, 1992
Bilde, *Kingship*	P. Bilde, T. Engberg-Pedersen, L. Hannestad, and J. Zahle (eds), *Aspects of Hellenistic Kingship.* Aarhus: Aarhus UP, 1996

Bilde, *Religion*	P. Bilde, T. Engberg-Pedersen, L. Hannestad, and J. Zahle (eds), *Religion and Religious Practice in the Seleucid Kingdom.* Aarhus: Aarhus UP, 1990
Bilde, *Values*	P. Bilde, T. Engberg-Pedersen, L. Hannestad, and J. Zahle (eds), *Conventional Values of the Hellenistic Greeks.* Aarhus: Aarhus UP, 1997
BMC Ptolemies	R. S. Poole, *A Catalogue of the Greek Coins in the British Museum,* xxiv: *The Ptolemies, Kings of Egypt.* London, Trustees of the British Museum, 1883
Briant, *RTP*	P. Briant, *Rois, tributs et paysans: études sur les formations tributaires du Moyen-Orient ancien.* Paris: Les Belles Lettres, 1
BSA	*Annual of the British School at Athens*
Bull. ép.	*Bulletin épigraphique* (annually in *REG*)
Bulloch, *Images*	A. Bulloch, E. S. Gruen, A. A. Long, and A. Stewart (eds), *Images and Ideologies: Self-definition in the Hellenistic World.* Berkeley, Los Angeles, London: Univ. of California Press, 1993
Burstein	S. M. Burstein, *The Hellenistic Age: From the Battle of Ipsos to the Death of Kleopatra VII.* Cambridge: CUP, 1985
CAH[1] vi	J. B. Bury, S. A. Cook, and F. E. Adcock (eds), *The Cambridge Ancient History*[1], vi: *Macedon 401–301 BC.* Cambridge: CUP, 1927
CAH[1] vii	S. A. Cook, F. E. Adcock, and M. P. Charlesworth (eds), *The Cambridge Ancient History*[1], vii: *The Hellenistic Monarchies and the Rise of Rome.* Cambridge: CUP, 1928
CAH[1] viii	S. A. Cook, F. E. Adcock, and M. P. Charlesworth (eds), *The Cambridge Ancient History*[1], viii: *Rome and the Mediterranean 218–133 BC.* Cambridge: CUP, 1930
CAH[2] iv	J. Boardman, N. G. L. Hammond, D. M. Lewis, and M. Ostwald (eds), *The Cambridge Ancient History*[2], iv: *Persia, Greece and the Western Mediterranean c.525 to 479 BC.* Cambridge: CUP, 1988
CAH[2] vi	D. M. Lewis, J. Boardman, S. Hornblower, and M. Ostwald (eds), *The Cambridge Ancient History*[2], vi: *The Fourth Century BC.* Cambridge: CUP, 1994
CAH[2] vii. 1	F. W. Walbank, A. E. Astin, M. W. Frederiksen, and R. M. Ogilvie (eds), *The Cambridge Ancient History*[2], vii. 1: *The Hellenistic World.* Cambridge: CUP, 1984
CAH[2] vii. 1, Plates	R. Ling (ed.), *The Cambridge Ancient History*[2]: *Plates to Volume vii Part 1. The Hellenistic World to the Coming of the Romans.* Cambridge: CUP, 1984
CAH[2] vii. 2	F. W. Walbank, A. E. Astin, M. W. Frederiksen, R. M. Ogilvie, and A. Drummond (eds), *The Cambridge Ancient History*[2], vii. 2: *The Rise of Rome to 220 BC.* Cambridge: CUP, 1989

*CAH*² viii	A. E. Astin, F. W. Walbank, M. W. Frederiksen, and R. M. Ogilvie (eds), *The Cambridge Ancient History*², viii: *Rome and the Mediterranean to 133 BC*. Cambridge: CUP, 1989
*CAH*² ix	J. A. Crook, A. Lintott, and E. Rawson (eds), *The Cambridge Ancient History*², ix: *The Last Age of the Roman Republic, 146–43 BC*. Cambridge: CUP, 1994
Cartledge, Constructs	P. Cartledge, P. Garnsey, and E. Gruen (eds), *Hellenistic Constructs: Essays in Culture, History and Historiography*. Berkeley, Los Angeles, London: Univ. of California Press, 1997
CHCL	P. E. Easterling and B. M. W. Knox (eds), *The Cambridge History of Classical Literature*, i: *Greek Literature*. Cambridge: CUP, 1985
Choix	F. Dürrbach, *Choix d'inscriptions de Délos*, i. Paris: Leroux, 1921–3
CIG	A. Boeckh *et al.*, *Corpus inscriptionum graecarum*. i–iv. Berlin: Officina Academica/Reimer, 1828–77
cos.	consul
CPC Acts 1	M. H. Hansen (ed.), *The Ancient Greek City-state (Symposium on the Occasion of the 250th Anniversary of the Royal Danish Academy of Sciences and Letters, July 1–4 1992)*. Copenhagen: Munksgaard, 1993
CPC Acts 2	M. H. Hansen (ed.), *Sources for the Ancient Greek City-state (Symposium August, 24–27 1994)*. Copenhagen: Munksgaard, 1995
CPC Acts 3	M. H. Hansen (ed.), *Introduction to an Inventory of Poleis (Symposium August, 23–26 1995)*, Copenhagen: Munksgaard, 1996
CPC Acts 4	M. H. Hansen (ed.), *The Polis as an Urban Centre and as a Political Community (Symposium, August, 29-31 1996)*. Copenhagen: Munksgaard, 1997
CPC Acts 5	M. H. Hansen, *Polis and City-state: An Ancient Concept and its Modern Equivalent*. Copenhagen: Munksgaard, 1998
CPC Papers 1	D. Whitehead (ed.), *From Political Architecture to Stephanus Byzantius: Sources for the Ancient Greek Polis*. Wiesbaden: Steiner, 1994
CPC Papers 2	M. H. Hansen and K. Raaflaub (eds), *Studies in the Ancient Greek Polis*. Wiesbaden: Steiner, 1995
CPC Papers 3	M. H. Hansen and K. Raaflaub (eds), *More Studies in the Ancient Greek Polis*. Wiesbaden: Steiner, 1996
CPC Papers 4	T. H. Nielsen (ed.), *Yet More Studies in the Ancient Greek Polis*. Wiesbaden: Steiner, 1997
CQ	*Classical Quarterly*
CR	*Classical Review*
CRAI	*Académie des Inscriptions et de Belles-Lettres: comptes rendus*
CUP	Cambridge University Press
DAI	Deutsches Archäologisches Institut
fr.	fragment
FGH	F. Jacoby, *Die Fragmente der griechischen Historiker*. Berlin: Weidmann, etc. 1923–58
Fraser	P. M. Fraser, *Ptolemaic Alexandria*, i–iii. Oxford: Clarendon, 1972

GMW i	I. Thomas (trans.), *Greek Mathematical Works*, i: *From Thales to Euclid*. London: Heinemann/Cambridge, MA: Harvard UP, 1939
GMW ii	I. Thomas (trans.), *Greek Mathematical Works*, ii: *From Aristarchus to Pappus*. London: Heinemann/Cambridge, MA: Harvard UP, 1939
Green, *HHC*	P. Green (ed.), *Hellenistic History and Culture*. Berkeley, Los Angeles, Oxford: Univ. of California Press, 1993
Gruen, *HW*	E. S. Gruen, *The Hellenistic World and the Coming of Rome*. Berkeley, Los Angeles, London: Univ. of California Press, 1984
Habicht, *Athens*	C. Habicht, *Athens from Alexander to Antony*. Cambridge, MA and London: Harvard UP, 1997
Harding	P. Harding, *From the End of the Peloponnesian War to the Battle of Ipsus*. Cambridge: CUP, 1985
Head²	B. V. Head, with G. F. Hill, G. Macdonald, and W. Wroth, *Historia Numorum: A Manual of Greek Numismatics*². Oxford: Clarendon, 1911
Hesp.	*Hesperia*
I. Cret.	M. Guarducci (ed.), *Inscriptiones Creticae: opera et consilio Friderici Halbherr collectae*, i–iv. Rome: Libreria dello Stato, 1935–50
I. Délos	*Inscriptions de Délos*. Paris: Académie des Inscriptions et Belles-Lettres, 1926–72
I. Didyma	A. Rehm, *Didyma*, ii: *Die Inschriften*. Berlin: Mann, 1941
IG	*Inscriptiones Graecae*. Berlin: de Gruyter
IGLS	L. Jalabert, P. Mouterde, and J.-P. Rey-Coquais (eds), *Inscriptions grecques et latines de la Syrie*. Paris: Geuthner 1929–
I. Olympia	W. Dittenberger and K. Purgold, *Die Inschriften von Olympia* (Olympia, 5). Berlin: Asher, 1896
I. Priene	F. Hiller von Gaertringen, *Inschriften von Priene*. Berlin: Königliche Museen/Reimer, 1906
ISE	L. Moretti, *Iscrizione storiche ellenistiche*, i–ii. Florence: Nuova Italia, 1967–76
JEA	*Journal of Egyptian Archaeology*
JHS	*Journal of Hellenic Studies*
JRS	*Journal of Roman Studies*
Kock, *CAF*	T. Kock (ed.), *Comicorum Atticorum fragmenta*. Leipzig: Teubner, 1880–8
Kuhrt and Sherwin-White, *Hellenism*	A. Kuhrt and S. M. Sherwin-White (eds), *Hellenism in the East: The Interaction of Greek and Non-Greek Civilizations from Syria to Central Asia after Alexander*. London: Duckworth, 1987

Lefkowitz and Fant	M. R. Lefkowitz and M. B. Fant, *Women's Life in Greece and Rome*. London: Duckworth, 1982
LSJ	H. G. Liddell and R. Scott, *Greek–English Lexicon*[9]. Oxford: Clarendon, 1940
LSJ Suppl.[2]	P. G. W. Glare, with A. A. Thompson, *Greek–English Lexicon: Revised Supplement*. Oxford: Clarendon, 1996
NEB	*The New English Bible with the Apocrypha*. Cambridge: CUP, [2] 1970
OCD[3]	S. Hornblower and A. Spawforth (eds), *The Oxford Classical Dictionary*[3]. Oxford and New York: OUP, 1996
OGIS	W. Dittenberger, *Orientis Graecae inscriptiones selectae*, 2 vols. Leipzig: Hirzel, 1903–5
ÖJh	*Jahreshefte des Österreichischen Archäologischen Instituts in Wien*
OUP	Oxford University Press
P.	papyrus: abbreviations not listed here can be found in E.G. Turner, *Greek Papyri: An Introduction*[2] (Oxford, 1980), or J.F. Oates *et al.*, *Checklist of Editions of Greek and Latin Papyri*[4] (Atlanta, GA, 1992)
PAE	Πρακτικὰ τῆς ἐν Ἀθήναις Ἀρχαιολογικῆς Ἑταιρείας
P. Col. Zen. i, ii	W. L. Westermann and E. S. Hasenoerl (eds), *Zenon Papyri: Business Papyri of the Third Century BC dealing with Palestine and Egypt*, i (equals *P. Col.* iii); ii (equals *P. Col.* iv). New York: Columbia UP, 1934
PCZ	C. C. Edgar (ed.) *Zenon Papyri*, i–iv (Catalogue général des antiquités égyptiennes du Musée du Caïre, 79, 82, 85, 90). Cairo: Institut Français d'Archéologie Orientale, 1925–31.
P. Enteuxeis	O. Guéraud, Ἐντεύξεις: *requêtes et plaintes adressés au roi d'Égypte au III*[e] *siècle avant J.-C.* Cairo: Imprimerie de l'Institut Français d'Archéologie Orientale, 1931–2
P. Hib.	B. P. Grenfell, A. S. Hunt, E. G. Turner, and M.T. Lenger (eds), *The Hibeh Papyri*. London: Egypt Exploration Fund, etc., 1906–56
P. L. Bat. 22	E. Boswinkel and P. W. Pestman (eds), *Les Archives privées de Dionysios, fils de Kephalas: textes grecs et démotiques. Texte* (Papyrologica Lugduno-Batava, 22[A]). Leiden: Brill, 1982
P. Lond.	T. C. Skeat, *Greek Papyri in the British Museum*, vii: *The Zenon Archive*. London: BM Publications for British Library Board, 1974
P. Oxy.	B. P. Grenfell *et al.* (eds) *Oxyrhynchus Papyri*. London: Egypt Exploration Fund, etc., 1898–
P. Rev	B. P. Grenfell and J. P. Mahaffy (1896), *Revenue Laws of Ptolemy Philadelphus*. Oxford: Clarendon

Petracos, *Amphiareion*	B. Petracos [V. Ch. Petrakos], *The Amphiareion of Oropos*. Athens: Clio, 1995
Préaux	C. Préaux, *Le Monde hellénistique: la Grèce et l'Orient de la mort d'Alexandre à la conquête romaine de la Grèce (323–146 av. J.-C.)*, i–ii. Paris: Presses Universitaires de France, 1978
Primo contributo	A. Momigliano, *Contributo alla storia degli studi classici*. Rome: Edizioni di storia e di letteratura, 1955
PSI	*Papiri greci e latini: Pubblicazioni della Società Italiana per la Ricerca dei Papiri Greci e Latini in Egitto*. Florence: Ariani, etc., 1912–
P. Tebt.	B. P. Grenfell *et al.* (eds) , *The Tebtunis Papyri*. London: Egypt Exploration Fund, etc., 1902–76
Quinto contributo	A. Momigliano, *Quinto contributo alla storia degli studi classici e del mondo antico*, i–ii. Rome: Edizioni di storia e di letteratura, 1975
RC	C. B. Welles, *Royal Correspondence in the Hellenistic Period: A Study in Greek Epigraphy*. New Haven, CT: Yale UP/London: Humphrey Milford, OUP/Prague: Kondakov Institute, 1934
RDGE	R. K. Sherk, *Roman Documents from the Greek East: Senatus Consulta and Epistulae to the Age of Augustus*. Baltimore, MD: Johns Hopkins UP, 1969
RE	G. Wissowa *et al.* (eds), *Realencyclopädie der klassischen Altertumswissenschaft*. Stuttgart: Metzler, 1893–1981
REA	*Revue des études anciennes*
REG	*Revue des études grecques*
Rostovtzeff, *SEHHW*	M. Rostovtzeff, *The Social and Economic History of the Hellenistic World*, i–iii. Oxford: Clarendon, 1941
SB	F. Preisigke, F. Bilabel, and E. Kiessling (eds), *Sammelbuch griechischer Urkunden aus Ägypten*. Strasbourg, Berlin, Heidelberg, etc., 1913–
Schürer² i	E. Schürer, *The History of the Jewish People in the Age of Jesus Christ (175 BC–AD 135)*, i. Edinburgh: T. &. T. Clark, 1973
Schürer² iii. 1, 2	E. Schürer, *The History of the Jewish People in the Age of Jesus Christ (175 BC–AD 135)*, iii. 1–2. Edinburgh: T. &. T. Clark, 1986–7
SEG	*Supplementum epigraphicum Graecum*. Leiden: Sijthoff, etc. 1923–
Sel. Pap.	A. S. Hunt, C. C. Edgar, and D. L. Page (eds) (1950), *Select Papyri*, i–iv (Loeb Classical Library). Cambridge, MA, and London: Harvard UP
SGDI	H. Collitz and F. Bechtel (eds), *Sammlung der griechischen Dialekt-inschriften*, i–iv. Göttingen: Vandenhoeck & Ruprecht, 1884–1915
Sherk	R. K. Sherk, *Rome and the Greek East to the Death of Augustus*. Cambridge: CUP, 1984

Sherwin-White and Kuhrt, *Samarkhand*	S. Sherwin-White and A. Kuhrt, *From Samarkhand to Sardis: A New Approach to the Seleucid Empire*. London: Duckworth, 1993
Staatsv. iii	H. H. Schmitt (ed.), *Die Staatsverträge des Altertums*, iii: *Die Verträge der griechisch-römischen Welt von 338 bis 200 v. Chr.* [nos 401–586]. Munich: DAI/Beck, 1969
Syll.[2]	W. Dittenberger, rev. F. Hiller von Gaertringen, *Sylloge inscriptionum Graecarum*[2], i–iii. Leipzig, Hirzel, 1898–1901.
Syll.[3]	W. Dittenberger, rev. F. Hiller von Gaertringen, J. Kirchner, J. Pomtow, and E. Ziebarth, *Sylloge inscriptionum Graecarum*[3], i–iv. Leipzig: Hirzel, 1915–24
Talbert, *Atlas*	R. J. A. Talbert (ed.), *Atlas of Classical History*. London and New York: Routledge, 1985
TAM	*Tituli Asiae Minoris*. Vienna: Österreichische Akademie der Wissenschaften, 1901–
Tarn and Griffith	W. W. Tarn and G. T. Griffith, *Hellenistic Civilisation*[3]. London: Arnold, 1952
Terzo contributo	A. Momigliano, *Terzo contributo alla storia degli studi classici e del mondo antico*, i–ii. Rome: Edizioni di storia e di letteratura, 1966
Tod	M. N. Tod, *A Selection of Greek Historical Inscriptions*, ii: *From 403 to 323 BC*. Oxford: Clarendon, 1948
UP	University Press
UPZ	U. Wilcken, *Urkunden der Ptolemäerzeit (ältere Funde)*. Berlin and Leipzig: de Gruyter, 1927–57
Walbank, *HCP*	F. W. Walbank, *A Historical Commentary on Polybius*. 3 vols. Oxford: Clarendon, 1957–79
Walbank, *HW*	F. W. Walbank, *The Hellenistic World*. London: HarperCollins, 1981, rev. 1986, 1992
W. Chrest.	U. Wilcken, *Grundzüge und Chrestomathie der Papyruskunde*, i. 2: *Chrestomathie*. Leipzing and Berlin: Teubner, 1912
Will	E. Will, *Histoire politique du monde hellénistique (323–30 av. J.-C.)*, i–ii. Nancy: Université de Nancy II, [1]1966, [2]1979–82
ZPE	*Zeitschrift für Papyrologie und Epigraphik*

LIST OF DATES

I have chiefly relied upon the tables in the *Cambridge Ancient History*. For more details, see Figures 2.1 (on 338–323 BC), 2.2 (on 323–301 BC), and 2.4 (on 298–277 BC). For dates of rulers, see also Appendix I.

Late fourth century BC

338	battle of Chaironeia: Philip II of Macedonia defeats southern Greeks, founds league of Corinth
336	assassination of Philip; accession of Alexander III (the Great)
334	Alexander invades Asia
331	Alexandria founded
	Agis III of Sparta leads revolt of Greeks
330	assassination of Darius III of Persia
324	Alexander's Exiles Decree
323	death of Alexander
	Ptolemy becomes satrap of Egypt
	outbreak of Lamian War (Greek revolt)
322	battle of Krannon: Antipater defeats southern Greeks
321	Triparadeisos conference: Antipater becomes regent
319	death of Antipater: Polyperchon becomes regent
	Ptolemy invades Syria and Phoenicia
317	Polyperchon proclaims Greek freedom
	Demetrios of Phaleron becomes ruler of Athens
	murder of Philip III Arrhidaios
316	Cassander ousts Polyperchon, executes Olympias, founds Cassandreia and Thessalonike, rebuilds Thebes
	Eumenes executed by Antigonos
315	Antigonos expels Seleukos from Babylon
	Tyre declaration: Antigonos Monophthalmos proclaims Greek freedom
	Ptolemy proclaims Greek freedom
315–314	Antigonos founds league of Islanders

313   Alexandria becomes capital of Egypt
312   battle of Gaza: Ptolemy and Seleukos defeat Demetrios son of Antigonos;
          Seleukid era backdated to here
311   peace between Antigonos, Ptolemy, Lysimachos, Cassander: Seleukos
          confirmed in his Asian possessions
310   murder of Alexander IV
308   (or 305) start of Seleukos's war against Chandragupta (to 303)
307   Athenian *ephebeia* made voluntary
          Demetrios son of Antigonos takes Athens, liberates Athens and deposes
          Demetrios of Phaleron
307–304   Cassander besieges Athens
306   naval battle of Salamis (Cyprus): Antigonos (I) and Demetrios (I) defeat
          Ptolemy and become kings
          Pyrrhos becomes king of Epeiros
305/4   Demetrios I fails to take Rhodes by siege but earns nickname Poliorketes
          ('Besieger')
          Ptolemy, Lysimachos, Cassander, and Seleukos become kings
304   Demetrios lifts the siege of Athens
302   Antigonos and Demetrios revive league of Corinth
c.302   Philetairos becomes governor of Pergamon on behalf of Lysimachos
301   battle of Ipsos: death of Antigonos I

Third century BC

300/299   foundations of Seleukeia-in-Pieria and Antioch
c.300–295 Lachares' rule at Athens
298   (or 297) death of Cassander
c.297   foundation of kingdom of Pontos
297–295   Demetrios I besieges Athens
295   Macedonian garrison installed in Piraeus
294   Demetrios I seizes Macedonia from Cassander's sons Alexandros and
          Antipatros
          Antiochos I becomes co-regent with Seleukos I
293   foundation of Demetrias
291   (or 290) Demetrios revisits Athens
288/7   Demetrios I expelled from Macedonia by Lysimachos and Pyrrhos, king
          of Epeiros
287   (or 286) Athens revolts from Demetrios
286   Demetrios captured by Seleukos
285   Ptolemy II Philadelphos becomes co-regent in Egypt
283   deaths of Demetrios I, Ptolemy I
          Pergamene era backdated to this year
281   battle of Koroupedion: death of Lysimachos
          assassination of Seleukos; Ptolemy Keraunos becomes ruler of Macedonia

280	Pyrrhos invades Italy
	death of Ptolemy Keraunos
	refoundation of Achaean league
280/79	war in Syria between Antiochos I and Ptolemy II
	Gauls repulsed from central Greece
279	festival of Ptolemaieia inaugurated at Alexandria
278/7	Gauls invade Asia Minor
277	Antigonos II Gonatas defeats Gauls and takes control of Macedonia
275	Pyrrhos defeated by the Romans
c.275	Arsinoë II becomes co-ruler in Egypt
c.274–271	'1st' Syrian war (Egypt makes gains)
271/0	Ptolemy II's procession at Alexandria
272	Pyrrhos invades Laconia, dies at Argos
268	death of Arsinoë II
268/7	(or 265/4) start of Chremonidean war (southern Greeks against Macedonia)
263/2	(or 262/1) Antigonos Gonatas captures Athens
260–c.253	2nd Syrian war (indecisive)
250s	battle of Kos?
259/8	'Revenue Laws' of Ptolemy II
c.255	Cappadocia breaks from Seleukid empire
251	Sikyonians, led by Aratos, expel Macedonian tyrant; Sikyon joins Achaean league
c.250	Baktria breaks with Seleukid empire; eastern satrapies lost to Parthians
c.249	(between 249 and 245) Alexander (Macedonian commander at Corinth) rebels
c.246	battle of Andros?
246–241	3rd Syrian war ('Laodikeian war') (Ptolemy III Euergetes takes towns in Asia Minor)
245	Aratos becomes general of Achaean league
	Antigonos Gonatas takes Corinth
c.244	accession of Agis IV of Sparta
243	Aratos expels Macedonians from Corinth
241	execution of Agis
c.240	Attalos I takes royal title
240/39	war breaks out between Seleukos II and his brother Antiochos Hierax
c.239/8–229	'war of Demetrios' (Athens against Demetrios II of Macedonia)
236	peace between Seleukos and Hierax
235	Megalopolis joins Achaean league
c.235	accession of Kleomenes III of Sparta
230–227	Seleukos II attempts to conquer Parthians
229	1st Illyrian war: Roman action against queen Teuta
	Athens revolts; Piraeus liberated

227	coup of Kleomenes III of Sparta; Achaean league declares war on Sparta
227/6	Rhodian earthquake
226-223	Attalos I of Pergamon takes control of western Asia Minor
223	accession of Antiochos III
223/2	Antiochos III gains territory from Pergamon
222	battle of Sellasia: Achaeans and Antigonos III Doson of Macedonia defeat Kleomenes
221	accessions of Ptolemy IV and Philip V
220	Achaios proclaims himself king of Asia
220–217	'social' war of Philip V against the 'allies' (Aitolia, Sparta, Elis)
219	2nd Illyrian war: Romans against Demetrios and Skerdilaidas death of Kleomenes in Egypt
219–217	4th Syrian war
218	Hannibal invades Italy
217	battle of Rhaphia: Egypt repels Antiochos III
216–213	Antiochos III's war against Achaios
215	Philip V's treaty with Hannibal
214–205	1st Macedonian war
212	(or 211) Rome's treaty with Aitolians against Philip
212–205/4	'Anabasis' of Antiochos III: he recovers eastern satrapies (temporarily)
c.210	Aigina sold to Attalos I
207	death of Machanidas, accession of Nabis at Sparta
205	peace of Phoinike
204	Antiochos III seizes rest of Pergamene territory
202–201	Philip V's campaign in the Aegean
202–200	5th Syrian war (Egypt gains part of Syria)
200	Romans and Attalos defend Athens and Piraeus against Philip

Second century BC

200-197	2nd Macedonian war
200	Philip V of Macedonia invades Attica
197	battle of Kynoskephalai: Rome defeats Philip V
196	Flamininus proclaims Greek freedom at Isthmian games
195	Roman war against Nabis
192	Aitolians attack Sparta, assassinate Nabis Philopoimen, Achaean league general, defeats Sparta; Sparta enrolled in Achaean league
191–188	'Syrian war' of the Romans against Antiochos III
c.190	(between 191 and 188) Athenians become allies of Rome
189	battle of Magnesia: Romans defeat Antiochos
188	peace of Apameia divides Asia Minor between Rhodes and Pergamon ancestral constitution of Sparta abolished

c.187–183	war of Eumenes II of Pergamon against Prousias I of Bithynia
184/3	Roman senate gives ruling about Sparta
183	Messene revolts from Achaean league
183–179	war of Eumenes against Pontos
182	murder of Philopoimen
	Lykortas recovers Messene for Achaean league
181/0	Achaean envoy Kallikrates urges senate to support its friends
179	Perseus becomes king of Macedonia
175	Jason becomes high priest at Jerusalem
172	Eumenes denounces Perseus at Rome
172–168	3rd Macedonian war
169–168	6th Syrian war: Antiochos IV invades Egypt
168	battle of Pydna: Rome defeats Perseus
	Q. Popillius Laenas forces Antiochos to abandon invasion of Egypt
167	Macedonia split into four republics
	Achaean hostages, including Polybios, taken to Rome
	Romans make Delos a tax-free port and give it to Athens
c.167	Menelaos becomes high priest at Jerusalem
166/5	Antiochos IV's procession at Daphne
c.166/5	Maccabees lead Jewish revolt against Antiochos IV
164	Rhodian treaty with Rome
163	Lysias, regent for Antiochos V, restores Jewish privileges
160/59	Attalos II becomes co-ruler in Pergamon
156–154	war between Prousias of Bithynia and Attalos
155	Ptolemy VIII bequeaths Egypt to Romans (not implemented)
155–153	Cretan pirates' war against Rhodes
152	Rome gives support to Alexander Balas
	Jonathan becomes high priest in Jerusalem
150	Achaean hostages return to Greece
150–145	Seleukids lose Media to Mithradates I Arsakes V of Parthia
149	revolt of Macedonians under Andriskos against Rome
	Attalos of Pergamon and Nikomedes depose Prousias of Bithynia
148	defeat of Andriskos
146	revolt of Achaeans; Mummius sacks Corinth; league disbanded
	Macedonia becomes Roman province
145	Ptolemy VIII and Demetrios II Nikator of Syria defeat Alexander Balas
143	Simon becomes high priest at Jerusalem
142	Diodotos Tryphon proclaims himself king of Syria
142	(or 141) Rome recognizes independence of Jerusalem
139/8	Tryphon defeated by Antiochos VII
135	John Hyrkanos becomes high priest at Jerusalem
134	Antiochos VII recaptures Jerusalem
133	Attalos III dies, leaving Pergamon to the Roman people
132–130	revolt of Aristonikos

131	eastern expedition of Antiochos VII
129	death of Antiochos VII while fighting Parthians; Judaea regains independence
129–126	M'. Aquillius organizes the province of Asia
124	end of civil war between Ptolemy VIII, Kleopatra II, and Kleopatra III
118	amnesty decree of Ptolemy and the Kleopatras
c.113	Mithradates VI of Pontos seizes power
108–107	Mithradates divides Paphlagonia with Nikomedes of Bithynia
102–100	war of M. Antonius against the Cilician pirates
101	(or earlier) Mithradates takes over Cappadocia (temporarily)

First century BC

96	Kommagene (Asia Minor) breaks from Seleukids
	Ptolemy Apion (illegitimate son of Ptolemy VIII) wills Cyrene to Rome; Ptolemy X Alexander I wills Egypt and Cyprus to Rome
89	outbreak of 1st Mithradatic war
88	Mithradates organizes massacre of Romans in Asia
	Athens abandons Rome, supports Mithridates; Athenion becomes hoplite general; Aristion then becomes 'tyrant'
87–85	Sulla besieges, then sacks Athens
84/3	last Seleukid monarch, Philip II, deposed by the Antiochenes; kingship handed to Tigranes of Armenia
83–82	2nd Mithradatic war: L. Murena's campaigns in Asia
80	Romans install Ptolemy XI: he is lynched
75	(or 74) Nikomedes of Bithynia leaves his kingdom to Rome
75/4	Romans annexe Cyrene
74	campaigns of M. Antonius against the pirates
73–63	3rd Mithradatic war
71	Mithradates held captive in Armenia by Tigranes
70	Lucullus reorganizes Asia Minor
69	battle of Tigranocerta; Lucullus briefly revives Seleukid dynasty, installing Antiochos XIII
68	campaign of Q. Metellus against Cretan pirates
67	battle of Zela: Mithradates defeats Lucullus
	Pompey's command against the pirates
66	Pompey defeats Mithradates
65–64, 62	Pompey reorganizes the east
64	Syria becomes Roman province
63	suicide of Mithradates
	Pompey captures Jerusalem
	Pompey suppresses Seleukid dynasty
57	Ptolemy XII Auletes takes refuge in Rome
55	Gabinius restores Ptolemy XII

*c.*55	Baktria falls to eastern invaders
53	battle of Carrhae: Crassus defeated and killed by Parthians
51	Parthians invade Syria
49	outbreak of Roman civil wars
48	battle of Pharsalos: Caesar defeats Pompey, who flees to Egypt and is assassinated there
	Caesar's war in Egypt, relationship with Kleopatra VII
47	battle of Zela: Caesar defeats Pharnakes of Pontos
	birth of Caesarion
45	Parthians invade Syria
44	assassination of Julius Caesar; Brutus goes to Greece
42	battles of Philippi
41	Mark Antony in Asia and Egypt
31	battle of Actium: Octavian defeats Mark Antony and Kleopatra VII of Egypt
30	deaths of Antony and Kleopatra; Egypt becomes Roman province
27	Octavian becomes Augustus
	province of Achaia created
25	province of Galatia created
22–19	Augustus in Greece and Asia
6	province of Judaea created

First century AD and later

17	province of Cappadocia created; Kommagene annexed
64–5	kingdom of Pontos added to Galatia
66	(or 67) Nero proclaims Greek freedom
	Jewish revolt
67	Nero at Olympia
70	Titus destroys the Temple at Jerusalem
116	Hadrian adds Phrygia to province of Asia
124, 128	Hadrian at Eleusinian Mysteries
131–2	Hadrian's last visit to Athens: Olympieion inaugurated, Panhellenion founded
132–5	Jewish rebellion under Bar-Kochva
143	consulate of Herodes Atticus
267	Heruli invade Greece; Dexippos defends Athens

1

APPROACHES AND SOURCES

The period and its problems

The period name 'hellenistic' is one of the most frequently discussed terms in the study of the ancient world.[1] It derives from the ancient Greek verb *hellênizô*, 'I behave like a Greek', 'I adopt Greek ways', or 'I speak Greek', and therefore ultimately from the Greeks' name for themselves, *Hellênes*. It is however, a modern coinage, based on the term *Hellenismus*, which the mid-nineteenth-century Prussian historian J. G. Droysen employed to describe the period when the spread of Greek culture to parts of the non-Greek world was given new impetus by the invasion of Asia by Alexander.[2] Droysen's work focused attention on the period as a distinctive phase of Greek culture;[3] sweeping views of a distinctive, unified hellenistic world-culture appear in more or less explicit forms in such magisterial treatments as those by Kaerst[4] and Beloch,[5] and are occasionally met with even now.[6]

In the period after Alexander the Great's conquests, *hellênizô* and cognate terms appear only rarely in documents, and usually with the limited meanings above. No ancient author refers to the Orient 'going Greek', as the modern term would seem to suggest, though Plutarch describes Alexander as having brought civilization to the peoples he conquered (*On the Fortune or Courage of Alexander the Great*, i,[7] 328 c–f, Austin 19). The search for an overall characterization of Greek–non-Greek interaction tends to presuppose a unified 'oriental' culture, quite at odds with reality.[8] Few, if any, scholars now suppose that the peoples of the Near East universally adopted Greek language and customs; there is no evidence that this happened. They prefer to paint a variegated picture of co-existence, interaction, and sometimes confrontation between newly settled Greeks and indigenous populations (some of whom had themselves migrated from elsewhere), and in a dynamic rather than static social context. Occasionally there is evidence of the active promotion of cultural interchange by rulers, but no single explanation fits all cases and each must be examined on its merits. The boundaries defining what it was to be Greek, or to be (as presumably a Greek would view it) non-Greek, were negotiable, not fixed, and had to be renegotiated as society changed – not least when generations of inter-marriage in Asia or Egypt raised issues of who was Greek and who was not.

What we call the 'Greek world' was never restricted to the area of the modern Greek state. In earlier times the Greek city-states had planted colonial settlements around the shores of the Mediterranean and the Black Sea, particularly in Sicily and southern Italy. Alexander conquered the Persian empire comprising Egypt and western Asia, but his short-lived empire was divided among his successors, eventually giving rise to three large kingdoms. Macedonia (including the Greek peninsula as far as the Isthmus, which Philip II had conquered in 338, but not the Peloponnese) was ruled by the Antigonid monarchs; Egypt by the Ptolemies; Asia (sometimes called Syria) by the Seleukids. The last was partly an agglomeration of separate principalities (such as Armenia and Cappadocia), as it had been under Persian rule. A fourth kingdom, Pergamon in north-western Asia Minor, broke from the Seleukids in the mid-third century BC, and various Seleukid territories became semi-independent or independent at different times (notably Baktria in the far east from the mid-third century on).

Pre-existing Greek city-states were incorporated into the kings' territories by a variety of methods, some of them remaining notionally independent even if informally subordinate. Within this new political context, Greeks were probably numerically dominant only within towns and cities, particularly in Alexander's new capital of Egypt, Alexandria, which became the largest city in the Greek world and distinctively multi-ethnic. From the late third century on, the rising power of Rome was increasingly influential; the Romans defeated Macedonia for the first time in 197 BC, expelled the Seleukid armies from Europe and imposed a damaging peace treaty (188), abolished the kingdom of Macedonia (168), defeated the confederation of southern Greek cities (146), and by stages took over the rest of the hellenistic world, notably gaining Egypt in 30 at the end of the Roman civil wars.

Despite the problems associated with the name 'hellenistic', it remains a convenient and clear label for the period beginning with Alexander, usually with his death in 323 BC but sometimes at other dates (notably the battle of Ipsos in 301 BC). The term is retained in this book, but purely as a chronological marker. Like all 'periods' in history, the hellenistic is a largely arbitrary construct. There is a particular difficulty in assigning a terminal date, and no attempt to do so can be completely convincing. Greek rule (which itself meant a variety of things) came to an end, generally in favour of Roman rule, at different dates in different places between 168 BC and AD 72; even then, the distinctive city-based culture of the Greeks, modified by centuries of interaction with non-Greek cultures, continued to evolve in new ways for many more centuries. With justification did A. H. M. Jones choose the thousand years beginning with Alexander as the chronological scope for his study of the later Greek city, which persisted long into the Christian era and after the division of the Roman empire into east and west.[9]

Given these difficulties, or fluidities, of definition – and particularly in view of the shorter definitions of the period that might be upheld (such as 301–146 BC) – it must be asked whether there is anything inherently distinctive about the period after Alexander. Given the plethora of alternative political or military events that could be chosen as termini, such an answer would better be framed in terms of society, economy, and culture. Provided we do not seek to torture the evidence in the search for fixed chronological boundaries or overnight transformations, the question can be treated as an investigation of the effects of Macedonian conquest upon Greece and the Near East. In addition, as subsequent chapters will reveal, the period beginning with Alexander saw an acceleration of contact of all kinds between different communities in and around the Mediterranean, in areas such as trade, travel, diplomacy, and the exchange of ideas.

A number of major issues have attracted the attention of historians in recent years. How did the classical city-state fare, and how did common people fare economically and in terms of political rights, within a world of monarchical military powers? How did Macedonia itself develop after the break-up of Alexander's empire, and what impact did rule by monarchs of Macedonian descent have upon Egypt and western Asia? How well did traditional forms of religion survive in Greece, and what changes took place in modes of religious practice and ethical systems? Outside Greece, in what ways did Greek culture and social organization interact with other societies? How did people, both in Greece and outside, deal with issues of gender and ethnicity in new social and political circumstances? What intellectual activities took place, and how far did they interact with, and contribute to, social life at large?

Evidence, from many angles, presents us with a period of rapid change. Despite earlier anxieties on the part of scholars, a consensus is growing that the Greek *polis* (city-state) continued to exist and in some respects to flourish and prosper; it seems clear that more cities were in some sense democratic than before, but that their freedom of action was limited. Many cities (*poleis*) had to come to terms with a new position of subordination to a king; but this was not a wholly new experience, for many had previously had to cope with rule by Athens or Persia. There are more worrying trends, however: in the Greek homeland at least, survey archaeology possibly indicates a gradual, though never total, drift away from small farmsteads to urban employment, perhaps supported by larger-scale estate farming in the countryside, carried out by increasingly rich landed aristocrats – though the evidence is not conclusive (p. 31).

There are also signs of social transformations, if gradual ones. Women are seen to play more prominent roles in public life, albeit within a male-dominated value system; certainly literature and public documents show signs of a more sophisticated view of women as persons.[10] There were new options in religion, especially in the areas of ruler-cult and newly introduced additional non-Greek cults in Greek lands, with greater prominence for healing cults and those concerned with individual destiny or salvation. In philosophy, there is an emphasis upon ethics and a person's role within a community. Literature, which had never stopped evolving (the alleged pinnacle of achievement in the fifth and fourth centuries only represents one snapshot), developed along new lines. Poetry is especially characteristic of the age, with its emphasis on the individual's life and his or her emotional and psychological states, rather than, as in classical Athens, an almost exclusive focus upon the citizen's duty towards his city. Finally, there were by any measure huge advances in scientific understanding, though not, as today, from a utilitarian or industrial point of view. Science was a cultural – almost philosophical and religious – activity, even a pastime for a leisured élite.

Every historical period can be seen to some extent as a mirror of our own, since it is the story of how people who were in most respects like us dealt with the problems they faced. The hellenistic period is no exception, and many writers have seen it as holding a key to the issues of their own day. W. W. Tarn, writing mainly between the two world wars in the heyday of the League of Nations, focused on the issues of racial and cultural confrontation facing Alexander and his successors, and on the nature of colonial rule in western Asia.[11] Mikhail Rostovtzeff, who left Russia to avoid the revolution, gave us a hellenistic world whose most important feature was the rise of a capitalist bourgeoisie (Alexander's successors are even 'self-made men').[12] Arnaldo Momigliano, an Italian Jew writing before and after the second world war, focused on intellectual history as an autonomous project, and also on problems of mutual understanding between races.[13]

More recently, in 1950s' New York, Moses Hadas painted an optimistic picture of the synthesis of cultures.[14] F. W. Walbank, a historian taking a materialist approach, writes in terms of political-military power and class relations.[15] Claire Préaux, a papyrologist whose work is informed by a social-historical approach, explores the economic system of Egypt and, in her later work, the interaction between kings and cities and between different cultures, taking a generally pessimistic view of the latter.[16] Others (such as the Quaker John Ferguson and the lifelong iconoclast Peter Green), writing in the age of late twentieth-century liberalism, have tended to see the hellenistic period in terms of (either healthy or déraciné) individualism, the breakdown of convention, and experiments with new modes of living and thinking comparable to those of the past thirty years in the capitalist West; Green, in particular, reflects a postmodern disillusionment with all institutions and political processes.[17]

Though some of these approaches have a stronger foundation in evidence than others, many of them could be shown to be historically relative, while some are excessively judgemental, selective, or exaggerated. Recent scholars are less often tempted to advance sweeping historical schemes.[18] It is important to understand the period using as many methodologically neutral terms as possible – wealth, groups, power, and so on – and, when using more determinate terms of analyses such as imperialism or economy, to define them closely. We can thus avoid imposing a rigid or judgemental scheme on what is surely the most complex of all periods of Greek history, and try to allow the diversity of cultures, social forms, and landscapes to emerge.

The literary sources

As soon as we try to understand the period we are faced with the problem of how to approach and interpret the data, which have a rather different character from those available for the preceding classical period.[19]

'Fragments'

A term often encountered when reading about hellenistic history, but rarely explained, is 'fragment'. Sometimes a fragment is just that, a broken piece of papyrus or the torn page of a medieval manuscript on parchment or vellum. Much more often, however, 'fragment' is used to describe a quotation or summary of a lost author in the works of a surviving author. The reason why these quotations are so important is that for some of the period after Alexander there is no contemporary, continuous narrative. Some works of history disappeared because they were re-read and copied less often in an age when a Roman reading public preferred summaries and compendiums (such as Justin's epitome of Trogus, below). Copies of older works preserved in libraries were thus more likely to be unique, so that whenever a library was destroyed an author's work might perish forever (on the destructions of libraries in late hellenistic and Roman Alexandria, see p. 235). We therefore depend on later authors who cite (or appear to be citing) lost works, often written centuries before their time.

One author who preserves the words and ideas of many lost originals is Athenaeus of Alexandria (c. AD 200), whose lengthy work *Deipnosophistai* (*The Philosophers' Banquet*) contains a string of anecdotes from earlier authors, including many from the hellenistic period. In this extract he preserves observations of natural curiosities by a second-century BC historian:

> Polybios of Megalopolis, in the thirty-fourth book of the *Histories*, when discussing the land of Lusitania in Iberia, says there are oak-trees growing in the depth of the sea, by eating whose fruit the tuna-fish grow fat.
>
> (Ath. 7. 302 e)

The first-century BC geographer Strabo (pp. 14–15) preserves what is clearly another part of the same passage:

5

But this oak produces so much fruit that, after it ripens, the sea-shore is filled with it both inside and outside the Pillars [*Straits of Gibraltar*], though those inside the Pillars are always smaller and more frequent. And Polybios says that this acorn is washed up even as far as Latium, unless perhaps, as he says, Sardinia and the neighbouring land are also producing it.

(Strabo, 3. 2. 7 (145))

The second sentence of this extract is placed alongside the quotation from Athenaeus in reconstructions of Polybios, book 34.

Other works which are rich sources of fragments include very late works of an encyclopaedic character. Stephanos of Byzantion's *Ethnika*, composed in the sixth century AD, survives only in an imperfect abridgement which preserves information mainly about the names of Greek cities.[20] The *Suda* (or Suidas), a historical encyclopaedia of about AD 1000 compiled from earlier reference works, contains many valuable fragments of lost writers; while other late compilations such as Pollux's *Onomastikon* (written in the second century AD but known only from a much later summary) contain many useful snippets of ancient knowledge.

The texts of authors whose work survives exclusively in fragments were collected by Jacoby in his (unfinished) work *Die Fragmente der griechischen Historiker*, each author being given a number (usually preceded by *FGH*, *FGrH*, or *FGrHist*).

Writings about Alexander

Though Alexander's invasion of Asia represents only part of the prelude to the hellenistic period, works written about Alexander during the early part of the period were influential in important ways, both on contemporary culture and on the writing of history. Alexander's importance to people of the next generation is confirmed by the number of works written about him, which are known only indirectly, from the use made of them by later, surviving historians, principally Arrian and Curtius.

The more reliable tradition was headed by Ptolemy, the first Macedonian king of Egypt, who wrote a personal memoir of the expedition, and by Aristoboulos (Aristobulus) of Kassandreia (*FGH* 139), who served with Alexander and later composed a rather too favourable portrait of the king. Both drew on the work of Kallisthenes (Callisthenes; *FGH* 124; p. 264), whom Alexander appointed as his official historian but later executed. The mainspring of the other, 'vulgate' tradition was probably Kleitarchos (Clitarchus) of Alexandria (*FGH* 137), who in the late fourth century wrote a history of Alexander, probably using first-hand accounts.

Surviving histories include an example of both historical traditions. Arrian of Nikomedeia (Lucius Flavius Arrianos Xenophon, *c.* AD 80–160), a

Greek from Bithynia who held office under the Romans, claims to have used the most reliable sources about Alexander and to have done so critically. His surviving works include the famous *Anabasis of Alexander* (*Alexander's Expedition to the Interior*), the foundation of all modern studies of Alexander, and the *Indikê*, an account of the voyage of the king's fleet back from India. Extensive fragments survive, on papyrus and in medieval manuscripts, of his *Ta meta Alexandron* (*What Happened after Alexander*, FGH 156; parts in Austin 22 *a*, 24), covering the first four years after the king's death.

In his account of Alexander in his seventeenth book, Diodoros (for whom see below) used Kleitarchos. The other main Alexander historian is a Roman, Quintus Curtius Rufus (first or second century AD), a rather shadowy figure writing in Latin who reflects the populist or 'vulgate' tradition. This gives his work a moralistic and rhetorical character, but he usefully complements Arrian for the period beginning in 333 (the earlier part of his work is lost). Elements of the vulgate tradition, deriving perhaps from popular traditions written down not long after the king's death, are reflected in the so-called *Alexander Romance*, a partly fabulous collection of stories surviving in late Roman and medieval versions (for more on these, see pp. 252–3).

Historiography of the hellenistic period

Historians were numerous in the hellenistic period, but few of their works survive. Local, regional, and antiquarian history flourished as genres, but most of the authors are no more than names to us (see Chapter 7). The lack of a continuous narrative is a problem for much of the period, particularly the early and mid-third century. The major third-century historians are all lost: Hieronymos, Douris, Timaios, Phylarchos, and Aratos of Sikyon. As Walbank remarks, 'There is strong evidence that it is these five who have stamped their character and their version of events on the surviving tradition.'[21] An equally lamentable loss is that of Philochoros, the last and greatest of the Atthidographers (writers of Attic, that is, Athenian, history), who covered contemporary as well as earlier events. The disappearance of these works is partly the result of the changes in Roman taste referred to above, but is also partly explained by a seeming lack of interest in the years *c*.301–*c*.229 on the part of later writers, who may have preferred not to focus on a time when the domination of the Macedonian dynasties had been virtually unchallenged. All these writers are discussed later (pp. 262–5); here I shall concentrate on authors who survive in part or whole.

For the period from 229 onwards we have the first near-contemporary narrative, fortunately of high quality. Polybios of Megalopolis (*c*.200–*c*.118) is the only hellenistic historian who survives in anything approaching a complete state. His text is mutilated, however; only one-eighth of the work (the first five of forty books) survives intact, the remainder being pieced together from shorter and longer 'fragments' (in the sense discussed above), especially an almost continuous précis of books 6–18.

Polybios witnessed important events and mixed with men who made history. His father was a prominent statesman in the Achaean league during the early second century. Polybios himself was one of the thousand Achaeans detained in Italy after the defeat of Macedonia; he enjoyed the company of Roman statesmen and literati while living there; he witnessed the sack of Carthage in the company of leading Roman commanders (146), and explored the Atlantic coast beyond the straits of Gibraltar. He wrote his history in order to explain how the Romans took over Greece between 220 and 167 (p. 369), and therefore included a prelude (books 1–2) on the rise of Rome, the early wars against Carthage, the condition of Greece under Macedonia, and the defeat of Sparta by Antigonos III of Macedonia. At the end he added an account of the effects of the Roman takeover of Greece (books 30–9). This takeover, not surprisingly, made a deep impression on him; he seems to have wanted both to explain to himself why the Romans' success was so total, and to communicate these reasons to his Greek readers so that they would accept the ineluctable new world order and make the best of it.

While it may seem almost unfair to lost historians to focus at such length on Polybios, we must assume that the reason his work survived was that it was widely read and copied, and therefore that it was thought excellent. With Thucydides, he stands as one of the two Greek historians who can, at least in terms of methodology and intentions, be called scientific – though both are literary artists, and far from dispassionate. He calls his writing *pragmatikê historia*, 'pragmatic history', based on written evidence, his own knowledge of events, the evidence of eye-witnesses, and so on. He arranges his material systematically: in the main body of his work he covers one year at a time, treating events in the west (including Africa), Greece, Macedonia, Asia, and Egypt, always in that order. He develops Thucydides' principles of explanation to a higher level of sophistication, which his insistence on the role of chance or Fortune (*tychê*, cf. pp. 173–5) does not invalidate. The corollary to his discussions of his own historical methods is his sometimes injudicious attacks on other historians' methods and biases, notably upon Timaios in book 12 (see pp. 262–3). He himself is clearly prejudiced, notably in favour of the Achaeans and against the Spartans; but the comment of one scholar that 'he was, though not of course neutral, honest' seems fair.[22]

The universal history by the Roman writer Livy (Titus Livius, probably 59 BC–AD 17) included many passages based on lost books of Polybios. Large portions of Livy's work survive, enabling scholars to fill gaps in Polybios. For Roman involvement in Greece down to 167 BC, Livy gives a detailed and valuable narrative in books 26–45.

A contemporary of Livy, Diodoros of Agyrrhion (Diodorus Siculus, 'the Sicilian'), wrote a *Bibliothêkê* (*Library*), a universal history to 60 BC. Books 18–20 are the only continuous narrative we have for the years 323–302 BC;

they rely heavily on the lost memoirs of Hieronymos of Kardia, Alexander's archivist and himself a military officer (p. 264). The remainder of Diodoros's work survives in fragments, but it is clear that for the history of his native Sicily down to the second quarter of the third century he uses Timaios, for Greek history of the later third and second centuries he follows Polybios closely, and for the period after 146 he uses the Stoic scholar Posidonius (135–51 BC). The books on events from 301 to 60 BC are fragmentary.

From 301 until Polybios's narrative sets in at 229 BC, there is no continuous account; the nearest thing we have to a narrative is a second-hand version of a lost work written in the late first century BC or early first century AD. Pompeius Trogus, a romanized Gaul from Gallia Narbonensis, wrote his *Philippic Histories* in the reign of Augustus. They survive in the form of an 'epitome' (précis) by Justin (M. Iunianus Iustinus), a writer of uncertain date, perhaps the later second century AD.[23] The summary occupies 262 pages of an English translation; the original was probably five to ten times longer. Summaries of individual books vary in length between one and nineteen pages, and are particularly short in the middle and later periods; books 26–35 (272–145 BC) occupy only thirty-four pages. The survival of the work is due to their popularity in the Middle Ages, when the epitome was read relatively widely along with a set of *prologi* (tables of contents) of uncertain authorship; these are independent of Justin, since they avoid some of his mistakes. Both their brevity and their relative accuracy are illustrated by the *prologus* of book 27, which covered no less than twenty years' history (246–226/5 BC). The following quotation retains the Latin spellings for names:[24]

> In the seven-and-twentieth book are contained the following. The war of Seleucus (II Callinicus) in Syria against Ptolemaeus Trypho, and likewise in Asia against his own brother Antiochus Hierax; in which war he was defeated at Ancyra by the Gauls. And how the Gauls, defeated at Pergamum by Attalos (I), killed Zielas the Bithynian. How Ptolemy (III) killed Adaeus whom he had finally captured, and Antigonus (III) at Andros defeated Sophron in a naval battle. How, put to flight in Mesopotamia by (Seleucus III) Callinicus, Antiochus escaped Ariamenes who was plotting against him, then afterwards escaped the guards of Trypho; when Antiochus was killed by the Gauls, his brother Seleucus also died, and Apaturius killed the elder of his (Seleucus's) sons.
>
> (Trogus, *Prologues*, 27)

An example of Justin's shortcomings, or of how his concerns are different from ours, is that in his much fuller epitome of the same book he fails to name the battle of Ancyra at all, and wrongly refers to Attalos of Pergamon as 'Eumenes of Bithynia' (27. 3. 1).

9

The work of Trogus covered the early Near East (books 1–6), Macedonia (7–12), the hellenistic kingdoms and their defeats by Rome (13–40), and the history of the Parthians (41–2); appended to it are the early kings of Rome (43) and the history of Spain and Carthage (44). The hellenistic sections included many episodes of Sicilian and Carthaginian history, and Justin's epitome of books 24–5 preserves a valuable account of the Gallic invasion of Greece (see pp. 52–4), as well as a remarkable story purporting to show how Ptolemy Keraunos ('Thunderbolt'), a son of Ptolemy I, tricked his sister (half-sister) Arsinoë II into marriage and killed her children so that he could take the city of Kassandreia from her (24. 2–3) – a rare example of a specific narrative about the early Ptolemies, though no more reliable for being rare. Justin is the main source for certain episodes, such as a coup at the Peloponnesian city of Elis in about 270 BC (26. 1. 4–10; in this particular case the epitome and the prologue scarcely overlap at all).

Justin's epitome is actually a personal selection rather than literally a summary, and can be shown to be inaccurate and confused in many points; but its stock has risen with the recognition that Trogus may have used Posidonius extensively (directly or via an intervening historian) and that Justin and the prologues are particularly important for western Greek and Carthaginian history.

The last major historian, particularly important for the later hellenistic period, is Appian (Appianos) of Alexandria (late first–mid-second century AD). A rough contemporary of Arrian, he worked as a lawyer at Rome and held a public post under the emperor Antoninus Pius. His history of Rome included several books describing particular peoples and how the Romans conquered them. Book 9, the *Makedonikê* (*Macedonian History*), is fragmentary, but the next three survive in their entirety. The brief book 10, *Illyrikê* (*Illyrian History*), focuses on Rome's involvements in north-western Greece in 230–119 and 50–33 BC. Book 11, *Syriakê* (*Syrian History*, usually called *The Syrian Wars*), details the war of Antiochos III against the Romans (chs 1. 1–7. 44) and summarizes later Seleukid history down to the Roman conquest and after (chs 8. 45–51, 11. 66–70). A digression on earlier events (chs 9. 52–11. 66) contains the famous sketch of Seleukos I and his achievements (for a quotation see p. 61). The twelfth book, the long *Mithradateios* (or *Mithridateios*; *The Mithradatic Wars*), narrates the three wars of Mithradates (or Mithridates) VI Eupator against the Romans, preserving key episodes such as the massacre of the Romans in Asia Minor (ch. 4. 22–3), the tyranny of Aristion at Athens, and Sulla's capture of the city (chs 5. 28–6. 41). Appian does more than just summarize his sources for us; he preserves material from lost works by Hieronymos of Kardia, Polybios, and notably the anti-Roman treatise *On Kings* by the first-century writer Timagenes of Alexandria (*FGH* 88).

For the period 69 BC–AD 46 we also possess books 36–60 (out of an original eighty books) of the *Roman History* by Cassius Dio (c. AD 164–after

229), another Greek member of the senatorial class from Asia Minor. The surviving books chiefly concern Roman history but contain important evidence for the later phases of Rome's Mithradatic wars (see Chapter 10).

Other sources with historical content

Non-Greek writers writing in Greek are an occasional but crucial source of evidence. For the history of the Jews under Seleukid rule, particularly the clash with Antiochos IV in the second century BC, the first and second books of the Maccabees, both in Greek, are a key source (pp. 266, 307), while Josephus (first century AD), another example of Jewish–Greek literature (p. 266), gives further insights into this and other episodes.

Babylonia and Egypt have one spokesman each. Sparse fragments survive of the *Babyloniaka* by the Babylonian priest Berossos (p. 261), which he reportedly dedicated to Antiochos I (r. 280–261). He is said to have set up a school for astrologers on the island of Kos, which was in the Ptolemaic sphere (Vitruvius, 10. 6. 2). In antiquity his work was read mainly in the form of a summary by Cornelius Polyhistor (first century BC). This, in turn, survives only in excerpts by Josephus (first century AD) and Abydenos (second century AD), and in an early fourth-century AD version by the Greek bishop Eusebios of Caesarea, in book 1 of his *Chronika*. Berossos first recounted (in rather poor Greek) the creation of the world and the revelation of the principles of civilization by the gods' messenger, Oannes:

> In the first year [*of the reign of Alorus*] a beast named Oannes appeared from the Erythraian Sea [*Persian Gulf*] in a place adjacent to Babylonia. Its entire body was like that of a fish, but a human head had grown beneath the head of the fish and human feet likewise had grown from the fish's tail.... It gave to the men the knowledge of letters and sciences and crafts of all types. It also taught them how to found cities, establish temples, introduce laws, and measure land. It also revealed to them seeds and the gathering of fruits, and in general it gave men everything which is connected with the civilized life.
>
> (*Babyloniaka*, 1. 1. 5)

The work then treated the history of the Babylonian kings and their successors down to Alexander, all rather briefly; this brought him criticism from Greek and Roman writers who expected more historical content. It appears, however, that Berossos's purpose was not so much historical as cultural: to provide Greeks, particularly the rulers of Babylon, with an outline of Babylonian culture and beliefs. Judging by later misrepresentations of that culture, his work had little influence.[25]

Better preserved than Berossos is an Egyptian author, Manethon (or Manethôs, or Manetho; *FGH* 609; see p. 261). It is uncertain whether he or Berossos

wrote first; they were near-contemporaries.[26] A priest, like Berossos, he dedi-
cated his *Aigyptiaka* (*Egyptian History*) to Ptolemy II. If it is true that Ptolemy I
asked him for advice when the cult of Sarapis arrived in Alexandria (Plutarch,
On Isis and Osiris, 28), he was an influential figure at the court of the early
Ptolemies. His book survives in the form of quotations and paraphrases in
Josephus, and quotations from a (lost) epitome preserved among the works
of late Roman and Byzantine authors such as the Latin chronographer
Africanus (third century AD), Eusebios (above; preserved in Greek and
Armenian), and the Greek monk Synkellos (eighth century).[27] Occasionally
we have extended summaries or paraphrases, as when Josephus criticizes his
account of Jewish history and customs (Manethon, fr. 54 = Josephus, *Against
Apion*, 1. 26–31. 227–87). A typical fragment, however, runs in the
following form (I reproduce three versions):

> Thirty-first dynasty: three kings of Persians. (1) Ôchos, in twentieth
> year of his own kingship over Persians, became king of Egypt for
> two years. (2) Arses, three years. (3) Dareios, four years. Altogether,
> years of Book 3: 1,050 [*editors suggest '850'*]. Thus far Manetho.
> (fr. 75 *a*, in Greek, from Synkellos citing Africanus)

> Thirty-first dynasty: three kings of Persians. (1) Ôchos, in twentieth
> year of his own kingship over Persians, holds Egypt for six years.
> (2) After whom Arses son of Ochos, four years. (3) After whom Dareios,
> six years, whom Alexander the Macedonian killed (!). These in the
> third (book) of Manetho. Thus far Manetho.
> (fr. 75 *b*, in Greek, from Synkellos citing Eusebios)

> Thirty-first dynasty, that of the Persians. Ochus, now in the twentieth
> year of exercising empire over the Persians, occupied Egypt and
> held it for six years. Thereafter Arses son of Ochus, four years. Then
> Darius, six years, whom the Macedonian Alexander killed. And
> these from the third [*'second' in the original Armenian version*] book of
> Manetho.
> (Manethon, fr. 75 *c*, Latin version of Armenian trans. of Eusebios)

The abundant discrepancies, particularly in chronology, illustrate the problems
afflicting all fragmentary sources of the hellenistic period, though this is an
extreme case. Nevertheless Manetho remains the foundation of pre-Ptolemaic
Egyptian chronology,[28] and another important (if rare) example of cultural
exchange between Greeks and non-Greeks.

Among the most valuable non-historiographical sources from later times
are the fifty biographies in Greek by Plutarch of Chaironeia (b. before AD

50; d. after AD 120), who also wrote copiously on philosophy and ethics. In these short, often brilliant accounts of individuals' lives he explores the roots of men's characters in their inherited and acquired qualities, as revealed by their actions, in order to make available to his readers a true understanding of character and morality. Forty-six of the lives form pairs – the *Parallel Lives* – in which a Greek statesman is explicitly compared with a Roman; in most cases, a third, shorter text known as the *Comparatio* accompanies the pair. Plutarch was a Boiotian from Chaironeia, but though he kept his roots there he, like Polybios and many other educated Greeks, benefited from intellectual contacts with, and visits to, Rome and Alexandria. The emperor Trajan bestowed honours on him. He was devoted to the ideals of classical Greece, which were being refashioned for a new audience during the period known as the Second Sophistic (*c.* AD 60–230), under the patronage of emperors such as Nero, Trajan, and especially Hadrian. Plutarch took seriously his responsibilities as holder of a priesthood at Delphi.

In the *Parallel Lives* Plutarch's general preference is for heroic figures from classical Greece who will match up to his chosen Romans; he seems to think less of Greece under and after Alexander. From late fourth-century Athens he portrays two victims of the Macedonian takeover of Athens, Demosthenes (compared with the Roman orator Cicero, himself a victim of civil war) and Phokion (alongside Cato the Younger, a similarly honourable victim). Otherwise, besides Alexander (juxtaposed to Julius Caesar), he gives us only seven hellenistic figures. From the years following Alexander's death he wrote just three biographies. King Demetrios I is his only royal subject from the generation of the successors of Alexander; he is compared with Mark Antony, another man to whom Plutarch attributes weakness of character revealed by circumstances. Eumenes of Kardia, the only non-Macedonian general among the Successors, is compared with Sertorius, a similarly talented and marginalized soldier. King Pyrrhos of Epeiros, who invaded Italy, is counterpointed with Marius. Plutarch's failure to include Ptolemy, Lysimachos, Seleukos, or any of their descendants – even men of such stature as the heroic reconqueror of the east, Antiochos III, or the aggressive Philip V of Macedonia – suggests that he had difficulty in elevating to exemplary status, even as negative models, Greeks who had oppressed other Greeks (Demetrios could at least be said to have liberated Athens twice). The resulting emphasis upon events before and after the mid-third century exacerbates the gap in our narrative sources.

Figures of the later third and second centuries among Plutarch's *Lives* include two Achaean generals. Aratos of Sikyon is treated in a free-standing biography, not one of a pair; Philopoimen, however, is paired with a Roman statesman involved in the conquest of Greece: Flamininus, the liberator of 197. Another *Life* is devoted to Aemilius Paullus, the victor over the last king of Macedonia; he is paired with Timoleon, a fourth-century Corinthian who overthrew tyrants in Sicily. The biographies of the reforming Spartan kings Agis and Kleomenes are written as a pair and are compared with a pair of Roman reformers, the brothers Gaius and Tiberius Gracchus.

Plutarch's *Lives* are, in default of other evidence, a major source of historical data; but they are moral biographies first and foremost, and only secondarily historical accounts. Although he uses his source material conscientiously, he often selects and rearranges it to highlight character traits and points of comparison. Sometimes he falls under the spell of tendentious sources, as in his biographies of Agis and Kleomenes, which are heavily reliant on the adulatory account of Phylarchos (see pp. 263–4), and in his portrayal of their enemy Aratos, in which he uses the Achaean leader's memoirs as a primary source, though he also criticizes him.

The subjects chosen by the Roman biographer Nepos (*c*.110–24 BC) for his collection of brief lives include the late fourth-century Athenian statesman Phokion (2 pages) and the Macedonian general Eumenes (9 pages). He also composed a page *On the Kings* (*De regibus*), one-third of which is a bare enumeration of the Successors. Though short on reliable fact, it has a certain interest, in so far as it confirms the bias of all our sources in directing attention away from the mid-third century:

> Furthermore, there were great kings among the friends of Alexander the Great, who seized empires after his death, among whom were Antigonus and his son Demetrius, Lysimachus, Seleucus, and Ptolemaeus. Of these Antigonus was killed in battle while he fought against Seleucus and Lysimachus. Lysimachus suffered a similar fate at the hands of Seleucus, for dissolving their friendship they waged war on one another. But Demetrius, when he had given his daughter to Seleucus, but the friendship between them had not thereby been able to remain secure, was captured in war and – the father-in-law a prisoner of his son-in-law – perished of disease. And not much later Seleucus was treacherously murdered by Ptolemaeus Ceraunus, whom he had given refuge, when he needed external support after he was expelled from Alexandria. But Ptolemaeus himself, after handing the kingdom to his son while he still lived, is said to have been deprived of life by the very same man.
>
> (Nepos, *De regibus*, 3. 1–4)

Geographical authors can also be invaluable.[29] Strabo, from Amaseia in Pontos (*c*.64 BC–after AD 21), is culturally and chronologically a hellenistic writer, though he is most often considered in relation to the Roman empire.[30] His surviving *Geographia* in seventeen books is not only one of the longest but also one of the most important sources from Greek antiquity, and he will be cited in the present work more often than any author except Polybios. The chief value of his work for hellenistic history lies in his topographical descriptions of the eastern areas of Alexander's empire which became

Roman provinces, but he also informs us about such matters as the history of the Attalids (see p. 312). His usefulness is all the greater for the fact that much of his geographical information was being drawn from authors of the third and second centuries; though out-of-date in his own day, it is relevant to hellenistic history. This is probably true of some of his information about Mesopotamia and the Seleukid provinces (there are many references in Chapter 8). His lengthy description of Alexandria, however (p. 215), is based on his own observations.

An equally important non-historiographical source, this time from the Roman period, is Pausanias (mid-second century AD), a doctor from Magnesia in Asia Minor (probably Magnesia-by-Sipylos), who composed a guidebook to the southern Greek mainland and its antiquities. His interest is limited, for the most part, to sights older than the defeat of the Achaean league by the Romans in 146 BC, but as a result he does include statues and other monuments of important figures in the third and early second centuries, some of which he uses as springboards for historical narrations. Book 1, on Attica, seems almost designed to introduce the reader to the history of the Macedonian monarchies, with its excursuses on the Gauls' invasion (ch. 4), the careers of Ptolemy I (chs 6–7), Attalos I (ch. 8. 1–2), Pyrrhos (chs 11. 1–14. 1), and Seleukos (ch. 16), events involving Mithradates and Sulla (ch. 20. 3–4), and the history of Athens from Philip to Cassander (chs 25. 3–26. 3), as well as a digression on Lysimachos which is one of our most important sources of information about the king (chs 9. 5–10. 5). Elsewhere there are sections on Spartan history (e.g. 2. 9. 1–3; 3. 6; 8. 27. 9–16) and an encomium of Philopoimen (8. 49–52); he is our prime source for the Roman sack of Corinth and the Roman settlement of 146 BC (7. 14–16).[31]

Finally, Athenaeus (p. 5) retails many anecdotes about hellenistic kings. His accounts of the entry of Demetrios I into Athens and of the Alexandria procession of Ptolemy II (respectively, Ath. 6. 253 b–f and 5. 201 b-203 e, Austin 35 and 219) are quoted elsewhere in this book. He is, by contrast, light on earlier material, perhaps because of the wealth of hellenistic sources on which he could draw.

Review of historical writings

Literary sources for events before the Roman takeover are intermittent, and with the exception of Justin there is a complete lacuna in the years 301–229. The most regrettable gap of all, perhaps, is the absence of detailed accounts of the careers of Lysimachos and Seleukos. Even for the third century, however, we can use inscriptions to reconstruct a narrative of sorts, and only isolated episodes remain seriously obscure. Historians have disagreed, for example, as to whether Antigonos II Gonatas of Macedonia ruled Athens for a period of years; there are uncertainties about the chronology of the Chremonidean war in the 260s; various battles, such as Kos and Andros in the mid-third century (p. 127), remain somewhat mobile in date; and there are famous unsolved puzzles, such as the revolt of Ptolemy 'the Son' in Ephesos in the 260s.[32] Other periods have problems too; the history of the later Ptolemies is represented chiefly by dynastic machinations, with some gaps only partly filled by events recorded in inscriptions and papyri; the sequence of native revolts is still a matter for discussion; not all the names and inter-relationships of the later Ptolemies and their queens are yet certain, just as with the later Seleukids. A particularly dire example of *terra incognita* is the history of the later Greek rulers of Baktria (northern Afghanistan), for some of whom the only evidence that they existed is in their coins; scholars tentatively restore a sequence of monarchs and estimate the lengths of their reigns from the numbers of coins that survive, a tenuous procedure providing no firm foundation for historical explanation (p. 456, n. 4).

In the light of what has been said above, it may be thought that the study of hellenistic history and culture is beset by insuperable problems, and that the paucity of sources accounts for, and perhaps justifies, the relative neglect of hellenistic history by modern writers, and its marginal place in university courses. Would the period look very different, however, if we had more literary sources? Would we be on firmer ground in trying to understand it?

It is not the lack of a continuous narrative that chiefly marks off this period from the preceding classical age, but the over-valuation of the preceding period and of particular categories of evidence. We can only begin to understand classical Greece fully when we liberate ourselves from the distorting presence of writers with strong world-views, such as Thucydides. The weight assigned to such 'classic' statements as theirs has not had an altogether benign influence. Historians of the classical period, as of the hellenistic, now rely crucially on non-literary evidence as well as historiographical sources; our understanding of the fifth-century Athenian empire and of the nature of classical Athenian democracy, once based on literary sources such as Thucydides and Diodoros, was completely transformed in the late nineteenth and twentieth centuries by discoveries of inscriptions. Again, there are many areas of classical history which literary and epigraphic evidence barely touches, and which we can scarcely begin to understand without approaching numismatic, artistic, and archaeological data; this is particularly true of social and economic history.

Similarly, the unevenness of the hellenistic narrative is partly the fault of ancient writers, whether surviving or lost, who concentrated on the wars and dynastic struggles of the immediate successors of Alexander, and on Rome's conquest of Greece, to the detriment of other aspects and periods. One possible reason for this may be inferred from Polybios, who at the outset of his history comments that

> in the times before these events [*of 220–216* BC], the events of the world happened, as it were, sporadically, since each of the things

16

that were done was, by initiatives, also by results, and by locations, at a remove from the rest. But from these times history happened, so to speak, in a corporeal form, and events in Italy and Libya are interwoven with those in Asia and of Greece, and the trend of all of them is towards one endpoint.

(Polyb. 1. 3. 3)

The relative neglect of some parts of the period may thus to some extent be inherent in the material, different historians treating different events without synthesizing a wider picture. It was exacerbated in the late hellenistic and Roman periods, when epitomes and digests entirely ousted parts of the narrative. It is far from certain that the rediscovery of a major literary work, such as the history of Hieronymos, would either change the narrative fundamentally or add to our understanding of key structures and social trends. What makes hellenistic history different and exciting, and may make it easier to achieve a balanced view of hellenistic society, is precisely the fact that *non-literary* evidence is so much more plentiful than pre-packaged narratives with their inevitably limited historical expertise and compromised viewpoints. Indeed, one of the themes of this book will be that there is no single 'hellenistic history', but a number of different histories.

Non-historical writings

The ancient tradition of historiography was closely focused on political and military matters, but for all periods of Greek and Roman history scholars are accustomed to making use of other classes of literary evidence to illuminate different aspects. Many contemporary works of creative literature, particularly poetry, contain evidence for society and culture; yet, like writings on religion, philosophy, and science, they have often been treated separately in general surveys of the period, or even left out of consideration. Such neglect is all the more unjustified since those who wrote about philosophy and mechanics saw themselves as literary artists.

Here only a brief enumeration of the sources will be given; more detail will be found in Chapters 5 (especially the section on philosophy), 7 (on literature), and 9 (on science).

The poetry of the hellenistic period, much of it written in a Ptolemaic milieu and sometimes referred to generically as Alexandrian, is well represented among extant works. Outside Egypt, but influenced by current styles, a major figure is Aratos of Soloi, author of didactic poems on astronomy and climatic signs (p. 245). Major early Alexandrian poets include Theokritos, the developer of bucolic poetry (poems about rural herdsmen), and his successors such as Moschos and Bion (second century BC) who are perhaps better described as pastoral (see pp. 237–9). The varied works of Kallimachos (Callimachus) place him in the forefront of third-century literature, alongside such luminaries as Apollonios of Rhodes, author of a new-style epic poem about the Argonauts. Among poets who to us seem minor figures, some were no doubt important to their contemporaries. Examples are the enigmatic Lyko-phron, with his seemingly interminable puzzle-poem *Alexandra* (pp. 247–8), and Nikandros (Nicander), whose surviving poems present the novel subject of poisons and poisonous animals. The *Mimes* of Herodas (pp. 249–51) came to light on papyrus only in the last century. Many hellenistic epigrams (not all of them Alexandrian) are preserved in anthologies, of which the first and most famous is Meleager's *Garland* (*c*.100 BC); leading exponents of the epigram included the third-century poets Asklepiades, Philetas, and Hedylos.

All this is directly of interest and value to the historian, and marks the hellenistic period as a golden age of Greek poetry whose practitioners easily measure up to the great lyric poets of the archaic age (*c*.700–480), who are so important for an understanding of the early development of élite society. Indirectly, if carefully interpreted, they give insights into social attitudes and practices to which classical sources rarely give us access.

Drama plays a smaller role than before, at least in extant literature. From the start of our period comes one of its greatest playwrights, the comic writer Menander of Athens, some of whose works are preserved on papyrus. His plays embody (and so encourage) new ways of presenting and discussing the life of the individual and the family. Apart from the mimes of Herodas, whose social context is the subject of debate, only fragments of new dramas survive. Although classical Athenian dramas continued to be performed, in a new political context they no longer had the same function of encapsulating the most heated debates of the day.

Our knowledge of philosophy and science is relatively full, both from contemporary and from later sources. From just before the start of the period we have numerous extant works by Aristotle of Stageira in Macedonia (384–322), head of the Lyceum at Athens and possibly tutor to the young Alexander. His treatises, perhaps based on lecture notes, cover subjects as diverse as logic, metaphysics, nature and life sciences, mind, ethics, politics, art, and poetics, and demonstrate how subject boundaries were fluid and how thinkers were willing to cross them. For the historian two works stand out. The *Politics* (*Politika*; a better translation of the title might be *Civics*), written around 330 BC, contains a wealth of information about the different Greek city-states. The *Constitution of the Athenians*, written by him or his assistants and discovered on papyrus in the late nineteenth century, is hugely valuable for Athenian history. Aristotle's wider *œuvre* had a greater impor-tance in later times, however; to medieval thinkers – perhaps to an excessive degree – he was the fountainhead of all knowledge of the cosmos.

Aristotle's successor, Theophrastos of Eresos in Lesbos, was equally multi-talented (pp. 179, 328, 341–4) and perhaps more firmly grounded in empirical data, as his many extant works show. Other works have fared less well: only one other survives complete, the philosophical treatise on harmony by

Aristoxenos, a younger associate of Aristotle. Burnt papyri and minor works of Epicurus have been found (p. 177), but for him and all other philosophers our main source is a later one, the ten books of *Lives and Opinions of Eminent Philosophers* attributed to Diogenes Laërtios (*c*. third century AD).

Besides the works of Aristotle and Theophrastos, extant contemporary sources for science (as opposed to philosophy in the narrower, modern sense) comprise works on astronomy by Aristarchos and Hipparchos, on mathematics and engineering by Archimedes and Euclid, on conic sections by Apollonios of Perge (*c*.200), and on physics by Philon (*c*.255) and Heron (later first century AD, but important for his recollections of his predecessors). All these writers were hugely influential, often establishing scientific terminologies still in use today.

Many details of scientific thought have to be filled in from later sources, particularly Greek and Roman writers of the imperial period. From the end of the hellenistic period, authors such as Strabo and the Roman architectural writer Vitruvius (both writing under Augustus) preserve many elements of hellenistic thought, often naming particular thinkers and inventors. So, too, does the Roman writer Pliny the Elder (first century AD) in his compendious *Natural History*.

Particularly problematic is the reconstruction of hellenistic medicine, for which we must rely on secondary sources. No primary works survive, though a long treatise *On the Material of Medicine* (*Peri hylês iatrikês* or *De materia medica*) by Dioscorides (Pedanius Dioscorides from Anazarbos in Cilicia), dealing with medicinal drugs, dates from the first century AD. It mainly covers sub-stances derived from plants but also from animals and minerals, and represents a major synthesis based on extensive travels, eye-witness experience, and research into earlier writers. Medical practice and theory are treated by the Roman writer Celsus (Aulus Cornelius Celsus, writing under the emperor Tiberius, AD 14–37), and by three authors writing in Greek: Rufus (later first century AD), Soranus (fl. under Trajan and Hadrian), the last two both from Ephesos, and above all the compendious works of Galen of Pergamon (AD 129–*c*.199). Parts of Galen and Rufus survive only in Arabic translations.

For astronomy, geography, and mathematics Claudius Ptolemaeus (Ptolemy; mid-second century AD) is a vital source (see pp. 349, 352, 354–5). Another is Pappos of Alexandria (p. 330), whose partially extant *Synagôgê* (*Gathering* or *Collection*) is a posthumous assemblage of his treatises; it includes commentaries on Euclid, Apollonios, Ptolemy, and other earlier writers, as well as useful information about Hipparchos. The extant works of three Neoplatonist philosophers play a similar role. Proclus (AD 401 or 412–485), from Lykia, wrote treatises on astronomy and commentaries on Euclid and Ptolemy. Ioannes (John) Philoponus of Alexandria (*c*. AD 490–570s) discussed Aristotle's physics and the nature of the universe. Also in the mid-sixth century, Simplicius of Athens wrote commentaries on Aristotle, preserving the substance of many discussions during the nine hundred years after his death.

Despite the gap in time, it is possible to place considerable weight on these late testimonies; Greek scientists were always conscious of their predecessors' work, and sought to validate their own contributions by referring back to them.

Literary and scientific writings are important evidence for the Greeks' view of themselves and for the nature of Greek society.

Non-literary sources

A striking feature of the hellenistic period, compared with the classical, is the very large number of non-literary texts that survive, and their preponderance over historiographical data. On one level, such sources – documentary papyri, inscriptions, coins and archaeology – give us a much more direct access to the period. On the other hand, these sources raise special problems of interpretation and require specialized skills in order to be appraised directly. They cannot speak to us in their own voice, as Thucydides or Polybios can; we must analyse them both internally and in relation to each other so that we can interrogate them rigorously, not subjectively.

Papyri

One of the most important classes of such data is that of the tens of thousands of papyri preserved in Egypt. However, since they are relevant almost exclusively to Egyptian history and not the Greek world in general, they are discussed in Chapter 6.

Inscriptions

The study of the period in general benefits greatly from the fact that a far wider range of inscriptions ('epigraphic' evidence) survives than from earlier periods of Greek history.[33] The present book quotes from many such documents. Whereas papyri often contain exact dates according to the Ptolemaic calendar, however, most inscriptions have to be dated interpretatively on the basis of their letter-forms. The shape of the lettering often indicates when and where a text was carved, within broad limits; a specialist epigrapher will typically be able to infer a date within a quarter-century or so. Assignment to a particular place may be based on the language of a text, which may be associated with a particular city. The limits vary, however; simple gravestones, invariably undated, may be hard to place within a century, while other inscriptions preserved out of context, with no archaeological provenance, cannot always be given a place of origin. At the other end of the spectrum, a decree naming a king, even without a findspot, can usually be dated to a particular reign – though since kings of a particular dynasty often had the same names, and were not numbered as they are now, it is not always certain which king is meant.

The most important class of epigraphic texts is that of civic documents of Greek *poleis* (city-states). Most cities selected certain public transactions for inscribing on stone, even when they were under the domination of Alexander and his successors (Fig. 1.1–1.4). Not only did the number of cities increase in this period, but they devoted increasing energy to the preservation of such records. The huge increase in the numbers of inscriptions from Greek cities of Asia Minor is one of the most striking features of the evidence, and in the absence of continuous narratives and papyri they are particularly valuable for the study of the western Seleukid empire. Among the evidence for the economic history of communities the inscriptions of Delos, especially the temple accounts of the curators (*hieropoioi*), are particularly rich in data (see e.g. Austin 104, from the accounts for 279 BC).[34] The archetypal document of the age, however, is the decree of the Council and People (e.g. *SEG* i. 363, quoted on pp. 78–9), which will often preserve the names of politically active citizens, or record a city's dealings with a king.[35] Numerically, however, gravestones are probably the commonest texts, a fact which in some cases has permitted demographic studies of urban communities such as Rhodes.[36] Gravestones, lists of names recorded for some collective purpose, and civic documents containing the names of politically active citizens offer many possibilities for prosopography (studies of the links between related individuals through time), which can in turn enable us to trace changes in political élites and elsewhere.[37] Another important class of documents (some of which are *polis* decrees, as already noted), is that of 'royal correspondence'.[38]

Coins

The historical evidence of coins is no less important than in the classical period. One of the most remarkable features of the evidence is the degree of standardization across the hellenistic world, which makes exceptions and deviations all the more significant.[39] Another is the emergence of smaller denominations, pointing to increased monetarization of the everyday economy, though it is likely that the majority of transactions were still in kind (see e.g. the third-century decree of the city of Gortyn about its new bronze coinage, *Syll.*[3] 525, Austin 105).[40]

Following the lead set by his father, Alexander the Great promoted a uniform currency across his empire,[41] though not to the exclusion of regional and civic issues, and adopted the Attic weight-standard of 17.2 g for the silver drachma. After his death this remained the norm except in Egypt, where Ptolemy I moved gradually to a lighter standard, fixed at 14.3 g by about 290 BC. Coins issued in the name of Alexander were minted by kings and cities for over two hundred years, while coinage in the name of cities, though it continued sporadically, occupied a less important place. Confusingly for the non-specialist, some cities at certain times issued coins in the name

Figure 1.1 Squeeze (paper impression) of honorific decree by an élite Athenian military corps for Demetrios Poliorketes, *c.*303/2 BC (*ISE* 7; *SEG* xxv. 149; see also p. 65 below). Note the *stoichedon* arrangement of the letters (in rows and columns), characteristic of classical Athenian public documents; its purpose is to make the text visually striking, a part of the monument, rather than simply to aid legibility. (Digital image courtesy of Centre for the Study of Ancient Documents, University of Oxford.)

of Alexander or in the name of the king of their region, rather than in their own name simply. Ephesos in Asia Minor, when under Ptolemaic rule, even struck both royal and civic issues on the Ptolemaic standard, which hitherto it had not used[42] (Fig. 1.5–1.10).

There are two principal aspects to the evidence of coins, the ideological and the economic, though they overlap. To issue coins, validated by one's portrait or name, is a way of claiming, and actually creating, both economic and political authority. Alexander's portrait was first put on coins by Lysimachos; to honour Alexander's memory was to endow oneself with legitimacy by asserting an inherited right to rule, but at the same time was an (admittedly only self-authenticated) certification of the metallic purity and commercial trustworthiness of the coins. Both these factors may explain the persistence of 'Alexanders' among new coin issues – just as they may account for the use of the image of Lysimachos after his death by the cities he had

Figure 1.2   Decree of the Samian *demos* for Metrodoros son of –inginos of Sidon, *c.*275 BC (W. G. Forrest, *Horos*, 5 (1987), 91–3). The beginning of the father's name is unrestorable; perhaps significantly, the cutter seems to have made two attempts at it, since line 10 is cut in a *rasura*, a recess in the stone due to an erasure. The letter-forms are typical of good stone-cutting in Aegean *poleis* in the third century BC. (Ashmolean Museum, University of Oxford, inv. 2.31; digital image courtesy of Centre for the Study of Ancient Documents, University of Oxford.)

ruled in the Propontis and Hellespont:[43] this perhaps gives the lie to the conventional image of Lysimachos as an unpopular ruler.

Figure 1.3 Squeeze of dedication from Itanos (eastern Crete), a Ptolemaic naval base, *c.*217–209 BC (*I. Cret.* iii. 4. 18). Lucius son of Gaius (a Roman citizen; the names are not enough to identify him) dedicates a nymphaeum and reservoir to Ptolemy IV and his queen, Arsinoë. The wide letters are characteristic of monumental texts. (Digital image courtesy of Centre for the Study of Ancient Documents, University of Oxford.)

Figure 1.4 Squeeze of manumission document from Sousa in Media of 183 BC (*SEG* vii. 17). A certain Kalliphon sets free an unnamed slave. The letters reflect manuscript forms as opposed to the monumental and public scripts characteristic of Old Greece. (Digital image courtesy of Centre for the Study of Ancient Documents, University of Oxford.)

To use one's own portrait, or those of one's ancestors, particularly on the same coin as Alexander's, was to go still further. Once the Successors became kings at the end of the fourth century, they gradually began to use their portraits on the obverse, retaining Alexander on the reverse, though some were issued in his name alone. Ptolemy I appears on coins before *c.*300 BC; Demetrios I of Macedonia, too, appears during his own lifetime. Seleukos I issued different coin types from other monarchies alongside 'Alexanders', and did not place his portrait on coins; Antiochos I was the first Seleukid to do so. The first Attalid ruler, Philetairos of Pergamon, though independent

Figure 1.5 Gold stater (16.81 g) in the name of Alexander. Magnesia-on-Meander, *c.*323–319 BC (*SNG* 2756). Obverse: head of Athena. Reverse: Nike. (Ashmolean Museum, University of Oxford.)

Figure 1.6 Silver tetradrachm (16.91 g) in the name of Alexander. Miletos or Mylasa, *c.*300–280 BC (*SNG* 2791). Obv.: head of Herakles. Rev.: Zeus. (Ashmolean Museum, University of Oxford.)

Figure 1.7. Silver didrachm (6.50 g). Samos, *c.*300 BC (J. P. Barron, *The Silver Coins of Samos* (London, 1966), p. 214, no. 2 *a*). Obv.: Lion's mask. Rev.: forepart of ox. (Ashmolean Museum, University of Oxford.)

Figure 1.8 Silver hemidrachm (1.74 g). Samos, *c.*300 BC (Barron, *Silver Coins of Samos*, p. 217, no. 5 *a*). Obv.: Lion's mask. Rev.: forepart of ox. (Ashmolean Museum, University of Oxford.)

Figure 1.9 Silver hemidrachm (2.39 g) of Aitolian League, *c.*220–189 BC. Obv.: head of Atalante. Rev.: boar. (Ashmolean Museum, University of Oxford.)

Figure 1.10 Bronze coin (6.34 g) of Antiochos IV. Apameia, *c.*169/8–164 BC. Obv.: head of Antiochos. Rev.: Zeus. (Ashmolean Museum, University of Oxford.)

from 284, did not at first take the royal title; he coined in Alexander's name and later that of Seleukos I, his nominal overlord. Only later did his successors put his image on coins,[44] and they never employed their own image as living rulers, even when they eventually adopted a distinctive coin of the realm (see below). This may be related to the pretence of civic status that the Attalid rulers kept up in relation to their home city of Pergamon.

For a city, to issue coins – not all cities were rich enough to do so, or were permitted to do so – was to claim and, by the very act, to some degree actualize an enlarged status on the world stage and express a real or fictive independence. It gave them an opportunity to play safe by declaring allegiance to a dynasty: indirectly by putting Alexander on the coins, directly by using the head of the ruler or his ancestors. The symbolic importance placed on *polis* coinage can be gauged from the fact that coin-forging was regularly a capital crime (see Austin 106, *Syll.*[3] 530, a list of convictions from Dymê in Achaea in the third century).

From a narrowly economic viewpoint, rulers might try to regulate economic activity by imposing standard issues, but the suggestion that they imposed their own coinages to the exclusion of all others is hard to verify. Even in Egypt, where there was little tradition of coin use before Alexander, it may be that Ptolemaic issues became standard almost by default, and the requirement that foreign traders exchange their coins (Austin 238, BD 84, *PCZ* 59021)[45] may have been merely a fiscal device, a way of creaming off a little silver on every transaction. In the Ptolemaic possessions outside Egypt, as in Seleukid areas, the simultaneous circulation of coins issued by different monarchies points to lively trade. In Attalid territory a lighter standard and a new type, the 'cistophoric' coinage (bearing an image of the golden basket of Dionysos), was introduced during the early second century (p. 316), but the Attic weights were not immediately abandoned, perhaps being minted for external transactions.[46] On the one hand, different kingdoms might represent more or less separate circulation spheres, with Alexanders dominant in Seleukid territory and coins of Ptolemaic weight in Egypt and the external possessions. In Egypt the use of Ptolemaic coins was certainly predominant and perhaps legally required; but in overseas possessions non-Ptolemaic coins circulated too, and in areas which changed hands from time to time, such as Hollow Syria, which the Seleukids recaptured in 200 BC, the existing Ptolemaic coins and the Seleukid coins of Attic weight continued to circulate together and some of the latter were even minted on the Ptolemaic standard. Generally, however, Seleukid provincial governors and Greek cities were not encouraged to mint, particularly in gold and silver.[47] The patterns of trade which the circulation of hellenistic coins illustrates are the subject of active investigation at present, and many old and new problems await an answer.[48]

On a narrower, documentary front, coins are sometimes evidence of particular historical events or of dynastic history. This is the spectacularly the case with the later Greek kings of Baktria (pp. 285, 456, n. 4).

Archaeology

The archaeology of the period is harder to characterize than that of the classical period, not least because of the huge geographical area involved. Architecture and sculpture have always loomed large in the consumption of hellenistic culture by western audiences, and references will be made in the following chapters to standing monuments of the period and to the results of excavation, particularly in the context of changes in urban form. In Chapter 3, coins and portrait sculptures will illuminate the self-presentation of rulers, and artistic representations will offer evidence for changes in the idea of the individual and of how identity was constituted, especially for women. A wider archaeological synthesis, however, is beyond the scope of this book.

In terms of the monumental remains of cities and sanctuaries, our knowledge of the foremost city of the Greek world, Alexandria, is frustratingly limited. In compensation, it is an easy matter to point to the grandeur of the acropolis of Pergamon with its great sculpted altar; to the stoas (open-sided colonnades) of the new marketplaces at Athens and Miletos; to new temples at sanctuaries like Didyma; to the excavated public and cultic complexes of new Greek towns of Asia, even as far afield as Ai Khanum in Afghanistan; and to the lavish dedications by foreign potentates at the healing shrine of Amphiaraos in northern Attica. At the level of domestic architecture, however, a rather limited range of case studies tends to be drawn upon, such as the fine houses at Delos and Priene and the visitors' residences at the aforementioned Amphiareion;[49] the period still awaits a synthesis of excavation results. (On town plans, see Chapter 3.)

The principal focus of art-historical research has been sculpture; it is primarily from sculpture that we take conventional artistic divisions of the period, such as J. J. Pollitt's 'rococo, realism, and the exotic', or Andrew Stewart's early (*c*.320–*c*.220), high (*c*.220–*c*.150), and late (*c*.150–30).[50] By contrast, standard works on hellenistic art devote relatively little space to mosaics, wall-paintings, and so-called minor art forms such as pottery, painted grave-stelae, mouldmade bowls, gems, coins, and cameos; yet those probably constituted the bulk of artistic production.[51] Much remains to be learned about the material cultures of different parts of Alexander's empire, though the analysis of sculpture itself is beginning to indicate the persistence and autonomous development of distinct local styles, particularly in the Aegean.[52] Quite possibly a greater quantity of objects is known than from the classical period, but an archaeological synthesis is still lacking. Artefact studies, indeed, are in a state of flux; many objects safely stored in museums lack any record of where they were found or excavated; the great majority of portrait statues of hellenistic rulers are lost (perhaps because they were made of bronze rather than the relatively less prestigious marble), and are known only from Roman copies. The number of excavated hellenistic sites outside Greece certainly exceeds that within Greece, but here too a general overview is lacking. The study of pottery typologies has so far produced only a few detailed corpora (bodies of material cogently dated and stylistically linked) against which new material can be tested.[53]

An artefact which contributes much to our understanding of trade is the stamped amphora handle. The amphora (*amphoreus*) or two-handled transport jar had a capacity of 20 to 25 litres and was typically used for oil, wine, and preserved foodstuffs. It often carried an impressed control mark on one handle, added before the jar was fired. Whereas the broken body-sherds of a jar may occasion little interest from excavators, stamped handles are easily recognized as items worth preserving. They usually indicate the origin of the jar, sometimes the date, and with due caution they can be the subject of statistical analysis. Many tens of thousands have been published from the Mediterranean and Black Sea areas, and study is beginning to reveal broad patterns such as the importance of Thasos as an amphora producer and the dominance of Rhodes in maritime transport (not necessarily of Rhodian produce), and to refine the chronology of other artefacts by association.[54]

Another area where archaeological evidence is beginning to illuminate new areas of hellenistic life is field survey, the systematic inspection, usually intensive and often without excavation, of the surface of a landscape in order to retrieve remains of abandoned settlements and other sites. The vast majority of finds are sherds (broken pieces) of pottery and roof-tile, with occasional 'small finds' such as inscriptions and coins. Consequently, the data illuminate a much wider range of site types and sizes than traditional archaeological methods, from substantial villages all the way down to rural storage huts and animal pens, from major rural sanctuaries to tiny cult places serving a restricted locality.[55]

Many of these surveys are as yet published only in a preliminary form. In addition, because of the state of pottery chronology there are variations in the dates assigned to the hellenistic period and its sub-phases. With those cautions in mind, the data can still help towards a provisional understanding of changes in demography, cultic landscapes, and the relationship between town and country.

The start of the period saw large-scale emigration from Greece, which may have led to reduced population at home and certainly brought about the settlement of Greeks and Macedonians in new cities and old, expropriated territories all across the Near East. The effects of these and other global changes upon the geographical and human landscapes of the old and new Greek worlds are only beginning to be understood, but it has become axiomatic among historians that no universal set of phenomena is to be expected. Demographic variability certainly seems to be borne out, even at a very local level, in the results of surveys within 'Old Greece'.

For cultic landscapes, a drop in activity at rural shrines has been inferred, suggesting a change in the relationship between urban and rural communities.[56] Rural settlement, however, seems to intensify in certain parts of mainland Greece and some islands. In the southern Argolid there is an increase in the numbers of small rural sites between c.350 and c.250 BC, as well as in the proportion of storage pottery at these sites; these data suggest agricultural intensification.[57] A similar pattern is seen slightly later in Aitolia,[58] an area whose cities banded together into a powerful federal state during the third century and may have prospered as a result. In Achaea, survey has revealed a significant recolonization of the rural landscape.[59] In Methana, site numbers increase in the early hellenistic period, a phenomenon the surveyors link to the existence of a Ptolemaic naval base.[60]

Conversely, in other areas there seems to be a less intensive use of the landscape. At this point, however, we should first consider a number of statements in the sources which appear to inform us about the economic and social condition of certain areas. In the early or mid-third century the author of a somewhat satirical description of central Greece describes Boiotian towns in positive terms:

> The city (of Tanagra) lies on a rocky height...The entrance halls of their houses and the encaustic paintings they display give the city a beautiful appearance. The city does not enjoy an abundance of agricultural produce, but it ranks first in Boiotia for its wine. The inhabitants, though wealthy, are plain in their style of living; they

are all farmers and not workmen. They know how to respect justice, good faith, and hospitality....

The city (of Thebes) lies in the heart of Boiotia.... Though an ancient city, its street-plan is modern in design ... the land is all well watered, green, and covered with hills, and has the largest number of gardens of any city in Greece.

('Herakleides of Crete', 1. 8–9, 12; Austin 83)[61]

In contrast, Polybios states that public affairs in Boiotia during the late third and early second centuries were at a low ebb, and that family fortunes were squandered on conspicuous consumption rather than passed on as inheritances (20. 6. 1–6, Austin 84). At first sight this indicates a turn for the worse in Boiotian society; but his account is almost certainly tainted by prejudice.[62] Likewise, his reference to the short-sightedness of the people of Elis in the north-western Peloponnese, who devolved civic functions such as the administration of justice to the countryside with the result that the rich neglected their life in the town (4. 73. 5–74. 2, Austin 85), seems rhetorically coloured and in any case refers only to the élite. Finally, it is hard to know what evidential status to attribute to statements by Polybios which imply that Greece in his day was suffering from a failure of family reproduction, resulting in a falling population (36. 17. 5–10, Austin 81).

It would be naïve to suppose that either of our authors can be relied on as scientific; even the seemingly optimistic 'Herakleides' must be suspected of having a rhetorical purpose – he devotes the conclusion of his work, for example, to demonstrating that Hellas proper extends as far north as Thessaly but no further, implicitly excluding Macedonia. Their statements about social change, while they must be considered seriously, should not be allowed to pre-determine the interpretation of archaeological data, to which we can now turn.

In Boiotia the survey data do indeed point towards a widespread abandonment of sites in or after the third century, including two towns;[63] but rather than being due to the moral inadequacy or folly of the locals, as Polybios might lead us to think, this could be the local effect of events such as the violent destruction and subsequent rebuilding of Thebes in the late fourth century.

Similar cautions must apply to Attica. The archaeological data for changes in rural settlement are hardly in a state from which reliable conclusions can yet be drawn, despite the optimism of some scholars. Epigraphic and textual evidence are generally held to indicate a slight fall in population, but the data are hard to interpret. There was certainly emigration to Alexandria, but the reduced numbers of inscriptions from demes (constituent villages of the Athenian *polis*) could be due to lack of funds rather than falling population. The fall in the number of Attic inscribed gravestones and those of metics (resident foreigners) might be explained by changes in commemorative practices, the reduced numbers of ephebes (élite military trainees) by changes in recruitment. Against the likelihood of net emigration, we must set the fact that the Athenians seem to have had no problem recruiting *bouleutai* (councillors), even when the *boulê* (council) was increased in size at the end of the third century.[64] On the archaeological front, much more work is needed before rural depopulation can be securely affirmed for Attica.

In north-western Kea the desertion of sites is clearly dated within the third century; the surveyors suggest that this may be due to the amalgamation of landholdings into larger estates, which promotes and is in turn promoted by the disappearance of the *polis* of Koressos.[65]

In Melos the picture is mixed; at the classical–hellenistic transition there is continuity at some sites but also a continuation of the classical trend towards nucleation; these changes may indicate rural depopulation and the increasing predominance of the main town.[66]

Finally, the data from the Laconia Survey indicate a slight drop in overall site numbers; but this generalization conceals two contradictory tendencies. Parts of the survey area closest to Sparta and the Eurotas plain yielded evidence of many small agricultural installations in the early and middle hellenistic period, while the part of the survey area furthest away from Sparta seems to undergo a concentration of settlement into smaller, more prosperous sites.[67] Here, too, local factors must be borne in mind, such as the decline in the Spartans' power and the gradual erosion of their territory in favour of the smaller towns of Laconia.

There seems to be no clear pattern in Greece, an area for which the data are relatively full. One might have expected, for example, that areas under Macedonian control behaved differently from others; this does not appear to be the case. Nor is it immediately transparent whether agricultural intensification in any given area is to be taken as a measure of prosperity or of crisis. The data certainly suggest that local factors sometimes took precedence over global trends.

Across the hellenistic world generally, from western Greece to Afghanistan, on the basis of some fifty survey projects there appears to be a broad trend – which may have been under way before the start of the period – towards increased urbanization, again with regional variations: here a static situation, there dispersal of population into rural settlements with agricultural intensification, elsewhere the concentration of population into towns and the relative neglect of the countryside.[68] The data are still the subject of analysis, however, and it may be many years before historians reach a consensus about how to read them and unravel their social implications.

Conclusion

This rapid review of the range of evidence will, I hope, have convinced the reader that, far from being the inferior historical period for which it has often been taken, the period after Alexander the Great is not only rich in evidence but poses crucial questions of historical interpretation which any society that calls itself civilized would do well to consider. No less than the classical period, this was a time of rapid social and cultural change. The changes in the location of political power and in how political and religious authority were constructed; the confrontation of (or, if you prefer, exchange of information between) supposedly alien cultures; the economic struggle between (or symbiosis of) town and country; the social roles performed by the creators of literature, philosophy, and of all kinds of learned writings; possible changes in the construction of the individual's role in civil society and as a member of a gender group – all these, and more aspects besides, make the hellenistic period more than usually worthy of investigation, and challenge us to examine our assumptions about how societies structure themselves and what factors are uppermost in their evolution.

2

ALEXANDER AND HIS
SUCCESSORS TO 276 BC

The hellenistic period embodies a paradox: the extension of the culture and influence of Hellas (Greece) into the non-Greek-speaking world took place after the decline of major Greek states such as Athens, Sparta, and Thebes, and as a result of the rise of what some southern Greeks considered a non-Greek kingdom, Macedonia. (Greek culture had, of course, spread to new areas earlier through colonization, but Alexander's conquests accelerated the process and gave it a new dynamic.) This chapter will first look back briefly to the condition of Greece before Alexander's reign, and then at his conquests and their effects. Wars among Alexander's successors led to the creation of new monarchies and dynasties. Two of Alexander's commanders did not become founders of dynasties, but their careers are for that very reason revealing and worthy of study in their own right: Eumenes and Lysimachos. There follows consideration of the other non-Greek enemy to penetrate the Greek world in this period, the Gauls, and of the possible effects of Alexander's campaigns and the wars of the Successors on the demography of Greece.

The fourth century and after

Classical Greece was a world of separate city-states (*poleis*), political communities of citizens based upon urban centres; it was not a system of territorial nation-states like the modern world. Despite this apparent fragmentation, the city-states formed a culture-sphere broadly united by language, custom, and religion, which embraced not only mainland Greece and the neighbouring islands but hundreds of Greek cities around the coasts of the western Mediterranean (notably Sicily and Italy), North Africa, Asia Minor, the Dardanelles and Sea of Marmara, and the Black Sea. The Greek-speaking world embraced a wide and diverse area; some of the most prosperous and powerful *poleis* lay far away from the Greek homeland, such as Syracuse in Sicily and Cyrene (Kyrene) in Libya.

Bordering on this 'Greek world' were large, powerful states such as the Carthaginian empire in North Africa, the ancient kingdom of Egypt, and the

Persian empire, with all of which the Greeks had extensive contacts, friendly and hostile. Other civilizations based on city-states were those of the Etruscans in central Italy and the Phoenicians in the regions later called Lebanon and Palestine. To the north were less well-known, semi-urbanized iron age societies such as the Thracians and Skythians.

The great majority of Greek *poleis* were not strongly democratic like fifth-century Athens; though many fourth-century *poleis* had a democratic constitution, this did not necessarily entail radical democracy. Some, indeed, had a limited, often property-based franchise or even an oligarchy (*oligarchia*, 'rule of the few'). Almost all of the city-states had cast off monarchical governments at an early date, though some, particularly in Sicily, were ruled by 'tyrants' (*tyrannoi*), dictators who seized power by force but were not necessarily uncultured or oppressive, even enjoying some popular support. Sparta, exceptionally among southern Greek states, retained a dual kingship, but its kings functioned mainly as military commanders and were subject to political control. In the north there were Greek-speaking monarchies such as Epeiros (Epirus), Illyria, and Macedonia; while in areas such as Thessaly (east-central Greece) and Karia (south-western Asia Minor) the fourth century saw the rise of powerful family dynasties ruling from an urban centre which was also a *polis*. Other cities, again, were at times subject to foreign kings, such as the Greek cities of Asia Minor, which for much of the classical period were forced to pay tribute to the Achaemenid kings of Persia.[1]

The cultural forms we associate most closely with classical Greece – literature, political systems, philosophy, and so on – developed in many different city-states, beginning in the archaic period (*c.*700–480); but the most spectacular developments had taken place in Athens during the late fifth century at a time when it ruled an empire incorporating hundreds of other Greek cities. The defeat of Athens by Sparta at the end of the Peloponnesian war in 403 did not mark a sharp break in political or cultural history; the Spartans did not destroy Athens, and in a few years it was once again a major power. There followed several decades of shifting alliances and wars, when, besides the already strong *poleis* of Athens, Sparta, and Corinth, a fourth, Thebes in Boiotia, was powerful for a time. With the help of the Persians the Spartans attempted to impose a peace treaty on the warring Greek states, which did not hold. The Thebans' power culminated in 371 when they defeated the Spartans at Leuktra in Boiotia; in the next few years a series of Theban-led invasions of the Peloponnese led to the liberation of Messenia (the south-western Peloponnese) from Spartan rule and a loss of Spartan influence, confirmed by an indecisive battle at Mantineia in eastern Arkadia (362). In these decades the fifth-century Athenian empire was revived in a new form, known today as the Second Athenian Confederacy; in theory it was less oppressive than its predecessor, but it fell victim to allied revolts.

Meanwhile, a new power in northern Greece was causing concern to the cities of the south. Philip II (r. 360/59–338) was building Macedonia into a military and economic power, and seeking to dominate mainland Greece. In 338, after two decades of warfare, he established his hegemony by victory at Chaironeia in Boiotia. He then inaugurated the league of Corinth, an alliance of all Greek cities (Sparta stood aloof) with himself as leader (*hêgemôn*); officially its purpose was to make war on the Persian empire, but it was also the instrument of Macedonian domination. Garrisons were installed in certain cities.

The wars among the Greeks in the early and mid-fourth century, and the Greeks' subsequent defeat by Macedonia, have often been seen as proving the obsolescence of the city-states system; the battle of Chaironeia has even been thought to mark the 'end of the *polis*', though others have placed this at different, later dates such as the end of the Chremonidean war in the 260s.[2] This is grossly premature. True, the fourth century brought the rise of federal leagues and the restoration of Persian power over the Greeks of western Asia Minor, so that from one point of view 'the independent city-state had declined long before the defeat at Chaironeia'; but it is clear that 'the *polis* in the true sense of the word existed and prospered throughout the Hellenistic and Roman periods' – the 'true sense' being that of a self-governing political community (whether wholly independent or not) that was also a state and had an urban centre.[3]

Not only does the fourth century have a better claim than the fifth to be the golden age of Athenian democracy, but one of the most marked features of Alexander's reign was the adoption of democratic institutions (promoted by him in Ionia: Arrian, 1. 17, Austin 4; Austin 5, BD 2, *Syll.*[3] 283, Tod 192). The trend continued under his successors. The characteristic political forms – popular assembly, magistrates elected or drawn by lot, representative council, and so on – spread to the majority of cities. Of course, form is not the same as content, and it often used to be claimed that democracy under the Macedonian kings was a sham. But as the 'epigraphic habit' spread across the newly enlarged Greek world, cities with democratic decision-making processes inscribed their public decisions on stone in ever-increasing numbers. The language of decrees, originally imitated from Athens, was adapted to express local variants of democracy; but broadly we see a standardized process, whereby proposals emanate from city officials, the council, or the assembly, and must be ratified by popular vote in order to take effect.[4]

Although, at certain junctures during the hellenistic period, popular participation in the government of Athens was restricted or even suspended, the city usually functioned as an active democracy till the second century and beyond. Even if the rich, as seems likely, dominated the democracy more strongly than in classical Athens – so that, as Aristotle put it, states with a democratic form could act more like oligarchies (*Politics*, 4. 1292 b 15) – it has been observed of Athens in the third and second centuries that 'The most lasting impression produced by a study of the inscriptions is that of a community regulating its affairs in exemplary fashion.'[5]

More generally, the hellenistic period was one in which participatory government was widely diffused. Strabo (writing in the first century BC but evidently looking back to a time when kings and cities were the main protagonists in Greek international relations) speaks of how kings manipulate cities through benefactions, not oratory: 'persuasion through words', he says, 'is not a characteristic of kings but of orators; we call persuasion royal when they bring benefactions and lead people in the direction they want to' (9. 2. 40 (415)). As Gauthier points out, this only makes sense if Strabo believes cities are governed by assemblies where rhetoric counts.[6]

From the fourth century on, there may have been increasing economic interaction among Greek *poleis* and between Greece and the outside world.[7] Civic administration also becomes increasingly refined, as we see from such documents as a harbour law of Thasos (Austin 108), Delian regulations on the sale of wood (Austin 109, *Syll.*[3] 975), and Athenian market regulations of the late second century (Austin 111).[8] From Pergamon (which, though in practical terms subject to a king, was every inch the Greek *polis* in its civic administration) we have a remarkable document of late hellenistic or Roman date which preserves the Attalid regulations for the upkeep of the streets, city wall, and water supply (Austin 216, *OGIS* 483).[9] In short, the *polis* flourished.

Alexander's legacy

Philip intended to follow up his success at Chaironeia by invading the Persian empire, centred on modern Iran and extending from the frontiers of India in the east to Asia Minor and Egypt in the west. This would have satisfied those fourth-century propagandists who wanted a 'panhellenic' leader (one 'of all Hellenes') to unite the Greeks by directing their energies against a common enemy; but in 336, when an advance army was already in Asia Minor, Philip was assassinated. His 20-year-old son Alexander – Alexander the Great – took up the task, but first had to subdue Macedonia's hostile neighbours, the Thracians and Illyrians. He then suppressed a Greek revolt, punishing the people of Thebes by razing their city to the ground (Arr. 1. 9. 9–10; cf. iii–3 Plutarch *Alexander*, 10. 6–11, Diodoros,. 17. 14, both in Austin 2; it was refounded by Cassander in 316). In 334 he crossed to Asia Minor with an army of Macedonians, Thessalians, and other Greeks.[10]

Victories in battles and sieges brought Alexander control of western Asia Minor (334), then Syria and Palestine (332) (Fig. 2.1). He rejected an offer made by the Persian king, Dareios (Darius) III, to surrender the western half of his empire, and seized Egypt. In 331 he captured Babylonia (roughly central Iraq), capturing the Persian royal treasury, which reportedly contained 50,000 talents (some 1,500 tonnes) of gold – a fortune of almost unimaginable size. Then, in quick succession, he took three of the four royal capitals: Sousa, Persepolis, and Pasargadai. At Persepolis the sixth-century palace built by Cyrus the Great was burnt down (Arr. 3. 18. 10–12; Diod. 17. 70–2, Austin 9); whether a deliberate act or an accident, he could present it as the Greeks' long-sought revenge for Xerxes' invasion in 481–479 and the burning of their temples.

When, in 330, Dareios was assassinated by Bessos, a pretender to the Persian throne, Alexander was undisputed 'lord of Asia' (*kyrios tês Asias*). That, indeed, is his title in a dedication from the city of Lindos on the island of Rhodes, probably dating from that year: 'King Alexander, having defeated Dareios in battle and become lord of Asia, sacrificed to Lindian Athena in accordance with a prophecy in the priesthood of Theogenes son of Pistokrates' (*Lindian Chronicle* (*FGH* 532), ch. 38, Burstein 46 *c*).

Alexander and his army were not content merely to return home laden with booty. Between 330 and 325 they marched through the eastern Persian empire, travelling even as far as the Punjab, where in 327 Alexander defeated king Poros but made him his ally. Now, however, the army refused to go further east and Alexander granted their wish (Arr. 5. 28–9. 1, Austin 12). Turning down the river Indus to the coast, he continued to sack cities and massacre the inhabitants. In 325, after an ill-judged and calamitous crossing of the Gedrosian desert (south-eastern Iran), Alexander seems to have decided to consolidate his empire for a time; but at this point his behaviour apparently became more autocratic. His treasurer, Harpalos, fled to Greece taking 6,000 mercenaries and 5,000 talents (Arr. 3. 6. 4–7; cf. Harding 120, Plut. *Lives of the Ten Orators*, 846 a–b = Philochoros, *FGH* 328 fr. 163).[11] There, plans for revolt were laid.

338	battle of Chaironeia
337	Hellenic league declares war on Persia
336	assassination of Philip at Aigai; accession of Alexander III
	accession of Darius III in Persia
335	sack of Thebes
334	Alexander crosses to Asia Minor
334–331	conquest of W. and S. Asia Minor, Egypt, Cyrene
331	foundation of Alexandria
	Alexander reaches Babylon, Susa
330–329	Alexander at Persepolis
330	Alexander at Ekbatana
	death of Darius
329–326	Alexander conquers Baktria, Sogdiana, invades India
326	Alexander's troops mutiny and he turns west again
325	crossing of the Gedrosian desert
324	Alexander at Susa
323	Alexander at Babylon; his death

Figure 2.1 The age of Alexander, 338–323 BC

Alexander may have wished to centre his kingdom upon the old heartland of the Persian empire, or perhaps Babylon. He persisted with attempts to reconcile the Macedonian élite to this idea, and to harmonize relations between them and the Persian nobility. It may be a sign of his readiness to be even-handed that in 325 two Macedonian commanders accused of perpetrating injustices against the population of Media were put to death (Arr. 6. 27. 3–5, Austin 13). At Sousa in 324 Alexander held a great banquet to celebrate their fusion into a single ruling people, marrying his officers to Persian women (Arr. 7. 4. 4–8; part in Austin 14). He had already taken as his first wife Rhoxane, daughter of a Baktrian king (Arr. 4. 19. 5–6); now he married a daughter of Dareios and possibly even a third wife, a daughter of Dareios's predecessor, Artaxerxes III (Arr. 7. 4. 4).

Both Philip after Chaironeia, and Alexander until late in his reign, avoided interfering directly in the affairs of the leading Greek city-state, Athens; probably there was no Macedonian garrison.[12] In 330 the Spartans led a rebellion which ended with king Agis's defeat at Megalopolis; Athens did not join. Perhaps to prevent further revolts in the homeland, Alexander ordered the city-states there to readmit political exiles, who, thanks to recent wars and upheavals, were a large group. Many may have been pro-Macedonians who, as Diodoros observes (18. 8; Austin 16), could provide a counterweight to revolt; but such direct interference in internal affairs, coinciding with Alexander's demand that divine honours be paid to his dead friend Hephaistion, gave his enemies a symbolic advantage. When, in June 323, he was taken ill after an extended bout of feasting and drinking and died at Babylon, the Greeks were presented with a chance to seize their freedom, while the Macedonians could now, if they wished, abandon their reluctant reconciliation with the Persians. The fact that Alexander had not indicated who was to succeed him, or had not indicated clearly, made matters worse.

Alexander's reign in many ways seems to foreshadow – and certainly helped to determine – the condition of the Greek world after his death. His relationship with the Greek cities, a blend of apparent deference to their traditions with thinly veiled autocracy, resembles what we see under his successors. He founded new cities, as did his successors. To accompany him on his expedition he took historians and other intellectuals, prefiguring the patronage of high culture by kings seeking to enhance their reputation. Perhaps most spectacularly, he developed a new style of Macedonian kingship, no doubt partly unconsciously but in many respects deliberately, which set the tone for later kings to emulate. Statues of Alexander idealized his good looks, his personal charisma inspired devotion in the army, and his own belief that he was descended from gods helped create a new religious code. He was the model against which later kings measured themselves – and, incidentally, became a folk-hero forever in the Near East and Mediterranean.[13]

Yet Alexander's unique achievements created problems for those who came after. He may have been more eastward-looking than his officers, and it seems he dreamt of a united Macedonian–Persian ruling class. The 'Last Plans' allegedly found among his papers after his death imply that he intended to conquer North Africa and western Europe, with the aim of uniting the various populations (Diodoros, 18. 4. 4, Austin 18; cf. Curtius, 10. 1. 17–18; Arr. 4. 7. 5; 5. 26. 1–2; 7. 1. 1–4, Austin 17).[14] Such grandiose ideas were unlikely to be followed through without strong leadership; because much of the success achieved by the expedition had attached to his own person, his disappearance left a vacuum. Perhaps he could have held the new empire together; but the very fact that his military successes were so rapid and unabating meant that, in effect, his armies had only cut a narrow track through the Persian empire. His Asiatic 'empire' can even be represented, by way of caricature, as little more than a thin strip of conquered land winding across Asia and back, leaving whole regions almost completely untouched by his passing. In such circumstances, and without the stability of a long reign, it was impossible for Alexander to make any permanent alteration to the greater part of his territory. Since his successors spent many years fighting each other, they were no better placed to create new administrative structures. It took more than a generation for the power-geography of the empire to settle down; when it did, it bore a marked resemblance to what had existed before Alexander reached Asia – and, indeed, to what had existed before the creation of the Persian empire under Cyrus the Great in the sixth century BC.

Neither Alexander's accession nor the death of the last Persian king wrought a violent transformation in Macedonia or Persia; nor did Alexander's premature death. We conventionally speak of a hellenistic or 'greekifying' period, but much of what we regard as characteristic of it had started before his reign. Many political trends began earlier, such as the rise of large territorial states and the revival of monarchical government in Greek lands. Widespread emigration from Greece in the half-century after 330 may have been partly the result of earlier population increase. The adoption of near eastern cults in Greek cities (Chapter 5) was nothing new in itself; while the paying of religious cult to living persons (Chapter 3) can be seen during the Peloponnesian war (431–404) and shortly after. Changes in 'high culture', such as the popularity of epigrams (pp. 253–5) and the increasingly domestic setting of comedy, were under way before Alexander's reign. Finally, changes in military formations and technology, such as the use of mercenaries and light-armed troops, and even the elaboration of new siege techniques and permanent defences, had begun before 400.

All these trends helped create a suitable climate for the conquest of western Asia. That conquest had repercussions in Greece, sometimes reinforcing these developments.

The Successors

The next few pages will concentrate on the actions of a military élite. A political–military narrative is a valid way of seeing the period, not least because that is how ancient writers presented it; in the ancient Greek and Roman world, powerful individuals made significant differences to the course of events. There are pitfalls, however. We should not exaggerate the roles played by individuals even if ancient authors do so. It is equally important not to retroject modern concerns, by ascribing to military commanders political, diplomatic, and strategic intentions that they may not have been able to formulate;[15] nor was it a world administered by economists and politicians schooled in complex bodies of theory. Finally, there is a danger of teleological thinking, of tacitly assuming that, because Alexander's empire was eventually divided up in one particular fashion, it was always bound to turn out that way.

The wars of the Diadochoi (323–276 BC)

A detailed strategic and diplomatic narrative of the half-century after Alexander cannot be written, given the patchy sources. Since, for a fifty-year period around the mid-third century, a continuous narrative is almost totally lacking, to pay undue attention to the events of 323–276 would produce an unbalanced picture of the hellenistic period as a whole. Only a brief outline is presented here, focusing on events significant in themselves or for later history, and without detailed source references. (A good imaginative reconstruction of events in the early years after Alexander's death is to be found in Mary Renault's novel *Funeral Games*.)[16]

The importance of this phase lies less in the often fragmented course of events than in how it sets the scene for cultural and political developments. Hence, though Eumenes and Lysimachos failed to establish themselves permanently in power, they merit discussion for their status in later sources and for their contributions to the process of establishing the final form of the empire. For the period after c.276 the narrative is carried on in the later chapters on different areas of the hellenistic world.

The commanders who inherited Alexander's empire are known as the Successors (*Diadochoi*; for chronology see Fig. 2.2). Alexander seems to have designated no heir unambiguously; when asked by Perdikkas, the senior cavalry commander, to whom he was leaving his kingdom, he may have said either 'to Krateros' (*tôi Kraterôi*) or 'to the strongest' (*tôi kratistôi*, Arr. 7. 26. 3), though this may be just a story. Strictly speaking, he did not have to name a successor, as the Macedonian army could be asked to choose one; but he had muddied the waters by getting rid of some likely candidates, and his friend Hephaistion, whom he might have put forward, was dead. If dynastic continuity were wanted, there was Philip III Arrhidaios, Alexander's half-brother; but he was allegedly mentally deficient – actually, perhaps, epileptic – and, in the eyes of some, unfit to rule. Alexander's Baktrian wife Rhoxane, however, bore a posthumous son, Alexander IV. These two heirs were recognized as joint kings but never exercised power, and the ensuing wars led to both being murdered within a few years.

Although Alexander's kingdom is often described as splitting into three parts after his death, the empire was not simply divided up; different areas were given to different commanders to administer, but Perdikkas was in overall charge; later it was redistributed by agreement or as a result of conflict. It was many years before the situation became stable, however, and it may be helpful to begin with a short summary before embarking on a fuller account.

323–322	Lamian war: Antipater suppresses Greek revolt
322	Perdikkas conquers Cappadocia; Eumenes becomes satrap
321	Perdikkas killed in Egypt
	Krateros defeated in Asia Minor
	Triparadeisos conference: Antipater made regent
319	death of Antipater: Polyperchon made regent
318	Antigonos, Cassander ally against Polyperchon
317	Polyperchon proclaims Greek freedom
	Cassander becomes regent
	Demetrios of Phaleron becomes ruler of Athens
	assassination of Philip III Arrhidaios
316	Olympias executed by Cassander
	Eumenes executed by Antigonos
315	Antigonos expels Seleukos from Babylon; he takes refuge with Ptolemy
	Tyre declaration: Antigonos proclaims Greek freedom
	Ptolemy proclaims Greek freedom
312	battle of Gaza: Ptolemy and Seleukos defeat Demetrios Poliorketes; Seleukos restored in Babylonia
311	peace treaty of Antigonos, Ptolemy, Lysimachos, Cassander
310	Alexander IV assassinated by Cassander
c.309/8	Antigonos expelled from Persia by Seleukos
307	Demetrios takes Athens from Cassander, expels Demetrios of Phaleron
306	Antigonos, Demetrios become kings
305/4	Ptolemy, Lysimachos, Cassander, Seleukos become kings
301	battle of Ipsos: Antigonos defeated and killed; Ptolemy takes Koile Syria

Figure 2.2   The age of Antigonos, 323–301 BC

In Egypt the situation was quickly settled: Ptolemy ruled continuously from 323. In Asia, Seleukos was not confirmed in control of his Asiatic provinces until 311. Macedonia was at first stable, then disturbed: after twenty years' rule by Cassander (see below), from 317 as regent and from 305/4 as king, his death in 298 or 297 was followed by a further two decades during which the kingdom changed hands every few years until Antigonos II Gonatas took over, permanently as it turned out.

In the aftermath of Alexander's death the work of adapting the Achaemenid administrative structure carried on without Greek–Iranian fission. Satraps (*satrapai*, the Greek version of the Persian word for provincial governors), a regent, and a viceroy of Macedonia were appointed. Perdikkas was made chiliarch (literally a commander of a thousand men, but often translated 'vizier') over the whole kingdom, and was in theory superior to other commanders. At the regional level, the elderly Antipater (Antipatros in Greek), viceroy in Macedonia, was confirmed as commander of the European territories (Fig. 2.3). Another general of the older generation, Antigonos, nicknamed Monophthalmos ('One-eyed'), was already satrap of Phrygia and was now put in charge of western Asia Minor. Ptolemy (Ptolemaios), a younger man related to Alexander, became satrap of Egypt. Lysimachos son of Agathokles, one of Alexander's *sômatophylakes* ('body-guards' or personal staff), received Thrace. Finally, Krateros was appointed representative (*prostatês*) of the kings.[17]

Disagreements about the assignment of satrapies and the powers of the regent soon led to open conflict. Perdikkas tried to exert overall authority; an alliance was formed against him, and in 321 he was assassinated while invading Egypt (Diod. 18. 37. 5). New negotiations, at Triparadeisos in Syria, made Antipater guardian of the young kings in Macedonia and Antigonos general of Asia (Diod. 18. 39. 5–7; cf. Arrian, *Ta meta Alexandron* (*FGH* 156), fr. 9. 34–8, Austin 24). Babylonia was assigned to Seleukos, former commander

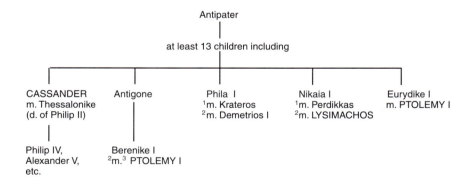

Figure 2.3 The family of Antipater

of Alexander's hypaspists ('shield-bearers'; they have been called 'a crack guards' regiment').[18] Even now, and for years to come, Alexander's kingdom was officially a single entity and no more divided than in, say, 325, when Alexander was in Afghanistan, Macedonia was governed by Antipater, and the various provinces of the former Persian empire were administered by satraps.

Rivalry soon turned into a blatant struggle for mastery over the whole empire. Antipater appointed as his successor a man of his own generation, Polyperchon (or Polysperchon), thus alienating his own son Cassander (Kassandros in Greek), who had aspired to become regent (Diod. 18. 48–50, Austin 25). As a result Cassander was receptive to overtures from Antigonos, who made an alliance with him and with Lysimachos and Ptolemy. There was no longer general agreement about who should rule which area; all was open to dispute, and much was disputed on the field of battle. (Some effects of the war between Cassander and Polyperchon are examined in Chapter 4.) Cassander became regent in 317 with the support of Eurydike, wife of Philip Arrhidaios. In the same year Alexander's aged mother, Olympias, invaded Macedonia and had Philip and Eurydike murdered. In 316, when Cassander re-entered Macedonia, she was condemned by the army and executed in her turn (pp. 118–19).

Antigonos sought to strengthen his position in Asia, expelling Seleukos from Babylon; this provoked the former allies and enemies of Antigonos to demand Seleukos's reinstatement. In the late 310s there were clashes between Antigonos and his opponents in various theatres of war including Karia, Thrace, and Palestine. One important result was the restoration of Seleukos to Babylonia in 312, an event in which Ptolemy played a leading role. In 311 a peace treaty implicitly recognized a four-way division of the empire. In theory Alexander IV, the posthumous son of Alexander the Great, was still due to become king (Diod. 19. 105; Austin 30),[19] but in 310 Cassander had him killed.

Nor did the treaty produce lasting peace; a confusing series of wars ensued. In 306 Antigonos's son Demetrios defeated Ptolemy at sea, near Salamis in Cyprus. Father and son were acknowledged as kings (*basileis*) 'by the multitude' according to Plutarch (*Demetrios*, 18. 1, Austin 36; Diod. 20. 53. 2–3; Appian, *Syrian Wars*, 54); the gesture may have been concocted by local political leaders. Before long Ptolemy, Lysimachos, Seleukos, and Cassander (Plut. l.c.; Just. 15. 2. 10–12) each adopted (or accepted) the title of king (*basileus*). In theory the Macedonian king had to be acclaimed by the army and nobles (p. 118 and n. 28), but each of the Successors now had only a part of the original Macedonian army, and few members of Alexander's original forces were still serving. Some historians have doubted that the act of calling oneself *basileus Makedonôn*, 'king of (the) Macedonians', amounted to a claim to rule the whole of Alexander's territory; but it is hard to see how such a title, at least initially, could fail to imply that other claimants were illegitimate.[20]

If there was one Successor who had his sights firmly set on reuniting the kingdom, it was surely Antigonos. After the capture of Cyprus, and having secured control of the Islanders' league, possession of the important naval power of Rhodes would give him total mastery of the Aegean. Demetrios besieged the city for over a year (305–304), employing massive forces and mechanical siege devices (for details of which, see pp. 338–40), but though the spectacular undertaking earned him his nickname of Poliorketes ('Besieger'), he failed to starve out the Rhodians, who received supplies from Ptolemy. They commemorated their survival by commissioning Chares of Lindos to build the Colossus of Rhodes, a bronze statue of Helios 70 cubits (32 m, 105 ft) tall, which may have stood at the mouth of the harbour. Its history is briefly told by Pliny (*Natural History*, 34. 41), and its construction is described in detail around 200 BC by Philon of Byzantion (*On the Seven Wonders of the World*, 4).[21]

Despite this failure, Antigonos pressed on. He set up a Hellenic league at Corinth in 302 on the model of Philip's in 338, with Demetrios as its *hêgemôn* (BD 8; lines 5–44 in Harding 138, lines 61–99 in Austin 42).[22] In 301, however, at the age of 81, he was defeated and killed at Ipsos in Phrygia by the combined armies of Cassander, Lysimachos, and Seleukos (the battle is described by Plut. *Demetr.* 29). Lysimachos now took charge of most of Asia Minor, while Ptolemy gained Palestine and south-eastern Asia Minor. Ipsos is often regarded as a turning-point in the history of this period.

Following his father's defeat and death, Demetrios retained a powerful fleet (for chronology see Fig. 2.4). We should not minimalize the significance of his campaigns after 301 just because he was eventually unsuccessful.[23] In reality, nothing was yet certain about the final shape of the empire, and with better luck Demetrios might have succeeded where his father failed. For a time he and Seleukos were allies, to their mutual benefit; but, just as the earlier friendship between Seleukos and Ptolemy had fallen victim to reality, so the new alliance proved temporary.

The death of Cassander in 298 or 297 tempted Demetrios to re-enter Greece, whereupon the others helped themselves to the Asiatic territories he had inherited from his father. Cassander's widow, Thessalonike (a daughter of Philip II) was now regent for their young sons. The eldest, Philip IV, soon fell ill and died. The second, Antipater I (or II), probably in his mid-teens, and the third, Alexander V, reigned jointly until in 294 Antipater murdered his mother and drove out his brother. Alexander made common cause with Demetrios but was reconciled with his brother; Demetrios then had him killed on suspicion of plotting against him. Antipater took refuge with Lysimachos but was soon done away with, no longer a useful ally. Demetrios was acclaimed king of Macedonia (294), but in attempting to regain his eastern possessions he was captured and imprisoned by Seleukos (288/7). He died eleven years later, allegedly of drink. (His character is examined at p. 62; see also Plutarch's *Life*.)

298/297	death of Cassander
294	Demetrios I seizes Athens, Macedonia
	Antiochos I becomes co-regent with Seleukos I
293	Lysimachos captured by Getai
288/7	Lysimachos, Pyrrhos partition Macedonia, expelling Demetrios
287	Athens revolts from Demetrios
286	Demetrios captured by Seleukos
285	Ptolemy II Philadelphos becomes co-regent in Egypt
283	death of Demetrios
	death of Ptolemy I
c.283	death of Agathokles, son of Lysimachos
281	Lysimachos killed at battle of Koroupedion
	death of Seleukos; Ptolemy Keraunos king of Macedonia
280	Keraunos killed fighting Gauls
280/79	Gauls repulsed from central Greece
279	Gauls set up kingdom of Tylis in Thrace
278/7	Gauls invade Asia Minor
277	Antigonos II Gonatas takes control of Macedonia

Figure 2.4 The age of Demetrios, 301–276 BC

Even though the Successors had been disputing the empire for a period longer than the whole of Alexander's lifetime, the overall political geography of the empire, outside Egypt, was still not fixed. Demetrios's disappearance led to the partition of Macedonia between Lysimachos and Pyrrhos of Epeiros. Later, Lysimachos established himself as sole ruler; he also controlled most of Asia Minor, and until now his centre of operations had lain east of Macedonia, on the European side of the Hellespont. In 281, however, at Koroupedion in Lydia, Lysimachos was defeated and killed by Seleukos. The aged victor tried to unite Europe and Asia by invading Macedonia, but was assassinated in 281 by an estranged son of king Ptolemy of Egypt, Ptolemy Keraunos ('Thunderbolt').

Alexander's last two surviving generals were finally dead, no fewer than forty-two years after the conqueror of Persia succumbed to his fever. Although the events of 323–281 can be reviewed in a few pages, many people born in the reign of Alexander will not have lived to see this denouement. To them, his death will have seemed as remote in time as the Suez crisis and the Hungarian revolution of 1956 did to someone looking back from the late 1990s. Chaotic as they may look, these four decades contained many periods of relative calm, and there were times when even the issue of who was to rule Macedonia may have seemed to be finally settled.

Ptolemy Keraunos died in 280 fighting the Gauls (see below), and it was not until three years later that Antigonos II Gonatas (r. 277–239) took control of Macedonia.[24] From that time until the Roman conquest of Greece in the second century BC, his descendants, the Antigonids, were the ruling dynasty of Macedonia.

Eumenes

At this point, with the sequence of events involving the main rivals established, the picture can be completed by describing the careers of other men who played a part in the struggles of the Successors and the administration of the empire. Besides the great names known to history there were many minor commanders, locally or briefly important. Some are known only from casual references in sources and documents, such as Eupolemos the Macedonian, who ruled part of Karia as a dynast in the 310s (Diod. 19. 68. 5–7, Austin 33).[25] In the following pages we shall consider two individuals who, though prominent, did not enjoy ultimate success. Lysimachos we have already met. First we focus on a figure who in the longer perspective might be considered a minor player, but who appears in ancient sources as a key figure of the years 323–316 (Diodoros, esp. 18. 29–32, 39–42, 53, 57–62; 19. 12–18, 21–34, 37–44; Plut. *Eumenes*).

As a citizen of Kardia on the shore of the Propontis (sea of Marmara), Eumenes, Alexander's secretary, was the only non-Macedonian appointed to a leading command in 323. He was assigned the task of expelling a local Iranian ruler, Ariarathes, from Cappadocia and Paphlagonia. He completed the task with the help of Perdikkas (Diod. 18. 16. 3, 18. 22. 1); but when Perdikkas was killed, the other Successors attacked Eumenes and condemned him to death in his absence – for killing Krateros, even though Krateros had attacked him.

During years of campaigning Eumenes repeatedly avoided defeat and, by clever ruses, kept his Macedonian troops loyal. One of the most colourful stories is preserved by Diodoros (18. 60–1). Eumenes wished to make his views count in the military council of his army, but reasoned that as a non-Macedonian he was liable not to be taken seriously. He therefore declared that he had had a dream in which he saw Alexander presiding over a council, and then persuaded his officers to set up an empty throne and place the royal insignia on it, as if Alexander himself were chairing their discussions. In this way, 'by placing himself on an equality with the other commanders ... he wore down the envy with which he had been regarded and secured for himself a great deal of goodwill among the commanders' (Diod. 18. 61. 2). Finally, however, he was besieged at Nora in Phrygia, captured, and put to death by Antigonos (Diod. 19. 44).

Both Diodoros and Plutarch make extensive use of the lost work of Hieronymos of Kardia (p. 264), who was attached to Eumenes' army after 323. As a result we know more about Eumenes than about almost any other Successor. Diodoros and Plutarch repeatedly stress that as the only non-Macedonian among the commanders he had to take care not to claim equal status; perhaps for this reason, he initially supported Perdikkas and the kings. Both authors, however, use his career as a moral fable about the fickleness of fortune (*tychē*). This emphasis may derive from Hieronymos – indeed, we may also be seeing a picture Eumenes wished to present to posterity – but it has been seized upon, and built up, by Diodoros and Plutarch under the influence of the ideas of their own times,[26] and we should not automatically take their valuation of Eumenes at face value. That does not mean, however, that they have exaggerated his power; he wielded considerable influence over events. The reasons for his failure to establish himself securely as a Successor are therefore worth considering.

Eumenes behaved much like any other Successor, and his career can serve as an exemplar of what was happening to Macedonian power. After the short regency of Perdikkas, who tried to hold the kingdom together, the armies of the Diadochoi were no longer in reality *the* Macedonian army, or sections of it, but mercenary forces attached to them individually by oath. Eumenes took care not to claim any legitimacy that properly belonged to Macedonians, yet he was defeated in the end. The cause of Eumenes' failure may lie, therefore, not (or not primarily) in any hostility he attracted from them – his own Macedonian troops were tenaciously loyal to him – but in the fact that in the final analysis he did not have a powerful enough army. As Briant says, neither the fact that he was non-Macedonian nor the fact that he remained loyal to the rightful kings can explain his failure.[27]

Eumenes is an interesting example of the mythologizing of the Successors by later authors, who sometimes follow contemporary sources. He appears as a trickster, a 'resourceful man' in the image of the epic hero Odysseus. His career becomes almost novelistic; like all good novels, it has a moral point to make, in this case about the instability of fate. Those are glosses, probably added later. Like any of the Diadochoi, Eumenes pursued his own interest. Like them, he represents a shift away from the Macedonian 'national' monarchy to a characteristically post-Alexander style of personal monarchy based on a mercenary army.

Lysimachos

Another figure worth focusing on, precisely because he did not succeed in establishing a dynastic territory with stable boundaries, is Lysimachos (Fig. 2.5). His long career is summarized by Pausanias (1. 9–10, Austin 45).

In 323 he was assigned the task of administering Thrace and defending it against the Odrysian Thracians, who forced him to a compromise settlement.[28] Involved in the major alliances against Cassander and Antigonos, he campaigned, like the other Diadochoi, on two fronts at once: to maintain his position in his province and increase his power, but also to protect Macedonia from attack by non-Greeks. His territory expanded to include most of Asia Minor and eventually Macedonia itself. He maintained close

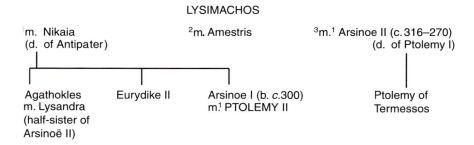

Figure 2.5 The family of Lysimachos

ties with the Athenians, for whom access to the islands of the north-eastern Aegean, and grain supplies from the Black Sea beyond, were perennial concerns. After Ipsos, Athens was no less valuable to Lysimachos in his diplomatic and military campaign against Demetrios, and he cultivated the city through generous benefactions. These were probably negotiated by the exiled Athenian Philippides of Kephale, a poet and author of political verses who lived at Lysimachos's court for many years and was honoured at Athens in 283/2 (Austin 43, BD 13, Burstein 11, *Syll.*[3] 374).[29]

Like other kings Lysimachos founded, or rather refounded, cities. In 309/8 Kardia, on the European shore of the Hellespont, became his new capital of Lysimacheia, well placed to control access to and from the Black Sea. He renamed Ephesos Arsinoëia after his third wife, Arsinoë II (sister of Ptolemy II Philadelphos of Egypt), removing the city to a new site, forcibly relocating people from the nearby *poleis* of Kolophon and Lebedos into the new city, and replacing the democratic constitution established by Alexander (Arr. 1. 17, Austin 4) with an oligarchy. He even caused the cult ceremonies for the city's patron goddess, Artemis, to be reorganized.[30] Such heavy-handed treatment may not have been to everyone's liking, but the citizen élite were no doubt quickly reconciled as long as they themselves retained political power. Lysimachos's memory was not tainted, for in the Roman period he was commemorated alongside other historical and legendary founders of the city.[31]

Lysimachos imposed a regional governor in Ionia, as any other satrapal ruler would have done; he arbitrated in disputes between cities such as Samos and Priene (BD 12, Burstein 12, *RC* 7, *OGIS* 13, of 283/2 BC). Nor does he appear backward in giving gifts to cities and temples. Like other Diadochoi, he probably received divine honours. He, too, had a kingly 'court' consisting of his *philoi* (friends), and despite the reported sneers of king Demetrios about their slave-like and licentious characters (Plut. *Dem.* 25. 4–6; Ath. 14. 614 f–615 a), these men were just as Greek and just as cultured as anyone's courtiers.[32]

Evidence for his alleged fiscal harshness towards Greek *poleis* is lacking though he may have been heavy-handed towards non-Greek populations (*laoi*), for example in Asia Minor. Like the other Successors he followed 'a policy fuelled by pragmatism rather than ideology which mixed incentives and deterrents in response to particular circumstances'.[33] He exploited his links with Alexander as they did; unlike some, he could boast of a long career in the service of Alexander, whose contemporary he was. He used visual imagery such as coins to reinforce his claims to power, retaining Alexander's coin types (Fig. 2.6). After Ipsos (301) he was the first to portray Alexander on coins, perhaps to show the king as his divine patron, while other Diadochoi chose Olympian deities as their emblems.

Lysimachos is sometimes presented in modern studies as an unintelligent, harsh ruler who did not deserve great success and did not achieve it; but the evidence is often over-interpreted. His military reputation may have suffered from the fact that in the late 290s he was captured by Dromichaites, chief of the Getai, a tribal people from beyond the Danube; but there is considerable evidence of his military acumen. As for his harsh rule, it may be largely a fantasy.

Many scholars have been tempted to see some truth in one feature of the mythology. Although Pausanias frames the story in purely personal terms and lets it be known that there were different versions, it seems certain that either Lysimachos or Arsinoë II procured the death of the heir apparent, Agathokles (the king's eldest son by his first wife, Nikaia):

> Human beings often suffer many misfortunes through love. For Lysimachos, being advanced in age, was considered blessed in his children, and Agathokles had children of his own by Lysandra. Lysimachos married Arsinoë (II) the sister of Lysandra. This Arsinoë, fearing for her children, lest when Lysimachos died they should be in Agathokles'

Figure 2.6 Silver tetradrachm (17.14 g) of Lysimachos. Pella, 286/5–282/1 BC (*SNG* 3755). Obv.: head of Alexander. Rev.: Athena. (Ashmolean Museum, University of Oxford.)

power, is said to have plotted against Agathokles. It has also been written that Arsinoë conceived a passion for Agathokles, but when she was rejected she plotted his death. They also say that Lysimachos later realized what his wife had dared to do, but there was nothing he could do any more since he was quite without friends. So when Lysimachos allowed Arsinoë to do away with Agathokles, Lysandra ran away to Seleukos and took her children and her brothers.

(Paus. 1. 10. 3–4)

The young man was a proven military commander, and according to the ancient sources his assassination sparked revulsion and provoked revolutions in the cities ruled by Lysimachos. This in turn caused the other Diadochoi to form a coalition against him, which led to his defeat and death in 281.

The claim that Lysimachos was an inadequate ruler may have no other basis than that he failed to establish a lasting kingdom and a dynasty – as if that was the sole measure or aim of the man's career. There is also a danger of circular argument. No evidence of his incompetence or brutality stands up to scrutiny; claims that he was senile, and Arsinoë's power excessive, are almost wholly worthless; even the death of Agathokles need not count against him if it was politically necessary. It has been suggested that 'Lysimachus' great error lay in a reluctance to recognise the claims of the coming generation which spelled out his own mortality',[34] but we may wish to seek a political explanation as well.

An earlier theory, that Agathokles was so popular that when he was killed the cities in Lysimachos's territory were outraged and called on Seleukos to help them revolt, cannot be sustained; but it may be that, in giving the impression of insecurity by being forced into ordering the death of his heir, Lysimachos provoked a crisis of confidence which opened the way for pro-Seleukid groups to advance their cause at his expense.[35] It may be that rivalry between Agathokles and Ptolemy of Termessos, Lysimachos's first son by Arsinoë II, led to a dynastic crisis which provoked Lysimachos into disposing of the heir apparent. As the survivor, Ptolemy of Termessos should have taken over the throne; but so total was the collapse of Lysimachean power that he was quickly expelled by Antigonos[36] and had to take refuge with Ptolemy II Philadelphos of Egypt. Alternatively, or in addition, the fact that Ptolemy of Termessos's mother now married her brother, none other than Philadelphos, may make one suspect that the Egyptian king had a hand in events. Such a move might be motivated by a desire to control the north-eastern Aegean; the Ptolemies were very active in the Aegean at this time, for example through the league of Islanders.

The dismantling of Lysimachos's power was not bound to happen; it was partly a matter of bad luck and partly the result of the disaster at Koroupedion (281), but for which we might now be talking of the Agathoclid dynasty of

Macedonia rather than the Antigonid. During his lifetime Lysimachos was just as successful as his rivals in playing in the role of a new-style king.

Other rulers

Rulers of lesser territories also adopted the title of king, notably in Asia Minor. The most important of these kingdoms was Pergamon in north-western Asia Minor, which was independent of the Seleukids from 283. Its rulers were known as kings from about 240, and its history is treated in Chapter 8 (pp. 312–19).

Other kingdoms enjoyed limited power but are important areas of Greek interaction with non-Greeks, since some remained under non-Greek rulers. The Thracian Zipoites ruled Bithynia, further east in north-western Asia Minor, from 297/6 to 279. His hellenizing aspirations are shown by the Greek name he gave his son, Nikomedes I (r. 279–250), who founded a Greek capital at Nikomedeia on the Propontis. The third king, Ziailas (r. 250–*c*.230), cultivated the friendship of the Ptolemies. In Pontos in northern Asia Minor, Mithradates I, perhaps a descendant of a Persian family which in the fourth century had ruled the town of Kios (Cios, Cius) on the Propontis, was proclaimed king in 281, though he backdated his regnal era to 297/6 (Diod. 20. 111). Unlike Bithynia, Pontos was generally allied with the Seleukids, and the second king, Mithradates II (r. *c*.250–*c*.220), married into the Seleukid royal house. In the mid-third century the mountainous central region of Cappadocia (Kappadokia), strategically important for control of western Asia Minor and therefore cultivated in Seleukid diplomacy, was ruled by an Iranian dynasty. The first ruler to be called king was Ariarathes III in 255, who married into the Seleukid royal family. Baktria (northern Afghanistan) achieved independence under Diodotos at some point in the mid-third century, perhaps in the 250s or later (p. 284). Euthydemos (r. *c*.226–186) became a king, a fact formally recognized by Antiochos III in 206 after the victory of Euthydemos over the 'barbarians' (Polybios, 11. 34, Austin 150).[37]

In the Greek west, the tyrant Agathokles of Syracuse took the royal title in 304, some twelve years after seizing power over his city from an oligarchic regime, 'since he thought that neither in power nor in territory nor in deeds was he inferior to them' (the Diadochoi; Diod. 20. 54. 1). (Diodoros, 19. 5–31. 17 *passim*, is our main source, mostly using Timaios.) Already exiled twice, Agathokles was apparently recalled by the people and, with Carthaginian help, returned in 319/8, becoming '*stratêgos* (general) with full powers over the strongholds in Sicily' (Parian Marble (*FGH* 239), B 12, Austin 21, Harding 1 *a*). Three years later he overthrew the six hundred oligarchs and became *strategos* in charge of the city, in effect a tyrant (Diod. 19. 9. 4). He tried and failed to uproot a Carthaginian province in western Sicily, being heavily defeated in Africa in 308/7; this left him in charge of the Greek cities of Sicily as before, but in his later years he was partially

51

successful in extending Syracusan power among the Greek cities of southern Italy, perhaps aspiring to unite the Greeks of Sicily with those on the mainland. Before he died in 289/8, his son Agathokles had been assassinated in North Africa by his own son Archagathos, whose ambition was to rule in Syracuse; whereupon the tyrant, rather than allow his grandson to succeed him, gave power back to the oligarchs. (In about 264, however, Hieron of Syracuse was recognized as king of the city after his victory over the Mamertini of Campania: Polyb. 1. 7–9.) In the long view Agathokles' achievements can be seen as no more than temporary; but modern opinion, no less than ancient, is divided about his abilities and his career.[38]

Although, for the leading Diadochoi, the title 'king of the Macedonians' at least initially embodied a claim to universal rule, a ruler who called himself *basileus* was only proclaiming his supremacy within his own territory, not the whole Greek world.[39] *Basileia* became, in effect, a rank rather than a formal claim to be the sole successor of Alexander, with whom many of these rulers had no direct connection.

The Gauls

The Greek world was not a self-contained entity, isolated from non-Greek peoples. A striking reminder of this fact came in the form of the Gaulish invasion of the early third century. For generations the Gauls or Celts (Galatai or Keltoi in Greek) had been migrating south and east from their homeland in north-western Europe; entire societies were on the move, perhaps as a result of population pressure at home. Gauls had even sacked Rome in the 390s, and Cassander and Lysimachos now had to defend northern Greece against raids by Gauls or by other tribes whom the Gauls had forced to leave their homelands.[40]

The death of Seleukos in 281 provoked a crisis in the north, which worsened when his assassin, Ptolemy Keraunos, was killed in battle against new Gaulish invaders.[41] One band of Gauls reached Delphi, where they were repulsed by the Aitolians and other central Greeks – aided by the god of the sanctuary, Apollo, who sent a snowstorm to stop them. The event is commemorated in a decree passed in 278 by the citizens of the island *polis* of Kos; the text is good evidence for the cult organization and, incidentally, for the continued prestige of the traditional Greek gods (cf. Chapter 5):

> Diokles son of Philinos moved:
>   Since, after the barbarian expedition against the Greeks and the sanctuary at Delphi, it is reported that the aggressors of the sanctuary have been punished by the god and by the men who came to defend it during the barbarian incursion; that the sanctuary has been saved and adorned with the spoils from the enemy; and that, of

the remaining aggressors, the majority have perished in combat against the Greeks:

So that it may be manifest that the people shares in the joy of the Greeks over the victory and is repaying thank-offerings to the god for manifesting himself during the perils which confronted the sanctuary and for the safety of the Greeks:

With good fortune, be it resolved by the people that the leader of the sacred embassy [*from Kos*] and the sacred ambassadors who have been elected should, on arriving at Delphi, sacrifice to Pythian Apollo an ox with gilded horns on behalf of the safety of the Greeks ... The sacred herald shall proclaim that 'the people is observing the day as sacred because of the safety and victory of the Greeks; and that all may be for the best for those who wore wreaths'....

(Austin 48, BD 17, *Syll.*³ 398)

A division of the Gauls led by Brennos came with 2,000 wagons, which implies he had a total complement (including non-combatants) numbering tens of thousands.[42] Justin (24. 6), summarizing Pompeius Trogus, says that 'when the defeated Macedonians had fixed themselves within the walls of their cities, the victorious Brennus ravaged the fields of the whole of Macedonia with no one to oppose him'. The total number of people on the move, including non-combatants, may have been as great as 300,000.[43] The Gauls' strength can be measured by their victories over Keraunos and his successor Sosthenes.

Some Gauls crossed into Asia Minor, partly at the invitation of Nikomedes of Bithynia, who made them his mercenaries (Memnon, *FGH* 434 fr. 11, Austin 140, Burstein 16).[44] They plundered the countryside, and there is a report of many hellenized inhabitants of north-western Asia Minor being captured by Gauls and ransomed by an official of the Seleukid king (Austin 142, Burstein 19).[45] They exacted tribute from cities and dynasts alike until defeated by Philetairos of Pergamon, and also by Antiochos I, in about 270. Antiochos established them in an area of northern Phrygia that became known as Galatia, 'Land of the Gauls', though permanent settlements may not pre-date the latter part of the third century. They continued to trouble Graeco-Macedonian rulers, but were probably not inherently aggressive, rather in search of a homeland.[46] They were available to be recruited as mercenaries, for example by Antiochos Hierax in 241 (p. 290). Philetairos's successful campaigns against them helped establish Pergamon as an independent state, and were commemorated, along with later victories over them, by the sculptures of Gauls fighting Greeks which decorated the acropolis of Pergamon (Fig. 8.6). Attalos I famously withheld the customary tribute from them, perhaps in order to provoke the confrontation which culminated in a great Pergamene victory. Still they were far from subdued; in 189 the Romans under Gnaeus Manlius Vulso were still driving

Gauls out of coastal regions of Asia Minor.[47] Eumenes II of Pergamon fought major campaigns in the 180s and 160s, and his successor Attalos II contemplated attacking them a few years later.

In Thrace, Antigonos II Gonatas wiped out a large Gaulish force in 277. There were no further raids into Greece, though the Gaulish kingdom of Tylis survived until c.212. The prestige of victory helped Gonatas take control in Macedonia (though he dated his reign from the death of his father Demetrios I in 283). This marks a turning-point in the global-political development of the hellenistic kingdoms: Gonatas, unlike previous Successors, was able to hold onto power, and the Antigonid dynasty ruled Macedonia until the Roman conquest. Here, then, as in Pergamon, opposition to the Gauls provided a lever for dynastic ambition.

Wherever they went, the Gauls instilled fear, or so the sources and documents claim. They represented a dangerous 'other', and became the archetypal barbarians, possibly the Greeks' most significant enemy since the Persians. Hammond attributes Macedonia's relative weakness after 277, at least in comparison with the other main kingdoms, to the long-term effects of the Gallic raids, which he sees as ruinous.[48] Actually, the Gauls may have been less of a threat to Greece than the Persians were in the early fifth century. Time and again, campaigns against them are exploited for propaganda purposes. Fear of the Gauls may have spurred the Greeks to uphold their own identity by demonizing them, and explains why we can see in Pausanias (1. 3. 5–4. 6; 10. 19. 4–23. 7) a strong colouring from Xerxes' invasion.[49] Their aggressive acts gave kings opportunities to show how Greek, how strong, and how meritorious they were; but in other circumstances they were not slow to use the Gauls' military weight in their own campaigns.

Armies and emigration

Our sources concentrate on the actions of a military élite. Posterity and fame (*kleos*) were important to aristocratic Greek men, but history is more than these things, and other factors were involved in drawing the map of the world after Alexander. As Claire Préaux puts it, 'Do the makers of history know where their action leads?'[50] Broader changes in society may have given added momentum to – and surely established the preconditions for – the setting up of a new political system. Why were Alexander and the Diadochoi able to raise such large armies?

Alexander faced a problem in the shape of the numbers of exiles from Greek cities. These were so numerous that according to Diodoros (18. 8, Austin 16; cf. 17. 109) more than 20,000 gathered at Olympia in 324 to hear his 'exiles decree' (p. 38). It seems likely that they were members of the hoplite class in their home cities – relatively prosperous men who could afford full infantry armour in the traditional Greek fashion – who had been expelled as a result of political troubles. The figure may comprise only a few men from each *polis*, though there may have been many more besides those at Olympia; but it is significant that the phenomenon of exiles was seen as general. An additional problem for Alexander was the large number of mercenaries laid off (at his command) by his satraps. Many thousands of them assembled in 324 at the sanctuary of Poseidon on Cape Tainaron in Laconia, a place where by tradition mercenaries were hired (Diod. 17. 111). Under the leadership of an outstanding Athenian general, Leosthenes, they made themselves available to Athens in preparation for a revolt against Macedonia.[51]

One possible demographic factor relevant to the fourth century was over-population, which could lead to emigration. Sallares has examined the long-term population trends of Greece from a biological and demographic point of view.[52] He detects a pattern in the sources which suggests that the human population peaked in about the fourth century and then, as biologi-cal populations are prone to do, overshot the carrying capacity of the landscape before falling back again in the hellenistic period. After the Mycenaean palace system came to an end in the twelfth century, it was likely that the human population of the Greek landscape would increase under its own momentum if it was not held back by accidents such as famine and invasion. Hence, in explanation of the frequency of Greek settlement over-seas during the so-called dark age (*c*.1100–*c*.900) and the geometric and archaic periods which followed it (*c*.900–*c*.480), one factor may well have been an excess (in some sense) of population, though people at the time would probably not have recognized it. The historian, however, has to analyse how such impersonal causes work through in actual social settings.

When considering the later fourth century, it is important to make explicit a possible link between demographic change and the numbers of political exiles; but people living at the time can have had no way of knowing that the population was rising, other than impressionistically and anecdotally, for there were few or no statistical data. What they will have been aware of is warfare and its casualties, disputes about land ownership, civil war resulting in expulsions, and so on. A possible consequence of a rising population may certainly have been more frequent civil strife, resulting in the expulsion of defeated parties.

As early as 380 (in his *Panegyrikos*), and as late as 342 and 338 (*Letters* 2–3: *To Philip 1* and *2*), the Athenian orator Isokrates called for a panhel-lenic expedition against Persia to sort out Greece's problems.[53] In the intervening years he made the same plea more than once: in 356 to king Archidamos of Sparta (*Letter 9: To Archidamos*), in 346 to Philip (*Oration 5: Philip*). On more than one occasion he highlighted among Greece's problems what he saw as the massive numbers of political exiles:

For although, by the nature of human beings, many evils exist, we ourselves have invented more than are necessary by engendering wars and civil conflicts for ourselves. Some people are being killed illegally at home, while others wander in foreign lands with their wives and children; and many, forced by a lack of daily necessities, meet their deaths fighting for their enemies against their friends.

(Isokrates, *Oration* 4: *Panegyrikos*, 167–8)

Similarly, in the oration *To Philip*, he wrote that 'it is easier to assemble a greater and more powerful army from those who are wandering than from those who belong to *poleis*' (section 96, cf. 120–1). Many of these people may have been political exiles, who were represented, or misrepresented, as a danger to Greece.

The Athenian occupation of Samos represents a special case of this phenomenon. In 365 the Athenians had brutally suppressed the *polis* of Samos and taken the island for themselves, sending Athenian citizens to settle as cleruchs (*klêrouchoi*, plot-holders, like those in the fifth-century Athenian empire) and farm the land. Many of the Greek exiles seeking to return home in 324 were the survivors and descendants of those Samians, pressing Alexander to re-establish their *polis*. Eventually he did so, though at first the Athenians did not obey his proclamation and only the Lamian war (p. 116) resolved the issue.[54]

Demographic factors may thus have made available a ready supply of troops for the Successors' armies, both through population increase and through political exile. Service in a king's army represented a route to social advancement – admittedly at the risk of not surviving at all – which was open to Greek exiles and non-citizens but also to regular citizens.[55] Recruitment generally led to settlement abroad upon retirement. It is difficult to view this as a purely demographic process; for a citizen, the choice between emigrating in the hope of a better life, and staying safely at home with fewer economic opportunities, may not always have been easy. Whether it is true, as some claim,[56] that a lack of other gainful employment was a factor encouraging emigration is uncertain; the economies of the city-states may not have been based on wage labour to any large extent. More probably, the increasing polarization of wealth classes and the growth of larger élite estates – a trend often seen in Greek history – was driving some citizen smallholders off the land and making them dependent on the rich for seasonal employment. To such men the chance of emigrating to a new city, or fighting for a king in the hope of rewards, or both, could be very attractive, giving the prospect of renewed land-holding status.

The sources give an idea of the scale of population movements. In 334, when he invaded Asia, Alexander took 12,600 southern Greeks with him, of whom 7,600 were from cities in the League of Corinth and the rest mercenaries. The remainder of his 37,000-strong army was made up of Macedonians, tribal levies from the north, and north-central Greeks such as Thessalians. He received about 65,000 new mercenaries during his expedition, of whom at least 36,000 were left behind as garrison troops or settlers.[57] Later some 23,000 Greeks (who may have included northerners and even Macedonians) were settled by Alexander in the 'upper' (eastern) Persian satrapies; on his death they revolted, wishing to return to Greece (pp. 283–4), and were massacred by the Macedonians (cf. Arr. 5. 27. 5, on the sending home of Thessalians from Baktria). After Alexander's death, the new rulers appear to have continued recruiting from Greece in ever larger numbers. Antigonos had 28,000 infantry and 8,500 cavalry in 317 BC (Diod. 19. 27, Austin 28); against him Eumenes fielded 35,000 infantry. Eleven years later Antigonos had 80,000 infantry (Diod. 20. 73). A century later Antiochos III was able to mobilize 70,000 infantry and 5,000 cavalry, of whom no fewer than 40,000 had been recruited from Greece and Asia Minor (Polyb. 5. 63–5, Austin 224); Ptolemy IV's force ranged against him in 217 BC included 5,000 Greek mercenaries including 2,500 Cretans. These are only selected examples, but they give an idea of the scale of emigration from Greece, even allowing for exaggeration and the difficulties of counting. Much of the emigration was from less urbanized areas such as Aitolia, Thessaly, and Crete rather than famous cities like Athens. Even in the relatively prosperous Ionian town of Magnesia-on-Meander under Antiochos I, however, citizens were willing to relocate to the new foundation of Antioch in distant Persis (Austin 190, Burstein 32, *OGIS* 233). Sparta is a special case: since the early fourth century Spartans had been earning money serving foreign potentates (see, for example, Plutarch's *Agesilaos*), and this continued.[58]

The ambitions of these thousands of men – many of whom may have endured relative poverty in their home towns – may have provided some of the motivation for Alexander's initial conquests and the territorial struggles of the Diadochoi. For soldiers the principal rewards of military service lay in plunder, booty, and ultimately land, so – aside from the risks to life and limb – it was important to carry on campaigning. Whether settling down in Alexandria-by-Egypt or in Alexandria Eschate (in modern Uzbekistan) was equally attractive is a moot point.[59]

One of a series of sketches of ethical traits by the late fourth-century philosopher Theophrastos gives a flavour of what was on offer for Athenians of the day – even if he is talking about a charlatan:

> On a journey he [*the fraudulent man*] is apt to put one over on a trav- elling companion by relating how he campaigned with Alexander, and how many jewel-studded goblets he got, and arguing that the craftsmen in Asia are better than those in Europe (he says all this even though he's never been out of town). He says that he's got no fewer than three letters from Antipater summoning him to visit Macedonia, and that he has declined a grant for the duty-free export of timber because he refuses to be prey to even one informer – 'The Macedonians should have been smarter than that!' And that during

the food shortage his expenses in giving to destitute citizens amounted to more than five talents — he just can't bring himself to say no.

(Theophrastos, *Characters*, 23)

Although the Macedonians here are a source of trouble — the passage implies that they liked to hire secret agents within cities — it is equally clear that making money in the king's service was something one could expect to hear people boast about, a recognized strategy for social advancement.

The personal leadership exercised by the Diadochoi over their troops represented a new social phenomenon, at least in its scale. Mercenary commanders had been used before by Greek cities and non-Greek potentates; in the early fourth century the Athenian Iphikrates, one of the most renowned of all generals, had served first his own city, then the Thracians, Persians, Spartans, and Macedonians. Members of old *poleis*, like Konon of Athens and king Agesilaos of Sparta in the early fourth century, had been employed, often with troops personally loyal to them, by potentates abroad. The sheer scale of the armies of the Diadochoi, combined with the personal oaths of loyalty sworn to them by the troops (to Eumenes, for example: Plut. *Eum.* 5. 3, cf. 7. 1, 12. 2; or to king Eumenes I, Austin 196, BD 23, *OGIS* 266),[60] increased the difficulty of reunifying the empire: too many individual commanders and soldiers had a stake in a different outcome.

The individual ambitions of Greek soldiers also had consequences for native populations in Egypt and Asia (Chapters 6, 8). The 'hellenistic' age was not a period when 'the Orient' became culturally Greek; but Greeks did settle in many parts of western Asia and Egypt and brought with them their culture, including military practices as well as religion, literature, and athletics — all the things that constituted their identity in their own eyes, and whose absence made barbarians of others. Emigration, exile, and mercenary service provided the main stimuli for the spread of Greek power to the Near East.

r, and lecturer with a
ional reputation. His
y and drumming with
on everything from
etry as an educational
nent and growth.

RC **sign up below**
Student Advocates

bout Rap and
etry in the LRC

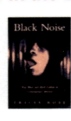

llege.ac.uk

3

KINGS AND CITIES

Claire Préaux's survey of Greek society and culture after Alexander, *Le Monde hellénistique*, takes as the title of its main part 'Les grands entités', subdivided into 'Royales' and 'Urbaines'. She sees kings and cities as the two major components of the period, and with good reason. New power centres arose in the persons of the kings, but the old cities were not swept aside and new ones sprang up. These two institutions will form the framework of this chapter.

The political changes of the period 338–276 entailed serious consequences for the old city-states of Greece. Kingship was anathema to the archaic and classical *poleis*; according to their mythology they had repudiated it very early, perhaps actually during the period we call the Dark Age (*c.*1100–*c.*900 BC). Apart from Sparta, whose two kings were in any case not particularly different from ordinary citizens, only barbarians like Persians had kings; in Greek ideology Xerxes and his successors embodied all that was worst about irresponsible sole power. In contrast, the city-state, whether democratic or oligarchic, was founded, in theory, on open debate between the citizens, be they a small or a large group. The revival of kingship therefore overthrew some cherished beliefs on the part of southern Greeks, though many Greek cities, such as those in Asia Minor, had long cohabited with monarchical regimes such as Lydia and Persia, sometimes paying monetary tribute. In the north, too, some cities had had to find a *modus vivendi* with the Macedonian kings, while some were even founded by Philip and his successors. The ideal model of the autonomous, self-sufficient *polis*, formulated by Aristotle and others, was not often borne out in reality.

In the longer term, the classical city-states system may be seen as an exceptional interlude in the history of the ancient Near East, which is dominated by monarchical government.[1] In the hellenistic period, as at other times, kings and cities had to find ways of coexisting. The relationship was not simply one of domination. While cities had to take care not to provoke hostility, kings also disdained *poleis* at their peril. Consequently the images of the rulers, whether created by themselves to present to their subjects or by their subjects in dealing with them, represented a compromise between change and continuity. Greek communities needed to counteract the negative terms in which they were used to framing ideas of monarchy, and habituate themselves to the new situation. It was natural for the kings – themselves culturally Greek – to employ and develop existing symbolic codes when presenting a public image to their subjects through coins, sculptures, and written documents. The cities did the same, in their petitions and in the honours they bestowed.

The kings faced three particular problems. The *poleis* had been governed by citizens well known to their fellows, whereas the new rulers were unfamiliar outsiders and political newcomers. Second, the old authorities were sanctioned by 'ancestral constitutions', whereas the military conquerors had to create their own legitimacy. Third, the *poleis* were urban centres with relatively small territories, whereas the areas controlled by the kings extended over vast distances. New supporting structures were therefore required, some of which will be examined below. The kings exploited the language of visual representation and ceremonial, and benefited indirectly from literary representations. Through the public image of the royal families, including women, and by the way in which their friends and associates developed into recognizable 'courts', kings sought to legitimate their power and to use it effectively. This presented some *poleis* with opportunities to work a situation to their advantage, by seeking privileges and benefactions. Such petitioning was often carried out through élite citizens who could use indirect or direct channels of communication with a king. Communication was two-way, however; it was vital for the king to keep a finger on the pulse of his allies and subjects.

Representations of kingship

Literary portraits

Our literary sources, both those written during the hellenistic period and later, derivative accounts, create and manipulate the images of kings and the ideals of kingship, representing a dialogue between the new holders of power and those on whom it was brought to bear or who were opposed to it. Some kings, notably the Ptolemies and Attalids, devoted enormous resources to preserving and elaborating Greek culture, such as by supporting libraries and writers (pp. 239, 329), this was another way in which kings could seek to mould their public image. The king benefited from being seen to exercise the almost sacred function of ensuring that the memory of the past was kept alive (see p. 242).[2] These activities were not mere 'public relations'; kings were, or wished to be seen as, Greek, and it was natural for them to use their wealth to foster the traditions and culture that defined Greekness. Once again, the difference with the past is more of scale than of kind.

Discussions of kingship and of individual kings can be found in many hellenistic writers, particularly historians and poets. Theokritos wrote a hymn (*Idyll* 17, part in Austin 217) to Ptolemy II (quoted, pp. 202, 238), which refers to the king's virtues: he is descended from Zeus, his late father Ptolemy I now sits among the gods, his birth was attended by signs from Zeus 'the preserver of illustrious kings', his Egyptian kingdom has 300,000 cities (a formulaic number), he rules many other lands and is 'sovereign of the seas', his wealth is greater than any, his territory is immune from attack, and he reveres the gods and gives gifts to cities and vassal kings. Poetic flattery it may be, but it encapsulates the royal attributes which were essential to success: divine ancestry, great power, a large territory, wealth, victory, generosity, and piety.

A similar range of characterization is given to Seleukos I in the portrait drawn by Appian:

> (55) And so it was that Seleukos became king of Babylonia, and also of Media, after he had killed in battle with his own hand Nikanor, who had been left by Antigonos as satrap of Media. He waged many wars against Macedonians and barbarians ... Always lying in wait for the neighbouring peoples, with the power to coerce and the persuasion of diplomacy, he became ruler of ... all other neighbouring peoples whom Alexander had conquered in war as far as the Indus. The boundaries of his rule in Asia extended further than those of any ruler apart from Alexander ...
>
> (57) ... He was tall and powerfully built; one day when a wild bull was brought to Alexander for sacrifice and broke loose from its bonds, he resisted it alone and brought it under control with his bare hands. That is why his statues represent him with horns added. He founded cities throughout the whole length of his empire ...
>
> (58) They say that when he was undertaking the foundation of the two Seleukeias, that of Seleukeia-by-the-Sea was preceded by a portent of thunder, and that is why he consecrated thunder as their divinity ...
>
> (Appian, *Syrian Wars*, 55, 57–8, Austin 46)

Appian says that even the attempts of the Magi (Persian priests) to conceal the most propitious hour for digging the foundations of Seleukeia-on-Tigris were thwarted by divine intervention; in other words, the gods were with Seleukos. The blend of royal propaganda, official flattery, and folk imagination well conveys the mystique with which kingly power was invested.

Polybios's discussions of the characters of the kings who feature in his narrative appear at first sight more factually based, even allowing for his prejudices and his reliance on second-hand information. Yet even he is working with an image of kingship and its responsibilities that reflects the attitudes of the age. Attalos I earns his praise for his pursuit of royal qualities, his benefactions, his achievements in war, and his personal decency (18. 41, Austin 199). His son Eumenes II receives a similar eulogy (32. 8, Austin 207). Philip V, however, falls far short of the ideal. Polybios, no friend of the Macedonians, regards him as wicked and in some respects insane, though on at least one occasion he behaved rationally and well. His army had invaded Attica, provoking an appeal from Roman envoys to withdraw: 'If he acted so, they added, he might consider himself at peace with Rome'. The army was indeed withdrawn, and Polybios approves 'Philip's truly kingly conduct, his magnanimity and fixity of purpose':

> for in his vexation at his recent losses and prompted chiefly by anger and indignation, he adapted himself to the situation with frenzied and almost inspired vigour, and by this means was able to resume the struggle against the Rhodians and king Attalos and achieve the success which ensued.
>
> (Polyb. 16. 28)

Polybios may be misreading the situation: Philip may have withdrawn for fear of provoking war with Rome. That does not matter; the point is that Polybios, though an analytical writer unlike Theokritos and a more critical historian than Appian, shares with them the presumption that a king ought to embody certain virtues. Philip's rational decision becomes, for Polybios, a sign of his *truly* kingly nature – even though on other occasions he shows himself to be inadequate. Another king who falls short in the eyes of Polybios is Antiochos IV Epiphanes, nicknamed Epimanes ('Crazy') because he allegedly mixed with common folk and was not above indulging in horseplay at the public baths (Athenaeus, 10. 439 a + 5. 193 d = Polyb. 26. 1 a–2, Austin 163 *a*; Livy, 41. 20, Austin 163 *b*; cf. Diodoros, 31. 16).

Plutarch's *Demetrios*, though written centuries after its subject's death and tinged with the moral and philosophical concerns of the day, embodies the same expectations of what a king should be. Demetrios is preternaturally handsome; his looks combine heroic attributes and royal dignity (ch. 2); he loves his father and is loyal to his friends (chs 3–4); he is decisive in strategy, brave in battle, and a resolute leader, and wages wars for the liberty of the Greeks (ch. 8); he is generous to defeated opponents (ch. 17). It is not his fault that the Athenians indulge in gross flattery; the flaw in his character is that he is a slave to pleasure and careless of his reputation. Plutarch is working with his own version of the 'ideal king', which Demetrios defines partly by contrast, and passes interesting but adverse comment on the significance of the adoption of kingly roles by Alexander's successors:

> Now this practice [*the adoption of the royal title*] did not involve merely the addition of a title and a change of fashion: it stimulated the men's pride and raised their ambitions, and made them arrogant

and obnoxious in their style of living and in their dealings with others. It is the same as with tragic actors who change their step, their voice, their posture at table, and their way of addressing others when they put on their costumes. They became harsher in their judicial verdicts and no longer concealed their power, which had often in the past made them more lenient and gentle with their subjects. Such was the power of a single word spoken by a flatterer, and so great was the revolution it brought about in the world.

(Plut. *Demetr.* 18, Austin 36)

Was it just a change of style? For Plutarch, evidently not; the new title altered these men's characters and therefore altered history. For Polybios, too, the personality of kings was a major determinant of their public actions, though he superimposes on the kingly imagery a further layer of analysis, believing that the most successful military leader is the one who is best at rational calculation. Different authors work with different conceptual frameworks and write for different audiences, but each assumes that kings owe it to their position and to their dignity to behave in certain ways.

A more problematic set of views emerges through contemporary philosophies, or the fragmentary accounts of them that we can reconstruct. In the classical period, authors critical of democracy such as Xenophon, Plato (in his *Politikos*, or *Statesman*), and Isokrates had developed theories of kingship as a form of government. Once monarchy was a reality and its own problems could be seen, philosophers continued to explore the concept and many works on kingship were written; none definitely survives, though the treatise *On Kingship* by Diotogenes, and another of the same title falsely attributed to the fourth-century Pythagorean philosopher Ekphantos, may possibly have an early hellenistic origin.[3] The effort of sustaining democratic decision-making in the face of royal power may have stimulated debate. To some extent those who elaborated ideas about kingship may have been trying to help Greeks to deal with the problems of a new political system rather than succumb to the prevailing top-down power relations or, alternatively, attempt to change them.

The Byzantine lexicon known as the *Suda* contains the following definition of kingship (*basileia*), thought to derive from a hellenistic source:

MONARCHY. It is neither nature nor justice which gives monarchies to men, but the ability to command an army and to handle affairs competently. Such was the case with Philip and the Successors of Alexander. For Alexander's natural son was in no way helped by his kinship with him because of his weakness of spirit, while those who had no connection with Alexander became kings of almost the whole inhabited world.

(*Suda*, s.v. *basileia*, Austin 37)

63

The philosophical work from which this probably derives apparently embodied the familiar Greek distinction between nature and convention; although the 'natural' right of kings to rule is not actually disputed, the traditional idea of a hereditary kingship is subverted, and by implication monarchy is a status that can be achieved by a powerful individual or attributed to him by others. At the same time there is the implication that a man may be unfit to be king, a view that may have arisen in a context of Greek opposition to the Successors and their descendants.

More radical critiques may be seen, notably among the early Stoic philosophers (Chapter 5). Zeno, the founder of Stoicism, may have taken a radical stance which his successors toned down once full independence was no longer within Athens' reach. Stoicism then came to be the predominant philosophy of the ruling élite in Greek states and later in Rome, who developed it from a general theory of moral perfection into a particular, narrow theory of ethical conduct for the ruler who would be just.[4] It, too, may represent an attempt to provide Greek élites with the conceptual tools which they needed in order to make sense of their relationship to the new outside powers, and to give them rhetorical justifications whenever they wished to press for fair treatment.

Cult and ceremony

The phenomenon of ruler-worship (Chapter 5), which became a regular feature of life, does not represent a violent uprooting of existing practice, but a refashioning of existing religious meanings in order to express and formulate the relations between urban communities and their new masters. Though its origins can be seen earlier, for present purposes it begins with the equation of Alexander with the Egyptian god Amun (*Ammôn* in Greek), indicated later by the addition of sacred horns to Alexander's head on coins of Ptolemy (Fig. 3.1).

Kings could modify their public image by adopting patron deities or divine ancestors. Coins of Attalos I carry bull's horns as a symbol of Dionysos, the

Figure 3.1 Silver tetradrachm (17.09 g) in the name of Alexander. Issued under Ptolemy I, *c.*319–315 BC. Obv.: head of Alexander. Rev.: Zeus. Alexander wears an elephant's scalp; the tip of a ram's horn projects beneath it. (Ashmolean Museum, University of Oxford.)

dynasty's chosen patron. After the repulse of the Gauls from Delphi, coins of Gonatas endow him with the horns of Pan, the god who was seen fighting against them (Fig. 4.3).[5] Seleukos I claimed Apollo as his ancestor, as is shown in a decree of Ilion:

> When Nymphios son of Diotrephes was *epimênios*, and Dionysios son of Hippomedon was president, Demetrios son of Diës moved:
>
> Since king Antiochos son of king Seleukos, having in the beginning taken over the kingship and pursued a glorious and honourable policy, has sought to bring back to peace and their former prosperity the cities of the Seleukis [*Seleukid Syria*] which were suffering from difficult times because of the rebels from his cause; ...
>
> and (since) now he has come to the areas this side of Mt. Tauros with all zeal and enthusiasm and has at once restored peace to the cities and has advanced his interests and the kingship to a more powerful and more brilliant position; ...
>
> be it resolved by the council and the people that the priestess, the temple-wardens, and the *prytaneis* [*senior magistrates*] should pray to Athena of Ilion, together with the ambassadors, that his presence [this side of Tauros] should be to the advantage of the king; ...
>
> and that the other priests and priestesses should pray together with the priest of king Antiochos to Apollo, the ancestor of his family, to Nike [*Victory*], to Zeus, and to all the other gods and goddesses....
>
> (Austin 139, BD 16, Burstein 15, *OGIS* 219)

This document neatly encapsulates the discourse within which both cities and kings had to operate. The king is the benefactor of his subjects and allies; he is successful; his kingdom is spectacularly wealthy; the city is unshakably loyal to him; both are pious and revere the gods.

The image of the king could be reinforced by a surname or nickname. Sometimes it is in Macedonian dialect and its meaning uncertain, as in the cases of Antigonos II Gonatas (p. 428 n. 24) and Antigonos III Doson. Sometimes the name is descriptive: Antigonos I is called Monophthalmos, 'One-eyed', though not in official documents. It can be a recognition of military success: as early as 303/2 Demetrios Poliorketes is addressed as Megas ('Great') in an honorific decree by an élite Athenian military corps who had fought with him (*ISE* 7).[6] Other names seem to derive from popular perception or satire, such as Ptolemy IX Lathyros ('Chickpea') and Ptolemy XII Auletes ('Oboist'). Many, however, are cultic. Antiochos I received (we are not told from whom) the title of Soter ('Saviour') for his victory over the Gauls (App. *Syrian Wars*, 65); it was already a cult title of deities such as Zeus and Asklepios. Occasionally the epithet is unambiguously divine, as with Antiochos II's title Theos ('God'), bestowed by the city of Miletos after he overthrew their tyrant. More than one king was called Epiphanes, which has the twin senses of 'eminent' and 'manifest', as of a god present here on Earth. In Egypt, indeed, the Ptolemies' surnames are often Greek renderings of traditional pharaonic titles.[7] When a title is used in documents during a king's lifetime, it probably reflects an image he was content to see advertised, whether or not it was done on his initiative.

The outward badges of kingship were not elaborate by the standards of modern European royalty. To judge from visual representations, kings wore military boots and a cloak, but the only emblem unique to them was the diadem (*diadêma*), a white (or purple-and-white) woollen headband (Fig. 3.2).[8]

Figure 3.2 Portrait of Demetrios Poliorketes from the Villa of the Papyri, Herculaneum (Naples, Mus. Naz. 6149). A good Roman copy. The king wears a thin, tubular version of the royal *diadêma* (headband); the Dionysiac attribute of small bull's horns are visible in the hair over his forehead (the right horn alone showing in this photograph, near the top of the *diadêma*). On these attributes, see Smith, *Hellenistic Royal Portraits*, 34–8 (diadem), 40–1 (horns). (Photograph: Deutsches Archäologisches Institut, Rome; neg. no. 83.1776.)

When in the 160s Eumenes II of Pergamon sent his doctor Stratios to persuade his brother Attalos not to desert him, Stratios

> represented to him that he was already practically joint king with his brother, and only differed from him in the fact that he wore no diadem and was not called king, though in everything else he possessed an equal and identical authority.
>
> (Polyb. 30. 2)

Though probably not lavishly dressed, kings were set apart by their lifestyle. For citizens of *poleis* the *symposion* (men's drinking-party) was, and probably remained, a central ritual of civic life. Under Philip II and his successors it took on a larger scale and a new meaning. Arrian describes a number of banquets at which Alexander revealed important policy decisions; for Plutarch and other biographers the feast is often the occasion on which a king's character is revealed most clearly. The 'banquet of the king and the wise men', in which the king posed questions to philosophers to test their wisdom, became a stock feature of popular sources (for similar episodes see Plutarch, *Alexander*, 64; *Pyrrhos*, 14, Austin 47 *b*).[9] Josephus, writing in the first century AD but using earlier sources, describes a similar scene in which Ptolemy III meets a Jewish moneylender (*AJ* 12. 175, Austin 276). These episodes may be tales that grew in the telling, but doubtless the kings could see the potential here for effective self-presentation.

Public ceremonies gave kings further opportunities to present themselves to a wider audience and consolidate their power.[10] A complex language of ceremonial, such as those of recent European monarchies, was not adopted, except perhaps in Egypt where each new king was crowned in accordance with pharaonic tradition.[11] Kingship was, however, increasingly associated with lavish festivals and exotic display, whether provided from the monarch's own resources or held in his honour.

The banquet was a visible demonstration of the king's great wealth, and it was obligatory for a leader to honour his subordinates by inviting them to his table. When Eumenes of Kardia was being besieged, even though he had no provisions other than grain and salt he invited his associates to dine with him, 'sweetening the common meal (*syssition*) with conversation of charm and friendliness' (Plut. *Eum.* 11). Greek tradition tended to frown on excessive luxury, so Eumenes' ability to make tolerable the inversion of the normally luxurious royal banquet redounds to his moral credit as far as Plutarch is concerned; Plutarch may be writing much later and has his philosophical agenda, but the story presumably has an origin in Hieronymos (p. 264). In showing hospitality the kings were upholding the traditions of Greek and Macedonian hospitality. The difference from earlier practice was, at least on most occasions, the scale and lavishness of the entertainment.

The king could bestow symbolic or real largesse while being fêted himself.

One such event was the occasion in 291 on which Demetrios I was welcomed into Athens and greeted with paeans, processional odes, and a hymn comparing him to the gods (pp. 160–1). Processions were a prominent feature of Greek religious practice, and the kings were not slow to engage with this civic tradition. The late author Athenaeus, drawing on the contemporary historian Kallixeinos, describes the great procession held by Ptolemy II at Alexandria in 271/0, which combined Greek and Egyptian elements. After a great number of exotic animals for sacrifice came a four-wheeled carriage bearing images of gods and statues of Alexander and Ptolemy.

> On a four-wheeled carriage ... the city of Corinth [*i.e. a personification*], standing next to Ptolemy, was crowned with a golden diadem.... This four-wheeled carriage was followed by women wearing expensive clothes and ornaments; they were given the names of cities, some from Ionia and the rest the Greek cities which were established in Asia and the islands and had been under Persian rule; they all wore golden crowns. On other four-wheeled carts were carried a *thyrsos* of gold 90 cubits long and a silver lance 60 cubits long, and on another one a golden phallus 120 cubits long, painted over and bound with golden fillets, with a gold star at its extremity, the circumference of which was 6 cubits.
>
> (Ath. 5. 201 b–f, Austin 219)

Then came exotic animals, more statues of gods, then over 57,000 cavalry and 23,000 infantry, lavishly kitted out. Rich prizes were offered for victors in contests, and presumably the population was treated to food and wine. The total expense was over two thousand talents, and the splendour of the occasion was no doubt intended to demonstrate the king's generosity towards the people of Alexandria, both Greek and non-Greek, to impress them with his power, and to emphasize the stability and continuity of his dynasty.[12]

The language of ritual, like that of art, was being used to express new social relations. In these and other ways the kings were adopting a Greek ceremonial code derived from the traditions of the *symposion* and of *polis* festivals. Indeed, the code of meanings and symbolic associations was one which they, as Greeks, shared; in time it becomes increasingly difficult to separate Macedonian identity from Greek. In this respect, as in others, the kings are from one viewpoint 'conservationists' who 'take on the job of upholding the values of the classical city'.[13] It was much more sensible than imposing one's will by force; but it would probably be wrong to imagine them taking conscious decisions to exploit existing ritual cynically. Rather than a calculated strategy, it may simply have seemed to them the most natural way of performing their role.

Visual representations

Particularly characteristic of the period from Alexander on, and partly new in Greek art, were the many royal 'portraits'. Greek culture was still, for the most part, oral. Literature flourished, and the public uses of writing were more extensive than before, thanks to the increasing tendency of cities to record their proceedings on stone and the kings' need for complex archives; but most men and women probably read little and wrote less. As in medieval Europe, statements about the religious and political order were often made through visual representation. Deities had earlier been shown in sculpture and on coins; now monarchs, too, were portrayed in this way.

The precedent was set by Alexander, who at an early stage became typified as a youthful figure with luxuriant hair (parted off-centre) and eyes upturned to heaven as if in recognition of his divine descent (Fig. 3.3).[14] In statues and in other media his standard portrait – not necessarily lifelike – is modified in various ways, such as by the addition of ram's horns to symbolize his link to his divine father Zeus-Ammon (for which see Arr. 3. 3–4, Austin 8). Not surprisingly, his portraits are the most numerous among royal statues, and provided a type upon which other statues were modelled. Lysimachos seems to have been the first to put Alexander's head on coins; others later did so to express continuity with the founder of the empire.

Statues of later kings are often harder to identify, partly because most of them are known from Roman copies; but it is clear that they drew not only upon images of Alexander in sculpture and other media, but also – like representations of him – upon the visual language of earlier Greek statuary. Kings were represented as warriors and horsemen, or simply as having athletic musculature. They were usually shown as young adults, certainly no older than early middle life; the portrait of Seleukos I was made when he was actually an old man.[15] They were made to seem godlike but 'separate from the traditional Olympians'.[16]

The first king depicted on coins during his lifetime seems to be Demetrios I. Coin portraits tend to be less stereotypical than statues, but it would be rash to read off individual personality traits from coins.[17] Coin portraits were not meant to be accurate renderings – given the lack of mechanically reproducible pictures, for example through engravings and photography, they could scarcely be so – but individual features could be included and presented as those of a particular king, a kind of signature. The Greek kings who ruled Baktria (pp. 284, 285–6) are often portrayed as mature, with 'realistic' faces and military headgear; did they really look like that, or was it a way of showing that they were good rulers?[18] Some portraits of the kings of Pontos give them small heads and large jaws;[19] these may be the recognized artistic signifiers of a royal family, or exaggerated resemblances to its founder. The issue is not accuracy, which there is no way of testing. Rather, coin portraits were probably meant to embody the virtues the kings wished

Figure 3.3 Portrait of Alexander (height = 0.35 m), found on the Athenian Acropolis (inv. 1331) near the Erechtheion; possibly the original of the 'Erbach Alexander' type and so dating to *c.*340–335, if not a later copy. Note the hairstyle, distinctive of Alexander portraits and imitations thereof, known as the *anastolê*, 'a quiff of hair standing up from the brow with a slightly off-centre parting' (Smith, *Hellenistic Royal Portraits*, 47). In this case Alexander looks straight ahead. Plutarch, *On the Fortune or Virtue of Alexander the Great*, ii, at 335 a–b, describes the heavenward look, which was actually characteristic only of portraits later in Alexander's life (possibly by Lysippos) and widely imitated. (Photograph courtesy of Deutsches Archäologisches Institut, Athens; neg. no. Akr. 2368.)

to project: courage, generosity, wisdom, justice, and so on. We have to ask what kind of statement was being made, by whom, and to whom.

It is important not to exaggerate the novelty of the royal statues; to erect statues of kings was not in itself an inversion of Greek norms, for cities had often put up statues of actual persons as well as of heroes and gods. In coinage, too, the kings were associating themselves – and being associated – with existing civic traditions. In both contexts the king is legitimated by being assimilated into the visual repertoire of Greek city traditions. The validation was thus mutual.

Royal women and the 'royal family'

Monarchy in this period, unlike tyranny in the archaic period, brought the female relatives of male dynasts to the forefront of public life. The term *basilissa* (queen) seems to have been applied to the wives of Macedonian kings only after 306/5, when the new monarchies came into being,[20] suggesting a more prominent role for royal women than in Alexander's lifetime. Some queens are thought to have become genuinely powerful by virtue of their own personalities, though it is likely that they were allowed this public status only in order to contribute to goals defined by men, who retained almost all official authority.

Olympias, the mother of Alexander, wielded enormous power in Macedonia after his death, waging wars in her own right and exercising royal prerogatives in Macedonia.[21] She can almost be considered one of the Successors; among royal women she was untypical in having so much freedom of action, yet typical in that ultimately she lost it. Eurydike, wife of Philip III Arrhidaios (Alexander's half-brother), who was defeated by Olympias and executed, is an example of a more common type: the royal woman who wields power only through her connections with her male relatives and associates and by exploiting her temporary influence over them.

After the wars of the Successors, royal women were more often the bearers of dynastic ambitions on behalf of men than players in their own right. Such a woman is Stratonike, wife of Seleukos I and later of his son Antiochos I. The episode was embellished as a love story by hellenistic writers, and is retold by Plutarch (*Demetrios*, 38) and Appian (*Syrian Wars*, 59–61), who give a sentimentalized account of how Antiochos fell in love with his father's young wife and was pining for her until a clever Greek doctor persuaded Seleukos to hand her over. None of this need be true; the story may well have its origin in propaganda designed to demonstrate the harmonious working relationship between father and son, concealing Seleukos's true purpose in sharing the kingship with his son to ensure a smooth succession.[22] Alternatively, the story need not have its origin in Seleukid propaganda, and may tell us nothing about royal policy, but may be the product of the rhetorical tradition of early imperial times.[23] Other women allegedly used as conveyors of political relationships include Berenike II, daughter of Ptolemy II, who was given to Antiochos II as part of a renegotiation of political relations between the two kingdoms. The resulting problems between Antiochos and his first wife, Laodike, led to the 'Laodikean' or third Syrian war (246–241; p. 289, see Fig. 6.4).

Not only women but sometimes the entire royal family came to be important signifiers of the health of a kingdom. The death of Lysimachos's son and heir may have held a special significance (pp. 49–50). More commonly the woman fulfilled the role successfully, as in the cases of Stratonike and particularly Arsinoë II (Fig. 3.4). It is customary to regard this Arsinoë, the sister and wife of Ptolemy II (r. 285–246), as the most successful royal woman of the early hellenistic period. Sister-marriage was something of a habit among the Ptolemies, following Egyptian precedent. Dynastically it was a safe move, avoiding the division of property or the kingdom and obviating the problem of choosing between other ruling families, or branches of the same family, when making new dynastic links – not to mention the difficulties which choosing a spouse from a Greek family resident in Egypt would entail. Arsinoë was even co-ruler from about 275 until her death in 268,[24] and was the first Ptolemaic queen to be portrayed on coins. The court poet Theokritos celebrates her piety towards the god Adonis in his fifteenth *Idyll* (pp. 238–9). Historians are perhaps too eager to see Arsinoë as a genuinely independent and powerful woman, and even as responsible for the growth of Ptolemaic naval power.[25] Ptolemy II might be content to state publicly that his policy was in accordance with the wishes of 'his ancestors and his sister' (Chremonides decree, p. 126); in actuality, while early queens like Arsinoë may have been influential in private, their public roles served mainly to reinforce the actions and status of their menfolk.

Later in the hellenistic period, particularly in the later Ptolemaic dynasty, there are prominent queens who genuinely seem to play independent roles in dynastic struggles (see Chapter 6). The most famous example is Kleopatra VII, mistress of Julius Caesar and Mark Antony.

A more typical example of the virtues hellenistic queens were supposed to embody, however, might be Apollonis, wife of Attalos I of Pergamon (r. 241–197), who in a decree of the mid-second century from Hierapolis in north-western Asia Minor is praised for her piety towards the gods and her parents, and for her harmonious relations not only with the beautiful, legitimate

Figure 3.4 Gold octadrachm (27.71 g) from Alexandria, *c.*261/0–240 BC. Obv. Ptolemy II and Arsinoë II, rev. Ptolemy I and Berenike I. (British Museum, London.)

children whom she bore but even with her daughter-in-law (Austin 204, *OGIS* 308). The construction of her virtues and achievements in terms so strongly linked to her roles as wife and mother is characteristic of the developing emphasis on the king and his relatives, particularly the Attalids, as a model family.

The negotiation of power

'Greek freedom' and the kings

Part of a king's duty was to be seen to uphold the freedom of the Greek communities within his territory. Documents record the efforts of generals and kings to persuade cities that they were fighting for their liberty. This claim, made in the fifth century by the Spartans and their allies when fighting against imperial Athens, was possibly first voiced in this period by the regent Polyperchon in 319. Diodoros (18. 55) reports that Polyperchon and his advisers, faced with an alliance of Cassander, Antigonos, and Ptolemy, decided

> to free the cities throughout Greece and to overthrow the oligarchies established in them by Antipater: for in this way they would best decrease the influence of Cassander and also win for themselves great glory and many considerable allies.

The change, however, was couched in terms of a decree of the kings, and really represented another invasion of city independence. The decree concludes:

> Let all the Greeks pass a decree that no one shall engage in opposition to us, and that if anyone disobeys, he and his family shall be exiled and his goods shall be confiscated. We have commanded Polyperchon to take in hand these and other matters. Do you obey him, as we also have written to you formerly; for if anyone fails to carry out any of these injunctions, we shall not overlook him.
>
> (Diod. 18. 56)

Several years later, in 314, in the most famous (but by no means the last) such declaration, Antigonos denounced Cassander at a general assembly of his army, referring to crimes against Alexander's family and stating that

> all the Greeks should be free, exempt from garrisons, and autonomous. The soldiers carried the motion and Antigonos despatched messengers in every direction to announce the resolution. He calculated as follows: the Greeks' hopes for freedom would make them willing

allies in the war, while the generals and satraps in the upper satrapies, who suspected Antigonos of seeking to overthrow the kings who had succeeded Alexander, would change their minds and willingly submit to his orders when they saw him clearly taking up the war on their behalf....

Ptolemy heard of the resolution concerning the freedom of the Greeks which the Macedonians with Antigonos had passed, and drafted a proclamation in much the same words to convey to the Greeks that he cared no less for their *autonomia* than did Antigonos. Each side saw that to gain the goodwill of the Greeks would carry no little weight, and so they vied with each other in conferring favours on them.

(Diod. 19. 61, Austin 29)

Similarly, in an inscription from Skepsis in the Troad (north-western Asia Minor), one of many copies displayed in different *poleis*, he makes sweeping claims about how he will treat the Greeks:

We have written a clause into the agreement that all the Greeks should join together in protecting their mutual freedom and *autonomia*, in the belief that in our lifetime they would in all human expectation be preserved, but that in future, with all the Greeks and the men in power bound by oath, the freedom of the Greeks would be much more securely guaranteed.

(Austin 31, BD 6, Harding 132, RC 1, OGIS 5)[26]

Autonomia (at least on one recent interpretation) meant more than merely 'autonomy', the freedom to pass laws: it meant real independence.[27] In such proclamations there was an irreconcilable disjuncture between freedom as a benefit from the king, and freedom from the point of view of the city and its ruling class, for whom liberty was not real if it was a thing to be granted and withdrawn at a king's whim, 'a passive condition'.[28]

Nevertheless the last sentence of the extract makes it clear that this was a two-way process, an observation that derives from Diodoros's main source for the Diadochoi, Hieronymos of Kardia. It is too simple to see the kings as deceitful; hostile cities were potentially very troublesome, and a king who was seen to be 'against' Greek liberty was bound to fare less well. To this extent the Greek cities were sometimes able to influence their destiny to good effect.

On occasions one may wonder whether the vaunted achievements of kings were welcomed by cities, such as when Lysimachos refounded Ephesos (p. 48). A lengthy document from the end of the fourth century (Austin 40, BD 7, *RC* 3–4, *Syll.*³ 344)[29] records the minute planning entailed by Antigonos I's scheme to 'synoikize' (synoecize) – combine into one city – the tiny *polis* of

Lebedos in Ionia and its larger neighbour Teos, and possibly to move Teos to a new site. As Austin remarks in his commentary, 'it seems clear that the plan was that of Antigonus himself, imposed on the reluctant communities, and in fact the synoecism was never carried out'.[30] Doubtless Antigonos's motives were a combination of strategic foresight and the desire to magnify his own fame by founding one more new city.

The military consequences of royal power were often calamitous.[31] Cities were sacked and razed during wars between rival kings. Kings would compel them to recall political exiles if it suited their purposes. Cities were generally no longer in a position to field their own citizen armies as in the classical period; there are only occasional examples of cities supplying citizen troops to a king's army, and mercenary service was now the rule. Macedonian rulers invaded their independence by installing garrisons, as Philip V did after his unprovoked seizure of Samos from the Ptolemies in 200;[32] in such cases much of the cost may have fallen on the host city, and there will have been the usual disruption and interference with normal life that result from the introduction of soldiers. That garrisons and the billeting of troops could arouse resentment is implied by the offer made by the city of Thasos to surrender to Philip V's general 'if he would let them remain without a garrison, exempt from tribute, with no soldiers quartered on them, and governed by their own laws' (Polyb. 15. 24). This case, incidentally, shows what one strong city-state could hope to gain from negotiating with a king.

Sometimes governors (*epistatai*) were imposed. They might be local citizens appointed to rule their own city; Douris of Samos is referred to as 'tyrant' of his city (on this term see also p. 34). An *epistatês*, indeed, was likely to be a go-between, negotiating with the king on behalf of the city; his role need not have been wholly repressive. He might secure a reduction of royal taxes or billeting.[33]

The exception proves the rule, however: cities normally expected that the king would require *phoros*, tribute. Cases of exemption include Erythrai in Ionia; the relevant inscription hints that a grant of immunity made by one king might not be assumed to hold good for his successor, and that to be on the safe side a city had better reapply:

> King Antiochos [*I or II*] to the council and people of Erythrai, greetings. Tharsynon, Pythes, and Bottas, your envoys, handed over the decree to us in which you voted the honours, and brought the crown with which you crowned us, and likewise the gold offered as a present, and they themselves spoke about the goodwill which you have constantly felt towards our house ... and also about the eminent position enjoyed by the city under the former kings ... And since Tharsynon, Pythes, and Bottas declared that under Alexander and Antigonos your city was autonomous and free from tribute, ... we shall help to preserve your *autonomia* and we grant you exemption

from tribute, including all the other taxes and the contributions to
the Gallic fund.... We also invite you ... to remember worthily
[those from whom] you have received benefactions ...

(Austin 183, BD 22, Burstein 23, *RC* 15, *OGIS* 223)

The passing mentions of regular and special taxes and of monetary levies are
revealing, as is the fact that the city, ironically, has to *buy* its tax immunity;
presumably there was thought to be a net saving, and the institution may be
explained by the king's preference for having a reliable source of cash rather
than farming out the tax collection to an entrepreneur each year. The
offering of crowns (often of gold, a further cost to the city) is another regular
feature of cities' dealings with kings (see further, on the Ptolemaic empire,
pp. 159, 195).[34]

Associates and advisers

The aura surrounding a king was enhanced by the presence of companions
and soldiers. The English word often used to describe a king's circle of officers
and supporters is 'court', no doubt rightly used to conjure up a mixed group
of adherents not linked to a particular location but travelling with the king.
While it recalls Persian, Egyptian, and medieval English monarchy rather
than anything Greek, it also resembles the elegant and cultured environment
of earlier Greek aristocrats, particularly the tyrants of the archaic period.
There are differences: the 'court' embraces a complex range of administrators
often running large territories, which was not a feature of earlier tyrannies.
The similarity is important, however, reminding us that while royal power
was in theory absolute or unconditional it depended on powerful and loyal
support.

Besides more or less functional assistants, the king was accompanied by
'Friends' (*philoi*), sometimes Macedonian but often from cities loyal to him.
They were chosen by him, and might not be retained by his successor. The
tradition had its origin in Macedonian monarchy, but was useful for administering new territories and satrapies. Those who were recruited from among
the élite of a *polis* had an important mediating role between city and king,
such as when the city had a request to make.[35] Athenians in this position
include Philippides of Kephale (p. 48) and probably the politician Demochares.
Recent work has shown how, over time, the Athenians by the mid-third
century came to view Friends of kings who were Athenian citizens as being
well placed not only to ensure the king's goodwill towards Athens, but to
exert positive influence over him in order to secure the Athenians' wishes.[36]
Sometimes Friends acted as a council of advisers which might meet formally;
when Polybios states that Antiochos III's *synedrion* met to discuss the revolt
of Molon (5. 41; Austin 147), he is probably referring to them. After distinguished service a Friend could be rewarded, for example with priesthoods in

cities under the king's control (see e.g. Austin 175, BD 132, *RC* 44, *OGIS* 244; Austin 176, *RC* 45; both concerning Seleukeia-in-Pieria).[37]

Sometimes the relationship was informal, as in the case of Demetrios of Pharos, the adviser with whom Philip V discussed how to react to Hannibal's victory over the Romans in 217 (Polyb. 5. 101). Some advisers gained a dark reputation. Agathokles of Samos and, especially, the king's guardian Sosibios are said to have exercised a sinister influence over Ptolemy V owing to his immaturity (Polyb. 15. 34–5). Polybios (7. 14. 6)[38] warns that few kings choose their advisers carefully enough; he is, of course, an opponent of kings. The influence of the Friends could, however, be represented as benign, as in a document recording the deliberations of Attalos, brother of Eumenes II of Pergamon, together with 'Athenaios and Sosandros and Menogenes but also others of my relatives' (*anangkaioi*, literally 'people intrinsically connected'; *RC* 61, lines 3–5), an interesting if possibly hyperbolic compliment.[39] From the viewpoint of a Greek city, a special connection with a king's Friend offered an incomparable channel of upward communication.

Negotiation with kings and between poleis

Cities were not necessarily powerless; the kings depended on them for practical and ideological support, and it was sometimes possible to make a trade-off. Cities, one may assume, vied with one another in giving gifts and paying compliments to kings; equally, kings could enhance their wider reputation by being seen to treat cities well. The following passage is from a fragmentary letter from Seleukos I and his son to an official at the sanctuary of Plouton (Pluto) and Kore at Nysa in Karia:

> King Seleukos and Antiochos to Sopatros, [greeting]. The Athymbrianoi [having sent] to us [as envoys] Iatrokles, Artemidoros, and Timotheos in the matter of their [right of receiving suppliants, their inviolability, and their tax-exemption], we have [...] the details and have written to you [that you may give them a formal] reply. [For our policy is always] through benefactions [to please] the citizens [of the Greek cities and] with reverence to join in increasing [the honours] of the gods, [so that we may be the object of goodwill] transmissible for all time [to those who come after us].
>
> (*RC* 9, *Syll.*[2] p. 467)

Sometimes the process is explicitly described in such a way that a mutually beneficial transaction is implied, as in a very long inscription from mid-third-century Smyrna (246–226/5 BC) of which the following is the opening:

Resolved by the people, proposal of the generals.

Since previously, at the time when king Seleukos (II) crossed into Seleukis, and many great dangers were threatening our city and territory, the people preserved its goodwill and friendship towards him, and was not daunted at the enemies' invasion and gave no thought to the destruction of its property, but considered every-thing secondary to the maintenance of its policy of friendship and to defending the king's interests to the best of its ability, as it initially promised:

and so king Seleukos, who shows piety towards the gods and affection towards his parents, being generous and knowing how to repay gratitude towards his benefactors, honoured our city because of the goodwill and zeal displayed by the people towards his inter-ests ...

(Austin 182, BD 29, *OGIS* 229)

It is striking that the city describes itself as a benefactor of the king! To assume the existence of what you want to bring about is good rhetoric.

Not only did it help the king to be able to claim that he was acting justly and piously, on occasion he had to prove it by dispensing practical justice. Since the archaic period, Greek cities in dispute with one another had often called upon a third city to arbitrate. To judge by the increasing frequency with which inter-state justice is recorded, it became quite an industry in the third century, even allowing for the greater frequency with which documents were inscribed on stone. There is no evidence that it was generally a successful procedure, but its popularity implies that it was sometimes effect-ive and certainly that it was generally commended.[40] One reason may be that to all intents and purposes cities could no longer put armies into the field against one another.

Often a city is thanked for sending a party of *dikastai* (jurors or judges) to resolve internal disputes in another city. The king could exploit the system: on one occasion the Ptolemaic admiral Philokles of Sidon arranged for Miletos, Myndos, and Halikarnassos to send dikasts to Samos who would resolve quarrels between citizens. The subsequent Samian decree in honour of the Myndian dikasts is preserved, and gives us an insight into the admin-istration of a city-state at this period.

Resolved by the council and the *dêmos*; proposal of the *prytaneis*:

Concerning the things about which the council took preliminary counsel, so that the dikasts who came from both Miletos and Myndos and Halikarnassos about the unresolved contracts might be honoured:

Whereas, when the citizens had differences from one another about the unresolved contracts, Philokles king of the Sidonians, wishing to be in concord as regards the *polis*, wrote that the *demos* of the Myndians should send a court that would reconcile the unresolved contracts; and the Myndians, affording every good will and eagerness towards the reconciliation of the citizens, selected respectable (*kalous k'agathous*) men and sent them to the *polis*, (namely) Theokles son of Theogenes (and) Herophantos son of Artemidoros; and these men (dealt) well and justly with all the cases brought to them, adjudicating some and reconciling others, preferring that those of the citizens who had differences should be reconciled and conduct their civic affairs in freedom from their charges against one another:

It has been resolved by the council and the *demos* that the *demos* of the Myndians be commended for their sending of the men, and that the men who came be commended, (namely) Theokles son of Theogenes (and) Herophantos son of Artemidoros, for having well and appropriately reconciled some of the cases and adjudicated others; and to crown them with a golden crown and to proclaim the crown at the tragic festival of the Dionysia; and that they be *proxenoi* of the *polis* and benefactors, and that citizenship be given to them on like and equal terms, and to allot them into tribe and thousand and hundred and *genos*[41] exactly as all other Samians; and that front-seat privilege be available to them at whatever contests the *polis* may arrange; and that access to the council and the *demos* be given to them in first place after the sacrifices and the royal rituals; and that they have the right of sailing in and out, in war and peace, without *sylê* and without truce; and that the successive established authorities look after them if they need anything;

And so that the *demos* of the Myndians may know what has been voted, (it has been resolved) to choose an envoy who, coming to Myndos, shall deliver the decree to the council and the *demos*; and to inscribe it on a stone *stêlê* (pillar) and erect it in the sanctuary of Hera; and the secretary of the council shall look after the inscribing, and the treasurer shall minister to the expense of the *stele* and the inscribing. And such expenses shall be available to the envoy as the *demos* may determine.

The envoy chosen was Aischylos son of Ampelides.

(Austin 135, *SEG* i. 363)[42]

We can observe the various magistrates of the Samians and their functions, and the way in which a middle-ranking *polis* inflates its importance by florid, repetitive, and legalistic language. Many of the phrases in the document are matched in similar decrees from Samos and elsewhere and became stock compliments in diplomatic exchanges. The way the document switches between the active and the passive voice, however, suggests a committee at work, or a series of amendments from the floor in a public assembly, each speaker trying to outdo the last in generosity.

In second-century Crete there may have been a system of common arbitration, *koinodikion*, for settling private disputes between members of different *poleis*.[43] Sometimes a city would arbitrate or mediate between two others, as when a Milesian panel of judges was called in to resolve a frontier dispute between Sparta and Messene (Burstein 80, *Syll.*[3] 683, *I. Olympia*, 52; cf. Tacitus, *Annals*, 4. 43. 1–6).[44] In other cases a king would be called upon to arbitrate. In the 280s Lysimachos was approached by Samos and Priene about their long-running argument concerning the territory of Anaia on the mainland of Asia Minor. Historical precedents were cited by each side in turn, and the king seems to have heard their envoys in person. He seems to express irritation with the Prieneans when he tells the Samians, 'If we had known that you had had this land in possession and use for so many years we should never have undertaken to hear the case' (BD 12, Burstein 12, *RC* 7, *OGIS* 13, lines 4–6), and he awards judgement to them. It is noteworthy that in subsequent flare-ups between Samos and Priene Lysimachos's judgement about at least one portion of the disputed territory was regarded as decisive.[45] Other examples of inter-city arbitration include the Megarian adjudication of the land frontier between Epidauros and Corinth around 240 BC (Austin 136, *Syll.*[3] 471);[46] like others of this kind, the inscription lists in detail the agreed boundary markers.

Notable exceptions to the generalization that dikastic missions became common are the two most powerful city-states of Greece, Athens and Rhodes, which never felt it necessary to call upon the citizens of other states, though Athenians often served as *dikastai* elsewhere.[47]

The growth of a 'diplomacy industry' can be seen in the number of documents which record that one city recognizes the *asylia*, or inviolability, of another city or cult place. Sanctuaries were inherently protected by divine sanction; technically, therefore, there was no need to grant them immunity. Beginning in the 260s BC, however, we have many inscriptions recording 'declared inviolability'. Recipient cities are typically in the Aegean and Asia Minor, though there are several from Boiotia: in the first known record the Delphic amphiktyony recognizes the *asylia* of the temple of Athena Itonia at Koroneia (*SEG* xviii. 240, *ISE* ii. 74).[48] Another characteristic example, the second earliest known, is from Delphi, and refers to a request initiated by the city of Smyrna and supported by a king:

GODS

[Resolved by the *po*]*lis* of the Delphians:
    inasmuch as king Seleukos (son) of king [Antioch]os, having sent a letter to the city, deems that both the sanctuary [of] Aphrodite Stratonikis and the *polis* of the Smyrnaians should be [sa]cred and

inviolable, himself previously having obeyed the oracle of the god and having performed the things he also deems that the *polis* should do, and has conceded to the Smyrnaians that both their *polis* and their territory should be free and not subject to tr[ib]ute, and confirms their existing territory and announces that he will restore their ancestral territory;

and (since) the Smyrnaians, having sent as envoys Hermodoros and Demetrios, think that the things conceded to them must be written up in the sanctuary, as the king deems also:

it has been resolved by the *polis* of the Delphians that both the sanctuary of Aphrodite Stratonikis and the *polis* of the [Smyr]naians are sacred and inviolable, just as the king has written [and] the *polis* of the Smyrnaians deems; and that it has been commanded to the sacred envoys (*theôroi*) who proclaim the Pythian festival that they praise king Seleukos on account of th[ese things] and his piety and his compliance with the oracle of the god, and that they sacrifice to Aphrodite: and that the *polis* is to inscribe this decree in the sanctuary of the god, and the [*i.e. king's*] letter on the wall in the archive.

(BD 28, OGIS 228)[49]

In this instance the interests of city, king, and sanctuaries worked together: the exchange of formalities allows the king's munificence to the city and his formal compliment to its sanctuary to be proclaimed to the Greek world at Delphi, reinforcing the prestige of the panhellenic centre in turn.

The fashion persisted throughout the hellenistic period. Antiochos III granted *asylia* to Teos in 204/3 as part of his wider attempt to revive Seleukid prestige (Austin 151, Burstein 33);[50] that the Romans, ten years later, matched his grant suggests a partly political motive (Austin 157, BD 87, Sherk 8, *Syll.*³ 601).[51] In AD 22 and 23, however, the Roman senate reviewed existing claims to the privilege by cities and sanctuaries in Asia, Cyprus, Crete, and possibly elsewhere (Tacitus, *Annals*, 3. 60–3; 4. 14. 1–2), and probably placed restrictions on future grants.[52]

Grants of *asylia* have sometimes been linked to religious decline (a phenomenon for which there is no real evidence; see Chapter 5) or to the desire to protect exiles, refugees, or criminals on the run; more plausibly, they have been seen as attempts to enlist military aid in times of trouble, or to limit piracy by peoples such as the Aitolians and Cretans. Some examples of piracy will now be reviewed before we return to *asylia*.

Piracy appears often in the sources, though the terminology varies and one writer's piracy is another's naval campaign. Menander, at any rate, dramatizes the seizure of a child and a slave by pirates, who then sell them at a slave-market at Mylasa in Karia (*The Sikyonian*, 3–15, Austin 86). A similar situation seems to be envisaged in the mid-third century when the city of Miletos concludes a treaty with Knossos, whereby a citizen of either *polis* may not purchase a free person or slave of the other; the inscription records that similar decisions were taken by nineteen other Cretan towns (Austin 89).[53] Also in the third century, the island city of Amorgos honoured two of its citizens for helping to rescue 'more than thirty girls, women, and other persons both free and slave' from pirates (*peiratai*; Austin 87, *Syll.*[3] 521).[54] In such cases the captors may be supposed to be doing what they normally do: making their living in a way traditional to them but less acceptable to the political communities of Greece. When, however, the Athenians in 217/16 honour a Cretan for rescuing people captured by Aitolians (Austin 88, *Syll.*[3] 535),[55] we may wonder whether this is not a case of warlike activity, perhaps connected with the war of Philip V against the Aitolians; it is worth noting that the term 'pirate' is not used in this decree. (A similar case is Austin 50, see p. 126.)

Measures against piracy had probably been envisaged in the charter of the Greek league set up in 302 by Antigonos I (p. 44). Later the Rhodians took on the role of restricting piracy, particularly by Cretan cities (for the exercise of Rhodian power in eastern Crete *c*.200 BC, see Austin 95, *Syll.*[3] 581, their treaty with Hierapytna).[56] The first Roman involvement in Greek affairs, in Illyria from 229 BC, was partly motivated by concern for Italian trading ships which were falling victim to Illyrian attacks. For the next two hundred years, campaigns against 'pirates' in southern Asia Minor, the Aegean, and the Syrian coasts were a periodic preoccupation of the Romans (see p. 393). Piracy of different kinds, then, though sometimes hard to distinguish from peripheral acts in military campaigns, was at times a hazard for travellers by sea and could involve individuals or communities in expensive ransom payments. On the other hand, it may often have flared up in the penumbra of wider conflicts, posing a danger to coastal settlements rather than ships at sea. Piracy, in the sense of robbery by ship, was a real phenomenon but not necessarily so widespread or homogeneous as to explain the generality of instances when *asylia* is sought or granted.[57]

A recent study points out that requests for military aid form a small minority of *asylia* documents; in most cases there is no convincing pragmatic explanation. To take an extreme case: when the people of Kos requested that the Greek city of Neapolis (Naples) in Italy acknowledge the inviolability of their Asklepieion, it is inconceivable that actual military assistance is envisaged. It seems likely, therefore, that what we are seeing is the exchange of recognition and prestige, things which, though on one level without practical efficacy, were important counters of value and might be expected to lead to intangible or long-term advantages as a result of the enhanced status they gave to cities and sanctuaries.[58]

As well as enjoying (to judge by the inscriptions) increasingly frequent diplomatic and ceremonial ties, cities may have become less impermeable in certain respects. They more often shared their citizenship with one another, for example through *sympoliteia* (e.g. Austin 134, *Syll.*[3] 647, between the

Phokian towns of Stiris and Medeon in the second century) or *homopoliteia* (attested only between the island *poleis* of Kos and Kalymnos in the late third century; Austin 133).[59] Shared citizenship is also recorded in the early third century between Hierapytna and Praisos in Crete (Austin 132).[60] Cities were readier to admit strangers and those of mixed parentage. In the later hellenistic period, as Roman domination led to the dilution of citizen values, women were sometimes allowed to act as quasi-magistrates and benefactors.[61]

Royal benefactions and monumentalization

The Greeks had long experience of constructing built environments for public use, in existing towns and sanctuaries or after the foundation of a new city. Early aristocrats and tyrants expressed their ambition and power by building lavish monuments for their cities; the most prominent of recent Greek dynastic monarchs, Maussollos (latinized as Mausolus), satrap of Karia in south-western Asia Minor, created a Greek-style palace at Halikarnassos. Philip II is credited with founding or modernizing a number of towns in northern Greece.

Kings, like their Macedonian and Persian predecessors, were expected to be rich[62] and to build lavishly. Ptolemy adorned Alexandria as the resting-place of Alexander and the new cultural capital of the Greek world. The Antigonids embellished Pella; later, the Attalids gave Pergamon its new acropolis; but the greatest founders of cities were the Seleukids, though Appian's list of the cities created by Seleukos (quoted, pp. 304–5) is an exaggeration. City foundations could have marked effects upon certain aspects of local cultures. In northern Syria the appearance of four major new cities (see Strabo, quoted on p. 288) brought about a new multi-cultural environment; the details of long-term cultural adaptations and borrowings from one culture to another, particularly in the cultic sphere, are not yet clear, but it has been noted that until the fourth century AD there are no documents or coins from this area bearing any Semitic scripts, only Greek (though many languages were indubitably spoken).[63] (On urban form, see further pp. 86–96.)

In Egypt, Alexander founded a new capital at Alexandria. In Asia, he and his successors created a relatively dense network of new urban centres, though the number of Alexander's foundations in the former Persian empire has sometimes been overestimated.[64] Not all were large cities – some were more like small market or garrison towns, typically settlements for veteran Macedonian soldiers – but they are a resonant statement of the power of the new order to transform the landscape. The construction of Ai Khanum in Baktria (p. 305 and Fig. 8.5), albeit incorporating elements from non-Greek architecture, is the most surprising – if only because the most far-flung – example of the imposition of Greek urban form upon an alien landscape.

Closer to home, royal intervention in the fundamental structures of cities could be materially and socially beneficial, if also a demonstration of power. Part of the city of Samos was twice replanned in the third century, with a new street alignment and new buildings; these operations may have been funded by the kings who ruled Samos, perhaps the Ptolemies on each occasion.[65] When Philip V responds to a request from the Thessalian city of Larisa in 217, he aims to reshape not so much the physical as the social form of the city:

> King Philip to the *tagoi* [*chief magistrates of the Thessalians*] and the city of Larisa, greetings. Petraios, Anangkippos, and Aristonous when they came on their embassy declared to me that because of the wars your city needs more inhabitants. Until I think of others who are deserving of your citizenship, for the present I rule that you must pass a decree to grant citizenship to the Thessalians or the other Greeks who are resident in your city. For when this is done ... I am sure that many other benefits will result for me and the city, and the land will be more fully cultivated.

The same inscription preserves a letter of 214 in which he complains that

> those who were granted citizenship in accordance with the letter I sent to you and your decree, and whose names were inscribed, have been erased .... That it is much the best state of affairs for as many as possible to enjoy citizen rights, the city to be strong, and the land not to lie shamefully deserted, as at present, I believe none of you would deny, and one may observe others who grant citizenship in the same way. Among these are the Romans ...
> (Austin 60, BD 31, Burstein 65, *Syll.*[3] 543, *IG* ix. 2. 517)

He aims to look like a concerned benefactor, but wishes to preserve the security of his territory. The document reveals both sides of royal power over Greek cities.

Royal intervention in the affairs of existing cities was not always unwelcome, particularly when cities encountered financial difficulties. The wars of the Successors may have caused economic problems among the élite; in Ephesos in the 290s, landowners were embroiled in major debt problems, their estates having been ruined during the conflict between Demetrios and Lysimachos (BD 9; *Syll.*[3] 364). Cities were sometimes compelled to raise public subscriptions for new buildings; examples from early in the period include the town of Oropos, on the Attica–Boiotia border, raising money for a fortification (Austin 101, *Syll.*[3] 544),[66] and Halikarnassos in south-western Asia Minor honouring those who contributed over 500 drachmas to a stoa built in honour of Apollo and king Ptolemy (Austin 100, *OGIS* 46). Istria in the early second century thanks a citizen for cancelling interest payments on a long-standing public debt to his father (Austin 102, *ISE* ii. 130), and in the mid-second century Krannon in Thessaly even attempts to solve debt problems by raising a public subscription (Austin 103, *ISE* ii. 199).

One possible by-product of such financial problems was that from time to time a city could find no citizen willing to incur the expense of public office;[67] reluctance was also, perhaps, natural when independence was limited by the need to adopt an appropriate posture towards a higher power, and where the political prominence one enjoyed within the city might be terminated by a hostile king. Sometimes a king temporarily took on a public role, such as chief magistrate or priest, which involved the funding of festivals and other public events. Alexander held such a position at Miletos in 334/3 (*Syll.*[3] 272), as did Demetrios in 295 and Antiochos in 280/79 (*Syll.*[3] 322). These crises seem particularly frequent during the wars of the Successors.

Cities would seek gifts from kings.[68] On other occasions kings might appoint city officials; a fragmentary letter of Eumenes I to the city of Pergamon (admittedly a city that enjoyed a unique relationship with a dynasty)[69] shows the close involvement of the king in the city:

[Eumenes son of Philetairos to the people of Pergamon, greetings. Palamandros, Skymnos, Metrodoros, Theotimos,] (and) Philiskos, [the generals appointed (by Eumenes) during the priesthood of ...], appear [to have discharged] their official duties [well in all circumstances]; for they have justly performed their duties and everything else, and] have [not only] administered [all the] revenues of the city and the sacred revenues [in] their period of office in a way that was advantageous to the people and the gods, but have also sought out (debts) passed over by the previous boards of generals ... We have decided ourselves to crown them at the Panathenaic festival, and we thought we ought to write to you about them, so that you might ... honour them as you think they deserve. Farewell.

(Austin 195 *a*, BD 67, *RC* 23, *OGIS* 267 i)

Rulers often made gifts to cities and sanctuaries. Particularly before the Roman conquest, these gifts might be in cash, though it could be more convenient for the ruler to donate in kind from the resources of his empire.[70] Antigonos I gave 150,000 *medimnoi* of grain to Athens in 307/6 (Plut. *Demetr.* 10, Austin 34), as well as timber to build warships; such a gift was clearly part of an effort to curry favour with an important ally. A number of wealthy rulers gave generously, both in cash and in kind, to the city of Rhodes after a devastating earthquake in 227/6 (Polyb. 5. 88–90, Austin 93). The Seleukid queen Laodike arranged similar gifts of grain to the city of Iasos in Karia, from which dowries were to be funded for daughters of needy citizens (Austin 156, Burstein 36, *c.*195 BC).[71] Gifts to sanctuaries might be made with the aim of putting a more general gloss on the king's standing in Greece, as when, in 160/59, Eumenes II and Attalos II of Pergamon gave money to Delphi for the purchase of wheat, the repair of the theatre, and the education of children:

> Resolved by the city of Delphi ...: since king Attalos (*II*) son of king Attalos (*I*), when we sent envoys to him ..., listened favourably to our requests and sent to the city 18,000 Alexander drachmas of silver for the education of the children and 3,000 drachmas for the honours and sacrifices, so that his donation might remain in perpe-tuity and the salaries of the teachers might be regularly paid and the expense for the honours and the sacrifices might be provided from the interest on the loan of the money: with good fortune, be it resolved by the city that the money be consecrated to the god ...
> (Austin 206, Burstein 89, *Syll.*[3] 672)[72]

It would be simplistic, however, to see these benefactions as pure public relations exercises; as Préaux pointedly remarks, 'authentic piety and disin-terested generosity are not necessarily excluded'.[73]

Civic society and socio-economic change

It has been suggested that the frequency of royal gifts to Greek communities led to a degree of economic stagnation, allowing cities to shirk the task of seeking to develop their economies.[74] This implies too modern a view of the administration of city economies; it is unlikely that city élites devoted much thought to economic 'development' in the modern sense. City economies probably remained largely unchanged except for the imposition of royal levies and, conversely, the intervention of kings through benefactions. Davies and others, in fact, point to signs of economic growth, partly explained by the increasing intensity of commercial interaction between different parts of the hellenistic world. Cities may have benefited indirectly from the Macedonian conquest and exploitation of western Asia, and from the general development of commercial institutions.[75] The economic base, of course, remained agricultural production in the rural territory (*chora*) of a city. (See Chapter 4 for the possible economic effects of Macedonian rule in Greece.)

Changes in urban form

The civic architecture and monuments of the hellenistic period are often easy to distinguish from earlier and later buildings; different architectural orders are inventively combined, and there is a general impression of grandeur. Institutions which gained new importance became architecturally more elaborate, such as the *gymnasion*, an educational centre where, in many cities, the adolescent sons of the élite were imbued with Greek culture. Inscribed laws about the administration of *gymnasia* are found in cities across the Greek world, such as Beroia in Macedonia (Austin 118),[76] Miletos (Austin 119, BD 127, Burstein 30, *Syll.*[3] 577), and Teos (Austin 120, BD 65, *Syll.*[3] 578), all from the second century (for the assumption that a *polis* needs, above all things, a *gymnasion* see Eumenes II's letter to a Phrygian community, p. 315). Older institutions such as agoras, theatres, and sanctuaries also became larger and more luxurious.

Yet many of these resplendent edifices were paid for by outside powers. At certain times, older cities like Athens appear to have been unable to fund major public projects from their own reserves, perhaps because they were no longer imperial powers but were dominated for shorter or longer periods by foreign rulers. Increasingly they relied upon external benefactors such as kings and their generals.

In Athens this trend began relatively late. There is a long gap in major public projects after 300/299, when the new Doric stoa at the sanctuary of Asklepios, on the south slope of the Acropolis, was voted in by decree (*IG* ii[2] 1685).[77] During the period of resistance to Macedonia and twenty-three years of direct rule ending in 229, no large commitments were made. Nevertheless after 229 the citizens were able to put in hand, presumably from public funds, a general renovation of city walls and of rural forts in Attica. To honour Diogenes, the general who liberated the Piraeus (Paus. 2. 8. 6), they inaugurated a cult, a festival, and a building, the Diogeneion (Plut. *Symposiaka problêmata*,[78] 9. 1. 1, 736 d); the last may have been part of the gymnasium complex probably founded about now in honour of Ptolemy III of Egypt, for which a new location has recently been proposed east of the Agora.[79]

At this point royal patronage starts to appear. In the early second century Eumenes II of Pergamon gave the city a great stoa on the south side of the Akropolis (Fig. 9.2); it is on a vast scale (163 m long) and is remarkable for its innovative use of arches. Eumenes may also have been honoured with a huge monument beside the entrance to the Akropolis (Fig. 5.2; p. 172). Between 175 and 164 the Seleukid king Antiochos IV also gave generously. The Olympieion, or temple of Olympian Zeus, had stood half-finished for over three centuries. On behalf of Antiochos, the Roman architect Cossutius finished most or all of the cella walls and columns (Vitruvius, 3. 2. 8).

Later, a sequence of alterations was made to the Agora and its surrounding area. Attalos II of Pergamon (r. 159–139/8) donated the stoa which, for the first time, gave the eastern edge of the Agora a defining façade: the famous 'Stoa of Attalos', reconstructed in the second half of the twentieth century (Fig. 8.8). To enable it to be built, a fourth-century lawcourt was probably demolished.[80] Around the same time, further stoas were erected in the south part of the Agora: the Middle Stoa with its triple colonnade, and the parallel

'Second South Stoa', which created an enclosed 'South Square' separate from the core of the old Agora (Fig. 3.5). Some time later the 'square' received two new temples. Meanwhile, in the main agora the existing Metroön, a building sacred to the Mother of the Gods which served as a city archive, received an elaborate new façade, while the main agora area was becoming increasingly filled up with statues of kings, their friends, and other bene-factors of the *polis*.[81]

The effect of these changes was to make the Agora less open and more structured, a process that was to continue in the Roman period. Within less than a century, the monumental character of the central public spaces of Athens had been transformed. Although Athens was no longer a major power, there was great cultural prestige to be gained by a king in attaching his name to its public monuments.

Recent study of the 'Tower of the Winds' (Fig. 9.1), also known as the Horologion (water-clock) of Andronikos of Kyrrhestos, east of the Agora, has revived the suggestion that the monument pre-dates the sack of the city by the Romans in 86 BC. It is therefore tempting to suppose that it, too, was

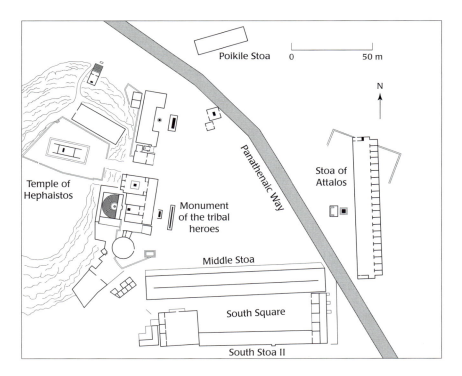

Figure 3.5   Plan of the Athenian Agora, showing hellenistic alterations including the 'South Square'. (Based on Travlos, *Pictorial Dictionary of Ancient Athens*, 23 fig. 31.)

donated by a king in the second century. When first erected (before the adjoining Roman Agora was constructed by Caesar and Augustus), the Tower dominated its surroundings from a prominent elevation, and stood in splendid isolation to serve as a market clock. Perhaps here, too, we have a case of a foreign ruler leaving his signature on Athens.[82]

The changes must be seen against the background of a new political order. Despite the continuance of wide participation in Athens and the near-universal adoption elsewhere of political structures of democratic type, radical democracy was a thing of the past even in Athens. Cities were increasingly reliant on foreign benefactors. While the new buildings which their generosity financed were an enhancement of civic amenities, were used by many people, and were no doubt particularly welcomed by those members of the citizen élite who were friends of the kings, the effect was to lay open the urban texture to the power – and tastes – of private, often non-citizen wealth. In Athens at least, this trend may have begun with the economic reforms of the 330s under the leadership of Lykourgos, which were designed to enforce financial stringency; there is evidence of the privatization, in effect, of corporate landholdings at that time, which may represent a partial withdrawal from the ethos of obligatory contributions to the public purse towards a system that relied on the goodwill of individual benefactors.[83]

Despite the role of non-citizen benefactors, the changes in urban fabric represent a continuous development from the classical past, not a radical break. Since the early archaic period, new towns had usually been laid out with a grid-plan of streets at right angles and with spaces reserved for temples, agoras, theatres, and so on. This system of planning came to be called 'Hippodamian', after Hippodamos of Miletos, an early fifth-century philosopher; the grid-plan long pre-dated him, but he may have given urban planning a theoretical grounding through his writings, which embodied a conservative social theory based on a tripartite division of society and territory (Aristotle, *Politics*, 2. 8. 1267 b–1269 a, cf. 7. 11. 1330 b).[84]

A planned urban centre was now *de rigueur* for any new city. Herakleides 'of Crete' (quoted, pp. 29–30) implicitly contrasts the fine urban layout of the rebuilt Thebes with the narrow, winding streets of Athens. A link between urban form and political health is made explicit by Strabo, who praises the city of Rhodes for having both excellent monuments and good government (14. 2. 5 (652–3), Austin 92).

Town planning in the hellenistic period took place within this existing scheme, though new monumental structures and the spaces reserved for them gave it a distinctive character. A good example from during or just before Alexander's reign is Priene, a small *polis* in Asia Minor which was moved to a new site (Fig. 3.6). Here a Hippodamian grid plan, with streets aligned north–south and east–west, was imposed upon a steeply sloping site, so that some streets actually consist of flights of steps (Fig. 3.7).[85] A similar idea is seen at Herakleia-under-Latmos.[86] Both are unusually strict examples of Hippodamian planning, and date from just before, or early in, the hellenistic period. In later foundations in western Asia Minor a more flexible approach is adopted, such as at Alinda, Assos, and above all Pergamon (below).[87]

Many cities demonstrate the range of adaptation applied to town-planning (in contrast, for example, to the almost wholly standardized Roman layout of later days).[88] Kassope, on the gulf of Arta, has natural defences in the shape of mountain crags; its walls enclose a network of housing blocks with long, narrow proportions; apart from the theatre near the top of the site, public buildings are restricted to a small area in the south-east. The

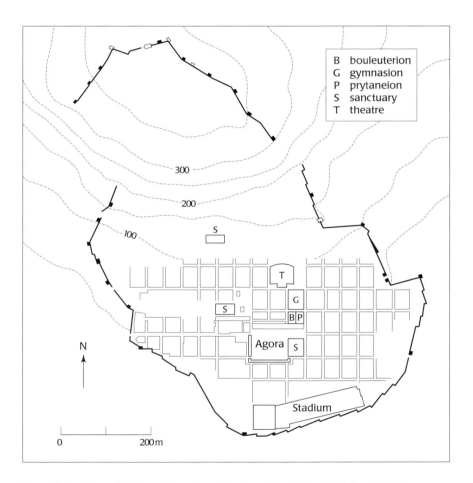

B	bouleuterion
G	gymnasion
P	prytaneion
S	sanctuary
T	theatre

Figure 3.6   Plan of Priene. (Based on Reinders, *New Halos*, 196 fig. 107.) Contours in metres.

Figure 3.7   A street in Priene. (Photograph by the author.)

layout of the town has aptly been described as utilitarian with no concessions to aesthetics[89] (Fig. 3.8). In Thessaly Gorítsa (possibly ancient Orminion), a small military town probably founded by Demetrios I to control the gulf of Pagasai, has a similarly functional appearance; but the city blocks are allowed to vary in size and proportions, perhaps because of the town's sloping situation on a ridge site (Fig. 3.9). The town never developed substantial public buildings, perhaps because of its relatively short occupation (less than a century).[90] At nearby Demetrias, in contrast, it was possible to adopt a completely uniform layout in a flat, coastal location; every block has the proportions 2 to 1, and substantial allowance is made for public buildings: an agora with stoas, a royal palace, and so on (Fig. 3.10). Though strategically located, Demetrias combines military functions with the attributes of a fully developed urban centre.[91] Finally, Halos (New Halos in the archaeological literature), on the west side of the gulf, which was occupied only from *c.*300 to 265 BC, had sixty-four house blocks of standard width but variable length (Fig. 3.11). The town had a primarily military function, like Gorítsa, but the fortified residential area is kept quite distinct from the military acropolis; both parts impose themselves upon the landscape with no concessions to contours.[92]

Even in these foundations with a mainly military purpose, allowance was made for the growth of a civic culture, where it was not actively promoted.

The Macedonian kings seem to have given their military architects free rein to adapt a basic scheme to terrain and circumstance; indeed, to experiment with new versions. They were conforming to a traditional ideal of the urban form, but also tuning themselves in to Greek cultural values. To found a *polis* was to display Greekness, but it was not normal practice to impose a pre-determined plan; variety and adaptation were part of the culture.

Outside Greek-speaking areas, a rectangular street layout can be seen as a conscious embracing of Greek style, a sign of the extension of Greek tradition to new environments. The urban form adopted was not always purely Greek; at Ai Khanum in Baktria, within a basically Greek town plan, the architectural complexes combined Greek and non-Greek styles (see p. 305; Fig. 8.5). The new capital of Egypt, Alexandria, was laid out on a grid plan for Alexander by the planner Deinokrates, with areas reserved for different groups of buildings (see further pp. 214–15).

Perhaps in order to rival the Egyptian city, the third-century rulers of Pergamon adopted an architectural scheme which exploited the steep terrain of the city's acropolis to best effect (Fig. 3.12). A Hippodamian plan was not imposed, no doubt because of the rugged contours, but, as in Alexandria, the public buildings were grouped in successive locations, in this case on different terraces mounting up the acropolis. Each terrace held an imposing group of monuments forming an architectural unity. The visitor moved from the grand lower agora to the gymnasium complex, followed by a sanctuary of Demeter, a second agora with, above it, the great altar to Zeus built by Eumenes II in the 170s to celebrate Attalos I's earlier triumph over the Galatai (Fig. 3.13). On the highest part of the acropolis were a grand sanctuary of Athena, a theatre, the library, the palaces of the kings, and military installations. No single structure dominates the city; instead, the series of architectural spaces is designed to impress the visitor by its increasing scale and elaboration, assisted by the view over the plain that opens up as one ascends.[93]

In many new towns an area was reserved for a palace. Hellenistic palaces can be divided into royal palaces (whether single buildings or complexes), governors' palaces, and private palaces (or palatial houses); the last two have been described as 'pale reflections' of the first.[94] In early hellenistic Macedonia (specifically at Vergína, Pella, and Demetrias), palaces are characterized by expansive terracing and wide colonnaded squares containing series of large rooms; at Pergamon and Alexandria, the palace quarter is set apart at one end or side, of the town; but at Demetrias under Philip V, the palace is rebuilt as a fortified acropolis, almost a town within a town.[95] Other palaces were built in all the major kingdoms as well as in Hasmonean Judaea (thirty-one have been identified), and provided a setting where the ruler could patronize architectural innovation and validate his or her status through conspicuous expenditure. As with town planning, there is no single model; not only is experimentation the norm, but in Asia the Greek and Macedonian elements are increasingly fused with native.[96]

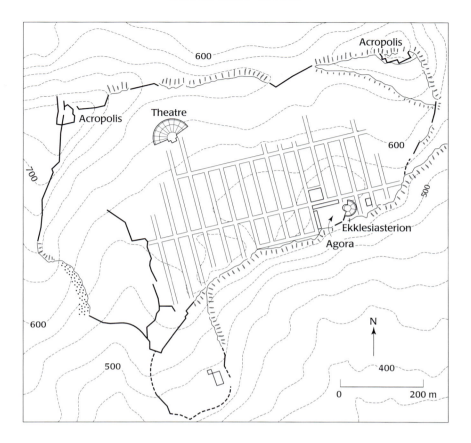

Figure 3.8. Plan of Kassope. (Based on Hoepfner and Schwandner, *Haus und Stadt*, fig. 95, and Owens, *City*, 76 fig. 21.) The 'ekklesiasterion' is the assembly building. Contours in metres.

Figure 3.9. Plan of Gorítsa. (Based on Owens, *City*, 78 fig. 23, and Reinders, *New Halos*, 49 fig. 21.) Contours in metres. (p. 94, top)

Figure 3.10. Plan of Demetrias. (Based on Owens, *City*, 79 fig. 24.) (p. 94, bottom)

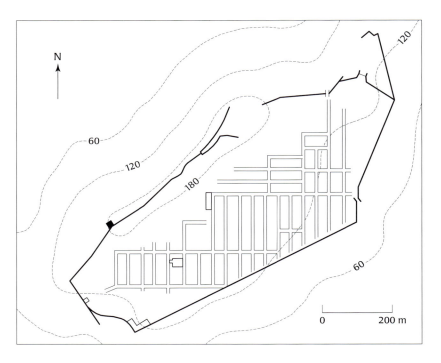

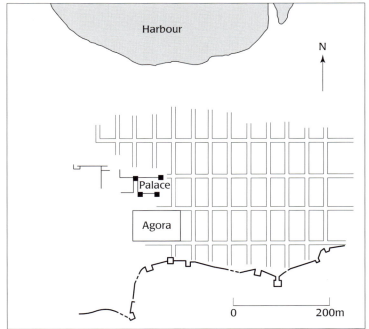

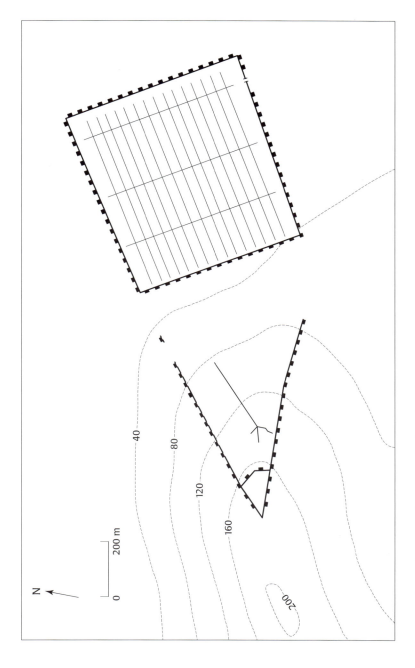

Figure 3.11   Schematic plan of New Halos. (Based on Reinders, *New Halos*, 35 fig. 12). Contours in metres.

Early Seleukid foundations, many built on unoccupied land or replacing native towns, have a broadly standardized layout, with a main street dividing the city lengthways, but in each instance adapted to the site; this is the case at Antioch-on-Orontes, Beroia, Apameia and its port Laodikeia-by-the-Sea, and Seleukeia-on-Tigris. Typically there was a separate palace zone and an acropolis. An axial street is seen in the little royal capital of Seuthes III of Thrace, Seuthopolis, which though barely 250 metres from end to end has its own agora and palace quarter. At Damascus, however, the need to compromise with the existing city layout brought about a mixed plan, with a central east–west street uniting the old and new quarters. Not all fusions of Greek and non-Greek towns were successful in architectural terms; at Doura-Europos some of the Greek-style construction projects, including the agora, were never finished.[97]

As well as expressions of hellenism, even of hellenization, and of the city ideal (but generally in a new, monarchical context), these outbursts of Greek-style urbanism represent the most spectacular demonstration of the ability of kings to monumentalize their power and change landscapes. The wealth and labour required to construct them were not to hand, but had to be mobilized. Not the least important aspect of city building in the hellenistic period is its economic implications. Urbanization depended on a combination of slave, military, and free labour – the last, perhaps, employed especially for the more skilled architectural and sculptural embellishments – and will have given employment to craftsmen and labourers, who may have migrated periodically to new projects. The resources to support these massive programmes will have come, like all the wealth of the kings, from a combination of the profits of war with trade tolls, revenues from royal estates, financial and manpower levies upon cities, and in short the extraction of wealth from the great mass of the population: Greek and non-Greek peasants, traders, and craftsmen themselves, together with slaves and other unfree groups. City foundation thus represented a redistribution of resources.[98]

Citizen euergetai

Royal benefaction was part of a larger phenomenon, for which historians have invented the term 'euergetism', coined from the Greek word for 'benefactor', *euergetês* (the surname of several hellenistic kings). An alternative name is the ancient Greek term *euergesia*, meaning both a single benefaction and the general practice.[99]

The practice was by no means new; classical Athens relied on rich citizens to fund festivals and public constructions. In the earlier part of the fourth century Xenophon, in his *Oikonomikos* (*Estate Manager*), outlined the duties of a landed gentleman:

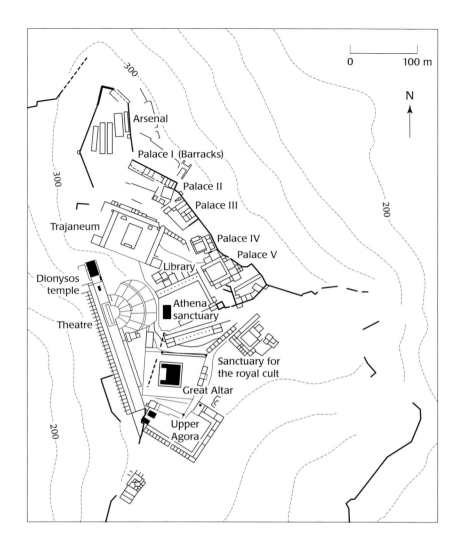

Figure 3.12. Plan of Pergamon. (Based on W. Radt, *Pergamon*, 84–5 fig. 10.)
Contours in metres.

You are bound to offer many large sacrifices; else, I fancy, you would get into trouble with gods and men alike. Secondly, it is your duty to entertain many strangers, on a generous scale too. Thirdly, you have to give dinners and play the benefactor to the citizens, or you lose your following. Moreover, I observe that already the state is exacting heavy contributions from you: you must needs keep horses, pay for choruses and gymnastic competitions, and accept presidencies; and if war breaks out, I know they will require you to maintain a ship and pay taxes that will nearly crush you.

(Xen. Oec. 2. 5–6)

In Athens it is possible that compulsory public benefactions (*leitourgiai*, 'liturgies'), were abolished by Demetrios of Phaleron (r. 317–307; pp. 120–1), in a move designed to placate the richest families who incurred the bulk of these expenses.[100]

The relative value of the largest benefactions may gradually have changed. There seems to have been a general polarization of wealth-classes, both generally and among the élite. A few individuals were so rich that they could serve the public good on a scale never before seen. A long inscription from around 200 (Austin 97, *Syll.*[3] 495) details the acts of Protogenes, a citizen of Olbia on the Black Sea, who helped the city cope with demands for protection money from a nearby non-Greek people, deal with corn shortages, and above all meet the cost of building a public granary and fortification walls. Perhaps a little later, the Black Sea city of Istria honoured its citizen Agathokles for similar services (Austin 98, Burstein 68, *ISE* ii. 131). In the same century the citizens of Paros honoured a man for his services, particularly as market superintendent (*agoranomos*), in which role he upheld the rights of both employers and workers (Austin 110).[101]

Another inscription, from the 240s, records a Samian decree in honour of a citizen, Boulagoras (Austin 113, BD 64, *SEG* i. 366; quoted, pp. 159–60). It details a string of his good works over a number of years. He represented his city in a successful petition to Antiochos Hierax concerning the perennially disputed estates of citizens at Anaia (see also p. 80). He acted on behalf of the *demos* in prosecutions for the misuse of its funds or property, and deputized for a gymnasiarch – president of (i.e. provider of funds for) the civic gymnasium – who found the cost of his office higher than he could meet. He advanced large sums to the city, enabling wheat to be bought for the citizens during a shortage, 'attaching the greatest importance to the common good and the enjoyment of abundance by the people'. He even lent money to 'the needy'.

We need not write Boulagoras into the role of a Victorian philanthropist; the poor people mentioned in the decree need not necessarily have been destitute, and may simply have been members of the landed class (or the citizen class as a whole, if they were now exclusively landowners) who were temporarily unable to fund the lifestyle to which they were accustomed. His

Figure 3.13 The altar of Zeus (or Telephos) at Pergamon, as reconstructed in the Pergamon Museum, Berlin. The sculptural programme comprised, round the entire outer frieze of the altar, a Gigantomachy (battle of the gods against the giants, symbolic of the victory of Greeks over barbarians) and, under the interior colonnade, an episodic narrative of the life of Telephos, legendary founder of Pergamon. (Staatliche Museen zu Berlin, Antikensammlung Pergamon OM 6921; © Bildarchiv Preussische Kulturbesitz, 1999.)

wheat benefactions may not be evidence of outright famine or a general grain supply problem. Major shortages had afflicted Greece during the years 331–324, when the city of Cyrene almost single-handedly made up the shortfall for some fifty Greek cities; an inscription from Cyrene (BD 3, Harding 116, *SEG* ix. 2, Tod 196) records their many benefactions, including the largest donation, of 100,000 *medimnoi* to Athens.[102] Cities regularly honoured foreigners for fair dealing in times of shortage; around 300 BC the Ephesians granted citizenship to a Rhodian importer (Austin 112, *Syll.*[3] 354), and another Rhodian was honoured by the citizens of Histiaia in Euboia in the late third century (Austin 115, *Choix* 50).

Boulagoras is more likely to have been dealing with a temporary shortage of wheat, which well-off citizens (or, again, citizens as a whole) desired in preference to the standard fare, barley.[103] He may have been trying to preserve the lifestyle of his fellow gentlefolk, not reduce social distress. Many references to a *sitônês* (wheat-buyer) in public documents may be signs of *euergesia* rather than of economic crisis (though there were crises, particularly in wartime). It is in this light that we should view, for example, the Delian honours for the *sitônês* sent to them by Demetrios II (Austin 114, *Choix* 48), and the famous Samian corn law of *c.*200 (Austin 116, BD 63, *Syll.*[3] 976).[104]

The wealth of Boulagoras and men like him may have come from seaborne trade, which flourished in the eastern Mediterranean world after Alexander, or from increased exploitation of those people, free and unfree, who owned no land. Many classical cities had a class of unfree, possibly ethnically distinct persons; Priene had its Pedieis ('plainsmen') who caused trouble in this period, while the Anaiitai of Samos, who lived at Anaia, may be a similar group. If, in addition, the land of free men was falling into the hands of big landowners, one can easily imagine how the rich became steadily richer.

Euergesia, whether internal or royal, allowed cities to enjoy a wider range of public services and amenities. Some cities appointed a public doctor, paid for from public funds – though he may have continued to charge fees. This is often seen in difficult times, as when the Cretan city of Knossos honours a doctor from Kos:

> The *kosmoi* and the city of Knossos to the council and people of Kos, greetings. Since, when the people of Gortyn sent an embassy to you concerning a doctor, and you responded with zealous eagerness by sending to them Hermias a doctor, and when there was a revolution at Gortyn and we came in accordance with our alliance to the battle [which took place at Gortyn] in the [city], and it happened that some of the citizens ... were wounded and that many [fell] seriously ill from [their] wounds, Hermias being a good man showed then all his zeal on our behalf and saved them [from] great dangers, and

otherwise he constantly gives assistance without stint to those who call upon [him] ...

(Austin 124, *Syll.*[3] 528)[105]

In another document the *demos* of Samos honours the public doctor Diodoros son of Dioskourides, who helped the citizens during Philip V's siege of the city and 'for many years in the previous period through his own skill and care looked after and cured many of the citizens and of the others in the city who had fallen seriously ill', distributing his services 'equally to all' following a series of earthquakes (Austin 125).[106] Once again, we should not import notions of modern public health care, free at the point of delivery.[107] Diodoros also appears in the list of contributors to the Samian corn law, suggesting that his profession was lucrative.

Euergesia was a way in which the citizens of Greek states, most of which no longer profited by making war against each other or against non-Greeks as they had done before, sought to maintain the privileges associated with citizenship. It was also a way for members of the élite to gain public credit and augment their political and civic standing. The elaboration and dissemination of this practice have sometimes been taken for a sign of decay in *polis* institutions, but this seems mistaken. On the one hand, *euergesia* can be portrayed as a replacement for the 'liturgy' (*leitourgia*) system of the classical city, whereby it was incumbent on rich citizens to take their turn in financing festivals, warships, and so on; on the other hand, we do not know that such a system was widespread outside classical Athens, or that this level of funding was widely available outside those classical cities that had large navies. Another explanation must be found than that *euergesia* simply evolved from liturgies.

It is generally accepted that the gap in wealth between ordinary citizens and the super-rich was widening; probably the wealth from trade flowing into *poleis*, particularly old ones, was accumulating mostly in the hands of men like Boulagoras. *Euergesia* may be a sign of continuing success (albeit unevenly distributed), not crisis. Boulagoras's greatest benefactions are not gifts, but loans or advances which are to be repaid; nor is there any reason to think he is using his wealth to make the whole *demos* into his client or build up a corrupt power-base.[108] Naturally, he may have hoped to earn public status and perhaps secure public office, but in a Greek democracy it was the people's right not to honour, not to elect him. It is also possible that his honours were delayed until the end of a distinguished career of public service, as sometimes happened in Athens.[109] The honours voted to him are modest; his actions conform precisely to the ideal of civic participation enunciated by Xenophon 150 years earlier.

Gauthier distinguishes between the early and late hellenistic periods. During the second century BC, under the influence of growing Roman power, the step-by-step limitation of participatory democracy by the Romans, and their patronage of élites friendly to themselves, *euergesia* becomes bound up with

political domination of one's fellow citizens; thus benefactors start to seem remote from the *demos*. Many benefactions are carried out without holding public office, often for the benefit of all the population, not just the citizens. *Euergesia* loses its strictly civic character.[110] The process is far from uniform or complete, however. Even in the late second century, Smyrna honours a citizen for good works very like those of Boulagoras in third-century Samos, and the honours are only a little more lavish: an annual crown, a front seat at the theatre for the man and his descendants, and a marble statue (Austin 215, *OGIS* 339); the tone is still very much civic.

Gender relations and individual identity

Various kinds of changes in civic society have been explored by historians: changes in class structure, in the distribution of wealth, in the role of the individual, and in gender roles. While literary representations of women need not be evidence of a radical turn-around in social relations (see pp. 249–50), there are changes in women's public status.

The fact that some royal women were powerful figures (pp. 71–3) may have affected the way in which other women were regarded. Plutarch's account of the role played by Spartan women in the third-century 'revolutions' (pp. 143–7) certainly seems to indicate a change in the way women were viewed, by comparison with, for example, classical Athens.[111] Spartan women had been thought unusual; Aristotle (*Politics*, 2. 6. 1265 b–1266 a) points out that they owned property and were politically active. Some of Plutarch's women exemplify the model Spartan character, like the mother of king Agis IV (r. *c*.244–241), Agesistrata, who on her way to her execution reportedly said, 'My wish is that this may be good for Sparta' (Plut. *Agis*, 20; see p. 146 for the events in question.) In the same episode Plutarch narrates the execution of king Kleomenes' mother Kratesikleia, and points up the courage of the unnamed young widow of Panteus, one of the king's bravest soldiers. The vivid details he gives suggest that for once this may be a real episode, described for Plutarch by his sources, albeit heightened in the telling and re-telling. In his hands, however, it becomes a proof of his own moral philosophy: 'thus Lakedaimon [*Sparta*], in equal competition making the women's action emulate the men's, demonstrated that in extreme circumstances virtue cannot be violated by Fortune' (*tychê*; Plut. *Kleomenes*, 39. 1).[112]

No less interesting is Agiatis, widow of Agis. Her husband had been killed at the instigation of Leonidas, father of the other king, Kleomenes III, and Leonidas had married her off to Kleomenes (p. 144). In Plutarch's account, owing much to a favourable memoir by Phylarchos (p. 263), she proves to be a reformer worthy of her late husband's memory:

> Agiatis was heiress to the substantial property of her father Gylippos, as well as being much more beautiful and lovelier than other Greek

women, and of equable temperament. The story is that … once married to Kleomenes, while continuing to detest Leonidas, she did make the young man a good, loving wife. For his part, as soon as he married he fell in love with her, and in a sense sympathized with his wife's devotion to Agis and her remembrance of him. Consequently he often asked about what had happened, and paid careful attention when she explained Agis's purpose and policy.

(Plut. *Kleom.* 1)

As Plutarch presents it, Agiatis is responsible for Kleomenes' later actions. It is difficult to sort out hard fact from the retrojection of later ideas about what Sparta was like in the third century. Agesistrata and Agiatis may genuinely have lived up to what they took to be the ideals of their society; our sources are unlikely to be totally wrong about the force of those aspirations. We can be reasonably certain, however, that these women, like royal women elsewhere, wielded influence only within a male-dominated value-system. Only, perhaps, in the late hellenistic period was the explicitly masculine image of the king compromised, as Ptolemaic queens exercised real power.[113]

Among non-royal women we hear of poetesses such as Erinna (Lefkowitz and Fant, nos 9–10), who recorded apparent reminiscences about her women friends; but little is known of her life, and it is even possible that some of her poems, like other works attributed to women in this period, were written by men.[114] Not for the first time in Spartan history, women's names appear in records of chariot-race victories at festivals (Lefkowitz and Fant, nos 45–7), indicating that they owned the chariot and team of horses (rather than that they were the charioteers).[115] Other prominent women include companions of philosophers, who are credited with wit and intellect. The story of Krates the Cynic and his wife Hipparchia is told by Diogenes Laërtios (*c.* AD 200–250) in his *Lives of the Philosophers*:

> She adopted the same dress, went about with him, and associated with him[116] in public; she went to dinner parties with him. Once, when she went to a dinner party at the house of Lysimachos, she put down Theodoros called the Atheist by using the following trick of logic: if an action could not be called wrong when done by Theodoros it could not be called wrong when done by Hipparchia. Therefore, if Theodoros does nothing wrong when he hits himself, Hipparchia does nothing wrong if she hits Theodoros.
> (Diogenes Laërtios, 6. 96–8, Lefkowitz and Fant, no. 43)

When Theodoros tries to humiliate her with a scornful reference to women's proper occupations, Hipparchia responds, 'Theodoros: you don't think that I have arranged my time badly, do you, if I have used the time I would have wasted on weaving for my education?' She was accounted a philosopher in

103

her own right, as was Leontion, the companion of the philosopher Epicurus, who even wrote on philosophy.[117]

We should not inflate the significance of these examples, as if they attest to an educational system that was widely available to women;[118] these examples appear in connection with anti-orthodox philosophies and lifestyles. There had occasionally been notorious educated women before, most famously Perikles' mistress Aspasia in fifth-century Athens. On the other hand, there are signs that it was now perfectly acceptable, if by no means commonplace, for a woman to be highly educated. Here, for example, is the first-century BC gravestone of a woman from Sardis, inscribed with a touching metrical epigram; stone and inscription were paid for by the community:

> This stone marks a woman of accomplishment and beauty. Who she is the Muses' inscriptions reveal: Menophile. Why she is honoured is shown by a carved lily and an alpha, a book and a basket, and with these a wreath. The book shows that you were wise, the wreath you wore on your head shows that you were a leader; the letter alpha that you were an only child; the basket is a sign of your orderly excellence; the flower shows the prime of your life, which Fate stole away. May the dust lie light on you in death. Alas, your parents are childless; to them you have left tears.
>
> (Lefkowitz and Fant, no. 49)[119]

Legal restrictions imposed on women include the *gynaikonomoi* (censors of women) appointed by Demetrios of Phaleron, whose function may have been to restrain excessive display of wealth and lavish parties. The ultimate purpose of such officials, however, may have been to control competition among male citizens (the ownership of women being one way of showing off wealth); what is more, there is no evidence that such institutions were common. Furthermore, while women may still have needed a male guardian (*kyrios*) for many legal transactions, there is plenty of evidence for Greek women generally enjoying a more public role, with rich women making benefactions to cities in their own names. Euxenia of Megalopolis in the second century served as priestess of Aphrodite, paying for the building of a wall round the temple and a guest-house for visitors. Phile of Priene (first century BC) 'dedicated at her own expense a receptacle for water and the water-pipes of the city' (Lefkowitz and Fant no. 48, Burstein 45). Pomeroy takes instances like these as evidence of the diffusion or dissolution of the former privileges of male citizenship, now that the political forum of the city was no longer so important in the world; van Bremen, however, detects no real change in women's legal position.[120] Nor was women's intrusion into the public arena the result of a lack of wealth among the élite; many men still had great quantities of money to do what they liked with.

The range of public activities open to women was wider than in classical Greece – or at least Athens, for other city-states may not have restricted women so severely in the classical period.[121] Literature and documentary evidence combine to suggest some relaxation of controls, at least at the élite level (the only one where we normally see women at all).

The rigid ideology, perhaps particularly strong in classical Athens, of an exclusively male political, social, and public life may have begun to break down; women could be discussed in new ways, at least in documents and literature. Just as the public ideology of civic virtue had to change to make room for kings and a new kind of *euergesia*, so it may have allowed women to enter in, in a controlled fashion. As the 'royal family' became an instrument of public self-presentation for kings, so did citizen wives for citizens, even as the content of citizenship was changing. These developments were not planned, nor are they wholly the product of the hellenistic period. Greek society was developing partly under the stimulus of, and partly independently of the powerful new monarchies.

The hellenistic period has sometimes been portrayed as a time when individual freedom increased and new opportunities arose for the fulfilment of personal destinies. This trend must not be exaggerated or rashly asserted in the absence of clear evidence; but there are signs of change. Increased numbers of statues and inscriptions naming individual men, women, and children, particularly in religious contexts, are evidence that, at least among better-off people, new kinds of commemoration were possible both during and after a person's lifetime.[122] This does not, perhaps, amount to any weakening of communal bonds, but is part of a growing body of evidence that individuals of both sexes were represented in new ways in public discourse.

New relations between individuals may be a precondition for new relations between the sexes. Archaeology offers some evidence. It has been suggested that the increasing similarity of men's and women's grave-goods in Attica from the fourth century on implies a new intimacy between the sexes; that artistic representations of Aphrodite, in addition to the more usual Hera, as patron of marriage are signs of a more relaxed demarcation between respectable women and *hetairai* (socially superior prostitutes); and that depictions of a woman or goddess bathing, or naked, are connected with a trend towards personal display of luxury and of signs of a leisured lifestyle, all of this tending to narrow the gap in status between the genders[123] – at least in Athens, and at least at a level of prosperity where individuals begin to be traceable in the archaeological record at all.

Many Athenians migrated to Delos when it came into their possession in 167. In this cosmopolitan society, the grave-sculptures both of Athenians and non-Athenians indicate altogether more conventional views of men's and women's roles than are indicated by non-funerary sculpture from the city of Delos itself and by funerary sculpture at Athens.[124] This would seem to be exceptional, however; a case, perhaps, of a prosperous, partly colonial society becoming more conventional than the society it left behind, and communicating its traditionalism to incomers from places other than Attica.

By the early Roman period, Plutarch's discourse *On Love* (*Erôtikos*) presents marriage as a partnership involving a measure of equal status and friendship for women, albeit a kind of participation in masculinity, and as a relationship which has important private aspects that had previously not been discussed. The family now has more than just a civic importance.[125] It is to be presumed that such changes in concepts of personhood took place piecemeal and gradually, and indeed that no 'steady state' existed. The renegotiation of social relations is a continuous process.

Beyond the *polis*?

The argument that the *polis* met its end at Chaironeia in 338 has been found wanting (p. 35). Many *poleis*, particularly in the Peloponnese and the Aegean, remained free of Macedonian domination and enjoyed diplomatic relationships with kings who, at least formally, treated them as sovereign states. The Rhodians and Aitolians alone remained continuously independent until the Roman conquest, and were thus able to make war and peace without restriction (one of the most notable inter-city wars was between Rhodes and Byzantion in 220 BC over control of access to the Black Sea trade; Polyb. 4. 46. 5–47. 6, Austin 94). Many cities, however, even when under the sway of kings, retained the power to organize their own defence. (For Byzantion's dominance over Black Sea trade, see Polyb. 4. 38, Austin 96.)

Ptolemaic and Antigonid power relied on keeping cities contented; it would have been impossible to impose loyalty across extensive territories and sea-based empires by military power alone. Being dominated by a king need not have only negative consequences. The causes of social problems in third-century Greece, too, are by no means clear-cut, and it would be rash to attribute them all to the influence of the monarchies. The city-states in an age of greater independence had created a good deal of social oppression, and the picture for the third and second centuries is not uniform.

Some may argue that the classical *polis* was not the *telos* (end or goal, in Aristotelian terminology) of Greek society, only an evolutionary stage on the road to federal states (see Chapter 4) or to territorial states as represented by the hellenistic kings and the Roman empire.[126] If this is meant as a functionalist argument – for example, that the *polis* had 'failed' to solve the 'problems' of Greece and was bound to succumb sooner or later to larger, more efficient administrations – we should reject it. The *polis* system, even as an element within territorial monarchies, proved itself flexible in managing resources and successfully channelling competition between individuals into social ends. The hellenistic monarchs were all too often selected by intrigue, assassination, or hired military forces, a system that would itself eventually prove insufficiently adaptable in the face of outside threats, as even the Roman empire did.

4

MACEDONIA AND GREECE

In this chapter the rise of Macedonia is traced, down to Alexander's expedition. Alexander's death thirteen years later led to a period of military conflicts during which power lay with a sequence of sometimes more, sometimes less 'legitimate' successors, until by 276 the kingdom settled under Antigonid rule. The Macedonians' sphere of influence extended far south into mainland Greece, but they could not control every area. Cities such as Athens periodically escaped from Antigonid control, sometimes with Ptolemaic assistance. Sparta provided a focus for revolt and was not suppressed until 222. The indirect effects of Macedonian rule can be seen even in the far-off Peloponnese; they may include the rise of the Achaean league as a military power. After 222 further Spartan attempts at recovery and reform were curtailed by Rome's Macedonian wars (211–168), the 'liberation' of Greece (197), and the incorporation of Sparta into the Achaean league (192).

Much of this chapter will focus on Athens and its development under, and in opposition to, Macedonian rule. This partly reflects the extremely large body of epigraphical data and the close attention paid to it by historians, notably Christian Habicht in a monumental series of studies. It is also because Athens was genuinely important. Though no longer capable of dominating southern Greece and the Aegean, given the power of the monarchies, it remained a significant military and naval power. Hence the Macedonians' determination to retain control of the Piraeus, Athens' port, as they did for much of the late fourth and third centuries, including a continuous period of sixty-six years from 295, and even at times when the city of Athens was itself free. Piraeus formed a key link in the chain of fortresses on the east coast of Greece which were garrisoned by the Macedonians. Control of Attica also gave the kings access (and prevented their enemies having access) to one of the major Greek sources of silver, in the mines of the Laureion district, whose principal value was as a source of bullion for coinage. Finally, by possessing Athens, a former imperial power and fountainhead of all that was prestigious in literature, visual arts, and philosophy, the kings could hope to gain cultural prestige by association and give some sort of legitimacy to their role as arbiters of Greek affairs.

Macedonia to 276 BC

The structure of the kingdom

As a geographical entity Macedonia can be defined as the drainage systems of the rivers Haliakmon and Vardar (ancient Axios) with their tributaries (Fig. 4.1).[1] Its central feature is the fertile coastal plain, one of the largest in Greece, behind which are mountainous areas forming upper Macedonia. Until mechanized farming prevailed, many parts of the plain were regularly flooded by the rivers bursting their banks and depositing silt; the plain thus offered spring and autumn pasture for sheep, goats, and horses, as well as deltaic and marsh products (salt, fish, and so on), while olives grew readily on the surrounding hills. The mountains are praised in ancient sources for their pastures and for products such as honey, wax, silk, and timber (Procopius, *On Buildings*, 4. 3. 27; Livy, 44. 43. 1; Tod 91 and 111), and many wild animals were hunted. In short, the landscape has an un-Mediterranean character, while the climate is more continental (cold winters, very hot summers) except in the Chalkidike peninsulas.[2]

The early kings had occupied 'the region by the sea now called Macedonia' (Thuc. 2. 99), but in the early fifth century Alexander I drove out neighbouring peoples along the fertile coastal plain and up the valleys to the north. The Persian satrapy of Thrace was probably taken over after the defeat of Xerxes' invasion of Greece. Until Philip II's reign, however, the kings were unable to establish permanent control of the mountainous hinterland. Philip's achievement is magnified in Alexander's speech to the army at Opis, as reimagined by Arrian five hundred years later:

> Philip found you wandering about without resources, many of you clothed in sheepskins and pasturing small flocks in the mountains, defending them with difficulty against the Illyrians, Triballians, and neighbouring Thracians. He gave you cloaks to wear instead of sheepskins, brought you down from the mountains to the plains, and made you a match in war for the neighbouring barbarians ... He made you city-dwellers and civilized you with good laws and customs.... He annexed much of Thrace to Macedonia, seized the most favourable coastal towns, and opened up the country to commerce, and enabled you to exploit your mines undisturbed.
>
> (Arrian, 7. 9, Austin 15)

Philip undoubtedly achieved much, but allowance must be made for the rhetorical character of this passage and its late date. He was not starting with a blank canvas; not only had his predecessors built up a flourishing kingdom, but there was already a deep-rooted civic tradition in Macedonian society.[3]

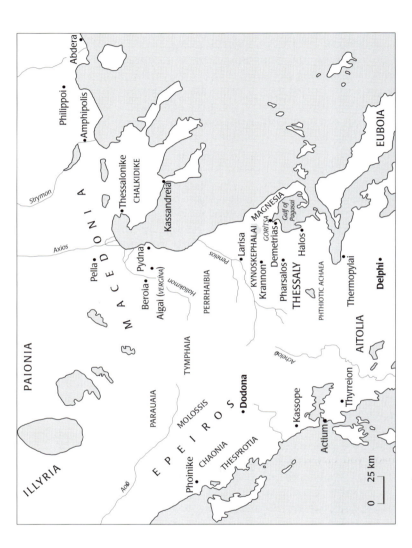

Figure 4.1 Northern Greece. (Adapted from Talbert, *Atlas*, 32.)

Philip not only conquered, he made new land. Drainage schemes were an important element of his work. Theophrastos (*On the Causes of Plants*, 5. 14. 5; for this work see pp. 343–4) wrote that after Philip took the forested and waterlogged plain of Philippoi from the Thracians, it changed into a drained, dried, and cultivated region.[4] Philip also established control of the coastal regions with the Greek cities, including the valley of the river Strymon east of the central plain, with the *polis* of Amphipolis, long disputed between the Macedonians and Athenians, before embarking on wider conquests of neighbouring 'barbarians' and eventually Greek lands to the south. The Arrian passage reminds us of an important fact of Macedonia's location: its neighbours – Thracians, Paionians, Epirotes, and Illyrians – were primarily non-urban peoples with more or less hellenized élites. To Greece as a whole, Macedonia seemed a bulwark against the 'barbarians'.

A debate has raged since antiquity about whether Alexander and his Macedonians were Greek. The coasts had long been within Greek consciousness; colonies had been founded in the archaic period, while rich Athenians like Thucydides had exploited the gold and silver resources of the hinterland. Before the fourth century, however, Macedonia may have been regarded as a fringe area, and during that century Athenian politicians were able to deny, when it suited them, that the Macedonians were Greeks. Once the Macedonians became a threatening power, some Greek writers represented them as in almost every way un-Greek.[5] It is likely, however, that the ruling Argeadai were more or less fully hellenized from at least the early fifth century, when we see them establishing cultural links with the southern Greeks. The kings claimed descent from Zeus; Alexander I took part in the Olympic games, apparently the first Macedonian to do so, persuading the judges of his Greekness by enumerating his ancestors back to the kings of Argos. There seems to have been a presumption that ordinary Macedonians, despite their dialect, were not as Greek as their kings – Herodotos describes Amyntas (*c*.500) as 'a Greek ruling over Macedonians' (5. 20)[6] – but despite ancient and modern controversies it seems clear that the Macedonians as a whole were Greek-speakers. While the élite naturally communicated with other élites in standard, probably Attic, Greek, the ordinary Macedonians appear to have spoken a dialect of Greek, albeit with loan-words from Illyrian and Thracian which gave ammunition to their denigrators.[7]

If proof be needed of the sophistication of Macedonia at this time, one may bring forward the fragments of the earliest surviving Greek literary papyrus, a carbonized book-roll found in a tomb-group of *c*.340–320 at Dervéni near Thessaloníki. It preserves parts of a philosophical text on Presocratic and Orphic cosmology composed around 400, and surely had a religious significance for the man in whose funeral pyre it was placed. The Dervéni roll provides evidence for a high level of culture among the aristocracy.[8]

Macedonia was a monarchy with a very large territory; its capital lay at Aigai. In many remote areas to which the kings laid claim it was hard to guarantee the loyalty of the local aristocrats. Thucydides paints a picture of a quasi-feudal society: 'The Lynkestians and Elimiots also belong to the Macedonians, as well as other up-country peoples; they are indeed allies and subjects of the Macedonians, but each has its own monarchy' (2. 99). By the late classical period, however, the whole kingdom, apart from the king's own land, was composed of civic territories generally based around an urban centre. In the 'new lands' beyond the Axios and Strymon, over which Philip II restored Macedonian hegemony, these might be grouped into *sympoliteiai* (joint polities). West of the central plain, beyond the mountains, associations of villages known as *ethnê* survived from earlier times (they are now regarded as geographically rather than tribally based). In the 'old kingdom' the dominant political form was the *polis*. Areas outside the core territory such as Thessaly, Thrace (which was governed by a *stratêgos*), and Paionia were not formally part of the kingdom. As a state, Macedonia both before and after Alexander could be described as a monarchical federal state, as opposed to the republican federal states arising in southern Greece (pp. 133–40).[9] The king exercised power through a council or *synedrion* whose members he was in theory able to choose; in practice, however, there was an 'inner cabinet' comprising the most powerful men, which other army commanders and delegates from *poleis* could be invited to attend.[10]

Macedonia possessed subject or 'allied' Greek cities, chiefly or exclusively on the coast (Fig. 4.1). Some were originally colonies of southern Greek states; under Philip they became subject to Macedonia. Their position was thus unlike that of southern Greek *poleis*, though they were not alone in having to cope with an external royal power while retaining their civic character. For the Macedonian kings, they represented more than just strategic strongholds and sources of tribute, tolls, and manpower. It was important for the prestige of the kingdom that they be seen to be real civic entities. An archetypal compromise is represented by Amphipolis, which under Philip retained a democratic form of constitution but also had a Macedonian garrison and superintendent (*epistatês*).[11] Philip's own foundation Philippoi (well known to Roman history as Philippi) had a democratic constitution; but foundations by his successors, such as Kassandreia (Cassandreia; see p. 114), seem to have had neither democratic institutions nor popular assemblies. They did, however, have magistrates such as archons (chief magistrates or a board thereof), treasurers (*tamiai*), and even generals (*stratêgoi*). We know little about how they were administered before the third and second centuries; it seems they could not take any major decisions without consulting the king, as in the case of the four cities (Kassandreia, Amphipolis, Philippoi, and Pella) which, in 242 BC, sought to recognize the sacred immunity of Kos, stating that their decision conformed to the king's policy (*SEG* xii. 373–4).[12] None the less they were considered *poleis* by the other Greeks and admitted to panhellenic festivals.[13]

The natural resources of Macedonia were varied. By virtue of its relatively wet climate the lowland area is able to support a wider range of arable and pastoral economies than southern Greece, while the extensive highlands had plentiful supplies of timber and pitch for building ships. One city was even called Xylopolis, 'Timbertown', and wood was regularly exported to southern Greek city-states for shipbuilding. Silver and gold were mined; proximity to the sources permitted the regular use (by the élite) of large silver and gold vessels such as those unearthed in excavations of fourth-century burials. Outside the *poleis* of the coastal strip the traditionalist element survived; settled pastoralist communities, rather than nomadic social units, were probably dominant even in upland areas.

Even before the hellenistic period the economy could almost be said to have been a 'royal economy'. The supply of timber and precious metals was probably a royal prerogative, and it seems taxes were paid on arable crops. In 334 Alexander granted the parents and children of the king's Companions killed at the battle of the Granikos 'exemption from tax raised on the land (*chôra*) and from all other services by the body (*sôma*) or special taxes (*eisphorai*) on properties (*ktêseis*)' (Arr., 1. 16. 5). The land tax was probably on the produce of land, whether private or belonging to the king; personal services may have comprised compulsory labour on city walls, roads, and other public works; levies may have been for emergency purposes only, in wartime. Plutarch describes Alexander assigning the revenues of particular ports and communities to individuals (*Alex.* 15, Austin 3 *a*), and there was probably a tax on the movement of goods.[14]

Whatever the actual degree of urbanization in the fourth century – there were over a hundred nucleated communities – Macedonia will have remained mainly rural, like most of Greece. Nor, despite the splendour of the palace at Pella and royal tombs like Philip II's at Aigai (or Aigeai; modern Vergína),[15] did it subsequently attain the splendour of the other kingdoms. The hellenistic world may have been the heir to Alexander's empire, but it was not ruled from Macedonia; the kings of Macedonia did not even rule Greece. Alexander and his father defeated the southern Greek alliance, but had not invaded all parts: the Peloponnese and the islands, for example, remained largely outside their control. Macedonian dominance was largely restricted to the area from the isthmus of Corinth northwards, and was maintained by the four garrisons later characterized by Philip V (according to Polybios, 18. 11. 5) as the 'Fetters of Greece' (*pedai Hellênikai*): at Acrocorinth (the mountain acropolis of Corinth), Piraeus, Chalkis on Euboia, and Demetrias in Thessaly (founded by Demetrios I in about 294). Possession of these strong-points guaranteed control of the sea route down the east coast of Greece.

Philip and Alexander

Philip II (r. 360/59–338) brought the Greek *poleis* of Macedonia under his control and established power over the mountainous regions. His main achievement, without which his conquest of southern Greece would not have been possible, was to force the submission of Macedonia's remoter neighbours, especially the Illyrians. To achieve this he created a new-style army with a new five-metre long thrusting-spear, the *sarissa*, which contemporaries saw as a key weapon but which was more than that. Since it partially replaced costly defensive armour, it allowed much wider participation in the army and consequently in political life.[16] From Alexander's accession or sooner, indeed, a common assembly of the Macedonians (as the army or the people) met on different occasions as a political body exercising juridical and civic functions similar to those of a city assembly.[17] An élite corps of Foot Companions (*pezhetairoi*) was created.[18] Techniques of military training were copied from southern Greek cities. The subjection of upper Macedonia was furthered by the fortification of existing market towns and strategic military strong-points. Philip made grants of conquered land to men whose support he wished to ensure. He established a common interest with the eastern Epeirote Molossian kingdom, marrying the king's niece Olympias, who gave birth to Alexander in 356. She was only one of seven wives, all of whom he evidently married to promote good relations with neighbouring kingdoms.

Arrian's (or Alexander's) statement that Philip made the Macedonians into city-dwellers is an exaggeration. King Archelaos (r. 413–399) had created a new capital at Pella in the lowlands; according to Thucydides (2. 100) he built fortifications and straight roads, and spent heavily on horses and new armour.[19] These changes must have permitted the more effective operation of royal power at a distance, even in remoter regions. Philip was not beginning with an empty landscape. Nor were all the new cities his creations. The two main foundations took place after Alexander's death and were initiatives of Cassander: the coastal *polis* of Thessalonike (modern Thessaloníki, Salonica) and Kassandreia, a new city replacing Poteidaia on the Pallene peninsula in Chalkidike. Both were synoikized from existing cities.

All the same, the scale of Philip's actions is impressive. There is evidence for a programme of city enlargements and population transfers; enlargements were often at the cost of the destruction of other settlements or the replacement of the previous inhabitants by Macedonian settlers. The small independent *poleis* of Galepsos and Apollonia were destroyed in the 350s (Strabo, book 7, fr. 34) and their populations were probably used to enlarge the foundation of Philippoi, while a nearby third city, Oisyme, was given to Macedonians to resettle. The independent *polis* of Methone, north of Pydna, was razed in 354 and its territory 'distributed to the Macedonians' (Diod. 16. 31 and 34), the existing population being sent away. Tens of thousands of captives from more remote areas of the Balkans were probably added to the free population of Macedonia: for example, 'more than ten thousand Sarnousians' in 345 and 'twenty thousand boys and women' from Skythia in 339/8 (Polyainos, 4. 2. 12; Justin, 9. 2). This accelerated urbanization under Philip need not have required a revolution from above, rather the redefinition and elaboration of existing settlements and the creation of new administrative structures.[20]

Although Philip did not completely reshape Macedonian society, he probably did make a reality of the already latent military power of his people (see below). This may explain the swiftness of the Macedonian conquests, both inside and outside Greece, between the 350s and 320s. Macedonia's power under Philip and Alexander was probably based more on the resources and manpower of the new Balkan and southern Greek territories which Philip had conquered than on any modern-style 'economic' restructuring of the kingdom. Allies and subjects could be taxed (Thrace, for instance, probably paid tribute, as it had previously done to local kings); trade tolls could be levied on the increasing number of coastal *poleis* within the kingdom, such as in Thessaly). Errington may be right to argue that Philip's main concern was the security of Macedonia; 'policies towards Greece initially took second place'.[21]

The senior commander Antipater is said – perhaps foreseeing the problems which Macedonian rule of the Near East would pose for Macedonia – to have advised Alexander not to undertake his Asian expedition until he had a son and heir (Diod. 17. 16). The expansion of Alexander's ambitions to include the conquest and rule of the Persian empire entailed a fundamentally new situation in Macedonia; but though this can be represented as undermining Philip's achievements, we should not forget that the campaign was planned by him.

The expedition against Persia did indeed profoundly alter the monarchy. As Errington observes, the growth in the army's personal devotion to the king undermined the traditional power of the aristocracy; the king's supporters were now loyal to him and to their own ambitions rather than to 'the interests of the Macedonian state as defined by Philip'.[22] One may doubt whether what Philip created was loyalty only to a state as such; he was just as charismatic a leader as Alexander, and it may only be because of Alexander's special place in the sources that his relationship with the troops appears closer than Philip's. On the other hand, Alexander's situation was very different from his father's: a Macedonian empire was now a fact, and he needed a new kind of support. Taking the army on a lengthy expedition outside Greece was bound to mean that individual nobles who could provide troops no longer had the same hold over him, and he was more reliant on the personal loyalty of troops and commanders.

Greeks of non-Macedonian origin had achieved high office before, such as under Philip, and non-Macedonian troops from the Balkans, such as Illyrians and Thracians, had regularly fought alongside Philip; Alexander found it necessary to elevate even non-Greeks to high positions, and to recruit Persians to the infantry phalanx. The Successors reacted against some of these changes, and after Alexander's death they attempted to rule collect-ively; but sheer force of circumstance in the new kingdoms meant that they themselves took on the new features of Alexander's kingship (see Chapter 3). Within Macedonia itself, more of the old-style monarchy remained, but the kings were forced to compromise to an extent with the public and cultural demands of hellenistic kingship (see below).

Macedonia under the Successors (323–276 BC)

Antipater, left in Macedonia as regent, had to deal with Greek revolts both before and after Alexander's death. Chief among these was the Lamian war of June 323 to early August 322 (Austin 26, Harding 123, *Syll.*[3] 317),[23] decided in the Macedonians' favour by the battle of Krannon in Thessaly.[24] (For places in Greece and the Aegean mentioned in this chapter, see Fig. 4.2.) For its part, Macedonia's population may by now have been somewhat depleted by the loss of supplementary contingents sent to Alexander from time to time. It is possible that the ensuing series of wars between rival leaders affected the country adversely, though the possible impact has prob-ably been exaggerated. There was emigration – thousands of Macedonians had gone with Alexander, and many had not returned – but the flow may have dried up after 323.

The successor whom Antipater chose in 319, the elderly Polyperchon, was ousted in 316 by Antipater's son Cassander, who retained control until his death in *c.*298, successfully forming alliances and waging wars against the other Diadochoi. Between the death of Cassander and the establishment of Antigonos II Gonatas as king (276), Macedonia had five rulers: Demetrios I (r. 294–288), Pyrrhos (288/7–285), Lysimachos (r. 288/7–281), briefly Seleukos I (281), and finally Ptolemy Keraunos (281–279).

Historians are prone to assume that 'dynastic instability' caused economic and social chaos; Macedonia is often said to have been in a 'shattered' condi-tion or a state of anarchy as a result of depleted manpower and military conflicts.[25] Yet not only did some of these kings rule for many years, but the rule of traditional or city law may well have continued to operate except at the height of actual crises, which were short-lived. There were invasions; but after Cassander attacked Macedonia in 317, besieging Olympias through the following winter in Pydna, there was no battle on Macedonian soil for nine-teen years[26] (Demetrios I in 302 only reaching Thessaly), though the army under Cassander was from time to time fighting outside Macedonia.

Only the period from the death of Cassander (*c.*298 or 297) to 277 could possibly be deemed a prolonged crisis for Macedonia. In 294 his sons Alexandros and Antipatros fought a civil war in which Alexandros was

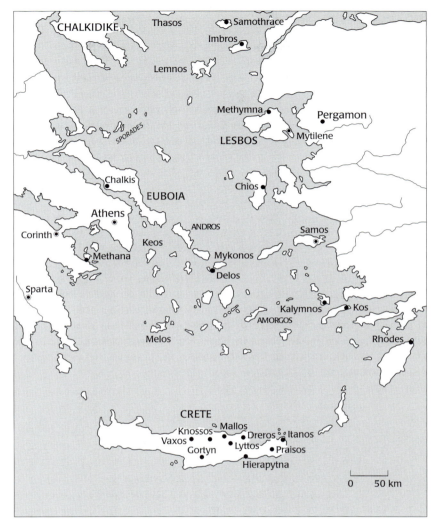

Figure 4.2 The Aegean. (Adapted from J. D. Falconer and R. J. A. Talbert, in Talbert, *Atlas*, 16.)

victorious, but the war provided Demetrios I with an opportunity to seize power – not before Alexandros had ceded to Pyrrhos of Epeiros the districts of Tymphaia and Parauaia. While Demetrios was campaigning in southern Greece in 288, Pyrrhos invaded southern Macedonia, dividing it with Lysimachos (based in Thrace) for three years until ousted by him. After Lysimachos's victory, Macedonia can almost be seen as a peripheral province of his kingdom, still centred upon Thrace. The death of Lysimachos on the battlefield of Koroupedion (281) was followed by Seleukos's invasion of

117

Macedonia and his assassination by Ptolemy Keraunos. The kingdom, dynastically speaking, now had its most legitimate king since Alexander's sons died: Keraunos was no upstart but a legitimate son of Ptolemy I and a grandson of Antipater.[27] He had ruled little more than a year, however, when he fell fighting the Gauls (p. 52). A certain Sosthenes, perhaps a former officer of Lysimachos, was made ruler, though he refused the title of king, and drove back that army of Gauls which had defeated Keraunos; the next group of invaders under Brennos learned the lesson, and made straight for the south. Pyrrhos remained a threat, invading again briefly in the late 270s; his successor Alexander II of Epeiros would do the same (see below).

Even at this time we should not assume widespread disruption or massive numbers of deaths. Ancient battles did not normally result in heavy casualties (exceptions tend to be reported prominently), and warfare for the most part did not entail large-scale destruction of property; during periods of violence, the greatest numbers of men may have been lost among the upper echelons of society. The king, normally an adult son chosen by the previous ruler, had to be approved by the army and leading nobles; if the succession was controversial or unclear, this was no mere formality.[28] Successive rulers and would-be rulers, therefore, took pains to win the support of other nobles and to eliminate opposition. It is likely that each leading nobleman could call on the support of people from his own locality. Many deaths occurred among the nobility during shifts in power. In 317, for example, Alexander's mother Olympias, returning to Macedonia at Polyperchon's instigation, wrought revenge on her enemies. Diodoros dramatizes the events vividly; note the role of Macedonian 'public opinion':

> But after Olympias had captured the royal persons and had seized the kingdom without a fight, she did not carry her good fortune as a human being should, but first she placed Eurydike and her husband Philip [*III Arrhidaios*] under guard and began to maltreat them. Indeed, she walled them up in a small space and supplied them with what was necessary through a single narrow opening. But after she had for many days unlawfully treated the unfortunate captives, since she was thereby losing favour with the Macedonians because of their pity for the sufferers, she ordered certain Thracians to stab Philip to death, who had been king for six years and four months; but she judged that Eurydike, who was expressing herself without restraint and declaring that the kingdom belonged to herself rather than to Olympias, was worthy of a greater punishment. She therefore sent to her a sword, a noose, and some hemlock, and ordered her to employ whichever of these she pleased as a means of death – neither displaying any respect whatever for the dignity of the victim whom she was unlawfully treating, nor moved to pity for the fate that is common to all. Accordingly, when she herself met

with a similar reversal, she experienced a death that was worthy of her cruelty. Eurydike, indeed, in the presence of the attendant prayed that Olympias might receive similar gifts. She next laid out the body of her husband, cleansing its wounds as well as circumstances permitted, then ended her life by hanging herself with her girdle, neither weeping for her own fate nor humbled by the weight of her misfortunes.

(Diod. 19. 11. 3–7)

More than a hundred prominent Macedonians who were friends of Cassander were assassinated (Diod. 19. 11. 8), but the queen's excesses apparently caused many Macedonians to turn against her even more strongly. The account is reminiscent of Plutarch's dramatization of the deaths of Agiatis and Agesistrata of Sparta (p. 102), but Diodoros or his source is more restrained in his moralizing.

In 316, as Eurydike had allegedly prayed, Olympias was in turn condemned to death by 'the Macedonians' after her capture by Cassander, who tried to drive her into exile and procure her death on the voyage.

As Olympias, however, refused to flee but on the contrary was ready to be judged before all the Macedonians, Cassander, fearing that the crowd might change its mind if it heard the queen defend herself ... sent to her two hundred soldiers who were best fitted for such a task, ordering them to slay her as soon as possible. They, accordingly, broke into the royal house, but when they beheld Olympias, overawed by her exalted rank, they withdrew with their task unfulfilled. But the relatives of her victims, wishing to curry favour with Cassander as well as to avenge their dead, murdered the queen, who uttered no ignoble or womanish plea.

(Diod. 19. 51. 4–5)

Once again the role of (élite) public opinion is interesting. Five years later, once his own position seemed secure, Cassander himself exterminated Philip II's line by doing away with Alexander's son, the young Alexander IV, and his mother Rhoxane (Diod. 19. 52; 19. 105, Austin 30).

This periodical loss of life among the aristocracy need not have had any serious consequences for the economy and society of Macedonia; it may, however, have encouraged peripheral territories to assert their independence.

Not all that happened in Macedonia under the Successors was bad. Cassander founded a new city (p. 114). There was the curious, philosophically sanctioned city of Ouranopolis (see p. 188). Thessalonike on the Thermaic gulf was formed by synoecism from several small settlements. Under Cassander Thrace was separated from Macedonia – he had to recognize the power Lysimachos wielded there – and following his defeat of Olympias Epeiros once again became a hostile neighbour; Cassander, however, succeeded in installing a pro-Macedonian king in 313. When the young Pyrrhos was made king of Epeiros in 306 by an anti-Macedonian faction, Cassander exerted indirect influence to have him replaced but did not intervene directly. In many ways Cassander, not surprisingly given his parentage, was an upholder of the traditional monarchy.

Demetrios I, who ruled from 294 to 288, falls into the same role: he had time to found the city of Demetrias in Thessaly, on the gulf of Pagasai, and continued to rule Attica and the limited Peloponnesian territories. He adopted his predecessor's relationships with foreign powers even where they conflicted with his own previous policies: hostility towards Aitolia and Pyrrhos, for example. His ambition, however, extended unrealistically to the reconquest of all Alexander's kingdom, and perhaps for this reason he failed to win the loyalty of the Macedonians, to judge from the stories in Plutarch (*Demetr.* 41–2: his defeats at the hands of Pyrrhos lowered his prestige, and his ostentatious lifestyle alienated traditionalists).[29] Macedonia was then ruled from outside by Lysimachos, Pyrrhos, and Ptolemy Keraunos until Gonatas took over in 277.

Greece under Macedonian domination

Athens and southern Greece, 323–276 BC

The business of suppressing the Greek revolt of 323 took Antipater a year. He then garrisoned the Mounychia hill of Piraeus and curtailed democratic rights at Athens, which had not happened in Alexander's lifetime. Similar measures were taken in other cities. Nevertheless, the revolt that led to the Lamian war was not an ill-judged adventure but a necessary gamble.[30]

In 319 Polyperchon, to secure his position in Macedonia against Cassander, abolished pro-Macedonian oligarchies in southern Greece, imperilling Macedonian control (Diod. 18. 55–7). In Megalopolis in 317 this had the paradoxical effect of enraging the normally sympathetic leading citizens into siding with Cassander against Polyperchon (Diod. 18. 68). It was a sort of second Exiles Decree, an attempt to woo support from Greek states. The Athenians hoped to regain Samos, but in the ensuing war Cassander attacked them, seizing the nearby islands of Salamis and Aigina and taking rural forts in Attica.

Cassander retained Antipater's authoritarian system of rule, but unlike his father he tried to win over pro-Macedonians rather than resort to force. The restoration of Thebes, from 315 on, was part of his bid for popularity. In 317, however, when a settlement was reached with Athens, he curtailed the democracy (though with a more generous minimum property qualification than under Antipater) and appointed Demetrios of Phaleron, an aristocrat with philosophical training, to rule Athens.

Demetrios may have been designated curator (*epimelêtês*), president (*epistatês*), or superintendent (*prostatês*); in 309/8 he also served as eponymous archon (the magistrate who gave his name to his year of office). His regime was characterized by strict supervision of other magistrates, but the conventions of democratic procedure were largely observed. The relative (though not total) lack of inscribed public documents from the years of his rule may be the result of the restrictions he placed on conspicuous consumption (an élitist, rather than populist, obsession in Greek politics), which also brought about the cessation of the series of splendid sculpted grave-monuments characteristic of fourth-century Athens. The austerity he promoted may have been in keeping with what circumstances demanded, rather than a result of his philosophical beliefs; alternatively, he may have been 'primarily a diplomat and a lawgiver' who was also a serious student of philosophy and a prolific and respected writer.[31] In external affairs the city was subject to the wishes of Cassander.

The southern Greek cities relied on the support of Ptolemy I for aid against Macedonia. In 308 he took Sikyon and Corinth 'and planned to free the other Greek cities also, thinking that the goodwill of the Greeks would be a great gain for him in his own undertakings', though when he received only lukewarm support in the Peloponnese he made peace with Cassander and retained only those two towns (Diod. 20. 37).

In the following year another Successor, Demetrios, sent from Asia Minor by his father, Antigonos, liberated Athens from Cassander's garrison of fifteen years' standing. Demetrios of Phaleron was deposed and democracy restored – though not the radical democracy of earlier days. Megara was also freed. The Macedonians razed the fort on Mounychia, and Demetrios and his father were voted golden statues and other honours by the Athenians (Diod. 20. 45–6; Plut. *Demetr.* 10). Altering constitutional structures that had been unchanged for three hundred years, the Athenians added two civic tribes, Antigonis and Demetrias, to the existing ten and increased the membership of the *boulê* proportionately from 500 to 600. Among other honours, cult was paid to Demetrios and Antigonos as saviour gods, and their statues added to the monument of the tribal heroes in the Agora. It was the first time such honours were paid in mainland Greece; but unprecedented achievement merits unprecedented honours.[32] The Athenians received back from Antigonos the north-eastern Aegean islands of Lemnos and Imbros, former possessions of theirs. Steps could now be taken to repair the city walls of Athens and Piraeus. The new democracy was active, the years of Antigonid occupation (307–301) seeing a resurgence of inscribed decrees.[33]

Athens and other Greek *poleis* had benefited from this phase of the wars of the Diadochoi, but were hardly in a strong position to fend off future Macedonian attacks. The aid given by Ptolemy and the Antigonids was not based on any belief in the inherent rights of Greek cities, and was conditional on their support.

After their victory over Ptolemy's fleet near Salamis in Cyprus in 306,

Antigonos and Demetrios were acclaimed kings.[34] In 304–303 Demetrios seized Chalkis in Euboia and won the support of the Boiotian league and Aitolia. Cassander, who on several occasions during this 'four years' war' (307–304) attacked Athens, Eleusis, and the Attic forts, finally besieged the city. In 304 Demetrios lifted the siege, restored the forts to Athens, and captured various other towns including Corinth and Sikyon:

> After Demetrios had moved the people of Sikyon into their acropolis, he destroyed the part of the city adjacent to the harbour, since its site was quite insecure; then, after he had assisted the common people of the city (*politikon plêthos*) in rebuilding their houses and had re-established freedom (*eleutheria*) for them, he received honours equal to the gods from those whom he had benefited; for they called the city Demetrias, and they voted to celebrate sacrifices and public festivals and also games in his honour every year and to grant him the other honours of a founder.
>
> (Diod. 20. 102, Austin 41)

As with other royal interventions in Greek *poleis*, it may well be that only one group among the citizens gained from the high-handed actions of Demetrios. He showed the same disdain for *polis* sensitivities in Athens in 304/3 and 303/2, making himself highly unpopular, if we can believe our sources, by his indulgent and immoral lifestyle. This translated itself into the political arena, for example when a young man persuaded the king to demand of the magistrates that they cancel a heavy fine which his father owed (Plut. *Demetr.* 24). On this occasion the citizens refused, but in 302 they were persuaded to rename a month temporarily so that the Eleusinian mysteries (the state festival of Demeter and Kore centred on Eleusis) could be repeated specially for Demetrios's benefit (Plut. *Demetr.* 26).[35]

In 302 Demetrios expelled Cassander's garrisons from Thessaly, but his success was cut short by the war against Lysimachos and Seleukos in Asia Minor, which ended with the defeat of the Antigonids at Ipsos (301). The Athenians declared that no king would ever be admitted to the city again (Plut. *Demetr.* 30. 4). They adopted a position of neutrality, not for the last time, and were rewarded with gifts of grain from both Cassander and Lysimachos in 299; but they probably lost Lemnos and Imbros.

It is uncertain whether Cassander made any active attempt to regain control of other southern towns. He played a part in suspending democracy at Athens, by encouraging Lachares, *stratêgos* of the foreigners and formerly (it is said) champion of the *dêmos*, to make himself tyrant[36] (Paus. 1. 25, Austin 23; see also *FGH* 275 *a*, Burstein 5, excerpts from a chronological papyrus of the second century AD). Lachares seems not to have interfered otherwise with the constitution; he may have arranged the much-needed grain donations, and perhaps the construction of the new stoa at the Asklepieion (p. 87).[37]

The death of Cassander in 297 gave Demetrios I the chance to lay siege to the city. The Athenians suffered terribly, paying 300 drachmas for a *medimnos* of wheat (normally costing around 5 drachmas) and eating mice while Demetrios laid waste the crops (Plut. *Demetr*. 33–4). In 295 they drove out Lachares and Demetrios gave them 100,000 *medimnoi* of grain. While the Piraeus and Mounychia were handed over to Demetrios, he went further than he was entitled to in garrisoning the Mouseion hill, south-west of the Acropolis (Plut. *Demetr*. 34); earlier it had been he who removed the garrison at Mounychia. Demetrios received fulsome honours to replace those that had been conveyed in 307 and later rescinded – a month named after him, a new festival of the Demetrieia created (Plut. *Demetr*. 12) – but while he claimed to be giving the Athenians the magistrates they wanted, he made the *boulê* an elected body rather than appointed by lot, and his fleet remained at Piraeus. An eponymous archon who unprecedentedly, and illegally, held office for two years running, Olympiodoros, was probably Demetrios's representative overseeing the city, just as the historian Hieronymos of Kardia was in Boiotia.[38] The later decree for Kallias of Sphettos (below) refers to this period as an 'oligarchy'.

On the other hand, before long the king was permanently absent, controlling large parts of the Peloponnese, exercising influence in Boiotia, and in 294 finally recovering Macedonia, which had been lost at Ipsos. In 291 or 290 he visited Athens, where the people fêted him as a god and appealed for his help against the Aitolians (p. 161), who had seized the sanctuary of Delphi. At Athens he set up a substitute for the Pythian games of Delphi (Plut. *Demetr*. 49. 7–8), but his invasion of Aitolia was repulsed by Pyrrhos of Epeiros. His ultimate aim, however, was the recapture of Asia and Egypt, and he commissioned five hundred warships from the dockyards of Piraeus, Corinth, Chalkis, and Pella (Plut. *Demetr*. 43); but in 288 his rule in Macedonia ended as a result of invasions by Pyrrhos and Lysimachos, and by Ptolemy's despatch of a fleet into the Aegean.[39]

In 287 or 286 Athens again revolted. Led by Demetrios's former puppet Olympiodoros, they stormed the Macedonian garrison. Many years later, in 270/69, the Athenian assembly passed a decree in honour of Kallias of Sphettos, which reveals the people's concern about the grain supply at the time:

> The people (crowns) Kallias son of Thymochares, of Sphettos....
>
> Resolved by the council and the people: ... since, at the time of the uprising of the people against those who were occupying the city, when the people expelled the soldiers from the city but the fort on the Mouseion was still occupied, and war raged in the countryside because of the (soldiers) from Piraeus, and Demetrios was coming with his army from the Peloponnese against the city, Kallias, on hearing of the danger threatening the city, selected a thousand of

the soldiers who were posted with him at Andros, gave them their wages and food rations, and immediately came to the rescue of the people in the city, acting in accordance with the goodwill of king Ptolemy (I) towards the people, and leading out into the country-side the soldiers who were following him, protected the gathering of the corn, making every effort to ensure that as much corn as possible should be brought into the city; ...

(Austin 44, Burstein 55)[40]

The rest of the inscription informs us that Kallias helped Ptolemy negotiate with Demetrios on behalf of Athens, and later (283/2) secured a gift of 50 talents of silver and 20,000 *medimnoi* of corn from the new joint king, Ptolemy II. Later Kallias led the Athenian sacred embassy to the first Ptolemaieia (for this festival see p. 139), and by 270/69, when he was granted by his fellow-citizens a gold crown, a bronze statue, and a seat of honour, he was permanently in Ptolemy's service.

The uprising of 287 or 286 did not achieve the liberation of Piraeus or the rural forts, still less an absolute break with Macedonia, but Demetrios conceded a measure of independence; his attention was probably on his forthcoming invasion of Asia. Piraeus had been garrisoned since 295, and would remain so (like Salamis) until 229; a second attack by the Athenians, once Demetrios's back was turned, proved futile. Eleusis was recaptured around 286/5, Rhamnous before 268; but Sounion remained Macedonian until 268. It may have been after the recapture of Eleusis that the Athenians introduced the system of two generals (*stratêgoi*), one based in Eleusis, the other with responsibility for eastern and southern Attica.[41]

Once again the Athenians' (relative) liberty depended on how mightier powers were inclined to treat them. Seleukos chose to return Lemnos to Athens in the last year of his life (having captured it recently from Lysimachos), but through the late 280s Antigonos II Gonatas, son of Demetrios I, retained control of Corinth, Chalkis, several Peloponnesian towns, and the Piraeus. After Koroupedion (281) the southern Greeks may have suffered as a result of the Gauls' invasion (pp. 52–3), but there were probably no long-lasting effects; only in Thrace, and later in Asia Minor, did the Gauls settle permanently.[42]

Whether out of sentimental respect for Athens' past or because of the danger of arousing opposition from rival forces, Athens was never ruthlessly suppressed, but marked the limit of attempts to extend Macedonian rule in southern Greece.

Rule and resistance under Antigonos Gonatas (276–239 BC)

After the assassination of Seleukos in 281, Antigonos II Gonatas (r. c.277–239; Fig. 4.3) was prevented by Ptolemy Keraunos from seizing

Macedonia at once. The battle of Koroupedion (p. 45) provoked a Greek revolt led by king Areus I of Sparta, who no doubt wished to restore Spartan hegemony in the Peloponnese. The rising petered out into a campaign against the Aitolians (Justin, 24. 1). Gonatas proved virtually untouchable because he inherited garrisons controlling Thessaly, the gulf of Euboia, Piraeus, and Corinth (cf. p. 113). Following Areus's failure he was free to invade Asia Minor, in what proved to be a last attempt to fulfil his father's and grandfather's ambitions. The Gallic invasion brought him back to Europe, however, and in 277 he inflicted on them their only heavy defeat, at Lysimacheia in Thrace.[43] Already in his forties, he was finally master of his kingdom.[44]

As a result of the death of Pyrrhos at Argos in 272, which must have been a blow to Greek (specifically Athenian) hopes,[45] Gonatas gained Argos, Megara, and bases in Euboia. The sources present his treatment of the Greeks as repressive, supporting tyrants and oligarchies, in contrast to the supposedly more pragmatic policy of Philip II and most of his successors. The reasons perhaps lay in his wish to maximize revenues, especially harbour dues, but the nature of Macedonian power stored up trouble. It gave Ptolemy II a pretext for intervening in Greek affairs, allowing him to appear a supporter of liberation. Epigraphic evidence, including the Kallias decree cited above, shows Athens assiduously cultivating its relationship with Egypt during the 280s and 270s.[46] Meanwhile the Aitolian league, still independent in central Greece, recruited new members from the west coast to the east, strengthening their control of the land routes from Macedonia southwards – hence the importance of Macedonian control of the 'Fetters'.[47]

When war came, in either 268/7 or 265/4,[48] it was based on an alliance made up of Athens (still independent) and a number of mainly Peloponnesian cities, aided by Egypt. Since the initiators were not under Macedonian rule, the war should not be seen as a revolt; they were attempting to free their fellow-Greeks. The earlier decrees of dynasts claiming to bestow freedom on

Figure 4.3   Silver tetradrachm (17.07 g) of Antigonos Gonatas, 277–239 BC (*SNG* 3260). Obv.: Macedonian shield with bust of Pan, possibly in the likeness of the king. Rev.: Athena. (Ashmolean Museum, University of Oxford.)

125

the Greeks evidently had repercussions, strengthening resistance to imperial takeover. Ptolemy II and his consort Arsinoë may have been the prime movers, alarmed by Gonatas's increasing domination of southern Greece.[49] The Aitolians were not involved, as we see from this inscription recording the Athenian decree whose proposer has given his name to the war:

> Chremonides son of Eteokles of Aithalidai moved. Since previously the Athenians, the Lakedaimonians [i.e. Spartans], and their respective allies after establishing a common friendship and alliance with each other have fought together many glorious battles against those who sought to enslave the cities; ...
>
> and now, when similar circumstances have afflicted the whole of Greece because of those who seek to subvert the laws and ancestral constitutions of each city; and king Ptolemy (II), following the policy of his ancestors and of his sister [Arsinoë II], conspicuously shows his zeal for the common freedom of the Greeks; and the people of Athens having made an alliance with him and the other Greeks has passed a decree to invite all to follow the same policy; ...
>
> be it resolved by the people that the friendship and alliance brought by the ambassadors between the Athenians and the Lakedaimonians, the kings of the Lakedaimonians, the Eleians, Achaeans, Tegeates, Mantineians, Orchomenians [of Arkadia], Phigaleians, Kaphyaians, and all the Cretans who are in alliance with the Lakedaimonians and Areus and the other allies, should be valid for all time....
>
> (Austin 49, BD 19, Burstein 56, Syll.[3] 434–5)[50]

The appeal to former alliances is mirrored in a decree honouring Glaukon, brother of Chremonides, who had served with Ptolemy II. The decree was passed between 261 and 246 in the name of the 'koinon of the Greeks', on the occasion of the Eleutheria or festival of Zeus Eleutherios ('of Liberty'), a panhellenic gathering at Plataia commemorating the Persian wars of 480–479 BC (Austin 51).[51]

Despite Ptolemaic support and Spartan attacks on Corinth, the Macedonian strongholds proved decisive, though independent Athens did not fall until 263/2 (or 262/1), after a siege and famine. Much of the action took place around Attica, probably including the use of a fort at Koróni by Ptolemaic naval forces (as attested by coins). A decree from the fort of Rhamnous in eastern Attica (Austin 50, SEG xxiv. 154)[52] honours a general who saved the local deme's harvest, paid for wheat imports, negotiated the release of prisoners, and dealt with marauding pirates. In 266/5 the Athenian demos honoured the ephebes (young élite officers) for their bravery during the previous year's fighting (Austin 117, Syll.[3] 385).[53]

The precarious nature of Macedonian rule was revealed during the

Chremonidean war. Alexander II, king of Molossia and son of Pyrrhos, invaded Epeiros while Gonatas was at Athens, causing the temporary loss of the homeland; but Gonatas quickly recovered his kingdom. Following the Greek war, new garrisons were established in Athens (on the Mouseion) and in various of its fortified rural demes. Gonatas appointed a virtual dictator, possibly none other than Demetrios of Phaleron, grandson of the earlier ruler of the same name. In 255 Gonatas is said to have given Athens its freedom, which may mean Demetrios was deposed; it certainly does not mean the garrison was removed. In most respects the history of the generation from 262 to 229 is poorly attested, owing to the loss of Phylarchos's history. Athens remained officially loyal to Macedonia, however, as many public inscriptions affirm. The democracy was tightly circumscribed: the archonship, hitherto filled by lot, was probably an elective office, and there is evidence that the ephebes and cavalry regiments were more socially exclusive than before.[54]

Although Gonatas defeated a Ptolemaic fleet in the crucial battle of Kos (probably during the 250s: Plutarch, *Moralia*, 183 c, 545 b),[55] and may have done so again in the battle of Andros (whose date is even more uncertain, possibly *c.*246; Trog. *Prol.* 27, quoted on p. 9; Plut. *Pelopidas*, 2),[56] his power over the southern mainland was never secure. The rise of the Achaean league under Aratos of Sikyon (pp. 137–8) resulted in the loss of Corinth, whose Macedonian governor, Alexandros, sided with the rebel Achaeans and proceeded to expel Macedonian garrisons from Euboia. Only Athens and Argos remained in Gonatas's hands, and they had to pay Alexandros to stave off attack. Warfare between the Achaeans and Aitolians in central Greece, however, offered Gonatas a chance to retake Corinth (245/4–243). Once again, in 243, Aratos expelled the Macedonians, capturing warships. He recruited more cities, and in 242 raided Attica to try to prise it from Gonatas's grasp and attach it to the league; but Gonatas was able to exploit divisions among the Greeks, and sent the Aitolians to raid the Peloponnese (241–240). A short-lived peace treaty was broken in 240 by an Achaean raid on Piraeus.[57]

In 239 Gonatas died at an advanced age after a reign of thirty-eight years. His personality dominates the mid-third century, though direct evidence for his reign is fragmentary. He has been the subject of divergent assessments ranging from Tarn's admiring biography (a book recently dubbed 'one of the most unreliable in the whole of Greek history')[58] to the trenchant criticism of Hammond that he unintentionally created a climate of resistance in southern Greece and strengthened a potentially dangerous ally in Aitolia.[59] He is often credited, however, not only with re-establishing the military strength of Macedonia but with emulating, as far as possible, the grandeur of the other monarchies. It may have been because he spent so much time in Macedonia that a sophisticated 'courtly society' developed. He certainly patronized Greek culture, and kept Macedonia on the map as far as royal prestige was concerned. As governor of Athens he had attended lectures by Zeno. Like earlier kings, especially Archelaos and his nearer predecessors Philip and Alexander, he invited intellectual and cultural figures to Pella, such as the poet Aratos of Soloi and the historian Hieronymos of Kardia.[60] He employed Greek architects for his new palace at Aigai (Vergína). His half-brother Krateros published an influential collection of Athenian historical documents. Gonatas was praised in later sources for his personal qualities[61] – he is supposed to have regarded kingship as 'glorious slavery' (*endoxos douleia*, Aelian, *Varia Historia*, 2. 20) – but there is no evidence that Zeno's universalist philosophy influenced his actual policies.

Perhaps it is best to tread a middle path between Tarn's idealization and Hammond's denigration. The achievements of Gonatas may have been exaggerated because of the supposed contrast with what went before; but I have suggested above that Macedonia was probably not devastated before 276, and it must be doubtful how much need for 'recovery' there was. His policy towards Greeks was not especially harsh; he was not the first to garrison cities. He may even deserve credit for not provoking the Aitolian league, which could have made it difficult for him to gain access by land route to southern Greece and thus required the maintenance of the 'Fetters'.[62]

In the final analysis Gonatas can be seen as continuing the traditional policies of Macedonian rulers since Philip: securing the frontier against attack without provoking potentially hostile neighbours, maintaining control of southern Greece for purposes of military security and revenue-raising, and keeping Ptolemaic power at bay. The negative press he has received in the sources may largely be due to the fact that he defeated the Athenians and Peloponnesians in war.

Political participation at Athens and elsewhere

The situation of Athens in these years might be thought to have undermined the nature of the *polis* as a participatory community. The democratic franchise was restricted first by Antipater, the minimum qualification being set at 2,000 drachmas; this may have excluded two-thirds of the voters. Full democracy was briefly restored in 318/7; a contemporary Athenian decree honours Euphron of Sikyon, who had helped the city during the Lamian war, and refers to the present time as one when 'the people has [come back] and has [recovered] its laws and the democracy' (Austin 26, Harding 123 *a*, *Syll.*[3] 317).[63] The franchise was restricted again under Demetrios of Phaleron (r. 317–307); after a census (Ktesikles, *FGH* 245 fr. 1 = Ath. 6. 272 c), the minimum property qualification was set at 1,000 drachmas, which may have cut out 5,000 of the 21,000 citizens.[64] Demetrios ended state payments to citizens for attending the assembly and juries, and subsidies for those attending the theatre; later, Cassander encouraged Lachares to seize sole power (p. 122); and Antigonos Gonatas, after his accession, may have continued to garrison the strong-points held earlier by Demetrios. The erection in 280/79 of a statue of the fourth-century anti-Macedonian orator Demosthenes implies that the Athenians thought themselves free from Macedonian control; but they were still dependent on powerful patrons, as when (in 280 or sooner) the Seleukid king Antiochos I gave them back islands with Athenian cleruchies on them, which he had taken from Demetrios in 288.

There are, it must be acknowledged, apparent signs of a weakening of democracy. There were real changes in the rules for citizenship, and real oscillations between oligarchy and democracy; there would be no return to the days when the assembly could be swayed by the views of landless rowers. The city's freedom of action in military matters was severely curtailed at various times, and the highest civic honours are now paid to orators rather than generals.[65] The comic plays of Menander might be thought to indicate major transformations in politics and society, and a dilution of earlier values; in his *Dyskolos* (*Ill-tempered Man*), for example, one character has land worth many talents and lives in the city, while poor men hire themselves out for wages. There is a certain depoliticization of literature: New Comedy is different from that of Aristophanes in the late fifth century, who engaged with a political society. Theophrastos in the *Characters*, written at the end of the fourth century, rarely alludes to politics.[66] It has been suggested that the propertied classes withdrew from politics.[67] Finally, in other cities under the domination of the kings, prosopographic studies of family relationships and genealogies during the third and second centuries suggest that politically active citizens may have been an increasingly small and wealthy minority.[68]

For each of these points, however, there is a counter-argument. The shift from military to rhetorical prowess is real, but is also a continuation of the increasing separation of roles in the fourth century;[69] and what could be more democratic than oratory? The restriction of voting rights, and the abolition of privileges which formerly allowed the landless citizen to influence decisions that affected him, do not imply that voters who retained their rights made less use of them. Large landed estates with absentee landlords were not new, nor was citizen labour; in the fifth century, politically active estate-owners spent much of their time in Athens, and there had always been landless men. The apparent depoliticization of literature does not mean that political debate was dead, only that the role of drama had changed. There is little or no evidence for the withdrawal of the élite; on the contrary, Chremonides and many other politicians were from the richest class in society, and his decree, apart from a passing reference to concord (*homonoia*, a very Stoic term), is inspired by the traditional ideology of *polis* liberty and resistance to monarchy. His role as a leader coming from a social élite is not at odds with his adherence to the philosophy of Zeno, even though Stoicism was originally an egalitarian, possibly non-nationalistic philosophy (pp. 185–7). Élite leadership was traditional; the élite were predominant even in the radical democracy of fifth-century Athens.

Developments in the Athenian *ephebeia*, a period of military service for young men, reflected the increasing dominance of an élite, but did not necessarily undermine the *polis*. By a law of 336/5 the *ephebeia* had been opened to all 18-year-olds, no doubt with the aim of increasing the pool of talent from which hoplites could be recruited into the citizen army. In 307, however, the institution was made voluntary and the term of service shortened to one year, perhaps as a cost-cutting measure; the evidence of lists of ephebes from now on shows that numbers were a fraction of their former level and that the institution became an élite preserve, designed to pick out future leaders of the city. During the Chremonidean war, as we have seen, the ephebes retained a military function. Only around 130 BC were more opportunities created for entry into ephebic training, but they may have been meant for rich citizens and foreigners; the corps was still clearly made up of the sons of the élite, who were required to attend academic lectures. The *ephebeia* had become a kind of finishing school for leaders of the *demos*. By the early first century it may have been even more exclusive, admitting as a member, for example, Ariobarzanes II of Cappadocia in 80/79.[70] Yet this domination may be seen in the same light as Chremonides' actions: at least until the mid-second century, they confirm that the élite were continuing to subscribe to the traditional political culture whereby they earned public honours serving the community.

Most tellingly, inscribed decrees from all over the Greek world show that assemblies continued to meet regularly, city councils continued to put proposals to the assemblies, and popular control over the choice of magistrates and popular voting on political decisions remained crucial.[71] This is not at odds with the increased domination of honours and offices by the rich. Only in exceptional cases like Delos, where the wealth of the panhellenic sanctuary of Apollo meant there was no real need for private funds to be used in the service of the *polis*, do we see wide participation in public office.[72] The essence of Greek democracy was generally not the equitable distribution of office between rich and poor, but the curbing of powerful interests and their redirection towards the good of the people as a whole. This essence seems to have been maintained by democratic forms of government, in Athens as elsewhere, even when *autonomia* was compromised.

Possible economic effects of Macedonian rule

Given the almost complete lack of continuous evidence for events and political developments in southern Greece, apart from the largely epigraphic evidence for the political history of Athens, it is hard to trace trends, but Macedonian rule will certainly have affected a city's economy to some extent. Contributions to royal coffers were expected, and no doubt exacted in different ways, such as through the presentation of crowns by cities or their rich citizens, or directly through tribute. Plutarch (*Demetr.* 27) tells a story that Demetrios required the Athenians to raise 250 talents and allowed his queen and her fellow-courtesans to spend it on cosmetics. The truth of the story cannot be tested, but it may imply that kings did exact money directly on specific occasions, and that this was resented.

The Macedonians' primary method of extracting wealth was through taxes and harbour dues. Given the un-institutionalized nature of the ancient economy, we cannot assume that this would make any difference to levels of manufacturing activity or to trade through, for example, the Piraeus. It is true that when the Romans made Delos a toll-free port the revenues of the rival commercial centre of Rhodes were hit hard; but there is reason to doubt the severity of these effects (p. 382), and in third-century mainland Greece any goods entering the Macedonian sphere by whatever route would presumably be taxed, so no particular harbour was worse off than any other. Piraeus and Corinth were still the most important disembarkation points for traders. We do not even know whether the king's harbour dues were added to the pre-existing city taxes or simply replaced them. More importantly, import and export trading should not be seen purely in terms of market forces and the balance of payments. Demosthenes in the late fourth century, for example, describes a trading loan in a way which implies that an exporter would import only what he could pay for in cash (*Against Phormion*, 6).

The spending élite of Athens derived their wealth mainly from their extensive landholdings, and would continue to buy imported and local luxuries for display and consumption, while exporting their surpluses of olive oil and other commodities. On them fell the main burden of special payments to the kings.

The real change may have been that the élite had less to spend on the city (compare Xenophon's civic prescription, quoted on p. 98). This was accompanied by a political change: in Athens the radical democracy no longer existed to compel the rich to spend on the public good, or at least not as generously as before. In cities outside Athens there are signs that an élite was less willing to serve its city at great expense. The very fact that rich *euergetai* are singled out for commemoration (pp. 96–102) suggests that such benefactions were harder to come by – not necessarily because of any economic change, but rather because the political demands on élite expenditure no longer carried the same force.

It is hard to detect any broader economic effects of Macedonian rule; rather we see political ones. Political changes, however, could have economic effects; it is in this light that we have to consider the evidence for increasing social distress in third-century Greece. We have already looked at the way in which cities relied increasingly upon wealthy benefactors; but this is not necessarily evidence of economic crisis so much as of political change (see above). There is possible evidence of poverty in Greece in the story of the Macedonian governor of Cyrene, Ophellas, who in 307 collected a mercenary force to help Agathokles of Syracuse against the Carthaginians:

Ophellas had married Euthydike, the daughter of a Miltiades who was named after the commander of the victors at Marathon [*490 BC*]. Because of this marriage link and the other signs of favour he had shown to the city, very many Athenians eagerly enrolled in the expedition, and not a few of the other Greeks were quick to take part in the venture, hoping to share out in land allotments the might-iest part of Libya [i.e. North Africa] and to loot the wealth of Carthage. For conditions all over Greece, on account of the contin-uous wars and the competitive behaviour (philotimiai) of the dynasts towards one another, had turned weak and straitened (tapeina); thus they understood that they would not only become masters of many good things but would also be liberated from their present evils.

(Diod. 20. 40)

This passage must be read with care. Diodoros directly attributes the hard-ship experienced by many Greeks to the effects of the actions of the Diadochoi, just as he makes the personal links between Ophellas and the Athenians a key factor. He is not necessarily describing an economic crisis. Greece had always experienced overpopulation, and Greeks had always resorted to emigration and colonization overseas.[73] The Diodoros passage certainly presupposes that there were men with no land, or not enough land, but when was it not so?

In this context we may examine some apparent references to class conflict within Greek states. In 316 Agathokles was able to raise support for his coup in Syracuse by promising cancellation of debts and redistribution of land to the poor (Diod. 19. 9, Austin 27 *a*). In the foundation charter of the Hellenic league set up by Antigonos and Demetrios in 302 there are frag-mentary references to traditional concerns of kings and city-states: '[Let care be taken ... to ensure that the] sea is clear [of pirates (?)] ... to use the ancestral constitutions ... nor with the purpose of revolution ...' (BD 8, Harding 138; later sections in Austin 42).[74] These phrases are reminiscent of earlier and later documents referring to the twin slogans of 'redivision of the land' (*gês anadasmos*) and 'cancellation of debts' (*chreôn apokopê*). At Itanos in Crete a third-century inscribed oath, probably sworn by those newly admitted to the (limited) citizen body, includes a promise not to 'initiate a redistribution [of land] or of houses [or of] dwelling-sites nor a [cancella-tion] of debts' (Austin 90, *Syll.*[3] 526).[75] In the late third century, local wars between Cretan *poleis* were accompanied by the prospect of, or actual, *stasis* (see, for example, the civic oath from Dreros, Austin 91, *Syll.*[3] 527).[76]

References to land and debt should not necessarily be seen in modern terms, as evidence of severe hardship or a proletarian underclass. This was a slave-owning society in which any free man was, by virtue of being free and a citizen, a privileged individual enjoying political and economic rights that set him above other men. His status *vis-à-vis* his fellow-citizens, and the loudness of his political voice, depended on his having land to farm, or to get others to farm, and on how much spare money he had for social display. Finley's work on Attic mortgage inscriptions has shown that debt was a problem not for the poor as much as for the élite who − like the estate-owners of Ephesos (p. 84) − borrowed large sums against the security of their land and then, for whatever reason, found themselves in trouble, perhaps losing their land. While men who never owned land may have been tempted to serve as mercenaries of the Diadochoi, the people most likely to call for redistribution were those who once had land but had it no longer. Civil strife within Greek cities, quite common in this period, is most likely to have been sparked off by disputes and rivalries among relatively privileged citizens. Calls for reform were, perhaps, not calls for revolution or a new social order, but for a new allocation of places within the existing order.

Leagues and 'federalism'

One of the strategies adopted by political élites was to promote what modern historians often call 'federalism';[77] more accurately, a particular kind of alliance or league for which the Greek term is *koinon* (simply 'thing in common', i.e. 'community').[78] To some extent the precedent was set by the kings: Philip II's league of Corinth (338) was a military alliance against Persia, with himself as *hêgemôn* (leader) and a council (*synedrion*) comprising delegates of the member cities in proportion to their populations. This in turn was modelled on the so-called Second Athenian Confederacy of the early fourth century, in which the liberty of member cities had been formally guaranteed in order to safeguard them from a revival of Athens' imperialistic ways. The league of Corinth was, of course, a tool of Macedonian domination, and some cities were garrisoned; but Philip needed to carry the potentially rebellious city-states with him.

In earlier periods there had been many such associations, often with a religious focus. One such was the Delphic amphiktyony, a sort of board of governors of the sanctuary of Apollo at Delphi appointed by the city-states of central Greece, sometimes from places as far away as Athens; in the time of Philip II this board wielded considerable political influence, but it had never been intended to subsume the *polis* communities whose delegates attended it. Other *koina* had been more like states, though invariably with a religious centre. Member-cities of the Boiotian confederacy, for example, which was formed in the sixth century, had developed in the fifth century a form of proportional representation and generally acted in concert. Thebes usually led the league, supplying four out of eleven 'boiotarchs' in *c.*386 BC. The confederacy survived the battle of Mantineia (362) and continued to play an important role until it was disbanded after Chaironeia (338), Thebes being destroyed by Alexander three years later.[79]

Some regions where the inhabitants, though based in a plurality of political

centres, identified themselves as belonging to a single *ethnos* (roughly trans-
latable as 'nation') had set up common political institutions and acted
together in military matters. The Arkadians set up a short-lived democratic
league in the aftermath of Sparta's defeat at Leuktra in 371.[80] In the
hellenistic period an old association of Ionian *poleis* in western Asia Minor
remained in existence; its honorific decree for Antiochos I is preserved
(Austin 143, BD 20, *OGIS* 222).[81]

This ethnic background is reflected in one of the major hellenistic
leagues, that of the Aitolians of west-central Greece. The Aitolians, well
known to the major states as providers of light-armed mercenary troops, had
set up a *koinon* which in 367 recognized the sacred truce at the time of the
Eleusinian mysteries in Athens (a member-city then violated it; see the
Athenian decree in Harding 54). By Alexander's time the Aitolians were
fully integrated into the Greek political world. He took account of them in
his Exiles Decree (324), by which they had to restore the inhabitants of
Oiniadai in Akarnania, whom they had expelled (Diod. 18. 8, Austin 16).
As a result they joined the Greek revolt leading to the Lamian war, by which
time they already included some of the neighbouring Akarnanian towns
(Paus. 1. 25, Austin 23).

By the third century if not earlier, the Aitolians were holding biannual
assemblies of adult males, and had an annual *stratêgos* (military commander)
and a large standing council (*boulê* or *synedrion*) which met between assemblies; the council was composed of city delegates, roughly in proportion to
each city's population. Within the council a central committee of *apoklêtoi*
('select men') administered day-to-day business.[82] In other respects Aitolians
were typical Greek town-dwellers and worshipped the Olympian gods. The
league itself had sanctuaries of Olympian deities such as Apollo's shrine at
Thermon, the central cult site of the *ethnos*. While all adult males belonged
to the 'Aitolian union', they remained citizens of their own *poleis* – some of
which were very small even by Greek standards (Fig. 4.4).

In the early third century the league expanded its power to include
Delphi, where it dominated the amphiktyony; the Aitolians took much of
the credit for defending the sanctuary against the Gauls in 278. In the 240s
the Chians, on the other side of the Aegean, honour them for granting their
city Aitolian citizenship and a seat on the amphiktyonic council:

> Resolved by the [council and people]; the [monthly president] of
> the polemarchs ... [moved]:
>   since the [Aitolian] league, because of the ancestral kinship and
> [friendship] which exist between [our] people and the Aitolians,
> voted previously to grant us citizenship [and] forbade all to plunder
> the property of [the Chians] from whatever starting-base [on] pain
> of being liable to prosecution before the [councillors] on a charge of
> harming the common interests of the Aitolians:

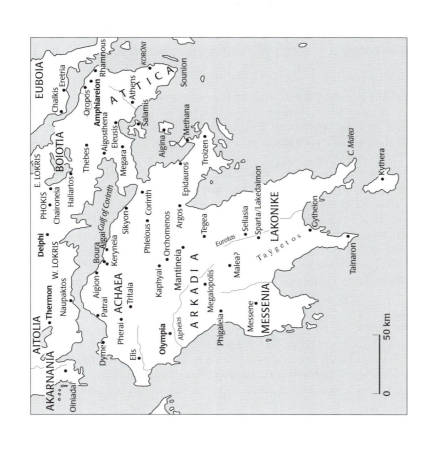

Figure 4.4   Central and southern Greece. (Adapted from Talbert, *Atlas*, 29.)

for this the people graciously [accepted] their goodwill and voted that the [Aitolians] should be citizens and share in all the rights the Chians share in, and decided that they should have priority [of access] to the council and the assembly, [and] be invited to seats of honour (*proedria*) at all the contests organized [by the city];

and now the sacred envoys and the ambassadors have returned and [reported] to the people the goodwill felt [towards our] city by the Aitolian league ...

therefore ... be it resolved by the council and people to praise the [Aitolian league] for the goodwill and zeal it shows on every occasion [towards our people, and] to crown it with the largest gold crown according to the law, worth 100 [gold Alexander] coins; ...

(Austin 52, *Syll.*[3] 443)

During the third century places even further afield were enrolled as, in some sense, members of the Aitolian *koinon*. Vaxos in Crete, Lysimacheia in Thrace, Kios in Asia Minor, and Kalchedon in the Black Sea are known to have enjoyed rights of *isopoliteia* ('equal citizenship') or *sympoliteia* ('joint citizenship').[83] This was not an empire; the *koinon* was perceived as powerful (it stood astride the Macedonians' land route to southern Greece, though it could be bypassed by sea) and attracted new member-states to take part in collective decision-making and, on some occasions, to pool military and naval forces. It was a major protagonist in Greek affairs during the advance of Roman power.

The other major league in the third century was the Achaean, originally based in the north-western Peloponnese[84] (Fig. 4.4). The second-century historian Polybios, a citizen of Megalopolis in the central Peloponnese, was the son of a leading Achaean commander. In his history he gives a rather partisan sketch of the league and its history:

Previously many attempts had been made to unify the interests of the Peloponnesians, but none had succeeded because everyone was anxious to secure his own power rather than the freedom of all. But in our time this undertaking has progressed and been completed to such an extent that not only do they have a common policy based on alliance and friendship, but they even use the same laws, weights, measures, and currency, and have the same magistrates, councillors, and judges. In general there is no difference between the entire Peloponnese and a single city except that its inhabitants are not included within the same wall ...

Why then is it that they [*the Arkadians*] and the remaining Peloponnesian peoples have consented to adopt both the constitution and the name of the Achaeans? ... In my opinion the reason is this: nowhere will you find a constitution and an ideal of equality, freedom of speech, and, in a word, of genuine democracy more perfect than among the Achaeans. The ideal found many willing converts among the Peloponnesians; many were won over by persuasion and argument; some who were forced to join when an opportunity suddenly arose were eventually made to acquiesce in their position.

(Polyb. 2. 37–8, Austin 53)

Polybios traces the history of the league, which until the early fourth century was an association of about twelve mostly small cities, through a period of disunity after Alexander, when Macedonian garrisons were placed in some of the member-cities, to its revival from about 280 when various towns expelled garrisons and tyrants. His patriotism leads him not only to exaggerate the degree of democracy in his own day – he may be writing before their defeat by Rome in 146[85] – but also to commit inaccuracy, since, though the cities issued common coinage, each kept its own laws. There was no federal mint; each city issued silver coins bearing the league's devices as well as its own, and bronze coins bearing its name in full as well as that of the Achaeans.[86]

It seems likely that both the *boule* and the assembly, at which all citizens were entitled to be present, met four times a year.[87] Like the Aitolians they had a *boule* and collective magistrates, including a chief *strategos* and ten *damiourgoi* ('people-workers', a common title for Greek magistrates). Whatever the theoretical limits on the power of these officials, it seems clear that the individual cities, though like all Greek states they will have had assemblies of some sort, were dominated by propertied élites who in turn dominated league politics. We shall see later how the self-interest of these leaders affected the behaviour of the league in the late third century.

Polybios glosses over the forced incorporation of cities, to which he himself attests elsewhere.[88] The rise of the league in the mid-third century was fuelled by the ambitions of Achaean cities and their leaders. The turning-point for the league was the enrolment of its first non-Achaean city, Dorian Sikyon. The Sikyonians, led by the 20-year-old Aratos, expelled their tyrant, Nikokles, in 251. This was not in itself an anti-Macedonian move – Aratos even appealed to Antigonos Gonatas for help (Plut. *Arat.* 4. 3) – but Nikokles was probably broadly pro-Macedonian. Megalopolis expelled its tyrant too, and one king gave Aratos twenty-five talents (Plut. *Arat.* 11. 2) – either Antigonos, to buy his loyalty, or Ptolemy II (who was later to become the patron of Aratos), to help the anti-Macedonian cause. The return of nearly six hundred Sikyonians exiled by Nikokles seems to have led to internal disputes; the decision by Aratos to enrol the city in the Achaean league may have been taken in order to stabilize the situation (Plut. *Arat.* 9. 3–4). In about 249 Aratos attacked Corinth itself, and the Macedonian governor Alexandros, as we saw, deserted to the rebels' side. Alexandros revived the league of Euboian cities and may have declared himself king.

137

Only now did the Achaean league become a focus for anti-Macedonian resistance by southern states. At the outset it seemed possible that Gonatas would support Aratos; a generation later Aratos would again turn to Macedonia. In the meantime the Achaeans, like *poleis* throughout this period, were dependent on assistance from outside powers, be they Alexandros or Ptolemy. Liberty may have been the slogan, but complete liberty was not possible.

Aratos became *strategos* of the league in 245, attacking the Aitolians who had earlier attempted a coup in Sikyon. They in return seized the territory of the Boiotians, now allies of the Achaeans. In the same year Antigonos Gonatas recaptured Corinth, suppressed the Euboian league, and garrisoned its towns (Plut. *Arat.* 17. 2). The Aitolians were trying to incorporate cities in the western Peloponnese, but Aratos restored Achaea's upward course by retaking Corinth in 243 by a surprise attack. The league now recruited Corinth, Epidauros, Megara, and Troizen, and elected Ptolemy III its *hegemon* (leader), probably an honorific position. Aratos attempted to bully Athens into joining, and made an alliance with Sparta. Even Polybios admits that cities were forced to join the league, and it is tempting to ask whether Aratos and his allies were seeking to create the biggest possible empire for their own ends, or to offer cities the chance of autonomous development and lift the fear of Macedonian rule. We must bear in mind that bringing a city into the league involved little more than the replacement of one ruling group with another, not outright warfare, let alone the enslavement of the population. Probably the two ambitions cannot be separated.[89]

To understand whether the Achaean league represented a Sikyonian empire or a collective strategy of resistance, we have to do more than look at the apparently democratic decision-making processes of the league; it is all too easy for a narrow group to dominate such a structure, and how this might happen may be readily imagined. It may also be helpful to ask whether the third-century leagues were like modern federal states, as is often claimed. The term 'federal', from the Latin *foedus*, 'treaty', indicates their origin in treaties, whether voluntarily agreed or imposed after military defeats. The regular Greek term, however, was simply *koinon*, a usage that went back to the early days of the *ethnos* and its common festivals.

Some leagues were instruments of domination. In 302 Demetrios I revived Philip II's league of Corinth (inscription, BD 8; part in Austin 42, cited above), specifically with a view to war against Cassander ('the common war'). Antigonos III Doson's alliance, founded after the defeat of Sparta in 222 (see below), incorporated both the Achaean league and many central Greek communities (Polyb. 2. 54, 65; 4. 9). The league of the Islanders ('*koinon* of the *Nêsiôtai*') was organized in 315–314 at the instigation of Antigonos I; here again there was a political reason, the Antigonids' enmity for Ptolemy. Ptolemy in turn took over the league in the early third century, and both he and his successor presented themselves as patrons of the islanders, as illustrated by the league's decree of around 280 agreeing to take part in the festival of the Ptolemaieia:

> [Resolved] by the delegates (*synedroi*) of the islanders:
>
> concerning the matters about which [Philokles] king of the Sidonians and Bacchon the [nesiarch (*commander of the islands*)] wrote to the cities, that they should send delegates to Samos to discuss the sacrifice, the sacred envoys (*theoroi*), and the contest which king Ptolemy (II) is instituting in honour of his father in Alexandria, to be equal in rank with the Olympic games, [and] (concerning which) Philokles and Bacchon have [now conversed] with the [delegates] who have arrived from the cities:
>
> be it resolved by the *koinon* of the delegates:
>
> since king Ptolemy (I) Soter has been responsible for many great blessings to the islanders and the other Greeks, having liberated the cities, restored their laws, reestablished to all their ancestral constitution, and remitted their taxes;
>
> and since now king Ptolemy (II), having inherited the kingdom from his father, continues to show the same goodwill and concern for the islanders and the other Greeks, and is offering a sacrifice in honour of his father ..., preserving his [piety] towards the gods and maintaining his goodwill towards his [ancestors] ...
>
> [to accept] the sacrifice and [to send] the sacred envoys at the [appropriate season for] all time to come, as instructed by the king; ...
>
> and to crown king Ptolemy son of king Ptolemy Soter with a [golden] crown for merit [worth] a thousand staters, for his excellence and his goodwill towards the islanders ...
>
> (Austin 218, Burstein 92, *Syll.*[3] 390)

Associations of this kind were designed with awareness of traditions of collective action, but had royal 'leaders' (*hêgemones*) and were obviously reflections of Macedonian and Egyptian power. Even a *koinon* acting independently of royal patronage, such as the Achaeans or the Aitolians, could choose a royal patron; the Achaeans chose Ptolemy III as their titular head (with few practical implications), and later the Aitolians chose Antiochos III as their *strategos* at a time when war with Rome was looming.[90]

Several leagues created in or before the fifth century were still active and developed further in the early hellenistic period. The Epeirote league, previously structured along tribal lines and made up of Molossians, Chaonians, and Thesprotians, took its new name around 300 and was a blend of monarchy, federalism, and tribal organization. The Thessalians retained their constitution until they were liberated from Macedonia and reorganized in 194; the federation lasted until Roman times, as did the early classical Phokian confederacy, which was absorbed by the Aitolians during 197–191 and then liberated (cf. Austin 134). The Akarnanian league, created in the fifth century, had a more chequered history: after its reorganization by Cassander in 314, when the Akarnanians agreed to concentrate into fewer, larger towns, it suffered domination by Epeiros and Aitolia and periodic dissolution, being refounded last around 230.[91]

New confederacies included those of the Magnesians in Thessaly, founded after the second Macedonian war (200–197) and based at Demetrias, and the Lykians, a hellenized people who had a federal structure by 200 BC. Finally, the four Macedonian republics set up by Rome in 167 had a federal structure, each having a representative assembly and a chief general.[92] By now it was less common to have a primary assembly with decision-making powers.

Membership of a league did to some extent limit the *autonomia* of member *poleis*; they undertook to fight alongside one another and to observe the constitution, and sometimes to mint coins to a common design. Perhaps unsurprisingly, there seem to have been no agreed procedures for withdrawing from a *koinon*; cities which tried to leave had to fight in order to do so, and might be forced back in. To this extent at least, sovereignty had been surrendered. Disputes among members were regularly submitted to arbitration by the governing body of the league, occasionally by outsiders. This was so, for example, in the case of the federation of Lesbian *poleis* (Mytilene, Methymna, Antissa, and Eresos) set up in the wake of the treaty of Apameia, following Antiochos III's defeat by the Romans (*IG* xi. 4. 1064, *SEG* xxiii. 491).[93]

Membership of the Achaean league may have entailed a democratic constitution. The accession of Arkadian Orchomenos in or soon after 235 is documented in a decree of the league from which it appears that the tyrant of the *polis* had abdicated, since he is now granted immunity from prosecution (Austin 54, BD 30, *Syll.*[3] 490).[94] Presumably each city could manage its internal administration, and even some kinds of relationship with outside *poleis*, without reference to the league. There was no formal intention to set up a unitary state in every respect, though *autonomia* in the sense of independence was incompatible with membership of a *koinon* of this kind.[95] Sikyon may have dominated the Achaean alliance, but it was an alliance that cities often wished to join – meaning, in practice, the majority of influential men, or the most powerful men from leading families within each city. They must have seen it as a sure protection against Macedonia. Unfortunately, as became all too clear, Sikyon was so powerful that its leaders could virtually dictate policy to other members, and a member-city was unlikely to be able to quit the alliance.

The Spartan 'revolutions' and their aftermath

Aratos of Sikyon tried to build up the Achaean league into a powerful alliance, partly to protect the southern Greeks, particularly the Peloponnesian city-states, from the league's enemy Macedonia. For Peloponnesians, however, the old enemy was not Macedonia but Sparta, the main town in the region which historians call Laconia (modern Lakonía) but was then known as *Lakônikê* (or sometimes *Lakedaimôn*). The third century saw attempts by the Spartan kings Agis IV (r. *c*.244–241) and Kleomenes III (r. 235–222) to re-establish their city's military power. They would ultimately be thwarted by Aratos and his allies, with aid from an unexpected quarter: the Achaeans' former enemy Macedonia.

Sparta after Chaironeia (338–c.244 BC)

Until 369 the Spartans occupied some three-fifths of the Peloponnese directly and dominated the rest through unequal alliances. In 369, following a crushing and unexpected defeat by the Thebans, they lost their territories in Messenia (Fig. 4.4). After Chaironeia (338), Philip II removed some inland frontier territories from their control and, more importantly, detached a number of the coastal *poleis* of the Perioikoi ('dwellers-around'), a class of citizens of the Lakedaimonian state who were not entitled to a political voice in Sparta.[96] Although the Spartans kept their port at Gytheion on the Messenian gulf, their territory now comprised little more than the Sparta and Helos plains, and the mountainous peninsulas of Tainaron (modern Máni) and Malea.

Spartan society was in some ways unlike that of other Greek *poleis*, though they shared important features. It was more traditionalist and rigidly struc-tured than most; it had two hereditary kings, and until part-way through this period it did not officially use coinage. Before the defeat at Leuktra (371) and the subsequent Theban invasions of Lakonike, Messenia, the south-western Peloponnese, had been farmed for the benefit of the warrior citizens (Spartiates) by the native Messenians, who had been made into helots (roughly 'serfs') in the eighth century. The labour of these people (who served loyally in the Spartan army and only rarely revolted) liberated the Spartiates from productive work and allowed them to devote their time to continuous military training, making them the most feared soldiers in Greece until the rise of Thebes and later of Macedonia.

Some helots remained in Lakonike after 369. Even before the loss of Messenia, however, the Spartiates had been declining in numbers, and relied increasingly on helots and Perioikoi to make up the army. This decrease in numbers, usually referred to as oliganthropy (from Aristotle's term *oligan-thrôpia*, 'shortage of people'), probably had a social rather than a biological cause: the Spartan inheritance system, which differed from those of other states in that women as well as men could inherit land, exacerbated the existing tendency of property ownership to drift upwards to the élite, who came to control more and more land.[97] After the loss of Messenia the situation became still worse. Since, to be a Spartan citizen, a man had to make his required contribution of agricultural produce to a common table, the skewing of the land-ownership profile resulted in the demotion of many citizens to the status of 'inferiors' (these had, of course, trained as Spartiates and were not disqualified from service in the army). By the 240s there were only about seven hundred full citizens (*Spartiatai*) and about a hundred families who owned land (Plut. *Agis*, 5, Austin 55 *a*). As well as the special problems caused by its unique social system, which were still working themselves through, Sparta shared in the contemporary difficulties experienced by other *poleis*, and perhaps in a higher degree, notably the polarization of land ownership and the monopolization of political power by an ever smaller number of entitled citizens.

Sparta had not fought alongside the other Greeks against Philip II at Chaironeia, and had remained outside his League of Corinth. In 331 Agis III with a joint Spartan and mercenary army, together with the less powerful Peloponnesian states, attacked the Macedonians in the Peloponnese but were defeated by Antipater at Megalopolis in the largest battle in Greece since the Persian wars. Many Spartans were killed and hostages had to be given to Antipater.[98] Perhaps for these reasons, Sparta did not join the Greek revolt of 323–322.

Under Areus[99] I (r. 309/8–265) the Spartans were again militarily active, helping their kinsmen at Taras (Taranto in Italy) against non-Greek neighbours (303). Lakonike was invaded by Demetrios I in 294, and in 281 Areus led the Boiotians, Megarians, and some Achaeans and Arkadians in an unsuccessful expedition to liberate Delphi from Aitolian domination. Once again heavy losses were suffered, no doubt exacerbating Spartan oliganthropy. Pyrrhos invaded in 272 but was deterred, ironically by a Macedonian mercenary force sent from Corinth.

Areus introduced Sparta's first coinage; some of his issues are modelled on Alexander's and bear the legend BASILEOS AREOS;[100] others have his head on one side and Alexander's on the other. In the Chremonides decree (above) he is named alongside the Lakedaimonians and without his fellow king. Sparta, or at least Areus, seems to have been taking on the language and style of the other monarchies when it suited. Areus might be blamed for failing to deal with the social problems; but a king, particularly a Spartan one, is the product, and perhaps the prisoner, of his society, and we know too little Spartan history in this period to apportion any fault.

The Chremonidean war ended in failure, with Areus dead. Between then and the accession of Agis IV in *c.*244 we know of only one event, an unsuccessful attack on Mantineia. Since Chaironeia the Spartans may have been ploughing their own furrow; but they were hardly guilty of isolationism. They have been criticized for not realizing that their days of glory were over and not acting accordingly; but to people living at the time, particularly in the Peloponnese, this may not have been obvious. A revolt against the Macedonians had more than a chance of succeeding, and success might bring renewed Spartan domination of the Peloponnese; though escape from

Macedonian rule would leave the city-states dependent on a new overlord in Egypt.

Agis and Kleomenes (c.244–219 BC)

The starting-point for the history of Agis and Kleomenes is the claim that the traditional military way of life had been put aside in recent times. Here we immediately encounter the major problem with our main sources, Polybios and Plutarch. Given Polybios's background as a military commander and the son of a prominent general of the Achaean league, he could hardly be expected to be anything other than passionately anti-Spartan. Plutarch, on the other hand, who uses Phylarchos of Athens (as does Polybios himself), takes a much more sympathetic view of the kings, which has influenced some modern writers (including Naomi Mitchison in her historical novel *The Corn King and the Spring Queen*; set mainly in late third-century Sparta and firmly founded on historical sources, it idealizes Kleomenes as a kind of proto-socialist).[101]

Polybios has his Achaean axe to grind, and for him the events of the two kings' reigns are nearly within living memory and have a resonance in his own day. Plutarch, however, is looking back from a second-century AD Greece situated within the Roman empire, at a time when earlier Greek history was being admired and refashioned for a new audience. His presentation of the Spartan kings partly reflects his and his contemporaries' views of the just, Stoic king and of the nature of threats to good social order; this may not be how people at the time saw the matter. Modern writers, similarly, tend to occupy different points on a spectrum; some see Agis and Kleomenes as reactionaries trying to put the clock back, while for others they are idealists aiming at citizenship for all.

As with the polarity in some modern presentations between Kleomenes as quasi-fascist or liberal socialist, the truth probably lies in between the Phylarchean and Polybian versions. The peculiarities of the Spartans' traditional society, and their desire to preserve their way of life and revive their military power, are not to be disparaged as eccentric anachronisms or treated as retrogressive instruments of class warfare (and Sparta was far from unique in having subordinate social classes), but should be viewed as a meaningful stance. When the kings claimed to be restoring the traditional Spartan way of life, which the Spartans believed had been instituted by an early reformer, Lykourgos, they were both right and wrong: they were reviving customs that were believed to have fallen into disuse, but were giving them a meaning which, strictly speaking, they had not had before. When they claimed to be bringing about a more just society, they were also, and by the standards of the age rightly, trying to make their *polis* powerful. There was propaganda value and the power of validation in appealing to the admired past.

Plutarch presents Agis IV (r. *c*.244–241) as moved by the poverty of the mass of citizens, who had lost their lands to the rich. He says they were clogging up the city and in a mood to revolt, though here his imagination seems to be coloured by episodes from late republican Roman history. What the young king (b. *c*.262) certainly did on his accession was to propose, through a supporter who was an ephor,

> that those who owed (money) should be released from their debts, and that the land should be divided up; the area from the water-course at Pellana to Mt. Taÿgetos and Malea[102] and Sellasia should be made into 4,500 lots (*klêroi*), and the area outside this into 15,000; that the latter part should be shared among those of the Perioikoi who were able to bear arms, and the inner area to the Spartiates themselves; and that the numbers of the latter group should be made up from those Perioikoi and foreigners (*xenoi*) who had participated in the upbringing (*trophê*) of a free man and who also had good bodily endowments and were in the peak of their years; and that these people should be arranged into fifteen messes (*phiditia*) by (groups of) 400 and 200, and live the life which the (Spartans') ancestors had.
>
> (Plut. *Agis*, 8, Austin 55 *b*)

Agis managed to force the other king, Leonidas, into exile when he opposed him; but having carried the abolition of debts he was foiled by the owners of large estates, who were only too happy to be freed from commitments but did not wish to lose their land. In 241 he was sent to help the Achaeans repel an Aitolian invasion (Plut. *Agis*, 13), and on his return he was executed – together with his mother and grandmother, who according to Plutarch were rich and, like Spartan women generally, influential (cf. p. 102).

Leonidas had been reinstated during Agis's absence, but made what seems at first sight to be a serious mistake, by marrying off the dead king's widow Agiatis to his own son Kleomenes (Plut. *Kleom*. 1). His aim was probably to bring Agiatis's fortune into his family by amalgamating the other royal house with his. According to the sources, Agiatis was no less committed to reform than her late husband, and before long the dead king's ideas began to work upon the new heir. Kleomenes also had as his tutor the Stoic philosopher Sphairos of Borysthenes (or of Olbia: Plut. *Kleom*. 2), who would later help him put his reforms into practice.

Six years later Kleomenes succeeded his father as king, whereupon the Achaeans started to put military pressure on Sparta in the hope of bringing it into the league. Kleomenes had other ideas: he was presented with several Peloponnesian towns by the Aitolians, and embarked on campaigns that caused a rift with Aratos. Eight years into his reign, in 227, probably on the death of his fellow king (Agis IV's young son), he invited Agis's brother to become king with him and struck at the ephors, whom he knew would oppose the reforms he planned. Four ephors were assassinated and their office abolished as 'un-Lykourgan'.

Kleomenes put forward similar laws to those of Agis, and set an example by ceding his own estates to be pooled among the citizens (Plut. *Kleom.* 11, Austin 56 *b*). Perioikoi were recruited as citizens and trained in Spartan fighting, and the training of the young men was reorganized under the supervision of Sphairos. Military successes against the Achaeans and other neighbours began to accrue. By way of reaction, Polybios says, Aratos induced the Achaean league to declare war (227; Polyb. 2. 46), and arranged that overtures would be made to the new Macedonian king, Antigonos III Doson (r. *c.*229–222, initially as regent for the young Philip V; Polyb. 2. 48–50).

Plutarch provides *prima facie* evidence of widespread social discontent which, he thinks, favoured the spread of support for Kleomenes from people wanting similar reforms in their own cities. He describes the situation in 225:

> The Achaeans were now in turmoil and their cities were on the verge of insurrection. The people in them were hoping for division of land and cancellation of debts; in many places the leading citizens were resentful at Aratos, while some were furious with him for inviting Macedonians to the Peloponnese.
>
> (Plut. *Kleom.* 17)

In his life of Aratos, based extensively on the commander's own memoirs, Plutarch says Aratos 'saw that the Peloponnese was shaking and that the cities were being moved towards revolt by those seeking change' (*Arat.* 39. 8); here he is under the influence of Aratos's own claims. (By contrast, in his life of Kleomenes, where he largely follows Phylarchos, he criticizes Aratos (ch. 16, Austin 57) for bringing in the Macedonians.) It may never have been Kleomenes' aim to spread social revolution, even among propertied élites in other cities. At Argos, says Plutarch, he failed to satisfy the demands of the people, and one citizen found it easy to persuade the people to support a revolt against Sparta, 'as they were aggrieved that Kleomenes did not make cancellations of debts as they were hoping' (*Kleom.* 20).

Polybios, by contrast, glosses over Kleomenes' real aims, simply saying that he 'revolutionized his country's traditional political system, and turned its constitutional monarchy into a tyranny' (2. 47). This judgement may be nothing but Achaean bias; but he is probably right to claim that Kleomenes' ambition was to rule the Peloponnese (surely not, as he claims at 2. 49, the whole of Greece: that had never been a Spartan aim, and was well beyond the city's capabilities).

The situation seemed important enough for Antigonos to bring an army down into the Peloponnese (224); presumably he perceived an opportunity to extend the Macedonians' domination into a region they had never controlled.

He inflicted a few setbacks upon Kleomenes (2. 54), but after Kleomenes' successes multiplied he confronted him directly and defeated the Spartans at Sellasia in northern Lakonike (222 BC; Polyb. 2. 65–9, a fine set-piece battle description).[103] Antigonos became the first invader to capture Sparta, reversed the reforms, and according to Polybios restored the 'ancestral constitution' (2. 70); that was a sham, for the kingships were abolished.

Kleomenes fled to Egypt; but Ptolemy III Euergetes, who had previously given him money, was succeeded by the young Ptolemy IV Philopator (r. 221–205), whose advisers considered that Antigonos was too strong and decided not to help Kleomenes regain Lakonike. In 219 Kleomenes and his followers launched a futile coup in Alexandria and were killed; once again Plutarch focuses on the sufferings and nobility of their executed womenfolk (*Kleom.* 38; cf. p. 102).

For Plutarch, writing in the second century AD, Kleomenes is an emblem of just kingship; his noble character makes him a 'true' king (*Kleom.* 13, Austin 56 *a*). The Spartan women, with their fortitude and their very Spartan gift for pithy, 'laconic' self-expression, symbolically personify the Greek spirit of the classical age admired by Plutarch and his readers. It is entirely fitting, in Plutarch's scheme of things, that signs of divine blessing should have gathered round the flayed and crucified body of the king (*Kleom.* 39), for kings rule by divine authority (like the Roman emperors of his own day) and Kleomenes embodied the true, Stoic virtues of kingship:

> And a few days later, those guarding the crucified body of Kleomenes saw an enormous serpent coiled about the king's head and concealing the face, so that no flesh-eating bird could land on it. As a result, a reverence of the gods and a fear fell upon the king (Ptolemy), and he offered the women an opportunity to begin rituals of cleansing, since he realized that a man had died who was loved by the gods and had a superior nature. And the Alexandrians fell to visiting the place, addressing Kleomenes as hero and child of the gods ...
>
> (Plut. *Kleom.* 39. 1–2)

Even Polybios, for whom Kleomenes is a tyrant, admits he was 'a man of outstanding gifts, ... formed by nature to lead and to rule' (5. 39). He is also a proof of the role of Tyche (Fortune) in human affairs (see pp. 173–5): but for chance, he would have escaped defeat and exile, for within a few days Antigonos had left to defend Macedonia against the Illyrians, and died soon afterwards (2. 70).

Agis and Kleomenes were not revolutionaries in the sense of expressing the masses' desire for progressive change. They did not enfranchise poor men, other than members of the community – Spartiates, Perioikoi (who were Lakedaimonians anyhow) – and élite foreigners; only in the desperate situation of 223/2 did Kleomenes sell citizenship to 6,000 helots in order to strengthen the army and raise cash (Plut. *Kleom.* 23). They were, however, more than just reformers; they pursued fundamental change and 'did, no doubt transiently and inadequately, revolutionize Sparta'.[104] That they based their appeal on supposedly ancient tradition allowed them (like the Gracchi, with whom Plutarch compares them) to enjoy upper-class support, and Kleomenes justified his actions by reference to 'respectable' philosophical teachings.

While it is true, as Cartledge suggests, that the slogans of cancellation of debt and redistribution of land cannot have had the same meaning in Sparta as elsewhere, Sparta's problems were in some measure those of Greece as a whole. There is no reliable evidence of mass hardship – Greek citizens hardly formed a social 'mass' in the twentieth-century sense – but rather of the loss of some land, and some privileges, by certain groups among the favoured class who formed the *politai*, or had once been *politai*. What the élites of the Achaean towns perhaps feared was not that the existing social order would be overturned by an enraged underclass, but that they and their friends would be deprived of political power by rivals – men much like themselves, but who would rely on the support of Sparta and thus permit the revival of Spartan power.

Neither the Spartans nor the Achaean leaders can be blamed for pursuing their own interests as they saw them. They may have judged that Macedonian power could never be absolute in the Peloponnese, and that the leadership of the region was there for the taking.

Sparta after Sellasia, and the reign of Nabis (207–192 BC)

Sellasia did not bring peace to the Peloponnese. There was violent political strife within Sparta; the kingship was revived; Philip V of Macedonia (r. 222–179) intervened several times; and for many years there were local wars. The shadowy king Lykourgos (early 210s) and the regent (or king) Machanidas (early 200s) repeatedly seized and lost former Spartan territories. Machanidas's death in a major battle at Mantineia in 207 brought a younger contemporary of Kleomenes III to the throne.

Nabis (r. 207–192), who probably reigned alone, made a new attempt at social and political reform. Like Areus, he put his image on coins; unlike Kleomenes, he kept a bodyguard of mercenaries and adopted the very un-Spartan trappings of contemporary monarchy, such as parade horses and a luxurious palace. It may be Achaean hatred of Sparta that makes Polybios (13. 6, Austin 63), followed by the Roman historian Livy, describe Nabis as a tyrant; at the same time, Nabis may have been consciously echoing the gloriously wealthy Sicilian tyrants of an earlier age. Like such a ruler, Dionysios I of Syracuse (r. 405–367), he is said to have given citizenship to 'slaves', probably meaning some (but not all) helots.[105] He seems to have encouraged Spartiates, perhaps for the first time since the archaic period, to engage in trade and commerce; he is named as benefactor in an inscription from the trading *polis* of Delos (*IG* xi. 4. 716). About now Sparta's first complete circuit of walls, some six miles long, was built, the water-supply was elaborated, and archaeology reveals an increase in artisan production, especially pottery workshops. Spartans even began to build monumental family tombs, a departure from the self-effacing norm of the classical period. Though it would be rash to credit Nabis with all these innovations, it does appear that, for whatever reasons, Sparta from the end of the third century on became increasingly like a 'normal' Greek *polis*.

Nabis cultivated diplomatic relations with the new power on the Greek stage – Rome – but had accepted the gift of Argos from Rome's enemy Philip V of Macedonia. After Philip's defeat in 197 (Chapter 10) the Roman commander Flamininus, to enhance Rome's standing among its Greek allies, betrayed the friendship of Nabis and invaded Lakonike on the pretext of liberating Argos, where Nabis had cancelled debts and redistributed land; once again social reform seems to have had pragmatic rather than idealistic aims, and opposition was motivated by the desire that one's friends should not be harmed. Sparta again lost much of its remaining perioikic territory. Nabis attempted to retake this in 193, but was assassinated. Sparta fell to the Achaean general Philopoimen, who had fought at Sellasia. Spartan ambitions were finally neutralized by its incorporation into the Achaean league in 192, and its independent history came to an end, though this, too, did not mean the end of trouble in the Peloponnese.

Athens and Macedonia after 239 BC

Athens from 239 to 192 BC

The description of Athens by 'Herakleides' (pp. 29–30) cannot be closely dated; even if it is accurate, it is hard to tell whether it belongs to a period of Macedonian rule or a time of freedom. Besides its classical monuments, says the author, the city has festivals to delight you, philosophers to entertain you, and top-class food, though in rather short supply (1. 1–2, Austin 83). Whatever its political fortunes, the city was riding high on its cultural reputation.

Having suffered from the Achaeans' attempts to separate them from Gonatas and his garrison (p. 127), the Athenians endured further assaults during the 'war of Demetrios', which lasted throughout the reign of Demetrios II of Macedonia (r. 239–229). What intermittent disturbance of Attic life this entailed may be imagined from the recorded disruption to festivals at Rhamnous on the north-east coast.[106] At Athens the cult of Antigonos Monophthalmos and Demetrios Poliorketes was given new life, but we cannot assume that the entire citizen body, or all members of the political élite, bore Macedonian rule cheerfully. Conversely, the Achaean raids may have been resented, for when Aratos was defeated (between 235 and 232) and rumours of his death reached Athens, there was premature rejoicing. The hostility he seems to have aroused – at least among some citizens – may explain why Athens would not support him against Sparta a decade later,[107] which must imply that a majority of politically active citizens opposed him.

Athens regained its freedom in 229. Upon the death of Demetrios II the Macedonian governor Diogenes, who may well have been an Athenian citizen put in charge of his fellows, handed over Piraeus, Salamis, and Rhamnous to the city. Aratos later claimed to have played a large part in this (Plut. *Arat.* 34; Paus. 2. 18. 6), but probably exaggerated his role.[108] The Athenians had been under direct rule for thirty-three years; perhaps a greater cause for celebration, however, was the freeing of Piraeus after no less than sixty-six years of occupation.

To preserve their freedom, the Athenians adopted an official neutrality; in reality they aligned themselves with their ally of the 260s, Ptolemaic Egypt, presumably hoping that this would deter Macedonian aggression.[109]

> The Athenians ... had by this time freed themselves from the fear of Macedonia, and considered that they had now permanently secured their independence. They accordingly adopted Eurykleides and Mikion as their representatives, and took no part whatever in the politics of the rest of Greece; but following the lead and instigation of these statesmen, they laid themselves out to flatter all the kings, and Ptolemy most of all; nor was there any kind of decree or proclamation too fulsome for their digestion: any consideration of dignity being little regarded, under the guidance of these vain and frivolous leaders.
>
> (Polyb. 5. 106. 6–8)

Polybios's vehemence may derive from a belief that the Athenians ought not to have remained neutral and should have joined the Achaean league, in which case Aratos would not have had to perform his notorious U-turn and call on the Macedonians for help. Self-interest, however, was the primary motive for the Athenians, no doubt rightly; besides, they had no love for Aratos after his invasions of Attica.[110]

Neutrality was tempered by diplomacy. In 226, as a decree attests (*ISE* 28),[111] the Athenians engaged the Aristotelian philosopher Prytanis of Karystos to negotiate with Antigonos, perhaps to seek recognition of their liberty; there is no evidence that their petition was successful. Within a short time, in response to the Achaeans' request for help, Doson revived the Hellenic league of Philip II and Demetrios I, which now included most of the central Greek states (*Staatsv.* iii. 507; cf. Polyb. 4. 25–6, Austin 58). Presumably as a reaction, the Athenians not long afterwards voted Ptolemy III honours hitherto matched only by those voted to the Antigonids in 307.

Among other awards, Ptolemy's cult was added to the pantheon, a new thirteenth tribe of Ptolemais was created, to consist of one deme from every other tribe and a new one of Berenikidai (named after his queen), and the *boulê* was increased to 650 members.[112]

Around the same time, the Athenians strengthened their city walls and those of their rural demes.[113] Their policy of neutrality, linked with the politicians Eurykleides and Mikion, spared them from involvement in the Macedonian and Roman wars of 222–205 (for which see Chapter 10), and even the Roman capture of Aigina in 210 and its handover to the Aitolians (who sold it to Attalos of Pergamon) did not cause them to take sides, but rather to join in unsuccessful mediation attempts under Ptolemy IV's aegis in 209 (Livy, 27. 30. 4–6). Although the city is named in the text of the peace of Phoinike, its name may be a forgery (p. 374). But in time neutrality became impossible.

In 201 a diplomatic clash with Philip V's allies the Akarnanians, perhaps rashly provoked by the Athenians, led to ferocious raids into Attica by the Akarnanians with Macedonian help. Livy sees its effects in grave terms: 'the army ... devastated Attica with the sword and with fire, returning to Akarnania with booty of all kinds' (31. 14. 7–10). Certainly anti-Macedonian opinion gained the upper hand among the Athenians. They declared war on Philip and abolished the two Antigonid tribes (as they had not done on those occasions when they had secured their freedom from Macedonia). References to the Antigonids were erased from public documents, curses upon the Macedonians were added to public prayers, and Macedonians were banned from Attica (Livy, 31. 44. 2–9). Since Attalos I of Pergamon was in Athens at the time to seek military aid against Philip, and since his appeal was successful, the Athenians took the opportunity to create a tribe of Attalis and a deme of Apollonieis (named after queen Apollonis), and to add the king's cult to the tribal pantheon. The currency of cult honours was becoming somewhat devalued, but feelings were running high and the Athenians could expect no mercy from Philip.[114]

The Athenians sent an envoy to Rome to seek aid. Later this would be used by the Romans to justify their entry into Greece, but it was not the primary motive or cause of their war against Philip. For the Athenians it was a wise move, for in 200 a Roman army provided their only reliable protection from the Macedonian armies which even reached the Academy, just outside the city walls (Polyb. 16. 27. 1; Livy, 31. 16. 2). Shortly afterwards, Philip himself almost penetrated the city at the head of his army; once more it was Athens' allies, this time Pergamene troops as well as Roman, that saved the day (Livy, 31. 24. 4–25. 2). Subsequently, however, the war moved to other theatres, and the Athenians reverted to a minor status among Rome's supporters. The tough settlement imposed on Philip in 196, and Flamininus's declaration that the Greeks should be free, marked the end of the Macedonian threat to southern Greece.

Throughout the second century the Athenians remained loyal supporters of Rome, probably becoming formal allies between 191 and 188. Not for a hundred years did the opposite view prevail. It was a remarkable century of peace for Athens;[115] which may really mean that those who wished to support Rome were consistently in the majority, perhaps more securely than in any other *polis*.

The last Antigonids (239–168 BC)

In Macedonia, the somewhat obscure reign of Demetrios II (r. 239–229) was heavily taken up with wars in Greece, including interventions in Akarnania, Argos, central Greece, and the north-west.[116] His premature death left Antigonos Doson (r. 239–221) as regent for the young Philip V. After successfully defending the kingdom against invasions from Dardanians, Aitolians, and Thessalians, Doson was made king with Philip as his adopted son and heir. He lost control of Athens at the outset, but supervised a reconstruction of the Thessalian league, restored influence in Karia in western Asia Minor (perhaps as a future province for Philip), and, as we have seen, launched a key expedition against Sparta which made Macedonia the decisive power in the Peloponnese. He appears to have learned from the experience of Demetrios II and made good administrative arrangements;[117] but at his death the handover of power to a 17-year-old was likely to change the speed and character of government.

Philip V (r. 221–179) earned his spurs fighting Macedonia's non-Greek neighbours, and then fought the 'social' war (i.e. war of the allies; 220–217) against the Aitolians, Spartans, and Eleians. His attempts to extend Macedonian influence to the Adriatic, and his alliance with Hannibal of Carthage, brought him into conflict with Rome, culminating in the first Macedonian war (211–205) against Rome and the Aitolians and the second (201–197) against a coalition of Rome, Egypt, Pergamon, Rhodes, Byzantion, and Aitolia. In both wars he was defeated and subjected to disadvantageous peace treaties. Although he became Rome's ally and was able to transform Macedonia's internal organization and rebuild its military power, he fell under suspicion, like so many of Rome's allies. After executing his younger son, Demetrios, for treason he quickly died, leaving the kingdom to Perseus (r. 179–168).[118]

Perseus in turn, earning traditional credit at home for campaigns in northern and central Greece, became an object of Roman fear; he was overthrown, and the kingship abolished, in the third Macedonian war (172–168); he died later in captivity in Italy.[119] The kingdom was divided into four republics, and in 146 it became a Roman province.

The limits of Macedonian power

The case for seeing Macedonia as impoverished at the outset of Gonatas's reign may not be as strong as historians have often assumed. Earlier (p. 54) it was suggested that, though the Gauls were the most significant invaders of Greece since Xerxes, the effects of their campaigns may have been exaggerated and that their importance may have been to provide kings with opportunities to demonstrate their military prowess. Antigonos Gonatas was not alone in making efforts to maintain a high cultural profile among their fellow monarchs. There was a long tradition of cultural and intellectual activity in and around the hellenized court. Philip V is said to have had a liking for epigrams and to have arranged for copies to be made of Theopompos's history of Philip II (*FGH* 115 fr. 31). There will have been new cult temples of city founders at Philippoi, Thessalonike, and Demetrias. By 187 a temple of the Egyptian god Serapis (see pp. 165–6) had existed for some time in Thessalonike (Burstein 72). The Antigonids made dedications at Delos, where by Philip V's reign there were enough resident Macedonians to form a *koinon* and dedicate a statue of the king, who built a stoa:[120]

> The *koinon* of the M[ace]don[ians] (honours)
> king Ph[ilip son of king]
> Demetrios for his v[irtue]
> and his goodwill [towards Apollo?]
>   (*Syll.*[3] 575; *Choix* 55)[121]

These isolated examples, some from after the 220s, give strength to the view that the Macedonian state after 277 was far from bankrupt. The difficulties of controlling southern Greece had more to do with the fragmented political landscape and the traditions of local independence than with any inherent weakness in the north. Even Philip II took twenty years to defeat the Greeks. The fact that after Demetrios Poliorketes half a century passed without a Macedonian army taking the offensive in Greece[122] does not mean the state was weak. Given the expense of preserving the 'Fetters', it would be surprising to find their armies also continually campaigning at great expense in the south. Nevertheless, some important Greek city-states remained independent for long periods.

The Macedonian kings did not over-exert themselves to establish complete control of southern Greece, and do not seem to have been overly concerned at the presence of Ptolemaic bases around the fringe of their territory. These considerations suggest that their interest was chiefly in excluding other kingdoms from gaining commercial or military advantage by having free access to Greece, and in preventing the growth or revival of potentially dangerous powers (Athens, Aitolia) within Greece. Well-placed garrison towns, and the use of puppet tyrants to rule cities, were efficient ways of stabilizing indirect control.

5

RELIGION AND PHILOSOPHY

Athens, the leading city of Old Greece, periodically lost its independence in the third century, but remained pre-eminent among Greek states for its philosophical schools, and on a number of occasions in the hellenistic period we read of philosophers involved in public life. This chapter aims to discover the social context of Greek philosophy in this period, but will first examine changes in other, older belief-systems.[1]

Since the days of the early thinkers, or Presocratics, philosophers had sought to relate the supreme divine controller of the universe in mythological and theological discourse to the observable world-order around them. Their arguments were framed largely within the terms of religion; it was appropriate that men should honour the gods with temples, statues, and games. Since then, philosophy had developed into a sophisticated discourse, while religion, too, continued to evolve as the *polis* developed.

In the hellenistic period religion and philosophy still influenced and took account of one another. Each discourse had to be adapted to cope with the existence of new monarchies, the changes in the role of the city-state, and the choices facing members of the élite. How was it fitting for citizens to honour the gods now, even supposing they were willing to do so? What duties did citizens owe to fellow-citizens, and to other members of the human race?

It has often been suggested that observable changes in religion and philosophy reflected fundamental and crucial changes of outlook, and many writers have assumed a breakdown of existing certainties in an age of rapid change. The archaeological, epigraphic, and literary evidence, however, suggests continuities rather than discontinuities. The position taken here is that the world did not change as radically as some have thought; neither, therefore, did religion and philosophy.

Religious change

The religious world of the classical *polis* has been the subject of intense investigation, and many new insights have been gained in recent years. Scholars emphasize the differences between ancient and modern religion, particularly differences from Christianity. Greek religion, which was polytheistic, was above all a religion involving practical transactions between the worshipper (or the community, or its representative) and divine powers. Gods had to be placated and honoured, and this had to be done in due form, with appropriate words and ritual actions (such as sacrifices). Belief, in the sense of a worshipper's emotional or philosophical commitment to a particular god's existence or a particular moral code, was not central as it is today; there was little debate (except perhaps among philosophers) about whether the gods existed, though there might be arguments about whether a particular god[2] was a 'true' deity or not. Nor did attachment to a particular cult exclude one from worshipping other gods. There were no sacred texts analogous to the Bible or the Koran. The earliest poets, Homer and Hesiod, were appealed to as authorities, in some sense, for the constantly evolving body of myths or legends (*mythoi*, 'stories'; *logoi*, 'tales') which expressed through narrative the relationships between gods and humans and in different ways provided models for action. Few if any cults offered an all-embracing moral code that was supposed to be valid for all humans. Particular cults did not imply particular theories about the creation of the world. Above all, religion was practical, though 'practice' could involve simply 'being there' while important rituals were performed, and taking part in festivities.

Central to classical religion were the twelve Olympian deities, from among whom the patron gods of particular cities were chosen: Athena in Athens, Apollo at Corinth, and so on. Often the patron deity went under a special title: Athena as guardian of Athens was Athena Polias (of the City), but appeared on the Acropolis as Athena Parthenos (the Virgin) and Promachos (the Front-line Fighter); at Tegea in the Peloponnese she was identified with a local goddess and became Athena Alea. The Olympians were honoured with stone temples and statues, though their sanctuaries (sacred enclosures) also contained monuments to other gods. The principal religious rituals of the classical city-states, too, were those involving the Olympians.

A second layer of classical cult practice involved 'heroes' of semi-divine status, ranging from the great figures of Homeric legend to actual (dead) persons elevated to cult status for conferring special benefits on the community, such as the founder (*oikistês*) of a city. A hero or heroine usually had a special connection with a particular city or region, as did the legendary first and last kings of Athens, Erechtheus and Kodros, and the Homeric figures Helen and Menelaos at Sparta.

To maintain both these groups of cults was to uphold the city's power and safety, and to construct a collective identity for the community. In theory at least, they commanded the allegiance and participation of all the male citizens and, when appropriate, of their women and children.

Finally, much of the social space within which Greeks moved was mapped out, more locally, by a whole geography of sacred spots and monuments, such as cults of the Nymphai at springs, or the stylized figures of Hermes which often stood at street-corners.

By contrast, the period after Alexander's death, perhaps more than any in Greek history, lends itself to (over-)interpretation as a time of religious crisis. In many general surveys of the period, one reads of a decline in traditional belief and a rise in scepticism, agnosticism, and atheism. Apparently oblivious to the contradiction, historians – even the same historians – discern increases in superstition, mysticism, and astrology as well as ruler-cult, Oriental cults, religions of personal destiny, and the worship of abstractions. These changes are interpreted as understandable reactions to the uncertainties of life in the Greek world after Alexander.[3] Religious and philosophical developments may even be presented as a logical step on the road to Christianity.

As a first note of caution, it is probably over-optimistic to suppose that we can generalize from the little evidence we have and speak of an age of uncertainty. Second, Greek religion, like philosophy, had always changed; foreign cults had been brought in, and while some were assimilated through the identification of the new deity with an Olympian god, others took their places alongside them in the calendar of religious ritual. Consequently it is not possible to reconstruct a definitive 'Greek religion' (such as by restricting Greek religion to gods with Greek names) or to declare any cult practised in Greek communities to be non-Greek. Third, there is a danger of imposing anachronistic or christianizing terms when describing even the most basic features of an ancient religion.[4] For example, Walbank in one passage appears to view changes in beliefs and rituals as a superficial phenomenon:

> Old certainties had gone and though ancient rites were still zealously performed in the conviction that what was traditional should be preserved, many people were at bottom agnostics or even atheists. The observance of established rituals must have meant little to many worshippers.
>
> (Walbank, *HW* 209)

We should not divorce belief and practice when talking about Greek religion, and it may be incorrect to view ritual as an epiphenomenon distinct from religious experience. Furthermore, terms like 'atheism' and 'agnosticism' may be thought to carry christianizing overtones, suggesting that religion was chiefly bound up with a sense of personal philosophy or even personal destiny. Today some atheists and agnostics prefer not merely to see themselves as denying certain propositions about the existence of God, but as making a positive statement about the relationship between human beings and the cosmos, believing that their position is more 'rational' and therefore more conducive to individual and collective happiness. The evidence for such ideas in Greek thought is extremely sparse; probably only a small minority among educated members of the élite who were in touch with the works of philosophers could even have formulated statements of this kind.

Nor should we seek to explain developments primarily in terms of, on the one hand, the emotional 'needs' of subjects or, on the other, cynical manipulation by their rulers. In his study of the Roman imperial cult Price has shown that neither an 'objective' explanation (in terms of ceremonies, resolutions, personnel, and so on) nor a 'subjective' one (in terms of emotional needs or manipulative calculations) is adequate by itself.[5] We should set out from the assumption that religious language and ritual have a meaning (albeit not a determinate one) for those involved, and examine new developments in terms of their social location and what they tell us about relationships within society.

Ruler-cult

One of the most frequently discussed features of the age, and supposedly one of the most visible signs of innovation and of a crisis in traditional religion, is ruler-cult. At the outset it is important to make two distinctions, one of which has to do with the nature of Greek religion, the second with the actual development of the phenomenon.

First, divine honours are not the same as deification, as Préaux shows particularly clearly.[6] The first known instance of divine honours being offered by a city to one of Alexander's successors is attested in the reply from the city of Skepsis to Antigonos's letter of 311 BC (cf. p. 74):

> So that Antigonos may receive honours worthy of his achievements and the people should be seen to be returning thanks for the benefits it has received, let it mark off a *temenos* (sacred enclosure) for him, build an altar, and set up a cult statue as beautiful as possible, and let the sacrifice, the competition, the wearing of the wreath, and the rest of the festival be celebrated every [year] in his honour as they were before. Let it [crown] him with a gold crown [weighing] 100 gold [staters] ...
>
> (Austin 32, BD 6, *OGIS* 6)

Here a living commander (not yet royal) is associated with an existing festival. This is some way short of deification; Antigonos is probably not being regarded as a god, but receives the same kinds of honours as gods and heroes. Similarly in a later era, when Attalos I's statue was placed next to that of Apollo in the agora of Sikyon (Polyb. 18. 16), that did not make him a god. Nor did sharing a temple with a god, as when Attalos III (r. 138–133) was honoured by his own city, Pergamon; most of the preamble explaining the king's benefactions is lost, but the start of the actual decree is preserved:

With good fortune, resolved by the council and people:

To crown the king with a golden prize crown, and to consecrate a 5-cubit statue of him in armour and standing on dogs in the temple of Soter Asklepios, so that he may be co-templar (*synnaos*) to the god; and to set a gold image of him mounted on a horse upon a marble column beside the altar of Zeus Soter, in order that the image may subsist in the most conspicuous position in the *agora*;

and every day the *stephanêphoros* ('crown-bearer', chief magistrate) and the priest of the king and the *agônothetês* (official in charge of festivals) are to sacrifice frankincense upon the altar of Zeus Soter to the king. And the eighth day (of each month), on which he arrived at Pergamon, shall be sacred for all time, and on it each year shall be realized by the priest of Asklepios a procession, the finest possible, from the *prytaneion* (chamber of the executive committee) to the sanctuary of Asklepios and the king, the usual persons co-processing.

(OGIS 332, lines 5–17)

The long list of honours continues (lines 17–62) with the participation of magistrates in the sacrifice and the funding thereof. The wording of the inscriptions to be carved on the statue and on the 'image' is laid down. The king is to be crowned each time he arrives in Pergamon ('our *polis*') by 'the *stephanephoros* of the Twelve Gods and of the God, King Eumenes' (note that the late king, not the living one, is held to be a god); the text includes the words of the prayers to be offered for his health, safety, victory, and strength and for the preservation of the monarchy, and of the official responses by prescribed personnel carrying or wearing appropriate items. Details are given of the sacrifices to be carried out on the anniversary of the king's arrival by each of the civic tribes, and of the funding thereof, again with specified prayers and responses. There are somewhat vague provisions for other sacrifices in his honour at the royal stoa, the altar of Hestia of the Council, and that of Zeus of the Council. The king is to be feasted by the generals. A copy of the decree is to be given to the king with (as it were) a fulsome covering letter; it is to be inscribed on a stele at the Asklepi(ei)on and incorporated into the city's laws.

Nothing here indicates deification as such; nor did the paying of cultic honours to individuals, whether during their lifetime or afterwards, necessarily imply that they were thought of as gods in the same way that Zeus and Athena were.

Second, a line needs to be drawn between 'civic ruler-cult', established (in theory voluntarily) by cities within the orbit of a king (especially in the Seleukid kingdom), and 'royal ruler-cult' promoted or set up by the king himself. For example, before the reign of Antiochos III there was no centrally organized cult of the Seleukid kings and queens, though there were local civic cults from Seleukos I on. No living Seleukid had yet been a god; kings established cults of their predecessors. Under Antiochos III, however, came a major innovation. Several stone copies of an edict of 193, evidently distributed throughout his empire, are preserved, including one from Laodikeia-Nihavend in western Iran (Austin 158)[7] and another from Eriza in Phrygia. In it Antiochos makes administrative arrangements for a new cult of Laodike, centrally organized but operating throughout the kingdom:[8]

> King Antiochos to Anaximbrotos, greeting.
>
> As we desire to increase still further the honours of our sister-queen Laodike, and as we think it important to do so because she lives with us lovingly and considerately and because she is reverently disposed toward the gods (*to theion*), we do on all occasions lovingly the things which it is fitting and right for her to receive from us, and now we have decided that, just as there are appointed throughout the kingdom chief priests of our cult, so there shall be established in the same districts chief priestesses of her also, who shall wear golden crowns bearing her images and whose names shall be mentioned in contracts after those of the chief priests of our ancestors and of us.
>
> Since, therefore, in the districts under your administration there has been appointed Berenike, the daughter of our relative Ptolemaios son of Lysimachos, see that everything is done according to what has been written above, and have copies of the letters, engraved on stelae, set up in the most conspicuous places, so that both now and in the future there may be evident to all in this matter also our policy toward our sister.
>
> (*RC* 36 (cf. 37), BD 131, *OGIS* 224)

We learn incidentally from this text that the king himself was already receiving similar honours. The list of dynastic cults inevitably grew longer as time passed; an inscription from Seleukeia-in-Pieria under Seleukos IV details a whole series of priesthoods of different, deceased members of the royal family (Austin 177, *OGIS* 245).[9]

The terms and concepts of religion had traditionally been used to distinguish outstanding men. Giving divine honours to humans was far from new. The reformer Lykourgos of Sparta (who, if he existed, may have lived in the early seventh century) was worshipped as a god, according to Herodotos (1. 66. 1). Founders of city-states were regularly worshipped as 'heroes' after their death, and occasionally while still alive. Examples invariably cited in the latter connection are the Spartan commanders Brasidas and Lysandros, honoured by cities newly allied to Sparta during and after the Peloponnesian war. It is also relevant that Greek kings in the classical period, such as in Sparta and Macedonia, claimed descent from the gods. It is possible to view ruler-cult as essentially a creation of the world of the Greek city-state; it was entirely consistent with traditional Greek religion.[10] The suggestion has sometimes been made that Seleukid ruler-worship began under the stimulus of near eastern practice; this has been rejected, since there is evidence that there was no 'native' worship of the Seleukids in Babylon and Iran, only the traditional prayers 'for the life of the king'.[11]

Now cult worship could be demanded by the ruler, and clearly it was a potent force to be exploited to the full. The only recorded opposition to divine honours was expressed during Alexander's lifetime. According to Arrian (4. 10–12, Austin 11), when Alexander desired that his lieutenants should prostrate themselves before him, Kallisthenes and the other 'court' intellectuals debated whether Alexander in particular, and humans in general, were worthy of divine honours. It is doubtful that we have here the record of a real debate.[12] The Athenian orator Hypereides protested in 323 that his fellow-citizens had been forced 'to see sacrifices accorded to men, (while) the statues, altars, and temples of the gods (were) disregarded' (*Epitaphios* (*Funeral Oration*), 6. 21); but like later objectors he was expressing displeasure at the present recipient's unworthiness rather than objecting to divine honours on principle. 'There is no sign of opposition based on the assumption that ruler-cult is in itself outrageous and sacrilegious'.[13]

Alexander appears to have believed he was a descendant of the semi-divine hero Achilleus, and later to have seen himself as a son of Zeus. It was not until well into the reign of Ptolemy I, however, perhaps in the 290s, that Alexander was honoured as a god.[14] At this stage no living king was a god, though kings had received godlike honours: the league of the Islanders had been the first (perhaps by 305/4) to vote Ptolemy I 'honours equal to those of the gods' (or so they claimed around 280: Austin 218, Burstein 92, *Syll.*[3] 390).

Deification of the Ptolemies began when Ptolemy II Philadelphos, after becoming sole king, proclaimed his late father, Ptolemy I Soter, a god. On the death of Soter's third and last wife Berenike in 279, Philadelphos set up a joint cult for them as Saviour Gods and inaugurated the festival of the Ptolemaieia in their honour. The importance of the Ptolemaieia can be seen from a decree of the Samians for a rich fellow-citizen, Boulagoras, in the 240s:

> and (since) during the present year a delegation of sacred envoys had to be sent to Alexandria, he [*Boulagoras*] – knowing that the people attaches the greatest importance to the honours paid to king Ptolemy (III) and his sister queen Berenike, since funds for their crowns and the sacrifices which the sacred envoys had to perform in Alexandria were limited, and there was no money to pay for the travel expenses of the leader of the sacred embassy and the sacred envoys who were to bring the crowns and perform the sacrifices, and no immediate source of money was available, and wishing that none of the honours previously decreed to the king, the queen, their

parents, and their ancestors should be omitted – promised that he would advance from his own resources the money for that purpose, which amounted to little less than six thousand drachmas; ...

(Austin 113, BD 64, *SEG* i. 366)

Later still, Philadelphos made himself and his sister-wife Arsinoë partners in Alexander's cult as Theoi Adelphoi, 'Sibling Gods' (*P. Hib.* 199).[15] This was the first time a living monarch had been made a god. Arsinoë was made a 'co-templar god' (*synnaos theos*) in all the temples of Egyptian deities, and certain royal revenues were creamed off to finance the cult (pp. 225–6).[16] Despite the royal initiative that lay behind these cults, there was Egyptian precedent for ruler-worship; so the royal cult of the Ptolemies, as practised and documented in native Egyptian temples, developed somewhat autonomously, adapting prior pharaonic practice to new requirements.[17]

In Athens, Antigonos I and Demetrios I were honoured as Saviours after capturing (or 'liberating') the city in 307. 'Saviour' is a title full of cultic resonance and is appropriate to Zeus, and now or soon after this they took, or accepted, the title of kings (Plutarch, *Demetrios*, 10, Austin 34). Further divine honours followed in 291 or 290, when Demetrios entered the city at the time of the celebration of the Eleusinian mysteries. He was met by choruses singing in his honour (Demochares, *FGH* 75 fr. 2 = Ath. 6. 253 b–c), and one of the hymns is quoted by Athenaeus, citing the contemporary historian Douris of Samos:

> How are the greatest and dearest of the gods
> present in the city!
> For here Demeter and Demetrios together
> are brought in by the season.
> She the solemn mysteries of Kore
> comes here to perform,
> but he is here joyfully, as befits the god,
> handsome and laughing.
> A solemn thing he appears, his friends all in a circle,
> and he in the middle of them,
> just as if his friends were the stars
> and he the sun.
> Child of the mightiest god Poseidon,
> and of Aphrodite, hail!
> Other gods, they either keep away
> or do not have any ears
> or do not exist or pay no heed to us;
> but you we see present,
> not made of stone, not made of wood, but real.
> We pray, then, to you:

first that you bring us peace, dearest one,
for you have the power.
That Sphinx who now subdues not Thebes alone,
but all of Hellas –
she's an Aitolian who, as she once did,
perches on a rock,
snatching up our bodies to carry them away,
and I cannot fight her:
Aitolians are always snatching things from neighbours,
but now things more remote –
above all, punish her yourself; if not,
find you some Oedipus
and he shall dash this Sphinx from the crag,
or turn her into ash.

> (Douris, *FGH* 76 fr. 13 = Ath.
> 6. 253 d–f, Austin 35, Burstein 7)

Some historians have confidently proclaimed that the hymn reveals a widespread disbelief in the existence of the gods. The substitution of a new god who is patently a mere mortal is held up as evidence of religious decline, irrationality, the cynical manipulation of religion for political ends, or – somewhat contradictorily – a combination of these. We should remember that the hymn survives only because a late author quotes it from a lost work of Douris, an anti-Macedonian author; there is no guarantee that it was performed just as Athenaeus says. Even if it was, and if Douris meant us to take it as evidence of scepticism (which is doubtful), can we be sure the poet was sceptical about the old gods, or was he just indulging in flattery? Even if he was a religious sceptic, were the members of his audience? If they were sceptics, were they representative of their age? Certainly not all Athenians accepted that it was right to have given such effusive honours to Demetrios in 306 and 302; Plutarch tells us that the poet Philippides of Kephale attacked the measures (Plut. *Demetr.* 12. 4, 26. 3).

The language of the hymn, in fact, contradicts the idea of a loss of belief. When the poet says 'or do not exist', he is hardly suggesting that *all* the gods may not exist: he invokes no fewer than four others, and implicitly makes Demetrios a god! Rather, just as some gods are far away or deaf or do not care, some may not be real gods. The language is that of traditional religion – just as the hymns of Kallimachos (Chapter 7), for all their self-conscious literariness and reframing of earlier myths, are still real religious expressions. Nor is the language necessarily more rational than earlier formulations; it is using a different rational framework. Finally, the key passage is surely the appeal for help against the Aitolians, who had taken control of the oracular shrine of Delphi and made an alliance with Thebes.[18] The hymn has a clear political import.

There is, admittedly, evidence that one could adduce in support of the idea that, while the common people still believed, members of the élite inclined towards atheism. A story sometimes used to support the idea of a sophisticated élite, cynically exploiting religious imagery to mislead gullible folk, is that of Eumenes and the empty throne (see also p. 46). Plutarch tells how Eumenes, fearing that his Macedonian lieutenants would betray him rather than be led by a non-Macedonian, told them that Alexander had appeared to him in a dream and said that, if they would erect a tent containing a throne for him, he would be present at their discussions and would guide them. Diodoros (18. 61) adds that sacrifices were made to Alexander and the commanders prostrated themselves 'as before a god',[19] while Plutarch (perhaps drawing on Hieronymos) characterizes their credulity as 'superstition' (*deisidaimonia*, *Eum*. 13). It is hard to believe that hardened military commanders who had served with Alexander were any more gullible than Eumenes himself; in suggesting this, Plutarch is surely indulging in Greek nationalism at the expense of 'mere' Macedonians. What the story suggests, rather, is that it was natural for both parties to accept that Alexander was some kind of divine, divinely inspired, or divinely favoured being (though not necessarily a 'god'). It may have made sense to believe that great military commanders, whose deeds far outstripped the achievements of the commanders of city-states, had at least divine support and probably divine parentage.

This perhaps explains why kings were able to exploit the forms of existing Greek ritual to legitimate their rule – though we must not see it solely as a political exercise. Nor can we claim that the impetus for setting up ruler-cult came largely from the worshippers,[20] as if it was a reflection of a lack of confidence in the old gods of the city-state, any more than we can view it purely as a royal propaganda device for promoting collective expressions of loyalty. When a city sets up a cult, we must presume, in the absence of evidence to the contrary, that there is more to it than political manoeuvring and certain groups trying to worm their way into the king's favour.

In third-century Pergamon and Macedonia there was no organized royal ruler-cult. In Macedonia this was perhaps because the kingship had its ritual and religious framework laid down earlier. In Pergamon, it may have been because the state was not so successful as an 'imperial' power as to require that kind of image-building. The compatibility of the traditional and the new is revealed by the case of the Rhodians, who on at least one occasion were guided by the Greek religious framework. Before they gave Ptolemy I the title of Soter (Saviour) for his help against the Antigonid attack in 305/4, they asked the advice of the oracle of Ammon in Egypt (Diod. 20. 100, Austin 39; Paus. 1. 8. 6 for the Rhodian origin of the name). Then, with the oracle's agreement, they dedicated to him a sacred enclosure (*temenos*) with adjoining stoas, naming it the Ptolemaion. Like hero-cult, a *temenos* is a wholly Greek religious feature.[21]

Inscriptional evidence shows that ruler-cult could be set up by groups and societies other than cities.[22] We have associations of mercenaries or veterans, the *basilistai* (not monarchists in the modern sense, but 'devotees of the kings') and *philobasilistai* ('lovers of devotion to the kings'), formed to celebrate the cult of the Ptolemaic kings and Egyptian gods together.[23] On Thera, where there was a Ptolemaic naval base, an association of *basilistai* made a dedication to Serapis, Isis, and Anubis (*IG* xii. 3. 443); at Thespiai in central mainland Greece there was a society of 'Philetairian co-sacrificers', *synthytai Philetêreieis* (*sic*), dedicated to the memory of the founder of the Attalid dynasty – founded, indeed, as the result of a benefaction by Philetairos himself (*OGIS* 311).[24] Later the hellenizing king of Pontos, Mithradates V Eupator (r. 120–63), gave a bronze vessel to a society of 'Eupatoristai from the gymnasium' (*OGIS* 367).

To judge from the last case, where the persons are members of a city's *gymnasion*, some of these cult societies were not expressions of simple piety on the part of ordinary folk, but part of an élite network of cult links not unlike the Panhellenion of the emperor Hadrian in the second century AD. Others were not necessarily for the élite. The Attalists of Teos in Asia Minor, who constructed a sanctuary, the *Attaleion*, near the theatre of that town (*OGIS* 326), were actors, part of the 'internationale' of performing artists of all kinds known as the craftsmen (*technitai*) of Dionysos. One of the main branches of the *technitai* was based in Athens. They were awarded privileges and protection by the amphiktyonic council which administered Delphi, as well as by states and kings; in the late second century they were involved in a dispute with the Isthmian guild of performers, which the Roman senate resolved in the Athenians' favour.[25] Royal patronage, which often helped fund city festivals, was extended to these groups of performers, who may have set up cult organizations to reciprocate the benefactions. The members of the Attalid royal family appear in one document as the patrons of the Ionian and Hellespontine branch of the artists (Austin 123, *Choix* 75).

Whatever the philosophical outlook of the individuals involved in such cult foundations, it is clear that Greek 'subjects' and hellenistic kings could only operate with the terms and concepts available to them. Religious expression was as potent a force as ever. Indeed, there may have been more religious practice and discussion of it than before.

'Oriental' and 'personal' religions

In general it was a time of religious change – like the classical period – in which the range of alternative religious practice was enlarged and extended. Some old cults spread to new places. At Rome, where Dionysos had been introduced in the fifth century and was well established, Asklepios was now received with the blessing of the Delphic oracle. Another trend, which Asklepios exemplifies, is the seemingly increased popularity of certain existing cults (the inscription quoted above, p. 157, shows the importance of his sanctuary in Pergamon). His major sanctuaries received costly new buildings. At Athens the Asklepieion, founded in 420/19, gained a huge two-storey stoa during Alexander's reign.[26] At Kos, where the fourth-century synoecism of the *polis* prompted the construction of an Asklepieion, foreign and local benefactors endowed it during the first half of the third century with new stoas, an altar, temples of Asklepios and Apollo, and a fountain-house; in the first half of the second century, a new temple, a monumental stairway, and two new halls were built. The newly adorned sanctuary may be the scene of the fourth *Mime* by Herodas, in which two poor women make their humble sacrifices to the god.[27] Grand though it was, the Asklepieion at Kos never had its own gymnasium, theatre, or stadium, unlike that at Epidauros, where many of the major buildings are as early as the fourth century.

A further indication of the elaboration of these sanctuaries comes in the form of epigraphic records of miraculous cures. The following inscriptions are from late fourth-century Epidauros:

> [Kleio] was pregnant for five years ... she came as a suppliant to the [god] and went to sleep in the innermost sanctuary. As soon as she came out of it and was outside the sanctuary she gave birth to a boy, who as soon as he was born washed himself from the fountain and walked about with his mother. After being granted this favour she wrote the following inscription on her dedication: 'It is not the greatness of the tablet that deserves admiration, but the divinity ...'
>
> A man with the fingers of his hand paralysed except for one came as a suppliant to the god, and when he saw the tablets in the sanctuary he would not believe the cures and was rather contemptuous of the inscriptions, but when he went to sleep he saw a vision. He thought that as he was playing dice below the sanctuary and was about to throw the dice the god appeared, sprang on his hand, and stretched out his fingers ... When day came he went away cured.
>
> Ambrosia from Athens, blind in one eye. She came as a suppliant to the god, and as she walked about the sanctuary she ridiculed some of the cures as being incredible ... But when she went to sleep she saw a vision. She thought the god was standing next to her and saying that he would restore her to health, but she must dedicate in the sanctuary as a reward a silver pig, as a memorial of her stupidity. Having said this he split open the diseased eye and poured in a medicine. When day came she went away cured.
>
> (Austin 126, *Syll.*[3] 1168)[28]

Recorded miracle cures of this kind, also found at Kos and at Lebena on Crete, possibly reveal the concerns and fears of ordinary people;[29] but we should be cautious.[30] There may be some truth in the alleged cures – among doctors today there is less scepticism than before about the effects of psycho-logical states upon the body – yet the documents are unlikely to be literal records of what ordinary folk wanted to say. Rather than being genuine, vernacular evidence of folk-belief and the life of 'ordinary' people, the stories were surely 'written up' by the priests in accordance with the rules of a genre of expression that required the achievements of the god to be proclaimed (just as Diodoros, 1. 25, is keen to insist that the god performs real cures). The emphasis on refuting the incredulous worshipper is patently designed to boost the reputation and wealth of the sanctuary.

More indicative of current folk belief, one might think, are the curses inscribed on lead tablets and dedicated at sanctuaries, many more of which are found than from earlier periods.[31] This may, however, simply reflect the nature of the archaeological record, and it would be rash to jump to conclu-sions about widespread literacy or about the antithetical relationship between personal religious expressions and 'official' cult; the curses are, after all, found at public sanctuaries. They may have been written mainly by the more privileged strata of society. It is false to assume that magic is the province of the unsophisticated, as the *Pharmakeutria* of Theokritos and the poems of Nicander show (Chapter 7).

Alongside the possibly increased popularity of pre-existing cults, there are signs of the vitality of religious sentiment in the worship of gods who were new to the Greek homeland or were taken up widely by Greeks in the new territories. Often they have been treated as a class of 'oriental' cults, but this is at once too broad a category and too limiting, for it is wrong to lump together the whole of Alexander's Asiatic and African conquests as if they formed a single cultural domain; there were many cultures and religions. A more rigorous yet still serviceable definition would be: cults with non-Greek names derived from cities and cult centres in Egypt or the Near East and newly introduced into Old Greece.[32]

Many such cults had already been introduced into Greece before Alexander's day: Plato's *Republic* (written in the mid-fourth century) opens with Sokrates going down to the Piraeus to see a new goddess, Bendis, ceremonially brought in (1. 327 a 1–3). A temple of Isis was founded in Piraeus by 333 at the request of Egyptians residing there (*Syll.*³ 380).[33] The Ptolemies organ-ized cult celebrations to Adonis in the palace at Alexandria (Theokritos, *Idyll* 15); Apollonios, financial minister of Ptolemy II, built a temple to the god Poremanres (a deified pharaoh) on his estate (*P. Mich. Zen.* 84).

One of the most important 'new' cults is that of Serapis (or Sarapis), whose name combines those of two Egyptian deities, Osiris and the Apis bull. The cult was not, as the Roman historian Tacitus (*Hist.* 4. 83–4, Austin 261) and the Greek biographer Plutarch (*On Isis and Osiris*, 28) were later to claim, invented by Ptolemy I or Ptolemy II in order to provide a point of union for their Greek and native subjects:[34] Serapis had received cult at Saqqâra by Alexander's time, and Macedonian involvement goes back to

Alexander's reign, for his officer Peukestas accorded protection to the sanc-tuary (Fig. 5.1)[35] and Graeco-Macedonian patronage is proved by finds of early Ptolemaic statues at the sanctuary. An anthropomorphic Serapis may, however, be a Greek innovation.

An example of the spread of the cult of Serapis within Egypt is the peti-tion from a citizen of Aspendos to the administrator Apollonios in 257 BC; the petitioner, who has undergone a miraculous cure, urges him to fund the building of a sanctuary of the god (Austin 239, *PCZ* 59034). Later Ptolemy III and Berenike, then Ptolemy V, are thanked by the Egyptian priests for protecting Apis and other divine animals in the land (see, first, the Canopus decree, Austin 222, BD 136, *OGIS* 56; second, the Rosetta Stone, Austin 227, BD 137, Burstein 103, *OGIS* 90). Royal patronage is only to be expected; the Seleukids, too, gave benefactions to native cults, particularly in Mesopotamia. What is unexpected, and may have helped foster the idea that the cult was invented only now, is its rapid spread. It is not surprising to find sanctuaries at places within the Ptolemaic sphere, such as Samos and other military bases where Egyptians served, but the cult quickly spread beyond the Ptolemaic domain. It is attested as far afield as Hyrkania, east of the Caspian Sea, in the reign of Antiochos I (281–261), in the following document from Gorgan in Iran. It records the manumission of a slave in the form of a letter apparently addressed to the governor of the satrapy:

> Euandros (sends) greetings to Andragoras (and) Apollodotos.
> We have set free Hermaios on behalf of king Antiochos and queen Stratonike and their offspring, (so that he may be) sacred to Sarapis; and we have set up in the sanctuary his release and that of his family.
> [...th (*day*)] of Gorpiaios. Farewell.
>
> (*SEG* xx. 325)[36]

One reason for the rapid diffusion of the Serapis cult may be simply that Egyptians were travelling far afield as mercenaries and traders; but the cult was patronized by Greeks, as is shown by Greek-style buildings and its installation within existing sacred spaces.[37] In many respects Serapis resembled Asklepios and other 'new' cult figures. He spoke to his worshippers in dreams and performed healing miracles; Strabo says the great Serapeion (or Serapieion; Serapeum in Latin) at Kanobos (Canopus) near Alexandria was patronized 'even by the most reputable men', who slept there or arranged for others to do so on their behalf (17. 1. 17 (801)). Like the Eleusinian mysteries, the cult involved initiation rites, which can be reconstructed from the Latin novel *Metamorphoses* (*The Golden Ass*) written by a north African author, Apuleius of Madaurus, in the second century AD. Like the mysteries, too, its appeal was universal – and not only among Greek-speakers, as was the case with Eleusis.

Another Egyptian cult taken up in the Greek world was that of Isis, sister

Figure 5.1 Military notice on papyrus, issued by the Macedonian general Peukestas. The texts reads Πευκέστου μὴ παραπορεύεσθαι μηδένα· ἱερείος τὸ οἴκημα ('From Peukestas. No one is to pass this point. The residence belongs to a priest'). Length of papyrus 0.358 m. (Reproduced from *JEA* 60 (1974), pl. 55 opp. p. 240, by permission of the Egypt Exploration Society.)

of Osiris, together with her son by him, Hôros (also called Harpokrates in Greek). The cult was known to Herodotos, who mentions foreigners (specifically Karians) taking part in her festival (2. 61). As with Serapis, detailed knowledge of the cult can only be inferred from later sources, Plutarch's *On Isis and Osiris* and Apuleius's novel; but it seems likely that it was in the hellenistic period, perhaps under Greek influence, that the Isis cult was endowed with Greek-style initiation rites and the goddess closely linked to the discovery of the techniques of civilization and the protection of marriage, social order, and of individuals in times of danger.[38] The main popularity of Isis, however, was under the Roman empire, when Diodoros wrote that the cult was known throughout almost the whole inhabited world (1. 25). This should be seen as another example of the Greek willingness to adopt foreign cults, rather than a sign of a fundamental change in Greek religion.

Other female deities 'imported' to the Greek world included the Syrian Goddess, Atargatis (related to Babylonian and Assyrian Ishtar and Phoenician Astarte).[39] By the early third century her worship had spread from Hierapolis in northern Syria to Egypt and Greece, later reaching Italy and the west. Her temple at Hierapolis was rebuilt by queen Stratonike around 300 and plundered by Antiochos IV (175–164); we happen to know of hellenistic sanctuaries in remote towns in Aitolia and Messenia, and on Delos. She was primarily a fertility goddess, though (like Ishtar) also equated with Aphrodite. (The principal sources are the second-century AD Lucian of Samosata's *On the Syrian Goddess*, and the *Metamorphoses* by Apuleius, 8. 24–30, where Lucius encounters her priests.)

Kybele (latinized as Cybele), called *Mêtêr Theôn* (Mother of the Gods) or *Mêtêr Megalê* (Great Mother), came from Pessinos in Phrygia to Greece soon after 400 and then to Egypt and Italy, where in 204 the Roman senate on the advice of the Sibylline oracles allowed her in; she became the 'Magna Mater' of the Roman empire. She, too, was a healing and protecting goddess, a guardian of fertility and wild nature. Her flagellant, self-mutilating followers are described by Lucian and Apuleius, and the Roman poet Catullus devotes one poem (63) to the legend of her consort Attis.

The busy port and cult site of Delos attracted merchants from all over the Mediterranean world; such was the commercial importance of the island that in the third quarter of the century its market was apparently capable of handling 10,000 slaves a day (Strabo, 14. 5. 2 (668–9), Austin 171). Here we can see in microcosm the processes of introduction and combination which characterize the rapid interchange of religious practices in the hellenistic world. Alongside a great variety of Greek cults we find epigraphic and archaeological evidence of a sanctuary area containing three shrines of Serapis, the earliest from *c*.275–250 and the principal one (known as Serapieion C) dating from the second century, having a colonnaded courtyard over 70 metres long, as well as the cults of three other Egyptian deities.[40] An inscription of c.215 BC records the introduction of the cult of Serapis (Austin 131, Burstein 102, *Syll.*³ 663).[41] There is ample evidence of a complex cult organization, and all four gods can appear together, as in this inscription from 109/8, when the island was ruled from Athens:

> Dionysios son of Zenon, of Kephisia [*the Attic deme*], having become deputy priest of Sarapis, dedicated the altars and the stairway to Sarapis, Isis, Anubis, and Harpokrates. In the priesthood of Apollophanes son of Dionysios, of Kephisia, and in the stewardship of the island of [—]imachos of Paiania, and of the officers of the sacred things Theon of Pa(i)onidai and Argeios of Trikorynthos.
>
> (*SEG* xvi. 452)[42]

Nearby was a sanctuary devoted to the Syrian gods, including Hadran, Hadad, and chiefly Atargatis, sometimes addressed as 'Holy Goddess' (*Hagnê Thea*) or identified with the Greek Aphrodite;[43] like Serapieion C, it is built in a wholly Greek style, with a theatre, stoas, monumental gateway, and so on. Again there was a permanent cult organization, with a priest sometimes appointed from Hierapolis and at other times from Athens. There was an association (*thiasos*) of worshippers which seems at first to have comprised only Syrian Greeks, probably merchants living in Delos, and later expanded to include others:

> The priest Nikon son of Apollonios, and the priestess, his wife, Onesako daughter of Xenon, made ready the existing house from which part was taken away for the temple of Sarapis, on behalf of themselves and their children, as a thank-offering for Hagne Thea. The following persons also contributed to the furnishing of the house: the *koinon* of the *thiasitai* of the Syrians who celebrate on the 20th day, whom the goddess brought together. [...] 50 Delian drachmas [...]
>
> (*BCH* 92 (1968), 359–74)[44]

Other near eastern deities to whom cult was paid at Delos include 'the Gods of Askalon', including Astarte Palaistine Ourania Aphrodite (*I. Délos* 1719), 'the gods of Iamneia' (Jabne in Palestine, *I. Délos* 2308–9), Kybele (many inscriptions) and probably Attis (*I. Délos* 2318), syncretistic versions of Greek gods such as Zeus Dusares (the latter is a Nabataean deity; *I. Délos* 2315), and other Arab gods such as Pakeidas and Oddos (*I. Délos* 2311, 2320). In one inscription (*I. Délos* 2321) an Arab ('Chauan son of Theophilos, *Araps*') dedicates to Helios, the Greek sun-god. Many of these testimonia come from two sanctuaries (known as B and C) on the north slope of Mt. Kynthos, which seem to have been designated as locations for non-Greek gods. A number of other small sanctuaries were identified by the excavators as 'oriental' on the basis of their ground-plans. Finally, a probable synagogue has been excavated, and literary and epigraphic testimonia confirm the presence of a Jewish community who called their god Theos Hypsistos (God the Highest).[45]

A notable feature of the profusion of cult activity at Delos is that it is not limited to ethnic Greeks, nor is there an absolute divide between the gods whom Greeks and non-Greeks worship. Syncretism, the conflation or identification of two deities from different pantheons into a joint or single cult, is important evidence – not necessarily of religious tolerance, but of the desire of particular groups and individuals to negotiate their relationships through the (often spontaneous) redefining of religious practice.

Isis, Kybele, and the Syrian Goddess suggest a pattern, but it would be wrong to draw sweeping conclusions, for example about changing views of womanhood; universal goddesses such as Demeter were widely worshipped earlier. Rather, these cults should be seen against the background of other universal and healing cults that were apparently growing in popularity, such as Asklepios and Dionysos, with which they had common features.[46] Dionysos, now as earlier, was a god of wildness and of the (temporary) subversion of civic norms; also, like Bakchos, of wine. He had no fixed body of ritual practice; his followers (male and female) apparently took to the hills, tearing apart sacrificial animals and eating them raw. The fifth-century tragedy *Bakchai* (*Bacchae*) by Euripides is a prime source, but it would be wrong to exaggerate the degree of popular or mass participation. It may be that his worship released social tensions, but presumably direct participation was restricted to a minority. A similar case may be that of the deities called the Kabeiroi (Cabiri), whose sanctuaries at Samothrace, Lemnos, and elsewhere received rich dedications from Macedonian kings, Ptolemies, and others. This cult, probably of Phrygian or Semitic origin, seems to have similarities with the Dionysos cult and the Eleusinian mysteries.[47]

The 'rise' of the 'new' cults therefore does not entail a 'decline' in traditional *polis* religion; on the contrary, the point is precisely that they were newly enrolled in the existing pantheon of the *polis*. Nevertheless it would be unjustified to see in this the emergence of a universalized and internationalized religious system;[48] there is too much continuity with the past. If anything is new, it may be the increased level of religious activity and celebration – assuming our records give a fair picture and we are not simply seeing more evidence than before. Surely the new cults were not, as is often asserted, the product of collective existential terror, but are an enrichment of religious experience. It may be that there was a demand for personal contact with deities;[49] but it would be rash to assume that this demand had been less strong in earlier Greek cult. The same people may have worshipped, or sought the aid of, many deities at once – old, new, Greek, non-Greek – whose powers often duplicated one another, something which was clearly not seen as a problem.

The new cults show that the demand for collective religious expression within the *polis* was very much alive; Préaux writes of 'a world continually celebrating festivals'.[50] Many victor-lists from such festivals are preserved on stone, as are innumerable statue-bases (the chariot of a Sidonian prince, for example, won the prize at the Nemean games: Austin 121,[51] *c*.200 BC); there were contests in acting (Austin 122, *Syll.*[3] 1080, from third-century Tegea)[52] and in the traditional athletic, musical, and other contests. The *polis* was still the *polis*, and though it evolved (Chapter 3), the signs of religious change may be less significant than the plentiful evidence of continuity.

The attachment to old city cults and temples showed no signs of abating. Consider the benefactions by many kings to old sanctuaries, such as the attempt by Antiochos IV (175–164) to complete the temple of Olympian Zeus at Athens (p. 87). Even under the Roman empire vast sums of money were spent on new monuments in old sanctuaries. The Roman consul Appius Claudius Pulcher initiated the building of a new monumental gateway at Eleusis in 54 BC;[53] two centuries later, the emperor Marcus Aurelius followed suit. The emperor Hadrian's huge investments in the monuments of Athens, and those of his Athenian contemporary Herodes Atticus in Athens and all over the Peloponnese, are well known.

Rural cults with a wide international reputation retained a strong hold on élite loyalty throughout the hellenistic and Roman periods, as instanced by the spectacular series of statue-bases at the oracular shrine of Amphiaraos near Oropos in north-eastern Attica (Fig. 5.2). Important persons who made dedications to the sanctuary include Lysimachos, who donated a statue of his sister-in-law: 'King Lysimachos (honours) Adeia, wife of his brother Autodikos, for her virtue and goodwill towards him. To Amphiaraos' (Petracos, *Amphiareion*, 45, no. 20). Also honoured were Ptolemy IV (221–205) with his queen Arsinoë, and other third-century worthies. Some of the statue-bases were recycled in the first century BC to carry honorific inscriptions for important Romans; not uncommonly the man is described as *patrôn* of the *dêmos*, a hellenization of the Latin *patronus* and an indication that the *dêmos* had received (and presumably expected to go on receiving) assistance or benefactions. The Romans so honoured run from the first half to the last quarter of the first century and include P. Servilius Isauricus (cos. 79), described as *euergetês*, and the Brutus who assassinated Julius Caesar, called *sôtêr* and *euergêtes*. Most notable are Appius Claudius Pulcher, the benefactor of Eleusis (above), and, from 27 BC or shortly after, Agrippa, the emperor Augustus's lieutenant: 'The *dêmos* (honours) Markos Agrippas, son of Leukios [*i.e. Marcus Agrippa son of Lucius*], thrice consul, its own benefactor' (Petracos, *Amphiareion*, no. 19).[54] The priests of Amphiaraos may have gone out looking for favours, but kings and leading Romans thought it was important to be connected with the shrine.[55]

Agrippa was also honoured with an equestrian statue placed atop an older monumental base which still stands beside the entrance to the Athenian

Figure 5.2   Statue-base of Lysimachos from the Amphiareion, near Oropos in Attica. (Photograph by the author.)

Acropolis (Fig. 5.3). The base originally carried a statue, possibly commemorating the victory of the chariot team of Eumenes II of Pergamon in the Panathenaic games of 178. More recently, it had been used for statues of Mark Antony depicted as 'New Dionysos', and of Kleopatra as Isis; their statues are said to have blown down in a storm in 31 BC (Plut. *Ant.* 60. 6; Cassius Dio, 50. 15. 2)[56] – just before the battle of Actium, which may mean the event is a fiction. The reuse of the monument for Agrippa is attested by an inscription with exactly the same wording as the one quoted above from the Amphiareion (*IG* ii² 4122).[57] Agrippa himself later gifted a concert hall (*ôdeion*) to the city of Athens, which was built in the middle of the Agora in about 15 BC and was known as the Agrippeion (Philostratos, *Lives of the Sophists*, 2. 5. 4).[58]

   All these dedications and rededications show that *polis* sanctuaries was no less significant than before. As for rural cult, it has been suggested that religion declined in the countryside of Attica, on the basis of the virtual cessation of deme decrees;[59] but the evidence is also consistent with a partial relocation of cult rather than any diminution of popular attachment, since there is a rise in cultic inscriptions at outlying garrisons such as Rhamnous

Figure 5.3 The monument of Agrippa below the entrance to the Athenian Acropolis (reused base of the chariot monument of Eumenes II). (Photograph by the author.)

and Sounion. Once again, cults of Olympians and heroes with a wide reputation, such as Amphiaraos, suffered no loss of clientèle.

Tyche

Historians lay particular stress on the religious phenomenon of Tyche, or Fortune. The Greek word τύχη (*tychê*), like 'fortune', had shades of meaning ranging from blind chance or accident to an active providence at work in the cosmos. In the latter guise *tyche* might work against you, and it was best to try to get it on your side, such as by naming your son Eutyches (Goodluck) or by invoking *agathê* ('good') *tychê*, as the fourth-century Athenian *dêmos* and others did at the start of their decrees. Playwrights and poets sometimes elevated *tyche* into a goddess: Pindar calls her the daughter of Zeus (*Olympian Ode* 12), and the fourth-century tragedian Chairemon makes her 'tyrant over the gods' (Stobaeus, *Florilegium*, 1. 6. 16).[60] Menander is quoted as referring to *tyche*'s 'divine breath or understanding that guides and preserves all things' (Stob. 1. 6. 1); but the abstract concept and the personified 'goddess' were not necessarily strictly demarcated (ancient Greek did not have separate lower-case letters and capitals, so there was no difference between the two words).

As a goddess to whom cult was actually paid, Tyche is found only occasionally. She had a sanctuary at Thebes, seen by Pausanias in the second century AD, with a statue of her carrying the infant Ploutos ('Wealth'; Paus. 9. 16. 1); the same author reports many similar cult sites in mainland Greece. In fourth-century Athens, Agathe Tyche received sacrifices alongside Eirene (Peace), and later there is evidence of cults at Antioch, Alexandria, and smaller towns.

Tyche was a subject of intellectual enquiry. Philosophers and historians tried to define it rigorously. Aristotle drew a distinction between *tyche* and simple accident, while the philosopher-dictator Demetrios of Phaleron wrote a treatise on *tyche* from which Polybios quotes. Referring to the fall of Persian power and the rise of Macedonia, Demetrios says that:

> Fortune – who makes no compact with our lives, causes events to happen in defiance of our expectations, and displays her power by surprises – is now, I think, demonstrating to all mankind that by establishing the Macedonians as colonists amid the prosperity of Persia, she has merely lent these advantages to them until she decides to do something else with them.
>
> (Polyb. 29. 21, *FGH* 228 fr. 39, Austin 20)

The idea of Fortune as a historical force was developed by Polybios, who says the Romans could not have conquered Greece without her aid. He may have been influenced by the Roman Fortuna, who was already worshipped as a goddess but was beneficent rather than capricious. He invokes *tyche* to 'explain' the incalculable element in warfare, observing that if Kleomenes III of Sparta had waited a few more days before offering battle, or before running away to Egypt, the Macedonians would have had to call off their invasion of Lakonike because of the news of an Illyrian attack on Macedonia. 'So it is', he says, 'that fortune always decides the greatest issues in human affairs in an arbitrary fashion' (2. 70). Polybios never resolves the contradictions in his use of the concept of Tyche, which is sometimes a guiding force in human affairs but sometimes simply the unforeseen element which we can only try to allow for as best we can. Walbank is surely right to conclude that 'how far men really personalized such an abstraction and whether they had any consistent view about it is a problem almost impossible to answer'.[61]

There seems to be little or no evidence for widespread participation in cult ritual for the goddess Tyche, as seems to be the case for the new universal goddesses. She had an official city cult in many places, but the personified goddess always seems to shade off into the city's own *tyche* or good fortune. The process of defining the historical and philosophical concept of *tyche* was probably quite independent of these cults. It is wrong to elevate Tyche, as many historians do, into a paradigm of hellenistic religion, a symbol of instability and socio-cultural breakdown; or to see the 'universal goddess' cults as sharing a 'common antithesis to the rule of Tyche/Fortuna'.[62] Tyche was not as important as that.

Religious decline?

In this period, it is often claimed, Olympian religion was under attack from scepticism, or eroded by the rise of other religions, or (somewhat contradict-orily) both at once. We have found reasons to doubt this; Apollo at Delphi was still able to repulse the marauding Gauls by exercising his power, as had been reported to the people of Kos when in 278 they voted gifts to the sanc-tuary and prayers and sacrifices in Kos itself (pp. 52–3).

Few major new temples to Olympian gods were now being built; but any religion has periods of active building and periods of quieter activity; most English cathedrals pre-date the Reformation, but afterwards the predomin-ant religious culture was still Christian. The dynasties made use of the Olympians as patrons or ancestors: Apollo for the Seleukids, Athena and Dionysos for the Attalids, Zeus and Herakles for the Ptolemies.

Perhaps it might be argued that these cults now had meaning only for kings and the increasingly narrow political élite? Even that would be a less radical change than we might think; most of the '*polis* cults' mentioned above were surely there because the aristocracy patronized them first, though participation in festivals was open to all. The very codification and systematization of the Olympians in the archaic period – such as their identification with local deities, such as Athena with Alea – implies a conscious effort by aristocrats in different cities to harmonize their ceremonial relationships, which were acted out not only in *polis* festivals but also at international gatherings like the Olympic games. In addition, the whole substratum of non-Olympian, non-hero religion, from local nymphs to gods of the street, presumably continued much as before and can truly be said to be the people's religion.

The prestige of Olympian cults, both urban and panhellenic, seems undi-minished. Manumissions of slaves were recorded on stone at second-century Delphi (Austin 127).[63] Cities continued to regulate their Olympian cults in detail (e.g. Austin 129, *Syll.*³ 1003, from second-century Priene) and inscribed calendars of traditional rituals (e.g. Austin 128, *Syll.*³ 1024, from Mykonos, *c.*200 BC). A traditional Attic cult association of *orgeônes* (sacrificing associates) recorded its administrative business in the usual way in 307/6 (Austin 130, *Syll.*³ 1097).[64] The evidence of new, 'official' patronage is no reason for supposing that the Olympian cults, and those of heroes, were not celebrated as enthusiastically as before.

There is clearly some change. The rise of 'universalist' cults has been pointed out.[65] The appeal of Dionysos and Asklepios, as of the Egyptian gods, was apparently not limited to people of one *polis* or ethnic group; Serapis and Isis found homes in many Greek sanctuaries. Some of these deities had been present before, but their cults now flourished. This, however, entails no diminution of allegiance to existing cults, only a broadening of options and religious modes of expression. One might even see it as a liberation of popular belief, which may have been constrained within the earlier Olympian–hero framework at a time when citizens – a narrow group, even among adult males – had more power.

The élite still played the leading role in formulating and coordinating public religion. Scepticism, often invoked by historians to explain religious change in any period of Greek history, probably flourished only among the literate class who have left us their words; but even there the increased numbers of cultic inscriptions and the construction of new sanctuaries and temples (albeit mainly for non-Olympian gods) suggest, if anything, an increase in élite activity. Religious practice certainly does not diminish. For popular belief the evidence is slim – limited almost entirely to curse-tablets and similar items – but again suggests no reduction in practical piety. New cults, as suggested above, may have attracted a genuinely popular following.

Historians may be prone to see Greek religion after Alexander in pessimistic terms because of their over-reverent attitude to the classical *polis* and their consequent feeling that the rise of Macedonian power was bad for Greece. If we insist on seeing religious change as a reaction to the supposed catastrophe of the *polis* or the existential uncertainties of the age, we may be deceiving ourselves about the age that preceded it, which was far from stable and harmonious. To emphasize the alleged decline in religion – a trend which some scholar or other has detected in almost any period of Greek and Roman history – may simply be to retroject a twentieth-century anxiety. If, additionally, we formulate our view in terms of increasing scepticism and/or rationality (which are not necessarily the same thing), we may be unconsciously privileging the views and actions of a minority élite group.[66]

Rival philosophies and common ground

Athens had been the centre of Greek philosophy for a century before Alexander's death, and remained so even when Ptolemaic patronage made Alexandria the main centre for literature and science (Chapters 7, 9). There were occasional disruptions. After the Antigonids liberated Athens in 307 and deposed the philosopher-tyrant Demetrios of Phaleron, popular opinion seems to have turned against philosophers, an attempt being made to bring them under state control. Only their departure *en masse*, led by Theophrastos, forced a rethink.[67] Athens was also not the only centre for philosophy; in the later second and first centuries there was a notable tradition at Rhodes, whose most famous son was the Stoic Panaitios (*c*.185–109). (For leading philosophers and their affiliations, see Fig. 5.4.)

The two main philosophical institutions, or groupings, before Alexander, Plato's Academy and the Lyceum (or Peripatos) of Aristotle, produced less innovative work in the hellenistic period and were overshadowed by the new fashions of Stoicism and Epicureanism. These are two of the so-called 'schools' into which philosophers of the period are usually classified, by modern writers as they were by ancient. Others include the Cynics, Sceptics, and Utopians. They vary, however, in the extent to which they were strictly defined associations with structures and formal membership. Many of the members of a particular school will have been taught by one philosopher and remained in his circle, one of them succeeding to the headship of the group; but in some cases the accepted labels may obscure not only the differences between members of the same school but also the overlaps between the teachings of different schools.

Our detailed knowledge of the work of philosophers after Aristotle and Theophrastos, and of their writings, is patchy. Some continuous passages of Epicurus are preserved on carbonized papyri from Herculaneum in Italy, buried in AD 79 by the eruption of Vesuvius; the books almost certainly come from the library of Philodemos, an Epicurean teacher who spent time at Herculaneum. Some letters and aphorisms (short, pithy sayings) of Epicurus survive. Of other philosophers we have only brief quotations, or lists of the titles of their books;[68] otherwise most of what we know comes from Diogenes Laërtios (p. 19). Fortunately, and perhaps significantly, he devotes more space to the founders of Stoicism and Epicureanism than to any philosopher except Plato.

The Academy, the Lyceum (Peripatos), and Scepticism

In the early fourth century Plato founded the Academy in Athens. Its name, Akademeia (or Hekademeia), had no connotations of ivory-tower scholasticism, as our word 'academic' does, but referred to a shrine of the Attic hero Akademos (or Hekademos) outside the city walls, where Plato's circle used to meet. In his early dialogues he elaborates the ideas of his mentor Sokrates, who left no writings and who was executed for impiety by the Athenians in 399. Plato argued for the existence of eternal truths and values, and imagined an ideal society ruled by philosopher kings. His 'idealism' was tempered by his successors, and under Polemon (head of the Academy from 314) the emphasis was on ethics – practical questions of right conduct. Plato had not neglected this area, but his philosophy proved hard to put into practice, and the main emphasis came to be on interpreting his work in the light of ethical philosophy. Platonism had a long after-life, culminating in the Neoplatonist work of Plotinus, a Greek of the third century AD.[69]

Aristotle (384–322 BC), from the Greek town of Stageira in Macedonia, studied at the Academy but broke away. He returned to Athens in the 330s and taught at the Lyceum (Lykeion, the area around the sanctuary of Apollo

The Academy

c.369 I **Plato** (Platon of Athens) (427–347) (Diog. Laërt. 3)
347 II Speusippos of Athens (c.407–339)
339 III Xenokrates of Chalkedon (c.396–314) – had left with Aristotle in 347
314 IV Polemon of Athens (Diog. Laërt. 4. 16–20)
270 V Krates of Athens (Diog. Laërt. 4. 21–3)
    VI Arkesilaos of Pitane (d. 242/1) (Diog. Laërt. 4. 28–45)
       Karneades of Cyrene (c. 129/8) (Diog. Laërt. 4. 62–6)
       Plotinus ('Neoplatonist', c. AD 205–270) – essays edited by Porphyry c. AD 301–5

The Peripatos or Lyceum

    I **Aristotle** of Stageira (384–322) (Diog. Laërt. 5. 1–35)
      Aristoxenos of Taras (c.370–after 322) – studied harmony, rhythm
322 II **Theophrastos** – formally established school (372/0–288/6) (Diog. Laërt. 5. 36–57)
288/6 III Straton of Lampsakos (c.328–270/67) (Diog. Laërt. 5. 58–64)

The Garden of Epicurus

307/6 I **Epicurus** (Epikouros of Athens, born on Samos) (341–271) (Diog. Laërt. bk 10)
      Philodemos of Gadara (c.110–40/35) – fragments and some epigrams survive
      Diogenes of Oinoanda (b. c. AD 150/60) – author of a long inscription summarizing Epicurean ideas

The Stoa

c. 301 I Zeno (Zenon) of Kition (c.333–c.261) (Diog. Laërt. 7. 1–160)
c. 261 II Kleanthes of Assos (c.332–232) (Diog. Laërt. 7. 168–76)
232 III Chrysippos of Soloi (c.280–c.206) (Diog. Laërt. 7. 179–202)
      Sphairos of Borysthenes (fl. 220s) (Diog. Laërt. 7. 177–8)
c. 206 IV Zeno of Tarsos
    V Diogenes of Babylon (c.240–c.152)
      Blossius of Cumae (fl. 130s)
c.152 VI Antipater of Tarsos (d. 129)
129 VII Panaitios of Rhodes (c.185–109)
      Poseidonios of Apameia (c.135–c.55)
      Epiktetos (c. AD 50–120) – works published by Arrian
      Marcus Aurelius (AD 121–80; emperor 161–80)

Sceptics

(n.b. Academy also adopts Scepticism under Arkesilaos)
      Pyrrhon of Elis (b. c.365) (Diog. Laërt. 9. 61–108)
      Timon of Phleious (c.320–230) (Diog. Laërt. 9. 109–16)
      Sextus Empiricus (late 2nd cent. AD)

Cynics
(not a formal school)

> Diogenes of Sinope (contemporary of Aristotle) (Diog. Laërt. 6. 20–81)
>
> Krates of Thebes (*c*.365–285) – influences Zeno (Diog. Laërt. 6. 85–93)
>
> Bion of Borysthenes (*c*.335–*c*.246) (Diog. Laërt. 4. 46–58)
>
> **Kerkidas** of Megalopolis, poet (3rd cent.)
>
> Teles (prob. late 3rd cent.)
>
> Menippos of Gadara (3rd cent.) (Diog. Laërt. 6. 99–101)

Figure 5.4 Leading members of philosophical 'schools'

Lykeios) or Peripatos (The Walk, after a gathering-place in the same area); the latter gave its name to the Peripatetic school of philosophy.[70] His concerns, like those of Plato's other successors, were more pragmatic than Plato's, as his works on ethics (such as the *Eudemian* and *Nicomachean Ethics*) demonstrate. Rather than attempting to formulate universal truths and derive rules of conduct from them, he took as his starting-point what people actually do, and why. His attitude is reflected in his numerous works on natural science; he was, for example, a pioneer of biological classification, an area in which his work was to prove immensely influential – perhaps excessively so – down to the Middle Ages and beyond.

Under Aristotle's successor Theophrastos (*c*.371–*c*.287), a citizen of Eresos in Lesbos, the Lyceum became a regular philosophical institute. Besides natural philosophy, Theophrastos wrote on rhetoric and literary style, poetry, comedy, and (in the *Characters*) human nature; he was also known, perhaps chiefly to his contemporaries, as a historian of philosophy.[71] (Theophrastos is discussed further at pp. 328, 341–4.) One of his associates was the Athenian dictator Demetrios of Phaleron (Diog. Laërt. 5. 75–85), who had a hand in helping Ptolemy I set up his library and Mouseion (Chapter 7) and is noted for having made the first collection of Aesop's *Fables*.[72] The successor of Theophrastos as head of the Lyceum, Straton, was a prolific researcher into natural phenomena, but none of his work survives. Information about the work of the Lyceum under Straton and his successors is scarce; in the first century BC, however, we hear of the rediscovery of Aristotle's manuscripts (p. 240), which prompted a renewed interest in his work.

Scepticism began to be developed by Pyrrhon of Elis (b. *c*.365) and Timon of Phleious (*c*.320–230); they looked back to the sixth-century philosopher-poet Xenophanes of Kolophon, who professed to undermine the conventional authority of Homer and Hesiod. Under Arkesilaos of Pitane (d. 241) the Academy moved towards this position; as a philosophy of knowledge, Scepticism asserted that certainty was impossible and that judgement should be suspended. A third-century AD Christian writer, however, tells us that:

> according to Timon, Pyrrhon declared that things are equally indistinguishable, unmeasurable, and indeterminable. For this reason neither our acts of perception nor our judgements are true or false. Therefore we should not rely upon them but be without judgements, inclining neither this way nor that, but be steadfast, saying, concerning each individual thing, that it no more is than is not, or that it both is and is not, or that it neither is nor is not. For those who adopt this attitude the consequence will be, first, a refusal to make assertions and, second, freedom from disturbance.
>
> (Eusebios, *Praeparatio evangelica*, 14. 18. 758 c–d)

If Eusebios accurately preserves the views of Pyrrhon, it appears he was not a nihilist denying the reality of the world we perceive, but sought the same thing as the Epicureans: happiness through the absence of disturbance (p. 182). The reader is not enjoined to disbelieve the evidence of the senses, but rather to avoid being misled into thinking that it is evidence of ultimate reality, a thing which is unknowable. This amounts to an attack upon attempts by philosophers such as Plato and Aristotle to understand the ultimate nature of the cosmos. As Diogenes Laërtios expresses it:

> We admit the fact that we see, we recognize the fact that we think a thing, but how we see or how we think we do not know. We say descriptively that this appears white, not being wholly certain that it actually is so.
>
> (Diog. Laërt. 9. 103)

A philosopher today might comment that it is hard to know what being white *could* consist in, other than being perceived to be white; but establishing whether the Sceptical approach is logically tenable is less important for present purposes than locating it within the culture of its age. Scepticism was a philosophical position, but it entailed certain attitudes on the part of the citizen if it was to be regarded as a justification for disengagement from public life.

Arkesilaos wrote nothing, perhaps to avoid the charge of appearing to have come to definite conclusions about the world. The second-century Academic Karneades followed his example, but many of his ideas are preserved by the Roman politician and orator Cicero (in his treatises *On the Nature of the Gods* and *On Divination*), to whom they were transmitted by his acquaintance Antiochos of Askalon, a member of the Academy; they are also discussed by Sextus Empiricus (*Against the Professors*), a Sceptic doctor-philosopher of about the late second century AD. As with many hellenistic philosophers, we rely on much later sources for detailed knowledge of the Sceptics' views. Karneades modified earlier Scepticism and argued against both Stoicism and Epicureanism by introducing a concept of probability: he observed that while sense-impressions cannot guarantee their own validity, we do in practice apply certain criteria to actual observations by which we assess how reliable they are.

> For example, as there exist in the place of judgement [*i.e. a lawcourt*] the thing that judges and the thing being judged and the medium through which the judgement is made, and separation and distance, and place, time, mood, disposition, and activity, so we judge the nature of each of these: the thing judging, lest its vision be impaired (for vision of that kind is incompetent to make judgement); the thing being judged, lest it be in too small a state; the medium through which the judgement is made, lest the air be in a dark condition; the separation, lest it be too large; the distance, lest it be compressed [*i.e. too small*]; the place, lest it be beyond measure; the time, lest it be (too) swift; the disposition, lest it be considered maniacal; and the activity, lest it be unacceptable.
>
> (Sextus, *Adv. math.* 7. 183 = *Against the Logicians*, 1. 183 (Loeb))

Karneades is well aware of the practical implications of his arguments; as Long observes, 'There is no reason to think that Karneades' scepticism was intended as a recommendation to behave with exaggerated caution in everyday judgements';[73] like other hellenistic philosophers, he aimed to provide educated people with the conceptual framework for achieving happiness.

The emphasis on formulating philosophies capable of practical application, rather than on developing confident world-models, may reflect political circumstances. Not that people were necessarily afraid in uncertain times, as some historians have alleged; rather, perhaps, élite citizens – those engaged in public life – had to find new concepts with which to define the political activity they felt entitled and able to undertake. At times of crisis there were, no doubt, risks in raising one's head too high; equally, in peacetime the power that accrued to a man active in local politics was more circumscribed than before, and the focus of ambition shifted to inter-*polis* diplomacy, negotiations with kings and their friends, and the cultivation of rhetorical prowess for political debate and *polis* ceremonies. Another focus of competition might be the promotion of particular religious cults, which may partly explain the seemingly pluralistic emphasis on newly adopted cults, including those speaking to personal destiny, alongside official Olympian deities.

Whether the reputation of the Academy and Lyceum actually declined, as is often claimed, is hard to know; what is perhaps revealing is that later generations have much more to say about two other 'schools' which developed only after the death of Alexander: Epicureanism and Stoicism, the Garden and the Portico.

Epicureanism

Epicurus (Epikouros in Greek) was the son of one of the Athenian colonists who occupied the island of Samos for forty-three years until 322. Born in 341, he migrated to Athens after the expulsion of the colony, studied philosophy, and set up his own school in about 307/6.

The central tenet of the Epicurean school was that in order to achieve happiness it is necessary to avoid trouble; the highest pleasure is 'the absence of disturbance' (*ataraxia*). Epicurus's elegantly expressed letter to Menoikeus, preserved by Diogenes Laërtios (10. 121–35), gives a good idea of this, but it is easy to see how his ideas could be misrepresented:

> So when we say that pleasure constitutes the goal, we do not refer to the pleasures of dissolute persons or the pleasures that subsist in enjoyment, as some people think who are ignorant, or do not agree with us, or represent us maliciously; but (we mean) neither suffering pain in body nor being disturbed in soul. It is not a succession of drinks and revels, nor the enjoyment of boys and women, nor of fish and the other things which a luxurious table carries, that give birth to the pleasant life, but sober reasoning, which investigates the reasons for every choice and avoidance and drives out those opinions by which the greatest turmoil possesses souls.
>
> (Diog. Laërt. 10. 131–2)

The emphasis on 'pleasure' (*hêdonê*), albeit in a rather rarefied form, gave rise to the taunt of 'hedonism' by Epicurus's opponents; this was unfair, for Epicurus was advocating a quiet, but civic, life. He justified his view by appealing to an atomic theory of the universe, which he claimed was an impersonal, mechanical system; even the gods, though they exist, are remote and uninterested in human affairs. Death is merely an end of sensation, a dissolution of atoms:

> Foolish, therefore, is he who says he fears death not because it will pain him when present, but because it pains him as something in the future. For that which does not annoy when present, pains only groundlessly when anticipated. The most fearful of evils, death, is nothing to us: for of course, whenever we exist, death is not present; but whenever death is present, then we do not exist.
>
> (Diog. Laërt. 10. 125)

Epicurus was no revolutionary – he took part in civic festivals, while arguing that men should avoid politics – but his views on society were unconventional. He urged people to set themselves free from the straitjacket of *paideia* ('education', i.e. Greek culture), and his followers' commitment to certain views involved a corresponding lifestyle, *truly* free. His home, situated between Athens and the Piraeus, was known as the Garden and housed a devoted community of adherents, including women and slaves; it was more a society of friends than a research institution, a commune rather than a college. It seems to have maintained itself for generations after his death, partly by observing communal rituals in memory of him. Like other philosophers, Epicurus seems to have placed great value on setting an example to others by his own behaviour, on living out the values he preached.[74]

It is sometimes asserted that Epicureanism was not an influential value-set; one author goes so far as to say that it 'never became wholly respectable (except for a short time at Rome towards the end of the Republic)', and that 'in both popularity and influence it was outstripped by the teachings of the Stoa', which became 'the most popular philosophy' under the Principate.[75] The idea that Stoicism was 'popular' will be examined in the next subsection; as for the notion of a 'respectable' phase of Epicureanism, it may be supported by pointing to upper-class Romans like Lucretius in the late second century BC, who sought to convert his readers (or to confirm Epicureans in their beliefs) by a reasoned statement of the materialist and moral philosophy in the form of a lengthy poem. It is unlikely, however, that Epicureanism was disreputable at any time except in the eyes of its philosophical opponents; indeed, Antiochos IV made it the official cult of his court.

It cannot be shown that any Epicureans were not respectable, and though the community included women and slaves its leaders, like most philosophers, belonged to the property-holding upper echelons of Greek society.[76] Such a cult of political withdrawal could perhaps only have been espoused by a social class that had the option of being politically active; the poor have no time to cultivate tranquillity.

The Epicurean prescription was not a life of indolence; it presupposed social organization, amenities, and the desire for self-perfection.[77] It gave much less moral and social justification for powerful groups and individuals to exploit one another, whereas Stoicism contained elements that could be used to justify the exercise of power. Both philosophies reflected, in different ways, the changes taking place in politics and society; but the magnitude and profundity of those changes should not be exaggerated.

Cynicism and Stoicism

Before looking at Stoicism, we should be aware that it had its origins in a much less 'respectable' ideology, Cynicism. This was never a formal philosophy, but there are key figures who shared similar views. The first is Diogenes of Sinope (404–323 BC), who was called *kynikos*, 'canine', because he rejected the conventions of society, tried to live without property, and advocated the flouting of common standards of behaviour. Today we might describe such a person as preaching an extreme anti-materialism. Diogenes Laërtios preserves numerous anecdotes, any or all of which may be unhistorical (6. 22–80). They include the famous encounter with Alexander, in which the king stands over him and tells him to ask for any favour he likes; 'Get your shadow off me', replies the Cynic. Many stories portray him as a debunker, relying on pithy wisecracks to puncture pretension.

Diogenes' views were taken up by his pupil Krates of Thebes in poems attacking luxury. Krates in turn taught Zeno, the founder of Stoicism, and though for ideological reasons ancient writers exaggerated the influence of the Cynics upon Zeno's most radical ideas,[78] we may suppose that it was his Cynic phase that gave Zeno the tools with which to criticize the existing social order.

In the third century we find other Cynics, such as the poet Kerkidas of Megalopolis, fragments of whose iambic tirades are preserved on papyrus. Kerkidas sounds like a revolutionary:

> [why did God not] choose that greedy cormorant wealthpurse,
> that sweet-scented out-of-control Xenon, make him a pathetic poor
>   man,
> and transfer to us who deserve it the silver that now
> is uselessly flowing away? What can there be to prevent the god –
> supposing you asked him the question – since a god,
> whatever comes into his mind, can easily get it all done,
> if a man is a turd of a loan-shark, a real old die-for-a-penny
> who squanders it all out again, one who's the death of his fortune,
> why can't God just empty this man of his swinewealth,
> and give to a thin-feeding, common-bowl cup-dipper
> all the man's damned expenditurette? Has the eye of Justice been mole-
>   blinded?
>
> (Kerkidas, fr. 2 in Loeb)[79]

The fragment continues with a veiled prophecy that Nemesis (divine vengeance) will catch up with the Macedonians 'who lord it over us'. That is not necessarily revolutionary talk. It is debatable whether this kind of poem (or song) was accessible to a mass audience or performed primarily in literary circles. Like Krates, Kerkidas adapted and parodied the classics; who but the educated élite would recognize it as parody? We may doubt that he had an expressly revolutionary purpose. One critic has argued that we should view Krates as a sympotic poet, writing songs with which people could entertain one another at dinner-parties, perhaps in competition with other songs, rather than as deeply radical[80] – more sung against than Cynic, one might say.

Besides poems, Cynic writers such as Bion of Borysthenes and Teles of Megara wrote *diatribai*. *Diatribê* literally means 'a whiling away of time', but came to denote speeches or discourses on moral themes. Stoic authors wrote *diatribai*, and the name implies nothing so furious as the English term 'diatribe'. Another third-century writer, Menippos of Gadara, is said to have combined seriousness with humour and to have mocked other philosophers; Roman satirists modelled some of their work on his. Once again, there is no way of conclusively detaching these authors (any more than one could detach Roman satirists) from an élite, literary context. The same must go for Sotades, who wrote scurrilous poems such as an apparent attack on Ptolemy II's marriage to his sister Arsinoë, from which comes the infamous line, 'You're sticking your prick in an unholy hole' (Plut. *On the Education of Children*, 11 a; Ath. 14. 621 a)[81] – apparent, because it is not at all clear whether this was some kind of genuine grass-roots protest of a kind that Ptolemy might have punished, or was the licensed lampooning of its day, like the satirical British television series of the 1980s and 1990s, *Spitting Image*. The sources agree that Sotades was punished, but differ in the details: he rotted in prison (Plutarch) or was thrown into the sea (Athenaeus). The discrepancy makes it uncertain whether Sotades suffered any penalty at all.

Since works like these do survive, we can only presume they were read by 'respectable' Greeks and scholars who possessed written copies. Bion is said to have moved from city to city, putting on a great show; 'in Rhodes he persuaded the sailors to put on student dress and accompany him', says Diogenes Laërtios (4. 53). We cannot build this up into a mass sentiment,[82] for the account continues with the words 'and bursting into the *gymnasion* with them he caught the eye of everyone'. The *gymnasion* is a place for respectable élite citizens.

The Stoic philosophy of Zeno (Zênôn in Greek) of Kition, as we have seen, had its roots partly in the Cynic rejection of conventional society, though Zeno also studied with Stilpon, head of the Megarian philosophical school (himself linked to the Cynics and a specialist in dialectic; see Diog. Laërt. 2. 113–20), and with Polemon, head of the Athenian Academy. Born at Kition on Cyprus, Zeno may have been an ethnic Phoenician, though his name and that of his father are Greek. Once he had formulated his own ideas independently of his teachers, he began to teach at Athens in the Stoa Poikile (Painted Stoa), from which the term 'Stoic' derives.

Zeno, according to ancient writers, held that the only real good is right action; everything else is neither good nor bad, but morally indifferent. The universe operates according to reason; as in Epicureanism, the gods are not active, but the wise man acts in accordance with their laws. Since he knows he is acting rightly, he is happy even in dire circumstances – 'happy even on the rack'.

Those, at least, are the central tenets of Stoicism, which had a long life and developed over five centuries. Zeno's own works do not survive. It is likely that his views were more radical than those of his successors. His main work was *Politeia* (*Constitution*; the title is the same as that of Plato's great dialogue which is, quite misleadingly, known as the *Republic*). He depicted an ideal society as living 'according to nature'; not an ecological commune, but a society with *rational*, hence 'true', values. Diogenes Laërtios preserves elements of Zeno's position in the shape of the attacks mounted upon him:

> Some indeed, among whom are the followers of Cassius the Sceptic, who in accusing Zenon say, first, that at the start of *Politeia* he declares the conventional education to be valueless; second, that he describes as foes, enemies, slaves, and strangers to each other all men who are not virtuous: parents to children, brothers to brothers, and friends to friends... Similarly, in *Politeia*, they say, he lays it down as an opinion that wives (are to be) communal, and around line 200 that neither sanctuaries nor lawcourts nor gymnasiums shall be built in the cities. And about coinage, they say, he writes that he thinks coinage need not be introduced either for exchange or for foreign travel. And he commands men and women to wear the same dress, and no part (of the body) to be completely hidden.
>
> (Diog. Laërt. 7. 32–3)

It appears that some homosexuality was to be acceptable; at least, we have the statement of Diogenes that the Stoics

> say that the wise man will feel desire for young men who demonstrate by their appearance a good natural disposition towards virtue, as Zeno says in the *Politeia*, Chrysippos in the first book of his work *On Ways of Life*, and Apollodoros in his *Ethics*.
>
> (Diog. Laërt. 7. 129)

Unlike Plato's ideal state, the commune would not necessarily be a city; Zeno was probably more concerned that it should embrace all wise men. They might live in cities, but these would not be typical Greek *poleis*.[83]

Zeno was not writing a prescription that could be put into practice, but examining a hypothetical situation. Although it is easy to see the role played by Cynic values, not to mention Platonic, in his thought, he has his own ideas and is not simply the product of his teachers.[84] Furthermore, since he was in demand as a teacher, or preacher, at Athens, his ideas must have struck a chord with his listeners and corresponded to their concerns. What were these concerns? If we wished to stress the idealism of Alexander the Great (as historians such as Tarn have done) and see him as aspiring to break down barriers between races, we could locate Zeno by reference to what would be seen as Alexander's failure and the chaotic legacy of his reign. Alternatively, we can play down Alexander's idealism (as scholars now do) and stress the instability of civic society in third-century Greece, particularly the frequency of civil disorder and class conflict, or the threat of it. One can certainly see Zeno as responding to threats, external and internal, to the *polis* of his day. His response certainly differed from Epicureanism in advocating positive action – political participation – rather than quietism. Some of his democratic ideas were of practical value, being adapted and used in the context of resistance to Macedonia at the start of the Chremonidean war (cf. the decree quoted on p. 126).[85]

Once Athens was defeated in 263/2, however – an event which coincided approximately with Zeno's death – Stoicism had to deal with the problem of creating the ideal state in a monarchical world. Under Kleanthes of Assos (*c.*261–232) and his successor Chrysippos of Soloi (232–*c.*206) the Stoa still seems to have remained a focus of anti-Macedonian theory. Sphairos of Borysthenes assisted Kleomenes III of Sparta in his reforms, and his links with Ptolemy III suggest that the destabilization of Macedonia was an aim they shared. Rome in the late third and early second centuries seemed a promising ally against Macedonia, but its influence shifted Stoicism in a more conservative direction. From the second century on, Stoicism was gradually adapted for use by a philosophy of the just ruler, and its more radical elements were toned down. Later Stoics even denied Zeno's authorship of the *Politeia*, or dismissed it as an immature work. 'The Stoa becomes transformed from a school largely critical of contemporary society to one which largely accepts it.'[86] It also remained what it had always been, a philosophy for the political élite.

Utopians

All these philosophical traditions reflect a problem that now faced educated Greeks: how to engage in the political activity that was a citizen's right, given the existence of the Macedonian monarchies. In different ways they all withdrew from confident philosophical theorizing and political commitment, with the exception of Zeno and the early Stoics.

While some philosophers theorized about ideal states, others described imaginary lands that might better be described as utopias. Euemeros (or Euhemeros) of Messene, who served with king Cassander from 311 to 298, wrote the *Hiera anagraphê* (*Sacred Narrative*), an imaginary account of a journey to a group of islands in the Indian Ocean where not only human nature but Nature has been made perfect. Eusebios cites a summary from a lost book of Diodoros, apparently quoting the latter's actual words:

> Euemeros, then, was a friend of king Cassander, and so had to carry out a number of royal missions and undertake long journeys abroad.

187

He says he travelled south to the ocean; starting from Arabia the Blessed he sailed for many days through the ocean, and came to islands in the sea. One of these was called Panchaia; there he saw the Panchaians who inhabit the island, men of great piety who honour the gods ... There is in the island, on a very lofty hill, a temple of Zeus Triphylios, founded by himself at the time when he was still among men and was king over the whole world.

(Diod. 6. 1. 4, 6, *FGH* 63 fr. 2, Austin 38)

It is a very Greek society, with three defined classes (as in the models of the fifth-century town-planner Hippodamos), though citizenship is universal. The Olympian gods are cut down to size: they were once nothing but great kings, now worshipped as gods by a grateful people, and are replaced by the sun, stars, and heavens, symbolizing the all-seeing eye of justice. Private property and money are absent, and the land is equitably divided among those who work hard. Alexarchos, brother of Cassander, may have tried to make reality out of fantasy by founding Ouranopolis (Heaven City) on the Athos peninsula in northern Greece[87] – he put the sun on its coins[88] – but Euemeros was hardly a political revolutionary; we must not forget that he was a military commander in the service of a king. More important than the philosophy was the city foundation, an eminently practical venture.

The 'philosophy' of Euemeros, in so far as it is one, should perhaps be seen as an attempt to provide a language in which to make sense of the new relationship between kings and cities. Its influence may be seen in the more idealistic book of Iamboulos (whose name suggests that he may have been a hellenized Nabataean Arab),[89] another fantastic journey probably written in the third century. The voyage took Iamboulos from Ethiopia to a happy island where he lived for seven years; again Diodoros preserves parts of the story (2. 55–60). The human and animal populations are even more preternaturally endowed than in Euemeros's tale: their bones are flexible, their bodies hairless and beautiful; they can imitate the birds, and can hold two conversations at the same time. Nature is positively bountiful, the crops ripening all year round. Again the Sun god is the ruler and guardian of justice, and society is run on communal lines with an even more egalitarian emphasis than in Euemeros, there being no mention of social classes:

They are said to live by kinship groups and constitutional units, not more than four hundred kindred persons being grouped together; and these people live their lives in the meadows, as the land has many things for their sustenance....

They do not marry wives, but have them in common; and they love as equals the children that are born, bringing them up as the children of all. While they are infants, the women who nurse them often exchange the babies, so that not even the mothers may know their own. For this reason, as no rivalry develops among them, they do not suffer from civil discord and always value concord most highly.

(Diod. 2. 57. 1, 2. 58. 1)

There is a rational system of monarchical inheritance, and euthanasia is practised for the incurable and those who reach the age of 150. This blueprint certainly reflects the social theorizing of the age, but for the most part it seems designed to entertain: there are extraordinary creatures on the island, including domesticated birds on whose backs infant children are placed to see if they can stand the rigours of flight and be deemed strong enough to be brought up. The inhabitants follow a strict and simple diet, and people perform community service on a rota.

In one respect it is perhaps justifiable to infer that there was more popular interest in this than in other philosophies, though it took a member of the élite to foment it. Aristonikos, claimant to the throne of Pergamon after the Roman takeover of 133, may have won widespread support by appealing to Iamboulos's book and naming his city Heliopolis (Sun City; Strabo, 14. 1. 38 (646), Austin 212); the Italian Stoic Blossius of Cumae was one of his supporters, and an inscription from Klaros, near Kolophon in Ionia, refers to Doulôn Polis ('Slavestown').[90] There is, however, no evidence of a revolutionary programme inspired by social philosophy, only of a political tactic at a desperate moment in his campaign.[91]

Even if they were evidence of popular interest, the Aristonikos episode and the foundation of Ouranopolis would be exceptions to the general rule. Although there was social discontent in third-century Greece, one should be wary of assuming that political culture spread very far down the social scale. It is possible (as Ferguson argues) that utopian ideals had some points of contact with practical Stoic politics.[92] Kleomenes of Sparta put the sun on some of his coins (like Alexarchos) and admitted resident foreigners to citizenship. The parallel with Aristonikos, however, is noteworthy: Kleomenes did not admit helots to citizenship until the crisis of 223/2 (p. 147).

Philosophy in society

Doctrinal change and the questioning of orthodoxy were not new to Greek thought; they are its hallmark from earliest times. Recent work on the new philosophies emphasizes their roots in fourth-century thought; they did not develop out of nothing, nor did philosophy make a quantum leap when Macedonia defeated the southern Greeks. (A similar case can be made for religious change as developing continuously; see above.) Of course, doctrinal change did not take place in isolation from the 'real' world, and will in some way have reflected (and affected) social and political changes. The mistake would be to locate the impetus to doctrinal change in the 'feelings' of individuals

189

about the world – of which we have no firm evidence – rather than in the process of debate and the transmission of ideas.

Hellenistic philosophy, particularly the rise of philosophies of withdrawal, is often held to be a response to the fears of people living in a new, uncertain age. Thus Tarn and Griffith: 'The two new philosophies ... were both products of ... the feeling that a man was no longer merely a part of his city; he was an individual, and as such needed new guidance.'[93] Even the more sober assessment by Long assumes that Alexander's conquests, 'in disrupting traditional patterns of life, ... made many people receptive to philosophies which stressed the self-sufficiency of the individual'. For Grant (as for many others) the philosophy of the period is 'the search for peace of mind', the literature sheer escapism.[94]

To appeal to the fears of individual men and women may be to project falsely onto antiquity a modern-day perception of the powerless 'little people' caught up in the vast, blind machinations of powerful states and economic forces. The *polis* was not in its death-throes. Politically the Greek world was, if anything, less chaotic than in the fifth and fourth centuries, when city-states continually fought wars, made and broke alliances, and for much of the time (with rare exceptions such as Athens) had little control over their own destiny. As for the terror of a vast new world, Greeks had always traded with, and colonized, Egypt, distant parts of the Mediterranean and the Black Sea, and parts of western Asia; now they could earn money for fighting there, and there were new opportunities for settling down with land and privileges.

The emphasis on ethics and withdrawal may reflect, not opting out or escapism, but a change in the political role of the social élite who are the real producers and consumers of philosophical discourse. Politics continued, though with different goals. Most philosophers of whom we hear were men from extremely privileged backgrounds for whom philosophy, though a passion, was also an indulgence or even, as Habicht terms it, 'a hobby for those affluent enough to dispense with paid careers'. 'Philosophers' often enter the stage as diplomatic envoys, as in the famous 'mission of the philosophers' to Rome, led by Karneades in 155; in Athens, at least three of the most important political leaders of this period are called philosophers: Demetrios of Phaleron (r. 317–307) and the 'tyrants' of the 80s, Athenion and Ariston.[95] But they may have been politicians first, and philosophers second.

World-views and society

The most important thing we can do in considering religion in this period is to accept the religious validity of the new cults. We should neither attribute excessive credulity to people of the time, nor exaggerate the evidence for scepticism or 'rationality'. In the case of philosophy, we should neither diminish new ideas by seeing them merely as reactions to collective fears, nor overstate the influence of systems of thought which were probably formulated by and for a political élite. The changes in both areas were at least as much the logical continuation of fourth-century developments as the product of a new world – which was not, after all, so very new. In both areas we have invoked the changing position of the élites within the *poleis*. City-states no longer involved (if they ever had) all citizens equally, and may have limited real power to a smaller group; conversely, élites had less power because cities had less freedom. This may have led to the formulation of new philosophical systems and at the same time removed restrictions on religious innovation. The chief new feature was the increased popularity of certain religions – not, it should be noted, all 'oriental', nor adopted by their adherents to the exclusion of other religious practices – religions that proclaimed a collective fulfilment and reached beyond one ethnic group. Even these were installed within the pantheon of the Greek city.

6

PTOLEMAIC EGYPT

In the next four chapters we move outside Greece and consider how Greeks and Macedonians imposed themselves upon neighbouring lands, and how they conceptualized their new relationship with the world through their cultural activities. We first consider one of the two largest kingdoms.

After outlining the landscape and pre-existing society of Egypt and the distinctive character of the Ptolemaic evidence, we shall review the history of the dynasty from its apparent glory days under the first two kings to the seeming chaos of the second and first centuries BC, when only the occasional documented event relieves the confusing sequence of dynastic scandals. Even the history of the monarchs, however, can be made to illustrate wider developments. Overviews of Greek society in Egypt, relations between Greeks and native Egyptians, and the nature of Ptolemaic economic administration are followed by a summing up of the possible long-term effects of Ptolemaic rule. Caution will be exercised, however, when attempting to assign the blame for decline, or even to identify the symptoms of decline; the kingdom survived far longer than its rivals, and there are signs of good government even in the last decades of the Ptolemies.

Land and people

As with other areas of the hellenistic world, it is important to be aware of the nature of the territory which Alexander conquered.[1] Ancient Egypt occupied an area not dissimilar in shape to the modern state of Egypt, which fills a block of land some 1,000 kilometres square, though like other ancient states it probably did not have neatly defined or policed land boundaries. As in Egypt today, the core territory was very long and extremely narrow. The main area of settlement, Upper and Middle Egypt, consisted of the Nile valley north of the First Cataract, below Syene (modern Aswan), c.800 kilometres inland; this fertile strip was generally 10–20 kilometres wide (Fig. 6.1). At its northern end the channels of the river Nile expanded to form the Delta, some 200 kilometres across at the coast, which linked Egypt to the Mediterranean world and was densely settled. The third main area of settlement

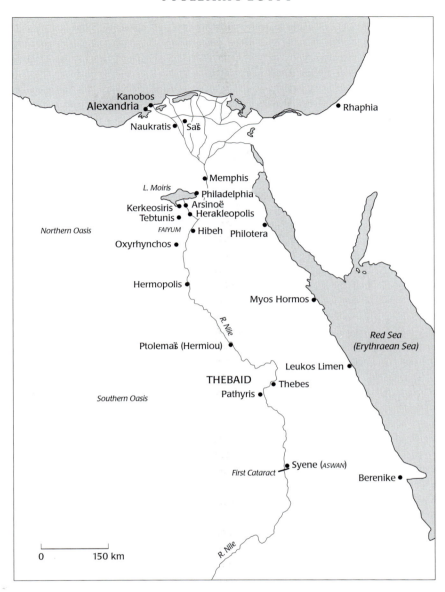

Figure 6.1   Egypt. (Adapted from J. B. Salmon in Talbert, *Atlas*, 76.)

193

was the Faiyum or Arsinoite nome (nomes, *nomoi* in Greek, were the administrative districts both before and after Alexander), a fertile depression some 850 square kilometres in extent today,[2] with Lake Moiris (Birket el-Qarun) to its north and the Delta to its north-east.

Although Egypt was hemmed in by inhospitable country, its population numbered several million, most of them living in small towns and villages. Until Alexander's invasion the capital was at Memphis, on the Nile not far south of the Delta, which in the Ptolemaic period had a population measured in tens of thousands[3] and remained a powerful religious and ceremonial centre even when Alexandria became the new capital.

Apart from the Faiyum, the land west of the Nile valley was desert relieved only by occasional oases, of which the largest were el-Bahriya and el-Kharga, the Northern and Southern (or Small and Great) Oases, each lying over 100 kilometres west of the Nile. The area between the Nile and the Red Sea, 100–150 kilometres to the east, consisted of barren hill-land rising to almost 2,000 metres above sea level; but there were quarries of granite, marble, and other excellent monumental stone in this eastern desert, and settlements on the coast such as Myos Hormos (Mouse Anchorage) and Leukos Limen (White Harbour), both of which may have existed previously and been refounded by Ptolemy II Philadelphos. The new port of Berenike was certainly founded by him, probably to shorten the crossing of the Red Sea:[4]

> The city [*Berenike*] has no harbour, but on account of the favourable lay of the isthmus has convenient landing-places. It is said that Philadelphos was the first person, by means of an army, to cut this road, which is without water, and to build stations, as though for the travels of merchants on camels, and that he did this because the Red Sea was hard to navigate, particularly for those who set sail from its innermost recess.
>
> (Strabo, 17. 1. 44–5 (815), Austin 277)[5]

Egypt is well provided with mineral resources. As well as a wide range of semi-precious stones and some gems, it has many stones for carving, building, and industrial purposes. The metal ores of the eastern desert, however, were not fully exploited until the Roman period,[6] and though there was a supply of gold in the far south it was difficult to work (Diod. 3. 12. 1–3, Austin 263).

As a result of the infertility of much of the land, Egypt was crucially dependent on the agriculture of the Nile valley, and the key feature of the agriculture was irrigation. The annual flood, which occurred reliably each year until the Aswan dam was built in modern times, provided Egypt with its greatest resource, the fertile silt of the valley and Delta, but created some of the greatest problems of organization. Water in the fields was controlled through a complex system of ditches and dykes, and villages and towns had to be protected by being squeezed into limited areas of higher ground. (A document from 257 BC preserves a contractor's tender for the repair of embankments at Memphis: Austin 242.)[7] The Ptolemies invested heavily in drainage projects in the Faiyum, cutting new channels in order to draw water from the marshland and bring new ground into cultivation.[8]

Like the Persian empire and its predecessors, Egypt was in many ways a traditional, hierarchical near eastern empire. It had existed as a kingdom since at least 3000 BC, though its territory varied in size; at its largest, it extended from Sudan to northern Syria. As in the palace states of bronze age Greece, the central administration extracted a large percentage of agricultural produce from cultivators and monitored it. After Alexander, Egyptian society remained extremely hierarchical, dominated by king and court, with the priests of the native temples forming a powerful secondary power centre with a virtual monopoly on (non-Greek) literacy.

As well as exploiting the heartland of Egypt, the Ptolemaic kingdom depended crucially for its wealth and security on the possession of external territories (see further pp. 205–7). Firm evidence for the economic role of the overseas possessions is somewhat limited, but they certainly contributed to the king's income: indirectly by absorbing the expenses of a Ptolemaic naval base, by supplying manpower to the armed forces, and through the regular Ptolemaic taxes of economic activities; directly by paying tribute, probably in the form of voluntary 'crowns' rather than compulsory charges.[9] The king's *dioikêtês* (chief finance official) closely supervised revenues and contracts in the empire (Austin 265),[10] and in 163 the commander of the garrison on Thera was directly responsible to him (Austin 266, *OGIS* 59).[11]

Egypt was an ethnically diverse country, the towns often being divided into different quarters and the army manned by foreign mercenaries. At Memphis, besides recent Greek immigrants and the descendants of earlier incomers such as the sixth-century Ionian mercenaries (known as Hellenomemphites), there were large numbers of Phoenicians, Karians (Karomemphites, less strongly defined as a community than in earlier times), Jews and other Semitic settlers, and Idumaeans (who probably came in the late second century). In the cities and the countryside security and public order were imposed by the presence of military garrisons.[12]

Egypt was seen in ancient times as a land of boundless natural wealth, thanks to its rich alluvial valley, and the vast majority of the population were Egyptian cultivators with smallholdings, who paid taxes in kind. It would be too simple, however, to imagine a mass of labourers exploited ruthlessly from the urban centres. The cultivators were legally free and entitled to justice, and slave-owning was mainly a feature of urban Greek society. This expectation of fair treatment was reflected in the tradition whose Greek name, *anachôrêsis*, means a 'going up' (from the valley into the desert), whereby aggrieved farmers would take themselves off, singly or *en masse*, to another region or a temple – a kind of strike action.[13]

The earlier history of Egypt suggests that if it was to have a single administration a strong central power was required; but overall control was hard to enforce, with the result that upper (southern) Egypt periodically became a separate entity. Egypt had had foreign rulers for much of the preceding three hundred years, most recently the Persians from 525 to *c*.404 and from 341 until Alexander's invasion; and the position of a pharaoh of foreign extraction had always raised in an acute form the problem of the relationship between king and people.[14] The king had to be in harmony with the gods of Egypt, or the stability of his rule would be jeopardized.

The temples, with their extensive landholdings and influential priestly hierarchy, represented an important parallel power-structure. At Memphis they occupied perhaps one-third of the area of the city and probably employed the largest number of people, acting as centres of redistribution and trade for the community at large. In Egypt before Alexander, the temples, though in some respects controlled by the crown, were major property-owners (by permission of the king) and collectors of taxes. Members of temple staff could be exempted from compulsory labour (see e.g. Austin 246, *PCZ* 59541). Diodoros preserves the claim that one-third of Egypt was given to the priests by the goddess Isis in order to pay for cult activities (Diod. 1. 21. 7, cf. 1. 73. 2–3); the second part, he says, is held by the kings to pay for wars, a splendid court, and gifts (1. 73. 6), the third by the military class (1. 73. 7).[15] Under the Ptolemies, crown income was diverted to the temples under two headings: *apomoira*, taxes paid on vineyards and orchards, was passed on for use in the royal cult (pp. 225–6), while *syntaxis* was a grant in support of the normal activities of temples. The latter was partly a replacement for the income that temples had previously collected from their own landholdings, parts of which were now controlled by the state while others were conceded back to the temples.[16]

The complexity and strength of Egyptian social organization mean that we should not expect to find a whole new system being imposed on a pre-civilized landscape by the 'rational' Greeks, or even to see rapid and far-reaching changes. Ptolemaic Egypt was not, to any marked degree, a 'top-down' creation of the Greeks and Macedonians. In many respects the period of Ptolemaic rule, though it lasted nearly three hundred years, did not bring a sharp break in society and economy; the agricultural population carried on much as under the Egyptian pharaohs and the Persians, and as it did later under Roman rule. Society was evolving, as societies always are, but structural changes took place gradually and not necessarily as a result of the Macedonian takeover.

Evidence

Uniquely among hellenistic states, Egypt has produced tens of thousands of records of day-to-day administration in the form of papyri, written in either

Greek (Fig. 6.2) or in Demotic, the written, somewhat formalized version of the Egyptian language.[17] Many are preserved because during the early Ptolemaic period it became common practice to recycle them into cartonnage, a form of papier mâché used in making mummy-cases. From those discovered in cemetery excavations, many important and lengthy papyri, including parts of literary texts such as plays by Menander (pp. 257–8), have been reconstituted. Other papyri have been recovered in their original form by the excavation of ancient settlements, such as the so-called Zenon archive from Philadelphia (p. 219). All this gives the social and economic history of Ptolemaic Egypt (and even the political history, particularly under the later Ptolemies), a level of detail not found elsewhere. Caution is needed, however, when generalizing from Egypt to the wider hellenistic world – this has been called the problem of typicality[18] – since some characteristics of the evidence may have been specific to this landscape and may indicate local political and cultural traditions different from those in Greece and western Asia.

Furthermore, the papyrus evidence, particularly in Greek, is unevenly distributed. Papyrus survives best in dry, undisturbed conditions; consequently, most finds are made where there is neither settlement nor cultivation today, such as on desert margins and in ancient cemeteries.[19] Because the desert later encroached on the Faiyum, this area has produced the majority of surviving papyrus documents of the Ptolemaic period. The rich and densely settled Nile valley has produced relatively few papyri, though there are important exceptions such as (among excavated papyri) the Serapeion archive from the Memphite nome and soldiers' archives from the Pathyrite, while finds of cartonnage include third-century texts from Hibeh and an important body of first-century material from the Herakleopolite nome (Abusir el Melek). Egyptian Thebes has produced a larger proportion of texts in Demotic. Faiyum papyri come mainly from villages, whereas many from the Nile valley are from urban contexts.[20] (Examples of documents from the Nile valley among those reviewed in this chapter included the cases of Peteharsemtheus and Dryton, p. 223.)

There are chronological variations. Some major sites, such as the western oases and the city of Oxyrhynchos in middle Egypt, have produced papyri mainly of Roman date. In many cases only a very short period is covered, since papyri often occur in the form of particular groups of documents, conventionally known as 'archives' (such as the Zenon archive). This is a misleading term, since documents were usually not catalogued or sorted in order to be archived, and may have survived together simply because they dealt with the business of one family, official, or community.[21]

Finally, thousands of papyri remain unpublished; this is particularly the case with those written in Demotic, since fewer scholars are equipped to read this language.[22] So while we have plenty of illustrative documents to draw upon, the task of generalizing from particular periods, social groups,

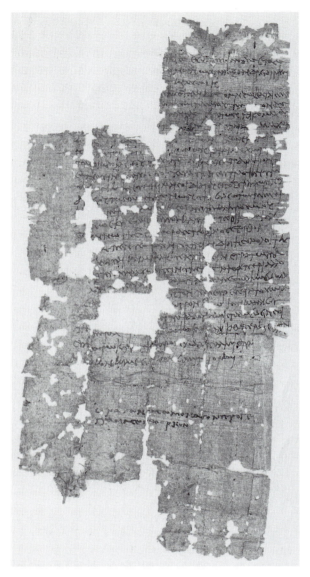

Figure 6.2   Greek papyrus (*P. Oxy.* 3777). The document, written by a scribe, starts:
'In the first year of the [reign of] Bere[nike], Goddess Manifest'. It dates from
between 2 and 31 August 57 BC, and is the first dated reference to the sole reign of
Berenike IV after the death of Kleopatra Tryphaina. It contains an oath sworn by
Straton (whose name appears in the middle of the preserved portion of line 6), a
senior cavalryman in the queen's service, to abide by a contract with Theon (line 8),
a man with the technical status of 'Persian' to whom he has ceded part of his land
allotment. Straton himself signs at the bottom. (Reproduced by permission of the
Egypt Exploration Society.)

and places to Egypt as a whole, let alone the wider Greek world, is often extremely complex, as regional variation must always be a likelihood.

Another important class of documents is that of ostraka, pieces of broken pottery (Fig. 6.3) which people would use for ephemeral communications and drafts, rather than waste costly papyrus. They survive in larger numbers from upper Egypt, but their distribution is less uneven than that of papyri, since their survival is not so dependent upon soil conditions . They have, in particular, helped scholars to build up a picture of Ptolemaic taxation.

Inscriptions make important contributions to Ptolemaic history, ranging from monumental public documents like the Rosetta Stone (p. 166) to the many Greek and Demotic grave-inscriptions from towns and villages. What is absent is the kind of civic documentation which we have from Athens and the other *poleis* of the Aegean world; that kind of political organization did not exist in Egypt, outside the Greek cities of Alexandria, Ptolemaïs, and Naukratis.

Among literary sources, we may single out Diodoros Siculus (first century BC), whose first book is devoted to Egyptian topography, customs, and history and draws extensively upon the late fourth-century author Hekataios of Abdera (p. 260) and on Agatharchides of Knidos (quoted, pp. 362–3).

The tendency to under-exploit Demotic sources is slowly being put right. In parallel with this development, it is beginning to be realized that in many respects Egyptian culture was bilingual. Many people, for example, had two names (pp. 216–17), and there was an entire Egyptian legal system functioning in parallel to the Greek law introduced with the Ptolemies. Contracts between Egyptians were still written in Demotic, using a complicated system of witnesses and multiple copies. By the late third century this was simplified, perhaps under the influence of Greek law, with up to sixteen witnesses listed on a single main copy (Greek contracts had only six witnesses). Finally, beginning in the third or second century, state *agoranomoi* ('notaries', not, as in Greece, market superintendents) could draw up contracts in Greek without any need for witnesses, while from the mid-second century registry offices (*grapheia*) kept copies of contracts; when the contract was in Demotic, a summary and the date were also recorded in Greek. Under these stimuli Greek began to oust Demotic as the normal language for these purposes. Nevertheless, the long-continued use of native legal forms, whose validity were accepted in Greek practice, will have played a crucial part in maintaining the Egyptians' own sense of identity.[23]

Because its survival is uneven in space and time, and because of the conditions of its creation, there is a danger that the fullness of our written evidence about Egypt may make historians over-confident. Papyri, ostraka, and inscriptions tell us chiefly about life in particular parts of the *chôra*, the rural territory outside the principal cities; the surviving literature and historiography (Chapter 7) are concentrated upon Alexandria and upon the world of court and king. Furthermore, there is a relative lack of archaeological

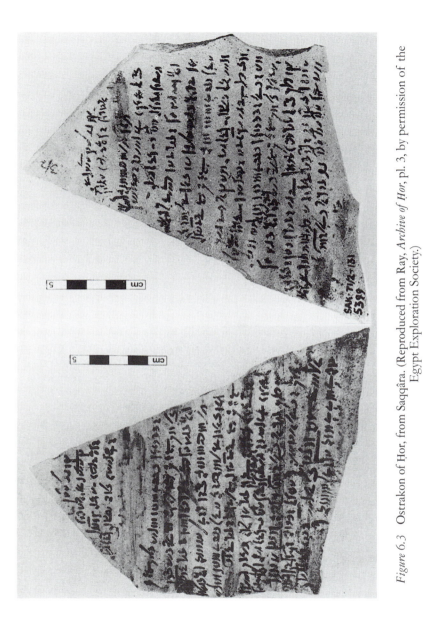

Figure 6.3 Ostrakon of Hor, from Saqqâra. (Reproduced from Ray, *Archive of Hor*, pl. 3, by permission of the Egypt Exploration Society.)

evidence from Alexandria, a city inhabited continuously since its foundation (though the picture is not so faint as a generation ago).[24] It would be wrong to generalize too easily from the economy and society of the Faiyum to life in the Delta and Alexandria, just as it would be to take the literature and science of the capital as typical of Ptolemaic Egypt as a whole.

The Ptolemaic dynasty

From Soter to the battle of Rhaphia (323–217 BC)

Ptolemy (Ptolemaios) son of Lagos (whence Lagidai and Lagids, alternative names for the dynasty), known to us as Ptolemy I Soter ('the Saviour', r. 323–282), took over as satrap in 323 on behalf of Philip III Arrhidaios.[25] Since c.331 Egypt had been governed by Kleomenes of Naukratis (or Alexandria), one of Alexander's appointees who had established himself as effective, or actual, satrap by the time of Alexander's death and presented Ptolemy with 8,000 talents when he entered into his satrapy. Kleomenes was evidently an efficient, not to say ruthless, administrator. The *Oikonomika* attributed to Aristotle tells how he manipulated the wheat price during a shortage, and tricked Egyptian priests into giving up temple treasures ([Arist.] *Oec.* 2. 2. 33. 1352 a–b). The contemporary Athenian courtroom speech *Against Dionysodoros* claims that he was responsible for artificially causing the price of wheat to rise ([Demosthenes], 56. 7).[26] At some time between 323 and 320, however, Ptolemy had Kleomenes killed, suspecting him of being sympathetic to Perdikkas the chiliarch (Paus. 1. 6. 3), who now had designs on Egypt (p. 42).

From Alexander and Kleomenes, Ptolemy inherited a tightly structured administration which controlled the work of the farming population and ensured the steady flow of taxes into the royal coffers; but he modified the existing administrative apparatus. To validate his rule he presented himself carefully to his populations, both within Egypt and in the outside world. To the native Egyptian population and its élite, priestly class he seems to have behaved from an early stage as the legitimate successor of Alexander; Diodoros (18. 14) says he behaved generously towards the natives at this time, which probably reflected the pharaonic tradition that each new ruler should publicly proclaim certain benefactions.[27] In the Greek–Macedonian context he took steps to make his position seem uniquely legitimate, seizing Alexander's mummified body while it was being taken to Macedonia for burial, and placing it in Memphis, the old sacred capital. Later he symbolically made clear the primary role of Alexandria by building a spectacular tomb for Alexander (later Ptolemy IV Philopator built around it a mausoleum, the Sema or Monument, to enclose the tombs of Alexander and all the Ptolemies).[28]

In the wars of the Successors Ptolemy seems mainly to play the role of onlooker, occasionally profiting from the conflicts of his rivals or influencing the outcome to his advantage. He took Koile Syria in 319, though Antigonos eventually conquered it. He helped Seleukos regain Babylon; but that was no guarantee of a permanent alliance. After Ipsos (301) he again seized part of Koile Syria and captured part of south-eastern Asia Minor. In the late 290s or early 280s the Islanders' league, founded in 315–314 by Antigonos Monophthalmos to control Aegean sea-routes, became Ptolemaic[29] and a *nêsiarchos* ('commander of the islands') was appointed (Austin 218, Burstein 92, *Syll.*[3] 390; and Austin 268, *OGIS* 43).[30] Ptolemy was clearly not content to stay at home and consolidate his family's power in Egypt; the reasons for his overseas ventures will be considered more fully below.

After ruling for thirty-eight years, in 285 Ptolemy promoted his son Ptolemy II, later called Philadelphos ('the Sister-loving', r. 285–246), to the status of co-ruler; he himself died two years later. The long-lived Philadelphos created, or enjoyed, a period of relative stability, during which the cultural reputation of Alexandria rose to spectacular heights (Chapters 7, 9). A detailed narrative of Ptolemaic foreign strategy for the mid-third century is not possible, but besides adding the important naval station of Samos to his Aegean possessions after the death of Lysimachos, Philadelphos gained territory in Asia Minor as a result of the first Syrian war of 274–271 (see Fig. 6.4 and p. 288).[31] These gains, or at least the spirit of ever-increasing empire, may be reflected in the list of the overseas possessions of Philadelphos given by the court poet of the early third century, Theokritos:

> Syria, Phoenicia, Libya yield their land.
> Arab and black-skinned Ethiop feel his sword.
> Lycia, Pamphylia, Caria call him lord,
> lord fierce Cilicia, sea-washed Cyclades.
> His ships proclaim him sovereign of the seas.
> (*Idyll* 17; cf. Austin 217)

Just before this, Philadelphos put down a revolt by his half-brother Magas in Cyrene (cf. p. 288 for Magas as a possible protégé of Antiochos II, aspiring to overthrow Ptolemy). In the 260s he supported Sparta and other Greek states

*c.*274–271	first Syrian war
260–*c.*253	second Syrian war
246–241	third Syrian (Laodikean) war
219–211	fourth Syrian war
202–200	fifth Syrian war
169–168	sixth Syrian war (Antiochos IV's invasion of Egypt)

Figure 6.4 The 'Syrian' wars.

in their unsuccessful revolt against Macedonia, the Chremonidean war (pp. 125–6), during or after which he suffered naval defeats off Kos and at Ephesos and may have lost control of the league of the Islanders.[32]

Soon after 261, the Seleukid king Antiochos II regained Samos and territory in Asia Minor as a result of the second Syrian war, which was brought to an end by his marriage to Berenike II, daughter of Philadelphos. That marriage in turn led to the Laodikean or third Syrian war (p. 289), in which Ptolemy III Euergetes ('the Benefactor', r. 246–221; also known as Euergetes I; Fig. 6.5) invaded Asia Minor and Mesopotamia, though his only permanent gains were in Asia Minor, plus Samos once more. (It was on his return to Egypt that he received the title Euergetes.) The invasion of Syria is told, ostensibly in the king's own name, in a fragmentary historical account preserved on papyrus (*FGH* 160, Austin 220, BD 27, Burstein 98). A more monumental text, very much in the style of traditional near eastern monarchs, lists his successes in Asia and takes credit for the recovery of sacred objects removed from Egypt by the Persians (Austin 221, BD 26, Burstein 99, *OGIS* 54; cf. the Canopus decree, Austin 222, BD 136, *OGIS* 56, line 11). A dedication by Ptolemaic mercenaries on service in Syria, perhaps at this time, has been found (Austin 274),[33] as has evidence for Ptolemaic regulation of livestock and slaves in Syria and Phoenicia in 260 BC (Austin 275, *C. Ord. Ptol.* 21–2).

The start of Ptolemy III's reign witnessed the first attested native rising in Egypt, but it seems to have been suppressed and not to have had lasting effects[34] (Fig. 6.6). Outside Egypt, both Philadelphos and Euergetes gave support to the Achaean league against the Macedonians. When Aratos struck a deal with Antigonos Doson (Chapter 4), Euergetes was willing to accommodate the exiled Spartan king Kleomenes III in Egypt but not to help him actively; he may have considered that Antigonos was now too strong to be worth opposing in this way.

The accession of Ptolemy IV Philopator ('the Father-loving', r. 221–205) is often presented, following Polybios, as a disastrous turning-point for Ptolemaic power. The young king and his supposedly wicked advisers

Figure 6.5 Portrait coin of Ptolemy III Euergetes, showing the king with radiate crown and other symbols of Egyptian–Macedonian royalty (*BMC Ptolemies*, pl. 12. 4). (British Museum, London.)

Sosibios and Agathokles are blamed for the loss of naval supremacy in the Aegean and for the catastrophic consequences of Antiochos III's invasion of Syria (in the fourth Syrian war, 219–211; cf. Polyb. 5. 67, Austin 148; Fig. 6.4).[35]

> To Ptolemy, immediately after these events [*the fourth Syrian war*], it happened that the war against the Egyptians occurred. The aforementioned king [*Ptolemy IV*], in arming the Egyptians for the war against Antiochos, acted admissibly for the present, but missed the mark as far as the future was concerned; for being filled with pride by coming first at Rhaphia, they [*the Egyptians*] were no longer able to endure what was prescribed for them,[36] but began to seek a leader and a personality, regarding themselves as capable of looking after themselves. And this they did in the end, not long after.
>
> (Polyb. 5. 107, Austin 225 *a*)

In 217 it had been necessary to recruit native Egyptians into the army in large numbers for the first time, in order to repulse Antiochos at the battle of Rhaphia near Gaza (Polyb. 5. 63, 65, Austin 224; for the Syrian forces see Polyb. 5. 79, Austin 149). As a result, Ptolemy gained the vital city of Seleukeia-in-Pieria; the charge levelled by Polybios and Justin that he failed to exploit his victory adequately is somewhat refuted by this acquisition, and by the quantities of booty captured.[37] However, Polybios blames the recruitment of native troops for the subsequent unrest.

Certainly there were turbulent episodes in the aftermath of Rhaphia. The one to which Polybios refers is the second known rising under the Ptolemies, and it was more serious than the first. Polybios does not name the leader but appears to mention the same revolt elsewhere (5. 87; 14. 12, Austin 225 *b*). It is alluded to in the Rosetta Stone (Austin 227, BD 137, Burstein 103, *OGIS* 90; above, p. 166), where it is stated that Ptolemy V Epiphanes punished men who had been rebel leaders under his father (lines 27–8, cf. 22–3). The Polybian chronology is self-contradictory, however, and it may be that the revolt took place well after Rhaphia rather than in its immediate aftermath. Furthermore, the Rosetta Stone records that among

245	first
217 ff.	second
197/185	lower Egypt
206–186	Thebaid
*c.*165	Thebaid
131–130	Harsiesis
88–86	Thebaid

Figure 6.6 Principal revolts in Ptolemaic Egypt.

the targets for the rebels' anger were native temples; perhaps they saw the priests as collaborators with the foreign ruler.[38]

On the other hand, the reign of Ptolemy IV has been reassessed as a time when Egypt's overseas influence was successfully maintained;[39] and the Ptolemies continued to reign for nearly two centuries more, considerably longer than their rivals. The causal link between the battle of Rhaphia and the unrest in Egypt is not strong. There is much else in the history of Ptolemaic Egypt in the intervening years, starting with a brief examination of the purposes of the kings' pursuit of overseas territories during the century after Alexander's death.

Ptolemaic ambitions

There was a Ptolemaic naval base on the island of Thera; more surprisingly, perhaps, others are to be found even on the Greek mainland, at Methana on the Saronic gulf (only about twenty-five miles from the Macedonian stronghold of Piraeus), on the island of Keos near Attica, and at Maroneia in northern Greece. Other possessions included Samos, Kos, and Cyprus. Itanos in eastern Crete was Ptolemaic from the time of the Chremonidean war (the town honoured Ptolemy III in c.246: Austin 267, Syll.[3] 463),[40] while other Cretan towns such as Gortyn enjoyed close diplomatic ties with Alexandria. A Ptolemaic enclave on the mainland opposite Samothrace brought the governor into contact with that island polis in the reign of Ptolemy III (Austin 269, Syll.[3] 602).[41] Parts of Asia Minor were captured from the Seleukids from time to time, and inscriptions attest to different levels of administration, and to Ptolemaic efforts to sustain a presence in the face of Seleukid opposition (Austin 270, BD 21, Burstein 95, RC 14; Austin 271, Burstein 100, OGIS 55; Austin 272, RC 30; Austin 273).[42] We have seen how successive Ptolemies strove to keep hold of parts of Syria, which seems odd only if one views Egypt as a self-contained geographical entity with secure natural frontiers.

Polybios is a key text:

> Because they ruled the territories of Koile Syria and Cyprus the earlier Ptolemies had always been able to put pressure on the kings of Syria both by sea and by land. Their sphere of control included the principal cities, fortresses, and harbours all the way along the coast of the eastern Mediterranean from Pamphylia to the Hellespont and the region around Lysimacheia, which gave them a commanding influence over the islands and the smaller kingdoms of Asia Minor; while their occupation of Ainos, Maroneia, and other cities even further afield enabled them to keep an effective watch upon the affairs of Thrace and Macedonia. Since they had extended their power to such remote regions and had long ago established such a

far-flung system of client states to protect them, the kings of Egypt had never felt anxiety concerning their rule at home, but had naturally attached great importance to the handling of foreign affairs.

(Polyb. 5. 34, Austin 223)

He is only one observer, he is not contemporary, and we expect him as an Achaean to be prejudiced against kings, particularly of Macedonian descent. He is probably close to the truth, however, in giving a plurality of reasons: to pressurize the Seleukids, to keep an eye on Macedonia, to ensure security, and (implicitly) to accumulate and wield power. It is a realistic amalgam of active and reactive strategies.

Much has been written in an often sterile debate about whether Ptolemy I and his successors coveted the whole of Alexander's empire (as, it is claimed, did Antigonos and Demetrios; cf. pp. 43–4; for Seleukos, see p. 287). A corollary of this is to ask whether the Macedonian kings or Seleukids had such an ambition. Even if the answer to any of these questions is affirmative, it is too simple to call Ptolemaic aggression 'defensive imperialism', as if it was a series of pre-emptive strikes aimed at preventing other powers expanding into the Aegean and eastern Mediterranean.

It seems unlikely that any such principle as a 'balance of power' was consciously observed.[43] Deterrence in the modern sense, too, is probably not in question. Troops were for action, and they expected regular rewards of booty and land. The king also had good reasons besides defence for displaying his strength: he had to prove himself as war leader and defender of the people; this may explain why at least four of the Syrian wars follow closely upon the accession of a Ptolemaic or Seleukid king. The creation of a naval empire was not merely a pre-emptive initiative, it was a necessary response to the demands made by the role of king, and to the power of Macedonian and Seleukid navies.

In any period, no ruler could hope to control Egypt without a line of forward defence. Cyprus was vital for controlling the sea approaches, as it had been in the fourth century and for Alexander.[44] In addition, valuable commodities for the maintenance of a navy and army – notably metals, timber, and pitch – could not be found in Egypt, or not in sufficient quantities, but were readily available in Koile Syria, Lebanon, and Cyprus. Cyprus could provide copious quantities of grain to relieve shortage in Egypt or elsewhere, as attested by the Canopus decree of 238 (p. 166), in which Ptolemy III buys wheat from it;[45] the Troödos mountains were a source of timber, and the copper ores of the foothills had been exploited for millennia. A military official with responsibility for the mines of the island was honoured by the *koinon* of the Cypriot *poleis* in the late second or early first century (*OGIS* 165). The island's silver deposits were probably exploited, too, to provide bullion for coins.

Strategically and economically Koile Syria, Cyprus, and Cyrene combined to perform a key role in preserving Ptolemaic power. They were administered in similar ways and belonged to the Ptolemaic currency sphere; political inter-ests preceded commercial, as was bound to be the case given the absence of a powerful export motive in ancient states. In the first place, the Ptolemies had an interest in assuring a continuous supply of key commod-ities not readily available in Egypt; this, indeed, was also a prime motivation in managing the internal economy, which alone could provide the revenues to pay for those commodities and sustain the military structures with which to ensure access to them. A second motive was political: the maintenance of Ptolemaic naval power in the eastern Mediterranean and Aegean was a vital strategic tool for containing Macedonia and preventing an Antigonid–Seleukid axis being formed against Egypt. Third, a show of power in Greek areas, including Macedonian areas of influence, like patronage of Greek culture in Alexandria, demonstrated the Greekness of Egypt and displayed the kings' commitment to Greek culture and tradition, justifying their right to a place in the Greek cultural orbit.

Until Rhaphia, Ptolemaic power extended far outside Egypt; it would not always do so again. The periods in the second and first centuries when Cyprus was not in Ptolemaic hands, and eventually the permanent loss of Cyprus and Cyrene in the first century, were major blows to the system, though the kingdom was still powerful throughout the second century.

Problems of the dynasty, 217–30 BC

Much of the recorded history of Ptolemaic Egypt consists of repetitious dynastic scandals and revolts, and needs to be balanced by the documentary evidence of inscriptions and papyri. Such a presentation in the literary sources does at least illustrate, among other things, the power of outside events to disrupt Egypt.

Even if Rhaphia did not immediately lead to wild unrest in Egypt, it seems that the generation after Philopator's accession witnessed the begin-nings of destabilization. Whereas the first revolt, early in Euergetes I's reign (p. 203), had led to no permanent disruption visible to us, native *anachoresis* now became increasingly frequent, and there were secessions in upper Egypt and Cyrene and disputes between rival claimants to the throne. In 205, late in Philopator's reign, an Egyptian leader whose name is probably to be transliterated as Haronnophris was crowned pharaoh at Thebes in the third attested revolt.[46]

Ptolemy IV was murdered by Sosibios and Agathokles. They tried to hold on to power under the young Ptolemy V Epiphanes ('the (God) Manifest', r. 205–180), and procured the murder of the queen mother, Arsinoë III (Polyb. 15. 25. 3–18, Austin 226). Sosibios, however, appears to have died shortly after Arsinoë, while Agathokles and his mother Oinanthe were lynched by the people of Alexandria, where Arsinoë had been popular. Polybios, while claiming, no doubt justly, to eschew extremes of sensationalism, nevertheless describes the gory scene vividly and at impassioned length (15. 26–36); its culmination suggests that he is far from unprejudiced about Egypt, be it Greek or native:

> A little later, first Agathokles appeared in chains. As soon as he came in, some people ran up and promptly stabbed him, doing the work not of enemies but of well-wishers: for they were thus responsible for his not meeting the mode of destruction he deserved. After him was brought Nikon [*a relative*], then Agathokleia [*Agathokles' sister, Ptolemy's mistress*] naked with her sisters, and succeeding upon these all their relatives. After the rest, they dragged Oinanthe from the Thesmophorion and came into the stadium, bringing her naked on a horse. All of them [*Agathokles and his relatives*] having been handed over together to the rabble, some people began to bite, others to stab, and others again to cut out their eyes. Each time one of them fell they would tear apart their limbs, until they had mutilated them all; for there is a terrible savagery in the people who live in Egypt when they feel angry passions.
>
> (Polyb. 15. 33. 6–10)

The early part of Epiphanes' reign continued to be troubled. Most of the Aegean and Asia Minor possessions were immediately lost to Seleukid and Macedonian aggression. Possibly under the terms of a secret agreement which he is alleged to have made with Philip V (Polyb. 15. 20, Austin 152), Antiochos III seized Koile Syria in 201–200 in the fifth Syrian war.[47] Epiphanes, guided by his adviser Aristomenes, ceded the territory and in 193 married Kleopatra I, daughter of Antiochos.[48] He matured into an effective ruler, putting down native revolts and a rebellion in upper Egypt. This event, or series of events, the fourth such revolt known in Ptolemaic Egypt, extended from perhaps 197 to 185 and included a siege by the king of the town of Lykopolis in the Delta. In Upper Egypt, Haronnophris was succeeded by Chaonnophris, who was not defeated until 186.[49]

About now, the Rhodians began to replace Egypt as the leading naval power in the Aegean and eastern Mediterranean. Under the terms of the peace of Apameia (188), which ended Rome's war with Antiochos III, they were granted control over parts of Asia Minor and effective power at sea.

Ptolemy V's son Ptolemy VI Philometor ('the Mother-loving', r. 180–145) tried to recapture Koile Syria in an all too well-signalled attack in late 170 or early 169. He provoked a spectacular response from his uncle Antiochos IV, who invaded Egypt in the sixth Syrian war (Fig. 6.4) and won a conclusive battle at Pelousion, seizing Cyprus and the whole of Egypt except Alexandria. Scholars disagree as to whether Antiochos was now crowned pharaoh or only instituted a protectorate in his nephew's name with himself as guardian.[50] In 168 Antiochos invaded again to besiege Alexandria, but in

July the Roman commander Gaius Popillius Laenas compelled him to abandon the invasion and give up Cyprus (for details see p. 292). The date of his departure is known from two Demotic ostraka in the so-called archive of Hor. The first carries a 'prophecy' of the king's departure (written after the event); in the first section or addresses Philometor directly:

> From Hor the scribe, a man of the town of Isis, lady of the cavern, the great goddess, in the nome of Sebennytos. The dream which told to me of the safety of Alexandria (and) the journeyings of 3tyks [*Antiochos*], namely that he would go by sail from Egypt by Year 2, Paoni, final day [*30 July 168*]. I reported the said matter (to) Hrynys [*Hellenios or Eirenaios?*], who was *stratêgos*, (in) Year 2, Paoni, day 11. Gryn3 [*Kleôn*], the agent of 3tyks, had not yet left Memphis. (But) the said matters were revealed immediately. He did not speak of them further, (but) he sent in the hour a letter. I gave it to the Pharaohs in the Great Serapeion which is in Alexandria, in Year 2, Epeiph, final day [*29 Aug. 168*]. For every matter which refers to this was compensation for you (at) the time in question (for) that which concerns me, namely, the greatness towards that which concerns the gods (in) your heart. I brought it before you, for I came to Alexandria with Tytts [*Diodotos?*] the *strategos*, namely [...]
>
> (Austin 165)[51]

(The characters *3* and *3* in the transcribed names represent a glottal stop in Egyptian.) The second ostrakon proclaims that Antiochos did leave on the day foretold.

Despite the possible implication of Antiochos's invasion that Egypt could no longer look after itself, the later part of Philometor's reign is a time when Egyptian power overseas is being reasserted. One sign of this is the restoration of a Ptolemaic garrison at Itanos in Crete in or after 163.[52] At this date the Romans do not seek to neutralize Egypt but to maintain it as a counterweight to Syria.

At the time of the invasion, the kingship was shared between the three children of Ptolemy V: Ptolemy VI Philometor, already king since 180; his brother, the long-lived Ptolemy VIII Euergetes II (r. 170–163, 145–116; nicknamed Physkon, see below); and their sister Kleopatra II (r. 170–145).[53] The two brothers were intense rivals and each sought support from Rome, Philometor eventually winning the senate's favour. Polybios astutely comments that:

> decisions of this kind are now very frequent with the Romans; they rely on the mistakes of others to increase and secure their own

empire in a statesmanlike way, by doing favours and appearing to confer benefactions on the offenders.

(31. 10, Austin 229)

Through an alliance with Pergamon, Philometor was able to meddle in the Seleukid royal succession – the royal families were related – and to capture Koile Syria in 147, only for it to be lost following his unexpected death two years later.

The period of co-rule in the 160s witnessed the fifth identified native rising. From about 165 the co-rulers at the time (Philometor, Euergetes II, and Kleopatra II) faced renewed unrest on the part of the Egyptian population. A certain Dionysios Petosarapis, one of the Friends of Philometor, led a futile revolt; when it went badly, he tried to mobilize native support (Diod. 31, fr. 15 a, cf. 17 b; Austin 228). Several papyri and two ostraka of the years around 160 allude to damage and casualties caused by rebels.[54]

Ptolemy VIII Euergetes II's first period of co-rule ended in 163. In 155, after an alleged attempt on his life, he made a will by which he left Egypt to the Romans if he should die without an heir (Austin 230, BD 43, Burstein 104);[55] It is the first known occurrence of such a practice, but like later instances it was probably intended only as a deterrent to assassination and was not activated.

In 145 Euergetes was ruling Cyrene when he was brought back to be king. Straightaway he murdered Ptolemy VII Eupator ('of the Good Father', r. 145), the child of his own elder brother Philometor by their younger sister Kleopatra, and married the doubly bereaved queen himself. (Notoriously, he also banished the intellectuals from Alexandria.) Later he additionally took as joint wife Philometor's daughter, his own niece, Kleopatra III (r. 116–101).[56] Such incestuous dealings, combined with Euergetes' stoutness, seem to have brought the monarchy into disrepute among Greeks, who nicknamed him Physkon ('Potbelly'). The surviving sources, such as Polybios, Diodoros, and fragmentary later writers, do not provide a full history, but after a power-struggle between the Kleopatras – the younger being niece, sister-in-law, and most importantly daughter to the elder – civil war followed in 132, Euergetes taking the part of the younger woman, his niece, stepdaughter, and co-wife. Dynastic strife was to remain a feature of Egyptian life for decades, with the Romans and the Alexandrian Greeks often playing king- or queenmakers; but on this occasion the king and his younger wife seem to have gained the upper hand within three years.

Less than a generation had passed since the previous known native rising when the Thebaid, its old religious centres protected by their distance from Alexandria, was again the scene of nationalistic protests. The revolt of Harsiesis (131–130), the sixth such attested, coincided with the war between Euergetes and Kleopatra II and is notable for its leader's being the last Egyptian to be elevated to 'pharaoh'. About now, the *polis* of Euergetis was founded to secure the southern frontier (133/2), and new troops were settled at Kerkeosiris in the Faiyum (130/29).[57] Other attestations of local troubles indicate a weakening of control from the centre; but while it is easy to portray the second century as a time of chaos, we should not exaggerate the degree to which remote dynastic problems may have affected everyday life.

The three combatants were reconciled in 124 and issued an amnesty decree in 118. This has been called 'almost the last major Greek papyrus document of the Ptolemies',[58] and is preserved on a papyrus written at Kerkeosiris by Menches (for whom see pp. 222–3). In this extract the spirit of reconciliation reflects the pharaonic tradition of *philanthrôpa* (benefactions):

> [King] Ptolemy and Queen Kleopatra his sister [and Queen] Kleopatra his wife grant an amnesty to all their subjects [in] the [kingdom], for involuntary and voluntary offences, [accusations, condemnations], and suits of all kinds up to the 9th of [Pharmouthi in the 52nd] year, except for [those] guilty of wilful [homicide] and sacrilege. They have also decreed that those who have fled [because they were charged] with brigandage and other offences shall return to [their homes], resume their former occupations, [and recover those] of their belongings [which were seized] for [these reasons] but which [have] not yet been sold. And [they remit to all] the arrears [for the] period [up to the] 50th year, in respect of taxes in kind and [money taxes] except for hereditary lessees who have provided a security.
>
> (Austin 231, BD 45, *P. Tebt.* 5)

There follows a long enumeration of different professions and social groups, from cleruchs to prophets, keepers of the granaries, peasants, weavers, and so on. The text combines generous provisions for debtors and workers in productive crafts with renewed concessions to temples and cleruchs, and attempts to set controls upon oppressive administration, which may, however, have been honoured in the breach.[59]

Euergetes II's death in 116 led to further strain between the two queens, who attempted to rule jointly. Next, Kleopatra III ruled with Ptolemy IX Soter II (r. 116–107, 88–81), known as Lathyros ('the Chickpea'), who may have been a son of Kleopatra II (rather than of Kleopatra III, as the sources have it). Our understanding of events in this period is hampered by often tendentious later writings. Pausanias, for example (1. 9. 1–3), presents the history of Ptolemaic Egypt as a moral drama dominated by the royal protagonists. Such authors seem unaware of the wider causes and consequences, which may have included administrative difficulties in the Faiyum and elsewhere.

In 107 Soter II was ousted by his half-brother (or brother), Kleopatra III's son Ptolemy X Alexander (I) (r. 107–96), who had been in charge of Cyprus. Soter now took over Cyprus, which thereby became detached from the kingdom, with a foreseeable impact on Egyptian revenues. Previously he had been ruling Cyrene; now it was given to an illegitimate son of Euergetes II, Ptolemy Apion. These changes of abode are more than the latest episode in a confusing narrative, for the eventual deaths of the two men changed the geopolitics of the eastern Mediterranean. In 96 Apion died and left his province to Rome; Alexander I did the same with Egypt and Cyprus.[60] To leave one's kingdom, or territory, to a non-Egyptian power was apparently preferable to prolonging dynastic strife; the precedent had been set by Ptolemy VIII in 155 (above), and perhaps unintendedly actualized in the case of Attalos III of Pergamon in 133 (p. 318), and it was better to leave it to Rome than to Syria. In the event the Romans did not rush to take up the legacy – Cyrene was claimed in 75/4, Cyprus not until 58–56 – but they exploited their now legitimate interest in Egypt and its possessions to manipulate the situation to their advantage.

Alexander allegedly killed his mother in 101, placing on the throne as his consort his niece, Soter II's daughter Kleopatra Berenike III.[61] When the Alexandrians deposed them both in 88, Soter returned once more and reigned with his now popular daughter (but did not necessarily marry her; father–daughter incest has pharaonic parallels but is unknown among the Ptolemies).[62] As on previous occasions, dynastic instability may have been a factor in Egyptian unrest, since in 88–86 another major rising took place, the seventh and last attested.[63] Although he dealt vigorously with the rebels, Soter showed greater sensitivity than Alexander through his concern for Egyptian cults.

The visit by the Roman general Lucullus in 87/6 may have made the Romans more aware of Egypt's tempting wealth. Only a few years later, when Soter II died, they did not hesitate to call the tune, installing Ptolemy XI Alexander II (r. 80), a son of Alexander I who had been living in exile at Rome. In keeping with recent practice he first married, then got rid of his late father's niece and wife – his own cousin and stepmother. Once again, however, public opinion (the more violent element) had a role: within three weeks he was lynched, which may have had as much to do with the part the Romans played in his elevation as with his domestic activities.

The last adult male Ptolemy to ascend the throne, Soter II's son Ptolemy XII, known as Neos Dionysos ('the New Dionysos') or Auletes ('the Oboist'; r. 80–58, 55–51) was brought back from Syria. (In 103 Kleopatra III had sent him to safety in Kos – showing surprising disinterestedness, if he was in fact Kleopatra II's son, not hers.) He had no option but to court the Romans, for example by sending gifts and supplies to Pompey during his campaigns in the Levant in 64/3, and later by paying to be recognized (in 59) as their ally. Like Euergetes II and Soter II, Auletes seems to have played a sensible hand inside Egypt by endowing many native temples. He fell foul of Roman politics, however, when the tribune Clodius proposed annexing Cyprus for the benefit of the Roman people, probably to support his grain handout scheme;[64] the prospect of losing Cyprus, Cyrene having gone the same way seventeen years earlier, provoked hostility to Auletes in Alexandria. He was deposed in favour of his daughter Berenike IV (r. 58–55), who ruled initially with her sister Kleopatra VI Tryphaina II,[65] then with her husband Archelaos (r. 56–55). The Romans, however, restored their compliant client after three years, and many Roman soldiers stayed on in Egypt for the first time.

Popular hostility in Alexandria to things Roman made Auletes' life difficult, and his reign is judged a time of poor government; but the strong Kleopatra VII (r. 51–30) proved to have her father's sure touch in dealing with the temples. She was also the first of the dynasty to speak Egyptian (Plutarch, *Antony*, 27). She was aged just 17 when she acceded with her 10-year-old brother (and husband) Ptolemy XIII (r. 51–47), who drowned during Caesar and Kleopatra's war against the nationalists; later she reigned with another brother, Ptolemy XIV (r. 47–44), as her consort, whose death she procured. She attempted to exploit to Egypt's advantage the political situation during the decades of Roman civil wars, and nearly succeeded. Her relationship with Julius Caesar in the 40s brought her not only Cyprus but also a son, known as Ptolemy XV Caesar (b. 47, r. 36–30) and nicknamed Caesarion (Kaisariôn, Little Caesar). Her dealings with Mark Antony in the 30s are too well known to detail here. At times it seemed as if the centre of the Roman world might shift east; but Caesar's heir Octavian defeated Antony and Kleopatra's naval forces off Actium on the west coast of Greece (31 BC). After he captured Alexandria, her pride left her no choice but suicide (on 12 August 30).[66]

Egypt finally became a Roman province, sixty-six years after Ptolemy X willed it to Rome. Pergamon had been Roman for a century; Pompey in the 60s, like a new Alexander, had redrawn the map of the eastern Mediterranean; only a few minor kingdoms in Asia Minor now remained (Pontos, Phrygia, Cappadocia). Though Egypt held out for much longer than the mighty Seleukid and Macedonian monarchies, and was not the powerless phantom that is sometimes portrayed, it was perhaps precisely its relative weakness that stayed the Roman hand. Philip V and Antiochos III could be represented as threats to Rome, and incurred military defeat; Egypt was not a threat, and Rome had supported it in order to nullify danger from Syria.

Greeks and Macedonians in Egypt

The position of the ruling Greeks and Macedonians *vis-à-vis* the Egyptian and other non-Greek inhabitants is different in certain respects from their position in other parts of the world; they formed a settler class as in Asia, but whereas in old Greece and the Seleukid territories Greek cities were numerous, in Egypt they were few. The old Greek port of Naukratis in the Delta, reorganized on the site of an earlier Greek foundation of the archaic period, remained important, but was overshadowed by Alexander's new capital. Various cities were renamed or refounded under a Greek name, but apart from Alexandria only one Greek foundation is recorded. Ptolemaïs Hermiou (or Ptolemaïs of the Thebaid) in upper Egypt was created by Ptolemy I on the site of an Egyptian village on the left bank of the Nile, and was perhaps intended as a counterweight to Egyptian Thebes (Austin 233, *OGIS* 48, is a decree of the city). Other foundations are known, such as Arsinoë, Berenike (p. 194), Philotera, and Alexandria Nesos. Ptolemaïs Theron (of the Beasts) was established on the east coast allegedly for the purpose of facilitating elephant hunts (Strabo, 16. 4. 7 (770)). (For Ptolemy II's interest in war elephants and exotic snakes, see Diod. 3. 36–7, Austin 278; for a dedication by elephant hunters under Ptolemy IV, at an unknown location, see Austin 279, *OGIS* 86.) Ptolemaïs Hermiou is the only substantial *polis* among these, enjoying formal autonomy and having the standard Greek institutions of *prytaneis*, *boulê*, and popular assembly, though its *prytaneis* were simultaneously holders of royal appointments, such as *epistratêgos* (additional general) of the Thebaid.[67]

Alexandria

The distinction between Alexandria (*Alexandreia*) as a Greek capital and its Egyptian setting may have been enshrined in official terminology, since documents of the Roman period refer to it as Alexandria-by-Egypt. Arrian describes how Alexander founded it, in terms which implausibly suggest an element of chance or whim, and eulogy, too:

> Alexander came to Kanobos, sailed round Lake Mareotis, and landed on the site of the present city of Alexandria, which is called after himself. The site seemed to him to be a most favourable one for the foundation of a city, and he thought that it would be prosperous. He was therefore seized with a longing for the task, and marked out himself the main parts of the city, the location of the agora, how many sanctuaries there should be and of which gods, those of Greek gods and of Egyptian Isis, and the course of the city-wall. He offered sacrifice over the plan, and the omens appeared favourable.
>
> (Arr. *Anab.* 3. 1, Austin 7 *a*)

Plutarch confirms that Alexander wished to found a city that would be 'large and populous'; he chose the site following a dream, and his advisers believed it 'would abound in resources and would sustain men from every nation' (*Alex.* 26, Austin 7 *b*). These statements need not be the product of hindsight; the site was an excellent one with natural harbours both on the seaward side and on Lake Mareotis. Like his successors, Alexander knew the value of cities as creators and gatherers of wealth.

The physical character of the city is less well known, for it has been continuously inhabited since its foundation; but the ancient layout can be traced in part from the modern street-plan, and we have a description by Strabo covering several pages (17. 1. 6–10 (791–5); part in Austin 232).[68] He admires the scale and depth of the harbour (a natural double harbour, improved by Ptolemy I), the lighthouse built on the island of Pharos (from which the architectural form took its name) by Sostratos of Knidos (completed c.280), the natural advantages of the site (resulting in a great inflow of wealth by land and sea), and the purity of the air.

> The whole city is criss-crossed with streets suitable for the traffic of horses and carriages, and by two that are very wide, being more than 1 *plethron* (30 m) in breadth; these intersect each other at right angles. The city has magnificent public precincts and the royal palaces, which cover one-quarter or even one-third of the entire city area. For just as each of the kings would, from a love of splendour, add some ornament to the public monuments, so he would provide himself at his own expense with a residence in addition to those already standing ... All, however, are connected with each other and with the harbour, even those that lie outside it.
>
> (Strabo, 17. 1. 8 (793), Austin 232)

He continues with a description of the Mouseion (see p. 241). Putting together the fragmentary archaeology with Strabo's description, something resembling the ancient city plan can be recovered (Fig. 6.7). The basic element was a squarish block of 330 by 278 metres, with an area reserved for a 'royal quarter', and its plan has been compared with that of Pella in Macedonia.[69]

Diodoros describes the Alexandria of his day as the largest city in the world (17. 52. 6), and states that its free inhabitants number three hundred thousand. If this included women but not slaves, or women but not military taxpayers, a total urban population of 400,000 to 500,000 seems likely, compared to the figure of seven million which Diodoros gives for the rest of Egypt 'in olden times' (that is, under the Ptolemies; 1. 31. 6–8).[70] The population had a different make-up from that of Egypt as a whole. Besides the many Greeks who emigrated in search of prosperity and city amenities, particularly in the half-century following the city's foundation, there were many Egyptians and Jews (many of the latter, apparently, originally prisoners of war). Citizenship was open only to Macedonians and Greeks, who were classified into demes on the model of Athens; they had a *boulê*, *prytaneis*, and assembly, though there is almost no evidence for the actual operation of these institutions, which may have been abolished in time.[71]

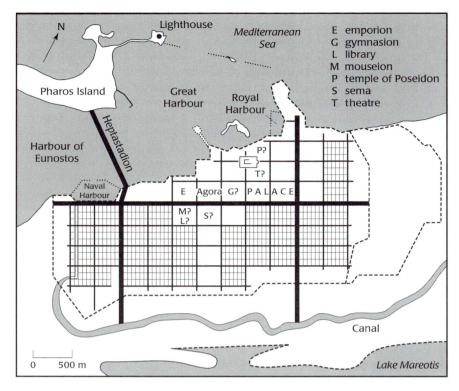

N

Lighthouse

Mediterranean
Sea

E emporion
G gymnasion
L library
M mouseion
P temple of Poseidon
S sema
T theatre

Pharos Island

Great
Harbour

Royal
Harbour

Harbour of
Eunostos

Heptastadion

Naval
Harbour

P?

C

T?

E Agora G? P A L A C E

M?
L?

S?

Canal

0   500 m

Lake Mareotis

Figure 6.7   Alexandria. (Based on Hoepfner and Schwandner, *Haus und Stadt*, fig. 225 opp. p. 238.)

The chôra

From 313 BC Alexandria represented the political capital of Egypt, as Memphis represented the religious centre.[72] Outside Alexandria the Ptolemies did not found cities, as the Seleukids did in Asia. The Nile valley and Delta had an ancient network of villages and roads, while among the existing cities were some that had at various times been capitals: Thebes, Memphis, and Saïs. The ancient provinces, nomes (*nomoi*) in Greek terminology, were retained, each being administered by a general (*strategos*); despite his title, a nomarch (*nomarchês*) was a man responsible for irrigation and reclamation projects under Ptolemies II and III, at least in the Faiyum. These men were assisted by *myriarouroi*, 'ten-thousand-*aroura* men', each of whom oversaw 2,500 hectares. Beneath the *strategos* were the royal scribes, then came the village scribe (*kômogrammateus*) or village officer (*kômarchês*, komarch); these men usually carried Egyptian names, though it is doubtful whether a name is a reliable indicator of ethnic identity. Many people used

216

two names, and in some professions it appears they employed whichever was felt more appropriate.[73]

During the later third century an intermediate level was inserted, the district or *toparchia* (a subdivision of a nome) under a *toparchês*. In parallel with these offices, a new financial hierarchy was imposed, comprising the *dioiketes* and the financial officer of each nome (*oikonomos*) with his staff. In addition, there was a hierarchy of collectors and auditors.

Although Greeks settled widely, we should imagine many of them living in villages rather than towns. Just as earlier pharaohs planted settlements of Greek mercenaries (such as the Ionians under Psammetichos in the sixth century: Herodotos, 2. 154), so the Ptolemies settled not only their own soldiers as a standing army, but also Greek (and Jewish) prisoners of war, on landholdings all over the country, particularly in the north. A reward in the form of land was a major inducement for Greeks abroad to sign up for military service. Though the new settlers were predominantly Greek-speakers, other nations were enrolled, such as Idumaeans from the area south of the Dead Sea and, especially in the third century, Jews. The settlers were known as cleruchs (*klêrouchoi*, cf. p. 56). At first their settlements were for life only; in a document of 239–238 BC (Austin 252, *P. Hib.* 81) the holdings of deceased cavalrymen are reclaimed by the crown. Gradually, however, their land allotments became permanent and heritable. In effect the settlers came to form a hereditary class of military reservists, facilitating government control; the system had a parallel in pre-Ptolemaic Egypt.[74] Soldiers occupying cleruchic land paid no rent, only certain taxes; those who rented royal or crown land were not exempt from whatever taxes were due on the land. A glimpse into their culture is afforded by a victor-list from a festival held in 267 BC in imitation of the Basileia ('royal festival') at Alexandria, founded recently in honour of the king's birthday (Austin 234); by holding, and commemorating, the festival the settlers proclaimed their Greekness and their loyalty to the king.[75]

Most settlers did not work the land but leased it to Egyptians; many lived as absentee landlords in Alexandria or a district capital. They could, however, be closely involved in the administration and economic exploitation of the farm. In 256 BC three men from one family, called 'Macedonians of the *epigonê*' (the meaning is uncertain), lease 100 *arourai* from the estate of Apollonios and agree to pay rent in return for seed corn and expenses (Austin 244, *P. Col.* 54). In the late second century we read of Dionysios son of Kephalas, from Tenis in the Hermopolite nome, a bilingual member of a Greek family which had become increasingly egyptianized. He and his female relatives took out loans of money and grain from other well-off soldiers and cleruchs in the area. The fact that they borrowed does not mean they were poor, for Dionysios had extensive farmland, leased from the crown, which was worked by others; probably he used the money and grain he had borrowed as capital to lend, in turn, to peasants at high rates of interest.[76] In a letter to the local *strategos* in 109/8 we see Dionysios protesting about the behaviour of a certain Admetos who, he says, is interfering with his sowing schedule:

> Therefore, as the land is in danger of going unattended and I am unable under present circumstances to take him to court over the contracts, I am forced to flee to you for refuge. I beg you, if you see fit, first and foremost to send an order to the police chief of Akoris not to allow the accused to interfere with me or my mother, and to give me guarantees [*to that effect*] in writing, until I am finished with the sowing and can settle accounts with him on all matters. If that is done, nothing of utility to the king will have been lost, and I will have been protected. Farewell.
>
> (*P. L. Bat.* 22, no. 11 = *P. Gr. Rein.* 18, lines 22–37)[77]

Dionysios draws a veil over the fact that he is several months late with repayments of a loan to Admetos, but is able to invoke a recent decree requiring crown tenants like himself not to be interfered with and distracted from their farming responsibilities.

There were social divisions among the cleruchs: the cavalry, for example, was almost exclusively Greek – or had Greek names. One man, who had hired his services to a Thracian with a Greek name, a settler 'of the first cavalry division' in the period preceding the Rhaphia campaign, complains about non-payment of his wages (13 January 218 BC):

> To King Ptolemy, greetings from Pistos son of Leontomenes, a Persian of the *epigonê*. I am wronged by Aristokrates, a Thracian, 100-*aroura* holder of the first cavalry division, one of the colonists in Autodike. For in the 3rd year, on the 8th of Audnaios, at Autodike, I [conclu]ded with him by contract [...] that I would accompany him on the military campaign, performing for him [the] services he required [...] and [bring] him back to Autodike, receiving from him as pay per month the sum agreed between ourselves. But when I performed the services [for him] and was without fault and brought him back to Autodike [...] contract, Aristokrates persists in owing me [10 drachmas] of my wages, (but) being petitioned by me he does not [render it] to me, despis[ing me because of] my weakness, but is likely to trick me. Therefore I ask you, King, to command Diophanes the *strategos* to w[rite to Pythi]ades t[he *epis*]*tatês* (that he should) send Aristokrates to him and, if the things I write are true, compel [him to] render the 10 dr. and cancel (?) the contract for me in order that I may not be tricked by him, so that through you, King, I may obtain assistance.
>
> (*P. Enteuxeis*, 119–21, no. 48)

Pistos has a Greek name and patronymic, but describes himself as a 'Persian of the *epigonê*'; the significance of this title is uncertain, but does not exclude Greek ethnic identity.[78]

Besides the cleruchs and career soldiers there was a class of prosperous non-military Greeks, many of whom started out with no wealth but made considerable fortunes. Those in the king's service received fine houses in Alexandria, sometimes large estates in Egypt, and even the revenues of towns in Asia Minor; they may have received salaries or supported themselves from whatever money they could extract from the people they were dealing with. Such a man was Kleon the royal engineer, responsible for public works in the Arsinoite nome (Faiyum), such as stone-quarrying and the upkeep of the irrigation system.[79]

A comparable case is that of Zenon, writer of one of the most famous 'archives' discovered in modern times, containing about two thousand documents and preserved at the site of his house at Philadelphia in the Faiyum, where it was discovered in the 1910s.[80] Much of his correspondence was with Apollonios, the *dioiketes* (for his title see p. 195). Having arrived from Karia and entered Ptolemy II's service in 261, five years later Zenon was put in charge of a 10,000-*aroura* (2,500 ha) estate granted to Apollonios by the king. This was clearly an exceptional post, but Zenon may not be unrepresentative of a whole class of Greek immigrants. Not all Greeks in Alexandria were well off, but for some Egypt represented an opportunity for advancement.

Separation versus integration

Further up the social scale the domination of Greek-speakers seems complete. The court was thoroughly Greek in culture, and particularly under Philadelphos and his successors no Egyptians are known to have held high office or military command (though caution is necessary in dealing with the evidence of names).[81] Active racial prejudice is hard to pin down, but a female character in the fifteenth *Idyll* of Theokritos seems to have a low opinion of natives. The poem is set in Alexandria, and depicts two women from Syracuse on their way to the festival of Adonis (cf. p. 239), who chat about their babies, the shopkeepers who cheat their husbands, the crowded streets, and the beautiful tapestries of the royal palace.

> Gods, what a crowd! How and when are we supposed to get through
> this terrible place? Ants, numberless and uncounted!
> Many good things, Ptolemy, have been done by you
> since your begetter's been with the immortals;
> no criminal now does his mischief, creeping up to someone Egyptian-
>   style,

the sort of games those bundles of deceit used to play before;
they're all just like each other, nasty tricks, all of them cursed.

(Theokritos, *Idyll* 15. 44–50)

Theokritos was a court poet, and the women he portrays are not poor since
they are accompanied by slaves. There can be no mistaking the attitude –
though we should bear in mind that Theokritos is not speaking in his own
voice but is assuming the outlook and diction of his character, a narrow-
minded Dorian woman from Syracuse; the humour may be partly at her
expense.

It would be interesting to know whether such scornful attitudes were to
be observed at lower levels of wealth. In one well-known example, a camel-
driver writes to Zenon with a complaint; presumably he employed a scribe
or interpreter to write this letter:

> You know that you left me in Syria with Krotos [*the agent of Apollonios*]
> and that I carried out all the instructions in connection with the
> camels and that I was blameless towards you. And when you
> ordered him to pay me my salary (Krotos) gave me nothing of what
> you had ordered. ... I held out for a long time waiting for you, but
> when I ran out of necessities and was unable to obtain these from
> any source, I was compelled to run away to Syria[82] to avoid dying of
> hunger....
>
> And when you sent me again to Philadelphia to Iason, and I did
> everything you ordered, for nine months now he gives me nothing
> of what you ordered, neither oil nor grain, except every two months
> when he also pays the (allowance for) clothing. And I am in distress
> summer and winter. And he tells me to accept ordinary wine for
> salary. But they have treated me with contempt because I am a
> barbarian [*i.e. non-Greek*].
>
> I therefore request you, if you please, to order them to let me
> have what is owed to me and in future to pay me regularly, so that I
> do not die of hunger because I do not know how to speak Greek
> (*hellēnizein*)....

(Austin 245, BD 114, *P. Col. Zen.* 66)

It is uncertain whether the camel-driver is Egyptian or belongs to another
ethnic group (the original editors suggested that he might be an Arab, like
other camel-drivers). Either way, the document seems to contain clear evidence for the existence of Greek prejudice against 'barbarians', since whether
or not the speaker's particular claims were true he must presumably believe
that his employer will recognize a legitimate ground of appeal. The last
sentence indicates that there could be practical disadvantages in not
knowing Greek.

Sometimes we see the relationship from the other side. In the second century a certain Ptolemaios, Macedonian by descent and a 'detainee'[83] in the Serapieion at Memphis (a temple staffed mainly by Egyptian priests), sends the latest in a long series of complaints to the local *strategos* about the non-Greek staff of the temple:

> As I have suffered grave injustice and my life has been frequently endangered by the temple cleaners whose names are listed below, I am taking refuge with you in the belief that in this way I would best secure justice. For on 8 Phaophi in the 21st year [*161/0* BC] they came to the Astarteion, which is in the sanctuary ... Some of them had stones in their hands and others sticks, and they tried to force their way in, in order to seize the opportunity to plunder the temple and to put me to death because I am a Greek....
>
> When these same men treated me in the same way in Phaophi of the 19th year, I immediately addressed a petition to you, but as I had no one to look after the matter further, they were let off scot-free and became even more arrogant. I therefore ask you, if you please, to order them to be brought before you, so that they may receive the punishment they deserve for all these misdeeds. Farewell.
>
> (Austin 257, BD 115, *UPZ* i. 8)[84]

Earlier, in 163/2, Ptolemaios had been attacked by the local bakers 'because I am a Greek' (*UPZ* i. 7).[85] These incidents were part of a pattern in the years after Antiochos IV's abortive invasion, when there was renewed nationalist unrest (p. 210). As with the camel-driver's complaint, however, it is not certain that the allegation of racial hatred was justified. Equally, hatred of Greeks may only partly explain events such as the burning of contracts (*P. Amherst*, ii. 30), which may also have been animated by a desire to destroy records of debt and thus sabotage the authorities. (For a case of archive-burning at Dymê in Achaea in 115 BC, punished by a Roman proconsul as likely to threaten good order and to lead to the cancellation of private debts, see Sherk 50, *Syll.*³ 684, *RDGE* 43.)

Earlier evidence may appear to suggest that Egyptian society at a local level was separate from others, Greek and non-Greek; but it must be interpreted with caution. In a study of twenty-one contracts made in 232/1 BC between Ptolemaic settlers in a (probably new) Faiyum village, it has been observed that different non-Egyptian ethnic groups — including Thracians, Jews, and Persians — were making contracts and (except for the Jews) inter-marrying, yet no Egyptian appears in any of the documents.[86] The apparent exclusion of Egyptians, however, may simply indicate that they were using their own separate legal system, not that they never made contracts with Greeks.

There is evidence of intermarriage between Greeks and Egyptians, particularly Greek men and Egyptian women, from as early as the third century and in the hinterland of Egypt. The adoption of Greek ways could be a passport to social advancement for upwardly mobile natives, and was most likely to be accomplished in places away from Greek-dominated Alexandria. It is likely that the Ptolemies, particularly from Soter on, actively promoted hellenization (or, more accurately, the use of Greek) through education and tax incentives.[87] At Egyptian Thebes, though Greeks appear to have been a strongly marked élite group of a few hundred or a few thousand families, there is evidence that from an early stage they formed close ties with the native Egyptian élite through professional connections and marriage links, which became increasingly frequent.[88] This is not to say that the Greeks were not the dominant partners; that they were so is suggested by the fact that Egyptian scribes began to learn Greek script at an early date.

Elsewhere, even in the highest circles, Greek society and Egyptian were far from being hermetically sealed off from one another. Some Egyptians attained positions of great responsibility, such as the general Nektanebo under Ptolemy I, grandson of a prominent commander of the early fourth century and great-nephew of one of the last pharaohs.[89] From the same period we have the example of the priest Manethon, who helped Ptolemy bridge the gap between Greek and Macedonian culture (pp. 11–12, 261). Some Egyptians have left their own claims to fame on their grave epitaphs, though it is possible that their achievements are inflated. Petosiris, from about the same period, who came from a rich landowning family and served as a high priest of Thoth at Hermopolis, boasts:

> I was favoured by the ruler of Egypt,
> I was loved by his courtiers.

Here again are the words of an Egyptian called Wennofer:

> I was a lover of drink, a lord of the feast day,
> It was my passion to roam the marshes,
> I spent life on earth in the King's favour;
> I was beloved of his courtiers.

Another man boasts, 'at the time of the Greeks I was consulted by the ruler of Egypt, for he loved me and knew my intentions.' Finally we may cite the grave-stele of Tathot; her grandson 'was in the king's service and transmitted reports to the magistrates; the king preferred him to his courtiers for each secret counsel in the palace'.[90] Turner doubts that such cases are anything other than exceptions;[91] but many Egyptians used Greek names in appropriate contexts, and may remain invisible to us.

One starting-point for hellenization was to be able to cite a Greek or Macedonian ancestor, as did Menches, a village scribe of the late second century. He and his father were 'Greeks born in this land' (*Hellênes enchôrioi*), which could mean Egyptians with at least one Greek ancestor, or Greeks who used Egyptian names when appointed to certain jobs; alternatively or as well, 'Hellene' may simply have denoted a privileged tax-status.[92] Menches had the Greek name Asklepiades, his father Petesouchos was also called Ammonios, and his brothers had Greek names. We may suspect that the family belonged more to the Egyptian side, but this cannot be certain. (For examples of Menches' work, see Austin 260, BD 68.)[93]

Another upward route for an Egyptian was to enter the army, particularly if he had a Greek ancestor. Lewis describes the case of Peteharsemtheus son of Panebkhounis and his relatives (mid-second century). Like his male relatives, Peteharsemtheus was a garrison soldier, which did not require him to give up his farming and business activities. Military service could elevate an Egyptian above his countrymen.[94]

The long life of Dryton of Ptolemaïs (*c*.195–*c*.112 BC), a career soldier probably of Cretan descent who served in and around Egyptian Thebes (renamed Great Diospolis or City of Zeus), is instructive. Transferred to a garrison in the Egyptian town of Pathyris around 152, he married Apollonia-Senmonthis, a woman from a hellenizing Egyptian family whose members bore dual names. That in itself suggests a family of high status, and the couple became major property-holders and lenders of money. Their descendants, however, living in an almost entirely Egyptian society, tended to use their Greek names less and less.[95]

As in earlier periods, the priestly class was set above ordinary Egyptians by virtue of its wealth and education, though it was not remote: on the contrary, priests in the agricultural regions of the country were farmers and heads of families, leasing plots of temple land and running their farms for three months out of every four; in the fourth month they served full-time in the temple. As Egyptians living for most of the time among Egyptians, they were potential representatives of their people,[96] and played an important role in the social unrest that seems increasingly to have plagued the kingdom (see below).

We have seen reasons to modify Préaux's view of Greek–Egyptian relations, that the two communities developed separately; that view itself represented a departure from earlier assumptions about cultural integration under the aegis of hellenization.[97] There seems, rather, to be evidence for the active building of multi-faceted social and economic ties from quite soon after Alexander's death – from the point, in fact, at which our papyrus evidence starts being plentiful. That is not to say that there was equality – the Graeco-Macedonian ethnic group, or groups, were clearly dominant in many respects despite being completely outnumbered by the Egyptians, perhaps by a factor of seventy to one.[98] Equally, it is not to posit harmonious relationships everywhere, still less to deny that communal relations appear to have worsened in the later third and second centuries.

Economic administration

The papyri testify to a detailed and highly interventionist administration; but it can be argued that we should not exaggerate the coherence or effectiveness of the system.[99] If that view is accepted, it has important implications for the purposes of Ptolemaic administration.

One of the most frequently cited documents is probably (though not explicitly) written by the *dioiketes* to an *oikonomos* (local administrator), telling him at some length the range of his duties and responsibilities. The subordinate is instructed to inspect

> the water-ducts which run through the fields, whether the intakes into them have the prescribed depth and whether there is sufficient space in them; the peasants are used to leading water from these to the land each of them sows. Similarly with the canals mentioned from which the intakes go into the above-mentioned water-ducts, (you must inspect) whether they are solidly made and whether the entries from the river are kept as clean as possible and whether in general they are in good condition.
>
> During your tour of inspection, try as you go about to encourage everybody and make them feel happier; you should do this not only by words, but also should any of them have a complaint against the village scribes or the komarchs about anything to do with agriculture, you should investigate the matter and as far as possible put an end to such incidents.
>
> (Austin 256, BD 85, Burstein 101)

In the remainder of the surviving portion of the document he is told to supervise the harvesting and transportation of crops, record royal and private cattle, inspect flax washeries, linen workshops, and oil-factories, audit village tax accounts, and regulate tree-planting. He will maintain records of royal properties, keep native soldiers and sailors in order, and generally prevent crime and extortion.

The document returns more than once to some of these themes, suggesting a series of additions and revisions to a standard text over many years. It reflects traditional scribal language and forms,[100] and the last section includes a formulaic exhortation to the *oikonomos* to 'behave in an orderly and upright way in your district, to avoid bad company, to steer away from all disreputable collusion, to believe that if you show yourself to be above reproach in these matters you will be held worthy of higher offices'. These sentiments are almost a literary genre. The document is probably not so much a description of what a typical *oikonomos* actually did on a day-to-day basis, as the kind of contractual letter each new incumbent would receive on being appointed. Detailed prescriptions on paper are not always carried out, and may be partly ritualized expressions of a superior's pious hopes for effective management and good shepherding of the people. It must be remembered that these officials were enormously privileged and socially remote from their subjects; for example, they were able to requisition vast amounts of produce from the local population for their own entertainment and lodging as they travelled about on business (Austin 254, of 225 BC, lists the lavish preparations for the impending visit of a *dioiketes*;[101] while *P. Tebt.* 758, of the early second century, contains an explosive rebuke from a superior to a local official, implying not only the desire to rein in excessive oppression but, at the same time, the relative freedom of action enjoyed by adminstrators at community level).[102]

Another famous document, the papyrus containing the so-called Revenue Laws of Ptolemy II, written in 259/8, might appear at first sight to reveal nothing less than a centralized, planned economy; but there are good reasons for thinking this is not the case. One section begins:

> [In the reign] of Ptolemy (II) son of Ptolemy [and his son] Ptolemy, year 27, [... the] sixth of the wine [produced ...], and from the [cleruchs] who are performing military service and who have planted their [own] holdings, and from the land [in the] Thebaid which requires special irrigation and from [... the] tenth.
> (Austin 235, BD 95, *P. Rev.*, col. 24; another part in Burstein 94)

There follow prescriptions about how the grape harvest is to be organized and monitored, how wine-growers are to register their business and sell their wine, how disputes are to be settled, and how the tithes or sixths are to be delivered to the royal treasury. Vineyards and orchards are to be registered and accounts kept. An earlier document, dated 263, was then copied onto the same papyrus:

> [King] Ptolemy (II) [to all the] generals, [cavalry commanders], officers, nomarchs, [toparchs], *oikonomoi*, checking clerks, royal [scribes], Libyarchs, and chiefs of police, greetings. We have sent to you copies of the [ordinance which] requires payment of the sixth to (Arsinoë) Philadelphos. [Take care therefore] that these instructions are carried out.
>
> (col. 37)

These texts were once thought to be evidence of a rational state economy, and were given titles accordingly; more recent interpretations emphasize that only a small part of the economy is being dealt with.[103] The king does not seek to 'manage' vine cultivation in a modern sense, only to ensure that all the taxable property and produce are declared and revenue collected. This regulation had a particular purpose: to guarantee the finances of the new cult of the deified Arsinoë Philadelphos by diverting the *apomoira*, the tax on orchards and gardens, to the cult (end of col. 33).[104] Thus there is evidence of centralization and control, but not of a planned economy. (A further point worthy of note is that cleruchs are charged a lower levy, one-tenth instead of one-sixth.) Similarly, the other section of the 'Revenue Laws' (Austin 236; BD 95, columns 38–56),[105] though it deals with oil monopolies and the revenues from them to the treasury (rather than to Arsinoë's cult), is still not evidence of a planned economy, rather of an attempt to use central organization to secure revenues.

Other documents (such as Austin 253, BD 87, of winter 239–238) concern the sowing schedule drawn up each year after the Nile flood, which laid down how much of each crop the landholder was required to sow. Regulations such as these should not be likened to the economic plans of modern states; rather, they were annual estimates to be reported upwards from the local level. As Austin remarks, 'they also show clearly the reluctance of the Egyptian peasantry to be restricted to the prescribed crops and the difficulties of enforcing the schedule in practice'.[106] In other words, production was not organized as such from the royal treasury, which for the most part was concerned only with specifying how tax revenues should be maximized and evasion prevented. Detailed methods of meeting the demand were worked out locally.

This explains why the king's officials are so often seen to write to their subordinates to urge that cultivation be maximized. Among the texts preserved in the Zenon archive is a letter from a doctor in Apollonios's service to Zenon's predecessor as estate manager:

> Artemidoros to Panakestor, greetings. As I was coming from Boubastis to Memphis, Apollonios ordered me to visit you if possible ... For he had heard that the ten thousand *arourai* were not being sown all over. He therefore instructed me to tell you to have the wood cleared away and the land irrigated, and if possible to sow the whole of the land, but if not that as much as [...] should be sown with sesame and that no part of the land should be left uncultivated.
>
> (Austin 241, *PCZ* 59816)

Like earlier rulers of Egypt, the Ptolemies continually sought to increase the amount of land under cultivation, which would have a direct impact on the amount of tax raised. A papyrus of 257 BC preserves a petition to Apollonios from Egyptian peasants brought in from another area to cultivate part of Apollonios's 10,000-*aroura* estate:

> After you gave us 1,000 *arourai* from the 10,000 and we had worked and sown these, Damis [*the local Greek nomarch*][107] took

from us 200 *arourai*, and when we objected he arrested three of our elders until he compelled them to sign an act of renunciation. And though we were willing to vacate the 1,000 *arourai* and asked him to allow us time to work and sow them, even then he would not agree but allowed the land to remain unsown.... And there are many mistakes in the 10,000 *arourai*, as there is nobody who knows anything about agriculture.

(Austin 240, P. Lond. 1954)

The core of the complaint seems to be not who should farm the land, but how it should be farmed. The Egyptians resent being asked to change traditional, presumably tried and tested, methods.

It is doubtful whether, in any meaningful way, the administrative hierarchy resembled a modern bureaucracy, as historians once believed. True, the degree of cross-checking and assiduous record-keeping is impressive. The daily correspondence of Apollonios the *dioiketes* often amounted to ten or more letters, each of which had to be logged with the date and time (Austin 247, BD 71).[108] Apollonios, the younger brother of Ptolemaios (the initiate at the Serapieion), kept a detailed record of his correspondence with officials about securing enlistment in the army; here the degree of bureaucratization is striking:[109]

From Demetrios, chief bodyguard and chief for supplies, I received four letters: one to Poseidonios, nome general, one to Ammonios, paymaster-in-chief, one to Kallistratos, secretary, and one to Dioskourides, king's friend and finance minister.... I received the order back from Ptolemaios his [Demetrios's] secretary, and the letter from Epimenes, and brought them to Isidoros, and from him I brought them to Philoxenos, and from him I brought them to Artemon, and from him to Lykos, and he made a copy of each, and I brought them to the correspondence bureau to Sarapion and from him to Eubios ...

(UPZ 14, quoted from Lewis, Greeks, 78)

It is a moot point whether or not these bureaucratic procedures were as inefficient as they seem to us. Certainly we need not take them as a sign of stifling totalitarianism, for which there is no convincing evidence; but it may be somewhat optimistic to claim, as does Lewis, that all this cross-referencing was an effective system for avoiding mistakes.[110]

At first sight, some Ptolemaic institutions appear to involve close control of the internal market. Historians often place emphasis upon the so-called royal monopolies, such as the strict control of all vegetable oil crops (dealt with in the later part of the 'Revenue Laws'), including the regulation of prices and points of sale. Mines, quarries, and salt were monopolies, while less rigid controls were exercised over linen, papyrus, and beer. Such controls were not ideological measures to create equality or economic growth in the state sector, as in the former socialist states of the twentieth century; nor were they like capitalist monopolies which seek to corner the market. As in many ancient empires, at least before the peak of Roman power, the aim was not to boost production in order to promote economic growth, nor was there a political goal: 'it was fiscal, not economic or socialistic'. Local bureaucracy, like central organization, was designed to increase the income of the state. The defence of Egypt entailed control of Cyprus and other island bases, and the capacity to intervene in Syria; revenues were essential for a strong fleet and army. Money in the treasury also allowed Ptolemy to be seen to live the proper life of a king, without which his credibility would suffer.[111]

It was for these reasons that active steps were taken to encourage trade through Alexandria and Naukratis and to build close relations with the Greek trading centre of Rhodes. Trade was also closely monitored. Not only were traders (as in modern states) required to change foreign coins for Ptolemaic currency; goods and commodities were, at least sometimes, registered in detail for tax purposes. The following extract is from a papyrus of 259 BC from the Zenon archive. A cargo imported for Apollonios the *dioiketes* is listed and taxed; the amounts on the left, in drachmas (dr.) and obols (ob.; an obol is one-sixth of a drachma), refer to an inland toll payable for transferring goods between Pelousion and Alexandria.

Valuation [at Pelousion] of the goods [imported] ... for [Apollonios] and the others on the boats captained by Patron and Herakleides. Year 27, Artemisios.

Belonging to Apollonios, [on the boat captained by] Patron:

2 dr. 3 ob.	5 [jars of] grape syrup @ 12 dr.	60 dr.
3 dr. 4 ob.	11 half-[jars] @ 4 dr.	44 dr.

And [on the boat captained by Herakleides:]

3 ob.	1 [jar] of filtered wine	12 dr.
1 dr.	[2 jars of] ordinary wine @ 3 dr.	6 dr.
[1 dr. 2 ob.]	[4 half-jars of grape syrup @] 4 dr.	16 dr.
[1 ob.; 1 dr. 3 ob.]	[1 half-jar of white oil]	30 dr.
[¼ ob.; 1 ob.]	[1 jar]	4 dr.
The 50 per cent tax on these goods, (total value)		[172 dr.]
The 50 per cent tax on this sum		86 dr.

(Austin 237, *PCZ* 59012)

The list goes on for many more paragraphs, detailing such luxuries as wine from Chios and Thasos, honey of different origins, various cheeses, dried and salt fish, wild-boar meat, Samian earth (a clay used in fulling), nuts from Pontos and elsewhere, a variety of other specialized foodstuffs, and even a large quantity of pure wool. Clearly this is trade and consumption at the luxury end of the market, bringing the kind of delicatessen fare that may have been demanded by Greeks in Alexandria and those in the upper echelons of the administration. Even though the goods are imported for a Ptolemaic official, contributions to the treasury under various headings are levied at very high rates, totalling over 1,300 drachmas.

Some observers have called the encouragement of trade 'mercantilism', but that term is more appropriate to early modern states. All ancient statesmen knew that a lively harbour makes a wealthy city, and it is true that the Ptolemies took measures to increase agricultural production; but these things were done (as far as we can tell) not to push exports into new, developing markets but, again, to increase revenue, this time from taxes on the growing trade in the port. An additional concern of the kings was to ensure the food supply of Alexandria and the availability of high-quality commodities for the Greek and Macedonian population.

The closed coinage system was probably not aimed at controlling the money supply, guarding against a negative balance of trade, or preventing fluctuations in exchange rates or inflation. It was, rather, both a statement of power and status and a way of ensuring a small net gain for the treasury on every transaction, since Ptolemaic coins were minted on a lighter standard than others and contained less silver. Furthermore, it now appears that the closed coinage system did not extend to the overseas possessions in Asia Minor.[112]

We should not overestimate the extent of innovation, as if 'rational', entrepreneurial Greeks came in and thoroughly modernized a stagnant, near eastern economic system. Ancient rulers rarely, if ever, sought to stimulate economic growth, at least in a modern sense, and in most respects Egypt was administered as before. For example, the entire system of collecting crops and transporting them overland or down the Nile (as in Austin 248, BD 93, a receipt from a boat captain for carrying 4,800 *artabai* of barley downriver to Alexandria)[113] was very probably a continuation of pharaonic practice, and the same is true of many other features of the economy.[114] The Ptolemies, like other monarchs, sought to maximize revenue in many ways.

On the other hand, it does appear that the early Ptolemies took steps to refine and enforce the system of taxation – itself a way of maximizing revenue. Evidence for the practical operation of tax-collecting suggests that the revised system worked well, though with varied results depending on the effectiveness of different collectors. A major step in this direction may have been the adoption of coinage even for small tax payments; a plethora of taxes, each one small-scale but together yielding huge sums, was the foundation of the economy.[115] Coinage made it easier to systematize and record payments and, no doubt, harder for individuals to avoid their obligations.

The results of Ptolemaic rule

It remains to account for the 'weakness' of the later Ptolemies. From the late third century onwards there were native revolts, sometimes associated with secessions of upper Egypt and with dynastic wars. The Aegean possessions were lost to the Rhodians or became independent. The kingdom increasingly suffered the consequences of events elsewhere. So was later Ptolemaic government oppressive? Merely inept? Was the rise of native pride after Rhaphia the main cause of decline, or are individual rulers to blame?

Polybios and others lay these problems at the door of weak kings like Philopator. For some modern commentators they are the direct result of the uncaring exploitation of Egypt and its people by Macedonian rulers and Greek settlers. Turner argues that from the start the peasants were too hard-pressed and the system inherently unstable; Walbank sums up the 'sorry tale' of Ptolemaic Egypt as a combination of 'a disastrous foreign policy, the loss of markets abroad, the wastage caused by internal unrest and civil wars, incompetent government at home, bureaucratic corruption and currency depreciation'.[116] Were the Ptolemies to blame for their own decline?

Already in the reign of Philadelphos there are signs of tensions between the Graeco-Macedonian ruling class and the native Egyptians, and as time goes by there is more and more evidence of the difficulties experienced by the state officials in running the economy. In 257 some peasants were complaining about new agricultural systems (pp. 226–7). From some time in the reign of Philadelphos we have a royal ordinance laying down what is to be done with runaway sailors (Austin 250, BD 103) and a letter from the king (Austin 249, BD 104) responding to complaints over billeting. Between 250 and 248 Zenon was short of cash, with the result that salaries and corn rations were reduced.

From early in Ptolemy III's reign (242/1) we have a memorandum from an official in the toparchy of Thebes about compulsory labour on maintaining canals and dykes. The writer uses 30 *naubia* per person (a *naubion* is a measure of volume, roughly a cubic metre) to reckon up the total available labour from all the persons liable for it, yielding a total of 32,460 *naubia*.[117] He then catalogues those persons who are either exempted or unable to perform it, in order to subtract their workloads:

the elders who guard the dams and embankments	53
the elders, the infirm, and the young	61
the inhabitants of Somphis who bury the cats	21
those assigned to the receiving measures of the state granaries	5
those who have discharged their obligations in the Pathyrite nome	15
those assigned to the fleet	2
among the Greeks	1

runaways	37
also the keepers of mummies	21
dead	7
subtract	282
whose *naubia*	8,460
this leaves as *naubia*	24,000

(*UPZ* ii. 157, Austin 251)

It is notable that in this example 37 out of a possible 1,080 persons (3.4 per cent of the potential labour force) are described as runaways.

The same period brought a major crisis in the shape of the Laodikean or third Syrian war (p. 289), from which Ptolemy III was recalled to deal with a native rising (p. 203).[118] It was during the early 230s that steps were taken to tighten up the sowing schedule (Austin 253, BD 87). All of this seems, at first sight, to be evidence of the start of economic difficulties. Yet if the economy was in some way malfunctioning, how did the kingdom hold together even as well as it did for a further two hundred years?

It is possible that the crises of the mid-third century were by their very nature temporary and were sometimes linked to the military exigencies of particular times. Even if too much surplus was being extracted through taxes and other impositions – and we have no way of knowing whether the amounts demanded were actually delivered – it need not have had 'economic' consequences, such as the breakdown of farming, let alone demographic or nutritional catastrophe; it might only result in resentment and social troubles, a shortfall in tithe collection, or both. And what would 'too much' extraction mean? There is no suggestion that increased pressure on cultivators resulted in 'over-farming', crop failure, or soil exhaustion, some of which are hard to imagine in a valley where the soil was renewed annually. It is true that people excused from paying certain taxes were often non-producers; Philadelphos exempted teachers of Greek, athletic coaches and victorious athletes, and probably artists of Dionysos (p. 163) from the salt tax, which from at least 263 was effectively a poll tax. In some circumstances registration as a Hellene ('Greek') entitled a person – whether or not they were ethnically Greek – to certain exemptions, which probably benefited a class that was already privileged. On the other hand, there were times when the salt tax itself was reduced for all payers; between 253 and 231 the rates for men and women were more than halved. There may have been a steady reduction of tax demands – which need not mean that less tax was collected, particularly from cultivators.[119]

To see the social unrest of Egypt and the military problems of the Ptolemies as the result of poor economic management is perhaps to adopt too modern a perspective. (It is also vulnerable to the counter-charge that previous rulers, including the independent pharaohs of the fourth century, had at times presided over what seems like chaos.)[120] The Ptolemies were primarily not managers but military dynasts, chiefly concerned with their own status and the defence of their territory. To look for evidence that intervention from above affected the agricultural cycle adversely – as opposed to provoking social discontent – may be to retroject analyses derived from modern capitalism and imperialism. What heavy taxation might engender was the abandonment of the land by cultivators who could not pay. This in turn would affect the amount of taxes collected.

The evidence for a deterioration in the practical management of agriculture in the second century (for example, the irrigation and drainage system) at a place like Kerkeosiris,[121] however, is not necessarily a sign of the oppressors reaping (so to speak) what they sowed. Complaints about the abuse of power by tax-collectors and others (see e.g. Austin 258, 156 BC; Austin 259, c.138 BC)[122] may, like social unrest, be as much a sign of the increasing difficulties which the authorities faced in controlling the population as of a genuine increase in injustice. It may be an example of passive, sometimes active, resistance by an increasingly assertive colonized population, rather than evidence of systemic mismanagement.

Similarly, evidence of persistent agricultural crises, such as the remarkable sequence of years from 51 to 48 that saw grain shortages, failed harvests, drought, and a low Nile flood,[123] need not signify fundamental ecological changes resulting from mismanagement; inter-annual variability is typical of Mediterranean agricultural systems. It may simply have been harder to cope with short-term changes at a time when central control was weakened.

An economic factor that had an increasing significance in the later stages of the dynasty was the power of Rome and the adverse effects of Rome's external and civil wars. The losses of Cyrene and Cyprus were blows to the Egyptian economy, but possibly no less damaging were the extravagant gifts, on several occasions totalling thousands of talents, given over several years, which were made to Rome and Roman commanders by Ptolemy XII Auletes. No doubt politically necessary, in all they exceeded an entire year's income for Egypt,[124] a figure which the contemporary observer Strabo puts at 12,500 talents (17. 1. 13 (798)).

Probably the Ptolemaic kingdom was neither a total success (what imperialistic venture is?) nor crudely oppressive. It is tempting to look for underlying causes of decline, even if it was not as swift or as total as some have thought. Some evidence of change has been outlined above. Large-scale immigration, both from Greece and elsewhere, dwindled after the early third century. Some scholars have pointed to the relative shortness of the spectacularly creative period of Alexandrian high culture (see Chapters 7 and 9), which occupied the first two or three generations after Alexander. In a new cultural and political situation, however, the predictable end of the first flush of enthusiastic innovation across a whole cultural field is not the same as the loss of creative energy, let alone of a wider socio-economic malaise. On the contrary, periods of cultural consolidation following phases of innovation (in the present case, the continuing exploration of existing literary forms and the amassing of new scientific discoveries on lines already mapped out) may be the best evidence of stable and prosperous times.

McGing has suggested that it is not possible to decide whether nationalistic sentiments or socio-economic grievances were more important in Egyptian revolts; indeed, there seem to be several factors pulling in the same direction. The nationalistic resentment of foreign rule does not account on its own for revolts when they happen. Besides the need for a strong and successful leader of a violent uprising, and sometimes the phenomenon of people in one area imitating successful actions by people elsewhere, there appears to be an opportunistic aspect, with revolts typically starting in the Thebaid at a distance from Alexandria, as and when the weakness of political authorities allows.[125] In other words, native revolts in themselves need not be evidence of increasing social discontent, rather of a general background of discontent combined with an increasing willingness to take action in response to grievances.

'Native unrest', the friction between different ethnic groups, cannot be divorced wholly from the military fortunes of the kingdom, but the mechanism by which one provoked another is not purely economic. Certainly the Egyptians who fought at Rhaphia were emboldened, and this may have a lot to do with the civil troubles in the ensuing decades; but the Egyptians, particularly the priests, the conscious guardians of tradition, were continually made aware that Egypt had had foreign rulers before – and were periodically provoked into revolt. During the fifth century, under Persian rule, the Egyptians rose up and held out from 487 to 485; they rebelled again briefly in 450; and from 404, with strong leadership, they secured freedom from Persia and remained free until the late 340s. Alexander arrived a few years later. Between 188 and 133, too, they may have taken heart from the overthrow of all the other major Greek powers (Syria, Macedonia, and Pergamon).

In the context of reinterpretations of twentieth-century empires, such as those by Edward Said, it is tempting to view difficulties in Egypt as partly the result of native resistance. Imperial subjects typically adopt a variety of stratagems, ranging from private literary expressions of resistance to outright violence; there is clear evidence of the latter, at least, from an early date. There was also a religious tradition of apocalyptic prophecy, exemplified by the 'Oracle of the Potter' from Roman Egypt (Burstein 106; the papyrus is third-century AD, the original text c.130–115 BC),[126] in which the downfall of corrupt Alexandria is foretold. We should not make too much of that particular prediction, even if we suppose it to have been made four or five centuries earlier than the date of the surviving copy; but it is part of a religious context that emphasizes the confrontation between Egyptian and foreigner.

The Ptolemies probably did not 'bleed Egypt dry'. But it may well be that, given the cultural self-awareness of Egyptians and their knowledge of their past, the agricultural system could not support their increased demands for taxation in pursuit of military ends without producing social unrest. Ptolemaic and Greek exploitation may have provoked stratagems of resistance and separatist ambitions, making the kingdom incapable of sustaining the Ptolemies' aims.

7

LITERATURE AND
SOCIAL IDENTITY

Writers in society

Greek culture gave rise to a large body of creative writing. Yet hellenistic writers have often been seen as poor relations of their classical forebears, a view fostered by the image of Alexandrian scholarship as a dry and dusty exercise in classification, and of the literature of the age as little more than inept imitations of earlier works of genius. These attitudes have now been abandoned, and scholars now recognize third- and second-century works of literature as important in their own right and no less 'classical' than the works of fifth- and fourth-century Athenians.

Unfortunately, many fewer of them survive, a fact that may lie at the heart of their undervaluation. We owe to the library of Alexandria the preservation of many classical texts which were recopied and disseminated from it. The effects of a major fire during Caesar's war against Pompey (Aulus Gellius, 7. 17. 3; Seneca, *De tranquillitate*, 9. 5; Orosius, 6. 15. 31–2) may have been offset by Antony's gift to Kleopatra of the substantial contents of the Pergamon library (Plutarch, *Ant.* 58); but disaster seems finally to have struck the main library when the palace quarter of Alexandria was destroyed during the Palmyrene occupation of the 270s AD, while its offshoot at the Serapeion fell victim to riots between pagans and Christians in AD 391.[1] To these sad losses are due many of the lamentable gaps in our knowledge of classical and hellenistic literature of all kinds.

Lack of preservation accounts for our virtual ignorance of the scholar who was reputedly the greatest poet of the early third century: Philetas (or Philitas) of Kos (b. *c.*340), tutor to the young Ptolemy II Philadelphos.[2] Later authors made him one of only two hellenistic writers in the canonical list of elegiac poets, but seem to have been much less interested in reading him than his contemporaries were, since only a few epigrams and some fragments of a prose work survive – a salutary warning about the danger of judging the significance of a writer in his own society from the fortunes of his works in after times.

Less poetry appears to have been written during the fourth century; this may be due to some change in élite society, which no longer needed or provided the same occasions for poetry, but it may be due to the taste of later generations and their choice of which poems to preserve. It is unlikely to be the result of a dearth of men and women capable of writing memorable poetry, though that impression is sometimes given in modern works. Similarly, in studying the hellenistic world we have to try to understand its writings in a social context. Writing and the performance of written works – in both prose and verse – were a social activity; therefore we would expect changes in literary output as Greek societies changed and as new purposes for writers evolved. Literature needs to be treated as a social and ideological practice, and to be examined from the points of view of who the producers and consumers were, what cultural needs it may have met, and what effects it may have had on society.

Literature is sometimes viewed, on an idealist view, as the 'informing spirit' of an age, or, on a narrowly materialist view, as something that happens outside the social order. Rather, it should be seen as part of the social order, acting upon it and being acted upon by it.[3] The very term 'literature' is, of course, problematic.[4] No single Greek word corresponds to it; there are words for different kinds of poetry, for music, rhetoric, philosophy, and history. Even with regard to the modern world it is hard to reach a definition of 'literature' that would satisfy everyone. Many would agree that the legend on a coin, or the notice in the railway station, are not (usually) to be regarded as literature, but most would accept that the works of Shakespeare are literature. Even there, however, things are not as simple as they seem; the 'literary' status attributed to certain writings, such as those of Shakespeare, may be a reflection not necessarily of any inherent quality – even if that could be objectively measured – but of the ideological and cultural purposes those works were intended to serve or were made to serve, and of the prestigious places they have been allotted within the social and political order of their day, or of our day.

A helpful definition of literature might be 'the circulated written works of a social élite, read or performed for enjoyment'. It is important, however, to define one's élite. In this book science, philosophy, and literature are treated separately, but for many practical purposes they were parts of the same set of social activities carried out by the same or similar individuals from the upper wealth-levels of society and their protégés who devoted their leisure to their chosen mode of cultural creation. With a few possible exceptions we cannot begin to see what popular writings may have been like; there may even have been an oral tradition of performed works (like the Atellan farces of republican Italy) of which no trace survives. This does not change the fact that the more élite writings have a special importance: they were circulated across the Greek world, and contributed to the formation, maintenance, dissemination, and development of a certain version of Greek culture. They were also known to Roman and later writers, who adapted them and referred to them in their own works.

'Writers' in earlier Greek times were almost invariably from the intellectual and wealth-transmitting social élite. Then, too, the boundaries between different literary genres and their practitioners were not strictly drawn. The sixth-century Athenian reformer Solon was not only a politician but a prolific poet, a successful military commander, and something of a philosopher. It is likely that no one chose to be a 'writer' as people do today; writing did not exist as a profession any more than being a politician or a sportsman. Similarly, in the fifth and fourth centuries the writers whom we still read probably possessed inherited wealth based on land-ownership, made money as military leaders, or both. As for the social background of hellenistic scholars and authors, there is little reason to suppose that things changed;[5] it is characteristic that Aristophanes of Byzantion, a Homeric scholar, was the son of a renowned mercenary commander (*Suda*, s.v.).[6]

Equally, the consumers of literature were a more or less narrowly defined élite; they saw, or may have seen, themselves as different from outsiders and their appreciation of literature as a crucial part of that difference. In classical Athens, likewise, the comedies of Aristophanes were written to be performed in front of a large audience, but that audience was, in the main, composed of a privileged group, the citizens.

This chapter will examine the new sites of literary production, and then look at how literary output may have been influenced by its imperial or colonialist context. It will consider the connection between literary writing and innovation. Were authors bound to try and write 'better' than, or differently from, their predecessors, and, if so, what was the purpose of such innovation? What is the significance of the new ways in which authors treat the apparently private or personal in what are ostensibly public writings, and how does the representation of women change? Finally, in what ways do changes in the city-state affect writing?

Sites of production

In older sites of literary output, such as Athens and other city-states of Old Greece, élite members of the community continued to write in old and new forms. In the new world, particularly in Alexandria, royal patronage gave rise to particularly interesting new forms of literature.

One result of royal patronage of authors was what is often described as 'court poetry', a famous example of which is a poem by Theokritos,[7] one of the hellenistic poets who is most widely read today. Born at Syracuse in Sicily, he moved to Alexandria around 270 but may have worked independently of the library and Mouseion (the Ptolemaic research institute). There is some internal evidence in the poems that suggests that, having failed to secure patronage from Hieron II of Syracuse, he found it at the court of

Philadelphos. His surviving poems, the *Idylls* (*eidyllia*, 'little pictures'), are mainly set in the countryside of Sicily and southern Italy, and can be regarded as the progenitors of pastoral poetry; but they do not share the prettiness of second-century pastoral poets such as Moschos and Bion, several of whose works are extant.[8] Many of the poems of Theokritos, though commonly regarded as pastoral, may be better described as bucolic ('about cowherds'; the word *boukolikos* is his, used by Thyrsis to describe his own song in Theokritos, *Idyll* 1, and by Lykidas in *Idyll* 7),[9] a term designed to convey that they have real roots in a tradition of rural song, though they also draw on earlier literary poetry. Written in a poetic form of the Doric dialect of his homeland, they appeal to that Alexandrian interest in getting a taste of the 'Other'. Theokritos makes efforts to emphasize the foreignness of his settings and characters;[10] even the herdsmen who compete in singing in several of the poems may partly be representative of a purer, older Greek way of life that appeals to the nostalgia of born-and-bred Alexandrian urbanites. One of his most memorable characters is not a human at all, but the gauche, one-eyed Cyclops, Polyphemos, victim of a distinctly anthropoid infatuation with a sea-nymph, Galatea (*Idylls* 6 and especially 11). Theokritos may be a bucolic poet, but his countryside is partly artificial, for the delectation of people for whom the Greek countryside was remote and only a memory.

Idyll 17 is not bucolic; it can fairly be described as a court poem. It praises Ptolemy II, and may have been written for a festival or a royal ceremony. Ptolemy's father sits with Alexander at the feast of the gods, as does his ancestor Herakles; his mother Berenike is the paragon of wifely virtue; signs of divine favour attended his birth on the island of Kos; he is master of wide, rich territories and the defender of his realm. Above all he is pious:

> Uniquely among men of former days
> and men whose warm tracks mark the dusty ways,
> Ptolemy has built shrines with pious care,
> proclaimed his parents gods and set them there,
> chryselephantine forms, as mankind's friends.
> On their fired altars as each season ends
> he and his consort burn fat oxen's thighs;
> she partners him in filial sacrifice.
> (Theokritos, *Idyll* 17. 121–8; cf. Austin 217)

('Chryselephantine' describes statues whose visible parts were made of gold and ivory.) The ode can be compared with other exercises in royal image-making (Chapter 3): the king must be wealthy, just, pious, and a successful warrior.

Idyll 15 (quoted earlier, pp. 219–20), contains an indirect tribute to Ptolemy. At the end, the women listen to a performance of a hymn to Aphrodite which is at the same time a tribute to Philadelphos's queen and the wealth of the city:

See how Arsinoë gathers all that's good
to lull Adonis, for whose love you pined
yearlong, O many-named and many-shrined.
Beside him pots of golden myrrh are placed
and fruit fresh from the tree, the season's best;
mouth-watering dishes; every kind of meat,
elaborate cakes and puddings, moist and sweet;
the world of fancies pastry-cooks devise
from honey and oil and coloured essences.
Green canopies of branches spread above,
where childish figures of the God of Love
open their wings like fledgling nightingales. ...
Let Samos and Miletos say with pride,
'Our looms have served Adonis and his bride.'
(Theokritos, *Idyll* 15. 110–27)

Nothing in such a poem can be taken as documentary, but it undoubtedly elevates Alexandria into the epitome of cosmopolitan sophistication based on imperial domination of the Aegean (perhaps here exaggerated). The rulers are depicted as pious and as the protectors of the realm.

Patronage was not, however, intended only to give rise to explicit celebrations of royalty. Much investment was devoted to the Mouseion and library at Alexandria.[11] Ptolemy I and the ex-tyrant of Athens, Demetrios of Phaleron, are credited with founding the library in the Brouch(e)ion at Alexandria. Ptolemy II added a second, smaller library at the Serapieion; some regarded him as the real founder. The contents of the library, or libraries, were thought to number several hundred thousand papyrus rolls, made up in part, it was said, of books which an edict of Ptolemy V forced ships docking at Alexandria to leave behind on departure.

In the mid- and late third century the Attalid kings of Pergamon emulated the Ptolemies by building a library and attracting artists and intellectuals away from Athens and Alexandria, such as Antigonos of Karystos (a sculptor and writer), Polemon of Ilion (a writer on art), and the philosopher and Homeric scholar Krates of Mallos in Crete, who lectured at Rome in 168. The Roman writer Pliny the Elder (*HN* 13. 17) says parchment was invented at Pergamon (in later Greek it was *pergamênê*, evidently from the name of the city) as a result of Ptolemy V's edict just referred to, which had the effect, or even the intention, of obstructing the growth of Eumenes II's library. (Vellum had been used since before Herodotos (5. 58), so what happened now was either a technical improvement or simply the revival of an older fashion.)

Nor should we ignore the Macedonian court at Pella as a centre of literary patronage, particularly from the time of Antigonos Gonatas onwards. Among notable writers who lived there for a time were the didactic poet and scholar Aratos of Soloi, the epic poet Antagoras of Rhodes, the scholar and playwright Alexandros of Aitolia, and philosophers like Timon of Phleious and Menedemos of Eretria. Unusually among historians (see p. 264), Hieronymos of Kardia spent time at Pella. The Cynic philosopher Bion of Borysthenes enjoyed the patronage of an Antigonos, probably Gonatas (Diog. Laërt. 4. 46, 54); Zeno, too, received an invitation from Gonatas but declined it, sending Persaios in his place (Diog. Laërt. 7. 6). The last king of Macedonia, Perseus, possessed a notable collection of books which was captured by the Roman general Aemilius Paullus (Plut. *Aem.* 28. 6).

Other kings, too, patronized Greek intellectuals. Ariarathes V of Cappadocia (r. 163–130) is credited by Diodoros with making his kingdom 'a place of sojourn for men of culture' (31. 19. 8). Cities like Rhodes and Athens were proud of their connections with the most prestigious thinkers and writers of the day.

Libraries in the Greek world before Alexander were a rarity, if they existed at all; the sixth-century tyrants Polykrates of Samos and Peisistratos of Athens owned large collections of books, according to Athenaeus (1. 4), but this is not confirmed by other sources and may be a retrojection from hellenistic times. Strabo, in an aside from his description of north-western Asia Minor, says Aristotle 'left his own library (*bibliothêkê*) to Theophrastos … and was the first man of whom we know to collect books and teach the kings in Egypt the arrangement of a library' (13. 1. 54 (608–9)). Aristotle died in 322, so the statement is literally false (if it refers to the Ptolemies); perhaps he actually advised Alexander, or perhaps this too is an invention by someone who remembered that Plato taught the Sicilian tyrant Dionysios II, and Aristotle (supposedly) the young Alexander. It is certainly possible that Aristotle's was the most notable book collection to date – a sort of university library for researchers. (In the same passage Strabo says Aristotle's own books finished up in the town of Skepsis, and that though the Pergamene kings tried their hardest they could not get their hands on them.)[12]

The organization of the library at Alexandria is not known, but we are told the names of the librarians. These men are also authors: they include Apollonios of Rhodes the poet (librarian *c.*270–245), Eratosthenes the geographer (lived *c.*285–194), Aristophanes of Byzantion the homerist (*c.*257–180), and Aristarchos of Samothrace the literary critic (*c.*216–144). The first librarian, Zenodotos of Ephesos (*c.*325–*c.*270, librarian from *c.*284), invented the marks written over Greek vowels to show the tonal accentuation,[13] and developed a science of textual criticism based on the comparison of different manuscripts, which must previously have been almost impossible. In time the library became the main source of reliable texts of authors such as Homer, who were increasingly acknowledged to be classics.

The Mouseion is briefly described by Strabo; the basic details may be the same as in Ptolemaic times:

The Mouseion also forms part of the royal palaces; it has a covered walk, an arcade, an *exedra*, and a large house, in which is the dining-hall [*Strabo actually uses 'syssition', the Spartan word for a communal citizen mess*] of the learned men [*or 'scholarly men': philologoi*] who are members of the Mouseion. This association of men shares common property and has a priest in charge of the Mouseion, who used to be appointed by the kings but is now appointed by Caesar [*i.e. the Roman emperor*].

(Strabo, 17. 1. 8 (794), Austin 232)

In the library and Mouseion the written record of Greek culture could be assembled, listed, and classified, an operation for which philosophers like Aristotle and Theophrastos had established a pattern. This in turn made possible the growth of what is often called 'scholarship'; but it is important not to infer that the prime motive was the progress of learning. Nor should we view the library and Mouseion as important only for what they gave to later culture, or as steps on the road to modern rationality. The collection and systematization of knowledge under the patronage of the kings created a new social site for literary output, which embraced not only what we would call imaginative or creative writing but everything from local history to philosophy and 'science'.

The Mouseion gave rise to scholarly in-fighting, which the following comment by Timon, from the perspective of another royal court, is thought to describe:

In the thronging land of Egypt
there are many that are feeding,
many scribblers on papyrus
ever ceaselessly contending,
in the bird-coop of the Muses.
(Timon, *ap.* Ath. 1. 22 d)[14]

He probably refers to the rivalries and polemics that were engendered among the intellectuals working in Alexandria. Kallimachos of Cyrene wrote catalogues such as *A Table of the Rare Words and Compositions of Demokritos* and, most famously, a 120-book *Catalogue of Persons Conspicuous in Every Branch of Learning and a List of their Compositions*, a sectionally arranged inventory of all the works in the library and the lives of their authors. It was perhaps the first Greek library catalogue, and though it is lost we indirectly owe to it most of what we know about lost classical works. Aristarchos of Samothrace responded with a treatise improbably entitled *Against the Library Lists of Kallimachos*, whose contents are not hard to guess. The apparently minute nature of the new scholarship is exemplified by works such as Aristophanes of Byzantion's treatise *On Words Suspected of Not Being Used by*

241

the Early Writers or the book of Ammonios *On the Fact that There Were Not More than Two Editions of Aristarchos's Recension of the Iliad.* The degree of inter-referencing that is going on is remarkable; it is really a case of writing books about books about books. Crucially, too, the creation of a designated place where literary work of many kinds was carried out made possible an increased separation between the performance and the book. (The common-place observation that the ancients always read aloud has been challenged. Silent reading was certainly practised in classical Athens, but there may still be room for a change of emphasis in the hellenistic period, as libraries became more common and inter-textual references more self-consciously literary.)[15]

These inter-referential writings which we call works of scholarship were themselves part of literature. The same is true of the works we call scientific. Scholarship, in the sense of reviewing existing written 'knowledge' in the light of new analysis, had become a state-supported profession on a large, organized scale for the first time in the Greek world; and a literature that becomes not only internally cross-referential but also sets itself in a certain alignment with respect to the body of earlier Greek writing is a distinctive hallmark of the period. The unpicking of canonical works, supported by funding from a higher authority, was an activity that itself created, then preserved and validated, a culture – a culture perhaps in search of an identity.

Collecting all known Greek texts and classifying them was not simply a way of making Alexandria spectacular; it was to make an almost sacred claim to be the guardian and controller of Greek culture for all Greeks. One function of libraries within all the new kingdoms was to guarantee the memory of the past (cf. p. 60).[16] Moreover, if knowledge is power, then control of the discussion and dissemination of knowledge gives redoubled power, not necessarily only cultural. This aspect of appropriation and control can be detected in many areas of intellectual life (as had been the case, in different circumstances, in classical Athens). To assemble the whole of Greek written culture was also to assert a particular relationship between Greek and non-Greek peoples, between the new Macedonian monarchy in Egypt and Greek culture in general, and between a ruling élite whose forefathers had scarcely been credited with belonging to Greece and the larger mass of Greek-speakers.

It is important, however, to put this largely Ptolemaic achievement in a wider context. Modern museums have been deconstructed in their imperial and post-colonial roles,[17] and the same can be said of libraries. There is a certain correlation, in history, between the creation of empires and that of collections: consider Rome, Vienna, London, Paris. A state library can be one expression of imperial success. This is not, however, a new feature of the hellenistic empires; the earlier empires of the Near East had libraries containing not only administrative archives but collections of sacred and 'literary' texts upon which scribes worked, even comparing different versions of the same text;[18] so it may be that what we see as a distinctively Greek creation was a fusion of the philosophical culture of fourth-century Athens with an older way of assembling and controlling the written word.

The assemblage of information also coheres with a change in the relationship between oral and written culture that has been detected in the second half of the fourth century. While Greek society, even in Athens, was still predominantly oral, the need was increasingly felt to ground collective memory in texts and documentary records. One symptom of this was the decision taken by the Athenians in the 330s, at the suggestion of Lykourgos, to preserve copies of the works of Aeschylus, Euripides and Sophokles in a public place (perhaps the Metroön in the Agora) and to require all those wishing to perform the plays to use the official texts (Plut. *Lives of the Ten Orators*, 841 f).[19] It is said that Ptolemy II borrowed the originals and never returned them. That explicit piece of appropriation, and the wider effort to amalgamate the totality of literary culture, can be seen as part of an attempt to demonstrate that Egypt was part of the Greek world. Without written transmission, such a transplantation of culture would necessarily be seen as incomplete.

Tradition and innovation

Tradition: innovation. Two words that in a way encapsulate the whole position of a Ptolemy: a new dynasty with a new capital, occupying an old kingship.

Of poetry in the narrow sense, excluding drama, Tarn opines that 'Poetry, by Alexander's day, had been almost crushed to death by the weight of the great masters; none could approach them, and it was hardly worth trying.'[20] This pessimistic view presupposes that poets were trying to write as well as, or better than, earlier poets; but to leave it there would be to ignore the social context in which they wrote. Préaux has a view not very different from Tarn's: she sees hellenistic literature as operating within a closed social milieu using a dead language, the language of a social class on the defensive.[21] It is true that one of the most marked features of the literature of the period is classicism, the elevation of a limited number of earlier works and styles to 'classic' status; and it is possible to view literature as becoming timeless and ignoring the present and the city.[22] While some examples may serve to illustrate these ideas, however, they may also lead us to question them.

Many of the most famous poets of Alexandria lived in the half-century after Alexander and were migrants from other parts of the Greek world. Kallimachos (Callimachus) of Cyrene (*c.*305–*c.*240),[23] whom we met before, worked at the library, though he was probably not its director as was once believed, and was remembered for a scholarly feud with his pupil Apollonios of Rhodes (pp. 255–6), though there is no contemporary evidence to confirm it. The scholar can be seen in the poet. Besides systematic bibliographical catalogues, he assembled lists such as *A Collection of Marvels in All the Earth According to Localities*; yet he was the author of poems like *Aitia* or *Causes*, a 7,000-line compendium of legends about Greek history and rituals, for example *The Lock of Berenike*, which combines court flattery with a dry wit. It commemorates the dedication of a lock of hair by Ptolemy III's wife, its disappearance from the temple, and its discovery in the northern sky (it is the constellation we still call Coma Berenices) by the astronomer Konon. The largest preserved fragment, from a papyrus, reveals how the stylized elegance appropriate to a piece of court flattery is offset by the original and witty entry of the lock of hair itself as an interlocutor:

> What can we locks of hair achieve when such great mountains give way
> to iron? May the race of the Chalybes be destroyed,
> who, raising it out of the earth – evil plant! – revealed it
> first and expounded the work of hammers.
> Me, recently shorn, my sister-locks were mourning,
> and at once the sibling of Memnon the Ethiopian
> rushed in, circling his dappled wings – he, the gentle breeze,
> the horse of violet-girdled Lokrian Arsinoë –
> snatched me with his breath, and carrying me through the moist air
> set me in the bosom of Kypris.
>
> (Kallimachos, *Aitia*, fr. 110 Pfeiffer, lines 47–56)

'Mountains giving way to iron' refers to king Xerxes' canal of 481 BC in Mt. Athos; the Chalybes are a people of the Black Sea region renowned for iron-working; 'the sibling of Ethiopian Memnon' is Zephyros, the south wind; 'Lokrian', used of queen Arsinoë, is an obscure play on the site of her temple; Kypris is a regular by-name for Aphrodite, from her temple in Cyprus, the island of her birth.

Many of Kallimachos's poems are full of such learning and mythological allusion, but they are also highly original. In his surviving *Hymn to Zeus*, while the overall form and language are those of the seventh-century 'Homeric' hymns, he introduces conversational exchanges, such as the discussion of the different versions of the birth of Zeus on Mt. Ida, when the god himself intervenes to declare that 'all Cretans are liars'. Kallimachos may be attempting to satisfy more than mere antiquarian interest, and to come to terms with a more sceptical milieu than earlier poets faced. His display of learning is done with the greatest economy and artistry and, more importantly, to a purpose beyond showing off; as in the following passage, where the nymph Rhea, having given birth to Zeus in Arkadia, is searching for water in which to wash:

> But Ladon was not yet in mighty flow, nor Erymanthos
> most limpid of rivers; still without water was all

Arkadia, though to be known for full abundance of water
later. For then, when Rhea loosed her girdle,
full many oaks above ground did moist Iaon
raise, and many carts did Melas carry,
and above Karion for all its water many
the snake that cast its nest, and a man could pass
on foot above Krathis and Metope full of pebbles
thirsty, though plentiful water lay underfoot.
(Kallimachos, *Hymn* 1: *To Zeus*, lines 15–33)

Here the geographical pointers are not entertaining puzzles to solve or dusty 'allusions' to earlier works; they enrich and, as Bulloch says, 'actualize the scene with an exactness that has the same purpose as the four details with which Arcadia's dryness is illustrated (oaks, cart-roads, snake-nests, a thirsty journey)'.[24]

One newly defined genre is didactic ('instructional') poetry, chiefly represented by Aratos of Soloi (in Cilicia) and Nikandros of Kolophon. It took the old and created new literary forms which paid homage to the canon. Aratos (*c*.315–before 240), who worked at Pella, wrote a wide variety of poems but is chiefly known for those on 'scientific' themes such as the *Astrika* (*On Stars*) and *Phainomena* (his only surviving work), both dealing with astronomy and meteorology. He was following in the footsteps of the eighth-century folkloric poet of religion and agriculture, Hesiod; of the more philosophical sixth-century poets such as Xenophanes; more recently, in poetry, of Empedokles of Sicily who wrote on nature (fifth century). Aratos was not the first to write a specifically astronomical poem, but his was read and studied most widely. More genuinely informative than other similar works, his work was closely based on the prose writings of the fourth-century astronomer Eudoxos of Knidos (Chapter 9), and can possibly be seen as part of the wider intellectual agenda involving the dissemination of knowledge; but 'popularization', Bulloch's term,[25] is too strong for a poem about such a recherché subject matter written in archaic Greek.

The two surviving works of Nicander (Nikandros; third or second century) are *Alexipharmaka* and *Theriaka*, the former dealing with poisons and antidotes, the latter with poisonous animals and the cures for their bites and stings. He is more literary and less informative than Aratos, and was, perhaps surprisingly, less widely read in antiquity. Bulloch suggests his work survived precisely because of the scholarly industry provoked by its 'sheer extraordinariness and literary perversity';[26] but this analysis surely underplays the impact of the social context in which Nicander was writing.

The importance of so-called didactic poetry probably lies not in any genuinely instructional purpose or effect – one can hardly imagine any but the most bookish (and leisured) reader sitting down with his Nicander, or even the (to us) more congenial Aratos – but rather in what they imply about the readership for whom they wrote: in the case of Aratos a readership in Pella as well as Alexandria. From one viewpoint they should be grouped together with the 'scientific' authors of Alexandria, with their passion for classifying the cosmos and presenting it to a Greek audience for consumption, as Herodotos had. They are works of true literary value.

Indeed, a notable didactic poet of the third century is Eratosthenes, who besides his scientific prose works (p. 327) published some of his ideas in verse, including a 1,600-line *Hermes* dealing with cosmology and the five zones of the earth, and the much-admired elegiacs of his *Erigonê*, retelling a Dionysos myth to explain the origins of three constellations.[27] The crossover between literature and science extends to Eratosthenes' prose works, too. His researches into historical chronology from the fall of Troy to his own day were adapted by Apollodoros (*c.*180–after 120; *FGH* 244), an Athenian of the Stoic persuasion, who worked in Alexandria until the banishment of the intellectuals (145), migrated to Pergamon, and finally returned to Athens in 138 or 133. He wrote four lost books of *Chronicles* (*Chronika*) in verse; these came to supersede Eratosthenes. (The *Library* or *Bibliotheke*, a study of hero myths still widely read today, is a first- or second-century AD work falsely attributed to him.) Apollodoros was used in turn by the Christian bishop Eusebios (*c.* AD 260–339) for his detailed world history; his tables of dates survive in an Armenian translation and a Latin version by St Jerome, and form the basis of the ancient chronology we use today – an example of the indirect importance of hellenistic scholarship, aside from what it may reveal about society after Alexander. Even as technical writing, however, Eratosthenes' work must be considered as literature, and literature of a new kind.[28]

'Tradition' is another of those pregnant words, at first sight straightforward but admitting of complex distinctions. We sometimes regard tradition as a given, a model to which individuals accommodate their behaviour as closely as they can. On the other hand, some traditions do not seem to work like that. Family Christmases are an example: almost no two families in Britain conduct the festivities in precisely the same way – some open presents on Christmas Eve, others on Christmas Day; they cut the Christmas cake at different times – yet most of them would say they are having a traditional celebration. The tradition admits of almost infinite creative variation. It can allow – even demand – a good deal of inspirational freedom. To regard the back-referencing of hellenistic literature as an artificial attempt to maintain an unchanging Greekness is an over-simplification. Innovation was not dilution; Greek culture was inherently innovative. Innovation *was* the tradition. Contrary to the suggestions quoted at the start of this section, literature was not dead, or defensive, or timeless.

From another point of view, particularly as regards its social role and the importance of patronage, some kinds of hellenistic literature represent a retreat from the specialized, *polis*-based, publicly sanctioned forms of classical Athens, particularly tragedy and comedy, and a return to earlier sites of production and performance such as the ruler as patron or the private, élite dinner-party or *symposion*.

Different audiences?

Some scholars see the Alexandrian poets as writing in an ivory tower. Is this fair, and for whom were they writing?

The evidence of papyrus finds from Egypt indicates that a very wide range of poets was being read in the various Greek-speaking communities. A recent corpus contains over a thousand papyrus fragments from the last four centuries BC, containing works by no fewer than 151 named poets and 285 of unknown identity (some of whom, of course, may be identical with members of the former group).[29] Papyri bear witness to the very wide popularity (not necessarily limited to those who could read or buy books) of Homer's *Iliad* and *Odyssey*, probably the literary works most widely read in Egypt; they also show the close standardization of the Homeric texts by the mid-second century, probably under the influence of Aristarchos of Samothrace.[30] A study of Roman papyri from Oxyrhynchos and elsewhere suggests that Herodotos was also widely read, particularly the parts of his book covering early Greek history and the Ionian Revolt.[31] Nothing is known about the organization of the book trade, but we are entitled to assume that the presence of Greek and Macedonian settlers created a demand for reading material, not limited to what were increasingly becoming the 'classics'. Besides these works, however, there were both more and less sophisticated literary products, and it is not easy to assess where their readerships might have been.

Perhaps the most 'allusive' poet, and the one who we might most readily dismiss as pedantic and academic, is Lykophron, sometimes called 'pseudo-Lykophron' to distinguish him from the author of a treatise on comedy who organized that section of the library in the early third century BC.[32] His only known work, one of those rare Alexandrian works surviving in their entirety, is the extraordinary *Alexandra*, a 1,500-line *tour de force* in mythological riddles. Internal evidence suggests it was written soon after 197, though an alternative date of *c.*275 (the lifetime of the author under whose name the poem is preserved) cannot be excluded. It purports to be a prophecy of the fall of Troy and all the history that flowed from it, spoken by Kassandra (Alexandra), the Trojan prophetess whose fate was that she would never be understood. Here she prophesies the wanderings of Odysseus and his companions:

> But others shall wander by Syrtis and the Libystic plateaux
> and the narrow convergence of the Tyrrhenian strait
> and the sailor-blasting lookouts of the half-beast,

she who formerly died at the hands of the Mekistean –
the hide-robed spademan, the cattle-driver –
and the rocks of the harpy-winged nightingales.
All of them, feasted on as raw meat,
will Hades hunt, he who keeps open house,
torn apart with all kinds of maltreatments,
leaving one as messenger of his slaughtered friends,
the dolphin-marked thief of the Phoenician goddess.
(Lykophron, *Alexandra*, 648–58)

'Libystic' is another form of 'Libyan'; the 'Tyrrhenian strait' is a circumlocution for the straits of Messana. 'The half-beast' is Skylla, 'the Mekistean' Herakles, who killed her at Mekistos in Elis. There follow references to the Augean stables and the cattle of Geryon; the monstrous nightingales are the Sirens; the last line contains coded references to Odysseus, his shield, and his patron Athena.

It is pretty indigestible stuff; most lines contain more than one word that is rarely if ever used elsewhere in the entire gamut of extant Greek literature. Lykophron may be assimilated to didactic poetry in some respects; but while at a line-by-line level his poetry is quite euphonious (at least in the original Greek), it is rather monotonous. It is hard to disagree with the view of quite a sympathetic critic that 'after a while Lycophron's very insistence on the awkward as a vehicle for virtuoso performance becomes perverse, and the poem falls exhaustingly flat',[33] albeit this reading is rather subjectivist. What kind of readership could stomach it? Voracious readers with a good education and time on their hands, to be sure. Like Kallimachos and others, Lykophron is probably writing for upper-class Greeks interested in the origins of Greek culture; he may also be seeking to monumentalize the effective end of Greek independence after the Roman victory at Kynoskephalai in 197 (the poem contains a striking tribute to the rising power of the Romans, who believed they were descended from the survivors of the sack of Troy).[34]

A fascination with formal aspects appears in many other places. Kallimachos and others experimented with new metres, and Lykophron devised the first known Greek anagrams: APO MELITOS, 'from honey', becomes PTOLEMAIOS, king Ptolemy; ION (H)ÊRAS, 'Hera's violet' (the H not being written in Greek), becomes ARSINOË, his queen.[35] Others designed riddling poems whose answer was revealed by their shape when written down, such as an altar or a double-headed axe. The best-known exponent of this trick is Simmias (or Simias) of Rhodes (early third century), whose *Wings*, *Axe*, and *Egg* are famous; a *Syrinx* (*Pan-pipes*) is attributed to Theokritos, an *Altar* to one Dosiadas (date uncertain).[36] Acrostics were invented: poems in which the initial letters of the lines spell out a name, like the signature NIKANDROS hidden in Nicander's *Theriaka* (lines 345–53). One cannot deny the outburst of collective imagination behind these experiments, though the likely readership is hard to assess.

The mimes of Herodas, a group of verse writings to accompany imitative movement and gesture, are the only extant examples of this important and ancient genre of Greek literature. The Spartans called the performers *deikê-liktai* in their dialect, and despised them (cf. Plut. *Agesilaos*, 21. 8; Ath. 14. 621 d–e);[37] in the changed atmosphere of the third century their popularity blossomed. The author's history is as uncertain as his name (Herodas, Herodes, or Herondas), but the consensus seems to be that he lived in Alexandria in the third century. There are no medieval manuscripts; the eight surviving mimes, each consisting of about a hundred lines of skazons ('limping iambics'), were discovered on papyrus in the late nineteenth century. Mimes seem to have been one-man stage performances, though we know of earlier examples circulated as texts. Herodas has something in common with the *Characters* of Theophrastos, though the low-life dramatis personae are little more than briskly sketched social types. An effeminate brothel-keeper prosecutes a sea-captain for assaulting one of his girls (*Mime* 2). A mother complains about her son's pranks and asks his sadistic school-master to thrash him within an inch of his life (*Mime* 3). Two poor, pious women encounter a sanctimonious temple-warden of Asklepios (*Mime* 4; the setting may be the actual Asklepieion in Kos; cf. Chapter 5). And so on.

Several sketches purport to take us into the private world of married women: one threatens her slave lover with punishment for sleeping with another woman; another visits a friend to discuss which cobbler makes the best leather dildoes; in the next mime she takes two friends to his shop, where he makes a boastful sales-pitch about his shoes and they bargain with him. The language is lively, the tone chatty and 'realistic', even down to the inconsequential asides and the passing disparagement of slave-girls:

Mêtrô:	Dear Koritto, you have the same yoke wearing you down as I. I too am a barking dog, snapping day and night at those unmentionable girls. But why I've come to you – [*here she shouts at the slave-girls*] get to hell out of our way, with your closed minds, only ears and tongues, but otherwise idleness! – I beg you, do not lie, dear Koritto: who was it stitched the scarlet dildo for you?
Koritto:	And where, Metro, did you see that?
M.:	Nossis, daughter of Erinna [*both are actual poets*], had it two days ago; ah, what a fine gift!
K.:	Nossis? From whom did she get it?
M.:	Will you blacken my name if I tell you?
K.:	By these sweet eyes, dear Metro, no one shall hear what you say from Koritto's mouth.
M.:	Bitas's Euboule gave it to her and said that no one should know.

249

K.:   Women! This woman will uproot me yet. I paid respect to her
        plea, and gave it her, Metro, before I used it myself. But snatching
        it like a windfall, she passes it on even to those who ought not to
        have it.

                                            (Herodas, *Mime* 6, lines 12–31)

Koritto describes how she wheedled the cobbler into letting her have one,
and then lapses into gossip:

K.:   Metro, what did I not do? What persuasion did I not bring to bear
        on him? Kissing him, stroking his bald head, pouring him a sweet
        drink, calling him papa, almost giving him my body to use.
M.:   But if he asked for that too, you should have given it.
K.:   Yes, I should have; but it is not decent to act unseasonably: Bitas's
        Euboule was grinding near us. For by turning our millstone day
        and night she has ruined it, to avoid setting her own for four
        obols.

                                                        (lines 74–84)

We should be careful not to assume that the scenes being described offer any
insight into how actual women behaved.[38] What we have is (apparently) a
man writing for a male actor who is performing to entertain a Greek audience that is, at least on the Athenian analogy, likely to be either
predominantly male or at least constrained by the ethos of a patriarchal
society; like Aristophanes' *Thesmophoriazousai* from late fifth-century Athens,
it may tell us less about women than about what men like to pretend they
think women get up to. With regard to the supposed impropriety of the
subject-matter, *Mime* 1 is revealing: an older woman invites a young wife
whose husband is away to meet a strapping young athlete, but the younger
woman will have none of it. Again as in Aristophanes, we are allowed to
peep into an imagined forbidden world of female scheming, but only to
glimpse it; marital propriety is, before long, restored.

    In *Mime* 8, Herodas, in the person of a farmer, narrates a dream which
signifies the poet's own savage treatment at the hands of his critics but also
predicts his ultimate fame. The interesting fact is (as we might have guessed
from the absence of a continuous manuscript tradition) that Herodas seems
not to have been much read by Greeks and Romans; he is hardly ever named
in later writings. Whether this is because of any literary shortcomings is to
some extent a matter of subjective judgement; it is true that the plots and
character are thin, the language a stylized imitation of the sixth-century
Doric dialect used by some earlier iambic poets.[39] Is it because this literature was felt to be 'beneath' educated notice, for example because he was
using the language of the common people?[40] Are the mimes a genuine literature of the lower classes? When and where they were performed we can only

guess. The fact that they seem to appeal to snobbish attitudes on the audience's part does not prove the contrary case; élite-produced literature is often enjoyed by those outside the élite. The literary dialect, the signs of innovation (such as the use of several characters), and in general the 'aesthetic mannerism'[41] of the pieces suggest that they are the product of an élite rather than a popular milieu. Their near-disappearance from literature cannot be attributed to any literary defects, or many less skilful poets would have perished; nor to their having been written for 'the people' rather than the upper-class reading public. Perhaps their popularity depended less on the silent text than on the live performance.

A popular audience is slightly easier to infer from the sensational content of some of the early Alexander historians. Onesikritos of Astypalaia, Alexander's helmsman, wrote an anecdotal account of the expedition. Kleitarchos of Alexandria wrote, perhaps under Ptolemy II, a factual account enlivened by more colourful passages and possibly a richer human dimension (he is used by Diodoros in book 17). Chares of Mytilene, Alexander's chamberlain, recorded court ceremonial and gossip. Given the frequency with which books purporting to be histories of Alexander appeared during the third century, it is possible that recitations or readings of mythologized stories about him were genuinely popular. If so, other kings may have had in mind the creation of a favourable image in the popular imagination when they encouraged books to be written about themselves.

Such memoirs may lie behind parts of the work known as the *Alexander Romance* or 'Pseudo-Kallisthenes' (after Alexander's historian, to whom it was misattributed). Alexander's life is here embellished with the stuff of rumour. His true father is the Egyptian pharaoh Nektanebo, who tricks Olympias into thinking he is a god (1. 4–11); Alexander later murders him (1. 14). He dies as the result of poison administered by his cupbearer, Iolaos (3. 31).[42] Alexander is a trickster like the Homeric hero Odysseus, sneaking into the Persian court disguised as a messenger (2. 13–14). Supernatural and magical elements abound: a river of Persia freezes so hard when snow falls that waggons can cross it, yet it melts in a few days (2. 14); he encounters 36-foot-tall men with hands like saws, spherical men 'with fiery expressions like lions', three-eyed beasts like lions, fleas as big as frogs, and a hairy giant who devours humans (2. 32–3). He tries to visit the sea-bed in a glass jar protected by a cage, but at 464 feet down a mighty fish seizes the cage and takes him to the shore (2. 38). The army explores a land of total darkness, and Alexander discovers (without knowing it) a spring that confers immortality, but does not drink from it (2. 39). He has himself carried up to the sky in a leather bag by giant birds, but a flying man warns him to return to earth (2. 40). Most of these tales, however, are fleetingly told and form only a small part of a chronological narrative in which the military campaigns dominate, albeit narrated by authors who seem to have no idea of ancient geography.

The stories survive in many manuscripts. The earliest, a Greek text, dates from the third century AD, but medieval versions occur across Europe in languages ranging from Magyar to Scots. By comparing different versions and seeing which episodes of the story they have in common, scholars have traced them to three probable ancestors. A fourth-century Latin and a fifth-century Armenian version derive from the third-century Greek text. A group of fourth- to eighth-century texts forms a separate tradition, represented by several good manuscripts. The third family has two branches: one, stemming from a tenth-century Latin text, includes the western European versions; the other, descended from a Syriac precursor, includes Arabic, Ethiopic, and eastern translations from which we can trace Persian, Afghan, and even Mongolian legends about Alexander.

In their earliest form, however, these tales probably originated not long after Alexander's death, and embody a combination of royal propaganda and popular discussion, perhaps formed in a multi-cultural environment, about the significance of the conquest of Egypt and Asia for Greek culture and identity. Papyri containing recognizable elements were current in the first century AD, and Josephus preserves elements of the later Jewish tradition about Alexander.[43] Written texts about Alexander may have circulated, perhaps in conjunction with oral performance, among ordinary Greeks in Old Greece and the Near East; many of the additions to the real Alexander's life may be folkloric elements taken from near eastern storytelling, rather than new inventions. The earliest fragments, however, contain few of the fabulous and unhistorical additions seen later; so if we wish to correlate supernatural elements with popularity, we should be cautious about positing too wide a readership too early.

In general we cannot discern the 'popular' Greek literature of the day with confidence, though stories about Alexander may be an exception. On the Egyptian side, however, the tradition of apocalyptic, apparently nationalistic prophecy has been mentioned (see p. 233 on the Oracle of the Potter). A wider tradition, apparently circulating widely, is represented by the *Demotic Chronicle* and other collected folk-tales evoking pre-Ptolemaic Egypt; the *Chronicle* was compiled as early as the mid-third century. These romances of Egyptian kings, queens, and heroic struggles have supernatural elements as well as divine characters. Though mass literacy cannot be assumed, they may have served as the basis for oral performance and thus fulfilled a similar function to the *Alexander Romance*, expressing the aspirations and collective retailing of Egyptian memory through which native Egyptians, perhaps at a popular level in the Egyptian *chôra*, asserted their identity over against the new ruling élite. Other native traditions include Instruction Texts, which include moralizing maxims apparently intended to remind audiences of their duty to their primarily Egyptian inheritance. In the Roman period, legends were translated and adapted into Greek, perhaps for a population that regarded itself as having at least partly an Egyptian ancestry.[44]

The public and the personal

The epigram is a literary form that often purports to embody personal sentiments and private concerns. It is a short poem, usually in elegiac couplets.[45]
Thousands survive in ancient literary collections and as inscriptions on stone
(cf. the gravestone of the woman from Sardis quoted at p. 104). The most
famous collection is the *Garland* by Meleager (Meleagros; late second–early
first century), which survives partly in the tenth-century AD *Palatine Anthology*
and in other manuscripts. As a form of writing the epigram, whose name
(*epigramma*) simply means 'inscription', is the earliest of all Greek writing:
short verse inscriptions were scratched on late eighth-century vases. Above
all, the epigram in the archaic and classical periods was a public poem, such
as the short poems by Simonides of Keos on the battles of the Persian wars,
which were inscribed on official monuments at Delphi and elsewhere.
Epigrams were often written for grave-inscriptions, and the fourth-century
philosopher Plato wrote epigrams that were much admired; it was a
distinctly aristocratic pastime. In the hellenistic period the form seems to
have been genuinely more popular than other forms of verse, to judge by the
numbers of known examples, though we must be careful not to assume that
all levels of society composed or even read them. A distinctive characteristic
of the hellenistic age is the presentation by poets of apparently personal
concerns; but one must be cautious about taking poems as documents of real
life, for poets adopt personas and voices other than their own – a fact which
misled ancient commentators no less than it misleads modern. It is hard to
exaggerate the degree to which epigrams are designed to show the author's
awareness and ability to reprocess stock themes, so that what appears to be
personal expression may be a piece of literary cleverness.[46]

Among the more famous literary epigrammatists was Asklepiades of
Samos, who besides inventing the metre that was named after him (the
Asclepiad) published epigrams combining the themes, traditional since the
sixth century, of love and drink:

> Wine is the proof of love. He denied his love to us,
> But the many toasts he drank convicted Nikagores.
> For he wept and hung his head, and quite downcast
> he looked, and, tight as it was, his garland wouldn't stay put.
> (Asklepiades, *Anth. Pal.* 12. 135)

Another Samian, by adoption at least, was Hedylos, whose mother Hedyle
was also a poet. He was the son of one of the Athenian settlers who occupied
the island in the mid-fourth century. In one epigram he reworks the same
story, as poets often did (though we cannot be sure which poem was written
first), giving it an overtly *risqué*, erotic flavour which perhaps suggests a
male audience:

Wine, and toasts that are so crafty, laid Aglaonike
down – and Nikagores' sweet desire.
From her there lie before Kypris, each still soaked
with perfumes, these moist trophies of virginal longings:
sandals, and soft sashes, uncoverings of breasts;
proofs of the sleep and snatchings that there were.

(Hedylos, *Anth. Pal.* 5. 199)

Whether Nikagores and Aglaonike were real people is unimportant; more
relevant is the possible occasion on which a song like this was sung (for it is
likely that many literary epigrams were written to be performed). The occasion
would probably be, in traditional Greek fashion, a *symposion* or men's drinking-
party.[47] However, while the subject-matter allows us to compare epigrams
with their classical predecessors, which were certainly often composed for
symposia, they do not allow us to make any deductions about sexual practice.
Epigrams often present women ironically, as may be the case here:

The Samian women Bitto and Nannion don't like to visit
Aphrodite according to her own rules,
but desert her for other things, not good. Cyprian Lady,
abhor these females exiled from your bed.

(Asklepiades, *Anth. Pal.* 5. 207; Gow and Page,
Greek Anthology, Asclepiades, no. 7)

The apparently lesbian women of this epigram by Asklepiades need not be
real people; and it is an open question whether the pointed, *risqué* wit is supposed to be appreciated by men, women, or both.[48] The subject can now be
discussed – with erotic details more or less explicitly suggested – and
preserved.

Other epigrams encapsulate a sentiment or a piece of philosophical
wisdom in a few well-turned lines. The epigram on friendship and death by
Kallimachos is justly famous in William Cory's translation,[49] but it may be
better to preserve the conciseness of the original:

Someone spoke, Herakleitos, of your fate, and brought me
to a tear, and I recalled how many times we both
set the sun with our talking. Well, somewhere you,
my friend from Halikarnassos, are four-times-long-since dust;
but your nightingales live, upon which the snatcher
of all things, Hades, shall not set his hand.

(Kallimachos, *Anth. Pal.* 7. 80)

The hellenistic epigram is sometimes taken, with other literature, as a
hallmark of the supposed individualistic concerns of the age; but poems had
been (ostensibly) personal since Archilochos in the seventh century. The new

features may be the emphasis on intimate details and a seeming realism; the latter parallels the shepherds of Theokritos and Apollonios of Rhodes's display of psychological empathy. It seems particularly rash on the part of some scholars to leap from new modes of expression (for all that these may imply a modified view of the individual) to grand conclusions about collective despair, escapism as a response to an awful political situation, an age of selfishness, and so on.[50]

The personal invades the poetic where one least expects it. Epic poetry in the manner, and on the scale, of Homer was traditionally a benchmark for Greek poets, though almost no post-Homeric epic survives. Kallimachos, for all his scholarliness, professed himself against overblown, clichéd heroic poems: one of his epigrams actually begins 'I detest the cyclic poem', a reference to the early post-Homeric epics; 'I loathe the common path' (fr. 28 Pfeiffer).[51] Everyone has heard his famous saying, *mega biblion mega kakon*, 'a big book is a big evil'.

The Muse of Kallimachos was 'slim', and he approved of Philetas and Aratos; he disliked epics like the only surviving one from this period, the *Argonautika* (*Voyage of Argo*) of Apollonios of Rhodes (Apollonius Rhodius).[52] Yet it is Apollonios, not Kallimachos, who is widely read in English today; and the nature of his poem is revealing. The *Argonautika* retells the legend of Jason's expedition in his ship *Argo* and the quest for the golden fleece of Kolchis. His originality lies in fusing a strong epic narrative with colourful elements derived from contemporary philosophy. Like all Greek poets when dealing with legends, Apollonios relies on the fact that the audience knows the story already, which gives him scope for innovation, and part of this innovation consists in relaying marvellous and wondrous things. He displays a characteristically Alexandrian liking for the curious and bizarre; ethnographic details of fantastical, distant places are deployed in a manner close to that of Herodotos. Most interesting, however, is his concern with individual character and emotion, which verges at times on a psychological study, as in the case of Medea. The examination of the symptoms of emotion was far from new – compare, from the sixth century, Sappho's famous fragment (31) exploring the feelings of the singer watching a girl whom she loves – but in Apollonios it is framed within an almost scientific discourse and an interest in causality. Combined additionally with a very visual sense of the domestic, it gives an exciting, novel mixture which is also strongly Homeric in colour:

> Night then brought darkness upon the earth, and at sea
> sailors looked to the Bear and Orion's stars
> from their ships, and sleep was now the desire
> of the traveller and gate-keeper, and a mother
> whose children had died was wrapped in deep slumber;
> dogs no longer barked through the city, no voice
> sounded – silence held the blackening night.

255

But no sweet sleep at all took Medea.
Many cares kept her wakeful in her desire for Jason,
dreading the bulls' mighty strength, by which he was likely
to perish with shameful fate in Ares' field.
Greatly the heart within her breast throbbed,
as a sunbeam quivers on the wall in a house,
coming back off water just freshly poured
in a basin or maybe a pail, and the beam wavers,
darting up and down in the quick eddy –
so in her breast trembled the girl's heart.

(Apoll. Rhod. 3. 744–60)

The simile of the reflection on the wall may be slightly laboured, and other elements from the passage can be paralleled from earlier poets (who themselves reused phrases and figures from *their* predecessors), but these justly famous lines illustrate the real originality of Alexandrian poetry. The emphasis on the feeling subject is particularly noteworthy, and is in tune with developments in philosophy. As to the poem's audience, again we can only suppose it to be an educated Greek élite, the kind of people whom the poet could expect to recognize the allusions and his originality. It is no longer acceptable to account the *Argonautika* a pale shadow of earlier epics. The numerous papyrus fragments suggest it remained widely read among educated Greeks for many generations, and its high critical standing is confirmed by Vergil's extensive use of it in his *Aeneid*.

Another poem exploring a psychological state is *Idyll* 2 by Theokritos, the *Pharmakeutria* or *Sorceress*, in which a jilted countrywoman, Simaitha, with the help of her maid Thestylis, casts a midnight spell to bring her lover back. Like Apollonios, Theokritos focuses on her inner turmoil as she recalls her passionate affair with Delphis, and the depiction of witchcraft is almost unique in contemporary or earlier literature, as is the attempt to explore a woman's emotional state. This poem again illustrates the Alexandrian fascination with the unusual and the 'pathology of unusual occasions',[53] as in these lines portraying a Bacchic-style frenzy of vengeance:

Next I light the bay-leaves. They crackle and flare.
When the flame has died no trace of ash remains.
Delphis wounds me. Then let the fire seize Delphis.
Shrivel his heart and burn along his veins
Turn, magic wheel, and force my lover home.

Now I throw on the corn-husks. Nothing holds fast
against you, Artemis, either on earth or in hell.
The town-dogs howl; the goddess is at the crossroads.
Keep us safe from her, Thestylis. Strike the bell!
Turn, magic wheel, and force my lover home.

Listen, the night is windless, the sea lies still;
only my turmoil interrupts the calm,
my love-gone-bad for a man in love with himself,
the thief of my happiness and my good name.
Turn, magic wheel, and force my lover home.
                                        (Theokritos, *Idyll* 2. 23–37)

We saw earlier (pp. 219–20) how his fifteenth *Idyll* portrays two women talking as they make their way through the streets of Alexandria to a festival. We may like to think that these poems are evidence of increased freedom of thought and behaviour for women, but Theokritos is a poet of the court, and a man. There seems to have been a wider range of public roles for women (pp. 102–6), and women were discussed in new ways; this, I suggested, may have had something to do with the reduced importance of male citizenship. We have to strike a balance between reading off changes in gender roles from literary depictions, and evaluating what substantive change in attitudes or behaviour may be attested by the readiness of poets and readers to depict women in a new way.[54]

Linked with this interest in what we might call psychological states is the presentation, in new ways and in new contexts, of the erotic. I suggested earlier that the mimes of Herodas construct women in the domestic environment according to an image that a male-dominated audience is willing to pretend it has of them. Herodas does not tell us anything directly about how women behaved, though he presents an explicit discourse about sex of which few if any earlier examples survive (the famous seduction scene in a song by the seventh-century poet Archilochos seems quite different in character; fr. 196a West).[55] Theokritos's Syracusan women going to a festival and his lovelorn *pharmakeutria* occur in poems which were surely written for an extremely select, court-centred readership among whom there may have been more opportunity for female self-expression or for the literary exploration of women's natures; they are not individual personalities.

Nor do women in the Attic New Comedy of Menander (Menandros; 342/1–c.290 BC) have individual characters. At the start of the twentieth century none of Menander's comedies survived in more than vestigial form; they had to be guessed at from later quotations and from the Roman comedies of Plautus and Terence, who reworked them a century later. Now large parts of several plays, some virtually complete, have been found on papyrus. They differ from the late fifth- and early fourth-century comedies of Aristophanes chiefly in their plots, which are centred on family dramas. Some of their events, though similar to those of television soap operas – the rediscovery of long-lost children, the rescue of kidnapped daughters – are too melodramatic to have been everyday experiences of those watching; perhaps their real purpose, by playing on the unconscious insecurities of the audiences, is to assert by implicit contrast the social values of normality and stability.

More revealing, at first sight, for attitudes to society and of the individual's place in it is the frequency in Menander of a love interest. In the *Perikeiromene* (*The Girl with her Hair Cut Off*), the mercenary soldier Polemon ('Man-of-war') cuts off the hair of the woman he lives with, Glykera ('Sweetie'), after hearing that she kissed another man. The following exchange may imply more freedom of action for women (or fewer restrictions on the portrayal of women's activities) than we might suppose existed in classical Athens:

Polemon: I've always treated her as my wife.
Pataikos: Don't shout at me! Who gave you her?
Polemon: Gave me her? She did.
Pataikos: Very good. She fancied you then, and now she doesn't. She's left you because you're not treating her properly.

(Menander, *Perikeiromene*, lines 239–43)

Pataikos urges Polemon that violence will not bring Glykera back. It is important to remember, however, that these are not real people but imaginary characters in a comedy performed in Athens, which was not a normal city; that Polemon is distanced from the audience by being a Corinthian; and that Menander was an associate of Demetrios of Phaleron, who introduced 'women's superintendents' (*gynaikonomoi*). Not surprisingly, social order is re-established: Glykera proves to be the daughter of Pataikos, the man she was kissing was only her long-lost brother, and she and Polemon get married.

The same cautions may apply to the so-called *anaischyntographoi* ('writers of shameless things'), a class of male authors ranging in date from the early fourth century to the time of Nero, who wrote what modern commentators sometimes call 'sex manuals' under female pseudonyms.[56] (The Roman poet Ovid's *Ars amatoria*, 'The Art of Love', is a parody of these books among others.) None is extant from, or explicitly dated to, the hellenistic period, but it is likely that some were written now; the cataloguing mentality was characteristically Alexandrian. In fact the works, which claimed to be didactic, covered all kinds of heterosexual erotic activity, and were not just enumerations of positions for sexual intercourse. One of them included a (no doubt literary) account of how a man should seduce a woman.

Works of this kind were attacked by philosophers including the Peripatetic Klearchos of Soloi (*ap.* Ath. 10. 457 d–e) and the Stoic Chrysippos (*ap.* Ath. 8. 335); not on the grounds that they mentioned any illicit pleasures – Greek culture was not overly prescriptive about what sex acts were or were not permissible – but because they encouraged self-indulgence and the over-elaboration of physical pleasures rather than the traditional philosophical (and 'manly') virtue of moderation.[57] These works, therefore, do not imply any post-classical 'liberation' but embody a traditional objectification of the female and adopt the standard 'male gaze'. There is nothing to indicate whether it was men or women, or both, that read them.

Why do we see more of the ostensibly personal and private made public? Is it simply that we know the titles of more lost works than for an earlier period? Is it a case of a different lens being held up to a society that was much the same as before? Or is it evidence of social change? Even if caution is appropriate, it does seem reasonable to suppose that if the lens has changed, then so has society; authors are expected to portray and discuss different things if they wish to entertain and illuminate their readers. Even if social practice has not significantly changed, its conceptualization has.

The loss of political freedom by some Greeks may have provoked a new subject matter for certain kinds of public discourse. No longer were issues debated in dramas performed at city festivals as in classical Athens. In places like Alexandria, politics was not really the citizens' business – though Polybios, in a different situation, would have wished it otherwise.

The 'Other'

This trend towards portraying the domestic – what Préaux calls *intimisme* – is linked by her to Greek exclusivity and the withdrawal of the Greeks into a kind of cultural *laager*.[58] Hadas, in contrast, links it to a lessening of the aggressive exclusivity of hellenism, now that the tightly circumscribed world of the *polis* was no longer the main seat of social power.[59] There is something to be said for both views, but we should be cautious.

In the first place, Menander's plays date from the generation after Alexander, before the political shape of the world had settled down. They cannot be taken as typical of hellenistic literature – a truly independent Athens was still a fresh memory and something to aspire to – but rather confirm that many of the developments of third-century Alexandrian literature were continuations of earlier trends, perhaps reflecting social attitudes whose origins can be traced to prosperous, democratic Athens rather than Ptolemaic Alexandria. The changes, if real, surely go back well before Menander's day; it may simply be that we are seeing sides of Athenian society that earlier audiences did not expect from a comic playwright.

Second, the degree of Greek exclusivity, at least in terms of culture, should not be over-stated. Greek culture in general had never been as exclusive or anti-barbarian as Aristotle, for example, implies in the *Politics*. He was writing in very specific circumstances, in a unique, even eccentric city (Athens), at a time when that particular *polis* had succumbed to a political threat and the problem if faced was how it should react or adapt. Greek societies had often interacted openly with non-Greek cultures, particularly in the cities of Asia Minor, the Black Sea, and the far west. We should think away the idea that Greeks and Macedonians always contemplated 'barbarians' with the kind of racial hatred we find in the modern era; what they perceived were cultural and military differences, and sometimes they felt superior. Alexander's captains may have gone back on his policy of 'fusion' with Iranians not so much for racialist reasons as because they had an opportunity to keep supreme power for themselves. Similarly, Lane Fox may be right to suggest that the maintenance of Greekness in literature was not 'a "culture of reinforcement" to keep up Greek morale abroad and to keep out barbarians', but rather 'marked social divisions between Greeks themselves'.[60] This remained the case even where there was originality in literary forms; these may not be the product of a new racial experience – as if Greeks saw themselves as living in beleaguered islands of hellenism surrounded by a barbarian sea, as some scholars have believed – but of new social, political, and cultural relations among Greeks. Not the least among the changes was the breaking down of boundaries around the *polis* (cf. p. 105).

In *Idyll* 15 of Theokritos (quoted, pp. 219–20) there is an apparent example of overt racial prejudice; but generally barbarians seem to feature less prominently than in classical Athenian writings, perhaps because they no longer represented a threat. Moreover, we see some signs of a tendency towards assimilating non-Greeks to Greek ways of thinking, in the way in which they are represented – much as, in the Roman period, Plutarch and Juvenal's writings about Egyptians *'integrate* what is distinct and separate in a way which is completely foreign to the imperial texts of the European empires. In Plutarch, Egyptian culture is made "ours".'[61] This is unlike the approach of Herodotos in the fifth century, who represented Egypt (unconvincingly) as in every way unlike Greek society (book 2). Now we have authors like Hekataios of Abdera (*c.*360–290, an adviser on Ptolemy's expedition in Palestine in *c.*320–318), who wrote an *Aigyptiaka* (*Egyptian History*) at the court of Ptolemy I,[62] drawing on Egyptian documents as well as earlier Greek writers including Herodotos. The first book of Diodoros shows us that Hekataios painted an idealized portrait of Ptolemy I and produced 'a work of propaganda portraying Egypt in a light which would appeal to Greek, and perhaps Egyptian, educated opinion'.[63]

The boundaries between history, geography, and ethnography were not yet explicitly drawn.[64] In a famous passage Hekataios describes the Jews in terms reminiscent of Spartans, and offers us a Moses somewhat like the Spartan lawgiver Lykourgos, at least in this extract:

> The lawgiver also devoted much attention to the arts of war, and he compelled the young to practise bravery and endurance, and in general to put up with every kind of hardship. He also made military expeditions against the neighbouring peoples, and acquired much land which he distributed in lots, making the lots equal for private individuals but larger for the priests, so that they might have more considerable revenues and so might devote themselves continuously and without interruption to the worship of God. Private individuals were not allowed to sell their lots, to prevent some from greedily

buying them up, and so causing hardship to poorer people and bringing about a decline in the population.
(Hekataios of Abdera, *FGH* 264 fr. 6 = Diod. 40. 3; Austin 166)

Hekataios presents the Jews as fundamentally un-Greek,[65] but in passages
like these, consciously or unconsciously, he seems to be trying to make them
accessible to Greeks by describing them in terms his readers can recognize
from their own history. (Mainland Greeks from at least the first half of the
third century may have come into contact with Jews, such as Moschos the
freed slave, who commemorated his liberation in stone at the Amphiareion
at Oropos after receiving a dream, probably from the hero Amphiaraos
himself: *SEG* xv. 293.[66] For actual Jewish–Spartan contacts see pp. 266–7.)
It has also been observed that part of Kallimachos's purpose in incorporating
Egyptian material into his poems may have been precisely to introduce
Egypt to a Greek audience and make the unfamiliar accessible.[67]

Later, probably in the early third century, Manethôn (or Manethôs, or
Manethô; *FGH* 609), an Egyptian priest, took up the project of Hekataios
and produced various works including a new 'official' *Aigyptiaka* or *History of
Egypt* from earliest times to 342. The original text is lost, but many fragments have been reassembled from later sources (p. 11), which make it clear
that Manethon did write a detailed narrative; unfortunately, none of the
original survives for the classical period.[68]

Perhaps in response to Ptolemaic initiatives like these, Seleukid
patronage led to works by Berossos (Bêrôssos; *FGH* 680), a Babylonian
priest who produced a *Babyloniaka*, or history of Babylonia down to
Alexander, written in Greek, one of whose aims was to make clear to Greeks
the difference between Babylonia and Assyria;[69] and by Megasthenes (*FGH*
715), a Macedonian commander who wrote about India from first-hand
knowledge but superimposed a Greek philosophical gloss upon his presentation of native cultures. Megasthenes' work survives indirectly in Diodoros's
description of India (2. 35–42).

It remains true that deciding whether to assimilate or differentiate
implies a position of cultural power. The imperial background is always
present and may influence writers consciously or subconsciously. In
Theokritos's *Idyll* 14 the lovelorn Aischines thinks of allaying his pain by
going and serving Ptolemy as a mercenary.[70] The possibility of going further
afield in the world was always present for late fourth- and third-century
Greeks. But while the hellenistic representation of the barbarian did help
construct Greek identity, we should not assimilate it too closely to modern
racism.

Historiography and the community

In order to sketch some general lines of approach to the social and cultural role of historians during the hellenistic period, the discussion will now focus on historians who wrote during the third and second centuries, whether or not their works survive. I shall not be dealing with sources written later, which are examined in Chapter 1. All contemporary histories are more or less completely lost apart from that of Polybios, and that survives only in part. The discussion will be concerned not with their accounts of events, but with their authorial purposes and characteristics.

To the reading public, history meant political and military history. Already in the classical period this entailed a strong emphasis on individual 'makers of history'; Xenophon, for instance, had written biographical portraits of men he admired, such as his *Education of Cyrus* and *Agesilaos*, even his *Anabasis of Cyrus* and *Hellênika* have a strongly biographical-cum-autobiographical flavour. The return of widespread monarchy to the Greek world accentuated this feature of historiography, though paradoxically it would be the most powerful individuals – kings like the Ptolemies, Seleukids, and Antigonids – that enjoyed the poorest literary record (see Chapter 1).

The biographical element was particularly marked in the work of Douris of Samos (*c*.340–*c*.270; *FGH* 76), a pupil of Theophrastos. Like his father, Kaios, he became tyrant of his city – they were not so much monarchs as military governors for the Antigonids[71] and later for Lysimachos. Douris's *Macedonian History* (*Makedonika*) covered the years 370/69 to *c*.281/0 and was heavily drawn upon by Diodoros and by Plutarch in his lives of Eumenes of Kardia, Demetrios I, and Pyrrhos. His history was sometimes viewed as sensationalist, and seems to have included scandalous anecdotes designed to show Macedonian kings in a poor light – even the Antigonids and Lysimachos (he may have composed his history after the death of Lysimachos and the end of the tyranny in 281/0). His life of Agathokles, tyrant of Syracuse, was equally hostile; it, too, is used by Diodoros. One study, however, has suggested that the predominant features of his writing were not scandal but 'myth, anecdote, moral lessons, marvellous stories, proverbs, poetry and etymologies'.[72]

A biographical and personal emphasis is seen in the work of Timaios (Timaeus) of Tauromenion in Sicily (*c*.350–260; *FGH* 566), who while living at Athens for several decades wrote a history of the western Greeks to the death of Agathokles (289/8) and an apparently separate account of the wars of Pyrrhos (to 272); he was Diodoros's main source for Agathokles. He, too, was hostile to Agathokles, who caused him to be exiled from Sicily; he was evidently prone to attack other historians, for which he was called Epitimaios, 'Slanderer'. Not all the lengthy criticism of him by Polybios (occupying the whole of book 12) is fair; he was an accurate investigator, and his investigations into synchronic dating were probably responsible for the adoption by historians of a standard chronology based on Olympiads (the four-year intervals between Olympic games: Polyb. 12. 11). He appears to have eschewed the more emotive tone of Douris; and was recognized as the first Greek historian to give due attention to Roman history, albeit from a western point of view (*FGH* 566, testimonia, 9 b–c).[73] Very few of the fragments concern Rome directly, but we know that he wrote about the Penates (the household gods of the Romans; fr. 59), gave a date equivalent to 814/3 for Rome's foundation (fr. 60), and probably stated that king Servius was the first to use stamped bronze as coinage (fr. 61). He famously remarked (fr. 139) that Alexander took fewer years to conquer Persia than Isokrates did to write his *Panegyrikos*, in which he demanded a panhellenic war against Persia.

An almost exact contemporary of Timaios, and like him resident in Athens, was Philochoros (*c*.350–*c*.260), himself a citizen of Athens and the last in a lively tradition of local Athenian historiography. His *Atthis* (the name, probably given by Kallimachos, is that of a legendary Attic princess) covered Attic history from mythical times, the last two-thirds (books 7–17) covering 320–261 BC. Unfortunately, because of the classical bias of later excerptors, almost all the surviving fragments are from the earlier books. Philochoros was distinguished by his antiquarian researches; he was 'perhaps the first scholarly historian'. Despite this, he typifies the involvement of hellenistic intellectuals and artists in public life, if only because he became embroiled in the politics of the Chremonidean war and was executed by Antigonos Gonatas as an Egyptian sympathizer.[74]

The next major, lost historian of the third century was Phylarchos of Athens or Naukratis (*FGH* 81), who wrote *Histories* extending from the death of Pyrrhos (272) to that of Kleomenes III (220/19) and used Douris extensively.[75] He, too, is criticized by Polybios (2. 56–63) for emotive writing and bias, though Polybios had plenty of inducements to misrepresent him since Phylarchos presented the Spartan kings Agis and Kleomenes favourably; it is this version that emerges strongly from Plutarch's lives of the two kings, and despite his criticisms Polybios draws on his work for the history of the Peloponnese down to the 220s. Whether or not Phylarchos was right about the Spartan kings, he seems to have had a particularly colourful and anecdotal style, which may explain why so many of his 'fragments' are quotations by Athenaeus, the third-century AD author of a vast collection of stories about dinner-parties and all kinds of luxury. The remarks of Phylarchos about Philadelphos are quoted in this manner:

> In his twenty-second book he says that Ptolemy, the second who was king of Egypt, who was the most respectable of rulers and devoted great efforts, if anyone did, to culture, was so deceived in judgement and so corrupted by his boundless luxury that he believed he would live for all time and said that he alone had found immortality.

So, being beset by gout for several days, when eventually he felt better and spotted through some windows the Egyptians eating their midday meal by the river and enjoying everyday things, and carelessly sprawled upon the sand, he said, 'Unhappy me! I can't even be one of them!'

(Ath. 12. 536 e, *FGH* 81 fr. 40)

A little further on, Athenaeus quotes an extended description by Phylarchos of the extravagant accoutrements of Alexander's court and its members (Ath. 12. 539 b–540 a = fr. 41). Phylarchos (again quoted by Athenaeus, 12. 521 b–e) is one of the prime sources for the fabled luxury of the people of Sybaris in Italy.

None of these three lost historians appears to have enjoyed royal patronage, and they were, on the face of it, able to write what they liked. Others were directly in the service of kings. Alexander had set the fashion by taking with him on his expedition a historian committed to his cause, Aristotle's nephew Kallisthenes of Olynthos (*FGH* 124); but in 327 Kallisthenes was executed for opposing the king's growing autocracy. Historians often served as archivist or *hypomnêmatographos* to kings, keeping records of diplomatic business;[76] it was a meticulous operation, to judge from the story that when Alexander burned the tent of his chief secretary Eumenes of Kardia, because he would not give him all his gold and silver, Eumenes was able to replace all the papers with duplicate copies kept by Alexander's satraps and generals (Plut. *Eumenes*, 2). The royal archive was a potential mine of important evidence: Philip V burned his to prevent it falling into the Romans' hands (Polyb. 18. 33), while Diodoros claims to have consulted the royal *hypomnêmata* of Alexandria (3. 38).

The most famous 'court historian' of the subsequent years was Hieronymos of Kardia (*c*.364–*c*.260; *FGH* 154), who was archivist to Eumenes (and possibly his nephew)[77] and later to Antigonos I, Demetrios I, and Antigonos II. Like Eumenes he was involved in affairs of state: at one time he governed Boiotian Thebes on behalf of the Macedonians. Despite these connections he is generally thought to have been a dispassionate historian, escaping even the censure of the caustic Polybios (at least in the extant parts of the latter's work); the charge of pro-Antigonid bias levelled by Pausanias (1. 9. 8, Austin 45) is hard to sustain. Hieronymos certainly reacted against Douris's propensity to retail scandal.[78] Though little read in later generations, he was among the historians most widely drawn upon by later writers on this period (Diodoros, Plutarch, Nepos, Arrian, and Trogus).

Hieronymos may not have been in the position of having to toe a particular line, but other kings certainly took a direct interest in shaping views of the recent past. Ptolemy I wrote up his memoirs of Alexander's expedition (*FGH* 138); they were used by Arrian, who rather strangely states (1. 1. 2) that they must be trustworthy because it is particularly dishonourable for a king to tell lies! Pyrrhos of Epeiros wrote his autobiography (*FGH* 229), as did Ptolemy VIII, both drawing on their official archives (Plut. *Pyrrh.* 21; *FGH* 234).[79] Attalos I of Pergamon kept a court historian, Neanthes of Kyzikos (*FGH* 84), and others used historians as their ambassadors more readily than philosophers, doctors, or lawyers.[80] Other historical works deriving from royal patronage included those of Hekataios, Berossos, Manethon, and Megasthenes.

Besides Alexander historians and the great historians discussed already, a plethora of writers composed histories of their local communities. Some are named in inscriptions, such as the Samians mentioned in connection with the land dispute with Priene (*I. Priene*, 37): Olympichos (*FGH* 537) author of a *Samiaka* (*Samian History*), and Ouliades (*FGH* 538), otherwise unknown. In Athens, Demosthenes' nephew Demochares wrote contemporary history. Diÿllos, son of an Attic historian, continued the work of the fourth-century historian Ephoros down to 297. Diÿllos's work was continued by Psaon (*FGH* 78), Psaon's by Menodotos (*FGH* 82). Nymphis, from Herakleia on the Black Sea (*FGH* 432), composed not only a history of Alexander but also one about his own city. Sosibios, the first Lakedaimonian historian (*c*.250–*c*.150; *FGH* 595), is slightly better known: from about thirty ancient citations we know that he composed a chronological account of early Spartan history and wrote on Lakedaimonian festivals and customs. Local historians from the island of Rhodes are named in the *Lindian Chronicle* (*FGH* 532, Burstein 46), composed in 99 BC, an example of a chronological record assembled for public display. Another is the *Parian Marble* of 264/3 BC (*Marmor Parium*, *FGH* 239; parts in Austin 1 and 21; Harding 1; Tod 205), a series of brief chronological lemmata such as 'From the time when a comet appeared, and Lysimachos [crossed over to Asia, 39 years, and Leostratos was archon at Athens]' (Austin 21, §25). Hellenized areas of Asia Minor had their historians too (Xenophilos of Lydia, *FGH* 767; Menekrates of Xanthos, *FGH* 769).[81]

Chronicles were a traditional Babylonian form, which was put to work in the service of the new order. Babylonian king-lists incorporate Alexander and his successors into traditional historical schemata, and provide important dating evidence for the Seleukid dynasty (Austin 138,[82] 141).[83] The so-called *Chronicle of the Diadochoi* includes retrospective 'prophecies' about Alexander and the Seleukids, perhaps reflecting Babylonian support for the new rulers as a result of the kings' efforts to find common ground with traditional culture.[84]

Greek prose works by non-Greeks include a remarkable range of Jewish literature.[85] The so-called *Letter of Aristeas*, probably dating from the second century BC, purports to be from an Alexandrian Greek courtier to his brother (part is Austin 262).[86] It describes the commissioning (which may be a real event) by Ptolemy II of a Greek translation of the Torah, the books of Jewish law which are the first five of the Bible. (The translation gave its name to the Greek version of the Old Testament, usually referred to as the

Septuagint; the name derives from the seventy-two Jewish scholars who translated the Torah for Ptolemy – in popular tradition the number was rounded to seventy, *septuaginta* in Latin.) The document tells how the scholars discussed kingship with Ptolemy at a seven-day feast, another example of the 'king meets philosopher' topos (p. 67).

'Jewish–Greek' literature took its origin from Greek versions of the narrative books of the Bible, especially Chronicles, and became a distinct strand in hellenistic prose writing.[87] It included translations and adaptations of other biblical texts, historical studies of Jewish history, philosophical treatises, and prophecies. While these texts served the needs of Greek-speaking Jews of the diaspora, they were also read by bilingual communities who needed to integrate with their Greek surroundings. The books of the Maccabees illustrate these different aspects. The first two books deal with the events of the second and third quarters of the second century; but while the first (written between 135 and 104) is translated from the Hebrew, the second (written between 124 and 63) is a paraphrase of a Greek original. The third and fourth books are partly fictitious, the fourth partly philosophical.[88] (The first two are often printed among the Apocrypha or non-canonical books of the Old Testament in the Christian Bible.)

An aspect of many of these works is the effort to connect Hebrew and Greek world-views in some way, as when Aristoboulos of Alexandria (*c*. late second century BC; not the Alexander historian) derived the ideas of Greek poets and philosophers from Moses. We read in Maccabees that the Jews claimed kinship with the Spartans and were acknowledged by king Areus in the mid-third century:

> Jonathan now saw his opportunity and sent picked men on a mission to Rome to confirm and renew the treaty of friendship with that city. He sent letters to the same effect to Sparta and to other places....
>
> Jonathan the high priest, the senate of the Jews, the priests, and the rest of the Jewish people, to our brothers of Sparta, greeting. On a previous occasion a letter was sent to Onias the high priest from Areus your king, acknowledging our kinship; a copy is given below. Onias welcomed your envoy ... We now venture to send and renew our pact of brotherhood and friendship with you, so that we may not become estranged, for it is many years since you wrote to us. We never lose any opportunity, on festal and other appropriate days, of remembering you at our sacrifices and in our prayers, as it is right and proper to remember kinsmen; and we rejoice at your fame. We ourselves have been under the pressure of hostile attacks on every side ... [but] we have the aid of Heaven to support us, and so we have been saved from our enemies, and they have been humbled. Accordingly, we chose Noumenios son of Antiochos and

Antipatros son of Jason, and have sent them to the Romans to renew our former friendship and alliance with them. We instructed them to go to you also with our greetings, and to deliver this letter about the renewal of our pact of brotherhood. And now we pray you to send us a reply to this letter.

This is a copy of the letter sent by the Spartans to Onias:

Areus, king of Sparta, to Onias the high priest, greeting. A document has come to light which shows that Spartans and Jews are kinsmen, descended alike from Abraham. Now that we have learnt this, we beg you to write and tell us how your affairs prosper. The message we return to you is, 'What is yours, your cattle and every kind of property, is ours, and what is ours is yours', and we have therefore instructed our envoys to report to you in these terms.'

(I Macc. 12: 1–23)

Later the Spartans responded to news of Jonathan's death and renewed their friendship with his successor Simon (I Macc. 14: 16–23). One exiled high priest, Jason (pp. 308, 309), even made his home at Sparta and died there (II Macc. 5: 9).

History was something which Greek élites (both in cities and in federal states) were more likely to wish to produce and consume than the subjects of the kings. This was particularly true for those wishing to write the critical kind of history done by Thucydides and the Attic historians of the fourth century. Other forms of literature needed patronage: funding from above was essential if the writing of scientific works, or diligent library research, was to be more than a pastime. For independent élites the feeling of political involvement was sufficient motivation for writing history.[89] On the other hand, a community's eminent status as a *polis* or league did not guarantee impartiality; historians independent of royal patronage could have axes to grind. Members of Greek élites may have wanted to read history because they saw their community as playing a part in the making of history, and in having played its part in forming the now 'classical' history of earlier times; they needed to know where they had come from. This partly explains the enthusiasm for local histories and antiquarian researches, now matters of public interest. Many such writers were extensively drawn upon in geographical works, which became more popular and played a large part in recording and constructing the horizons of the Greek world after Alexander.

One of the most partisan writers of the third century was Aratos of Sikyon (271–213; not to be confused with the didactic poet), general of the Achaean league for much of the period 245–220. Though 'rough in style and marred by significant omissions',[90] his memoirs, essentially an apologia for his own actions, were Polybios's main source for the period down to 220. Polybios was polemically pro-Achaean and anti-Spartan, not surprisingly in view of his origins (Chapter 1); the same must have been true of Aratos, despite Polybios's claim that the memoirs were 'honest and lucid' (2. 40, Austin 53). Not surprisingly, the view taken of Kleomenes III by these authors was very different from that offered by Phylarchos. Both Aratos and Polybios exemplify the historical work of an independent Greek élite, though Polybios has far larger horizons than a *polis* historian.

Military history, though not unique to historians from the world of Greek politics, was no less important for them than it was for kings. Battles and wars, for us a specific aspect of history to be subsumed within larger social and cultural questions, were for ancient writers the structure of history. Battles become literary set pieces,[91] one of the most carefully designed kinds of writing. Polybios devotes detailed narratives to battles like Sellasia (2. 63–71) and Rhaphia (5. 80–6), always endeavouring to provide a cogent explanation of how the outcome was bound to be what it was, allowing for the element of Tyche (Fortune).

Thanks to the use made of *polis*-based histories in works by later writers like Diodoros, we have a somewhat greater knowledge of these than of royal histories. The former were perhaps more likely to survive, directly or indirectly, and more likely to be written. Alexandrians did not have the same incentive to inquire into their past, because they had no voice in matters of state and no *polis* history comparable to those of Greece; and kings' histories did not hold the same intrinsic interest for Romans either, or for Greeks under the Roman empire, as histories of the Greek states.

It remains to explain why historians have largely disappeared. It is too simplistic to allege, like an earlier observer, that 'The chief reason for the disappearance of so much Hellenistic prose is to be found in its lack of attention to style',[92] though it may be that the militant adoption of fourth-century Attic Greek style in later times caused some third-century works to fall out of fashion. Partly we may adduce the loss of hellenistic writing in general. The great length of historians' works is sometimes cited by later writers:[93] Diodoros complains of those historians who pad out their work with excessive passages of direct speech, leading some readers, 'wearied in spirit by the historian's wordiness and lack of taste, [to] abandon the reading entirely' (20. 1). Pausanias implies that historians of the kings had long since ceased to be read (1. 6. 1). The histories of the Seleukids and Ptolemies may indeed have been unobtainable by the time of Plutarch, who has left us no biographies of them; alternatively, these men may have been unsuited to be his heroes.[94] Prolixity is not unique to hellenistic historians; it may explain the disappearance of much of Livy and Diodoros. The increasing popularity of the précis and of abridged versions (such as Justin's outline of the histories of Pompeius Trogus) is another reason for the loss of complete works.[95]

Furthermore, so few works of Greek historians survive from any period that the existence of the few that do (Herodotos, Thucydides, Xenophon, and Polybios) implies a positive selection, whether deliberate or unconscious.

We come back to 'classicism', the elevation of certain texts to canonical status, concomitantly with their use in Greek and Roman education. Only this, perhaps, could ensure that enough copies of a work existed to maximize its chance of surviving; the loss of many works may owe much to their deselection.

As a footnote to this survey of the purposes of historiography in the Greek world after Alexander, we may briefly mention poetic history. Besides verse works by astronomers and natural scientists (see above, 'didactic poetry', and Chapter 9), it was not unknown for history to be written in epic form. Rhianos, a Cretan-born ex-slave (b. *c.*275), wrote (probably at Alexandria) epics on Greek ethnic histories, most importantly the *Messêniaka* (*Messenian History*) in six books, used by Pausanias (4. 6, etc.) for the early history of Sparta. It should perhaps be classed alongside *polis* history; it must have been a source of pride to the Messenians, giving them the history they lacked during centuries of Spartan occupation down to 369. Other poetic histories concerned the deeds of kings: besides the verse originals of the *Alexander Romance*, a certain Pytheas (not the explorer of Chapter 9) wrote a poem about Eumenes II's victory in 166, and historical poems about Philetairos of Pergamon were inspired by his victory over the Gauls (*Choix* 31).[96] It is a salutary reminder that we risk distorting Greek literature if we pigeonhole it too neatly; as was noted before, history often overlaps with geography and ethnography, and either verse or prose could be the medium.

Conclusion

In evaluating the place of Greek literature in society, it is important to ask where the Greeks were who read these works. It is axiomatic that only a minority of the Greek population in any one society may have been functionally literate,[97] while fewer still had the leisure to read what we call 'literary' works. Still, it is easy to point to Athens, Alexandria, and Pergamon as centres of literary production and consumption, and no doubt in these and other old Greek cities there was a relatively wide educated group (when schools are mentioned in classical sources, even in quite minor cities, they have a hundred or more boys in them).[98] A narrower range of philosophical and literary works may have been read in the newer Greek communities of Egypt proper and the Seleukid empire; from such evidence as we have for the teaching of Greek in Egypt, it appears that the educational canon embraced earlier works such as Homer, Attic tragedy, and New Comedy, while among contemporary literature only some Alexandrian poetry was employed.[99]

Outside the towns of Old Greece the scraps of evidence are few but suggestive. The reversed imprint of a papyrus text of a Greek philosopher has been found in the soil at Ai Khanum;[100] in the same Greek architectural environment, someone inscribed Delphic maxims brought from Greece by a philosopher named Klearchos, probably Klearchos of Soloi (Austin 192,

Burstein 49).[101] The work of Berossos implies a literate circle in Seleukid Mesopotamia whose existence we might not have suspected, though if Burstein is right to regard his style as inferior we may wonder whether the book was widely circulated. Beyond cases like these we can only infer, from the existence of Greek towns and *katoikiai*, that there were *gymnasia* to ensure the reproduction of Greek culture through the teaching of Homer and the 'classics' (see Austin 255, *P. Enteuxeis*, 8, for an example of privately maintained *gymnasia* in Ptolemaic Egypt). Whether much of the new literature penetrated so far is open to doubt.

Sherwin-White and Kuhrt take a relatively optimistic view of cultural interaction between members of Greek and non-Greek élites. Against scholars like Préaux who have asserted that Greek culture was exclusive in Egypt and the Seleukid empire, but without going as far as those scholars such as Hadas who posit extensive hellenization, they show that the evidence for strict non-permeability of Greek and 'barbarian' society cannot withstand scrutiny; there was some pro-active hellenization by the kings. Nevertheless, for Greeks in the east – and for any hellenizing natives allowed to join in – Greek *paideia* meant above all the maintenance of Greekness, not the creation of a new hybrid. Only in places like Alexandria did Greek culture, while building upon the old as Greek culture always had, create new forms to satisfy new needs. Even here, however, we must not lapse into considering interaction only from the Greek point of view; it was a two-way process.

The social role of Greek literature is not a simple one. It generally defined an élite, but there are hints of popular consumption too. The representation of the non-Greek sometimes creates Greek identity by distancing it, and sometimes asserts Greekness by appropriation and assimilation. The personal and the public coexist, and modes of patronage appear that may be compared to those of archaic Greece. Writers engage with tradition, yet (in traditional manner) they innovate, experimenting with new ways of describing human concerns and constructing the human personality. Historiography both describes the new, multipolar power system and upholds civic identity, according to need. The common thread in all this is the prolific replication of literary forms, testifying to the continuing role of reading and performance in cultural debates and self-reflection among Greek élites.

8

THE SELEUKID KINGDOM AND PERGAMON

The Seleukid empire was the largest of the Successor kingdoms. Unlike Macedonia and Egypt, it was not a geographical unity populated mainly by one ethnic group, but embraced many landforms and cultures. It offered the greatest opportunities for interaction between Greeks and non-Greeks; it is the part of the Greek world after Alexander where we can most often see 'hellenization' at work, through city foundations. At the same time, because of its size, it presented particular problems of control and imposed crucial constraints on the aims of its rulers. Other aspects of the empire have been discussed earlier; here the emphasis will be on landscapes and resources, and on issues of military, economic, and other forms of management and control. Following a geographical outline and an examination of military problems within a narrative setting, the techniques and structures with which the Seleukids ruled their empire will be considered. A recurrent theme in these sections is the degree to which the Seleukids built a new structure or inherited an existing system for exploitation; to a large extent the ground had been cleared for the Seleukids, since the Persians over two centuries had selectively targeted the more profitable parts of the empire, particularly Asia Minor and the lowlands, creating an infrastructure of communication, fiscal administration, and military control which was not overthrown by Alexander. Finally, a brief examination of the history of the Attalid dynasty will lead on to a scrutiny of the causes of imperial decline for the Seleukids.

The sources for Seleukid history are somewhat different from those we have met hitherto. While there are thousands of Greek inscriptions from Asia Minor and other western parts of the empire – notably the royal letters collected by Welles – for places further east we depend on documents in non-Greek languages, which are still in the process of being integrated into general historical accounts. In particular, there are important Babylonian astronomical diaries and a range of other cuneiform texts (e.g. Austin 138, a list of kings from Alexander to Antiochos IV).[1] Archaeology has tended to focus on urban sites (especially those in Asia Minor) and the recovery of works of art and documents, many of which lack proper contexts; detailed field survey work has not progressed far except in Mesopotamia,[2] though the

Balboura survey in Lykia is beginning to illuminate processes of hellenization at a town founded in about the early second century BC.[3] Though contemporary histories are lacking for much of the third century, we have the later Alexander narratives for places affected by his campaigns as well as works by historians such as Appian (*Syrian Wars*, *Mithradatic Wars*, and so on) and Justin. For economy and landscapes we can use geographical authors such as Strabo. The biggest difference from Egypt is that no papyri are found within the empire; while for reconstructing some aspects of dynastic history, particularly in Baktria and India, we depend almost entirely upon the elusive evidence of coins.[4]

Land and resources

A glance at a sufficiently small-scale relief map shows that the highland region extending from Turkey to Afghanistan forms a block which more or less cuts off Arabia and Mesopotamia from India, China, and the western Asian steppes (Fig. 8.1). The lowlands of the Levant or 'Fertile Crescent' are confronted on the north-east by the continuous wall of the Zagros mountains; these are the 'hard lands' which the Persians of Cyrus's day, in the Greek story (Herodotos, 9. 121), chose not to leave for fear of losing their special toughness. The heart of the Persian empire was located in the area where the mountain block and the lowlands meet, with four royal capitals situated in the Zagros range: Ekbatana (the old Elamite capital, modern Hamadan), Sousa, Persepolis, and Pasargadai. The first two are in its gentler, western part which gave access to the rich agricultural lands of the west: Mesopotamia, Egypt, Syria–Phoenicia, and western Anatolia. In addition, the Tauros range formed a near-impenetrable barrier; even the easiest pass, known as the Cilician Gates, was formidable.[5]

The descriptions that follow are intended to illustrate the wealth and diversity of the Seleukid territories and their economic resources, and to give some sense of the landscapes, which can rarely be obtained from general books about the period. They also point to the historical questions of how the kings managed to govern their territories, and to what extent they managed to unify them.

The empire can be divided into four main topographic units.[6]

Western Anatolia

Western Anatolia (western Asia Minor) consists mainly of a plateau 500–1,500 metres above sea level[7] (Fig. 8.2). The whole peninsula measures *c*.800 kilometres from west to east, and is bounded on three sides by seas, but on the east by the Tauros massif, which is continuous with the north-westward extensions of the Zagros mountains (see 'Eastern Anatolia, the northern highlands, and inner Iran' below, pp. 279–81). Not only are access

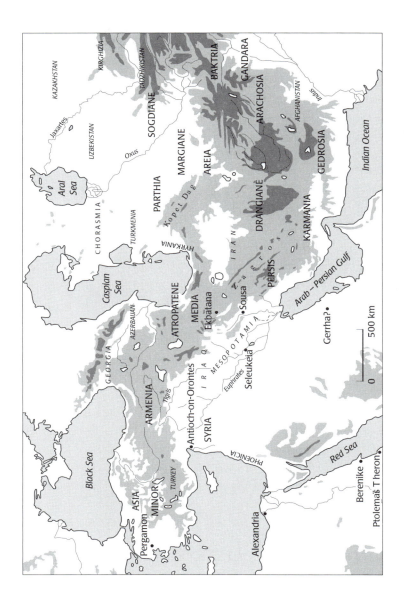

Figure 8.1 The Seleukid empire. (Adapted from Kuhrt and Sherwin-White, *Hellenism*, fig. 1.) The shaded areas represent land over 1,000 and 3,000 m.

and egress at the eastern end difficult, but in general the west coast offers more points of easy access.[8] This fact, and the topographic divisions, have tended to discourage political unification.

The comparatively limited agricultural potential of the plateau – attributable to climate rather than relief – has meant that cities in most periods have been mainly on and near the coasts. Hellenization of the interior had not proceeded far by the late fourth century, and Alexander did not have time to conquer every part – several areas of the interior and north, such as

Figure 8.2   Western Asia Minor. (Adapted from J. B. Salmon in Talbert, *Atlas*, 73.)

Kommagene and Pontos, were not conquered by him and were never firmly within Seleukid power[9] – but the narrow coastal plains of the north and west were fringed with Greek *poleis*. The most famous were on the west coast: from Pergamon in the Troad, via Aiolis and then Ionia with towns such as Ephesos and Miletos, to the partly Hellenic areas of Karia and Lykia in the south-west, where Halikarnassos was situated. Inland from Ionia lay the Persian satrapy of Lydia with its capital, Sardis. Parts of western Asia Minor were famous for wines, fruits such as figs, and generally animal products such as sheepskins and woollen textiles.[10]

While the Greek cities enjoyed a typical mix of trade and agriculture – some, like Priene, dominating a territory inhabited by non-Greek peoples reduced to quasi-serfdom – the inland areas, though partly urbanized, were generally less prosperous. Further east the peninsula was divided into Bithynia, Phrygia, Pamphylia, and Paphlagonia (a mountainous hinterland behind the north coast). While not all these were Seleukid satrapies, most were within the Seleukid sphere of domination. (Pontos is included in the 'Eastern Anatolia' section, below, p. 279.)

Though the urbanized regions west of Tauros were capable of producing substantial revenues, the region was naturally hard to control from the east and became the theatre for intra-dynastic wars and secessions, even though one would have expected the kings to have devoted considerable efforts to holding onto it. In the third century the Greek cities oscillated between Ptolemaic and Seleukid control. Distance alone seems an inadequate explanation of these difficulties, since Seleukeia-in-Pieria (to name but one of the Seleukid capitals) is no further from the wealthier parts of Asia Minor than it is from western Iran; the distance is smaller by sea. The problems were probably due partly to the geographical and political fragmentation of Asia Minor, partly to the traditions of Greek city independence, but very largely to the proximity of Egypt and Macedonia, whose rulers periodically tried to destabilize Seleukid power.

The Levant or 'Fertile Crescent'

This lowland zone embraces modern Israel, Jordan, Lebanon, Syria, and Iraq (Fig. 8.3), and its south-western areas were continually disputed with the Ptolemies. It is with good reason that these regions are together referred to by modern writers as the Fertile Crescent; indeed, their fertility may have been greater in antiquity.[11] They remained a major source of wealth, not least because they had the greatest concentration of large cities in the whole empire. Many were already ancient, such as Babylon and Uruk in Mesopotamia, and the Phoenician ports of Tyre and Sidon.

Mesopotamia (the north-eastern two-thirds of Iraq) is a low-lying area some 35,000 square miles in extent, formed by the combined river plains of the Euphrates and Tigris. In mitigation of the extreme temperatures

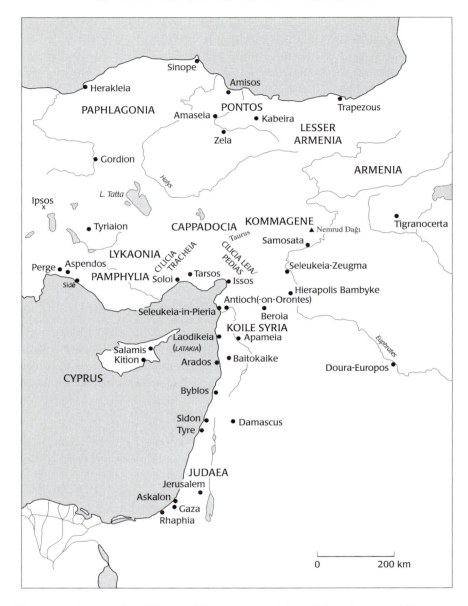

Figure 8.3 Eastern Asia Minor and Syria. (Adapted from J. B. Salmon in Talbert, *Atlas*, 74.)

associated with a continental climate (cold, dry winters; hot, dry summers),[12] the plentiful meltwater of the Tigris and Euphrates flooded annually like the Nile, permitting the complex irrigation schemes which Strabo describes (16. 1. 9–11 (740–1)). Alexander entertained the idea of renovating a canal downstream from Babylon, so that in the dry season it could be more easily dammed and the Euphrates remain full:

> Where the stream of the Euphrates was diverted into the Pollakopas, he decided to shut off the outlet firmly; but going forward about thirty stades the earth appeared somewhat rocky, such that, if it were cut through and linked to the old channel along the Pollakopas, it would not permit the water to flow through because of the hardness of the ground, though the diversion of the water could be carried out easily at the appointed time. For these reasons he sailed to the Pollakopas and navigated down it to the lakes in the direction of the land of the Arabians. There he saw a certain place in a good spot, and founded a city and walled it, and in it he settled certain Greek mercenaries, some of whom volunteered while others were unfit for war through age or wounds.
>
> (Arrian, *Anab.* 7. 21. 6–7)

The fertility of the area was legendary:

> The land produces barley in quantities that no other land does, even, they say, threehundredfold. Its other requirements are provided by the palm-tree, namely bread, wine, vinegar, honey, and grain-meal; and all kinds of textiles come from it; and the bronzesmiths use the kernels in place of charcoal, and these when soaked are fodder for oxen and sheep which are being fattened.
>
> (Strabo, 16. 1. 14 (742))

In addition to agricultural produce, the cities of Mesopotamia probably earned tolls from the overland caravan trade.[13] Agriculture and trade kept their contribution to the royal treasury at a high level. The best land was where the two rivers approached one another. Here, opposite Babylon, Seleukos I founded a new city, Seleukeia-on-Tigris, which became a nodal point for routes into Asia; Strabo describes how it grew larger than Babylon and took over from as a capital (16. 1. 5 (738), Austin 188). It was created partly for political reasons, as is suggested by the opposition to the scheme by the Magi, 'not wishing such a fortress (*epiteichisma*) to come into existence to their disadvantage' (App. *Syrian Wars*, 58).[14] The Assyrian silk of Pliny the Elder's day (*HN* 11. 75) may be a post-Seleukid development, but his Babylonian papyrus (13. 73) could be a hellenistic legacy; it is particularly unfortunate that soil conditions have not allowed papyri to survive.

Sherwin-White and Kuhrt argue that the core of the empire was here. The area had been urbanized since the third millennium BC, and was the setting for pre-Persian empires such as the Babylonian and neo-Assyrian. Babylon on the Euphrates had a highly developed system of law, commerce, and bureaucracy; the priests of the city, from long experience, had even developed ceremonies with which to welcome new conquerors![15] The hills of northern Mesopotamia produced timber, building-stone, and minerals, but the river plains of the south had the richest concentration of agricultural land.

Syria and Lebanon offered supplies of timber and pitch, essential to naval power; Diodoros (19. 58. 2–5) describes how Antigonos had a fleet built with timber from Lebanon and set up shipbuilding centres in the ports of Phoenicia and elsewhere.[16] Syria had relatively large amounts of good arable.[17] Strabo describes additional resources in the water-meadows of the river Orontes:

> And here Seleukos Nikator maintained his five hundred elephants and most of his army, as did those who were kings later. And it was once called Pella by the Macedonians, because most of the Macedonians who served in the army settled there, and Pella, the homeland of Philip and Alexander, had become like a *mêtropolis* (mother-city) for the Macedonians. And here were the military finance office and the stud, with more than thirty thousand royal mares and three hundred stallions. And here the colt-breakers, hoplite trainers, and all the other educationalists in military matters drew their salaries.
>
> (Strabo, 16. 2. 10 (752))

Daphnai, the garden suburb of the new foundation of Antioch (Antiocheia in Greek), had groves of trees, and Damascus was well watered. Syria was also a key land of passage: it afforded the shortest link from the Mediterranean to inner Asia, leading to the middle Euphrates via the low plateau of Aleppo (ancient Berrhoia or Beroia).[18] The independent coastal cities had grown rich on trade in early Greek times, and the sea off Tyre yielded an income from purple dye. Understandably, Alexander and his successors strove to keep them loyal; hence the recurrent disputes between the Ptolemies and Seleukids for control over this area. The Ptolemies, in fact, controlled Phoenicia much of the time.[19] Before the reign of Seleukos the principal settlements were Phoenician Arados and an unfinished Greek *polis* at Antigoneia (which Seleukos destroyed); probably, too, some of the Macedonian place-names listed by Strabo had been assigned before Seleukos,[20] though he was active in founding cities which grew to great prosperity.

Adjacent to Syria on the north was Kilikia Leia (Smooth Cilicia; also called 'Cilicia Pedias', the plain of Cilicia), well watered from Mt. Tauros; in Roman times it grew flax for the linen-makers of Tarsus (Dio Chrysostom, *Oration* 34. 21–3). To the south, Palestine (Palaistine) had arable, good pasture, sometimes relying on irrigation. Date palms and balsam trees flourished in inland valleys of the lower Jordan (Diod. 19. 98); asphalt was gathered from the shores of the Dead Sea and used in Egypt for mummification.[21] Transjordania was fertile, with partly volcanic soil; the area of Gilead had copious springs, deciduous woodland, and grazing. Some of the lands adjoining the Fertile Crescent could not be easily ruled directly, and traditional gift-exchange relationships were sustained with the semi-nomadic Arabs of the Syrian desert and northern Arabia.[22]

Eastern Anatolia, the northern highlands, and inner Iran

This topographical region (Fig. 8.4) is a chain of mountain ranges extending all the way from Kilikia Tracheia (Rough Cilicia), Lykaonia, and Kommagene via Pontos and ancient Armenia (modern Armenia plus north-eastern Turkey) and Atropatene (Azerbaijan) into Iran (which is not an ancient name). There it includes the Zagros range and the component parts of inner Iran: Media, Sousiane, Persis (southern Zagros, the Persians' homeland), Karmania, and Paraitakene (in other words, roughly modern Iran without its highest, eastern part).[23] It forms a physical barrier between lands connected to the Mediterranean and those looking east towards India and China, and those looking north-east towards the great plains of the central Asian republics of Turkmenistan, Uzbekistan, Kirghizia, and Kazakhstan. Iran itself is a plateau or basin (mainly 500–1,500 metres above sea level) ringed by mountains: the steeper face of Zagros overlooks it from the west and south-west, Mt. Elburz (or Alburz) and Kopet Dag adjoin it on the north, and to the east and south lie the westward extensions of the Himalaya–Kara Koram chain. Iran also has two coasts, the Caspian and the Arab–Persian gulf.

Kommagene is described by Strabo as 'quite a small land', with its former (i.e. Seleukid) royal residence at Samosata, a city with 'an extremely fertile, but small, territory surrounding it' (Strabo, 16. 2. 3 (749); also 12. 2. 1 (535), implying that it is extensively planted with fruit trees); but it may not have been brought under direct satrapal rule before the campaigns of Antiochos III. Large parts of Kommagene were steppe lands, and Lake Tatta was saline.[24] Cappadocia was known to Strabo for its orchards (in one area, Melitene, at least: 12. 2. 1 (535)). Silver mines are known from earlier and later times, as is a source of ruddle (12. 2. 10 (540)). Pontos in northern Asia Minor had timber resources; its fertile areas included Amaseia, Strabo's homeland (12. 3. 15 (547)). Fruit-trees flourished; silver, iron ore, and various minerals were mined in north-eastern Pontos and other areas of northern Asia Minor (12. 3. 40 (562)). Coastal cities exploited the fishing grounds of the Black Sea.[25]

Armenia, which Alexander probably conquered, 'abounds in fruit and cultivated trees and evergreens, and even bears the olive' (Strabo, 11. 14. 4 (528)), the last presumably in the valleys. Silver and iron were mined, and it was noted for its cavalry horses; but its mountains rise to 17,000 ft (5,200 m) at Mt. Ararat, and unlike the Zagros they do form a major obstacle. Armenia is further isolated by its severe winters:[26]

Figure 8.4   The central and eastern Seleukid empire. (Adapted from J. B. Salmon in Talbert, *Atlas*, 70–1.)

> Chorzene and Kambysene are the northernmost districts (*eparchiai*) and suffer the most from snow, adjoining as they do the Kaukasian mountains, Iberia, and Kolchis. Here, they say, in the mountain passes, entire caravans are often swallowed up in the snow when particularly severe snowfalls occur; and that the inhabitants have staves against these kinds of dangers, which they push up to the surface to enable them to breathe and to obtain help from those who pass that way, so that they can be dug out and saved.
>
> (Strabo, 11. 14. 4 (528))

These conditions do not fully account for the lack of active interference by the Seleukids, for Armenia is accessible from Mesopotamia via a relatively low pass to the headwaters of the Euphrates.[27] It was occasionally a thorn in the side of the Seleukids, aiding their enemies on several occasions in the third century. It was divided into two areas, both under Iranian dynasts who seem to have been content to be 'subject' to the Seleukids; only later on did the king intervene directly, ousting Orontes, the last of his dynasty, in favour of another ruler.[28]

Mountainous Atropatene (modern north-western Iran and Azerbaijan, on the south-western shore of the Caspian) remained semi-independent under its former satrap Atropates (whence the ancient and modern names) and his successors, of whom the most powerful was Artabarzanes in the reign of Antiochos III. It had some productive slopes, aided by rain-bearing winds from the Caspian.[29]

Inner Iran is largely made up of hill-land and mountain, and is noted for its harsh, continental climate, but like Mesopotamia it enjoyed plentiful water from rivers fed by snow from the mountains. The Persian aristocracy had a reputation for making 'gardens' (perhaps, rather, parks and game reserves) with orchards of apples and peaches (cf. p. 299). Alfalfa was grown as fodder for horses, and Strabo (11. 13. 7 (525)) mentions Greater Media as an area of horse-rearing – Ekbatana's mint-mark was the forepart of a feeding horse. Media was home to many cattle. Parts of the territory that are now salt desert may have been lakes in antiquity; even in recent times there have been fertile valleys such as the Teheran plain in Greater Media and around Isfahan (which is in ancient Media Paraitakene, eastern Media). The bitumen from a well in Sousiane (Hdt. 6. 119), however, may not have been extensively exploited, and the hard-wearing Persian carpets mentioned by the elder Pliny (*HN* 8. 191) were perhaps a curiosity rather than a prime export. Overall, Iran was probably not wealthy or highly productive, and the landscape is geographically disunited, though there are easy passes through the encircling mountains.[30]

The largely village-based population of inner Iran must have made its living from a mix of pastoral and small-scale arable production – hardly the basis for great prosperity but, given the size of the territory and the probable population numbers, the area was a potential source of much tribute. Large cities did exist, such as Ekbatana on the trade-route from China to Syria, the old palace capitals of Sousa, Pasargadai, and Persepolis in the Zagros, and new foundations like Laodikeia. Media's main centres were Rhagai and Ekbatana; Sousa was refounded by Seleukos I as Seleukeia-on-Eulaios.[31] The Seleukids ruled pro-actively in inner Iran,[32] as evidenced by the installation of garrisons and of new towns such as Laodikeia (Nihavend) in Media. However, while areas of the old Persian heartland like Media, Sousiane, and Persis were directly governed by satraps, some parts remained under semi-independent rulers. The hills between the Tigris and Zagros, for example, were a satrapy, but Zagros itself was controlled through gift-exchange with mountain villages.[33] The value of western Iran to the Seleukids must generally have been based on negotiated relationships with the existing nobility, who could ensure that taxes were paid and military forces raised when necessary.

The eastern satrapies: outer Iran and beyond [34]

The lowlands of the north-east

Beyond the Elburz lay the small satrapy of Hyrkania (now Gurgan) on the south-eastern shore of the Caspian. Beyond the mountain range of Kopet Dag was a compact group of north-eastern lowland satrapies: in present-day Turkmenistan were Parthia, Margiane (astride the river Oxus), and Areia (the last covering north-eastern Iran and north-western Afghanistan). Further east, around Marakanda (modern Samarkhand in Uzbekistan), lay the most remote Seleukid area of all, Sogdiane (also called Transoxiana by scholars) (see Fig. 8.4).

Hyrkania is an area of hill settlements favoured by rain-bearing winds from the Caspian, and is not known to have received any foundations under Seleukid rule.[35] To its east lay Parthia, which later wielded great power but grew only slowly (below, p. 320; for its origins see Strabo, 11. 9. 2–3 (515), Austin 145);[36] through the third century, at least, it remained formally a vassal of the Seleukids. The adjacent region of Areia, a fertile satrapy, was probably Seleukid throughout the third century; like other parts of Iran it suffers extremes of temperature, but cities were supported by irrigation of rivers fed by meltwater in spring.[37] The same was true of Margiane to the north, whose fertility Antiochos I so admired, according to Strabo (11. 10. 2 (516)), that he refounded Alexander's new city as Antiocheia (near modern Mary, formerly Merv, in Turkmenistan).[38] Much wealth will have been gained from the existence of the overland trade route to China.

Finally, Sogdiane, further north, lay open (like Margiane) to attacks from still more remote steppe peoples, but formed a valuable satrapy in conjunction with Baktria. Sogdiane has been described as 'a region of rich fields and beautiful gardens', richer in natural resources than Baktria, and the irrigated river soils of Baktria, Sogdiane, and Margiane made these areas together 'the Babylonia of the East'.[39] Sogdiane actually had more mountain land and more desert than Baktria, but a greater number of fertile oases, such as the main town of Marakanda. Seleukid intervention here mainly took the form of founding cities and smaller military settlements. The city of Alexandria Eschate (Alexandria the Furthest), refounded by Antiochos I as another Antiocheia, testifies to the kings' active interest, and there is evidence of other new city foundations, like the Greek constructions at Marakanda.[40]

The eastern highlands

Beginning in central eastern Iran, this area comprises Drangiane in east-central Iran and southern Afghanistan, Arachosia in southern Afghanistan, Baktria in mountainous north-eastern Afghanistan, and Karmania in south-eastern Iran (see Fig. 8.4).

Drangiane was a fertile region irrigated by the river Helmand, and probably remained Seleukid throughout the third century despite a gap in the evidence.[41] It was noted for its tin mines (Strabo, 15. 2. 10 (724)). The eastern, desert part of Arachosia was ceded to the Mauryan king Chandragupta (p. 287) by Seleukos I. Arachosia was then annexed by Demetrios of Baktria after the death of his father Euthydemos c.189, along with Paropamisadai (the slopes of the Hindu Kush, north-east of Areia) and probably Areia and Drangiane. Western Arachosia, like other areas described here, has extreme temperatures and relied on irrigation. In the far south Karmania (modern Kerman) was not only a fertile valley but also produced gold, silver, copper, ruddle, salt, and vines (Strabo, 15. 2. 14 (726–7)).[42]

Baktria is often marginalized in general accounts because it was separate from the Seleukid kingdom from the mid-third century; but it was by no means cut off from the west (see Fig. 8.4). It has been argued that a southward expansion of Parthian power did not cut the Seleukids off from Baktria-Sogdiane; not only is there an alternative route linking central Iran with Baktria, but the evidence for the rapid rise of Parthia is insubstantial – until this time Parthian power was probably restricted to areas in and north of Kopet Dag.[43] Furthermore, complete cultural separation of Baktria after the political breakaway under Diodotos is inherently unlikely; the known wealth of Baktria-Sogdiane (which formed a single satrapy) made it an important area of concern for the Seleukids.

Baktria was reputedly a rich land, famous for its cavalry and its transit trade along the caravan roads, but poor in silver and gold; Tarn declares that 'the wealth of Bactria lay in, and not below, its soil'.[44] Like other areas of the eastern empire it depended on irrigated agriculture and the plentiful rivers running off the mountains, in this case the rivers of the Oxus (Amu Darya) basin. The irrigation system was extensive, and according to Strabo (11. 11. 1 (516), Austin 191, Burstein 51 c (a)) Apollodoros described Baktria as 'the ornament of all Ariane' (i.e. eastern Iran). In addition to the agricultural base, the inhabitants probably drew on the silver resources of the Hindu-Kush. So legendary was the wealth of Baktria that ancient sources claimed it had a thousand cities; if the category of *poleis* may be stretched to include the small urbanized 'village' settlements that were often called *poleis* in Greece, this may not be far from the truth.[45]

The satrapy was strategically important[46] because of the Asiatic steppes to the north. Like the Achaemenids, the Seleukids and the subsequent Graeco-Baktrian dynasty had forts on the river Jaxartes (Syr-Darya). Alexander had founded Alexandria Eschate in Sogdiane; Seleukos added Antioch-in-Skythia, and Antiochos I further military settlements centred on Antioch-in-Margiane (Merv).

Baktria was lost to the Seleukids at some time during the mid-third century; but to call this a secession implies too legalistic a break, as if the

United Kingdom were to leave the European Union. A revolt in the far east had begun before Alexander's death (Diod. 17. 99. 5–6) and resumed later:

> Those Greeks who had been settled by Alexander in the so-called upper satrapies were missing Greek culture (*agôgê*) and the Greek way of life (*diaita*), but had been cast away in the furthest reaches of the kingdom. While the king lived they gave in out of fear, but when he died they revolted. They put their minds together and chose as general Philon the Ainianian and put together a substantial force: for they had more than twenty thousand infantry and three thousand cavalry, all of them with frequent experience of the struggles of war and notable for their bravery.
>
> (Diod. 18. 7. 1–2)

Perdikkas ordered the Macedonian army to massacre them, though according to Diodoros the commander in the field was happy not to do so, and it was only the Macedonian soldiers (and presumably subordinate commanders), greedy for booty, that carried out the order (Diod. 18. 7. 5–9). All this provided the preconditions for revolt in the late 240s or early 230s under Diodotos, who took the title of king. Sherwin-White and Kuhrt make a powerful case against seeing this revolt as the result of neglect by the Seleukids, whose determination to hold Baktria-Sogdiane is well demonstrated by their city foundations and is supported by the fact that Seleukos I sent Demodamas of Miletos, at an uncertain date, to intimidate the steppe nomads beyond the river Jaxartes (Pliny, *HN* 6. 49; see also below, pp. 285, 306–7. A certain Patrokles (*FGH* 712) explored the Caspian region on behalf of Seleukos while in charge of Baktria-Sogdiane around 280 (Strabo, 2. 1. 2–9 (67–70), *passim*; 11. 7. 3 (509); cf. 2. 1. 14 (73) for probable information from Patrokles).[47]

The farthest east

More remote areas, such as Gandara (a former Persian satrapy along with Sind),[48] Gedrosia (Baluchistan: a desert table-land at *c*.5,000 ft, 1,500 m),[49] and the areas around the cities of Taxila and Pushkalavati[50] in the Indus valley, were ceded to Chandragupta (see Fig. 8.4). His Mauryan empire was powerful in its own right and a potentially dangerous neighbour of the Seleukids. Under either his successor Bindusara or the next king, the renowned Aśoka, it expanded to embrace most of the Indian subcontinent apart from the extreme south, western Arachosia included. Aśoka was a convert to Buddhism (the religion was founded in the sixth century) and attempted to propagate his religion in areas of Greek settlement; he sent missionaries to Greek kings, and has left us a remarkable series of rock-cut inscriptions (the Rock Edicts) in which he sets forth moralizing pronouncements (though the texts as we have them are versions edited by local officials and are adjusted to the culture of the areas to which they were presented).[51] In a bilingual Greek–Aramaic inscription from Kandahar he similarly set out his achievements; here is a translation of the Greek version:

> Ten years having been completed, king Piodasses [Aśoka] made piety known to men, and afterwards more pious he caused men to be and things to flourish throughout the whole land; and abstinence the king practised from animate things, and also other men and all who were hunters or fishermen of the king have ceased hunting, and if there were some incontinent men, they have ceased from their incontinence to the extent possible, and they are obedient to their father and mother and the elders in contrast to before, and in the future more profitably and better in every way will they live by doing these things.
>
> (Burstein 50)[52]

Trade with India, particularly in luxuries like hardwood, spices, and precious stones continued under the Seleukids.[53] Without doubt the kings encouraged it, both for the things it made available and for the tolls they could levy. Seleukos sent Megasthenes (p. 261) to report on India, perhaps with a view to military action; he appears to have thought better of that, but Megasthenes' work remained an important addition to Greek ethnography of non-Greeks.[54] Demodamas (the one who campaigned beyond the Jaxartes, above) wrote about India (*FGH* 428).

Conquest of at least the north-western frontier of India was never achieved by the Seleukids, but had to wait for the expansion of the Graeco-Baktrian kingdom in the mid- and later second century, particularly under the so-called Indo-Greek (or Graeco-Indian) kings Demetrios II (*c*.185–175?) and Menandros (Menander, r. *c*.155–*c*.130). Demetrios II was the first Graeco-Baktrian king whose title, 'Aniketos' (Unconquered), was rendered into an Indian language on coins. Buddhism remembers Menandros as Milinda: he converted to Buddhism and is said to have debated doctrine with a monk (see e.g. Plutarch, *Precepts of Statecraft*, 821 d–f).[55] From this point on, however, the Graeco-Baktrian and Indo-Greek kings are almost lost to history. Coins of about twenty later rulers are known; probably several dynasties are represented. The Graeco-Baktrians appear to have ruled beyond the Oxus until *c*.140, about which time the Chinese pushed Skythian peoples across the river; these, defeated by Mithradates I (or II) of Parthia, settled in Drangiane for several generations. After Menandros, coin hoards suggest a chaotic period in the eastern and southern parts of the Greek territories. By about 100 the Yuëzhi had taken Baktria itself; they, in turn, were forced out by the Saka people coming from the Pamirs and by the Skythians, now known as Skytho-Parthians, moving north from Drangiane.

The last known king, Hermaios, is believed to have tried to unify the Baktrian and Indian branches of the Greek kingdom; but by about 50 BC the various invaders had carved up the Greek territories among themselves.[56]

The whole area described in the preceding four sections is made up of four main relief zones, but covers a wide variety of landforms. Though more or less naturally defined by geographical barriers on every side, it could hardly be said to form a natural unit. For the eastern part alone (Iran, Afghanistan, and central Asia):

> it is clear that there could be neither unity nor large populations here like the Nile and Tigris–Euphrates River basins. Vast areas, for the most part, could only be ruled for a short time by either nomadic or tribal states, or by some kind of feudal alliances. The problems of communication and holding allegiances were enormous ...
>
> (Frye)[57]

How well the Seleukids faced up to these problems, and those of the rest of their empire, is an important question. They had a head start, for they inherited from the Achaemenids a system that had controlled the entire area more or less successfully for two hundred years. In the study of the Seleukid empire, it may be better to assume the success of their rule unless there is evidence of failure, rather than concentrate exclusively on what has been dubbed their decline.

Crises and continuities in Seleukid power, 312–164 BC

Seleukos I and Antiochos I (312–261 BC)

Seleukos I (r. 305–281) was appointed to Babylonia on Alexander's death. Expelled by Antigonos, he was restored in 312 with the help of Ptolemy. Antigonos remained a powerful enemy, and, since Seleukos had initially not been appointed to govern the whole of Alexander's eastern conquests, if he wanted more provinces he would have to fight for them, both against Antigonos (whom he finally defeated in Babylonia in 308)[58] and against local rulers appointed by him, such as Nikanor in the small area of northwestern Iran known as Media. In addition to Media, Seleukos took the extensive tribute-producing lands of Sousiane and adjacent regions (Diod. 19. 100), probably including Persis. He now 'wrote to Ptolemy and his other friends about his achievements, already possessing a king's stature and a reputation worthy of royal power' (Diod. 19. 92). Diodoros may be writing with hindsight, knowing that before long Seleukos joined the others in adopting the royal title; but the connection between victorious military campaigns and royal status is clear. By Ipsos (301) or soon after, he had added the further territories of Outer Iran, all of which had in some sense belonged to the Persian empire and were conquered, or at least passed through, by Alexander.

Before Ipsos, Seleukos invaded north-western India from Baktria, making war on Chandragupta (Sandrokottos in Greek), who had recently established an extensive and powerful Mauryan kingdom, presenting himself as an anti-Macedonian ruler after Alexander's satraps and their replacements had been killed in India. Here, too, Seleukos could claim to be restoring Alexander's inheritance; but this time he made a treaty, ceding territory in return for war-elephants.[59]

The aftermath of Ipsos brought further gains when Seleukos received wealthy Koile Syria and Phoenicia by treaty. He immediately lost parts of them to Ptolemy, but soon captured northern Syria, northern Mesopotamia, Armenia, and southern Cappadocia; he also asserted suzerainty over Kommagene.[60] He was now master of virtually all Alexander's conquests outside Greece, apart from Egypt and parts of Asia Minor – in effect, the former Persian empire with all its tribute-bearing lands.

At the end of the 280s Seleukos finally defeated Lysimachos at Koroupedion and invaded Macedonia (p. 45). A Babylonian document from this time actually refers to his wish to reconquer 'Macedonia, his land', whereas the Greek sources refer only to his 'longing' (*pothos*) to see his homeland again.[61] In practice the Successors were compelled to compromise if they had any deep-seated desire to reunite the whole of Alexander's empire (compare Ptolemaic ambitions, discussed on p. 206); but this episode suggests that a latent desire resurfaced in Seleukos when an occasion presented itself.

His assassination caused no crisis, for his son Antiochos I (r. 292–261) had been co-ruler since 292. This was not a division of the kingdom prompted by deep-seated problems, nor does there seem to have been a formal distribution of powers.[62] A co-regency was a clever public statement of dynastic stability, an intelligent innovation in the light of experience, perhaps most notably the aftermath of Alexander's death.

Probably to symbolize their cooperation and safeguard the succession, Seleukos handed on his wife Stratonike to his son Antiochos (see p. 71). Antiochos was in the far east when Seleukos died, and it is known that parts of the empire now revolted, including 'the cities of Syria' (decree of Ilion, Austin 139, BD 16, Burstein 15, *OGIS* 219; quoted, p. 65), probably Seleukos's own foundations; the trouble was perhaps provoked by Ptolemy II.[63] Evidence for non-Greek unrest, however, is tenuous,[64] and Antiochos's campaigns over the next few years are best viewed as a restatement of sovereignty over areas conquered by Seleukos I, or assigned to him after Koroupedion, rather than the quelling of a rebellion.

By *c.*270 Antiochos had defeated the Gauls (see p. 53), and his standing was high in Asia Minor. This perhaps helped preserve the loyalty of Cappadocia (under a *stratêgos*) and of the governor of Pergamon, Philetairos, previously an officer of Lysimachos. There was probably a clash with Ptolemy II, known as the first Syrian war, in which Ptolemy seized some of Lysimachos's former possessions in western Asia Minor and the Aegean. It is possible that Antiochos hoped to depose Ptolemy and place on the throne of Egypt Ptolemy's brother Magas, ruler of Cyrene, with whom he made a pact; if so, it came to nothing. After a decade of military action, Antiochos's territories from Asia Minor and Syria to the east were now loyal and intact.

The reigns of both Seleukos and Antiochos are distinguished by active city-building in Iran and Asia Minor. Their projects may include Ai Khanum and Ikaros (p. 305). Stability was ensured by strong, prosperous urban foundations such as the four Syrian cities founded by Seleukos after Ipsos, described by Strabo:[65]

> (4) Seleukis is the best of the aforementioned parts [*of Syria*], but is called Tetrapolis [*The Four Cities*], and is such according to the outstanding cities in it, of which there are quite a few; but the largest are four, Antioch [*Antiocheia*] near Daphne, Seleukeia-in-Pieria, Apameia, and Laodikeia, which used to be called sisters of one another because of the concord between them. They are foundations of Seleukos Nikator.[66] ... (5) Moreover, Antioch is the *mêtropolis* of Syria, and the king's residence (*basileion*) was founded here for the rulers of the land, and in power and size it is not far short of Seleukeia-on-Tigris and Alexandria-by-Egypt ...(6) Daphne lies above Antioch by forty stades, a settlement of moderate size, but also a large, shady grove dissected by waters from springs; in the middle is an inviolate sanctuary and temple of Apollo and Artemis.... (8) Towards the sea from these is Seleukeia and Pieria, a mountain ... The city is a remarkable fortification, mightier than (any) force.... (9) Then comes Laodikeia, a city most beautifully built upon the sea and with a good harbour; it has a territory rich in wine in addition to its other fertility. It provides the greatest part of their wine to the people of Alexandria, and the mountain lying above the city is covered in vineyards almost as far as the summits ... (10) Apameia also has an acropolis that is mostly well defended; for it is a well-fortified hill in a hollow plain. The Orontes makes it like a peninsula, as does a large lake lying round it which discharges itself into wide marshes and exceedingly large meadows for oxen and horses. And thus the city is securely located ... and it enjoys an extensive and blessed land through which the Orontes flows, and dependent towns occur frequently in it.
>
> (Strabo, 16. 2. 4–6 (749–50), 8–10 (751–2), Austin 174)

Syria was familiar to Greeks, particularly as a great centre of trade, but this network of new foundations was a bold and successful attempt to impose a new framework of military and economic control.

Like his father, Antiochos resorted (in 279) to the device of co-regency to secure the succession, but deemed it necessary to execute his son Seleukos in the early 260s (Trogus, *Prologues*, 26).[67] The new heir was his younger son, the future Antiochos II.

Events in the reigns of Seleukos I and Antiochos I had established Syria as a zone of friction between Asia and Egypt. They had also (apart from a hiatus in 281) allowed the kings and their administrators to accumulate half a century's experience of consolidating imperial power and building a stable dynastic unity.

Antiochos II and Seleukos II (261–226 BC)

The reigns of Antiochos II (261–246) and Seleukos II (246–226) are sometimes portrayed as periods of major crisis threatening their control over the eastern empire. Musti presents the Iranian possessions as increasingly marginal to 'the economic and political unity which was growing up in the Syro-Mesopotamian heart of the state',[68] but the westward emphasis is debatable. The rulers of Baktria seized their independence about now, but there is no detailed evidence for other events in the east; for any given area it may be safer to assume continuity of Seleukid rule unless it is disproved. In this light, the fact that no Seleukid king is known to have visited Iran between the 260s and c.230[69] may be a sign of confidence and stability rather than weakness. Baktria remained in some sense attached to the empire, which had need of its resources and strategic protection; the key issue is what belonging to the empire entailed, and we will return to this. Eventually Greek Baktria fell to nomadic invaders in about the late second century; perhaps the rulers left while ordinary folk remained and paid allegiance to new masters.[70]

Early in his reign Antiochos II (r. 261–241) fought the second Syrian war against Ptolemy II, who was seeking to gain territory in Asia Minor and the Aegean but instead lost to Antiochos some Greek towns in Ionia, islands such as Samos, and coastal areas of Cilicia Tracheia and Pamphylia. What then followed may be seen as either a compromise or a diplomatic victory for Antiochos: he divorced his queen, Laodike, and married Ptolemy's daughter Berenike. The deaths of both kings in 246 were quickly followed by a further mutual test of power, the third Syrian or Laodikean war (246–241), in which Ptolemy III invaded Asia Minor hoping to secure the succession for Berenike's son by Antiochos. She and her son were assassinated, however, and the throne passed to Antiochos's chosen successor, his son by Laodike, Seleukos II. Despite this setback Ptolemy's invasion actually penetrated as far as Babylon, though in the end he gained or regained only certain

Mediterranean strongholds, including Seleukeia (the port of Antioch) and various areas in Cilicia Tracheia, Pamphylia, and Ionia.

Seleukos II (r. 241–226/5), like his predecessors, used the device of an early co-regency to secure control over the empire; but his co-ruler was his brother, Antiochos 'Hierax' (Hawk), and their rivalry soon spilled over into war (c.241–c.239; cf. Strabo, 16. 2. 14 (754), Austin 144). Attalos I of Pergamon was soon engaged in a war with Hierax, who was now calling himself king; after intermittent campaigns Attalos defeated him in 227 and now ruled much of Asia Minor; but in the broader picture (if we accept that the centre of the empire was not in the west), the loss of territory to Pergamon was perhaps not so serious. More important for Seleukos was control over the north-east; around 230–227 he was fighting the Parthians, perhaps with an eye to reasserting control over Baktria.

The thirty-five years of the reigns of Antiochos II and Seleukos II had witnessed losses of territory and dynastic struggle, suggesting that the empire might be more vulnerable to disruption than before. A combination of accident and design would prolong the series of crises after the death of Seleukos II.

Seleukos III and Antiochos III (226/5–187 BC)

Seleukos II died early, and his son Seleukos III (r. 226/5–223) was assassinated while campaigning against Attalos I. He was succeeded by his brother Antiochos III (r. 223–187), aged 19 or 20, who would be the longest-lasting and most successful member of the dynasty since the founder. His accession was followed in 221 by those of two even less mature men in the rival kingdoms: Ptolemy IV in Egypt and Philip V in Macedonia, a historical coincidence not lost on Polybios (2. 71, cf. 5. 34; Austin 223). Their reigns would see a complete reordering of the global politics of the eastern Mediterranean, assisted by Rome's intervention.

First, however, Antiochos III had to fend off other threats. On Seleukos III's death the army had acclaimed as king Achaios, a grandson of Seleukos I; but he turned down the throne in favour of Antiochos III and continued to lead the campaign against Attalos (Polyb. 4. 48, Austin 146). Polybios tells us that Antiochos's chief minister Hermias dominated the young king. Molon, commander of the eastern satrapies, revolted in 222, allegedly provoked by fear of Hermias's power. Hermias was assassinated and Molon was defeated, but not before he had invaded the western empire. Soon afterwards Achaios assumed the royal title in Asia Minor, a region which was from time to time the focus of separatist ambitions. For a time Antiochos was content to leave him alone, but in 213 Achaios was captured, mutilated, and impaled, the same punishment as the Persian kings had traditionally meted out to traitors.

Antiochos's western campaigns had already led him to invade Egypt, where he was defeated at Rhaphia (p. 204). Now (212) he took Kommagene and northern Armenia, and exacted arrears of tribute from the ruler of southern Armenia. Continuing east, he embarked on the eight-year series of campaigns (212–205/4) that became known as his *anabasis* or 'ascent' (like Xenophon's *anabasis*, 'journey to the interior', with Cyrus the Younger in 400–399), in which he restored Seleukid suzerainty in the eastern satrapies. His reported attack on the Parthians is to be seen as the expulsion of cross-border raids from north-eastern Media rather than an invasion of their territory proper, since the Parthians, as their coins show, still acknowledged Seleukid overlordship;[71] he earned himself the title of Megas, 'the Great'. He attacked Euthydemos of Baktria as a rebel and usurper, but eventually recognized his kingship; according to Polybios, Euthydemos pleaded their mutual need for security from the large numbers of nomads threatening both kingdoms (Polyb. 11. 34. 1–10, Austin 150, where we learn that he came originally from Magnesia, probably the Lydian town of that name). The stereotypical representation of non-hellenized pastoralists as dangerous barbarian hordes is typical of ancient rhetoric, and may be genuine rather than Polybian, since this would probably be well calculated to appeal to a Greek ruler in western Asia.[72] The senior king, anyway, granted kingship to his vassal.[73] Antiochos renewed links with Mauryan India, traversed the eastern Iranian satrapies, and made a treaty with the Arabs of Gerrha.

The *anabasis* must not be seen as a temporary and unsuccessful attempt to rebuild the eastern empire – it had never broken apart – but as a necessary, and for near eastern empires traditional, periodic reassertion of overlordship. The expedition was much more than a momentary pause interrupting an inexorable decline.

Despite his various successes, the event for which Antiochos III is best remembered is his war against the Romans between 192 and 189, culminating in his defeat at Magnesia in western Asia Minor (early 189). By the peace of Apameia (188) he gave up most of Asia Minor, which was divided between Rhodes and Pergamon. Within a year he died. These are often seen as fatal blows for the Seleukid empire, the beginning of the end; it remained a large kingdom for another century,[74] but had lost one of its most valuable possessions, Asia Minor.

From Seleukos IV to Antiochos IV (187–164 BC)

Historians and students usually concentrate on Seleukid and Attalid history down to 188, but the later parts of their stories are important and well documented, and reveal much about the nature of the two kingdoms and the reasons for their demise. The likely reasons for the collapse of the Seleukid kingdom centre upon the Romans and what seems to have been their deliberate policy of destabilization. After Magnesia, without attempting to take over the western half of the empire, they were able to influence events enormously through diplomacy and military action.

Antiochos III's son Seleukos IV (r. 187–175) is portrayed as weak by the sources, but it is hard to know what credence to give this, since the situation in which he found himself did not offer many opportunities for vigorous rule. He fell behind with indemnity payments, and seems to have maintained only the minimum of diplomatic contact with Rome; more actively, he arranged marriage alliances with Prousias of Bithynia and Perseus, king of Macedonia. He sent his chancellor, Heliodoros, to raise funds from the Temple at Jerusalem; when the mission failed, Heliodoros encompassed the king's assassination (II Macc. 3: 4–40). Perhaps because Seleukos had distanced himself from Rome, the Romans' ally Eumenes II of Pergamon helped Seleukos's younger brother Antiochos secure the throne in the face of opposition from the late king's son Demetrios, who was a hostage at Rome. A decree (probably from Athens) praises Eumenes and his queen Apollonis for helping Antiochos (Austin 162, Burstein 38, *OGIS* 248). It is uncertain whether the Romans were genuinely offended at this usurpation of the throne; they may have even connived at it, and it gave them an excuse to interfere later.[75]

This younger brother of Seleukos, Antiochos IV (r. 175–164), was known as Theos Epiphanes ('the God Manifest'). He has a reputation for eccentricity (p. 62), but seems to have been an effective ruler. Controversy rages about his treatment of the Jews in the 160s (pp. 307–12), but in his early years he paid off the indemnity to Rome (Livy, 42. 6. 7), was active in diplomacy and gift-giving towards Greek cities, notably at the sanctuary of Olympian Zeus in Athens (p. 87). As king in 168, however, he submitted to the Roman demand that he desist from his invasion of Egypt during the sixth Syrian war, which had been going well (pp. 208–9). On this infamous occasion the Roman commander Gaius Popillius Laenas presented him with the Senate's demand, and actually drew a circle in the sand around the king, telling him to give his answer before he stepped outside it (Polyb. 29. 27, Austin 164).[76] It did not take Antiochos long to comply, despite the facts that Rome was exceeding the terms of Apameia, that it had been Ptolemy VI who attacked him and not the other way round, and that his empire was still powerful and wealthy. He may have had an understandable fear of the Roman army, which had earlier defeated Antiochos III and was now fresh from victory over Macedonia.

Far from being disheartened or unbalanced by his humiliation, Antiochos undertook military campaigns in the east. Before setting out, he demonstrated his empire's continuing power by organizing an enormous procession to the sanctuary of Apollo in Daphne, near Antioch, in 166/5. Behind 36,000 soldiers (many with gold weapons and accoutrements), 500 gladiators, about 9,500 cavalry (many of the horses having gold or silver trappings and the riders in purple coats with golden decoration in animal forms), 140 chariots drawn by 760 horses, two elephant-drawn chariots, and 36 elephants, came about 800 youths in gold crowns, about 1,000 oxen for sacrifice, and a further 300 oxen and 800 elephant tusks presented by foreign states.

> The mass of statues is impossible to describe; for images of all the gods and guardian spirits who are named or honoured by men were carried, some gilded, others clothed in gold-embroidered garments. All of these were accompanied by the appropriate legends, executed according to the traditional narratives in expensive materials. Following these were an image of Night and one of Day, of Earth and Heaven, of Dawn and Midday. One may comprehend how great was the mass of gold and silver objects in the following way: one thousand slaves belonging to Dionysios, the king's secretary, walked in procession bearing silver vessels, none of which had a weight less than 1,000 drachmas. There were royal slaves numbering six hundred, bearing golden vessels; then came about two hundred women sprinkling (the spectators) with perfumes from golden urns. Behind these processed eighty women in golden-footed litters, and five hundred in silver-footed, richly dressed. And these were (only) the most spectacular things in the procession.
>
> (Polyb. 30. 25–6 = Ath. 5. 194)[77]

Antiochos then went east (165–164) and restored Seleukid rule in Greater Armenia, which, like other eastern satrapies, had asserted its independence after 188. He tried to do the same in parts of Iran, but succumbed to a fatal illness. If his strategic aim was to hold up the Parthians' advance, it was at least temporarily achieved, and he may be accounted one of the more successful Seleukid kings.[78]

Methods of control

Unity versus regionalism

The Seleukids faced problems of geographical distance and ethnic diversity, of traditional and new power-centres; but they ruled with forceful ambition and exploited the resources of their empire with considerable success. In this section we shall see that they had learned from their Achaemenid predecessors to rule by means that did not involve the expensive over-use of force.

When Alexander defeated Dareios he took over the existing system of provinces ruled by satraps, usually Persian men though sometimes local nobles. Alexander appointed both Macedonians and occasionally Persians; Seleukos continued the practice.[79] The Persian system had been designed to ensure the loyalty of a province – meaning, in effect, its ruling élite – as a reliable source of tribute and, when necessary, military manpower on the rare occasions of a major levy. The limited design meant that the Persians did not have to create a complex, interventionist administration; indeed, they seem to have had no aspirations to change the economy or society of a province, desiring to get out of it only what they wanted. The system, however, offered the satrap many opportunities to further his own power, even to the extent of refusing to pay the tribute and claiming independence. If this happened, a province could only be won back by military action on the part of the king, so a satrap might be able to avoid paying tribute for a long time. The best tactic for the king was to pick his satraps carefully and keep a close eye on them by having centrally appointed officers within the provincial palace.

Herodotos, in the fifth century, gives a useful indication of the government's potential income when he records the amounts of tribute supposedly received by Dareios I in the late sixth century from each district of his empire (3. 89–95), and though we do not know whether the amounts are accurate, or whether they are the sums actually delivered, his account indicates which satrapies were seen as most important. Of areas that later formed part of Seleukid territory, the one paying the most was Babylonia-Assyria (1,000 talents of silver), followed by the Persian gulf (600), Cilicia (500), Media (450), and the Greek and neighbouring areas of western Asia Minor (400), though the whole of Asia Minor excluding Cilicia paid 1,060 talents. Phoenicia, Syria, Palestine, and Cyprus are listed as paying only 350 talents between them, but this may be because they provided warships; it may be, too, that in relation to the populations of these small areas their contributions were high. Interestingly, Baktria on its own paid 360, but the Parthians, Chorasmians, Sogdians, and Areians together only 300. Assuming that there had been no radical socio-economic change in these areas, Herodotos's figures may be taken as a broad guide to the relative importance of different Seleukid satrapies.

The principal features of the Persian satrapal system are mirrored in the Seleukid empire: the close scrutiny of prospective satraps, prolonged periods of non-intervention, and occasional military expeditions by the king to remind the local ruler of his duty. Along with a variety of landscapes went a variety of local administrative systems – local kings and native 'dynasts', centrally appointed satraps, and independent Greek cities – just as in the Achaemenid empire. The main concerns of the king and his advisers were, apart from resisting attack, to maximize the inflow of tribute in whatever form and the capacity to raise a major army when needed. A corollary of the system is that, as under the Persians, 'independence' for a province rarely meant outright hostility or a military threat to the king; a satrap might still formally recognize suzerainty, for example through his coin types. If he defaulted on the tribute, calling himself king, then the greater king would have to act, as Seleukos II did against Diodotos; but it is noticeable that when Antiochos III attacked Euthydemos of Baktria he did not press home his victory to the point of extinguishing the satrap, but came to a diplomatic compromise. Only in cases where a member of the royal family or a general of the king broke away, posing a threat to the dynasty, were cruel measures taken following victory, as against Achaios.

Another important facet of the empire was the use of old near eastern languages in administration. Scholars no longer believe that Greek was promoted as the sole official tongue. The bureaucracy was just as complicated as under the Persians, and most of it was left to run in the same way as before. In non-Greek areas, scribal languages such as Aramaic remained in use for official records, while cuneiform Akkadian was also used, as in the building inscription of the temple of Ezida founded by Antiochos I at Borsippa near Babylon in 268:[80]

> Antiochos, the great king, the mighty/legitimate king, king of the world, king of Babylon, king of lands, caretaker of Esagila and Ezida, first son of Seleukos, the king, the Macedonian, king of Babylon, am I.
>
> When I decided to build Esagila and Ezida, the bricks for Esagila and Ezida I moulded with my pure hands (using) fine quality oil in the land of Hatti and for the laying of the foundation of Esagila and Ezida I brought (them). In the month of Addaru, on the twentieth day, year 43, the foundation of Ezida, the true temple, the house of Nabû which is in Borsippa I did lay.
>
> (O) Nabû, lofty son, wise one of the gods, the proud one, worthy of praise, most noble son of Marduk, offspring of Erua, the queen, who formed mankind, regard (me) joyfully and, at your lofty command which is unchanging, may the overthrow of the countries of my enemies, the achievement of my battle-wishes against my enemies, permanent victories, just kingship, a happy reign, years of joy, children in satiety, be (your) gift for the kingship of Antiochos and Seleukos, the king, his son, for ever.
>
> [*Another prayer follows, then a third*:]
>
> (O) Nabû, first son, when you enter Ezida, the true house, may favour for Antiochos, king of lands, (and) favour for Seleukos, the king, his son, (and) Stratonike, his consort, the queen, be in your mouth.
>
> (Austin 189)[81]

The Seleukid kingdom resembles modern empires in certain respects – an ethnically defined ruling group, economic exploitation of conquered territories (in this case mainly through taxation, tribute, and military service), and so on – but no attempt was made (as in the British and Soviet empires) to homogenize law or standardize economic production. Among its peculiarities were that the Graeco-Macedonian rulers were, in effect, exiles from their ethnic homeland, and that they were both the creators and the heirs of empire. Centre–periphery (or core–periphery) theory, often used in the analysis of modern global-political relationships (based on the idea that economic systems draw wealth from disadvantaged outlying areas into a dominant central zone), can illuminate certain aspects but cannot be transferred whole-sale into the ancient context, not least because the empire did not have a single centre – one modern discussion names five places as capitals under the Seleukids: Antioch, Seleukeia-on-Tigris, and the older Achaemenid centres of Ekbatana, Sousa, and Sardis[82] – or an economic or administrative centre. Diversity and lack of centralization were the hallmarks of this tributary landscape. In a sense the 'core' was wherever the king was; Antiochos III still dealt with routine business during his *anabasis*. In 210, from somewhere in Iran, he wrote to Zeuxis, viceroy of Asia Minor, about the appointment of a priest, as we learn from Josephus, Jewish historian of the first century AD:

> King Antiochos to Zeuxis, his 'father', greetings. If you are in good health, it is well; I too am in good health.
>
> (149) On hearing that the people in Lydia and Phrygia are in revolt, I thought this required great attention on my part, and after discussing with my Friends what ought to be done, I resolve to move two thousand Jewish families with their chattels from Mesopotamia and Babylonia to the strongholds and the most strategic places. (150) For I am convinced that they will be loyal guardians of our interests because of their piety to God ... I wish therefore to transfer them, although this is a laborious task, with the promise that they shall use their own laws. (151) When you have brought them to the places I have mentioned, you will give them each a place to build a house and a plot of land to cultivate and plant vines, and you will grant them exemption from taxes on agricultural produce for ten years.... (153) Show concern for their people as much as possible, so that it may not be troubled by anyone.
>
> (Jos. *Jewish Antiquities*, 12. 148–53,
> Austin 167, Burstein 29, cf. 35)[83]

From another point of view, the 'core' of the empire is defined vertically (in terms of social class) rather than horizontally (in terms of geographical regions), and consists of the Graeco-Macedonian ruling élite.[84]

Land and taxes

A passage near the beginning of book 2 of the *Oikonomika* attributed to Aristotle, but probably written by another scholar after Aristotle's death, analyses 'royal' and 'satrapic' management (*oikonomia*) in a way that suggests the writer has in mind the Seleukid empire.

First let us look at royal management (*basilikê oikonomia*). While this is totally powerful, it has four departments, concerned with the management of coinage, exports, imports, and expenditure. Taking each of these in turn, I say that the management of coinage is whether to make large or small denominations and when. The management of exports and imports is which of the things received from the satraps it will be advantageous to dispose of and when. The management of expenditure is which ones are to be limited and when, and whether coinage, or things that may be sold for money, are to be given out against expenditure.

Secondly, satrapic management (*satrapikê oikonomia*). There are six kinds of revenues for this: from land; from his own property [*or 'special things'*] in the country; from merchandises [*or 'merchants'*]; from taxes; from cattle; and from other things. Of these, the first and most important is revenue from the land; this is what some call *ekphorion* and others 'tithe'. The second is that from his own property [*or 'special things'*]: here gold, there silver, there copper, and in any given place whatever things there may be. The third is that from merchandises [*or 'merchants'*]. The fourth is that which comes from taxes on land and from sales taxes. The fifth is that from cattle, called 'first-fruits' or 'tithe'. The sixth is that from other things, referred to as poll-tax and *cheirônaxion* [*a craft-tax?*].

([Arist.] *Oikonomika*, 2. 1. 2–4, 1345 a–b)[85]

It should be emphasized that the author is describing two aspects of a single system, not two alternative systems. The extract neatly brings out the different interests of different parties: the king receives things from the satraps and desires to maximize the income to his treasury; the satrap is concerned with gathering revenue at the grass-roots level and with directly regulating economic activity in his province, but also has private estates upon whose produce he can distrain. The satrap was perhaps also responsible for the upkeep of the 'royal road' system which Herodotos so admired (5. 52).

Within a province, however, at least in the western part of the empire, the king had direct responsibility for certain economic arrangements. Forests and mines, for example, probably belonged to the king. The sales taxes mentioned in the text just quoted imply royal control of fairs and markets (see also the inscription Austin 78, BD 40, Sherk 21, *Syll.*³ 646).[86] Royal control of fairs and markets is implied by a letter from a king Antiochos (probably I or II) to an official about the important sanctuary of Zeus of Baitokaike near Arados in Syria:

A report having been brought to me about the power of the god Zeus of Baitokaike, I have decided to concede to him for all the time the sources of the god's power, namely the village of Baitokaike,

formerly held by Demetrios son of Demetrios, grandson of Mnaseas
..., together with everything that appertains and belongs to it
according to the existing surveys, and including the revenues of the
present year ... Fairs exempt from taxation are also to be held every
month on the 15th and 30th; the sanctuary is to be inviolate and
the village exempt from billeting ...

(Austin 178, *RC* 70)[87]

Evidently the king or a predecessor had once 'granted' the village to Demetrios,
perhaps a Greek or Macedonian in his service;[88] presumably the beneficiary
received taxes or tithes paid by cultivators, craftsmen, and tradesmen. The
passing references to 'surveys' (*periorismoi*: registrations of *horoi*, boundaries),
annual revenues, and billeting are noteworthy; but the document, like
others quoted in this chapter, should be viewed in the context of pre-
Alexandrian practice – just as, much later, Augustus was somehow involved
in a decision by the city of Arados to permit the tax-free transit of goods and
animals for sale at the twice-monthly fairs held at the sanctuary (the city
reported its decision to him and a copy of the decree was inscribed immediately below the text quoted above).[89] There is an important distinction
between ultimate ownership, which lies with the king, and the usufruct of
the land, which he may give to someone else.[90]

Few details of the fiscal economy of the Seleukids are known, but the
administration of land taxes must have varied according to local custom.
Centrally imposed 'royal' taxes were probably more uniform. One of the rare
sources for the second group is a letter of Antiochos III to Ptolemaios,
governor of Hollow Syria, following his conquest of the area; it is preserved
by Josephus. After thanking the Jews for their support and granting them
aid in restoring the city, recently destroyed in war (cf. p. 307), the king sets
out his intentions:

> (142) All the people of the nation shall govern themselves in accord-
> ance with their ancestral laws, and the senate, the priests, the
> scribes of the temple and the temple-singers shall be exempted from
> the poll-tax, the crown-tax, and the salt-tax. (143) To hasten the
> repeopling of the city, I grant to the present inhabitants and to
> those who come back before the month of Hyberberetaios [*c.
> October*] freedom from taxes for three years. (144) We also remit for
> the future one-third of their taxes to make good the injuries they
> have sustained.
>
> (Jos. *AJ* 12. 142–4, Austin 167, Burstein 35)

Later the passage mentions remission from taxes on agricultural produce
(§151). Demetrios I, in a letter to the Jews of 152 BC (I Macc. 10: 29–30),
writes of a land tax, 'tributes' (the salt tax and crown tax?), and of the price

tax on salt, as well as tithes, tolls, and 'cattle tributes'. The salt tax was prob-ably related to salt-pans, which, like mines, quarries, and fisheries, were probably crown property. The poll tax is self-explanatory. It is certain that customs and harbour dues were levied, and probably a tax on the use of the royal roads and the main waterways.[91]

The Seleukids' main concern, like that of their Persian predecessors, was to maximize revenues, and this should be understood as lying behind certain measures which may at first sight look like something more ambitious, the promotion of economic growth and innovation. (See pp. 344–5 for royal experiments with new crops and animals.) Whether or not he claimed a parcel of land as his own, the king exercised traditional rights of ownership in many places. From the Persian kings the Seleukids inherited large estates of 'royal land' (*basilikê chôra*); Greek sources refer to *paradeisoi*, 'paradise gardens' or rather parks, scattered across the empire from Sardis to Baktria.[92] Since the king could control the productivity of his own estates, if of no others, he had an opportunity to try out new crops or varieties of live-stock. In so doing the Seleukids were following the practice of the Assyrian and Persian kings,[93] displaying their fairness and compassion and revealing that they could take the long view.

Elsewhere it is likely that new land was brought into cultivation. Antiochos III's letter to the Babylonian Jews speaks of giving each settler 'a place to build a house and a plot of land to cultivate and plant vines'; after ten years they would become liable to taxes (Jos. *AJ* 12. 148–53; Austin 167; Burstein 29 + 35).[94] Even if the land was not vacant at the time, a change in its use seems to be envisaged, which will produce revenue in due course.

In both these documents there is mention of tax immunity, a piece of good 'public relations' the Seleukids often exploited. Neither document, however, is evidence of any attempt to change economic organization in detail at a local level, only of the reassignment of local control over revenues.

Further details of land tenure organization come from a famous inscrip-tion from Ilion in north-western Asia Minor (again, we cannot extrapolate from this peripheral area to the former core areas of the Persian empire). The dossier begins with a letter from Meleagros, satrap of the Hellespontine area, who is forwarding to the 'council and people' of Ilion three letters from Antiochos I and urges them to vote honours to the king. Copies of the king's letters are inscribed below his:

(1) King Antiochos to Meleagros, greetings.... We have given to Aristodikides of Assos 2,000 *plethra* of arable land, to be attached to the city of Ilion or Skepsis....

(2) King Antiochos to Meleagros, greetings. Aristodikides of Assos came to see us requesting that we give him in the Hellespontine satrapy Petra, formerly held by [*another*] Meleagros, and in the territory of

Petra 1,500 *plethra* of arable land and a further 2,000 *plethra* of arable land from the territory bordering on the portion we had already given him.... Do you therefore investigate whether this Petra has not been previously given to someone else, and designate it with its neighbouring territory to Aristodikides. And from the royal land which neighbours on the land previously given to Aristodikides, give instructions to measure out and assign to him 2,000 *plethra* and to allow him to attach it to any city he wishes in the country (*chôra*) and the alliance. Should the royal peoples (*basilikoi laoi*) from the region of Petra wish to live at Petra for their own security, we have given instructions to Aristodikides to allow them to reside there. Farewell.

(Austin 180, BD 18, Burstein 21, *RC* 13, *OGIS* 221)

The third letter responds to an apparent complaint from Aristodikides about a subsequent delay, and confirms the previous instructions. Once again, the assumptions behind the texts are at least as revealing as the details of the transaction. The king decides, apparently unilaterally, to reassign land previously granted to a Greek or Macedonian man (not the satrap) to a citizen of Assos, who furthermore has the right to 'attach' the land to a nearby *polis*; the measure amounts to a benefaction to the city as well as the individual (cf. Austin's n. 5). In addition there is mention of 'peoples', *laoi*, belonging to the king; these may be non-Greeks inhabitants of quasi-serf status who are attached to the land, like the Pedieis of Priene (p. 100).[95]

In 254/3 Antiochos II transferred estates to his ex-wife Laodike; again peasant villages and their revenues are bought and sold (Austin 185, BD 25, Burstein 24, *RC* 18–20, parts in *OGIS* 225). A similar case is attested in an inscription from Sardis, detailing the grant of an estate comprising a number of native villages to one Mnesimachos, who also receives a loan from the temple of Artemis at Sardis (Austin 181, *c*.200 BC).[96] In yet another case from western Asia Minor, a Greek *polis* expresses thanks to Seleukid officials after securing the revenues from 'sacred' villages which are possessions of the city (Austin 187, date uncertain).[97]

For the eastern two-thirds of the empire there is no Greek evidence for land tenure, but it seems likely that the land was under a mixture of ownerships and *de facto* possession through use. Besides 'royal land', there was land that had been granted to temples or other Greek and non-Greek communities, often in accordance with ancestral arrangements,[98] to individuals, or to military *katoikiai* (p. 304) and Greek cities.

The king's concern with revenue-raising could even entail royal *euergesia*, as a document from Lykia illustrates. The king involved is Eumenes II of Pergamon, but it may be supposed that similar things happened in the Seleukid domains:

King Eumenes (II) to Artemidoros. I have read the comments you appended to the petition submitted by the settlers in the village of the Kardakes. Since after investigating you find that their private affairs are in a weak position, as their trees are not yielding much fruit and their land is of poor quality, give instructions that they may keep the piece of land they bought from Ptolemaios [*probably not a king*] and the price they did not pay because most of them have no resources left, and give instructions not to exact the money; and since they must pay for each adult person a poll tax of four Rhodian drachmas and an obol, but the weak condition of their affairs makes this a burden to them, (give instructions) to exempt them from the arrears for the sixteenth year [*182/1*] and from 1 Rhodian drachma and 1 obol from the seventeenth year ... and that they may repair the fort they previously had, ... while I myself will pay for a skilled craftsman. Year 17, the 4th day from the end of the month of Dios.

(Austin 202)[99]

It is rare that historians see the effects on ordinary people of rulers' acts, and rarer that the kings show concern and compassion; we benefit from governmental reliance on documentary communications.

Image and ideal

As in the fiscal sphere, so in the area of royal image and ideology, the Seleukids largely took over the traditional elements. Like the Achaemenids, they cooperated with the priests of Babylon, even funding new constructions. To validate their own position as lords of Asia the kings from Antiochos I on took steps to promote ruler-worship. Antiochos III was the first to organize a royal ruler-cult (the term used by Sherwin-White and Kuhrt) of the royal family, but Antiochos I had established a cult of the late Seleukos I[100] without the central organization implied by the later measures (see Chapter 3 on divine honours and the deification of kings). The divinely favoured, and eventually divine, status of Seleukos and his heirs was emphasized by stories that grew up early on, making Seleukos a descendant or even a son of a god. A decree of Ilion in honour of Antiochos I from early in the latter's reign states that the priests and priestesses of the city shall sacrifice 'to Apollo, the ancestor of his family' (Austin 139, BD 16, Burstein 15, *OGIS* 219). In the 240s Seleukos II, thanking the people of Miletos for honours, refers to the benefactions of his ancestors and father (Antiochos II) 'because of the oracles given out from the sanctuary there of Apollo Didymeus' (of Didyma, the sanctuary near Miletos) 'and because of kinship to the god himself' (Austin 186, *RC* 22, *OGIS* 227).

Like previous rulers of the region, the Seleukids exploited the visual language of royalty. Beginning with Antiochos I, the reigning king's portrait appeared on coins; the king probably approved his own portraits, though this does not allow us to treat them as lifelike (see p. 69).[101] Oddly, no sculpted image of a Seleukid is securely identified.[102] The love stories surrounding the handing on of Stratonike by Seleukos I to his son (p. 71) may reflect an attempt, whether directly sponsored by the kings or not, to circulate favourable tales about them. A string of anecdotes about Seleukos I appears in Appian:

> His great successes in war earned him the surname of Nikator ['*Victor*'] ... He was tall and powerfully built; one day, when a wild bull was brought to Alexander for sacrifice and broke loose from its bonds, he [*Seleukos*] resisted him alone and brought him under control with his bare hands. That is why his statues represent him with horns added....
>
> They say that when he was undertaking the foundation of the two Seleukeias, that of Seleukeia-by-the-Sea was preceded by a portent of thunder ...
>
> They also say that for the foundation of Seleukeia-on-Tigris the Magi were ordered to select the day and the hour when the digging of the foundations began, but they falsified the hour as they did not wish to have such a stronghold threatening them. Seleukos was waiting for the given hour in his tent, while the army ready for work kept quiet until Seleukos should give the sign. Suddenly, at the more favourable hour, they thought someone was ordering them on to work and sprang up; not even the efforts of the heralds could hold them back.
>
> (App. *Syr.* 58, Austin 46)

These stories, which Appian must have taken from hellenistic sources, neatly encapsulate several aspects of the image the Seleukids wished to cultivate: the tactful use of native priests (the story of the attempt by the Magi to sabotage the foundation need not be historical), the pious observation of religious ritual for the good of the governed, the manifest proofs of divine intervention in his favour, and the performance of superhuman feats.

Hellenization and urbanization

Large numbers of Greek and Macedonian soldiers were settled in the Near East by Alexander and his Successors (pp. 56–7). In the first of his two discourses *On the Fortune or Courage of Alexander the Great*,[103] Plutarch makes an explicit link between the foundation of cities and the bringing of civilization to Asia:

But if you consider the effects of Alexander's instruction, you will
see that he educated the Hyrkanians to conduct marriages, taught
the Arachosians to till the soil, and persuaded the Sogdians to
support their parents, not to kill them, and the Persians to respect
their mothers, not to marry them. [*He specifies how Greek literature
and religion were taken up in the far east.*] ... Alexander founded over
seventy cities among barbarian tribes, sprinkled Greek institutions
all over Asia, and so overcame its wild and savage manner of living.
... Those who were subdued by Alexander are more fortunate than
those who escaped him, for the latter had no one to rescue them
from their wretched life, while the victorious Alexander compelled
the former to enjoy a better existence. ... Alexander's victims would
not have been civilized if they had not been defeated.

(Plut. *Moralia*, 328 c–f, Austin 19)

Not only, however, is the figure of seventy exaggerated – Alexander was not
single-handedly responsible for all the urban foundations[104] – but we may
legitimately doubt that his motives and those of his successors were so
noble.

At any rate, Seleukos I and Antiochos I were the most active city founders
in the east.[105] Some areas of the empire, such as Iran, were mainly non-
urban. According to Arrian (*Indikê*, 40. 8), Alexander founded towns in
order to turn the Iranians from nomads into cultivators, but it can be shown
that they were already becoming widely sedentary, and it seems likely that a
predominantly village-based society existed already and continued to
exist.[106] Pre-Alexandrian society in the Near East, however, included some
of the oldest urban entities in the known world, and their roles remained
largely unchanged under Seleukid rule. Such seems to be the case at Uruk,
where no Greek influence is visible throughout the whole Seleukid period;
while Babylon, though it probably received an additional Greek-speaking
community, did not change its name or status.[107]

An example of more pro-active hellenization is the old Lydian–Greek
town of Sardis in western Asia Minor, where Greek buildings and institutions were added and the street-plan relaid on a 'Hippodamian' grid pattern
after the devastation of the city by Antiochos II in a siege. Elsewhere a
Greek population, a Greek name, and *polis* institutions were bolted on to an
existing non-Greek town, such as Berrhoia (formerly Alep), and perhaps at
the 'Antioch' which Antiochos IV wished to make of Jerusalem; during the
third century the old Elamite and Persian capital city of Sousa received
Graeco-Macedonian colonists and was refounded as Seleukeia-on-Eulaios.[108]
Some *poleis* were created out of nothing (or from a small non-Greek site) and
given Graeco-Macedonian citizens; this happened at Apameia-on-Orontes,
Seleukeia-in-Pieria, Doura-Europos, and others (for a fragment of the constitution given to Doura-Europos, see Austin 179).[109] Sometimes an existing

city was replaced with a new structure, possibly on a new site, as at Antioch, where Seleukos I destroyed an existing city, Antigon(e)ia, founded by Antigonos (Strabo, 16. 2. 4 (749), Austin 174), and moved its Greek émigré population to the new site. Sometimes a new city was placed beside an old capital, as in the case of Seleukeia-on-Tigris, built opposite Babylon (above).[110]

In many places the Seleukids founded veteran colonies with an expressly military purpose, often called *katoikiai*, 'settlements', mainly of Graeco-Macedonians. Though some were founded as garrisons and others as colonies in their own right, they typically had an ethnically homogeneous population. Greek culture was promoted through the *gymnasion* (see, for example, the new royal letter from Tyriaion in Phrygia, pp. 315–16), which admitted only selectively; but in a settlement that was a *polis* the native population would become members of the city. Cohen points to *realpolitisch* motivations for this active colonization programme – trade, military security, sometimes local political circumstances – and rejects the suggestion that hellenization was a policy of the kings, an idea which we find in the fourth-century AD orator Libanius of Antioch:[111]

> The other kings have exulted in destroying existing cities; he, on the other hand, arranged to build cities which did not yet exist. He [*Seleukos*] established so many over the earth that they were enough to carry the names of towns in Macedonia as well as the names of those in his family .... Moreover, if one should wish to compare him with the Athenians and Milesians, who are supposed to have sent out the greatest number of colonies, he would appear to be the greater colonizer, for he so much outstripped each of them in the magnitude of his works that one of his cities was worth ten of theirs. One can go to Phoenicia to see his cities, one can go to Syria and see even more and greater cities of his. He extended this noble work up to the Euphrates and the Tigris; and surrounding Babylon with cities, he scattered them everywhere, even in Persia. In short, there was no place suitable to receive a city that he left bare; rather, by hellenizing the barbarian world he brought it to an end.
>
> (Libanius, *Oration* 11. 101)

With Cohen's caution in mind, we may nonetheless accept that Libanius was not far from the truth in his encomium on Seleukos, which reveals how great was the posthumous reputation of Alexander's Successors. Hellenization, however, was largely an indirect effect of colonization.

The naming of cities after members of the royal family was a further contribution to dynastic propaganda.[112] Appian, in his famous eulogy of Seleukos (*Syr.* 52–63, Austin 46), attributes thirty-four cities to Seleukos: sixteen named Antioch (Antiocheia in Greek), nine named Seleukeia, five named Laodikeia after his mother Laodike, and four Apameias named after his wife. Appian may be conflating the foundations of Alexander and Antiochos I with those of Seleukos, but the message is the same.

> The others he called after places in Greece or Macedonia, or after his own achievements, or in honour of Alexander the king. That is why there are in Syria, and among the barbarians inland, many Greek and many Macedonian place-names: Berrhoia, Edessa, Perinthos, Maroneia, Kallipolis, Achaia, Pella, Europos, Amphipolis, Arethousa, Astakos, Tegea, Chalkis, Larissa, Heraia, and Apollonia; also in Parthia Soteira, Kalliope, Charis, Hekatompylos, and Achaia; among the Indians Alexandropolis; and among the Skythians Alexandreschate. Also, called after the victories of Seleukos himself there are Nikephorion in Mesopotamia and Nikopolis in Armenia, very near to Cappadocia.
>
> (App. *Syr.* 57, Austin 46)

During Seleukos's reign some twenty cities were founded across the empire from Cilicia to Iran, of which the four most famous are the Syrian 'tetrapolis', none of which is more than 50 kilometres from the Mediterranean: Seleukeia-in-Pieria, Antiocheia-on-Orontes, Apameia (also on the Orontes), and Laodikeia-by-the-Sea. In north-eastern Syria, on the upper Euphrates, he founded Seleukeia-Zeugma, and on the opposite bank (joined by a bridge) another Apameia; further downstream were Doura-Europos and Berrhoia. In Mesopotamia he founded Seleukeia-on-Tigris and others. Definite foundations of Antiochos I include Antioch-in-Persis and the refoundation of Antioch-in-Margiane.[113]

That Baktria was far from marginal to Seleukid policy[114] is borne out by the new city constructions there, of which the most famous is at Ai Khanum on the river Oxus. It was built in the late fourth century and destroyed by the Sakai invading from the east around 150. It has Greek-style buildings such as a theatre, cult sanctuary, *gymnasion*, and long stoas enclosing public spaces, plus a grand house, a garrison installation in the citadel, and a large fortification, though buildings and architectural elements reminiscent of Achaemenid architecture were also found. It is hard to be certain where Greeks and non-Greeks, respectively, lived – or whether there was a spatial divide between them (Fig. 8.5).[115] Other notable Seleukid foundations include the excavated settlement of Ikaros, on Failaka island at the head of the Arab-Persian gulf. A probable pre-Seleukid trading-post with a pre-Greek cult complex, it may not have had *polis* status.

Places like these, whether autonomous *poleis* or not, sometimes had a royal governor. Most of them will have had the normal Greek civic institutions of public assembly, council (*boulê*), and elected magistrates, but the texture of civic and political life is obscure. Despite the formal procedures according to which the king treated the *polis* as his equal in status, it is often clear that it

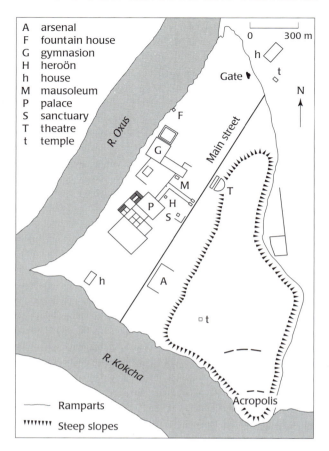

A	arsenal
F	fountain house
G	gymnasion
H	heroön
h	house
M	mausoleum
P	palace
S	sanctuary
T	theatre
t	temple

Figure 8.5 Ai Khanum. (Adapted from A. Bereznay and R. J. A. Talbert in Talbert, *Atlas*, p. 69.)

is his decisions that count. When the city of Magnesia-on-Meander in western Asia Minor requested that its new festival be recognized as 'iso-pythian' (equal in status to the Pythian games at Delphi), it was the king who had to accede to the request and instruct his officers to see that other cities did likewise (Austin 184, BD 128, *RC* 31, *OGIS* 231).[116]

Old Greek cities were less often subjected to a radical reshaping (though cf. pp. 87–9), and under the Seleukids, as under the Ptolemies, they were gener-ally treated respectfully; in theory, indeed, they were still independent entities with which the kings had to negotiate a relationship. A famous example of successful negotiation of its position by a minor city is the case of Demodamas of Miletos, member of the council and proposer in 299 of a decree in honour of Antiochos I (Burstein 2, *OGIS* 213),[117] who had agreed to pay for a stoa in the sanctuary of Apollo at Didyma, and of another decree in honour of his mother Apame. We have already met Demodamas as a general of Seleukos (p. 284), but he is also an example of a chain of influence stretching from a city via one of its prominent citizens all the way up to the king.

Besides illustrating how Seleukos developed the image of a harmonious ruling family (as with the story of Stratonike), the documents exemplify how a local community, particularly an old Greek *polis*, could exploit personal contacts with the centre of power, playing upon its own history and upon the desire of the king to appear generous. This is all the more striking when we consider the geographically marginal position of Miletos within the kingdom and the vast distance between it and the probable location of the court at any given time.[118]

There were many purposes behind city foundations, and many varieties of *poleis* in different landscapes, but the uniformity of administrative structures that resulted is one of the political landmarks of the hellenistic period.

The Seleukids and the Jews of Jerusalem

The Seleukids' most notorious confrontation with a non-Greek community, and the one most often cited by modern writers in connection with the issue of hellenization, was with the Jews of Jerusalem in the second quarter of the second century.[119] A record of a kind is preserved in I and II Maccabees (pp. 11, 266), covering, respectively, the years 175–135 and 175–160, not always in chronological order. The book of Daniel, which took its final form around 165, contains retrospective 'prophesies' of events at that time. Josephus (*Jewish War* and *Jewish Antiquities*) narrates some episodes, not necessarily reliably. Both he and Maccabees also include direct quotations from contemporary correspondence.[120] Unfortunately, almost every detail of the chronology and causes of the events remains controversial, and no more than an overview can be given here.[121]

Down to 200 Jerusalem and its territory were Ptolemaic possessions, but hostility to Ptolemaic rule arose in some quarters, as expressed in the Greek book of Ecclesiastes ('The Preacher', *c*.250 BC) which is preserved among the books of the Bible. It seems that Ptolemy IV unwisely attempted to popularize Greek cults such as that of Dionysos, though details are uncertain. Antiochos III captured southern Syria from Ptolemy V in the fifth Syrian war (202–200), and in traditional near eastern fashion proclaimed toleration of local culture. The letter to Zeuxis (p. 296) details his encouragement of the Jewish 'nation' (*ethnos*) to live by its own laws while paying the appropriate taxes, though considerable tax concessions are granted. In a document quoted by Josephus, Antiochos gives contributions towards their sacrifices including animals, wine, oil, and frankincense to the value of 20,000 silver pieces, 1,460 *medimnoi* of wheat, and 375 *medimnoi* of salt, and promises materials for rebuilding the Temple (Jos. *AJ* 12. 140–1, Austin 167, Burstein 35).

The king clearly had a key role in appointing the high priest of Jerusalem, as happened in 175:

> But when Seleukos (IV) departed this life and the kingdom was taken by Antiochos (IV) called Epiphanes, Jason the brother of Onias usurped the high priesthood by illegitimate means, promising the king in a petition 360 talents of silver and 80 talents of other revenue. He undertook beyond this to pay a further 150 talents if he were granted permission to establish by his own authority a gymnasium and a corps of ephebes and enrol those in Jerusalem as 'Antiochenes'.[122]
>
> When the king agreed and he gained the office, he immediately set about converting his fellow-countrymen to the Greek way of life. Abolishing the existing royal privileges ... and the legitimate institutions, he brought in illegal customs. For he saw fit to establish a gymnasium below the acropolis and lead there the most athletic of the ephebes wearing sunhats (*petasoi*). There was such a flowering of hellenism and advance of gentile customs through the over-whelming wickedness of the impious Jason – no true high priest – that the priests were no longer conscientious over the duties concerned with the sacrifice, but, despising the Temple and neglecting the sacrifices, they hastened to take part in the unlawful exercises in the palaestra as soon as the sound of the discus summoned them.
>
> (II Macc. 4: 7–14)

The author employs the term *hellênismos*, possibly used here for the first time in Greek, to denote 'the Greek way of life' (4: 13; it is opposed to *ioudaïsmos* at 2: 21).[123] It appears Jason was not alone but was the leader of a group of 'hellenizers':

> In those days came forth from Israel a lawless generation who persuaded many others by saying, 'Come, let us make a treaty with the peoples around us, since many evils have fallen upon us from the time we separated from them.' This proposal seemed good in their eyes, and some of the people eagerly went to the king, who granted them permission to practise the customs of the heathen. And they built a gymnasium in Jerusalem in accordance with the customs of the nations.
>
> (I Macc. 1: 10–14, Austin 168)

This ought to mean that the impulse for hellenization in the late 170s and early 160s arose initially within Jerusalem, but received royal approval; it would be normal for a community wishing to build *gymnasia* and generally alter its institutions to try to secure royal support, including financial aid. A near-contemporary parallel is provided by a newly discovered inscription from Phrygia of the years after 188, by which Eumenes II of Pergamon grants a small community the status of *polis* and allows it to build a *gymnasion* (quoted further, pp. 315–16). At the same time, there seems to be no abandonment of old ways: I Maccabees specifically implies that the rituals at the Temple continued, though in the eyes of some they were no longer properly respected. Combined with evidence which can be interpreted to mean that hellenization had proceeded more slowly in Judaea than in other parts of the Near East,[124] this raises the question whether, at this stage, the hellenization of Jerusalem was being imposed from above or was, rather, the product of internal cultural politics. Needless to say, both views have been held.

At some point (possibly in 167 or earlier), Jason was replaced as high priest by one Menelaos. Under him there was internal oppression and civil war (II Macc. 4: 26–5, 27); but it is not certain that he had anything to do with the 'hellenizers'.[125] At the time of Antiochos's humiliation by Popillius Laenas in Egypt (p. 292), rumours of the king's death (II Macc. 5: 5) provoked civil war in Jerusalem; this may be why Antiochos intervened to restore order, and perhaps to save face. Many people were killed and Jason was expelled. Perhaps unwisely, Antiochos robbed, or allowed his soldiers to rob, the treasures of the Temple before garrisoning the town (I Macc. 1: 20–36, Austin 168). It is not clear that this had anything to do with the earlier introduction of Greek customs.

Soon, however, there was active persecution of the Jews of Jerusalem; the chronology is disputed,[126] particularly the timing in relation to the invasion of Egypt. Menelaos's role is also uncertain; equally uncertain is whether the oppression was part of the attempt to introduce Greek *polis* customs by the 'hellenizing movement'. What is not disputed is the statement that the king 'issued a proclamation to the whole of his kingdom that they should all form one people and that they should each give up their own customs' (I Macc. 1: 41). The same author goes into considerable detail:

> The king also sent letters by messenger to Jerusalem and the cities of Judaea that they should follow customs alien to their land, banish holocausts, sacrifices, and libations from the sanctuary and profane the sabbaths and festivals, defile the sanctuary and the holy men, build altars and sacred enclosures and temples of idols, sacrifice pigs and unclean animals, leave their sons uncircumcised, and defile themselves with every kind of impurity and abomination, so as to forget the law and change all their ordinances. Anyone who did not confirm to the king's edict would be punished with death.
>
> (I Macc. 1: 44–50, Austin 168)

As usually interpreted, and even making allowance for the polemical tone, this means that Antiochos banned Jewish religious and social practices outright (which incidentally confirms that they were still being observed; neither the earlier hellenization moves nor Menelaos's appointment, it appears, was intended to stop the observance of Jewish law and custom). The Roman historian Tacitus puts it more strongly: 'king Antiochos attempted to abolish superstition and introduce Greek ways' (*demere superstitionem et mores Graecorum dare*), but was prevented from improving that vilest of races (*taeterrimam gentem*) by the war against the Parthians' (*Histories*, 5. 8. 4).[127]

The author of I Maccabees also says that Antiochos built 'the abomination of desolation' on the altar of the Temple (I Macc. 1: 54, Austin 168).[128] The precise meaning has been endlessly debated; one suggestion is that this refers to the building of an altar of the Syrian god Baal-Shamen,[129] which, if true, would tell against an active hellenization policy by the king, though in favour of the promotion of a monotheistic alternative to the Jewish god. Alternatively, if we take a consensus of sources from different dates (Dan. 11: 39; II Macc. 6; I Macc. 1; Diod. 34/35. 5. 1; Jos. *BJ* 1. 34), the king may have polluted the altar of the Temple by sacrificing a pig.

Late sources also refer, with less certainty, to the erection in the Temple precinct of cult statues of Zeus Olympios, and possibly of Antiochos himself and Athena (Jerome, *On Daniel*, on 8: 14–15 and 11: 31; Synkellos, p. 531 Dindorf). Olympian Zeus, however, was a god with whom Antiochos IV was closely identified, for example because of his benefactions to the construction of the Olympieion at Athens and of another temple at Priene. The Byzantine author Ioannes Malalas (pp. 206–7 Dindorf) even states that the Temple was rededicated to Zeus Olympios and Athena; this is quite possible, since the possibly non-Jewish community at Mt. Gerizim successfully petitioned the king to rededicate their sanctuary to Zeus Xenios (II Macc. 6: 1–2; cf. Jos. *AJ* 12. 258–63, Burstein 42).[130] If true, it points to an attempt to substitute Greek polytheism for the worship of the Jewish god; but not all scholars accept this evidence, and some prefer to interpret the events, including the possible rededication of the Temple, as part of the gradual grass-roots hellenization of Judaea and the (inferred) emergence among the peoples of the region of a preference for a single 'highest' god, whatever one's culture.

If the line taken here is correct, however, there is no evidence that Antiochos was promoting monotheism; he simply decided to impose Greek cult on the Jews, for reasons we cannot definitely discern but which were evidently political. The attempt to suppress even customs such as dietary restrictions tends to confirm that this was not simply a religious campaign. Perhaps during his invasion of Egypt, events at Jerusalem under Menelaos led to disturbances the king could not ignore (these disturbances were not necessarily to do with opposition to Greek ways, since the innovations were not apparently undermining Jewish tradition). Given the unusual strength of Jewish identity and custom, the king may have decided that unusual measures were required to bring the city back into line.

The long-term results of the attempt to bring Jerusalem to heel were dire. Perhaps as early as 166/5, a group led by Mattathias and his son Judas Makkabaios ('the Hammer') began armed resistance to the suppression of Jewish law, eventually recapturing Jerusalem and defeating the governor of Syria in battle. Once Antiochos was at war in the far east and short of cash, however, he issued an amnesty and announced a return to the law (II Macc. 11: 27–33, 164 BC). After his death in late 164, the regent Lysias, in the name of the young Antiochos V, reversed the earlier decree:

> King Antiochos to his brother Lysias, greeting. Now that our royal father has gone to join the gods, we desire that our subjects be undisturbed in the conduct of their own affairs. We have learnt that the Jews do not consent to adopt Greek ways, as our father wished, but prefer their own mode of life and request that they be allowed to observe their own laws. We choose, therefore, that this nation like the rest should be left undisturbed, and decree that their temple be restored to them and that they shall regulate their lives in accordance with their ancestral customs. Have the goodness, therefore, to inform them of this and ratify it, so that, knowing what our intentions are, they may settle down confidently and quietly to manage their own affairs.
>
> (II Macc. 11: 22–6; Burstein 43)

He was simply recognizing the *status quo*, however; the Jews had already retaken the Temple, which was reconsecrated at the end of 164.

By the end of the 160s the Jews had forged an alliance with the Romans (II Macc. 8. 22–32, Burstein 44), who no doubt welcomed an opportunity to destabilize Syria. Despite victories over Seleukid armies, Judaea henceforth did not become independent immediately but cultivated a close and respectful relationship with the Seleukid kings. In 152, for example, when king Alexander Balas invaded, Jonathan Makkabaios acknowledged his suzerainty, was appointed Friend, and was sent a purple robe and gold crown (I Macc. 10: 15–20). From 142, however, the descendants of Mattathias ruled as high priests (and kings from 104–103), gradually expanding Judaean territory at the expense of the increasingly divided Seleukid kingdom. In 139, during his war with Diodotos Tryphon, Antiochos VII was forced to confirm earlier remissions of tribute and make other concessions (I Macc. 15. 1–9, Austin 172). He later captured Jerusalem, but after he died fighting the Parthians in 129 Judaea became independent (Just. 36. 1. 10). This lasted until Pompey's reconstruction of the Levant in 63, though the dynasty continued thereafter to the time of Herod the Great and beyond.[131]

The short-lived suppression of Jewish culture had far-reaching effects for the history of the region in the centuries that followed.[132] By attempting to outlaw a culture with such internal strength, the king provoked a reaction which left Judaea more assertive and ambitious than before, and thus boosted further the already strong spirit of independence among the Jews. If the interpretation followed here is correct, however, the episode carries no general lesson about the weakness or inadequacy of Seleukid rule, or the unwisdom of pro-active hellenization.

The Attalid dynasty (283–133 BC)

An early breakaway, and the most important, from the Seleukid empire was the town of Pergamon in north-western Asia Minor. As the empire lost, by stages, its power in Asia Minor, Pergamon was to become its principal successor on the mainland and, as such, the main focus of Rome's attention, with consequences both good and bad.

Pergamon, hitherto a relatively obscure town whose existence is attested only from the end of the fifth century, was administered on behalf of Lysimachos from c.302 by Philetairos, whose post was probably that of *gazophylax* or keeper of the treasury. He was the son of a Macedonian, Attalos; Strabo (13. 4. 1–2 (623–4), Austin 193) summarizes the history and chronology of his descendants, the Attalids. Although no member of the family was proclaimed king before c.240 (in Austin 197, Burstein 85, *OGIS* 273–9, of c.238–227 BC, 'king' Attalos I dedicates booty from his military victories), the official regnal period was backdated to 283, the date when Philetairos (who had held office at Pergamon since c.302) offered allegiance to Seleukos I instead of Lysimachos. It is assumed that henceforth he held a more exalted post than that of treasurer. His name appears on coins of the city, along with the head of Seleukos. When Seleukos died in Europe, Philetairos delivered his ashes to the new king, Antiochos I (App. *Syr.* 63). Already the city's influence, though not its direct sovereignty, extended across a wide area; Philetairos made benefactions to Kyzikos (Austin 194, *OGIS* 748) and other cities, and probably refounded the sanctuary of Meter (the Mother Goddess) at Mamurt-Kaleh, some 30 kilometres from the city. He also won a victory over the Gauls at around the same time as Antiochos I (on the Gauls, see Chapter 2). While other local rulers in Asia Minor broke with Lysimachos, none enjoyed the success of the Attalids.

Eumenes I (r. 263–241), Philetairos's nephew and adopted son, governed as dynast rather than king. Pergamon, already a distinguished *polis* because of the nearby sanctuary of Meter, gained further prestige. Within two years of taking office, Eumenes defeated Antiochos I in battle and asserted greater independence; by now he was *dynastês* of the territory around the city, a role he may have claimed at the time of his accession. His coins bear the head of Philetairos instead of Seleukos, representing a denial of the previous relationship of subordination. By now Pergamon controlled the harbour town of Elaia, and its rulers had probably built a fleet.[133] Eumenes was succeeded by his cousin (once removed) and adopted son, the long-lived Attalos I (b. 269, r. 241–197).

In the first few years of his reign Attalos refused to pay the protection money which dynasts of western Asia Minor periodically gave to the Gauls (Livy, 38. 16. 14); he defeated them in Mysia, taking the royal title (Polyb. 18. 41. 7–8).[134] The war was commemorated with sculptures symbolizing Pergamon's championing of hellenism against barbarians, including the famous combat scenes such as the Gaul killing himself and his wife, and the Dying Gaul (they are known only from Roman copies; Fig. 8.6).[135] The change of policy regarding the tribute is taken as a sign that Attalos had built up a strong army, his predecessors having relied more upon mercenaries (see e.g. Austin 196, *OGIS* 266, an agreement between Eumenes I and his mercenaries).[136]

In probably separate campaigns Attalos defeated Gallic mercenaries of Antiochos Hierax, gaining much Seleukid territory from the pretender as a result (p. 290). These new lands were retained in the face of attacks from Seleukos III (r. 226–223), but were probably lost for a short time to Achaios (p. 290). The two may have reached an accord before Achaios proclaimed himself king in 220, since in that year the Byzantines appealed to both parties for aid in their war with the Rhodians (Polyb. 4. 48. 1–3); Attalos was willing but unable to respond since he was confined to Pergamon

Figure 8.6   The 'Dying Celtic Trumpeter' from Pergamon (Roman copy of an original of *c.*220 BC). (Photograph: Deutsches Archäologisches Institut, Rome; neg. no. 70.2117.)

(Polyb. 4. 48. 11), but the appeal implies that he was no longer actually at war with Achaios. In 218, however, when Achaios was in Pisidia, Attalos took the opportunity to retake Aiolis and Mysia (Polyb. 5. 77–8). Two years later he made a pact with Antiochos III against Achaios (Polyb. 5. 107. 4), probably following it up before 212 with a formal alliance (referred to retrospectively at Polyb. 21. 17. 6; App. *Syr.* 38). It was a turning-point in Attalid–Seleukid relations: possibly for the first time, the Seleukids recognized the sovereignty of their former possession.

In the first Macedonian war, though probably not formally an ally of Rome, Attalos supported Rome and its allies. This may have been partly the result of close ties with the Aitolians; Attalos now served as their general. During the war he gained possession of Aigina (*c.*210; for details, see p. 374). Pergamon was named among Rome's friends in the peace of 205. Later Attalos was granted Andros by the Romans (199; Livy, 31. 45. 7) and briefly held a town in Euboia.[137]

The means by which Pergamene power was exercised in north-west Asia Minor is worth focusing on. In Pergamon, now and already under Eumenes I, the king exercised *de facto* power by appointing the *stratêgoi* (generals) of the *polis* (Austin 195, *RC* 23, *OGIS* 267), a system that was probably extended to other cities only after 188. In recovering Aiolis and Mysia in 218, Attalos probably re-established a relationship in which Greek *poleis* did not enjoy independence but only internal autonomy; those in Aiolis probably paid tribute, while those in Mysia, mainly non-*polis* settlements, may have contributed troops. Territories away from the core were probably dominated less formally, by a sort of protectorate.[138]

Attalos was instrumental in bringing the Romans into Greece again, against Macedonia, and in securing help for them from Athens, Achaea, and even Sparta. A symbolic pinnacle was scaled when, in 200, he defended the Piraeus against the forces of Philip V. His visit to Athens is described by Polybios (16. 25–6, Austin 198). As well as receiving civic honours (p. 150),[139] he may now have dedicated on the summit of the Akropolis, immediately above the theatre of Dionysos, the statues of mythical figures commemorating Greek victories over barbarian enemies (giants, Amazons, Persians, Gauls) which are known as the Small Pergamene Dedication (again only Roman copies survive).[140] He may also have paid for a stoa at Delphi and fortifications for the Aitolians.

Polybios's assessment of Attalos is favourable (18. 41, Austin 199). Pergamon was now visibly ensconced at the heart of Greek civic consciousness. It had enjoyed a century of independence, thanks to its distance from the Seleukid heartlands, its fertile territory, and the long-established wealth of the Greek towns of western Asia Minor. The length of Attalos's reign may have promoted stability, and in terms of resilience and rising status his reign may, in a sense, represent the peak of Pergamene success; for though the decades after his death witnessed the most spectacular monumentalization of the citadel of Pergamon and massive territorial gains, these brought problems in their train.

Eumenes II (r. 197–159) maintained his father's close links with the states of southern Greece, assisting the Achaeans' campaigns against Sparta (195, 192) and making lavish endowments at Delphi. Livy explicitly comments that 'all the states of Greece and many rulers were obligated by the benefactions and gifts of Eumenes' (42. 5. 3). Despite the earlier friendship with Antiochos III, however, Pergamon suffered attack in 198. This drove Pergamon firmly into the Roman camp, and it became Rome's principal ally in the war against Antiochos.[141] By the peace of Apameia in 188, Pergamon gained the Seleukid part of northern Asia Minor and became the most powerful kingdom in the area.

A remarkable new epigraphic find contains a very public profession by Eumenes of his indebtedness to Rome. It is his response to a petition from a small community in Phrygia, probably a mixture of Greek and Gaulish settlers, who in the aftermath of 188 BC sought the status of *polis*:

WITH GOOD FORTUNE

King Eumenes to the inhabitants of Toriaion [*i.e Tyriaion*], greetings.

The men from among you, Antigenes, [B]rennos, and Heliades, whom you sent to congratulate us on achieving all our aims and reaching this place in good health, on account of which things, indeed, you rendered thank-offerings to the gods and presented the fitting sacrifices, and to request, because of the goodwill which you bear towards our affairs, that there be granted to you a *polis* constitution (*politeia*) and your own laws and a *gymnasion* and as many things as follow from these, have spoken to these matters with great enthusiasm ...

And I considered, on the one hand, that granting your requests was in no small way significant for me, relating to many greater matters; for now (a favour) given to you by me would be lasting, as I have gained full authority [*over the land*] through having received it from the Romans, who prevailed both in war and by treaties, whereas this favour decreed by those who had no such authority would not be (lasting), for this favour would rightly be judged by all as empty and deceitful.

But because of the goodwill which you bear towards us and have demonstrated at the opportune time, I concede both to you and those living with you in (fortified) places (*chôria*) that you be organized into a single citizen body (*politeuma*) and use your own laws. If you yourselves are content with some of these (laws), refer them to us so that we may assess whether they contain anything contrary to

315

your advantage. If not, inform us and we shall give you the men capable of establishing a council and magistracies and dividing the *dêmos* and distributing it into tribes and, after making a *gymnasion*, of supplying oil to the young men....

(*Epigraphica Anatolica*, 29 (1997), 3–4, lines 1–11, 17–34)[142]

In a subsequent letter the king promises to arrange for revenues to be earmarked in support of the oil supply. He explicitly links his obligations to the Romans with the obligations he has as a ruler to treat his new subjects well.

Although Pergamon had gained a considerable amount of territory, Pontos remained independent in the north-east of Asia Minor. On the borders of Pergamon were the kingdoms of Bithynia, Celtic Galatia, and Cappadocia, of which only the last was friendly. From about 187 to 183 Eumenes was at war with Prousias of Bithynia, who though pro-Roman had lost territory to Pergamon by the settlement of 188, and with the Gauls. Roman threats forced the issue in favour of Eumenes. (Among Prousias's commanders was the exiled Hannibal, whom Prousias was forced to surrender in 183 and who then committed suicide.) Victory over the Gauls led the Greeks of Asia Minor to call Eumenes 'Nikephoros' (Bringer of Victory), and in 181 he inaugurated a panhellenic festival of Athena Nikephoros at Pergamon.

Eumenes' war against Pontos and its allies (183–179) was likewise won with the help of Roman diplomacy. As in the peace of Phoinike (p. 374), other states were in some sense accessories to the peace, including Greater Armenia and certain Greek cities of the Propontis and Black Sea (Polyb. 25. 2. 12–13). The power of the kingdom was at its height, not entirely through its own efforts, and this was reflected in the further elaboration of the already grand acropolis complex and by Eumenes' gifts of grain and architectural monuments to cities such as Athens (the Stoa of Eumenes, Fig. 9.2). This was the period during which the new 'cistophoric' currency (p. 27) was introduced to celebrate the

Figure 8.7　Silver cistophoric tetradrachm (12.40 g) of Eumenes II of Pergamon (r. 197–158). Pergamon, *c.*180s–160s BC. Obv.: cista in ivy wreath. Rev.: bow-case entwined by serpents. (Ashmolean Museum, University of Oxford.)

dynasty's achievements (and its new political distance from the Seleukids), perhaps immediately after Apameia (Fig. 8.7).[143]

When Eumenes supported Antiochos IV's bid for the Seleukid throne (p. 292), he may have felt invulnerable; but his support for Rome against Perseus (172–168), and the ensuing defeat of Macedonia, removed the very reason why Rome needed him. It was not long before the senate was finding reasons to suspect his loyalty and show favour to his brother Attalos (Polyb. 29. 22; 30. 1–3). The senators even refused to give Eumenes a hearing (Polyb. 30. 19. 12). They encouraged the Gauls to rebel (so Polybios implies, 30. 3. 7–9; 30. 30. 6), then declared them free (30. 28) – an action they had no legal power to take. Conversely, Pergamon's hostile neighbours, such as Prousias II of Bithynia, found a hearing in Rome. Eumenes received widespread sympathy in Asia Minor for his treatment at the hands of the Romans (Polyb. 31. 6. 6).[144] Tributes paid to the king, such as the lavish honours he accepted from the Ionian league in 167/6 (Austin 203, BD 41, Burstein 88, *RC* 52, *OGIS* 763), reflect his reputation. (His war against the Gauls, 168–166, is mentioned by Attalos in a letter to the town of Amlada: Austin 205, *RC* 54, *OGIS* 751.)

The Rhodians, too, had fallen from grace, losing not only territory but also the leadership of the Islanders' league. Their friendship with the Romans was only partly repaired by a treaty in 164.[145] Rome allowed some Karian towns to choose allegiance to Rhodes, but elsewhere the Rhodians' power to control piracy was successfully challenged by the Cretans (155–153). The decline in the military power of Rhodes coincides with its rise as a cultural centre with a renowned philosophical school.[146]

The accession of Attalos II in 158 brought no real change; he had to defer to the Romans, even though he had been their favoured candidate. An extraordinary, and apparently genuine, document from his private correspondence, published on stone a century later, records high-level, secret discussions about a possible attack on the Gauls. It is a letter to a Galatian priest:

> King Attalos to Attis the priest, greetings.... When we came to Pergamon I called together not only Athenaios, Sosandros, and Menogenes but also many others of my 'relatives', laid before them what we had discussed at Apameia, and told them what we had decided. A very elaborate discussion ensued, and to begin with everybody inclined to the same view as we did; but Chloros was extremely insistent in emphasizing the Roman factor and advising that in no way should anything be done without consulting them. At first, few shared his point of view; but after this, as we kept examining the matter day after day, his advice made a greater impression on us, and to go ahead without consulting them seemed to involve considerable danger....
>
> (Austin 208, BD 42, Sherk 29, *RC* 61, *OGIS* 315 *c* vi)

As Habicht remarks, this clearly shows that the kings of Pergamon believed that Rome meant them to have no independent policy.

Attalos was able to repel an attack from Prousias in 156–154; the senate, seeing no danger to Roman interests, backed him. Conversely, or consistently, when Attalos, together with Ariarathes of Cappadocia, attacked the Greek city of Priene which had caused them trouble, the senate again prevented any change to the *status quo*.[147] Attalos was, however, able to connive at the deposition of Prousias by his son Nikomedes in 149, and to put down the ravages inflicted upon Greek towns by Thracian soldiers in the next few years. He supplied troops to support Rome's wars against Andriskos and against the Achaeans (Paus. 7. 16. 8).[148] Pergamene power and wealth were still on a grand scale. As well as new edifices at home, Attalos founded or refounded cities within his territory and endowed cities elsewhere with spectacular gifts, most famously the stoa in the Athenian agora that bears his name (Fig. 8.8).

As Ptolemy IV is to Ptolemy III, so Attalos III stands in repute compared with his father. The sources for his short reign blacken his name, but the alleged crimes may be inventions. He was certainly unusual in apparently having a genuine and active interest in the arts and sciences. There is evidence that he performed the regular administrative duties of a king (such as the correspondence about a priesthood in Austin 210 *a–b*, *RC* 66–7, *OGIS* 331 ii–iv), but he may have delegated them to officials, and it does not prove he was a competent ruler. His negative press may simply reflect – but could also be justified by – his unexpected action in leaving his kingdom to the people of Rome in his will.[149] The reasons are unknown, but since he died prematurely, and childless, his will may not have been intended as a permanent solution but as, for example, a temporary device to prevent Aristonikos, his (alleged) illegitimate brother, from playing the heir presumptive. The king's death had unforeseen consequences at Rome, where the tribune Tiberius Gracchus used the bequest to fund his land reforms (see Plutarch, *Ti. Gracchus*; Appian, *Civil Wars*, book 1). The decree of the Roman senate

A   B

Figure 8.8   The reconstructed Stoa of Attalos II in the Agora at Athens: (*a*) exterior; (*b*) interior. (Photograph by the author.)

recognizing Attalos's acts, and hence his will, as valid has survived in a fragmentary copy from Pergamon (Austin 214, Sherk 40, *OGIS* 435).[150]

In Pergamon, Aristonikos proclaimed himself king Eumenes III (we know this only from his coins).[151] Our sources paint him a kind of Greek Spartacus who mobilized slaves and poor countrymen, but he probably did this as a last resort after failing to attract more powerful support (see also p. 189). Just after Attalos's death the citizens of Pergamon granted citizenship to various military groups resident at Pergamon but excluded persons who had left, or might leave, the city and its territory:

> In the priesthood of Menestratos son of Apollodoros, on the 19th of Eumeneios: resolved by the people, motion of the generals.
>
> [Since] king Attalos Philometor and Euergetes, having [departed] from among men, left our [native city] free, having attached to it also the [civic] land which he designated, and (since) it is necessary for the will to be ratified by the Romans, and it is [essential] for the safety of all the [undermentioned] classes (of men) should share in citizen rights because of the [complete] goodwill which they have shown towards the people; with good [fortune, be it resolved] by the people to grant citizen rights to the [undermentioned classes]: ...
>
> (Austin 211; part in Burstein 91, Sherk 39; *OGIS* 338)

This is presumably connected with the revolt of Aristonikos; apparently the *polis* is attempting to drum up support from non-citizens. The decree may also be intended to impress the Romans. Similarly, at this time either Pergamon or Elaia resolved to celebrate its close relations with Rome with a festival which included a sacrifice to the deified goddess *Rhômê* (Austin 213, Sherk 44, *Syll.* [3] 694).[152] The kingdom's dependence upon the Romans is obvious.

A widely based coalition, including cities and kings of Asia Minor as well as Rome, faced up to Aristonikos. A Roman consul and the king of Cappadocia lost their lives, but Aristonikos was defeated in 130 and his last followers in 129. Thereupon a senatorial commission created out of the Pergamene kingdom the Roman *provincia* of Asia (comprising only part of Asia Minor; Strabo, 14. 1. 38 (646), Austin 212). Thus they continued the process of deliberate romanization by direct action. After 150 years of soundly based independence, Pergamon found it impossible to survive the friendship, and the suspicion, of the Romans. Its disappearance left the attenuated Seleukid empire as the main focus of Rome's attention in the east. How Syria fared in the face of growing Roman power in and after the mid-second century is the subject of the next section.

Seleukid decline

From Antiochos V to Pompey (164–64 BC)

During the century after Antiochos V's expedition to Iran, the Seleukid kings found it increasingly difficult to hold the parts of the kingdom together. Roman interference caused further instability, and as success eluded one king after another they became more and more often the victims of court plots and rebellions by those who, perhaps, thought they could do a better job.

On Antiochos III's death in 164 his infant son Antiochos V Eupator was installed on the throne, with a regent, Lysias. In the same year, Roman ambassadors 'approved' concessions which Lysias had granted to the Maccabaean faction in Jerusalem, though they had no legal right to do so (II Macc. 11: 34–8); in the following year they ordered the partial destruction of Antiochos's armed forces, which were in excess of those allowed under the treaty of Apameia. Rome preferred an infant king to an adult (so Polybios speculates, 31. 2. 7), and refused to help Demetrios, the son of Seleukos IV ousted in 175 (Polyb. 31. 2, Austin 169); he therefore escaped from Rome and seized power as Demetrios I Soter (r. 162–150), executing Antiochos V and Lysias.[153] Demetrios was active in dealing with internal rivalries, cultivated good relations with states in Asia Minor, and recovered Babylonia and other eastern satrapies once more for the Seleukids (App. *Syr.* 47, cf. Diod. 31. 27a). His intervention in a dynastic dispute within Cappadocia, however, was undermined by the senate (158–157 BC; App. *Syr.* 47, cf. Diod. 31. 19. 6–8; 31. 32; Polyb. 31. 3; 32. 10); later he seems to have lost the initiative in Asia Minor and to have antagonized Ptolemy VI by attempting to subvert Ptolemaic rule in Cyprus (Polyb. 31. 5).

With Ptolemaic and Pergamene help, Rome (Polyb. 31. 18) successfully backed another supposed son of Antiochos IV, Alexander Balas (r. 150–145; also called Epiphanes, e.g. I Macc. 10: 1), who first overcame and killed Demetrios and then defeated Ptolemy VI Philometor, recovering Hollow Syria in 145.[154] For the first time a Seleukid king was indisputably the puppet of foreign rulers (who in 146 became the undisputed rulers of Greece). Alexander's reign saw the unavoidable recognition of Jonathan Makkabaios in Judaea and the loss of two satrapies: Media to Mithradates I (Arsakes V) of Parthia (r. *c.*171–*c.*128), a non-Greek kingdom whose power probably grew slowly in the third and early second centuries,[155] and Sousiane to the local ruler of Elymaïs.

Perhaps because Alexander was inactive in foreign affairs, his erstwhile allies in Pergamon, Cappadocia, and Egypt did not oppose the young Demetrios II Nikator (r. 145–140, 129–126/5), a son of Demetrios I, in his two-year campaign to win the throne. Ptolemy VI used force to decide the war in his favour (Diod. 32. 9 c; I Macc. 11: 1–13; Jos. *AJ* 13. 109–16), exacting Koile Syria and Palestine as his reward; but when Ptolemy died of battle wounds Demetrios reneged on the deal, broke with Egypt, and forced Jonathan to acknowledge his suzerainty (Polyb. 39. 7; Diod. 32. 9 d and 10. 1; App. *Syr.* 67; etc.).[156] He soon gained a reputation as a harsh ruler (Diod. 33. 4, Austin 170), and antagonized many of his subjects by disbanding his regular army. Their protests were quelled with the help of the Jews, but continued under the leadership of a certain Diodotos, who proclaimed Alexander's two-year-old son king Antiochos VI (r. 145–142). Diodotos forged an alliance with the Jews but discarded both it and his royal protégé when success followed, killing both Jonathan and Antiochos. As Diodotos Tryphon Autokrator (r. 142–139/8) he was the first Seleukid ruler not of the royal blood.

The death of Jonathan left the way open for his successor as high priest, Simon, to secure the independence of Jerusalem with Demetrios II's help (142 or 141); its independence was recognized by Rome (I Macc. 14: 40).[157] In 140/39 Demetrios invaded Mesopotamia in an attempt to retake Babylonia, which had fallen to Mithradates, but he was captured in Media. His brother Antiochos took up the standard against Tryphon and was proclaimed Antiochos VII Sidetes (r. 139/8–129; nicknamed from having lived in Sidê as a young man) in 139/8. With the help of the Jews, he defeated Tryphon, who committed suicide.

Now that Antiochos VII no longer needed the support of the Jews, he invaded Judaea and restored Seleukid sovereignty after a siege of Jerusalem (135–134). Trogus observed of the Jews that 'their strength was such that henceforth they tolerated no king of the Macedonians, but lived by their own authorities and plagued Syria with great wars' (Just. 36. 1. 10). While Pergamon was being turned into a Roman possession after 133, Antiochos attempted to preserve Seleukid hegemony in the east against Mithradates' successor Phraates II (r. 138–c.128). He launched an expedition in 131, but after reconquering Babylonia, Seleukeia, Sousa, and Sousiane he was defeated and killed in Media (129). Although Demetrios now escaped from captivity and reigned for a few years, Seleukid rule in the east was never restored. The kingdom was reduced to Cilicia and northern Syria. (The Jews regained their independence under John Hyrkanos.)[158]

The Seleukids had repeatedly tried to recover their lost lands, and more than once they temporarily succeeded. Antiochos VII almost defeated the Parthians, so it is hard to argue that failure was due to any inherent military or structural weakness in the empire. It is possible, however, that over several decades the interference of Rome distracted the kings from their urgent task of holding onto Mesopotamia. Nevertheless, to call the death of Antiochos VII 'the catastrophe of hellenism in continental Asia'[159] is to misrepresent the situation. It was certainly a disaster for the Seleukids (and the casualties suffered against the Parthians were immense), but we may doubt whether they saw themselves in any large sense as hellenizing Asia, and whether many things changed for the inhabitants of Babylonia when their rulers changed, since the Parthians kept the existing administrative structures and even extended Seleukid irrigation systems in the eastern provinces.

After the death of Demetrios II, allegedly murdered by his wife Kleopatra Thea (widow of Antiochos VII), what remained of the kingdom was disputed between different members of the royal family. Along with fragmentary sources, brief narratives of these events are given by Appian (*Syr.* 68–9) and Trogus (Just. 39–40), but it is hard to sift facts from legends.[160] The heir to the throne, Seleukos V, was soon killed by his mother. His brother Antiochos VIII Grypos (r. 126/5–96) first disposed of her (121) and then disputed the kingdom with his half-brother Antiochos IX Kyzikenos (r. 114/3–95), younger son of Antiochos VII. Though the territory was split between them, Grypos's long reign seems to have been relatively peaceful. His assassination in 96 left Kyzikenos briefly in overall control, but one of the five sons of Grypos, Seleukos VI, overthrew him within a year, only to be immediately overthrown by his victim's son Antiochos X Eusebes. There followed a decade of warring between Eusebes and Grypos's four younger sons, all of whom (Antiochos XI, Philip I, Demetrios III, and Antiochos XII Dionysos) ruled part of the kingdom at one time or another (the first two, as twins, jointly for a time). Antiochos XI was defeated by his cousin Eusebes, who was in turn defeated by the Nabataean Arabs, with further loss of territory. Demetrios III was captured by the Parthians. Antiochos XII died fighting the Nabataeans, resulting in the loss of Damascus. When in 83 Philip II (son of Philip I) became embroiled in civil war against Antiochos XIII (son of Eusebes), the people of Antioch, tired of internecine strife, handed the kingship to Tigranes of Armenia (see further Chapter 10). The dynasty was extinguished for fourteen years, to be revived briefly in 69 before its final suppression by Pompey in 63.

Neighbouring peoples – Jews, Nabataeans, and Armenians – gained territory and power at the expense of a declining Seleukid empire. This is not to be seen as the result of nationalist (in the sense of anti-imperialist) feeling on the part of colonized 'natives', or of an inherent failure of Seleukid control; still less as the Seleukids' just deserts for their generations of wicked oppression. These and other satellite states, normally semi-independent under both Achaemenids and Seleukids, would surely have resumed sending tribute to the great king if the Seleukids had beaten the Parthians. So far were they from wishing to throw out the foreign oppressor that some of these monarchies imitated the Seleukid court; in Kommagene, for example, Seleukid dynastic names were employed and Iranian and Greek elements were adopted into the culture of the kingdom even though it had been increasingly independent since the mid-second century.[161]

Causes of 'decline'

In some modern accounts the problems of the empire spring from the idea that a small, non-native ruling class could hardly keep control over a sprawling patchwork of nations; but this is exactly what the Persians had done for over two centuries. Accounts that emphasize 'nationalist' ambitions on the part of local rulers and peoples are too heavily coloured by modern views of the nation-state.[162] The suggestion that the Seleukids 'failed' to standardize law-codes, introduce new technologies, or improve conditions for their subjects falls to the objection that these were not the purposes of ancient imperialism. Equally, the idea that, as Rostovtzeff argued,[163] the Seleukids fostered their Graeco-Macedonian population as a bulwark against Iranian unrest, chiefly by means of city foundations, now seems too simple.

It has been argued, on the basis of about 250 names of Seleukid officials over three centuries, of which 97.5 per cent were Greek, that the Seleukids actively excluded non-Greeks from authority.[164] Sherwin-White attempts to disparage the sample's value because it is restricted to the upper echelons of the adminis-tration, which we would expect to comprise mainly Macedonians and Greeks';[165] but this is simply to gloss over the very possibility that the Graeco-Macedonians did monopolize these real positions of power. A more serious observation would be that Habicht's sample is biased by the fact that the known names occur in Greek documents and literary texts, which will be more likely to mention Greek than non-Greek officials. Furthermore, non-Greeks may have taken Greek names as alternatives or given their children Greek names.[166] So Sherwin-White's main contention on this point still stands: 'What goes on at levels immediately below [the top positions] ... is more revelatory of policy towards non-Greek subjects.'[167] Cases like those of Banabelos (his name is Babylonian), administrator of the land of a high-ranking Seleukid official named Achaios (related to the later viceroy of Asia Minor; see Austin 142),[168] and of Bagadates (Iranian by name), put in charge of a major sanctuary of Artemis by the people of Amyzon in Karia in 321 on the proposal of no less a figure than the Macedonian satrap Asandros, could hardly have arisen had there been systematic prejudice against non-Greeks.[169]

The fundamental argument of Claire Préaux's survey of hellenistic society is that the Graeco-Macedonians pursued their own imperial interests and kept the non-Greek peoples at a distance; to describe the situation she uses the word *étanchéité*, 'impermeability'.[170] There is little direct evidence in favour of such a phenomenon, and there is now some against it. In settlements like Ai Khanum and Ikaros (Failaka), there is no evidence of spatial segregation of Greek and non-Greek houses.[171] Opposition to the Seleukids did not come exclusively from non-Greeks; as Sherwin-White and Kuhrt remark, 'It is also possibly anachronistic (if fashionable) to expect opposition from subjects to empire and monarchy.'[172] (In Chapter 6 we saw similar evidence of integration in Egypt.)

An issue that is hard to resolve is whether Seleukid rule had any noticeable economic effect on the empire, adverse or favourable. There is no direct evidence that taxation or military practices impoverished the territories. In the light of Walbank's comments about the disastrous consequences of Ptolemaic rule for Egypt,[173] one might be tempted to suppose that the effects of having a non-Asian ruler in the former Persian eastern empire were pernicious. A similarly pessimistic assessment is given by Kreissig, who convincingly minimizes the degree to which Hellenic socio-economic forms were introduced, and reasonably assesses the relationships of production as a combination of old 'oriental' forms (his term) with decreased political freedom for the producing cultivators, but less persuasively sees the situation in marxist terms – a fundamental contradiction between oppressed farmers and labourers on the one hand, a privileged class of Macedonians and Greeks on the other.[174] It is probably difficult to substantiate such broad generalizations.

It seems the Seleukids mostly adopted existing mechanisms of control and exploitation. Where they modified them, such as by imposing new ownership of land, introducing new crops, or increasing the use of coinage,[175] they were doing no more than the Achaemenids had. One may doubt whether they could have made any fundamental shift in the economy, given the size of the kingdom, the lack of sophisticated communications and other means of imposing change at a distance, and the tiny administrative superstructure. It is important to stress the difficulty of distinguishing general effects across such a vast and disparate landscape, particularly given the fragmentary nature of the evidence.

A subtler argument about Seleukid weakness might centre around the problem of controlling provinces at a distance. In Herodotos's day it took three months for a message to reach the Aegean from Ekbatana, and this may still have been a handicap; distance could be held up as an underlying cause of the loss of Baktria and other eastern provinces. Distance, however, was not the only factor; culture and politics could mitigate or magnify its effects. Asia Minor was hard to control, despite its relative proximity to the imperial capitals (no less distant than Iran in miles, it was effectively brought closer by sea travel); nor is there any direct evidence for Greek regional separatism as such; when Asia Minor was a separate kingdom under Achaios, it had nothing to do with cities' resentment of Macedonian rule, and much to do with Achaios's own view of the new king and his advisers. Conversely, the satrapies of outer Iran were attached to the Seleukid kingdom in some fashion almost continuously until after the reign of Antiochos III.[176]

The rise of outside powers, above all the Parthians and Romans, may account for the difficulty of keeping possession of territories. These exogenous factors explain the increasingly chaotic succession disputes after 188. It would have been possible for the Seleukids to hold onto the extensive and variegated territories of the old Persian empire only if the Romans had not chosen to subvert the stability of the dynasty.

The burden of the study by Sherwin-White and Kuhrt is that historians have underestimated the Seleukid debt to the Achaemenids. As in the preceding Persian empire, there are important exchanges of cultural information. The empire was like its predecessor in being neither paralysed by distance and ethnic confrontation, nor emasculated by single military defeats in one area (compare Xerxes after 480, or the Seleukids after the breakaway of Pergamon and Baktria in the mid-third century, and after Magnesia).

It would be wrong to give the impression that the Seleukid kingdom was just a second Achaemenid empire. There were innovations and alterations, and the superstructure of the empire was principally Greek in its language, customs, and aspiration. The conquerors' homeland was no longer within the empire; Seleukos I never gave up (or perhaps, late in his life, revived) his ambition of ruling Macedonia, and nearly succeeded. There was no *a priori* reason why he and his successors could not have held onto both kingdoms; the Persians under Xerxes had nearly taken Greece, and only wishful thinking says they could never have done so: the outcome in 480–479 was determined by the better organization, tactics, and perhaps technology of the Greeks, just as it was Roman military accomplishment that gained them power in the east in the second century. In the fullness of time, an eastern empire would indeed occupy Greece for a period of centuries. This said, it would be wrong to imagine the Macedonian rulers of Asia as being tortured by a chronic longing for home, a kind of inverse of the *pothos* ('longing') for new horizons which Alexander is supposed to have felt. Such an assumption has perhaps inclined historians to overstate the western preponderance of Seleukid interests, which were centred as much in Mesopotamia as in Syria.

The military erosion of the empire lasted from the mid-second century to the campaigns of Pompey – hardly an overnight phenomenon. As far as the Roman takeover is concerned, this too was a gradual process, culminating in the deposition of Antiochos XIII Asiatikos and the Roman annexation of Syria in 64.[177] Nevertheless the process was fairly relentless, even if for the Romans the takeover of the empire would by no means have been inevitable had the Seleukids defeated the Parthians, as seemed likely at times. What made it irresistible in the end was the power of the Roman army. Apart from the superiority of the Roman legions, why were Rome and Pergamon able to interfere so disastrously in the decision-making of still-powerful Seleukid kings? Why was Popillius able to draw his circle in the sand? Probably it was fear of the Roman legions – which had already defeated Seleukid and Macedonian armies – that made Antiochos knuckle under in 168. On the day Popillius took his vine-stick from under his arm, a new and disturbing aspect of Roman power was made manifest.

The empire could have expanded under Seleukos and later, but military factors and chance (as in 281) prevented it. Culturally the power structures were Greek-dominated but owed much to their Achaemenid predecessors. Neither ethnic confrontation nor the 'exile factor' can account for the long erosion of territory and military power. No inherent instability, but Roman and Parthian power, put an end to the long Seleukid adventure.

9

UNDERSTANDING THE COSMOS

Greek 'science' after Aristotle

Greek thinkers in their society

There is no exact equivalent in Greek of the term 'science'.[1] The semantic field of the English word itself is varied, including not only an objective branch of knowledge, based on systematic observation, experiment, and tests and aimed at understanding the material world – the primary sense of the word today – but also a number of other classes of systematized knowledge (such as 'political science').[2] Despite this difficulty of definition and translation, we can justify using 'science' – with all due caution – as an analytical category even though members of a past society would not have recognized it; for in order to explain the past in satisfactory terms we have to make it meaningful to the present, being clear at the same time about the differences between how we conceptualize things and how the ancients did. Here, then, 'science' will be used to cover a range of investigations and theories about the workings of the material world (natural philosophy, as distinct from ethical and political philosophies); but part of the aim will be to clarify how ancient investigations differed from modern, with no presumption that they had features in common.

On a related point, we must avoid purposeless judgements and comparisons. Many published surveys of hellenistic history include an evaluation of the 'achievements' of hellenistic thinkers, essentially in terms of how interesting they were – almost as if Greek culture were competing in a talent contest. Rather than adopt this approach, we should seek to understand hellenistic thought and invention in scientific areas against the background of the society (or societies) that gave rise to them. In taking this approach we shall be following above all the work of Geoffrey Lloyd, whose extensive writings have redefined the whole subject of Greek science.[3]

Nor should we evaluate hellenistic science (as is often done) according to how well it foreshadowed, or led to, later discoveries. It has been noted, for example, that Poseidonios (fr. 49 Edelstein–Kidd (fr. 28 Jacoby) = Strabo, 2. 3. 6 (102), cf. 1. 4. 6 (65)) deduced, perhaps from Eratosthenes, that by sailing west beyond the pillars of Herakles (the straits of Gibraltar) one would reach India. A similar idea appears in a tragedy by a Roman aristocrat of the first century AD:

> There will come an age in the far-off years when Ocean shall unloose the bonds of things, when the whole broad earth shall be revealed, when Tethys shall disclose new worlds and Thule not be the limit of the lands.
>
> (Seneca, *Medea*, 375)

Some scholars have opined that these ideas led to the discovery of America;[4] but it took no revolution in thinking to make that hypothesis, and even if Christopher Columbus was aware of these ideas it would not help us understand the practice of science in the hellenistic period, or the significance of Poseidonios's proposition at the time when he made it. The search for the origins of modern knowledge risks becoming an essentially anachronistic inquiry if it ignores the terms, aims, and transmission of ancient investigations.

Above all, we should not assess the thinkers of this period on the basis of how far they fell short of what they might have achieved, or why they did not do the things they did not do.[5] Rather, our aim must be to understand sociologically what was investigated, by whom, for whom, and for what purposes — purposes framed in the terms of ancient discourse, not assessed and graded by the standards of modern science.[6]

In modern westernized societies, scientists are salaried professionals holding titled posts, funded by government or industry, and possessing acknowledged public qualifications. They may pursue a lifelong career teaching or researching into one branch or sub-branch of knowledge. These branches have become increasingly specialized: today we have not only chemistry, metallurgy, and physics but inorganic chemistry, the metallurgy of semiconductors, and theoretical particle physics. In the Greek world there were no formal educational qualifications; and while broad disciplines such as philosophy and mathematics were explicitly distinguished one from another, they were not subdivided as finely as today. Moreover, scientists in their investigations often crossed over what we might see as subject boundaries.[7] Eratosthenes of Cyrene (275–200), who studied at Athens under the Stoic philosopher Ariston before moving to Alexandria, wrote about geography, mathematics, astronomy, history, and literature. The entry on him in the Suda tells us that 'because he ranked second in every branch of culture (*paideia*), though touching the heights, he was named "Beta"' — the second letter of the Greek alphabet, meaning Number Two[8] — though the anecdote may also be ironic, implying that he was in fact regarded as the greatest scientist overall.

For large areas of science we depend on Greek and Roman authors of the imperial period; the interpretation of these poses particular problems (as discussed in Chapter 1). In some areas, however, extensive writings survive.

Theophrastos of Eresos in Lesbos (372/1–288/7 or 371/0–287/6) succeeded Aristotle and remained the head of the Peripatos from 322 until his death (see also p. 179). He wrote numerous books (mostly short pamphlets, in all likelihood) on a wide range of subjects. Among his extant works are treatises on metaphysics, the senses, plants, odours, fire, stones, winds, meteorology (this is preserved only in Syriac and Arabic versions), and last but not least his famous sketches of *Characters* (quoted, pp. 57–8); a list is given by Diogenes Laërtios (5. 42–50).[9] Some of these, no doubt, were sections of larger writings and were not free-standing, full-scale monographs; but they illustrate the wide range of interests one man could pursue. The multi-disciplinary nature of his activity is far from being without parallels in Greek history. Men like Thales of Miletos (early sixth century BC) combined the pursuit of original ideas about the world with a thoroughly aristocratic – and presumably intensely competitive – role in politics and public leadership. He learned how to predict eclipses, but was also a military leader and a political theorist. In the hellenistic period we have the example of Douris of Samos (p. 262), historian, tyrant, and pupil of Theophrastos. Nor were 'scientists' restricted to intellectual activities: doctors appear as private advisers to kings (as earlier under the pharaohs and Persian kings), while they and other thinkers serve as diplomatic envoys.[10]

The thinkers of this period were mainly, perhaps all from the educated élite; there is no clear evidence of the kind of upward social mobility offered by a career in science in the modern world.[11] Archimedes of Syracuse (*c.*287–212 or 211) was related to the ruling family of his city, and his father Pheidias was an astronomer. Their names hint at their origins: compound forms like Archi-medes (Ruler of Persians), Erato-sthenes (Lovely in Strength), and Hipp-archos (Horselord) are more likely to belong to a landowning élite; humble men in this period, when mentioned at all, often have simpler names such as Zenon ('Zeusman'), Neon ('Newman'), and Zoïlos (perhaps 'Lively'). A partial exception to the social generalization is Ktesibios (*c.*270 BC), inventor of various mechanical devices described at length by the Roman architectural writer Vitruvius (9. 8. 2–5; 10. 7. 1–8. 6); he was the son of a barber at Alexandria (Vitruv. 9. 8. 2). Though detailed evidence is lacking, it is likely that the majority of investigators were men with private means, who depended on their own resources and leisure time to be able to carry our their work, while only a minority of less well-off men like Ktesibios received substantial help from rich or royal patrons.[12]

These considerations help us to understand why the social position of the scientist was, like that of the philosopher, not very similar to that of the modern chemistry professor and closer to that of the successful novelist. Not only did thinkers attempt to write works which had literary merit in their own right (sometimes even writing in verse), but the scientist was not so much a useful servant of government or business as a purveyor of cultural discussion and intellectual entertainment for a literate élite, and could even be a transmitter of moral wisdom. He – for most, perhaps all, writers on these matters were male – wrote for people like himself, who were educated and had leisure time in which to read, or be read to. They were interested in being able to talk knowledgeably to their social equals about new ideas.

The hellenistic period brought many writers and scholars to Alexandria under the aegis of Ptolemaic patronage. Since literature and science were not situated in watertight compartments, we find scientists in the same places as writers and scholars: the library and Mouseion founded by the early Ptolemies. They enjoyed access to one another and were probably fed and housed at the king's expense. Royal funding and the emphasis on research differentiate the Mouseion from the earlier Academy and Lyceum at Athens;[13] we can only speculate as to whether, without royal assistance, these men would have had leisured, contemplative conditions in which to think, debate, and write. It seems at least possible that they would; Lloyd cautions against assuming 'that every scientist who is recorded as having worked in Alexandria (and they include almost all of the important names in third- and second-century science) was subsidized by the Ptolemies'.[14] It is quite likely that various kinds of intellectuals earned their living wholly or partly by lecturing to paying audiences (in the manner of fifth-century sophists at Athens) or, if they possessed practical wisdom in mechanics or medicine, by selling their services. Lloyd is probably right to suggest that most investigators did not expect to live by pursuing scientific inquiries alone; they were probably well-off before they started. The majority came from city-states outside Egypt, like Eratosthenes of Cyrene and Aristarchos of Samos. Most or all of them will have been born into the social élite, even if at the start they may have enjoyed patronage from, or been somehow under the tuition of, an established master.

Royal patronage, where it existed, of course, enhanced the prestige of a king. The Ptolemies, and later the Attalids, sought to make their capital cities into intellectual centres of world-wide renown. (It is important to remember that Ptolemaic and Seleukid patronage of literature and science closely mirrors the practices of earlier near eastern monarchies.) The motives behind Ptolemaic patronage of intellectuals were examined in Chapter 7. They apply equally to the sciences, with one important difference: some things that scientists did had practical benefits for the kings. In the Greeks' representation of their own history there was a tradition of the outstanding individual who combined the roles of statesman, wise man, 'first discoverer' (*prôtos heuretês*), and benefactor of mankind. The kings adopted and refurbished this model through their patronage of intellectuals. The fruits of patronage were not for their consumption alone; we can imagine that knowledgeable citizens of Alexandria and Pergamon took pride in innovations – which would further enhance the king's prestige.

The modern distinction between pure and applied science is not exactly paralleled in Greek thought, though the theoretical–practical distinction is made, for example by Pappos of Alexandria, a geometrician writing in about the early fourth century AD and clearly following hellenistic sources:

> The mechanicians of Heron's school say that mechanics can be divided into a theoretical (*logikon*) and a manual (*cheirourgikon*) part. The theoretical part is composed of geometry, arithmetic, astronomy, and physics. The manual part is composed of work in metals, architecture, carpentering, and painting, and anything involving skill with the hands.
>
> (Pappos, *Collection*, 8. 1–2, *GMW* ii. 615)[15]

Plutarch seems to express a slightly different distinction, and a prejudice widely shared by Greek and Roman élites (not just of his own period), when he says that Archimedes regarded the practical applications of his mathematics in the fields of engineering and warfare as 'ignoble and vulgar', and valued only those pursuits 'the subtlety and charm of which are not affected by the claims of necessity' (*Marcellus*, 17. 4). Despite all this, one may reasonably doubt that Archimedes, as a prominent citizen of a famous Greek *polis*, would have scorned the practical contribution he could make to the safety of his fellow-citizens. Plutarch may be writing for Greek and Roman readers of his own time who expect him to say this kind of thing, though they may well be benefiting economically from such rude practicalities as trade, agriculture, and building techniques. Modern works on hellenistic science perhaps unwittingly embody the same relative evaluation of pure and applied science, in treating the pure before the applied. If we want to understand the place of the scientist within society, we would do well to look first at the inventions and practical applications of which both kings and other Greeks will have been aware in their lives.

Engineering, mechanics, and physics

Entertaining an élite

In his early life, according to Plutarch, Archimedes invented anti-siege engines 'mostly as incidental works (*parerga*) to a playful geometry' (Plut. *Marc.* 14. 4). The combination of scientific, particularly mechanical, inventiveness with the theme of amusement is characteristic of many areas of hellenistic science. Vitruvius's descriptions of the inventions of Ktesibios switch easily between utility and pleasure:

> Ktesibios, therefore, after observing that, by the transmission and expulsions of air, sounds and tones arose, used these principles and

was the first man to invent hydraulic machines. He also explained the expulsions of water and self-powered machines and many kinds of entertainments (*deliciae*), among which were the preparation of clocks run by water.

(Vitruv. 9. 8. 4)

Vitruvius describes water-powered musical organs, in such a way as to imply that Ktesibios was a pioneer (10. 7–8): we do not know when or where such instruments were used.[16] Élite amusements intersect with serious astronomy in the person of Archimedes, who besides his many other achievements made a planetarium, perhaps to entertain his fellow-aristocrats (described by Cicero, *De re publica*, 1. 14. 21–2).

A key text in this connection comes from the aforementioned Pappos, who enumerates the arts 'most necessary for the purposes of practical life'. The first three items in his list are not surprising: the art of making pulleys, the art of making engines of war such as catapults, and the construction of engines to raise water from a great depth. For a modern reader it is more unexpected, and consequently more illuminating of the purposes of science in the age after Alexander, to find in the fourth place

the wonder-makers (*thaumasiourgoi*), of whom some ply their art through pneumatics, as Heron in his *Pneumatika*; others appear to imitate the movements of living creatures through strings and ropes, as Heron in his *Automata* and *Balancings*; others through things carried on water, as Archimedes in his book *On Floating Bodies*; or through clocks operated by water, as Heron in his *Hydreia*, which appears to share common ground with the art of sundials.

(Pappos, *Collection*, book 8, preface, 2; *GMW* ii. 617–19)

Finally, he says, comes the art of making spherical models of the heavens. Pappos is not surveying any actual past society, but reviewing the range of extant scientific works known to him. Nevertheless it is reasonable to guess that his order of priorities broadly reflects those of kings and mathematical engineers in the third and second centuries, since he refers to authors of that period.

The extant treatise *Pneumatika* by Heron (*Hêrôn*, or Hero) of Alexandria, though written in the second half of the first century AD, reflects a typical hellenistic mix of theory and the manufacture of amusements – 'wonders' – for the élite at play.[17] It was partly based on the work of Straton, Theophrastos's successor as head of the Lyceum. Heron ostensibly proves the principles of Aristotelian physics by the results of simple experiments involving metal spheres; but he describes numerous gadgets for trick effects, such as drinking-vessels and a device that has been described, somewhat misleadingly, as a 'proto-turbine' – it was simply a metal sphere with bent tubes

331

attached, which rotated on a pivot as a result of the action of steam expelled from a cauldron underneath (Heron, *Pneumatika*, proem, 16. 23–4). It was probably conceived as a 'wonder', with no functional purpose save that of demonstrating the inventor's ingenuity.

Civic applications

Some inventions had a communal benefit. Pappos's reference to 'instruments for raising water' probably denotes the Archimedean screw or 'snail' (*kochlias* in Greek, *cochlea* in Latin), which may have been used to pump out ships and drain fields after the Nile flood (Diod. 1. 34; 5. 37). Athenaeus (5. 208 f) refers to 'the *kochlias*, which Archimedes invented', while Vitruvius (10. 6) describes a similar machine, without attributing it to him. There is a tradition that Archimedes actually invented it in Egypt, and a 'snail' in use is depicted on a late hellenistic terracotta relief from Alexandria.[18]

Another new mechanical device with an agricultural application was a water-mill (Vitruv. 10. 4–5; Antipater of Thessalonike, *Anthologia Palatina*, 9. 418; Strabo, 12. 3. 30 (556); cf. Pliny, *Natural History*, 18. 97),[19] while third-century papyri attest the limited adoption in Egypt of metal ploughshares and other tools. Two Zenon papyri (*PCZ* 59782a, 59851) refer to the consumption of large quantities of iron (including *c.*100 talents) on the estate, while another (59849) is a receipt for mattocks.[20]

Archimedes devised the compound pulley, an improvement on the simple pulley known before. The tradition of benefactor of mankind is perhaps reflected in the story that with the aid of his compound pulley system he single-handedly launched the *Syrakosia*, the flagship of the tyrant of Syracuse, Hieron. It was supposedly on this occasion that he told the king, in the paradoxical way beloved of Greek thinkers (as they are represented to us) showing off their divinely inspired wisdom, 'Give me a place to stand and I will move the earth' (this version appears in Pappos, *Collection*, 8. 11. 19, *GMW* ii. 35; also in Johannes Tzetzes' twelfth-century verse *Book of Histories*, ii. 130, *GMW* ii. 21); Plutarch has him boasting that 'if he had another earth and crossed over to it, he would move this one', and bringing ashore a three-masted merchantman single-handed (Plut. *Marc.* 14. 7–9). The importance of the story (whose truth or falsehood is unknowable and irrelevant) lies in the presentation, once again, of the inventor as benefactor of the community.

Ktesibios (p. 328) invented water-clocks, of which Vitruvius (9. 8. 2–5) gives an extended account. After describing the toothed gearing which is set in motion by a rising float, Vitruvius explains the adjustment of the machine for different seasons:

> The hours are written either on a small column or on a pilaster, and
> a figure emerging from below points to them with a wand throughout

the day. Additions or extractions of wedges effect shortenings and lengthenings of the pointers for particular days and months. For the purpose of adjustment, devices to hold back the water are to be constructed.... But if by the additions and subtractions of wedges the truncations or lengthenings of the days are not shown to be happening (accurately), because wedges often have errors, it is to be solved as follows. Let the hours be written on a small column, crosswise in accordance with the diagram (*analêmma*),[21] and let the monthly lines be marked on the small column. And let this column be allowed to revolve, so that in turning continuously to the figure and the wand with which the figure as it emerges shows the hours, the column makes the shortenings and lengthenings of the hours for each particular month.

(Vitruv. 9. 8. 6–7)

The precise mechanism is hard to visualize from this description alone, but the passage is one of many pieces of evidence for the complexity of mechanical devices and for the degree of patient trial and modification that went into their design. The passage from Pappos cited earlier names Heron as an inventor of water-clocks.

A descendant of Ktesibios's invention can be seen in the late hellenistic Tower of the Winds, built by Andronikos of Kyrrhestos in, probably, the late second century, which overlooks the (slightly later) Roman forum at Athens (Fig. 9.1). The tower, which Vitruvius purports to describe but may not have seen for himself, is decorated with reliefs depicting the eight winds; on the roof stood a weather-vane in the form of a figure with a wand which would point to the appropriate relief; inside the tower was a water-clock and sundials adorned its outer walls. The placing of the tower on an elevation above the east side of the Athenian Agora emphasizes its civic function of public timekeeping.[22] As such it superseded a water-clock of the second half of the fourth century, built in the south-western part of the Agora, which was itself converted during the hellenistic period from a simple outflow clock by the addition of a superior inflow mechanism, probably in the light of technical advances such as those made by Ktesibios.[23] (A very similar structure to the latter, probably also late fourth-century, can be seen in the Amphiareion at Oropos.)[24]

Vitruvius also describes Ktesibios's invention of a pump for raising water to a reservoir from which a fountain can be supplied; it seems, from his account, to depend on animal or human power continuously turning a capstan. This is another example of mechanics being applied to the enhancement of the urban environment.

In this connection we may mention the introduction of improved mortarwork in public masonry, and of the first true arches and vaults; the Greeks may have learnt the new forms as a result of Alexander's Persian campaigns.

Figure 9.1   The Tower of the Winds and the Roman Agora at Athens. (Photograph by the author.)

Examples of vaults are known from the late fourth century onwards, including the entrance tunnel to the stadium at Nemea in the Peloponnese (*c*.325) and a third-century vaulted cistern on Delos. In mainland Greece they appear in the rear wall of the Stoa of Eumenes at Athens (mid-second century)[25] (Fig. 9.2). A further example of innovative experimentation for civic improvement is offered by the discovery of an underfloor heating system of middle and late hellenistic date in the baths of the sanctuary of Asklepios at Arkadian Gortys,[26] a probable ancestor of the Roman hypocaust; as so often, the Romans seem to have taken over existing Greek terminology (*hypokauston*, 'fired underneath'). The sighting instrument known as the *dioptra*, improved by the astronomer Hipparchos during this period (p. 351), was useful in the context of activities such as public construction and land surveying; Polybios (10. 45–6) describes a technique for using it to spell out words transmitted by signals. These and other inventions locate some activities of hellenistic scientists within the context of the city, and are a further sign of the continued success of the *polis* as a social institution.

Military techniques

Military technology, owing to the increasingly vast expenses it entailed, was the province more of kings than of *poleis*; but it brings together a number of developments in engineering. Sieges and the building of strong fortifica-

Figure 9.2   The surviving rear wall of the Stoa of Eumenes at Athens. (Photograph by the author.)

tions – sometimes to assert status and aspiration to power, not purely for defence – had long been features of city life (compare the walls built by Polykrates, the sixth-century tyrant, around the acropolis of Samos), and became more common in the Peloponnesian war of the late fifth century. Only exceptional *poleis* resisted the trend, such as the Spartans; and though they found it necessary to throw up a ditch and palisade when Cassander threatened to invade the Peloponnese, in or soon after 319, it was not until the reign of Nabis (207–192) that permanent brick-and-stone walls were erected.[27]

The fourth century gave rise to a new genre of literature, the treatise on military matters. An extant book by a mid-fourth-century Arkadian general, Aineias (Aeneas the Tactician or Aeneas Tacticus), commonly known as the *Poliorketika* (or *How to Survive under Siege*), is the prime example.[28] Although the work contains sections of considerable technical interest (such as on opening locked gateways and sending secret messages), the author's main concern is with the political management of a city population at a time when treachery is an ever-present threat; the techniques of defence which he discusses are almost wholly non-mechanical. Already, however, there had been developments in siege techniques such as those implemented by the tyrant Dionysios of Syracuse, who commissioned catapults which hurled arrows. In the 330s Alexander used missile-throwing machines at the siege of Tyre, and his engineer Diades invented the *korax* or boarding-bridge for use in naval encounters (a similar device is described in detail by Polybios, 1. 22. 3).[29] Royal patronage was an important factor in the development of these arts; we know of an Athenian engineer, Epimachos, who assisted Demetrios I at the siege of Rhodes, and of the architects Kallias and Diognetos who defended the city (Vitruv. 10. 16. 3–4). A certain Biton dedicated a short treatise on *Constructions of Engines of War and Projection* to 'king Attalos'.[30] Among surviving sources is the *Mechanical Collection* (*Mechanikê syntaxis*, 'Mechanical systematic treatise') of Philon of Byzantion (also known by the latinized name of Philo), written around 200 BC, book 4 of which was entitled *Belopoiika* (*Artillery*, or *On Making Missiles*).

The development of these and similar machines is an important demonstration that Greek scientists were not, as is often asserted, fixated on abstract theory and incapable of practical experimentation. Philon informs us that Alexandrian engineers, with royal help, made systematic trials of different designs of catapults, adjusting the design until they achieved the right results:

> In the old days, some engineers were on the way to discovering that the fundamental basis and unit of measure for the construction of engines was the diameter of the hole.... It was impossible to obtain it except by experimentally increasing and diminishing the perimeter of the hole.... Later engineers drew conclusions from former mistakes, looked exclusively for a standard factor with subsequent experiments as a guide, and introduced the basic principle of construction, namely the diameter of the circle that holds the spring. Alexandrian craftsmen achieved this first, being heavily subsidized because they had ambitious kings who fostered craftsmanship. The fact that everything cannot be accomplished by the theoretical methods of pure mechanics, but that much is to be found by experiment, is proved especially by what I am going to say.
>
> (*Belopoiika*, 50. 14–26 with omissions)[31]

Key points in this passage are, first, the alleged contrast between earlier, haphazard experimentation and later investigations based on the search for a constant factor; second, the role of royal patronage. Among the principal artillery designs described by Philon is the catapult invented by Ktesibios which was powered by bronze springs and compressed air (Philon, *Bel.* 67. 28–72. 23)[32] (Fig. 9.3).

Weapons of attack could be weapons of defence; the inventor could be the benefactor of a city as well as a king's servant. Archimedes invented grapnels and catapults that helped the Syracusans keep the Roman ships at bay for three years (described at length by Plut. *Marc.* 15. 1–17. 3), and allegedly devised mirrors which would focus the rays of the sun so as to set ships on

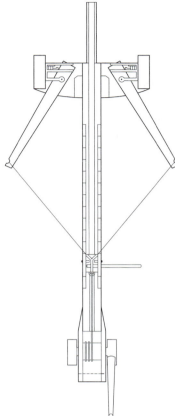

Figure 9.3. Ktesibios's bronze-spring catapult. (Closely based on Marsden, *Greek and Roman Artillery: Technical Treatises*, 174, diagram 8; reproduced by permission of Oxford University Press.)

fire (Tzetzes, *Chil.* 2. 118–27, *GMW* ii. 20).[33] The importance of anti-siege tactics, and the close connection between mechanical experimentation and public safety, are well brought out by the variety of imaginative ruses which cities adopted,[34] particularly those involving machines of defence which hurled hurling missiles, scythes, and nets, or tipped noxious and impeding substances onto the heads of the attackers. It is indicative of hellenistic and Roman thinking, therefore, that Vitruvius, heavily imbued with hellenistic ideas, should end his work *On Architecture* with chapters on weapons of attack and stratagems of defence (10. 10–16).

Some of the most visible responses to the new tactics are the surviving remains of fortifications, which took increasingly complex, tactically sophisticated layouts from the second half of the fourth century onwards. The fort of Eleutherai in north-western Attica (Fig. 9.4) has a wall-plan designed to hamper attackers, with complex gateways of different shapes and deflections

Figure 9.4   The north fortification wall at Eleutherai in north-western Attica.
(Photograph by the author.)

in the walls to allow defenders to fire at attackers from the side.[35] Until
1981 the tallest surviving work of Greek architecture was the south-east
corner tower of the fort of Aigosthena at the head of the Gulf of Corinth (the
topmost courses of masonry were dislodged as a result of earthquake damage;
the fort may be linked with Demetrios I or another of the Successors, but
has also been tentatively attributed to the Athenians and dated to the 340s[36]
(Fig. 9.5).

Unprecedented military power demanded constructions on an unprecedented scale.[37] Just as royal patronage gave rise to gigantic architecture, so it
produced huge military devices such as the famous Helepolis ('Take-city') of
Demetrios Poliorketes. He used one of these against the city of Salamis in
Cyprus in 306 (Diod. 20. 48. 2–3); it had ballistas capable of throwing
missiles weighing three talents (*c*.80 kg), but the citizens set it on fire
(20. 48. 6–7). During the siege of Rhodes in 304 a larger version was built:

> So, having prepared a mass of all kinds of material, he constructed a
> machine called the *helepolis*, which in size exceeded by far those that
> were before. He caused each side of a square platform to be almost
> fifty cubits long, put together from squared timbers bound with
> iron. The interior space he divided up with beams about a cubit
> from one another, so that there would be standing space for the men

338

Figure 9.5   The south-east tower at Aigosthena in the Megarid in 1980.
(Photograph by the author.)

who would propel the machine forward. The whole structure was
wheeled, supported by eight solid, huge wheels; for the thicknesses
of their rims measured two cubits and were shod with strong plates
of iron.... The whole edifice being nine storeys high, the first floor
measured forty-three *akainai* [*4,300 sq ft, c.400 sq m*] (in area), the
topmost nine *akainai* [*900 sq ft, c.80 sq m*]. He covered the three
visible sides of the machine with riveted iron plates on the outside,
so that nothing should be harmed by fire-throwers. The floors had
windows on the front, corresponding in sizes and shapes to the peculiarities of the weapons that were to be launched. These windows
had shutters which were drawn up mechanically, by which the men
on each floor who were busied about the launching of the missiles
might receive protection; for the shutters were stitched together
from hides and were filled with wool, for the purpose of absorbing
the impact of the artillery.

(Diod. 20. 91. 2–6)

Other accounts are given by Vitruvius (10. 16. 3–8) and by later authors.
The machine was propelled by 3,400 men, those on the outside being
protected by lean-tos and covered passages. When the *helepolis* was brought

up to the walls, accompanied by battering rams and loaded with artillery (Diod. 20. 95. 1–2), it seems to have proved its value, since parts of the Rhodian walls were overthrown (95. 5); later it was damaged by fire when its metal plates were dislodged, but the fires were extinguished (96. 4, 7). Eventually, however, the siege was abandoned (99. 1), and such oversized contraptions seem to have fallen out of favour.

Other sources tell of huge warships built for Antigonos Gonatas and Ptolemy Philadelphos, which had, respectively, twenty and thirty banks of oars; these are known from a dedication by Ptolemy II found in the sanctuary of Aphrodite at Paphos on Cyprus: 'King Ptolemy (honours) Pyrgoteles son of Zoës, architect of the thirty-bank ship (*triakontêrês*) and the twenty-bank ship (*eikosêrês*)' (*OGIS* 39). Athenaeus (5. 203 d–e; Austin 219) lists Philadelphos's exceptional ships, mentioning the 'twenty' and the 'thirty'. The trend towards gigantism in the display of royal power reached its apogee in the forty-row ship of Ptolemy IV,[38] of which we have a description by Kallixeinos:

> Philopator constructed his forty-bank ship with a length of 420 feet; its beam from gangway to gangway was 57 feet; its height to the gunwale was 72 feet. From the top of the stern-post to the water-line it measured 79½ feet. It had four steering-oars, 45 feet long, and the oars of the topmost rowers, which are the longest, measured 57 feet; these, since they carried lead on the handles and were very heavy inboard, were yet easy to handle in actual use because of their nice balance.... It was extraordinarily well proportioned. Wonderful also was the adornment of the vessel besides; for it had figures at stern and bow not less than 18 feet high, and every available space was elaborately covered with encaustic painting ... Rich also was the equipment in armament, and it satisfied all the requirements of the various parts of the ship. On a trial voyage it took more than 4,000 men to man the oars, and 400 reserves; to man the deck there were 2,850 marines ...
>
> (Athenaeus, 5. 203 e–204 d)

It can only have been a kind of floating fortress, may never have seen action, and perhaps was not intended for action.

Most of the military innovations of the hellenistic period took place outside Greece; that is not surprising, since most of the opportunities for trying them out took place outside the world of the *polis*, now that cities conducted few campaigns. Garlan, however, points to a 'fossilization of the military art in the Hellenistic kingdoms' in technical matters, blaming this for the defeats of Macedonia by the Romans and of the Seleukid empire by the Parthians.[39] He points to the rigidity of the phalanx and the over-elaboration of manoeuvres under the influence of abstract modelling. His account is perhaps unduly influenced by Polybios, who, he says, laments the mediocrity of some aspects of military practice (Polybios discusses problems of the phalanx at 18. 28–32; part in Austin 67). Nevertheless, it seems true that kings and generals preferred to rely on the tried and trusted formulae – though in which age, until the most recent times, has this not been true? – and may have been slow to adapt in the face of new enemies with new tactics. Kings were not afraid to innovate where wealth could be thrown at a problem, for instance by commissioning technological improvements in military hardware, or by building grandiose – and no doubt often effective – fortifications. Possibly the scale of the monarchies, compared with the city-states, was not conducive to rapid experimentation and limited their capacity to adapt in the face of new threats from the west.

Understanding life-forms

Increasing sophistication and increasing complexity of description are features of Greek philosophical and scientific writing both before and during this period. Another feature is the effective specialization of different sciences, though not of scientists.

Botany and zoology

The principal botanical author is Theophrastos (pp. 179, 328), one of the few authors on life-sciences whose works survive in a reasonably full form.[40] There is not enough space here to discuss the copious works of Aristotle in the area of life-sciences,[41] and we can do no more than note that Theophrastos's equally wide-ranging work springs directly out of that of his immediate predecessor. There is also debate about the extent to which he saw himself as challenging rather than extending Aristotle's achievement.[42]

Theophrastos drew on earlier writers and on new evidence gathered by the scientists who accompanied Alexander's expedition;[43] his two books remained the key texts in botany thereafter. He does not seem to have carried out experiments, but his work is classified according to an Aristotelian rationality and eschews, for the most part, the attribution of magical properties to plants.[44] He is part of the gradual reaction against the magical interpretation of natural species.[45]

The earlier *Enquiry concerning Plants* (or *History of Plants*) was written around 300.[46] Book 1 deals with the structure and classification of plants; the brisk, rigorously impersonal tone is set from the start:

> In considering the distinctive characters of plants and their nature generally, one must take into account their parts, their qualities, the ways in which their life originates, and the course which it follows in each case (conduct and activities we do not find in them, as we

do in animals). Now the differences in the way in which their life originates, in their qualities, and in their life-history are comparatively easy to observe and are simpler, while those shown in their 'parts' present more complexity. Indeed, it has not even been satisfactorily determined what ought and what ought not to be called 'parts', and some difficulty is involved in making the distinction.

(Thphr. *HP* 1. 1. 1)

Later books deal with (2) propagation, especially of trees, (3) wild trees, (4) trees and plants of particular regions, (5) timber, (6) under-shrubs, (7–8) herbaceous plants, and (9) juices of plants and medicinal properties of plants. These books are rich in description and enumerate many hundreds of observations of particular species. Sometimes classification and specific data go together:

As to cultivation and tending, some requirements apply equally to all trees, some are peculiar to one. Those which apply equally to all are spadework, watering, and manuring, and moreover pruning and removal of dead wood. But different trees differ in the degree. Some love moisture and manure, some not so much, as the cypress, which is fond neither of manure nor of water, but actually dies, they say, if it is over-watered when young. But the pomegranate and vine are water-loving. The fig grows more vigorously if it is watered, but then its fruit is inferior, except in the case of the Laconian variety, which is water-loving.

(Thphr. *HP* 2. 7. 1)

That extract exemplifies the way in which Theophrastos relies on reports from around the Greek world, usually specified with 'they say' or a similar phrase. The systematic nature of his classification, like Aristotle's, is generalized from experience of the world, not imposed on reality by *a priori* reasoning. Other passages display his or his correspondents' close attention to detail – whether or not their classification and explanatory framework match those of today:

The tree found about Mount Ida, called *koloitia*, is a distinct kind, and is shrubby and branching with many boughs; but it is rather rare. It has a leaf like that of the 'broad-leaved' bay, but rounder and larger, so that it looks like that of the elm, but it is more oblong: the colour on both sides is green, but the base is whitish; in this part it is very fibrous, because of its fine fibres which spring partly from the midrib, partly between the ribs (so to call them) which run out from the midrib. The bark is not smooth but like that of the vine; the wood is hard and close, the roots are shallow, slender, and spreading (though sometimes they are compact), and they are very yellow. They say that this shrub has no fruit or flower, but has its knobby winter bud and its 'eyes'; these grow alongside the leaves, and are very smooth, glossy, and white, and in shape are like a winter bud. When the tree is cut or burnt down, it grows from the side and springs up again.

(Thphr. *HP* 3. 17. 3)

Such enthusiastic and systematic recording, and the desire to find comparisons with known data, are characteristic of hellenistic science.

A work often printed together with the *History of Plants* is Theophrastos's surviving treatise *On Odours*, which also deals with spices and perfumes. With book 9 of the *History*, it gives invaluable data about the practices of ancient herbalists, and illustrates the absence of experimental testing:

Of cyclamen the root is used for suppurating boils; also as a pessary for women and, mixed with honey, for dressing wounds; the juice for purgings of the head, for which purposes it is mixed with honey and poured in; it also conduces to drunkenness, if one is given a draught of wine in which it has been steeped. They say also that the root is a good charm for inducing rapid delivery and is a love potion; when they have dug it up, they burn it, and then, having steeped the ashes in wine, make little balls, like those made of wine-lees which we use as soap.

(Thphr. *HP* 9. 9. 3)

There are, however, surprising gaps for anyone familiar with Mediterranean cuisine today: garlic (*skorodon*), for example, is mentioned only as a precaution against poisoning taken by those digging up hellebore (9. 8. 6). Theophrastos tells us little of his methods of collecting data.

The later treatise *On the Causes of Plants*, from the last decade of Theophrastos's life,[47] is more abstract and seeks explanations of common and uncommon characteristics of plants in general. It deals with (books 1–2) spontaneous processes intrinsic to plants (generation, sprouting, flowering, etc.), (3–4) processes resulting from human intervention (chiefly agriculture), and (5) the unnatural ill effects of agriculture and the special effects of human artifice. Book 6 deals with flavours and odours, as did book 7 (now lost). The more explanatory aim of much of this work is shown here:

Another problem is this: why, when the cereal is plump and one might say dry (as it were), rain, far from improving the crop, makes it worse; but cereal that has been reaped and heaped into piles gets plumper and so improves, and some farmers even sprinkle the pile?

> The reason is this: in the first case the cereal gets drenched and
> the sun comes out again and removes the native fluid with the rain,
> and so shrinks the kernels; in the second case dampness is produced
> in the pile and the vapour that arises, which is thin and like *pneuma*
> [*warm, expansive gas*], penetrates the kernels and makes them plumper.
>
> (Thphr. *CP* 4. 13. 6)

(Contrast the more descriptive passage about the same practice at *HP* 8. 11. 4.)

Knowledge of plants was a focus of attention for writers about agricultural techniques. None of the many agricultural works of this period survives; but much material was later taken over by Roman writers on estate management such as Varro (*De re rustica*, published in 37 BC), who lists over fifty earlier writers, almost all Greeks of the hellenistic period (1. 1. 8).

Agriculture and pastoral production were objects of royal interest, particularly in Egypt and Asia, where there was a Persian tradition of kingly encouragement for experimentation with new species; the late sixth-century letter of Dareios I to his satrap Gadatas in Ionia (ML 12) is a famous early example of this concern. Innovation did not normally take the form of the scientific breeding of new varieties, but involved, rather, the transplantation of crops and animals into new environments, either with the aim of enhancing the quality of life for members of the élite or in the hope that they would increase royal revenues. Already in the archaic period powerful men had been introducing new domesticated animals from other countries, such as the sheep, hunting-dogs, and goats introduced by Polykrates, tyrant of Samos (late sixth century; Ath. 12. 540 d–e).[48] In the hellenistic period, a combination of good public relations and concern for royal revenues is reflected in the agricultural interests of monarchs. Hieron II of Syracuse and Attalos III of Pergamon are listed as authors of treatises on agriculture (Varro, *RR* 1. 1. 8; Columella, *RR* 1. 8; Pliny, *HN*, indexes of authors cited in books 14, 15, and 18).

Most of the evidence for royal intervention concerns Egypt. We are told that Ptolemy I made a personal approach to Theophrastos (Diog. Laërt. 5. 37; he gives no details, however). Many changes were made to existing patterns of cultivation.[49] We have the evidence of the Zenon archive (p. 219) that Ptolemy II personally authorized various measures on the Apollonios estate for the promotion of agriculture. These included new varieties of fruit trees from the king's botanical gardens; Apollonios arranged for six different kinds of fig trees to be planted, as well as pomegranates and apricots (*PCZ* 59033, 257 BC).[50] A three-month wheat was to be planted on irrigated land (*PCZ* 59155, 256 BC), and special breeds of sheep from Miletos and Arabia (*PCZ* 59195, 255 or 254 BC; 59430, undated).[51] Apart from the quick-harvesting wheat, the transplantations of which we hear tend to be of luxury crops, like the vines introduced to Babylonia by the Seleukids:

The vine, which was not grown there [*in Sousis*] formerly, the Macedonians planted both there and in Babylon, not digging trenches but only thrusting into the ground stakes with their points covered in iron, then removing them and immediately putting down the young plants in their place.

(Strabo, 15. 3. 11 (731))[52]

Also from the Zenon archive comes a striking document of 257 BC on the promotion of viticulture. An agent writes to Apollonios the *dioikêtês* about his huge vineyard in Galilee, at a time when it is under Ptolemaic rule:

Glaukias to Apollonios, greeting.
About the things you instructed me to report to Nikanor and Antiochos, we reported them. Know that they are conforming to them. The other things we will report to you whenever we arrive. Arriving at Baitanôs [*Bethaneth*] and taking Melas with me, I visited the plants and all the other things. Well, they seem to me to be satisfactorily cultivated, and he said the vineyard was 80,000 (in number). He has also constructed a well and a satisfactory dwelling. He gave me the wine to taste, and I did not distinguish whether it was Chian or local. So you are doing well, with good luck in all things.

(*P. Lond.* 1948)[53]

From its scale this would seem to be a commercial undertaking, albeit aimed at the luxury end of the market.

Attalos III was devoted to botany for the purpose of cultivating medicinal plants, and is said by Celsus, Galen, and Pliny to have discovered various remedies.[54] Sometimes more machiavellian motives may have been present; Plutarch informs us that 'Attalos Philometor made a habit of cultivating poisonous herbs, not only henbane or hellebore but also hemlock, aconite, or dorycinium' (*Demetr.* 20; cf. Pliny, *HN* 25. 6. 28. 64; 25. 8. 55. 99; Justin, 36. 4. 3), and Galen reports that these were used on criminals.[55]

Sometimes an interest in flora and fauna may have had a combination of political aims with the desire to enhance royal prestige, as when Ptolemy II included exotic animals in his great procession (Kallixeinos *ap.* Ath. 5. 201 b–c; Austin 219; see p. 68), and when Seleukos I sent an Indian tiger to Athens (Ath. 13. 590 a, quoting the comic playwrights Philemon (fr. 47; Kock, *CAF* ii. 490) and Alexis (fr. 204; Kock, *CAF* ii. 372)). When Ptolemy VIII – no friend of the Mouseion – imported exotic birds with which to adorn his court (Ath. 14. 654 c), do we assume his motives were limited to a desire for luxury? When Philetairos took an interest in stockbreeding, was he merely playing the intellectual, promoting the cultural standing of his kingdom, taking a proper interest in the revenue-raising potential of the land, or seeking to avail himself of the best possible textiles for the court? Motives can be hard to disentangle. Sometimes a commercial interest may be present (again partly directed towards keeping revenues up), as with Seleukid and Ptolemaic attempts to acclimatize spice- and perfume-bearing plants;[56] but we cannot discount the same prestige considerations as lay behind the patronage of literature and the arts.

Medicine

Medicine, like other areas of science, did not undergo a fundamental transformation, but evolved from what was there before. The main centres of teaching and research were the island *polis* of Kos, with its healing sanctuary of Asklepios, and the new cultural capital in Alexandria. As with other sciences, medical investigators set out with differing philosophies and views of the material universe. Like philosophers, they grouped themselves into 'schools' with rival ideologies and possibly competing approaches to medical practice, though we should not exaggerate the differences.[57]

An important figure who stands at the beginning of hellenistic medicine is the rather shadowy Praxagoras of Kos. In the second half of the fourth century he gained a reputation as an anatomist and teacher and made important discoveries, modifying the earlier Hippocratic theory of bodily humours.[58]

Among the pupils of Praxagoras was one of the two most renowned doctors of the third century, Herophilos of Chalkedon (*c*.330–*c*.260 BC). He discovered the nerves, distinguishing between sensory and motor nerves and identifying those in the brain and the optic nerve, as well as defining different parts of the eye. He described the liver, and parts of the male and female reproductive and cardiovascular systems. Although he theorized about imbalances in the 'humours'[59] as a cause of disease, he regarded all explanations as provisional. He is most famous for analysing the character and variation of the pulse, which he used as a diagnostic tool. In short, Herophilos's work was among the most fertile of any Greek scientist, stimulating a wide range of approving and hostile discussions in many later writers, medical, philosophical, and religious.[60]

Erasistratos, from Ioulis on Keos (*c*.315–*c*.240 BC), made important discoveries about the heart valves and introduced a single theory uniting breathing, blood, the nervous system, the muscles, appetite, and digestion, based on the transmutation of inhaled air into 'vital *pneuma*' (literally 'breath') and ultimately blood, though the blood was thought to occupy only veins, not arteries. The same model was used to explain diseases, including those of women (which were held not to be specific to them). Erasistratos is remarkable for his readiness to carry out experiments, dissecting animals and humans to test his theories.[61]

Both Herophilos and Erasistratos belong to the group of so-called

Dogmatists (the name may be a later invention), who asserted the value of dissection; indeed, the two are the only ancient medics known to have performed dissection systematically. The 'Empiricists', on the other side, urged that the doctors should avoid theorizing about the body or about diseases and consider only symptoms.

While they often devoted great energy to the investigation of the human organism, medical writers would usually interpret what they saw only in such a way as to uphold their existing model of how the body worked. The main difference between medicine and other sciences was that most medical writers were practising doctors, so that most of the medical investigation was carried out by men who depended on their art for their livelihood. They were frequently the recipients of public honours, and their social status was high, as one might expect. In Cyrene their political independence was guaranteed in the refoundation charter of Ptolemy I:

> Whosoever of the citizen body is serving in a public capacity as doctor, gymnastic trainer, or teacher of archery, horse-riding, or hoplite fighting, or as herald in the council chamber, let him not participate in the offices proper to the Ten Thousand (citizens). Whosoever of these men shall be chosen by lot shall resign from his office.
>
> (Austin 264, Harding 126, *SEG* ix. 1, lines 42–5)[62]

It is possible that this is a restriction upon lower-status professions; but the key word is *dēmosiâi*, 'in a public capacity', perhaps implying that a potential conflict of interest is being averted, or that these groups are being exempted from public service as a recognition of the contribution they are already making.

Some medical investigation went on at the upper level of society, alongside other sciences. Ptolemaic patronage is implied by the Roman medical encyclopaedist Celsus, who preserves much of our knowledge of hellenistic science and is no sensationalist:

> Furthermore, since pains and various kinds of diseases arise in the internal parts, they [*those who profess medicine founded upon reason*] believe that no one can bring remedies to them if he does not know the parts themselves, and that therefore it is necessary to cut open the bodies of dead persons and inspect their viscera and intestines. They believe that Herophilos and Erasistratos did so in by far the best manner. They received from the kings wicked men brought
> · from prison, and cut them open when alive; while breath remained in them, they examined things which nature had previously enclosed, their location, colour, form, size, disposition, hardness, softness, relationship, also the projections and depressions of each one, and if one is inserted into the other or receives part of another

into itself.... Nor, they believe, is it cruel (as the majority of people suggest) to seek in the punishments of wicked men, and only a few at that, remedies for innocent persons of every future generation.

(Celsus, *De medicina*, *prooemium* (Preface), 23–4, 26)

Celsus disapproves of vivisection, but his dispassionate tone gives him credibility. More sensationally, around AD 200 the Christian author Tertullian, probably following Soranus, referred to Herophilos as 'that doctor or butcher who cut up innumerable human beings so that he could study nature', and specifically alleges vivisection (*De anima*, 10. 4).[63]

Although this evidence is tainted by anti-pagan bias, that of Celsus makes it likely that scientific dissection of humans was being practised, perhaps for the first time, and possibly vivisection.[64] One may wonder whether the different ideological groupings among doctors somehow reflect the varying availability of royal funding; it would not be surprising if those to whom anatomical material was not available asserted the primacy of external observation. Royal patronage may even have had the effect of polemicizing the medical profession.

There were important new discoveries, mostly attributed to Herophilos and Erasistratos. In the nervous system the sensory and motor nerves,[65] sinews, tendons, and ligaments were first clearly distinguished by these two men. Modern writers often parade the errors of Greek medicine, but given the theoretical standpoint available to the ancients their conclusions were often entirely reasonable, such as when Erasistratos, following earlier doctors, concluded that in the arteries (as opposed to the veins) there flowed not blood but air. Erasistratos also investigated the digestive system with great intelligence, while Herophilos created an elaborate system for reading the health of the patient from the pulse.[66] The desire to systematize knowledge into a schema that could then be applied to actual cases reveals that medicine was no more the prisoner of theory than any other science was.

Medicine and religion cross over at various points. Already in the fourth century the popularity of the healing god Asklepios had begun to increase, as witness the fourth-century Asklepieion at Athens. His cult was not a focus of civic ceremony, but is rather an example of one to which the individual would go in the hope of personal guidance from the deity (cf. pp. 164–5).[67] A person suffering from an illness or injury not responding to treatment would sleep in the sanctuary (a process known as incubation) hoping that a cure would be communicated to them in a dream. The medical efficacy of the cult is hard to assess from the surviving documents. Ptolemaic patronage of the Asklepieion on the island of Kos, where there was a medical school reputedly founded by Hippokrates, is well known and is attributed to Philadelphos's gratitude to the island of his birth, his mother having been sent there in 309/8 when pregnant with him (Parian Marble (*FGH* 239), B 19, Austin 21).[68] Royal patronage of medicine is not to be attributed to any desire to improve the health of the king's subjects, though he could bask in the reflected glory of new discoveries and association with healing gods.

Just as medicine, even more than other sciences, had a practical aspect, so it had a political and cultural context. This is not to deny the humanism of its practitioners, exemplified perhaps in the famous Hippocratic oath. Of uncertain date, it is generally assumed to belong to the late classical or early hellenistic period. It was probably not a universal declaration by doctors but specific to one group, for besides standard injunctions not to administer poison, not to use a pessary to cause an abortion, and even (apparently) to respect confidences it includes an undertaking never to operate invasively ('I will not cut, not even those suffering with the stone'), something many doctors certainly did. Its injunction to respect one's master and to pass on one's learning do, at least, conform to the general structure of fourth- and third-century medicine.[69]

One of the most famous ancient medical writings is the fourth-century treatise *On Airs, Waters, and Places* attributed to Hippokrates.[70] It advises the doctor to take account of local winds and climate and thus to anticipate the kinds of diseases he is likely to encounter in any given region, and classifies different nations according to their intelligence, political character, and military spirit. The equable climate of Asia is held to be the cause of the stagnant mental and physical attributes of its inhabitants (ch. 16), whereas the varied and changeable conditions of Europe have made its inhabitants warlike, courageous, and willing to take risks – though the author explicitly assigns a prominent role to cultural traditions as well (ch. 23).

A development of the same construct appears in Aristotle's *Politics*:

> For the nations (*ethnê*) in cold places and about Europe are full of spirit, but rather lacking in intelligence and skill, because they live free on the whole but are ungoverned and unable to rule their neighbours; and those around Asia are intelligent and skilled of soul, but spiritless, because they live under another's rule and as slaves; but the race (*genos*) of Hellenes, as it occupies a middle place in spatial terms, thus shares in both characters. For it is spirited and intelligent, because it lives free and is better governed and able to rule all people once it acquires a single constitution.
>
> (Arist. *Pol.* 9. 7. 1327 b 23–1328 a 33)

The idea reappears in the Stoic author Poseidonios (*c*.135–*c*.55 BC), who is the probable source of a passage in the *Tetrabiblos* (for which see pp. 354–5) written by the second-century AD astronomical writer Claudius Ptolemaeus, commonly known as Ptolemy. The civilized region has now expanded to include the Egyptians and Chaldaeans. One extract must serve for the whole passage:

The inhabitants of the region between the summer tropic and the Bears, however, since the sun is neither directly over their heads nor far distant at its noonday transits, share in the equable temperature of the air, which varies, to be sure, but has no violent changes from heat to cold. They are therefore medium in colouring, of moderate stature, in nature equable, live close together, and are civilized in their habits. The southernmost of them [*the Egyptians and Chaldaeans*] are in general more shrewd and inventive, and better versed in the knowledge of things divine because their zenith is close to the zodiac and to the planets revolving about it.

(Tetrabiblos, 2. 2. 55–8)

In the late first century BC the hellenistic idea was reworked by Vitruvius; in his scheme, however, it is the Italians that occupy the most favourable climatic zone and therefore have superior endowments:

For the races in Italy are very well moderated in both respects, both in the limbs of their bodies and in the strengths of their minds towards bravery.... Italy has praiseworthy characteristics which are moderated by combinations from either side, between the northern and southern (regions). Thus by its policies it restrains the courage of the barbarians, but by a strong hand the calculations of the southerners. Thus the divine mind has allocated the polity of the Roman people an outstanding and moderate region, so that it may obtain empire over the world.

(Vitruv. 6. 1. 11)

The theories of medical writers, though often contradictory, reveal social and cultural assumptions. Vitruvius was able to convert the idea for his own propagandistic purposes, and flatter a Roman readership by transferring Aristotle's eulogy of Greek characteristics to them, because hellenistic science could posit a causal connection between a landscape or climate and the nature of the organisms in it.

Mathematical speculation

Astronomy and astrology

Traditional Greek astronomy goes back to the use of the stars and planets to mark calendrical points, seen in Homer and Hesiod. In the early sixth century Thales of Miletos is said to have predicted an eclipse, though this may not have been possible before Meton of Athens, in the late fifth century, discovered the nineteen-year cycle that links the movements of the sun and moon. Fifth-century cosmologists and philosophers posited that the earth was spherical, and that eclipses were caused by the moon passing in front of the sun (though this idea may not have gained wide currency), but were vague about the number and names of the planets. Only in the fourth century did either Plato or Eudoxos of Knidos (who was a geometrician as well as an astronomer) theorize that the motions of the heavenly bodies were to be accounted for geometrically, develop the notion of concentric spheres, and distinguish the five naked-eye planets clearly. (On Eudoxos, see Diog. Laërt. 8. 86–91.) Only the most basic astronomical instruments were in use. Apart from Meton, Eudoxos may have been the first to make use of Babylonian concepts, which are seen in his descriptions of constellations.[71]

Thus hellenistic astronomy did not break new ground in drawing upon near eastern observation and theory, though there was now easier access to Babylonian data. Developments in astronomy are continuous with earlier inquiry into the cosmos and, like other scientific pursuits, spring directly out of fourth-century work, though the most rapid advances were made in the second century, somewhat later than in other areas of science. Two strands can be distinguished: the desire to catalogue the visible heavens, and the desire to explain the observed movements of the sun, moon, and planets. Often the two projects went hand in hand.

Hipparchos of Nikaia (c.190–after 126 BC), known as the inventor of trigonometry, may also have devised an improved *dioptra*, apparently adjustable for the inclination of the north pole (Archimedes, *Sand-reckoner*, 1. 11; Heron, *On the Dioptra*, 3; Ptolemy, *Almagest*, 5. 14; Proclus, *Outline of the Astronomical Hypotheses*, 4).[72] Other improvements to measuring instruments took place: Hipparchos may have used the armillary astrolabe, a set of concentric rings rotating round one another to simulate the relative movements of the sun, moon, and planets.[73] Similar instruments are described by Ptolemy (*Almagest*, 5. 1; 5. 12). With the aid of sighting and modelling instruments of this kind, Hipparchos produced the first comprehensive catalogue of stars, surpassing that of Eudoxos. Some of the data had a Babylonian origin, though Hipparchos also built upon observations by early third-century astronomers at Alexandria, such as Timocharis and Aristyllos (Ptolemy, *Almagest*, 7. 1).[74]

In the area of explanation, Hipparchos discovered the precession of the equinoxes, which we now describe as an effect of the slow gyration of the earth's axis every 25,000 years, which causes winter constellations to become summer ones and vice versa. Since, without modern instruments, this phenomenon can be observed only by comparing astronomical observations over many decades, it is a testimony to the detail and care of these astronomers that Hipparchos's calculation for the length of the cycle, 36,000 years, is of the right order of magnitude – though it would not matter if his error were far greater, for it is not the accuracy but the method that is the point. This is one more rebuttal of the idea that Greek thinkers were bound up with theory to the exclusion of actual experiment, observation, and measurement.

This desire to catalogue and name the heavens may be seen as part of a larger ideological project, which might be said to have begun (in a very different form) with the historian Herodotos in the fifth century and culminated in the maps and universal geographies of the Roman period. Both Greece and Rome were, so to speak, outward-bound cultures, and the discourse within which the élite (and others) operated was coloured by a desire to identify and symbolically appropriate the peoples and lands with which they came into contact.[75] Seen in this context, and against the background of Alexander's conquests, the project of enumerating and cataloguing the earthly and heavenly worlds gains particular coherence.

There are close links between the cataloguing aspect of astronomy – astronomical exploration, so to speak – and terrestrial measurement. Hipparchos was probably the first to design an elaborate system of latitude and longitude, though the basic concepts were already known to Eratosthenes (p. 361). Our main source for Hipparchos's work is Ptolemy's *Mathematike syntaxis*, 'mathematical systematic treatise' (known by its Arabic title *Almagest*, reflecting Greek *megistê*, 'greatest'), a huge manual of astronomy in thirteen books written in the second century AD. Perhaps the most ambitious project linking the two was the attempt to measure the size of the earth (pp. 360–1). Aristarchos of Samos (fl. 280 BC), followed by Poseidonios, calculated the distance of the sun from the earth. Others assigned names to new celestial objects. Konon of Samos (later of Alexandria) discovered the small constellation of Coma Berenices (or designated it as a constellation, for its constituent stars were visible with the naked eye), naming it in honour of the queen (p. 244).

One of the Greek astronomical theories most often cited today is the 'heliocentric hypothesis' of Aristarchos.[76] Today we see the earth as just one of the planets that revolve around the sun, and the apparent movement of stars and sun across the sky as illusory, the result of the earth's rotation. The orthodox view in antiquity was that the earth stood still at the centre of the universe while the sun, stars, and planets revolved around it. Aristarchos's alternative hypothesis, that the earth does indeed revolve around the sun, is described by Archimedes in an extant treatise:

> Aristarchos of Samos produced a book based on certain hypotheses, in which it follows from the premises that the universe is many times greater than the universe now so called. His hypotheses are, that the fixed stars and the sun remain motionless, that the earth revolves in the circumference of a circle about the sun, which lies in the middle of the orbit, and that the sphere of fixed stars, situated about the same centre as the sun, is so great that the circle in which he supposes the earth to revolve has such a proportion to the distance of the fixed stars as the centre of the sphere bears to its surface.
>
> (Archimedes, *Sand-reckoner*, 1, *GMW* i. 3–5)

Although we cannot know whether Aristarchos actually believed this to be the case, we have no good grounds for doubting that he meant his hypothesis seriously as a possible mathematical solution to how the heavenly bodies moved.[77] It did not find general favour: Plutarch says that after Aristarchos only one astronomer adopted it, a certain Seleukos of Seleukeia-on-Tigris, a Chaldaean or Babylonian of c.150 BC, 'the former only hypothesizing this, the latter also asserting it' (*Platonic Questions*, 1006 c).[78]

Historians sometimes express regret that this hypothesis, which we now know to be closer to the truth than the orthodoxy at the time, was rejected for centuries afterwards. Such reactions miss the point. Given the views of the material world generally held at the time, Aristarchos's theory was, if not untenable, at least impossible to prove. Plutarch records an objection on religious grounds: he says the Stoic philosopher Kleanthes 'thought that the Greeks ought to indict Aristarchos of Samos on a charge of impiety for putting in motion the Hearth of the Universe' (*On the Face on the Moon*, 923 a);[79] no less an authority than Aristotle (*De caelo*, 2. 13) had declared that earth did not move. Then there is the fact of what we call gravity: to every appearance the earth is the centre towards which all things move. Next, there is the argument that the air and moving objects should be visibly affected if the surface of the earth were moving rapidly. Finally, if the earth is circling round the sun every year, then the stars should seem to move from side to side as our viewpoint shifts – the phenomenon now known as stellar parallax. Aristarchos was aware of this, but explicitly assumed that the stars were infinitely far away from the earth so as not to have to build a defence against this argument. Given the low degree of precision available in directional measurement, however, it would have been impossible to demonstrate stellar parallax.[80] Préaux, indeed, attributes the rejection of Aristarchos's hypothesis chiefly to this lack of precise measurement; but we do not know that anyone thought of testing it in this way. Rather, the terms of the prevailing discourse were so overwhelmingly against Aristarchos that there were no compelling reasons why other astronomers should feel obliged to refute his theory through observed data; there were plenty of other grounds for dissent.

This case study is an example of Greek scientists 'getting it wrong' for perfectly good reasons, which means that we ought not to convict them of error. Since current theory seemed to explain the phenomena, there was no incentive to correct it. In no way does the case of Aristarchos imply a lack of rationality, or any desire to twist the facts and obscure the truth. It does reveal the way in which it was hard to escape from an existing world-view – which perhaps even Aristarchos did not intend to do.[81] We also have to consider who the consumers of astronomy were.

Similar considerations apply to the theory of epicycles and eccentric circles which was used to explain irregularities in the observed motions of the sun, moon, and planets. This model was adopted in preference to the earlier theory of Eudoxos that the heavenly bodies moved on fixed spheres with the earth at the centre. It involved attributing to the sun, moon, and planets a complex motion made up of a combination of circular movements and differing speeds of rotation. The theory is best known from Ptolemy but was probably first enunciated in detail by Apollonios of Perge (active at Alexandria in the second half of the third century), the other dominant figure in hellenistic astronomy. We now know that the irregularities are due to the shape of planetary orbits, which are not circular but elliptical; but in its time the theory was flexible and could give 'economical and often tolerably accurate accounts of some highly complex astronomical phenomena'.[82] For these excellent reasons it remained the dominant model of the heavens for many centuries, being enhanced by Hipparchos and later taken up by Ptolemy, then becoming the medieval orthodoxy until the time of Tycho Brahe.

A few words should be said about astrology, the science of interpreting the motions of the heavenly bodies and their influence on human affairs. There was no firm boundary between astrology and astronomy; the function of the latter was frequently to serve the former, and the practitioners were often the same people. Recent scholars concur in seeing astrology, in so far as it became a systematized body of thought, as an intrinsically post-classical phenomenon, and point to the virtual absence of astrological ideas in fourth-century Greece. Whether (as Préaux argues) it was also an intrinsically Greek creation, a logical extension of classical science, rather than (as earlier scholars saw it) an 'oriental' borrowing, is less clear. Probably it should be regarded as a combination of different materials. Systematic astrology as such was entirely in tune with other aspects of Greek science. On the other hand, a considerable stimulus was offered by newly available astronomical data from Babylon, which were not readily accessible to earlier Greeks,[83] and by the new data that continued to come out of Babylon. Horoscopes containing astronomical and other data for the day of a person's nativity were being cast in Babylonia from at least the early fourth century BC. An Egyptian contribution can even be seen, in the calendrical system used in Greek astrology. While no single culture created astrology, *Greek* astrology probably took form in Alexandria, where Babylonian data and astrological methodology were systematized by Greek scientists.[84]

A distinction between two kinds of procedure is made explicit by Ptolemy at the start of his astrological work *Apotelesmatika* (*Influences*) or *Tetrabiblos* (*The Four Books*):[85]

The more observant farmers and herdsmen, indeed, conjecture, from the winds prevailing at the time of impregnation and of the sowing of the seed, the quality of what will result; and in general we see that the more important consequences signified by stars are usually

known beforehand, even by those who inquire, not by scientific means
[*physikôs, 'by (the laws of) nature'*], but only by observation.

(Ptolemy, *Tetrabiblos*, 1. 2. 4)

Ptolemy's distinction between natural enquiry and mere observation should
not mislead us. He is not saying that hard data are of secondary importance
– as compared, for example, with abstract reasoning – but that there can be
scientific astrology and less scientific astrology. The better sort combines
philosophical expertise and wide empirical knowledge; the worse sort
embraces both casual observation by ordinary people and the erroneous
claims of charlatans. He inveighs against the purveyors of irrational astrology,
who 'for the sake of making money, claim respectability for another art' (he
means low-grade astrology, in effect) 'in the name of this one, and deceive
ordinary persons by seeming to predict many things, even those that have no
capacity' (*physis*, literally 'nature') 'of being foretold' – since everyone knows
that some things can be foretold (1. 2. 6). This distinction, like that
between predicting the movements of the heavenly bodies and predicting
their influence on events, was framed – could only, indeed, be framed – in
terms of their relative accuracy, not in terms of the lack of any rational basis
for astrology.

The passage immediately before this illustrates the distinction. Ptolemy
points out that everyone knows that the sun and moon influence life on
earth. In Greek thinking, the moon was widely held to influence the
weather and the behaviour of certain plants and animals, and Poseidonios
correctly linked it to the tides.[86] Ptolemy notes the connection (1. 2. 4),
observing that certain plants and animals are affected by the moon.[87] From
this it is no more than a small step to infer that the lesser heavenly bodies
have an influence, albeit a more subtle one, on human affairs. For Ptolemy,
then, there is a scientific astrology, even if there is also an irrational one.
Even today one hears rationalizations of astrology – for example, in terms of
the supposed effects of the minuscule gravitational forces exerted by the
planets upon the developing human embryo. Implausible as this may seem,
in the absence of refutation by rigorous scientific evaluation it would be a
rash person who refused to keep at least a partly open mind. All the more so
should we be willing to credit scientists of the hellenistic and early Roman
periods with being able to think rationally, albeit within the terms of a
discourse and cosmology different from ours.

Greek astrology came into its own in the Roman empire, when it was
much in demand from élites and ordinary folk alike; Ptolemy's work is
evidence of its importance in the second century AD. We can only guess how
widely it was practised in the hellenistic period; but it would be reasonable
to guess that it started with the Greek élite, particularly in Alexandria,
where most of the known astronomers were working.

Mathematics, pure and applied

Mathematics had made some advances before the late fourth century, when Eudemos, a pupil of Aristotle, compiled a history of arithmetic and geometry. The Pythagorean philosophers had discussed the properties of numbers in a semi-mystical way, but a rigorous tradition of geometry had begun to develop by the end of the fifth century. It is uncertain how much of this the Greeks inherited from second-millennium Mesopotamia or early iron age Egypt, and how much they invented independently; but it is likely that the notion of proof was theirs. Major steps forward in surmounting logical problems were made in the fourth century by Eudoxos, who probably put geometry on a firm footing in advance of Euclid. Thus, in mathematics as in other areas, the third and second centuries represented a continuation of what went before, not a radical departure.[88] The third-century achievement in mathematics has been characterized as the greatest of any science.[89] This may be true, but one should not only compare mathematics with other sciences, or with mathematics before and after; the role of mathematical speculation in society and culture also needs to be considered.

There is no denying the excellence of Greek writing in the field of pure mathematics. Its sophistication can be grasped immediately by a glance at almost any passage (such as in the Loeb selection, *Greek Mathematical Works*). The name of Euclid (Eukleides in Greek), who worked in Alexandria around 300 BC (his birthplace is uncertain), is still familiar to students of mathematics, principally because of his work on geometry. Although it is difficult to establish how original his contribution was, he may have broken new ground simply by systematizing existing knowledge more comprehensively than his predecessors. It seems likely that he also refined the basic notions of axiom (first principle) and hypothesis, and added new axioms, such as that all non-parallel lines will eventually meet. In accordance with the traditions of Greek philosophy, he starts from first principles, of which the following extract gives a flavour:

> *Definitions.* (1) A point is that which has no part [*i.e. is indivisible*]. (2) A line is length without breadth. (3) The extremities of a line are points. (4) A straight line is a line which lies evenly with the points on itself. (5) A surface is that which has length and breadth only. (6) The extremities of a surface are lines. [*Another seventeen follow.*]
>
> (Euclid, *Elements*, 1, *GMW* i. 437–9)

To an almost unique degree among ancient mathematical works, Euclid's ideas, with some modifications by later writers, formed the basis of a whole branch of the subject, geometry, until the twentieth century. His proofs are laid out exactly in the manner of modern textbooks, using letters of the alphabet to designate points, and are accompanied by diagrams in the surviving manuscripts. Here is the start of one of his propositions (the so-called 'method of exhaustion'; Fig. 9.6):

> Circles are to one another as the squares on the diameters.
>
> Let *ABCD, EFGH* be circles, and *BD, FH* their diameters. I say that, as the circle *ABCD* is to the circle *EFGH*, so is the square on *BD* to the square on *FH*.
>
> For if the circle *ABCD* is not to the circle *EFGH* as the square on *BD* to the square on *FH*, then the square on *BD* will be to the square on *FH* as the circle *ABCD* is to some area either less than the circle *EFGH* or greater. Let it first be in that ratio to a lesser area *S*. And let the square *EFGH* be inscribed in the circle *EFGH*; then the inscribed square is greater than the half of the circle *EFGH*, inasmuch as, if through the points *E, F, G, H* we draw tangents to the circle, the square *EFGH* is half the square circumscribed about the circle, and the circle is less than the circumscribed square; so that the inscribed square *EFGH* is greater than the half of the circle *EFGH*.
>
> Let the circumferences *EF, FG, GH, HE* be bisected at the points *K, L, M, N*, and let *EK, KF, FL, LG, GM, MH, HN, NE* be joined; therefore each of the triangles *EKF, FLG, GMH, HNE* is greater than the half of the segment of the circle about it ... [*The proof continues for another two pages.*]
>
> Therefore circles are to one another as the squares on the diameters; which was to be proved.
>
> (*Elements*, 12. 2, *GMW* i. 459–61)

Among many other legacies of hellenistic mathematics, we may mention Apollonios's detailed investigation of the conic sections (parabola, hyperbola, and ellipse; the names may go back to the fourth century, however).[90] Much of the groundwork for calculating areas and volumes was done by writers like Heron (in his *Metrika*), while Euclid used his geometrical knowledge to build on earlier works on optics and harmonics. Here the work of mathematicians came close to the solution of practical problems.

Archimedes, despite the wide-ranging ingenuity of which we have seen many and varied examples, was chiefly known as a mathematician. He calculated a more precise value of pi (π, the ratio of a circle's circumference to its diameter), and regarded his highest achievement as the calculation of the relative volume of a sphere to that of an exactly enclosing cylinder. Like others he ranged widely; his works include *On the Sphere, Quadrature of the Parabola, Spirals*, and so on. One of his odder and more playful exercises is *The Sand-reckoner*, in which he tries to find a way of expressing the largest number anyone might want to express. His answer, in modern notation, is

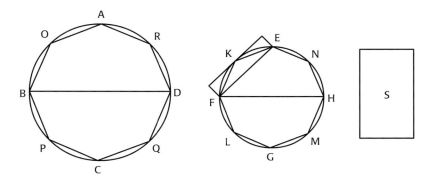

Figure 9.6 Euclid's proof by the method of exhaustion. (Based on Thomas, *Greek Mathematical Works*, i. 461.)

10 followed by 80,000 million million zeroes, or 10 to the power (8 × 3 10^{16}). Hampered not in the slightest by the lack of a modern numerical notation, he devises a system for expressing this number economically in words: 'a myriad myriad units of numbers of the myriad myriadth order[91] of the myriad myriadth period' (i.e. 10 to the power 10^8, all to the power 10^8). He also shows that the number of grains of sand that the universe could hold is less than 10^{63}.

This, of course, was an exercise in pure speculation, with little possibility of practical application. Archimedes considered pure numbers in his *Method of Mechanical Theorems*, where he formulates what we would call a model for integration.

For applied mathematics we stay with Archimedes, usually remembered today as the man who discovered how to measure the specific gravity of a solid body. For this story, we turn once more to Vitruvius. The tyrant Hieron of Syracuse wished to check whether a golden crown was made of the pure metal. When the idea of how to ascertain the density of the crown came to Archimedes as he got into the bath:

> he did not delay, but moved by joy he jumped out of the bath and, making his way home naked, he communicated in a loud voice that he had truly found what he sought; for as he ran he was shouting repeatedly in Greek, '*Heurêka, heurêka*' ['I've found it'].
>
> (Vitruv. *On Architecture*, book 9, preface, §10)

Archimedes' method was to compare the amount of a fluid displaced when the body whose specific gravity (density) is unknown is immersed in it with the amount displaced when a body of equal weight and known composition is immersed. Though the narrative is doubtless fictionalized and the science probably inaccurate,[92] the story is interesting not least for what it reveals about the link between scientist and patron, and in having a practical consequence. In his mathematical writings Archimedes, more than other mathematicians of the age, tended to consider problems of solid bodies in an abstract way, in contrast to the earlier, pseudo-Aristotelian *Mechanika* with its practical orientation.[93]

At the same time, others were applying mathematics specifically to practical, mechanical problems. Heron discusses the different forces needed to move a given weight using pulleys, levers, and toothed or cogged wheels (*Dioptra*, 37; *GMW* ii. 489–97). The screw was widely investigated and widely applied for the first time (as in the Archimedean screw; see p. 332). In an ancient shipwreck (now dated not later than the 60s BC) off the southeastern Peloponnese was found the so-called Antikythera Mechanism. It is an astronomical device, made up of more than thirty toothed wheels, which enabled calculations to be made, including the positions of the sun and moon (Fig. 9.7).[94] This rare surviving example of an ancient machine demonstrates the capacity of hellenistic mathematicians to devise useful applications for their work, when the need was felt.

Exploration, empires, and economies

The history of Greek 'science' may be understood, from one angle, as associated with an increasing sophistication of society and culture. From the archaic period on, we see a differentiation of poetry from prose, the emergence of distinct genres of writing within each, and the rise of rhetoric as an art with rules. The sophistication of the spoken and written word allows for new techniques of persuasion and description; the human and geographical worlds are described and symbolically manipulated.

Hellenistic culture included two kinds of geography, which we may call 'theoretical' and 'descriptive'. The former has many points of contact, as already noted, with astronomy and mathematics; indeed, the same men were often the practitioners of all three. The latter often represents the descriptions of their travels by official (royally sponsored) and private voyagers, who appear not to have moved in the same 'scientific' milieu. Little of their work survives; we rely almost entirely on later compilers such as Strabo, Diodoros, and Ptolemy. With all those authors, particularly Strabo, we must make allowance for the fact that they are looking back from a period when Roman culture was prone to appropriate all others and interpret them in the light of Rome's imputed destiny as world-ruler.[95]

Much of the work of scientists in this period can be related to the desire for a conceptual framework to match the (actual or desired) mastery over the newly settled territories. Alexander wanted to know how far he had travelled and how big his empire was, and was accompanied by bematists (pacers),

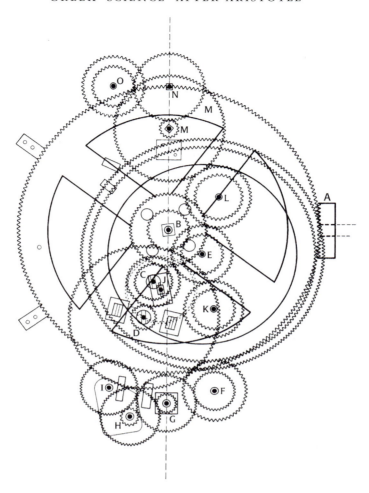

Figure 9.7   The Antikythera Mechanism. (Closely based on B. Pope's drawing in Price, *Gears*, 37 fig. 29; reproduced by permission of the American Philosophical Society.)

surveyors who measured land distances. The scholars who travelled with him (such as Kallisthenes, Nearchos, Onesikritos, and Aristoboulos) left accounts of the regions through which they travelled. Around 300 BC the philosopher Dikaiarchos, reportedly with royal assistance (Pliny, *HN* 2. 162), made a map of the world and calculated the heights of mountains.

Dikaiarchos may have estimated the earth's circumference. In this he was followed by Eratosthenes, librarian at Alexandria under Ptolemy III and tutor to the young Ptolemy IV,[96] who neatly exemplifies the link between royal power, science, and imperial ideology. He measured the difference in angle between the shadows cast at noon on the summer solstice by the pointers in the bowls of sundials at Alexandria and at Syene (Aswan), which was reckoned to be 5,000 stades (c.920 km) further south. Here is the culmination of the long proof which a later author painstakingly set out:

> Whatever ratio, therefore, the arc in the bowl of the sundial has to its proper circle, the arc reaching from Syene to Alexandria has the same ratio. But the arc in the bowl is found to be the fiftieth part of its proper circle. Therefore the distance from Syene to Alexandria must necessarily be a fiftieth part of the great circle of the earth. And this distance is 5,000 stades. Therefore the whole great circle is 250,000 stades. Such is the method of Eratosthenes.
> (Kleomedes, *On the Circular Motion of the Heavenly Bodies*, 1. 10. 52)[97]

The fact that a figure of 250,000 stades (c.46,000 km) for the earth's circumference (Strabo, 2. 5. 34 (132) gives 252,000 stadia) is close to the correct figure of c.40,000 kilometres is of secondary importance; the point is that the attempt was made logically according to the discourse of his day.

Eratosthenes expounded a theory of the world's layout, asserting that Asia, Europe, and Africa, together formed one 'island'. This and the preceding discovery were probably published in two separate works, *On the Measurement of the Earth* and *On Geography*; they are summarized at length by Strabo in books 1–2 of his *Geographika* (see also Pliny, *HN* 13. 13. 53). Eratosthenes may have been the first scholar to work fully with the concepts of latitude and longitude, later elaborated by Hipparchos (pp. 351, 352). Dikaiarchos used a central parallel of latitude (Straits of Messina–Cape Malea–Rhodes) and a meridian (north–south line) through Lysimacheia on the Hellespont; Eratosthenes had about thirteen parallel meridians on his map. Strabo (2. 1. 35–6 (87–8)) quotes Hipparchos as refining Eratosthenes' map and proposing the addition of regularly spaced north–south divisions.

Geographers enjoyed royal sponsorship for the purposes of exploration and military campaigns, a tradition inherited from the Persians and earlier rulers.[98] We know the names of expedition commanders who left records of their explorations, such as the Seleukid officer Patrokles (p. 284), who explored the Caspian (Strabo, 2. 1. 17 (74); 11. 7. 3 (509)) and wrote about north-western India and other eastern areas of the empire. The Ptolemies sent many expeditions to the south, partly in the search for war-elephants. The tradition of exploration on behalf of the rulers of Egypt went back to the pharaohs; in the fifth century Herodotos (4. 42) describes an expedition sent by Necho which circumnavigated Africa.[99]

Literary accounts of upper Egypt and the Red Sea are due to Greeks such as Eudoxos of Kyzikos. An upper-class citizen (for, as Strabo tells us, he served his *polis* as a sacred envoy, *theôros*) of the late second century, he attempted to circumnavigate Africa with Ptolemaic patronage (Strabo, 2. 3. 4–5 (98–102), follows Poseidonios but is sceptical). Eudoxos allegedly financed his westward journey towards Gibraltar by 'everywhere noisily proclaiming his scheme' (presumably in order to get financial donations) 'and making money by trafficking'. Another explorer, Hippalos, is recorded in the anonymous first-century AD *Circumnavigation of the Erythraian Sea* (the Red Sea) as having discovered the sea route to India; the work is often known by its Latin title of *Periplus maris Erythraei*, and places particular emphasis on the commercial resources of the places described.[100]

These stories are sometimes told to illustrate the discovery of the monsoon 'trade winds', but more importantly they reveal the nexus of links between Greek élites, royal interest in trade revenues, and the literary conceptualization of distant parts. This nexus is also seen in Agatharchides of Knidos (*FGH* 86), who lived from *c*.215 to after 145 and wrote an earlier *Periplous of the Erythraian Sea* under Ptolemy VIII.[101] His work, too, relates to trade with India. Diodoros quotes Agatharchides for the cause of the Nile flood:

> The nearest approach to the truth has been made by Agatharchides of Knidos. His explanation is as follows. Every year continuous rains fall in the mountains of Ethiopia from the summer solstice to the autumnal equinox; and so it is entirely reasonable that the Nile should diminish in the winter when it derives its natural supply of water solely from its sources, but should increase its volume in the summer on account of the rains which pour into it....
>
> As to his own statement, he adds, testimony to its truth is furnished by what takes place in certain regions of Asia. For on the borders of Skythia which abut upon the Caucasus mountains, annually, after the winter is over, exceptionally heavy snowstorms occur over many consecutive days; in the northern parts of India at certain seasons hailstones come beating down which in size and quantity surpass belief; about the Hydaspes river continuous rains fall at the opening of summer; and in Ethiopia, likewise, the same thing occurs some days later, this climatical condition, in its regular recurrence, always causing storms in the neighbouring regions. And so, he argues, it is nothing surprising if in Ethiopia as well, which lies above Egypt, continuous rains in the mountains, beating down during the summer, swell the river, especially since the plain fact itself is witnessed to by the barbarians who inhabit those regions.
>
> (Diod. 1. 41. 4–8)

Thus Agatharchides supports his theory by appealing to comparative evidence for the behaviour of rivers in Skythia, northern India, and Ethiopia, which appears to derive from sources known to him or even from autopsy.

Élite Greeks could apparently explore on their own initiative too, though we should not suppose that their motives were purely scientific. In about

320 Pytheas, a sea captain from Massalia (now Marseilles), claimed to have sailed to Britain and 'Thoule, which Pytheas says is six days' sailing from Brettanike towards the north, and is close to the frozen sea' (Strabo, 1. 4. 2 (63)) – Thoule (Thule) is Shetland, Iceland, or perhaps the Faeroe islands[102] – and wrote a geographical work touching on longitudes and latitudes. His work, though now accepted as well founded, was the subject of controversy, Polybios and Strabo both pouring scorn on the veracity of his account. Polybios's criticisms are preserved in Strabo's paraphrase (2. 4. 1–5 (104–7) = Polyb. 34. 5–7). Pytheas claimed to have reached an arctic region where

> there was no longer any proper land nor sea nor air, but a sort of mixture of all three of the consistency of a jelly-fish, in which the land and sea float; this medium, in which one can neither walk or sail, holding everything together, so to speak.
>
> (Strabo, 2. 4. 1 (104) = Polyb. 34. 5. 3)

Polybios found it incredible that 'a private individual and a poor man' 'should have traversed such vast distances on shipboard and on foot' (Strabo, 2. 4. 2 (104) = Polyb. 34. 5. 7); but presumably Pytheas, a literate ship captain, was not poor, just not aristocratic like Polybios. Strabo rebuts Polybios's criticisms of Pytheas's calculations of distance. Polybios may have been moved to dismiss Pytheas's claims because they might have outshone his own achievements in sailing beyond the straits of Gibraltar, perhaps as far as southern Morocco, under the aegis of Scipio Aemilianus (if this is the sense of Pliny, *HN* 5. 9).

Roman generals, like Greek kings, had their own reasons for wanting to gather knowledge of distant parts and of their potential for trade and plunder. At the same time, the polemics between Greek writers on geographical subjects, which are at least as violent as in any area of intellectual work, indicate the extent to which expert knowledge was bound up with élite status and international reputation.

Conclusion

Experiment versus speculation

This chapter has already alluded to the view that Greek thinkers were too fond of theorizing and insufficiently dedicated to the experimental process which would have been necessary to test their theories. It is quite true that labour was too cheap for there to be any widespread programme of exploiting technology and restructuring production.[103] To imagine, however, that things could have been otherwise, or to regret that they were not, is anachronistic: it would have been hard to find an educated Greek who thought slavery or the exploitation of non-Greek *laoi* unjust. The claim is also refuted by the evidence of experimentation and technological innovation,[104] which allowed an increasing degree of control to be applied to the environment and the materials that made it up. The late classical period had its share of these; Theophrastos, for example, describes recent discoveries such as the means of producing red ochre and the extraction of cinnabar (*On Stones*, 53, 58–9). Besides Philon's systematic trials of catapults (p. 336), we have the famous statement of Erasistratos, reported by Galen, about persistence in investigation:

> The man who is used to inquiry tries every possible loophole as he conducts his search, and turns in every direction; and, so far from giving up the inquiry in the space of a day, does not cease his search throughout his life. Directing his attention to one idea after another that is germane to what is being investigated, he presses on until he arrives at his goal.
>
> (Galen, *On Habits*, 1)

There is no doubt that the fourth-century ferment of experimentation was continuing, and accelerating.

It would be unreasonable to complain of a failure to disprove incorrect theories when, compared with today, very few kinds of measuring instruments were available or conceivable. Precise data were not neglected: there are many examples of new calculations and improved instruments.[105] Hipparchos was aware of the need for more precise directional instruments, but used perfectly valid procedures to measure the duration of the lunar month to within a second (Ptolemy, *Syntaxis*, 4. 2. 270–1) and to calculate the distances of the sun and moon. According to Pappos he also saw the need for further measurements with which to determine with increased accuracy the moon's distance from the earth.[106] We have already noted improved devices for measuring time, for sighting and levelling, and for measuring the heavens.

While scientists could be aware of the need for precise measurement, they were understandably less willing to throw over long-held beliefs. Science is a social activity; then as now, one had to justify one's views to others.[107] Explanations of natural phenomena by argument from analogy, or in terms of sympathetic effect (*sympatheia*), were quite acceptable. For astronomers it was desirable to explain movements of planets in terms of circular motion, since earlier philosophers such as Plato had demanded it; hence the adoption of the epicyclic theory. Astronomers were accordingly more inclined to refine old models than to seek new ones – just as most scientists, in most periods, have been.

The prevailing discourse did often stifle alternative views, as happens to a greater or lesser degree in any culture; Aristarchos's heliocentric hypothesis was rejected. Thomas Kuhn, in his *Structure of Scientific Revolutions*, has explored the way in which 'paradigm shifts' – wholesale substitutions of fundamental, new terms of reference, such as relativity or quantum theory – have been necessary for major advances in scientific understanding.[108] Some changes in the science of the hellenistic period could reasonably be described as paradigm shifts, like the substitution of epicycles for the heavenly spheres or the ways in which magic came to be criticized by scientists even while it continued to be practised in society at large. Perhaps these two examples are untypical, but there were many other refinements and systematizations of theory and observation. It is possible to be logical while using the terms of a discourse whose rationality is different from ours.

An 'age of achievement'?

The early part of the hellenistic period, roughly the third century, does give us the names, and sometimes the personalities and writings, of a larger number of really significant individuals applying their creative minds to the natural world with greater success than in any other period of Greek or Roman antiquity, as is clear from the debt owed to them by later ages. It is even a tenable view that some areas of science stagnated after 200;[109] perhaps, however, not because standards declined but because fewer men were engaged in 'research'. What does this suggest about Greek society?

The scientific thought of the hellenistic age can be best understood if it is contextualized within social and political change, and against the background of long-term continuities in élite culture. The man we call the scientist was of the élite and wrote for members of the élite, including kings. We should resist any temptation to see him as a disinterested soul, single-mindedly devoted to his calling; still less a monk-like figure, shielded from normal life within his ivory tower, or a poor writer struggling to break the shackles of the irrationality and prejudice of those around him ('One day they'll understand me!'). Whether or not it is true, as in the famous anecdote, that Archimedes died at the hands of an ignorant Roman legionary while distractedly drawing a geometrical diagram in the sand, the evidence suggests he had actually spent the preceding months helping his fellow townsmen defend their *polis*.

Science, then as now, could serve imperialist and ideological interests, not all of them benign. Some work by hellenistic thinkers was done in the spirit of the ideal citizen, to be conspicuous in benefiting other members of the privileged community (like Ischomachos, who stands for Xenophon in the *Oikonomikos*); some was done to please a king. These aims are not incompatible. If members of the élite chose to devote their leisure to investigating the cosmos, they did so as representatives of a fundamentally colonialist civilization which saw the non-Greek world as being there to be catalogued, named, and if possible tamed. They also belonged to a particular social and religious culture in which, to be worthy of one's social position, one had to fulfil certain expectations. To tell one's fellow-citizens about the nature of the universe was partly a sacred activity, and most Greeks remained within the religious culture they had inherited. The cultural self-regard of the élite depended on continually having new things to say about the world.

Lloyd has argued[110] that the rise of science in the archaic and early classical periods was due to the combative, argumentative nature of *polis* society. Conversely, one might infer that the apparent slow-down in intellectual creativity after the third century happened because the location of political contestation had shifted away from the *polis*. One could argue that this shift began on the day when Alexander razed Thebes to the ground. How far had the process gone? It is true that Alexander left Pindar's house standing (he was a highly educated man), and that his successors used their wealth to patronize the arts and sciences, taking the initiative away from *polis* assemblies. One could speculate that after a few generations, perhaps by the Chremonidean war, the élite had lost its view of itself as a primarily political body and the accompanying culture of political dialectic had become watered down. Once the social setting for this critical spirit was gone, dialectic and debate could no longer serve the same cultural purposes, and the original reasons for men's interest in natural philosophy may have evolved into something else. The scientist in Alexandria, indeed, was no longer a free member of a political class, but was vulnerable to the whim of the king: Ptolemy VIII even expelled the members of the Mouseion at a time when he was in conflict with the Alexandrians (Menekles of Barka, *FGH* 270 fr. 9 = Ath. 4. 184 b–c, Burstein 105).[111]

On the other hand, despite the global-political changes and the foundation of the monarchies, Greek culture remained city-based; citizen status within a *polis* remained the primary component of Greek identity, and the culture created by the *polis* system persisted among élites even into the Roman period.[112] What was perhaps exceptional in the third century was the role of Alexandria[113] and later of Pergamon, both of which offered facilities and hospitality to élite thinkers. This was not done from any noble motives by kings wishing to encourage pure speculation – the Ptolemies did not, one supposes, offer scholarships to gifted but poor Greek boys – nor was it from any desire to find and bring together men of talent who might otherwise lie undetected. Élite Greek thinkers were surely drawn by royal patronage, and perhaps by the sense of a new world to colonize. It may rather be the military and political problems of the monarchies in the second century that account for the decline in intellectual output – not that it dried up, for it did not.

While there were many practical applications, and considerable interaction between theory and practice, the more general lack of development may have been due to the comparative isolation of writers on mechanics, who could have developed practical applications of theories and inventions, and to a lack of systematic support attributable to the dominant values of society.[114] Préaux identifies an absence of *enracinement*, 'rootedness', pointing out that in hellenistic culture 'The ideal human type is not the "researcher", but *the orator* who is effective in the king's councils' (original emphasis).[115] I would go further and suggest that there were no 'researchers' in the modern sense, nor any firm dividing line between the 'orator' – be he politician, administrator, or 'man of action' – and the so-called scholar, who was no less paradigmatic a member of the Greek élite. 'Science' was something in which educated (that is, prosperous and leisured) Greeks often took an interest. They were interested, but did not regard science as a thing that could impact upon the forces of production and upon living conditions for society as a whole, except indirectly through public amenities such as water-clocks or machines that would promote success in war. That was the normal attitude of the time, and it would be unreasonable for us to criticize their outlook as irrational or a distortion. Aristarchos's work was in demand as much as Theokritos's because both men's creations, and the social situation of their production, embodied a satisfying and justifying world-view. This is not to deny the real achievements of hellenistic scientists, the fact that some investigators were laying claim to 'a new kind of wisdom', or the high standards of evidence or proof that were sometimes required.[116]

10

ROME AND GREECE

The Roman takeover of Greece is not a separate part of history from the hellenistic period, nor even the end of hellenistic culture – though the continuing story of Greek culture within a mature Roman empire (and later the eastern Roman or Byzantine empire, to AD 1453 and beyond) cannot form part of the present account.

The conquests of Syria and Egypt and the takeover of Pergamon have been examined in Chapters 6 and 8. This chapter will show how, between 229 and 30 BC, almost all the remaining parts of Alexander's empire apart from the eastern Seleukid territories became parts of the Roman empire. The process reveals how Roman imperialism evolved. It also illustrates the weakening of Greek political culture, based on the city-state and allowing for a greater or lesser degree of democratic participation, which for up to 250 years after 323 BC allowed the propertied classes – for better or worse – to compete, as they had previously, for control of their cities, to negotiate key issues of *autonomia* and external allegiance, to represent their cities' interests as they saw them, and to vie for honours. When the worst of times, particularly the early and middle first century BC, came to an end for the Greek cities of Greece and Asia, and they began to flourish once more economically and culturally, they did so as administrative units in a very different system. City élites, though adequately rewarded for docility, no longer had a role in determining key issues regarding the fate of their communities. It was the Roman conquest, not the Macedonian, that fundamentally altered the nature of the *polis*.

The fairly detailed narrative in this chapter reflects the relatively plentiful source evidence; indeed, the relevant pages of Livy down to 167 (books 26–45) are one of the fullest narratives for any period of Greek history, and in terms of interest and illumination they well repay the effort of reading them. These passages of Livy and the partly fragmentary history of Polybios contain many implicit and explicit insights into the nature and practice of Roman imperialism in Greece down to 146. Limits of space preclude a discussion of the nature and causes of Roman imperialism in the late republic.[1] While eschewing a detailed discussion of alternative views, the pages that follow will attempt to draw out the political and moral implications of key moments in the actions of the Romans.[2]

For the period after 146, particularly the Mithradatic wars, we are again well provided with sources, though not always complete and never contemporary in the manner of Polybios. He, in an oft-quoted passage near the start of his work, sums up the purpose of his history as being to explain

> how, and under what kind of constitution, almost all inhabited parts of the world, in not as many as fifty-three years, fell under the single rule of the Romans, something that is not found to have happened previously.
>
> (Polyb. 1. 1. 5)

He has in mind the years 220 to 167, from the start of the second Punic war (against Hannibal) to the end of the Macedonian monarchy. He writes from the viewpoint of a Greek who knew Roman aristocrats at first hand and came to believe that their rule could be made into something of benefit to conquered peoples. His own explanation of Roman success was framed in terms of the superiority of the Roman constitution, with its theoretically tripartite blend of monarchy (the two consuls), oligarchy (the senate), and democracy (the popular assemblies). This does not satisfy modern commentators, who prefer to look at the structure of Greek and Roman society and the strengths and weaknesses of their political systems.

It has been suggested that Roman expansionism was fundamentally the result of the nature of Roman politics. Roman élite society was totally geared to military achievement; political success depended on commanding armies that were successful in the field and thereby earning popularity with people and senate. The system depended, however, on individual commanders not achieving too much to the detriment of other aristocrats' careers. The senate learned how to take a long view while turning situations to its advantage, and Roman policy and behaviour evolved – some contemporaries said for the worse – as the Romans grew used to the exercise of power in new places. Intensifying competition between aristocrats, it is argued, combined with an ever-increasing reservoir of manpower, meant that the temptation to exercise power by sending an army to the next place, and then the next, was almost irresistible.[3] There is much truth in all this, but any explanation in terms of social structure needs to be backed up by a sympathetic viewing of Roman perceptions. The invasions of Italy by Pyrrhos in 280–275 and by Hannibal in 218 may have conditioned the Romans to take the initiative in aggression rather than let potential invaders act first.

Rome in the third century

The city-state of Rome lay on the west (more properly south-west) coast of Italy – the side away from Greece. It was an expansionist power long before it came into conflict with the Greeks. In the fifth century BC the Romans dominated the Latins and Etruscans of west-central Italy. After expanding their territory at the expense of Samnium and Campania (where there were Greek colonies) in the fourth century, and subduing a great revolt of the Latins in 341, the Romans came to control the whole of northern and central peninsular Italy by 300 through a combination of conquest, military alliances, road-building, and the foundation of colonies. The broadly oligarchic state of Rome maintained its hold on the regions by giving support to local élites, giving them an interest in preserving the *status quo*.[4]

Greeks had settled in Italy and Sicily since the eighth century BC, and religious and cultural contacts between Rome and Greece are attested as far back as the early fourth century, when the Romans made a dedication in the treasury of the people of Massalia (modern Marseilles) at the sanctuary of Apollo in Delphi.[5] It is hard to overstate the prestige which must have attached to Greek culture in the eyes of the Latin-speaking aristocrats of central Italy. Centuries of proximity to the Greek towns of Campania such as Cumae and Pompeii, generations of trading contacts with Syracuse and other Hellenic cities around the shores of the western Mediterranean, travellers' tales of the architectural splendours of the early *poleis* of the eastern Aegean, of classical Athens, and latterly of the metropoleis of the Macedonian kings will all have served to elevate this most recent eastern Mediterranean culture to a position comparable, perhaps, to that with which the early Greeks endowed Egypt and Persia. (Another appropriate analogy might be the admiration felt by imperial Russian aristocrats of the nineteenth century for the commerce and culture of France and the German states.)

From the late third century or earlier, many Roman aristocrats were imbued with what was already seen as a classical culture. Roman aristocrats adopted Greek surnames as early as the later fourth century.[6] In the third century Livius Andronicus (probably a Greek freedman from Tarentum) composed, presumably for an élite readership, the first Latin poems in Greek forms and translated the *Odyssey* into Latin verse. Romans were allowed to take part in the Olympic games of 228, and were not the only non-Greek people with whom a 'common origin' was postulated in that century (Plutarch, *Flamininus*, 11. 4). The Romans consulted the Delphic oracle after their defeat by Hannibal at Cannae in 216. The senator Quintus Fabius Pictor, who was part of that mission, later wrote the first history of Rome, and wrote it in Greek, partly to show how Greek a city Rome was and partly to convince the Greek world of the merits of Roman policy.[7] Cato the Elder (234–149) opposed the over-ready adoption of Greek culture (though not Greek culture as a whole) as well as excessive involvement in eastern wars;

yet, although his *Origines*, a history of Rome from its foundation (begun in 168 and never completed), was the first such work in Latin, it was clearly inspired by Greek historiography.[8] By now, philhellenism had become a valuable instrument of Roman policy. The Romans' stance as guarantor of Greek freedom, proclaimed in the 190s (below), helped recruit support against Philip V, but was emphasized less strongly in later wars as their domination spread further east.[9] The Roman state that came into conflict with successive hellenistic kingdoms and leagues, therefore, was far from being a representative of a wholly alien culture. Whether the Greeks knew as much about Rome is a question often discussed.[10]

Macedonia and the southern Greek states were not within easy reach of Roman territory; the kingdoms of north-western Greece were, and it was a king of Epeiros, Pyrrhos, who in 280–275 invaded Italy and Sicily at the invitation of the people of Tarentum, already in conflict with Rome (the main source is Plutarch's *Pyrrhos*).[11] He defeated the Romans more than once, threatening their domination of Italy. The Romans' final victory in 275, a shock to observers in the Greek east, was followed in 272 by the capture of Tarentum; their control of peninsular Italy was virtually complete. By 241 they had defeated Carthage for the first time and taken control of Sicily with its Greek cities, which became the first *provincia* or conquered territory. Sardinia followed in 238. Then a local affair in north-west Greece led to Rome's involvement with Macedonia, in a roundabout fashion.

Rome's wars against Macedonia and Syria

The Illyrian wars and first Macedonian war (229–205 BC)

It was in north-western Greece that events occurred which attracted the attention of the Romans: the extinction, through a combination of accident and federalist traditions, of the royal house of Epeiros in 232, the recruitment of Illyrians by Antigonos Doson of Macedonia to harass the Aitolian league, and the incursion into the western Peloponnese by one party of these raiders. All this created a context for the naval defeat of the Illyrians and Akarnanians by the Aitolians and Achaeans at Paxos in 229.[12] Not least because Illyrian ships were attacking Italian trading vessels in the Adriatic, these events cannot have escaped the notice of the Romans, leading them to involvement first in Illyria, then indirectly in Macedonia.

In 229 the senate resolved on military action against the Illyrian queen Teuta – the 'first Illyrian war'[13] – perhaps partly under the stimulus of the Italians' appeals for help, but probably also because she had ordered the murder of a Roman envoy appealing on behalf of a Greek town which she was besieging. The accounts of Appian (*Illyrian Wars*, 2. 7–8) and Polybios (2. 2–12) may appear to contradict, but in fact complement each other here.[14] The Romans may have been prompted not only by fears of a possible invasion in the long term, but also by the desire not to be seen to let down their Italian allies, whose trading ships would be in danger from unchecked Illyrian 'piracy', actually a part of normal economic life for Illyrians as for other north-western Greeks. As the experiences of other imperial powers confirm, involvement in one area can lead to commitments further afield.

In a brief campaign (229/8), several Greek towns were liberated, setting the tone for future actions. The Romans tried to establish competing power centres in north-western Greece, which were intended to keep an eye on one another; but their client ruler, Demetrios of Pharos, feathered his own nest by establishing close links with both Illyria and Macedonia, and Illyrian troops helped Antigonos Doson defeat Sparta in 222 (pp. 145–6).

In 220 Demetrios and another Illyrian leader, Skerdilaidas, raided the Peloponnese as a way of harassing the Aitolians, who were at war with Philip and his allies, including the Achaeans, in the 'social' war (220–217, from the Latin *socii*, 'allies'). This provoked the Romans into sending another army into the Balkans, in the second Illyrian war (219). Demetrios fled to Macedonia (Polyb. 3. 19), where he may well have become influential over the new king, Philip V. During the negotiation of the peace of Naupaktos in 217, at the end of the social war, Agelaos of Naupaktos warned of the danger from Rome, inviting Philip to become the protector of the Greeks:

> This occasion and this conference were the first to involve the affairs of Greece, Italy, and even Africa. For no longer did Philip or the Greek leaders make war or peace with each other solely by reference to Greek affairs; they now all had their eyes on objectives in Italy. And the same soon happened to the islanders and the peoples of Asia: those who were displeased with Philip and some of those who had grievances against Attalos no longer inclined to Antiochos or Ptolemy or looked to the south or the east, but from this time cast their eyes to the west, some sending embassies to Carthage and others to Rome. Rome did the same with the Greeks, alarmed at Philip's audacity and fearing that he might join the attack on them in their present situation.
>
> (Polyb. 5. 103–6, Austin 59)

In the light of this it is no surprise that in 215 we find Philip making a treaty with Hannibal of Carthage, who had invaded Italy and defeated the Romans in the field. The treaty (Polyb. 7. 9, Austin 61), which may not even have been ratified at Carthage,[15] does not imply that Philip had designs on Rome – it may have been purely for his own safety – but in such a situation, and remembering Pyrrhos's invasion sixty years earlier, the Romans could hardly ignore the potential danger.

Thus began the first Macedonian war (214–205). The action took place outside Macedonia, in areas where the Aitolians hoped to extend their power. During the war, in 212 or 211, the Romans made a treaty with the Aitolians,[16] who had recently been at war with Philip and his allies including the Achaeans in the 'social' war of 220–217. The text of the treaty is summarized by Livy (26. 24. 7–15, Austin 62 *a*) and partially preserved in an inscription from Thyrreion in Akarnania, important evidence for the development of Roman imperialism:

> And if the Romans capture by force any cities of these peoples, let it be permitted to the Aitolian people to have these cities and their territories as far as the Roman people is concerned. And [whatever] is captured by the Romans apart from the city and its territory, let the Romans have it.
>
> > (Austin 62 *b*, BD 32)[17]

The specification of how any rewards of joint military action are to be divided is revealing; the Aitolians, like the Illyrians, were habitual raiders (cf. p. 82), but in the present case it is not booty but the cities that they are to get. The Romans are allowed to seize not only material but also living plunder. The typical conduct of the Roman army after a siege in this period is described by Polybios, in his account of the sack of Nova Carthago (New Carthage) in Spain in 209:

> Scipio, when he judged that a large enough number of troops had entered the town, let loose the majority of them against the inhabitants, according to the Roman custom; their orders were to exterminate every form of life they encountered, sparing none, but not to start pillaging until the word was given to do so. This practice is adopted to inspire terror, and so when cities are taken by the Romans you may often see not only the corpses of human beings but dogs cut in half and the dismembered limbs of other animals.
>
> > (Polyb. 10. 15)

New Carthage, of course, was a town which the Romans wished to make an example of; in the Macedonian wars, they sometimes did not kill the population of a captured town but enslaved them, as at Achaean Dymê in about 208:

> The Dymaians had recently been captured and plundered by the Roman army, and when Philip had given orders that they were to be re-purchased from wherever they were in servitude, he had restored to them not merely their freedom but their homeland.
>
> > (Livy, 32. 22. 10)[18]

The treaty with the Aitolians illuminates the way in which the Roman army stood to profit by war while avoiding long-term commitments and seeming generous to their allies. In other respects, too, the treaty was a continuation of the Romans' earlier policy of not directly seeking conquests across the Adriatic; but it did commit the Aitolians to attacking Philip by land, and the Romans to supporting them with warships.

In the first Macedonian war various Greek towns were freed from Philip, including Aigina which was sold to Pergamon *c*.210 and became an Attalid naval base (Polyb. 22. 8. 10; see also Austin 209, *OGIS* 329, a decree of the Aiginetans in honour of their Attalid governor in the mid-second century). The list of those with an interest in Roman success was evidently not confined to Greece. After a time the Romans left the main fighting to the Aitolians, being concerned with their own war against Carthage; but in 206 the Aitolians, tired of waiting for Roman help, made peace with Philip after he attacked their common sanctuary at Thermon.[19] In 205 the Macedonian war was ended by a somewhat indecisive peace treaty concluded at Phoinike in Epeiros, of which we only have Livy's summary (29. 12. 11–16, Austin 64). Philip was allowed to retain most of the territories he had conquered in north-western Greece, apart from certain peoples who had earlier been allies of Rome, and two towns which were to become Roman possessions. The loss of Polybios's account makes it hard to interpret with certainty an appendix to the treaty (Livy, 29. 12. 14, Austin 64) which appears to make a wide range of other states and peoples parties to it in some sense; but they include Pergamon and Sparta, which may have wished to demonstrate their alignment with the Romans, perhaps to secure protection from Philip. The names of Ilion and Athens, if no others, may be interpolations by a first-century BC author.[20] Be that as it may, the peace of Phoinike crystallized Rome's widening influence over the Greek world.

The second Macedonian war (200–197 BC)

The respite was temporary. Roman influence soon grew, both in mainland Greece and in the Aegean. Five years later they attacked Macedonia itself, inaugurating the second Macedonian war (200–197).[21] In 202 and 201 Philip had ventured into the Aegean, using an independent Aitolian commander to raise funds by attacking allies of the Aitolians and naval bases of the Ptolemies and Rhodians. His capture of several non-aligned Greek towns, and his enslavement of the people of Kios in western Asia Minor (Polyb. 15. 21–3), caused alarm and made him widely unpopular. He besieged Chios but suffered a major naval defeat there against the combined fleets of the three most powerful naval cities in the Aegean: Rhodes, Pergamon, and Byzantion (Polybios, 16. 2–10, describes the battle at length). Later (or possibly earlier) he defeated the Rhodians and attacked Pergamon, where he was accused of violating shrines of the gods (Polyb. 16.

1).[22] Macedonian rule was established over several Karian towns, Samos was captured by force (App. *Macedonian Wars*, fr. 4; see the inscription quoted on p. 101), and Philip may have formed with Antiochos III a secret pact to seize Egypt, perhaps with the real intention of neutralizing Antiochos.[23]

In the autumn of 201 the Rhodians and Attalos of Pergamon sought help from the Romans (Livy, 31. 2), who issued an ultimatum to Philip (Polyb. 16. 27. 2–3). The determination of the people of Abydos in the face of Philip's siege is evocatively portrayed by Polybios (16. 30–1, Austin 65). The vote for war took place early in 200. The Athenians abolished honours voted earlier to Philip V (Livy, 31. 44. 2–9, Austin 66), and created a new tribe of Attalis in honour of the king of Pergamon, who helped defend the city and the Piraeus against Philip's troops (Polyb. 16. 25–6, Austin 198).[24]

The interests of Roman commanders, ambitious for triumphs, coincided with the interests of many Greek communities and the Romans' perception that Philip must not be allowed to flout the earlier settlement engineered by Rome. The second Macedonian war had more far-reaching effects than the first, and involved many states on the Greek mainland and in the Aegean. The Roman commander Titus Quinctius Flamininus focused his energies on Philip's possessions in southern Greece, presenting Rome as the liberating power. When direct confrontation came, Philip was on the receiving end of the first major defeat of a Greek army by Roman legions, at Kynoskephalai in Thessaly (197; described, Polyb. 18. 19–27).

In 196 the senate imposed a severe treaty confining Philip within Macedonia, requiring the surrender of his garrisoned towns in Greece and Asia Minor, and confiscating his fleet (Polyb., 18. 44–5, 47, part in Austin 68). Of particular long-term significance were the requirement that 'all the other Greeks, both in Asia and in Europe, were to remain free and use their own laws' (Polyb. 18. 44. 2; Austin 68), and the proclamation made by Flamininus at the Isthmian games of 196, in which he reiter-ated the theme of Greek freedom:

> The senate of the Romans and Titus Quinctius the proconsul, having defeated king Philip and the Macedonians in war, allow to be free, ungarrisoned, not subject to tribute, and using their ances-tral laws the Corinthians, Phokians, Lokrians, Euboians, Phthiotic Achaeans, Magnesians, Thessalians, and Perrhaibians.
>
> (Polyb. 18. 46. 5, Austin 68)

This announcement, says Polybios, was received with rapture by the crowd, among whom some distinguished men had been expecting the Romans to retain control of key places (18. 46. 1). In the context of Macedonian aggression it is easy to understand why Flamininus had such a warm reception; but Rome's victory irrevocably changed the lives of the Greeks, and the new superpower brought, as superpowers do, a combination of benefits and hazards for those who had recourse to them.

Rome against Antiochos III (197–188 BC)

Another remarkable feature of the settlement of 196 was the fact that the Romans claimed the right to determine the fate of Greeks in Asia. Some cities, indeed, already placed their hopes in Rome. The people of Lampsakos in north-western Asia Minor sent an embassy to Flamininus's brother Lucius, himself a Roman commander; through him they 'urged and besought them [*the Roman people*], since we are kinsmen of the Romans, to take thought for our city so as to bring about whatever seemed advantageous to the people' (Austin 155, BD 33, Sherk 55, *Syll.*³ 591),[25] a reference to the city's efforts in 196/5 to preserve its independence from Antiochos III, who was attempting to recover Seleukid possessions on the coasts of Asia Minor (Livy, 33. 38, Austin 153), opposed by the Rhodians.

In a meeting with Roman envoys in 196 Antiochos argued that he was merely recovering his ancestral possessions (Polyb. 18. 49–51, Austin 154); but as these could be held to extend into Europe, where he had recently seized towns in and near the Chersonese and was rebuilding Lysimacheia, he was in effect denying the Romans' right to pronounce upon Greek affairs even there, not only in Asia.[26] From his point of view the Romans were the intruders. In 195 and 194 he campaigned in Thrace. Livy preserves details of a conference between Antiochos's envoys and members of the Roman senate in 193, in which Flamininus warned him that friendly relations with Rome depended on his staying out of Europe and allowing the Greeks of Asia Minor their autonomy (Livy, 34. 57–9).[27] It is an example of the Romans' increasing tendency to regard other people's business as their own, seeing events in areas bordering on their sphere of influence as events upon which they were entitled to voice an opinion. The possession of irresistible power tends to lead to such arrogance; in this respect, thus far, it might be hard to portray the Romans as less imperialistic than Philip and Antiochos.

A recurrent pattern of events in this period is the way in which former allies become objects of Roman suspicion, are cast by the Romans in the role of potential enemies, and feel themselves increasingly threatened to the point where they conclude they can survive only by opposing Rome. How cynical a view one should take of Roman behaviour depends on one's view of Roman imperialism.[28] Another of the striking characteristics of these years is the way in which the Romans quite clearly take a long view in diplomacy and war, which perhaps entitles one to judge them severely if they appear on occasion not to deal straight.

Rome's earlier manipulation of different parties in Greece was the origin of the war against Antiochos, but a more important factor was the enormous confidence the Roman senate now felt in its military power. The Aitolians had rejoined the side of Rome in 199,[29] but were inevitably suspect thereafter. In 192, disappointed at not receiving Greek territories from the settlement, they attempted to seize Sparta (where they assassinated Nabis), Chalkis, and Demetrias and called upon Antiochos 'to liberate Greece and to arbitrate between the Aitolians and the Romans' (Livy, 35. 33. 8). Antiochos did invade Greece, landing at Demetrias, but found little support; as Errington remarks, 'most Greek states since 196 had enjoyed greater practical independence than at any time since the middle of the fourth century'.[30] In evaluating the choices of the Greek cities, we must remember that most or all southern Greek cities had democratic constitutions, and that the choice a city made depended upon one group among the political leaders being able to create majority support. If we then ask what the élite and common people would have thought of a Seleukid warlord intent on ruling them as tributary possessions, we must conclude that he might well have seemed scarcely preferable to an aggressive Macedonian king. Roman professions of support, such as the letter from L. Cornelius Scipio and his brother to the people of Herakleia-under-Latmos (Austin 159, BD 38, Sherk 14, $Syll.^3$ 618),[31] are a sign of the high hopes which some cities placed in them. The unfortunate, if (to the people of the time) unpredictable, outcome was that the alternative to Antiochos – the Romans – would prove no better, perhaps worse.

Antiochos was heavily defeated in spring 191 at Thermopylai, again in 190 in a naval battle off Myonnesos in western Asia Minor, and shortly afterwards at Magnesia-by-Sipylos (Livy, 37. 40–4, part in Austin 160, enumerates the Seleukid forces at Magnesia; for the events of the war, see Polybios, books 20–1; Livy, books 35–8).[32] The treaty made at Apameia in Syria in 188 freed all Seleukid territory in Asia Minor west of the Tauros mountains, but gave the northern part to Pergamon and the remainder to the Rhodians (Polyb. 21. 43, Austin 161). This was despite the Rhodians' request to the senate (a self-interested request, claimed Eumenes) that the Greeks of Asia be liberated (Polyb. 21. 22–3, Austin 200). Liberation, therefore, did not necessarily mean freedom; the former tributary cities of Antiochos in northern Asia Minor were excused from paying tribute to Pergamon only if they had fought against Antiochos, and remained subject to Pergamon (Polyb. 21. 46) – though in particular cases they might enjoy tax remission and other benefits (as did an unnamed Hellespontine city in Austin 201).[33] Many towns welcomed the Rhodian takeover, but some which feared the break-up of local spheres of control were not so warm. In Lykia, which had supported Antiochos, armed resistance to the Rhodians lasted a number of years (Polyb. 22. 5).

In Greece, the Aitolians became the first Greeks to have their independence formally taken away (for Roman treatment of Aitolia in 191 and 189, see Polyb. 20. 9–10 and 21. 32, Austin 69–70), and lost to the Thessalians their dominance over the Delphic amphiktyony (Austin 72, $Syll.^3$ 613 a).

Roman power in a Greek landscape (188–179 BC)

Confident from extraordinary success – victories over Carthage and the two most powerful hellenistic kingdoms within fifteen years – the Roman senate began to display yet more arrogance. Several episodes in the years after 188 revealed the Romans' ability to misrepresent situations to their advantage and with impunity. They took a view about whether Sparta should remain within the Achaean league (it had been enrolled by Philopoimen in 192: Livy, 35. 37. 2), even though it was strictly an internal matter for the league (the Spartan constitution was abolished in 188: Livy, 38. 34, Austin 71). They instructed the Boiotians to take back an exile who had helped Flamininus (Polyb. 22. 4. 5). They lent a favourable ear to envoys from cities appealing against Philip V's continued rule, even where the Romans had implicitly recognized his right over them (Polyb. 22. 6, in 188/7 BC; Livy, 39. 25–9, in 185 BC); both Polybios (22. 18. 10) and Livy (39. 23. 5) situate the origins of Rome's war against Perseus (171–168) in Philip's resentment at this.[34] Philip, meanwhile, set about restoring Macedonian military power (Livy, 39. 24. 1–4, Austin 73; cf. Austin 74, Burstein 66, *ISE* ii. 114, if it dates from this time).[35] In the winter of 188/7 a Roman envoy exceeded his authority in pronouncing about the Achaeans' treatment of Sparta (Polyb. 22. 10; Pausanias, 7. 8. 6; 7. 9. 1). Four years later, another made no attempt to cloak the mailed fist when arbitrating between the two parties (Livy, 39. 35–7):

> Then Appius [*the Roman commissioner*] said that he seriously advised the Achaeans that, while they were still at liberty to do it of their own free will, they should come to terms, lest they soon have to do it unwillingly and under compulsion.
>
> (Livy, 39. 37. 19)

Finally, in Rome that winter (184/3) the Achaeans were forced to accept the senate's ruling about disputes at Sparta (Polyb. 23. 4), including their recommendation that the Spartans be allowed to restore their city wall (Paus. 7. 9. 5). When Messene seceded from the Achaean league, the Romans again arrogated to themselves the power to determine outcomes (Polyb. 23. 9. 8–10). Narrating the forcible restoration of Messene to the league by the Achaeans in 182, Polybios formulates the Romans' position explicitly: having previously disclaimed any *locus standi* in the matter of Messenia, they now claimed they had banned exports of grain and weapons to the rebels (Polyb. 23. 17. 3).

> From this they were fully revealed to all observers: so far from dodging and overlooking items of foreign affairs that were of minor importance, they were on the contrary annoyed when reference was

not made to them on every single matter, and if all was not carried out in line with their view.

(Polyb. 23. 17. 4)

The mentality of supreme power appears once more; or, if one prefers, one may see it as the mentality of the world's policeman.

The question of Sparta's membership of the league was raised again, and in Rome in 181/0 the Achaean envoy Kallikrates urged the senate to show that it backed its upper-class supporters in Greek cities, in order to force its populist opponents to capitulate. 'If an indication of disapproval came from the senate, even the political activists would quickly transfer to the Roman cause, and the populace (*hoi polloi*, "the many", the common people) would follow them out of fear' (Polyb. 24. 9. 5). The assumption that the majority of the population were now anti-Roman is revealing. As a result the senate

> for the first time embarked on the policy of weakening those in the various states who were working for the best, while building up those who, whether justly or unjustly, appealed to it for help. As a result it came about by degrees, as time went on, that the senate found it had lots of yes-men but was short of genuine friends.
>
> (Polyb. 24. 10. 4–5)

Polybios's view is no doubt coloured by the fact that his father, Lykortas, was one of the Achaean leaders at this time who wished to deal with Rome on a basis of mutual respect. Kallikrates and other hyper-pragmatists, however, made their careers out of advocating obedience to Rome as the supreme good.[36] Polybios goes so far as to say that Kallikrates 'did not realize that he had become the inaugurator of great evils for all the Greeks, but especially the Achaeans' (Polyb. 24. 10. 8).

Greece suffered a tumultuous few years,[37] further weakening its resistance to Rome. The Achaeans debated whether to resume normal relations with Macedonia (Livy, 41. 23–4). Internal disturbances erupted in Aitolia, Thessaly, and Crete. In Lykia, the senate in 178/7 had arbitrarily reversed its earlier assignment of the region to the Rhodians following representations from the people of Xanthos:

> Finally they [*the Xanthian envoys*] worked on the senate to the extent that they sent envoys to Rhodes who were to explain to the Rhodians that reference had been made to the memoranda made by the ten commissioners when they were in Asia sorting out matters regarding Antiochos, and the Lykians had been found to have been given to the Rhodians not by way of a gift, but more as friends and allies. When such a resolution of the matter was announced, it did not altogether please many people. For the Romans seemed to be

379

playing the umpire in the question of the Rhodians and Lykians, wishing to bankrupt the stores and treasuries of the Rhodians.

(Polyb. 25. 4. 5–7)

Polybios goes on to say that the senate's motive appeared to be revenge for the rapprochement between the Rhodians, Seleukos IV, Perseus, and Prousias of Bithynia (25. 4. 8). Soon the dispute between the Lykians and Rhodians flared up again (Livy, 41. 25).[38]

The ending of resistance to Rome: the third Macedonian war

When Perseus succeeded Philip as king of Macedonia in 179, he began cultivating support both there and in southern Greece (Polybios calls it *hellênokopein*, 'cutting (a) Greek', perhaps a metaphor from minting coins, 25. 3. 1). It was suspected that he might have instigated trouble between two tribes to his north. Since this is not certain, it is a measure of the Romans' supreme confidence in their own right to determine the outcome of Greek affairs, and possibly of an extreme defensiveness, that a report of the suspicion seems to have been enough to make them apprehensive about a war with Macedonia (Livy, 41. 19. 4; 175 BC). When Perseus restored Macedonian rule over Dolopia to the south – possibly in breach of Rome's instruction that the Macedonians were to remain within their ancient frontiers – and his envoys were said to have visited Carthage, the Romans assumed he was preparing for war.

In 172, Eumenes II of Pergamon (r. 197–159/8) denounced Perseus in Rome (Livy, 42. 11–13). When Perseus was alleged to have contrived an assassination attempt upon him (42. 15–17), the Macedonian was declared an enemy of Rome. Livy enumerates the considerations weighing with the different Mediterranean powers as they watched the approach of war (42. 29, Austin 75). A rhetorical version of the grievances against Perseus is preserved in a letter from the Romans, or a Roman official, to the Delphic amphiktyony (Austin 76, Sherk 19, *Syll.*[3] 643).[39]

This was the start of the third Macedonian war. According to Livy, Perseus now had a larger army than any king since Alexander the Great (42. 51, Austin 77). He was tricked by an offer of negotiations (42. 39–42), which gave the Romans time to prepare for war and gather support in Greece (42. 47). Some senators – the older ones, it should be noted – disapproved of such duplicity, 'the new and excessively scheming wisdom' (42. 47. 9). It is not unknown for the prolonged enjoyment of extraordinary success to engender ethical laxity in a governing élite.

When Perseus won a cavalry battle in Thessaly (Livy, 42. 58–61) but found his peace terms rejected (Livy, 42. 62; Polyb. 27. 8), there was an outburst of pro-Macedonian feeling among the states of Greece. This change of heart must mean, in practice, a shift in the balance of power within the political leaderships of cities. It was not shared by the Athenians, who were not only grateful allies of the Romans but had more reason than most to fear the wrath of Macedonians (see p. 150). Elsewhere, however, according to Polybios, 'this feeling on the part of the populace (*hoi polloi*) suddenly shone out like a fire' (27. 9. 1), a sign that public opinion, at least in numerical terms, had shifted or had become too strong to be stifled. Livy confirms that the common people backed the Macedonians, though their leaders were divided (42. 30. 1–7, Austin 75).

Popular support for Perseus can even be offered as evidence that Rome was waging class war,[40] but one may doubt whether ordinary people consistently believed that their interests were better served by Macedonia, or would have been right to do so. Philip V had enslaved the people of Kios a generation before (p. 374); cities like Lampsakos had appealed to the Romans for protection against the Seleukids. All imperial powers need friends among the economic élite of subject states, and cultivate and favour their friends; Macedonia may have been no better in this respect. It may be, then, that the propertied class, who invariably occupied the positions of leadership, had always been divided into pro-Macedonians and pro-Romans, each group deriving its cohesion largely from personal affiliations, the two commanding popular support turn and turn about. At one juncture it could be prudent for a city to call on Rome to save it from Macedonia; at another time the tables were turned. At certain times Rome, at others Macedonia would play the 'freedom and justice' card. Neither master, one suspects, would have left ordinary people particularly worse or better off, economically or politically. The ulterior aim, or aspiration, for a Greek community was *autonomia*, and it was a hope unlikely to be fulfilled in either case.

In 170 the Roman praetor Hortensius dealt with the people of Abdera in the same way Philip V had dealt with Kios, but the senate ruled him out of order and commanded the restoration of those enslaved (Livy, 43. 4. 8–13). There were other incidents; safeguards were put in place; but support for Rome was eroding even in the Achaean league and among pro-Roman groups in Aitolia. The situation was rescued by gentler Roman diplomacy, but it was a dangerous time for Greek states. In the early part of the war the Boiotian league was dissolved. After Perseus was defeated by L. Aemilius Paullus at Pydna in 168, a thousand Achaeans were deported to Italy and indefinitely detained, 550 leading Aitolians were put to death, and 150,000 people were sold into slavery from Epeiros, which had supported Perseus. It was in this same year that Gaius Popillius Laenas delivered his ultimatum to Antiochos IV (p. 292).

The kingdoms of Epeiros and Macedonia were abolished and Macedonia was split into four federal republics. None had its own name – they were simply parts of Macedonia – and they were set up in such a way that they could not unite or collaborate: marrying across state lines was forbidden, as was owning property in more than one republic (Livy, 44. 29. 3–30, 32.

1–7; Austin 79).[41] The Rhodians, perhaps mischievously encouraged, had put themselves in the Romans' bad books by attempting to mediate between Rome and Perseus; they were punished by the removal from their control of the Karian and Lykian territories assigned to them in 188 (Polyb. 29. 19. 5).

The Athenians seem to have done well out of the settlement – perhaps because their city was relatively unimportant in strategic terms. They successfully petitioned the senate to be given back Delos and Lemnos, which they had possessed before. More controversially, they received the land of the people of Haliartos in Boiotia, where the Romans in 171 had enslaved the population and obliterated the town (Livy, 42. 63. 11–12; Strabo, 9. 2. 30 (411)). The envoys were told to ask the senate to restore the Haliartians, but, if this request was not granted, to ask for the land themselves; Polybios criticizes them unduly for this (30. 10. 1–9). In awarding Delos to Athens in 167 and making it a tax-free port (Polyb. 30. 20. 7; cf. 30. 31, Austin 80), it is traditionally supposed that the Romans set out to ruin the Rhodian economy. A Rhodian speaker in Polybios (30. 31. 9–12) appears to claim so in 165/4, asserting that the value of the Rhodians' harbour dues, *when farmed out*, had fallen by 85 per cent. The effect may have been temporary, however, and the report tells us nothing about changes in trade. The decision may have been intended as a favour to Rome's friends on Delos and in Athens, rather than as a punishment of Rhodes.[42]

So secure were the Athenians in the friendship of the Romans that they were able to maintain active diplomatic contacts with the Attalids until 133 and with the Ptolemies and Seleukids throughout the second century. Despite Antiochos III's defeat, or perhaps because of it, his successors Seleukos IV (r. 187–175) and Antiochos IV (r. 175–164) were generous to the city and its temples, most notably that of Olympian Zeus (p. 87). Not to be outdone, Eumenes II (r. 197–159/8) and Attalos II (r. 159/8–139/8) donated splendid stoas on the south slope of the Acropolis and the east side of the Agora, respectively (see Figures 8.8 and 9.2), in return for which the Athenians erected statues of both kings above the theatre of Dionysos (Plut. *Antony*, 60. 6; quoted below, p. 443 n. 56).[43]

In short, Athens (or its élite) prospered, as is suggested by the popularity of its New Style coinage (Fig. 10.1), which was introduced probably after 168 and was minted for about 120 years. It became one of the most widely used currencies in the eastern Mediterranean and was granted a privileged status by the Delphic amphiktyony, perhaps around the mid-second century (Austin 107, *Syll.*[3] 729).[44] It has been suggested that, as the Laureion silver mines of Attica are thought to have been less productive now than in the classical period, the silver for this new coinage may partly have derived from melted-down Macedonian coins.[45] On the other hand, the two attested slave revolts in the Attic mines, in 133 (Orosius, 5. 9. 5, using Livy) and shortly before 100 (Posidonius, *FGH* 87 fr. 35) may indicate an intensification of mining and silver-processing.

The new coinage is commonly found on Delos, which had close economic ties with Athens. Members of the aristocracy in both places are often related to one another, and the relative independence of Delos seems to have made it attractive to rich Athenians with business interests. A building programme on the island, and the concomitant need for temple accounts to be inscribed, almost certainly provided employment for letter-cutters who had previously been kept busy making inscriptions in Athens.[46] Prosperous non-Greek traders migrated to Delos, putting their sons through the local version of the *ephebeia*, which they eventually dominated. In the late second century, with Delian prosperity reaching its height and increasing numbers of Italians resident there, members of the élite, who knew they owed their prosperity to Roman favour, began to dedicate votives to 'the people of Rome' jointly with the *demos* of the Athenians. It was around the same time (*c*.119 BC) that honorific statues of distinguished Romans began to be erected in Athens itself.[47]

From Pydna to the sack of Corinth (168–146 BC)

For the years 167 to 150 our sources are incomplete: Livy is lost, Polybios fragmentary. Although there is little evidence, it is possible that this is because it was genuinely a quiet time, at least at first. The Romans supported Kallikrates at the head of the Achaean league, but kept the Achaean prisoners until Polybios helped secure their return in 150 (Plut. *Cato the Elder*, 9 = Polyb. 35. 6). The senate also continued to intervene willingly in local disputes, such as between Sparta and Argos, or between Athens and the Delians expelled after 167 (Polyb. 32. 7; in this case the judgement went against Athens in 159/8). The senate also appears to have overruled the Athenians in a matter concerning a Delian private priesthood of Sarapis (Burstein 75, Sherk 28, *Syll.*³ 664).[48]

Rome sought to weaken the Achaean league by detaching cities from it (Paus. 7. 11. 1–3). In a revealing comment, Polybios (32. 13) reports that the senate feared the Roman army would lose its fighting edge if it were not used, and therefore eagerly embraced a brief war in Dalmatia in 156. The

Figure 10.1 'New Style' silver tetradrachm (16.75 g). Athens, *c*.125 BC. Obv.: head of Athena. Rev.: owl on amphora. (Ashmolean Museum, University of Oxford.)

revolt of Andriskos in Macedonia, who sought to recreate the kingship and gathered considerable support from within the four republics, gave the Romans a reason for full-scale intervention in 149–148.

In southern Greece in the late 150s, a persistent argument between Athens and the Achaean league, over Athenian possession of Oropos on the Boiotian border, led to a rift between Sparta and the league: a Spartan general, Menalkidas, was said to have cheated Kallikrates out of his share of a bribe paid by the Oropians (Polyb. 32. 11. 5–7, fragmentary; Paus. 7. 11. 4–7. 12. 9; cf. also Austin 137, *Syll.*[3] 675, recording mediation by an Achaean).[49] Though Kallikrates died in 150, Menalkidas and the Achaean Diaios went to arbitration in Rome (149/8), but this was overtaken by events. With Kallikrates out of the way, the league was less easily reined in. Diaios persisted with military action against Sparta's Perioikoi, despite having agreed to await a senatorial commission, and Menalkidas behaved equally provocatively (Paus. 7. 13. 2–8). Frustration with Achaean obstinacy led the senate to announce that Sparta, Corinth, Argos, and other places were to be removed from the league, whereupon relations with the league broke down and the Romans declared war in 146 (Paus. 7. 14. 1–15. 1).

As in 172, there was wide support for the anti-Roman cause, futile though it may have seemed. Polybios makes a notable remark, even if it is tainted by class prejudice, about the composition of the Achaean league assembly in spring 146, where Roman envoys attempted to mollify the delegates:

> When they heard this, the populace (*hoi polloi*) were not at all prepared to put up with it, but jeered at the envoys and with uproar and shouting threw them out. For there had gathered together a mass of labouring persons and artisans such as never was seen before; for all the cities had caught a cold,[50] but the city of Corinth was doing it *en masse*, indeed probably more than the rest. A few people, however, very much liked what they heard from the ambassadors.
>
> (Polyb. 38. 12. 4–5)

As Walbank remarks, such a spectrum of representation was unlikely at a (mere) council meeting;[51] presumably this was a plenary session of council and assembly jointly (cf. p. 137). Corinth was one of the two major centres of manufacturing in Greece, and probably the 'hooligans' were largely local men and not council members. This was no takeover by working-class radicals, but it indicates the sense, and strength, of popular feeling, which had a rare opportunity to show itself because of where the meeting took place.

Defiance proved futile, and perhaps it was as foolish as Pausanias declared three hundred years later (7. 14. 5–6). The Romans defeated the league forces on three occasions (Polyb. 38. 14. 3; Paus. 7. 15. 4–6); after the third defeat, in August or September 146, Diaios (in the view of Pausanias) could have reached Corinth and forced Mummius into an interminable siege (Paus. 7. 16. 4). Instead, Corinth surrendered. Two days later the city was burned; most of the citizens were murdered; the women, children, and slaves were sold; and antiquities including religious votives were looted (Polyb. 39. 2; Paus. 7. 16. 8, Austin 82). Some of these ended up in Pergamon, which had supplied troops in support of the Romans (Paus. 7. 16. 1 and 8).

Macedonia was made into a single *provincia* with a Roman governor. Pausanias describes the political settlement imposed on the Achaean league:

> In those cities that had made war upon the Romans, Mummius destroyed their walls and took away their weapons, even before commissioners were sent by the Romans; but when the men arrived to be his advisers, then he put a stop to democracies and installed governments based on property classes. Tribute was fixed for Greece, and those who had wealth were prevented from external acquisition. The various league councils of national groups, that of the Achaeans, those of the Phokians or Boiotians, or anywhere else in Greece, were similarly dissolved, every one.
>
> (Paus. 7. 16. 9)

Pausanias does observe, however, that the rights of federation were later restored, and some of the indemnities imposed by Mummius were cancelled (7. 16. 10).

Once again Athens, as a friend of the Roman people and no military power, benefited from the senate's generosity at the end of a conflict. Although Oropos may have been given to Eretria, Athens may have received some of the Sporades islands instead. Although the few epigraphic records of official sacrifices to the Roman people pre-date 146, they are not likely to have been interrupted. Documents from the last quarter of the century refer to the Romans as 'the common benefactors', that is, benefactors of all the Greeks, and Athenian–Roman relations were never warmer.[52]

Trade with Rome may have been the intended scope of a decree dating from around 112/1, which not only standardizes units of sale in Attic markets – as in this extract:

> Those who sell Persian nuts (walnuts), dried almonds, hazelnuts of Herakleia, pine-nuts, chestnuts, Egyptian beans, dates, and any other dried fruits that are sold with these, and lupines, olives, and pine kernels shall sell them with a measure of a capacity of three half-*choinikes* of grain levelled off, selling them with this *choinix* heaped up, with a depth of five fingers and a width at the rim of one finger ...

but also introduces a new *mina* (one-sixtieth of a talent) for certain kinds of transactions:

> The commercial *mina* shall weigh 138 [drachmas of wreath-bearing (*i.e. New Style*) silver] according to the weights at the mint, and a make-[weight] of 12 drachmas of wreath-bearing (silver), and everybody shall sell all other goods with this *mina* except for those expressly specified to be sold according to the silver (coin standard), and they shall place the beam of the scales level at a weight of 150 drachmas of [wreath-]bearing (silver) ...
>
> (Austin 111, *IG* ii² 1013)

The interpretation of the document has been much debated. The difficulty may arise from the combination of two separate measures in one decree: a simple updating of market regulations (as in the first extract) together with a revision of the standard unit of weight. A *mina* of 150 drachmas (*c*.646 g) would weigh almost exactly two Roman *libri* (*c*.655 g). The first extract, too, may envisage bringing the Attic *choinix* in line with Roman units of dry measure. It is possible, therefore, that the purpose is to facilitate the exchange of Athenian and Italian commodities.[53]

Once again, however, we must consider the possibility that such a measure may have served the interests of only one section of society, and that there was a variety of views about Rome (as there presumably was among citizens of other *poleis*), even if for the moment some voices were silenced.

Mithradates

The rise of Pontos and the first Mithradatic war (113–84 BC)

It was only a few years later, in 133, that Pergamon, still a prosperous kingdom and once Rome's ally, succumbed to Roman power; the fortuitous death of Attalos III left Rome in the position of sorting out the administration of western Asia Minor. We have already seen (in Chapter 6) how Roman influence upon Egypt grew during the second century, until in 96 Ptolemy Apion left the kingdom to the Roman people; thereafter the Romans played the kingmaker on several occasions in Alexandria, until the civil wars brought about Egypt's annexation as a province. Finally, with the Seleukids, too, Rome played the kingmaker during the mid-second century, but the main beneficiaries were the Parthians and other eastern neighbours, who reduced the kingdom to a fraction of its former size, a remnant in Syria and Cilicia (Chapter 8).

Nevertheless, the Roman takeover of the east did not proceed altogether smoothly, and there were times when Roman power looked vulnerable. Resistance came from the lesser kings of Asia Minor.

Early in his long reign, Mithradates Eupator ('the Great') of Pontos (r. *c*.113–65) built a Black Sea empire. Later he expelled the Romans from Asia for a time. His career takes us from the demise of an independent Pergamon to the last phase of the Roman civil wars, and illustrates both the looseness of Roman rule at this time and the overwhelming military resources which, in the end, decreed that Rome would triumph.[54] The sources for his career are reasonably full, including Appian's *Mithradatic Wars*, Plutarch's lives of *Sulla* and *Lucullus*, a few passages of Justin (notably books 37–8), and political speeches by the Roman orator Cicero (*Pro Flacco*, *Pro Murena*, *Pro lege Manilia*).

The ancestors of Mithradates were local Iranian dynasts who governed part of north-western Asia Minor in the mid-fourth century. Mithradates Ktistes ('Founder'), expelled by Antigonos Monophthalmos in 302, appears to have established a new kingdom in Pontos in north-eastern Asia Minor in or around 297. He and his successors gradually gained wider influence and sometimes territory from Paphlagonia, Bithynia, Cappadocia, Galatia, and Phrygia. Strictly speaking, their fertile, well-watered territory was called 'Cappadocia by the Euxeinos' (Polyb. 5. 43. 1) or 'by the Pontos' (Euxeinos and Pontos are the ancient names of the Black Sea: Strabo, 12. 1. 4 (534); for resources of the region see p. 279). Culturally it was a combination of Greek cities with their distinctive political traditions and a village-based society with temple centres, overlain by a well-established Iranian aristocracy.[55] The kings, however, were not only Iranian by descent but were closely aligned to the Seleukid royal family through marriage alliances. The identities of the members of the dynasty are not all certain, but notable gains were made by Phraates (r. *c*.189–*c*.159), who was made to cede territory by the Romans but gained Sinope and the suzerainty of Armenia Minor. Like other eastern kingdoms, Pontos came to be heavily influenced by Roman policy, which first maintained it in friendship and then undermined it.

Mithradates seized the throne in about 113. He is said to have spent years up to this point in exile in the mountains of north-eastern Asia Minor, cultivating bodily prowess and, apparently, building up a resistance to the poisons every king feared:

> Celestial manifestations had also predicted his future greatness. For both in the year in which he was born and in that in which he first began to reign, a comet lit up so strongly for seventy days on each occasion that the whole of heaven seemed to be burning. For both by its size it had occupied a fourth part of heaven, and by its brightness it had vanquished the power of the sun; and while it arose and set it consumed a duration of four hours.
>
> While a boy, Mithridates suffered attacks by his guardians, who ... beset him with poisons. Fearing this, he quite often drank antidotes and thus protected himself against attacks, seeking out stronger

preventive remedies, with the result that as an old man he was
unable to die by poison even though he wished to.

(Just. 37. 2)

Such legends are partly the product of his mythologizing by eastern and
especially Roman authors; for Mithradates became in Roman consciousness
an archetypal enemy alongside such luminaries as Hannibal and Perseus.

Early in his reign Mithradates accepted suzerainty from the king of Armenia
Minor and annexed Kolchis, a major port on the eastern shore of the Black
Sea (Fig. 10.2). By helping Chersonesos against its Skythian neighbours, he
gained control of the Crimea; he gave military assistance to Olbia and
Apollonia in the north-west, and became master of virtually the whole sea.
This alarmed the Romans, particularly when his expansionism affected
regions just outside their sphere of influence. In 108–107, with Nikomedes
of Bithynia, he seized Paphlagonia; ignoring a Roman order to withdraw, he
instead occupied part of Galatia. An attempt to persuade the senate to ratify
his gains was unsuccessful. He and Nikomedes fell out over Cappadocia,
earlier ruled by Mithradates' sister and arguably part of his sphere of influence; by about 101 he had deterred Nikomedes by a massive invasion of
Cappadocia and installed a puppet king there. When, a few years later, the
dispute flared up again, the senate ordered Mithradates out of Cappadocia
and Nikomedes out of Paphlagonia, later establishing a new king of
Cappadocia chosen by the local nobles.[56]

Mithradates exploited the death of Nikomedes in 94 as an opportunity to
take Cappadocia and Bithynia, which he did in 91/0 through his son-in-law,

Figure 10.2   The Black Sea. (Based partly on Austin xv, fig. 1.)

Tigranes I ('the Great') of Armenia (r. 96 or 95–*c*.56). Once again he yielded to Roman demands and withdrew, but when the king of Cappadocia, restored by Roman commissioners and encouraged by them to recoup their costs, attacked Pontos, Mithradates first protested against this and then retook Cappadocia, prompting the first Mithradatic war (89–85; see esp. App. *Mith*. 15. 50–58. 240; also Plut. *Sulla*, 11–14, *Luc*. 2–4), which was essentially started by the Roman commissioners in the field, led by M'. (Manius) Aquillius, rather than by the senate. (The depth of Mithradates' reserves and the stamina of his fighting armies are demonstrated by the scale of their sustained efforts.) Defeating the Romans four times in 89, he gained Bithynia, Phrygia, Mysia, Lykia, Pamphylia, and Ionia, dismantling the Roman province of 'Asia'. When Aquillius was captured, he was cruelly executed:

> Not long afterwards he also captured Manios Akylios, the man chiefly responsible for this diplomatic mission and this war. He had him tied to an ass and led around, (with a label) proclaiming his name, Manios, to onlookers, until in Pergamon he poured molten gold down the man's throat to express the shameful bribe-taking of the Romans.
>
> (App. *Mith*. 21. 80)

Many Greek cities welcomed the end of Roman rule, though resistance in Karia, Rhodes, and elsewhere was born out of earlier benefactions and current privileges granted by Rome. When L. Cornelius Sulla, the future dictator of Rome and former proconsul of Cilicia, received from the senate the command of the war, Mithradates embarked upon his most savage and most daring of exploits, nothing less than the ethnic cleansing of Asia Minor. Probably in the first half of 88, by secret arrangement at thirty days' notice, the authorities in every city in Asia Minor put to death all resident Italians – free men, freedmen, women, children – on a single day (App. *Mith*. 22. 85–23. 91). Plutarch says 150,000 were killed (*Sulla*, 24), but even if the lower total of 80,000 given by other sources is still an exaggeration, this calculated atrocity had a staggering impact. The atrocity points to the unpopularity of Rome's official representatives, especially among propertied Greeks in Roman areas who paid the costs of the colonial administration. It will also have fossilized the loyalties on both sides ('it ensured that no city that did his bidding now could ever hope to be received back into Roman allegiance')[57] and stiffened the resolve of the Roman senate.

Although, within Greek cities, there may have been popular support for the attack, a change of ruler may, as so often in Greek history, have been engineered by one group among the propertied élite in order to out-manoeuvre their political opponents. There may have been no increase in freedom; in some places dictators (*tyrannoi*) wielded power on behalf of Mithradates. In 88 Mithradates besieged Rhodes, the last serious bastion of opposition and a focus of loyalty to Rome, but was forced to withdraw. It was his first serious setback; Appian (*Mith.* 26. 103–27. 105) blames it on the collapse of Mithradates' giant siege-engine.

In Old Greece, reactions to Mithradates' 'liberation' of Asia Minor were varied, though the Achaean league and most of the Boiotian cities joined his cause, as did Sparta. At Athens, support for Rome had previously been the majority sentiment; in 102–100, for example, ships had been sent in support of M. Antonius's campaign against the pirates of southern Asia Minor; and the fact that in 109/8 a dispute between Athens and Sikyon could be settled by a third party without reference to Rome suggests that the hand of Roman rule was not always heavy.[58]

Now, however, an anti-Roman party gained ascendancy, apparently with popular support (Paus. 1. 20. 5 refers to 'the disruptive element' of the citizenry). Athenion, an Aristotelian philosopher – surely riding on the support of the propertied classes, not only the poor – returned from a diplomatic mission to Mithradates bearing the king's pledge of support for debt reforms and democracy, and was elected hoplite general. Mithradates may even have been made eponymous archon of the city for 87/6. This striking reversal of Athens' previously pro-Roman stance is perhaps to be explained by a combination of resentment at Roman creditors and disapproval of Rome's treatment of Mithradates. One wonders whether changes in the economic interests of the élite may not lie behind a change in political calculus: Habicht points to the rise of *nouveaux riches* with commercial interests in Delos, who in the late second century began to overshadow the older landowning aristocracy.[59] Another probable factor in the Athenians' choice is the fact that Mithradates controlled the Hellespont, always at the front of their minds because of their interests in the north-eastern Aegean and the Black Sea grain supply.

About Mithradates, not all Athenians were of one view. Our main source for Athenion, the Stoic Poseidonios (*FGH* 87 fr. 36), ridicules him, probably to use him as a moral example and to demonstrate the irrationality of the Athenian *demos*.[60] Even the head of Aristotle's Academy, Philon, took refuge at Rome, and the island community of Delos defected from Athens. An Athenian expedition against the island, led by another Peripatetic philosopher, Apellikon, was easily quashed by a Roman force, but shortly afterwards Mithradates' general Archelaos seized the island and presented it to Athens, reportedly with the loss of 20,000 Italian lives (App. *Mith.* 28. 109). An Athenian named Aristion, a philosopher of the rival Epicurean school, had accompanied Archelaos and now became 'tyrant' of Athens (though some believe Athenion and Aristion to be the same man)[61] and helped Archelaos prepare Greece for the Roman attack.

Sulla arrived in early 87 and besieged Athens and Piraeus (Plut. *Sulla*, 13–14; App. *Mith.* 30. 118–38. 150). Though he eventually gave up the siege of Piraeus, in Athens the citizens endured dire conditions. Eventually, in the spring of 86, they yielded:

Learning that those in the town were pretty hard pressed and had slaughtered all their cattle, boiling the hides and skins and sucking what nourishment they could get from them, and that some had even laid hands on the dead, (Sulla) ordered his army to dig a ditch round the city so that no citizens might slip out unnoticed, even one at a time. And when he had taken this measure, he brought up ladders and at the same time began to excavate the wall. The men inside being weak, a rout at once took place.

He burst into the city, and straightaway there was a great and pitiless massacre: for they were unable to escape because they were starving, neither was there any pity shown to children or women. Sulla ordered the killing of anyone who was found. He was angry that they had so rapidly and senselessly changed sides and joined the barbarians, showing nothing but hostility towards himself. At this point most of the people, learning of his order, threw themselves into the path of their slayers; but a few weakly found their way to the Acropolis. Aristion fled with them, after setting fire to the Odeion so that Sulla would not have a ready supply of timbers for the assault on the Acropolis. Sulla prohibited the torching of the city, but gave it to his army to plunder. In many buildings there were found portions of human flesh made ready for consumption.

(App. *Mith*. 38. 148–50)

Some weeks later, those on the Acropolis surrendered and were put to death.

During the siege of Piraeus, Sulla demolished the Long Walls linking Piraeus to Athens and used sacred trees from the Academy and Lyceum for timber (App. *Mith*. 30. 121); he also expropriated treasures from the great Greek sanctuaries at Epidauros, Delphi, and Olympia (Paus. 9. 7. 5). When Archelaos abandoned the Piraeus, the Romans burned the town and destroyed its naval base (App. *Mith*. 41. 157). Roman soldiers robbed the Stoa of Zeus Eleutherios of votive shields commemorating the dead of past wars (Paus. 10. 21. 5–6). Archaeological traces of the sack of Athens include damage to buildings in the Agora and the abandonment of the procession building (Pompeion) at the Dipylon gate, where missiles have come to light.[62] Sulla had many works of art shipped to Italy, including columns from the unfinished temple of Olympian Zeus which were placed on the Capitol at Rome (Plut. *Publicola*, 15. 4). It is possible that the fine statues known as the Piraeus Bronzes, discovered in the harbour in 1959, were lost while being taken to Rome, perhaps from Delos.[63] Pliny the Elder reports that a painting by the fifth-century artist Zeuxis was lost at sea (*HN* 36. 45). The library of Aristotle and Theophrastos, which Apellikon had purchased after its discovery in Skepsis, was sent to Rome (Strabo, 13. 1. 54 (609); an alternative story is given by Ath. 1. 3 a–b, however).[64]

The constitution of Athens was modified to give more weight to the propertied classes and elected magistrates rather than those appointed by lot. The new regime seems not to have encouraged political debate, judging by the paucity of public documents from the mid-first century. On the other hand, the Athenians were allowed to keep Delos, though it never recovered its prosperity, and probably Salamis.[65]

A few months later, the forces of Mithradates were nearly annihilated in two great battles in Boiotia, at Chaironeia and Orchomenos, in which many tens of thousands of his soldiers are reported killed. Sulla ravaged the towns of the district as a punishment for their disloyalty. With Archelaos, however, he agreed that Mithradates could retain his kingdom if he gave up his recent acquisitions, surrendered large numbers of fully armed warships, and paid a large indemnity.

In Asia, Mithradates was the subject of increasing opposition in Asia during 86 and 85. He cruelly captured Chios, deporting its population to the Black Sea (they were rescued by the people of Herakleia Pontica). Other Ionian towns which revolted were ruthlessly suppressed, while his pledges of generosity to others had little effect. In 85 a Roman army (under a rogue commander) won victories in Bithynia; but the Greeks of Asia must have wondered which military power was the more lethal, for the Romans plundered captured cities and their territories and slaughtered the people of Ilion even though they had opened their gates. At a conference at Dardanos in the Troad, Mithradates was forced to accept the terms offered earlier (Plut. *Sulla*, 24; App. *Mith*. 56. 227–58. 240). Sulla, distracted by civil war at home, may have been anxious not to provoke him further by excessive demands; he was also buying time to arrange the future disposition of Asia. He remained there until 84, and then spent a winter in Athens before returning to business in Italy.

With the exception of steadfast allies such as Rhodes, Chios, some cities of south-western Asia Minor, and Ilion, the Greek towns of Asia were dealt with abysmally in Sulla's settlement, paying huge indemnities and the expenses of the occupying army (Plut. *Sulla*, 25). Those who resisted were massacred, others enslaved, and some town walls were demolished (App. *Mith*. 61. 251). Including tax arrears the indemnity totalled 20,000 talents, a figure not beyond conceiving – Alexander had captured 50,000 talents of gold from Darius – but far beyond the means of the already impoverished cities. The burden was still being felt a generation later, for many communities fell victim to Roman investors and tax-farmers (*publicani*), some of whom returned after escaping with nothing from the bloodbath of 88 and now lent at extortionate rates of interest and under harsh terms. Public buildings had to be sold or mortgaged (App. *Mith*. 63. 261), while individual landowners who could not meet their repayments lost their lands.

At the same time, such wealth as remained in the cities seems to have accumulated in fewer hands, judging by the occasional reference to super-rich men, one of whom was Hieron of Laodikeia:[66]

Laodikeia, formerly a small city, enjoyed growth in our time and that of our fathers. It was damaged during a siege under Mithridates Eupator, but the quality of the land and the good fortune of certain of the citizens made it great. First there was Hieron, who left to the people a legacy of more than 2,000 talents and adorned the city with many dedications. Then there was Zenon the orator and his son Polemon; the latter, because of his great courage, was deemed worthy of the kingship [*of Pontos and the Bosporos*] by Antony and subsequently by Caesar Augustus.

(Strabo, 12. 8. 16 (578))

Though there had been grand civic benefactors earlier, the scale may be new. Men like Hieron may have profited from the misfortune of lesser landowners. The economic consequences of Sulla's disposition of Asia Minor would pre-occupy later Roman commanders.

Another consequence of the harsh settlement of Asia may have been the increase in piracy in the eastern Mediterranean. Appian implies a connection with the Roman settlement of Asia Minor, for he refers to it immediately after describing the financial desperation of the cities:

Thus the money was brought together for Sulla, and Asia had her fill of evils. And large numbers of pirate bands sailed openly against her, resembling navies rather than raiders. Mithridates had been the first to launch them upon the sea, when he was despoiling all the places on the grounds that he would not possess them much longer. They had multiplied especially at that time, and began to assault openly not only seafarers but also harbours, settlements, and cities. Thus Iasos, Samos, and Klazomenai were captured, and Samothrace, though Sulla was there present, and the sanctuary of Samothrace was plundered of valuables worth 1,000 talents, it was estimated.

(App. *Mith.* 63. 261–3)

Later (92. 416–93. 427) he retraces the rise of the pirates, blaming Mithradates for inciting them at the outset but attributing their persistence to their 'having been deprived of livelihood and nationality by war' (92. 417). Piracy will have been fuelled by the large numbers of dispossessed citizens, freed and escaped slaves, and former soldiers and rowers whom the mayhem of recent years had cast out of the city-states; on one view, though partly the fault of Diodotos Tryphon and his use of pirate fleets, it was exacerbated by the destructions of Carthage and Corinth and the Romans' increasing liking for slaves (Strabo, 14. 5. 2 (668–9), Austin 171). Piracy was another problem the Romans would have to deal with later.

The second and third Mithradatic wars (c.83–63 BC)

An ambitious Roman commander, Licinius Murena, provoked Mithradates into defending himself (the second Mithradatic war, c.83–81; App. *Mith.* 64. 265–66. 281); and after Sulla's death the senate refused to ratify the peace of Dardanos. Though Mithradates observed its terms for a number of years, it is not surprising that he began preparing for war; there were men at Rome who spied opportunities for themselves in a renewal of hostilities. In 78–77 the Romans created a 'province' of Cilicia, in reality a command against the pirates of southern Asia Minor; but if they saw Mithradates as the real problem it may explain why they built a military road from Sidê in Pamphylia almost as far as Cappadocia.[67]

The third Mithradatic war[68] (73–63; App. *Mith.* 68. 289–113. 555) was occasioned by the death of Nikomedes of Bithynia (c.75), who left his kingdom to the Roman people. The senate made it a province and appointed L. Licinius Lucullus, who had earlier behaved decently towards the Greek cities as governor of Cilicia, to take charge of the war which they already expected (for Lucullus's conduct of the war, see Plut. *Luc.* 7–35). In 73, as earlier, Mithradates opened his campaign by inflicting a major shock on the Romans in battle, this time at sea, but during 73 and 72 Lucullus cleverly focused his military resources on control of the sea and avoided a set-piece confrontation, eventually picking off parts of Mithradates' army and navy and capturing key ports on the Black Sea. In 72 and 71, having forced Mithradates to retreat, Lucullus attacked Pontos directly while the Roman fleet won a series of naval encounters. In a battle near Kabeira (71) Lucullus forced Mithradates to withdraw and turned a retreat into a massacre (Plut. *Luc.* 11). The king betook himself to the court of Tigranes in Armenia, while Lucullus reorganized Pontos. After the Roman demand for Mithradates' surrender was refused (70), Lucullus invaded Armenia and won a great victory at Tigranocerta (October 69), receiving the submission of neighbouring peoples and principalities and restoring the erstwhile Seleukid king Antiochos XIII (p. 322) to the Syrian throne.

While Lucullus continued in 68 to campaign against Tigranes and dismantle his kingdom, Mithradates produced yet another miraculous revival. In 67 the Romans were soundly beaten at Zela in Pontos, and Lucullus's tired legions coerced their commander into withdrawing. Mithradates and Tigranes re-entered their kingdoms, and Lucullus set about restoring the cities devastated by Mithradatic or Roman assaults: Kyzikos, Sinope, and Amisos (Plut. *Luc.* 12, 19, 23; App. *Mith.* 83. 370–4). Later another proconsul organized the restoration of Herakleia, where Roman tax-collectors had been murdered (the story is told by Memnon of Herakleia, *FGH* 336, of whose local history, written in about the second century AD, extensive fragments survive). Lucullus alleviated conditions in Asia Minor generally by fixing interest rates and regulating debt repayment (Plut. *Luc.* 20; App. *Mith.* 83. 376).

In 68 the Romans resumed operations against Cretan pirates, now active around Italy; in 67 they resumed their Cilician campaign. Soon, over the heads of the existing proconsuls, Cn. Pompeius secured massive military resources from the senate, with which he nullified the pirates' forces in a mere three months. In 66, amid political controversy at Rome, he received the prestigious command against Mithradates and Tigranes, again in place of the existing commanders. Cicero, in his speech *On the Command of Gnaeus Pompeius* (*De imperio Gnaei Pompeii*), exaggerates the Mithradatic threat to Roman revenues and Italian profits in the province of Asia. Within months Pompey had defeated Mithradates in battle and secured the surrender of Tigranes. Mithradates attempted to rebuild his forces from a base in the Crimea, but was frustrated by a revolt by his son Pharnakes (63). Immune to poison, he reputedly ordered a Celtic officer to kill him. (The sources for these events include Plutarch's *Pompey*, books 36–7 of Cassius Dio, and App. *Mith.* 94. 428–111. 539.)

Mithradates' ultimate failure represents, perhaps, the end of serious resistance to Rome's power in Asia Minor. Whether he could have survived by working for coexistence with Rome is doubtful; there were lessons to be learned from the fate of earlier kings, and Mithradates may have had little choice but to prepare war once more. Choices existed for his subjects, too. As so often in wartime, many individuals and communities were forced to take sides who might rather not have done so, with serious consequences for those who were unlucky enough to back the loser. Fortunately, perhaps realizing that Sulla's settlement had made the condition of Asia worse rather than better, Pompey took a different line.

Like Sulla when dealing with Mithradates, Pompey allowed Tigranes to retain his kingdom but confiscated his conquests. This was a crucial step in the disassembly of the hellenistic kingdoms of the east, but it was only a part of Pompey's design. He followed up his victories with a campaign against the Albanians and Iberians in the Caucasus, virgin territory for a Roman army; glory and political success at Rome were probably his main aims, rather than the development of Italian trade and financial activity (which was concentrated in western Asia Minor) or the suppression of piracy as such. In 65 he took Kolchis and returned to the Caucasus; the Albanians submitted but kept their lands.

During the rest of 65 and most of 64 Pompey administered the confiscation of Mithradates' vast treasury, reorganized Pontos, and recognized or established existing and new rulers across Anatolia (perhaps through his deputies). He had induced the Parthian king Phraates to attack Tigranes of Armenia by the promise of territory; Phraates kept his side of the bargain in 66, but Pompey appears to have gone back on their agreement during 65, perhaps preferring to alienate Phraates rather than build him up. In late 64

Pompey captured Kommagene and met the latest Seleukid claimant, Antiochos Philadelphos, at Antioch. Deeming Antiochos to be incapable of holding onto power in face of increasingly independent Arab and Jewish states, he made Syria into a province – perhaps as a bulwark against the Parthians rather than to suppress pirate bases, though he eliminated them too.[69] In Judaea in 63, faced with a dispute between rival claimants to the high priesthood, Pompey took Jerusalem by a siege of three months' duration, entering but not desecrating the sanctuary of the Temple (Josephus, *Jewish Antiquities*, 14. 29–79; *Jewish War*, 1. 127–57). Jewish territories acquired by the Maccabaean kings were assigned to Syria, which was thereby strengthened.

Pompey's reorganization of Anatolia and the Levant was not radical, but it reveals how the Romans now sought to strike a balance between security and state profit – or at least the recouping of military costs. The kings of Cappadocia, Kommagene, and Galatia were made 'friends and allies of the Roman people', and Mithradates' son Pharnakes was even allowed to keep Crimean Bosporos. In Kommagene king Antiochos I (r. *c*.69–*c*.36) created one of the most remarkable cultic monuments of this period, thousands of feet above sea level on the mountain of Nemrud Dağı. In inscriptions on the backs of sculpted colossi representing himself and the gods, he proclaimed his own divinity identifying himself as 'Great king Antiochos the God, the Just, the Manifest, Roman-lover and Greek-lover' (*basileus Megas Antiochos Theos Dikaios Epiphanês Philorhômaios kai Philhellên*), boasted of his piety and the rewards it had earned him, and described the images 'of Zeus Oromasdes and of Apollo Mithras Helios Hermes and of Artagnes Herakles Ares and of my fatherland, all-nurturing Kommagene' which he had set up here (Burstein 48, *OGIS* 383).[70] It is not only one of the most remarkable instances of syncretism under royal sponsorship, and proof of the partial cultural fusion that had taken place in Asia Minor, but also testament to the importance henceforwards of identifying Rome's interests with one's own.

Under Pompey's settlement the province of Cilicia was extended and some ruined Greek cities were revived (App. *Mith*. 115. 561–2), including Soloi, renamed Pompeiopolis. In Bithynia, Greek cities were allowed to administer territories; in Pontos, now part of a joint province with Bithynia, this entailed the dismantling of Mithradates' district governorships. Local government had become the backbone of Roman power in the provinces, though it was democracy only in name since city councils (*boulai*) were filled through nomination by superior magistrates. Tribute payments were not imposed except upon local dynasts in Pontos, Syria, and Judaea, but the farming of taxes was made less exploitative.[71] A further reorganization of Judaea took place a few years later under the governor Gabinius, after a recurrence of civil war. The high priest was stripped of political authority and, as elsewhere, towns became the building-blocks of Roman regional government (Jos. *AJ* 14. 91, *BJ* 1. 170).

The culmination of Roman hegemony

After 86 Athens was once more an ally of Rome, and it officially remained free for a further fifty-nine years. There was a brief formal interruption when the Roman tribune Clodius (not the Roman senate) awarded the consul Piso a *provincia* that for the first time included Attica; this was tantamount to declaring it sovereign territory of the Romans, and the purpose was to make it easier for Italian creditors to sue Greek cities. The violation of independence did not outlast Piso's command (58–55).[72] The adverse effects of the Sullan settlement of the cities of Asia may have been felt in Greece, and may explain the cancellation in 58 of taxes imposed by Sulla upon Delos.[73]

In the east the Romans suffered humiliation in 53 at the hands of Parthians, when the senior statesman Crassus was killed; the defeat halted the eastward advance of Roman power for generations, and led to the Parthian invasion of Syria in 51. Greece was one of the battlegrounds of the civil wars, where Pompey was defeated by Caesar at Pharsalos in 48. A few weeks later Pompey was assassinated at Alexandria; Caesar followed him there, and was embroiled in Egyptian dynastic politics and trapped in Alexandria for a few months. At this time his relationship with Kleopatra VII developed; their son Ptolemy Caesar ('Caesarion') was born after his departure. In 47 he campaigned in Asia, defeating Pharnakes of Pontos at Zela, and returned to Italy, where he was assassinated in 44.

Within the space of ten years Athens was ruled by Pompey, Julius Caesar (48–44), Brutus (44–43), and Antony. It is unclear whether they interfered with the constitution; Antony's evident love for Athens is no proof that he did not adjust the nominal democracy. As in the pre- and post-Sullan eras, the *polis* was dominated by wealthy families; the leading priests, the eponymous archons, and other leading magistrates were related to one another. In the 40s the Areiopagos council remained a key centre of power.[74]

By his victory at Actium (31) Octavian became master of the eastern Roman world. He had Cassius, one of Caesar's murderers, put to death in Athens in defiance of sacred Greek custom, since the man had sought asylum there.[75] The official freedom of Athens came to an end when the *provincia* of Achaia was created in 27; it included most of mainland Greece, which till now had not formally been a province. As the emperor Augustus, Octavian made provinces out of Galatia (25 BC) and Judaea (6 BC). The last fragments of Greek Asia Minor were absorbed under his successors.

The effects of Roman rule

Increasing numbers of Italians made Athens their home during the later second and first centuries. While some were exploitative businessmen, many no doubt genuinely admired Greece's antiquities and cultural legacy. Greece became almost the equivalent of the eighteenth-century Grand Tour. After

Sulla's capture of Athens, Philon and other philosophers returned to the city. Cicero was deeply moved when he first visited Athens. He mentions the *gymnasia* and academic life of Athens in his dialogue *De finibus* (5. 1), where his cousin Lucius is especially struck by the *exedra* (here a sort of lecture hall) where Karneades had taught, and comments that 'There is no end to this in Athens; wherever we set foot, we tread upon some bit of history'. Like Sulla in 84, Cicero sought initiation into the Eleusinian mysteries, and he spent the next two years studying philosophy and rhetoric in Athens and Rhodes; he made the effort to celebrate the mysteries again when he had the opportunity nearly thirty years later.[76]

On the other hand, the city of Athens was in debt, like those of Asia, and relied on Atticus and other rich men for gifts of cash, such as Cicero's friend Titus Pomponius, nicknamed Atticus ('Athenian') in 50 BC (Cic., *Letters to Atticus*, 6. 6. 2). The depredations of the rogue proconsul Verres, later prosecuted by Cicero, included the removal of the remaining gold from the Parthenon (Cic. *Verrine Orations*, 2. 1. 44–5; 2. 4. 71). For over two centuries, Greek kings had paid for the grand projects the city could no longer afford, but few kings remained. In the mid-second century the Middle Stoa may have been a royal gift; in the later second century there were contributions from Ptolemy IX, Mithradates V, Mithradates VI the Great, and John Hyrkanos of Jerusalem. In the early first century Ariobarzanes II of Cappadocia contributed to the new Odeion and was honoured by the Athenians (Vitruv. 5. 9. 1; *IG* ii² 3426–7), but thereafter it was mainly Roman aristocrats and commanders who competed with one another in this kind of generosity.[77] Pompey in 62 (Plutarch, *Pompey*, 27. 3), and Julius Caesar and Appius Claudius Pulcher (p. 171) about a decade later (Cic. *Att.* 6. 1. 25), gave vast sums for new buildings. Large parts of Appius's monumental gateway for the sanctuary at Eleusis are still visible, as is his name on an architrave inscription. Caesar's gift was used for a new agora or forum, completed by Augustus.[78]

Alcock has successfully unpicked the old notion that Greece under Roman rule was in a ruinous condition.[79] That misplaced stereotype, reflected in earlier studies of late hellenistic and Roman Greece,[80] derives from rhetorical exaggerations such as the account of the state of Greek cities by Servius Sulpicius Rufus in a letter to Cicero in 45 (Cicero, *Letters to Friends*, 4. 5). The results of urban and rural archaeology are starting to show that the change was longer-term and subtler. There was (in places) a trend towards larger rural settlements and the enlargement of the rural estates of the élite, exemplified by greater differentiation of buildings in the countryside and the probable growth of urban populations in parts of Greece.[81] In towns, Roman intervention could result in the radical reshaping of urban monumental centres, as when the temple of Ares from the Attic countryside was brought into the Agora of Athens and re-erected, or when the emperor Nero attempted to cut a canal through the Isthmus of Corinth.[82] Work continues on the imperial road network of Greece; and there are spectacular examples of political reorganization such as the creation of new cities (*coloniae*), one of which was Corinth under Julius Caesar.[83]

Under the Roman principate the different areas of the hellenistic world grew more alike in character, as the *poleis* finally ceased to be, even in theory, the political entities that gave structure to the landscape but became essentially administrative and fiscal units in the larger imperial system. Members of civic élites in Greece, Asia Minor, and the Levant looked to Rome, or at least to provincial governors, for patronage and benefactions. In some ways the international networking of Greek élites continued as in the classical and hellenistic period, but the stage on which to display one's status was now a wider one: we may note the international cult network established by the emperor Hadrian (r. AD 117–38) under the name Panhellenion;[84] the patronage made available to upper-class Greek *literati* like Arrian and Plutarch; and the opportunities to hold the now purely ceremonial office of consul at Rome. This honour was granted in AD 129 to the administrator and historian Arrian; earlier, in 114, to the prince of Kommagene and honorary Athenian citizen Gaius Iulius Antiochos Philopappos, whose monument surmounts the Hill of the Nymphs. Some of the most spectacular monuments of Roman Greece are due to Hadrian himself, such as the temple of Olympian Zeus at Athens, finally completed now.[85]

The other benefactor whose works strike the eye today was an Athenian: Herodes Atticus (Lucius Vibullius Hipparchos Tiberius Claudius Attikos Herodes), son of the first Greek consul at Rome and himself consul in 143. He used his vast inherited wealth to adorn many Greek towns and sanctuaries, rebuilding the stadium at Athens, building the famous Odeion (concert hall) that bears his name, a lavish nymphaeum at Olympia, and so on.[86] Such egotistical displays were not always received without controversy, but are typical of an age when the exercise of ceremonial and political power through wealth was no longer constrained by the demands of a wider community. Monuments may speak to all, but they did not necessarily speak for all. The Roman conquest had wrought a change upon the Greek *polis*.

APPENDIX I

Dynastic chronologies

See also figures 2.1–2, 2.4, 6.4 and 6.6.

Note: Relationship to other rulers; s. = son of; d. = daughter of; [1], [2] = first, second periods of rule.

1 *Rulers of Macedonia*

360/59–336	Philip II	
336–323	Alexander III (the Great)	s. Philip II
323–317	Philip III Arrhidaios	s. Philip II
323–310	Alexander IV	s. Alexander III
317–316	Olympias	mother of Alexander III
315–297	Cassander (king from 305)	s. Antipater (regent)
297	Philip IV	s. Cassander
297–294	Antipatros and Alexander V	ss. Cassander
294–288	Demetrios I Poliorketes ('Besieger')	s. Antigonos I Monophthalmos
288/7–285	Pyrrhos of Epeiros	
288/7–281	Lysimachos	
281	Seleukos	
281–279	Ptolemaios Keraunos ('Thunderbolt')	s. Ptolemy I
c.277–239	Antigonos II Gonatas	s. Demetrios I
239–229	Demetrios II	s. Antigonos II
c.229–222	Antigonos III Doson	nephew of Antigonos II
222–179	Philip V	s. Demetrios II
179–168	Perseus	s. Philip V

Note: Strictly speaking, Antigonos II should be Antigonos I (Antigonos Monophthalmos was never king in Macedonia) and Antigonos III should be Antigonos II, but the numbering given above is conventional.

2 The Ptolemaic dynasty

304–283	Ptolemy I Soter ('Saviour'; governor from 323)	
285–246	Ptolemy II Philadelphos ('Sister-friend')	s. Ptolemy I
246–221	Ptolemy III Euergetes ('Benefactor')	s. Ptolemy II
221–204	Ptolemy IV Philopator ('Father-friend')	s. Ptolemy III
204–180	Ptolemy V Epiphanes ('(God) Manifest')	s. Ptolemy IV
180–145	Ptolemy VI Philometor ('Mother-friend')	s. Ptolemy V
170–163	[1]Ptolemy VIII Euergetes II Physkon ('Potbelly')	s. Ptolemy V
170–164, 163–116	Kleopatra II	d. Ptolemy V
145	Ptolemy VII Neos Philopator (with Ptolemy VI, and briefly after the latter's death)	s. Ptolemy VI
145–116	[2]Ptolemy VIII	
139–101	Kleopatra III	d. Ptolemy VI, wife of Ptolemy VIII
116–107	[1]Ptolemy IX Soter II Lathyros ('the Bean')	s. Ptolemy VIII, Kleopatra III
107–88	Ptolemy X Alexander I	s. Ptolemy VIII
101–88	[1]Kleopatra Berenike	d. Ptolemy IX
88–81	[2]Ptolemy IX	
80	[2]Kleopatra Berenike	
80	Ptolemy XI Alexander II	s. Ptolemy X
80–58	[1]Ptolemy XII Neos Dionysos Auletes ('the Piper')	s. Ptolemy IX
58–55	Berenike IV (at first with her sister Kleopatra Tryphaina)	d. Ptolemy IX
56–55	Archelaos	husband of Berenike IV
55–51	[2]Ptolemy XII	
51–47	Ptolemy XIII	s. Ptolemy XI
51–30	Kleopatra VII Philopator	d. Ptolemy XI
47–44	Ptolemy XIV	s. Ptolemy XI

3 The Seleukid dynasty

305–281	Seleukos I Nikator ('Victor'; ruler from 312)	
281–261	Antiochos I Soter (co-ruler from 294 or 293)	s. Seleukos I
261–246	Antiochos II Theos ('the God')	s. Antiochos I
246–226/5	Seleukos II Kallinikos ('the Glorious Victor')	s. Antiochos II

226/5–223	Seleukos III	s. Seleukos II
223–187	Antiochos III Megas ('the Great')	s. Seleukos II
187–175	Seleukos IV Philopator	s. Antiochos III
175–164	Antiochos IV Epiphanes	s. Antiochos III
164–162	Antiochos V Eupator ('of the Good Father')	s. Antiochos IV
162–150	Demetrios I Soter	s. Seleukos IV
150–145	Alexander Balas (Epiphanes)	's.' Antiochos IV
145–140, 129–126/5	Demetrios II Nikator	s. Demetrios I
145–142	Antiochos VI Epiphanes	s. Alexander Balas, Kleopatra Thea
[142–139/8	Diodotos 'Tryphon', pretender (*CAH²* viii. 367 n.)	
139/8–129	Antiochos VII Sidetes	s. Demetrios I
126/5–123	Kleopatra Thea ('Goddess')	wife of Demetrios II
126/5–96	Antiochos VIII Grypos	s. Demetrios II
126	Seleukos V	s. Demetrios II
114/3–95	Antiochos IX Philopator 'of Kyzikos'	s. Antiochos VII
95	Seleukos VI	s. Antiochos VIII
95	Antiochos X Eusebes ('the Pious') Philopator	s. Antiochos IX
95–88	Demetrios III Philopator Soter (at Damascus)	s. Antiochos VIII
95	Antiochos XI Epiphanes Philadelphos (in Cilicia; twin of Philip I)	s. Antiochos VIII
95–84/3	Philip I (in Cilicia)	s. Antiochos VIII
87	Antiochos XII Dionysos (at Damascus)	s. Antiochos VIII
84/3	Philip II	s. Philip I
69–63	Antiochos XIII Philadelphos	s. Antiochos X?

4 *The Attalids*

283–263	Philetairos (not king)	
263–241	Eumenes I (not formally king)	nephew of Philetairos
241–197	Attalos I Soter	cousin and adopted s. Eumenes
197–159/8	Eumenes II Soter	s. Attalos I
159/8–139/8	Attalos II	s. Attalos I
139/8–133	Attalos III	s. Eumenes II
[133–129	Aristonikos ('Eumenes III')]	

5 *Rulers of Baktria*

256–248	Diodotos I	
248–235	Diodotos II	s. Diodotos I

(henceforward, dates are all approximate)

235–200	Euthydemos I
200–190	Euthydemos II
200–185	Demetrios I
195–185	Antimachos I
185–180	Pantaleon
185–175	Demetrios II
180–165	Agathokles
171–155	Eukratides I (usurper?)
155–130	Agathokleia and Menandros
…	
75–55	Kalliope and Hermaios (last known rulers)

Some twenty other names are known. For details see the tables in *CAH*^{2} viii. 420–1.

APPENDIX II

Genealogical tables

(1) THE ANTIGONIDS

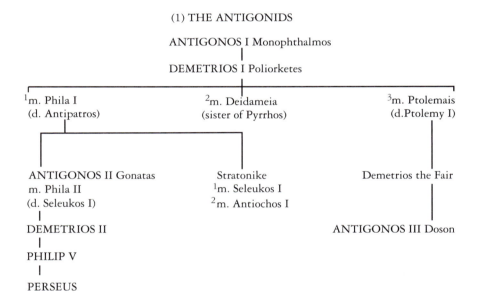

Figure A.1   The Antigonids

Note: d. = daughter of; m. = married; s. = son of

See also Figure 2.3 and 2.5.

(2) THE EARLY PTOLEMIES

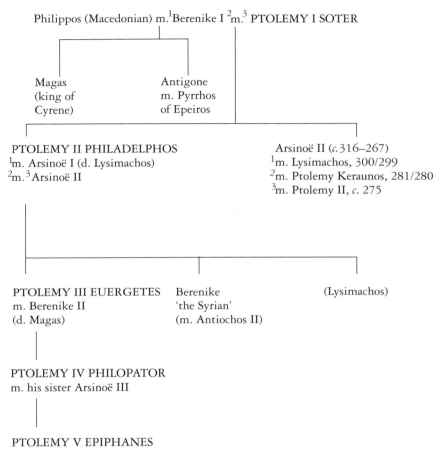

Philippos (Macedonian) m.[1]Berenike I [2]m.[3] PTOLEMY I SOTER

Magas
(king of
Cyrene)

Antigone
m. Pyrrhos
of Epeiros

PTOLEMY II PHILADELPHOS
[1]m. Arsinoë I (d. Lysimachos)
[2]m.[3]Arsinoë II

Arsinoë II (c. 316–267)
[1]m. Lysimachos, 300/299
[2]m. Ptolemy Keraunos, 281/280
[3]m. Ptolemy II, c. 275

PTOLEMY III EUERGETES
m. Berenike II
(d. Magas)

Berenike
'the Syrian'
(m. Antiochos II)

(Lysimachos)

PTOLEMY IV PHILOPATOR
m. his sister Arsinoë III

PTOLEMY V EPIPHANES

Figure A.2   The early Ptolemies

Note: Before Berenike I, his third wife, Ptolemy I also married (secondly) Eurydike I, by
whom he had Ptolemy Keraunos (see above). The remainder of the Ptolemies were
descended from his marriage to Berenike I (granddaughter of Antipatros), who was
Ptolemy's mistress before she was his wife.

(3) THE EARLY SELEUKIDS

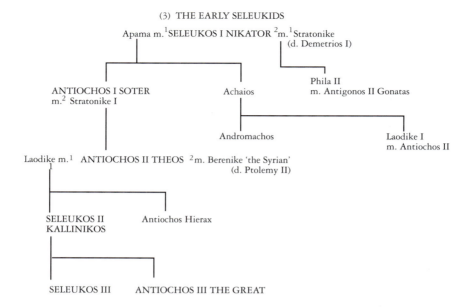

Figure A.3   The early Seleukids

FURTHER READING

After sections on general works and sources, Further Reading is arranged by numbered sections corresponding to the subjects of Chapters 1–10. Except under 'General' and 'Sources', the emphasis is first upon introductory and general works on a topic, then on specialized treatments not cited in the notes. Publication details are abbreviated; full details may be found in the Bibliography.

GENERAL

The best general synthesis of recent times, though chiefly devoted to social and cultural themes down to 146 BC, is Préaux, *Le Monde hellénistique*, unfortunately not translated into English; it has very full bibliographies (at i. 13–76). The best in English is Walbank, *The Hellenistic World*, which is a reliable guide but takes a rather more materialist historical approach than the present work and covers considerably less ground; like Préaux, its emphasis is pre-146.

J. Ferguson's readable *Heritage of Hellenism* gives an inspiring though somewhat idealized picture. The cultural chapters of Tarn and Griffith, *Hellenistic Civilisation*[3], are still useful and interesting, assembling a wide range of information in a small compass. Green's *Alexander to Actium* is a massively documented and illustrated compendium, but its interpretations are often eccentric (see various critical reviews, e.g. those by Austin, Shipley, and Potter cited in the Bibliography). Some of the ideas in the present work are foreshadowed in Shipley's review, and in Parkins and Shipley, 'Greek kings and Roman emperors'.

Companion volumes in the same series as the present work provide excellent introductions to adjacent periods and regions: see Cornell, *Beginnings of Rome*; Hornblower, *Greek World 479–323 BC*; Goodman, *The Roman World*; and Kuhrt, *Ancient Near East*.

Until recently, specialized works tended to be massive and not in English, but some may still be consulted with profit and are cited in later sections. Pride of place must go to Rostovtzeff, *Social and Economic History of the Hellenistic World*, though his modernizing approach should be borne in mind.

The *Cambridge Ancient History* deserves special mention, though it tends to conceal the primary evidence. In the second edition, *CAH*[2] vii. 1, *The Hellenistic World* (ed. Walbank *et al.*), covers the first half of the period and key topics for the whole. The studies are mostly well related to one another, but tend to treat political history and culture separately and to underplay the latter, though Davies's masterly chapter on culture, society, and economy is an outstanding exception. See also the chapters by Garlan (warfare), Heinen (Syrian wars, Asia Minor), G. E. R. Lloyd (science), Meister (Agathokles), Musti (Syria and Seleukids), Thompson (agriculture),

407

Turner (Egypt; somewhat general), Will (political history of the Successors, two chapters), Winter (buildings and town planning), and especially Walbank (four chapters on sources, monarchy, and Macedonian–Greek history). All the above chapters are listed in the Bibliography. Ling's *Plates* volume forms an excellent companion, superbly integrating monuments, artefacts, and historical essays.

CAH^2 vii. 2, *The rise of Rome* (ed. Walbank *et al.*), contains a good chapter by Franke on Pyrrhos. CAH^2 viii, *Rome and the Mediterranean* (ed. Astin *et al.*), contains key chapters, notably by Derow (final stages of Roman conquest), Errington (Rome's involvement from 229 to 188; two chapters), Habicht (later Seleukids and Roman imperialism), Narain (Baktria and India), and Rawson (hellenization of Rome). CAH^2 ix (ed. Crook *et al.*), on the late Republic, includes chapters by Hind (Mithridates), Rajak (Jews under Hasmonean rule, A. N. Sherwin-White (Pompey in the east), and esp. D. J. Thompson (later Ptolemies). Each volume contains vast bibliographies, date tables, and family trees.

For the fourth-century background, including Alexander, CAH^2 vi, *The Fourth Century* (ed. D. M. Lewis *et al.*), is invaluable; see especially the essays by Austin (society and economy), Bosworth (Alexander, two chapters), J. R. Ellis (Macedonia, two chapters), Garlan (warfare), Hammond (Illyria and NW Greece), Hornblower (sources; Asia Minor; Persia; general epilogue), A. B. Lloyd (Egypt), G. E. R. Lloyd (medicine), Maier (Cyprus and Phoenicia to 311), Ostwald and Lynch (philosophy), Picard (Carthage to 308), Pollitt (classical and hellenistic art), Purcell (S. Italy), Rhodes (the *polis* and alternatives), Stolper (Mesopotamia to 330), and Westlake (Sicily to 330).

The first edition of *CAH* is still useful, particularly the masterly chapters of Holleaux, Rostovtzeff, and Tarn, as well as other sections on cultural aspects, which are less well covered in CAH^2. CAH^1 vi, on the fourth century (ed. Bury *et al.*), contains three chapters by Tarn on Alexander and Greece. CAH^1 vii, on the hellenistic monarchies and Rome (ed. Cook *et al.*), includes Barber (literature), W. S. Ferguson (philosophy), W. H. S. Jones and T. L. Heath (science), and the outstanding studies of history and institutions by Holleaux (Rome and NW Greece), Rostovtzeff (Egypt, Syria), and Tarn (Macedonia; Greece; the new kingdoms; Egyptian–Macedonian relations). In CAH^1 viii, on Rome and the Mediterranean (ed. Cook *et al.*), are three excellent essays by Holleaux (Rome against Antiochos and Philip V) and three by Rostovtzeff (Bosporan kingdom; Pergamon; Rhodes, Delos, and trade). CAH^1 ix includes Tarn on Parthia.

Recent years have seen a steady increase in the number of accessible papers in English, notably in the excellent collections edited by Bulloch *et al.*, *Images and Ideologies*; Green, *Hellenistic History and Culture*; and Cartledge *et al.*, *Hellenistic Constructs*, a volume in honour of Walbank. All three are published or co-published in the increasingly authoritative 'Hellenistic Culture and Society' series from Berkeley. For others in the series, see the Bibliography entries for Ager, Annas, Bar-Kochva, Billows, Bracht Branham and Goulet-Cazé, Burton, Canfora (less good), Clauss, G. M. Cohen, Dillon and Long, Eckstein, Errington, Green (three works), Kallet-Marx, Mikalson, Reger, Rigsby, Stewart, and Tracy (*bis*); I have not yet seen those by S. D. Cohen, Feldman, Gruen, Gutzwiller, Holt, or Scholten. The series includes parallel editions of Kuhrt and Sherwin-White, *Hellenism*, and Sherwin-White and Kuhrt, *Samarkhand to Sardis*.

Further important work appears in 'Studies in Hellenistic Civilization' series from Aarhus, comprising (to date) five collective volumes of papers in English, edited by Bilde and others, and monographs by Engberg-Pedersen, Gabrielsen, and I. Nielsen. 'Hellenismestudier', also from Aarhus but in Danish, includes *Aspekter af hellenismen*, *Fra Xenophon til Augustus*, and works by Østergård, Tortzen, Zahle *et al.*,

Engberg-Pedersen (three edited volumes), and Bilde (two edited volumes); also Briant, *Alexander den Store*. 'Studi ellenistici' from Pisa, by Virgilio and others (see Bibliography, also under Campanile, Del Monte, and Franco), contains good papers, mainly in Italian.

R. W. Wallace and E. M. Harris (eds), *Transitions to Empire* (Festschrift for Badian), contains a wide range of essays on the period down to 146 BC.

Besides works cited in the notes to Chapter 1, additional studies of modern scholars' contributions include Finley, 'The historical tradition: the *Contributi* of Arnaldo Momigliano'; Reinhold, 'Historian of the classic world: a critique of Rostovtzeff'.

1 APPROACHES AND SOURCES

(a) Translations

Among collections of translated sources the most brilliant is Austin's *Hellenistic World*, which has extensive notes and covers historical sources as well as inscriptions and papyri but lacks a detailed table of contents. Bagnall and Derow, *Greek Historical Documents: The Hellenistic Period*, is less ambitious but stronger on papyri.

The Cambridge series 'Translated Documents of Greece and Rome' is invaluable. Harding's *From the End of the Peloponnesian War to the Battle of Ipsus* and Burstein's *Hellenistic Age* include fragmentary historians not available elsewhere; later events are covered by Sherk's *Rome and the Greek East to the Death of Augustus* and *The Roman Empire: Augustus to Hadrian*, the former based on Sherk's *Roman Documents from the Greek East*, which does not include translations.

In works on hellenistic history, inscriptions in older collections are customarily cited by the numbers they bear in those works (in which they are often untranslated and sometimes have commentaries in Latin): e.g. *Choix*, *IG*, *OGIS*, and *Syll.*[3]; note also 'Tod'. In the present work, where there is such a reference, it is given in the text. One of the earliest works to translate all documents is still a standard text: Welles, *Royal Correspondence*. None of the above collections attempts to illustrate literature, philosophy, or science.

Penguin Classics translations (not normally listed in the Bibliography; published by Penguin Books in Harmondsworth or, more recently, London), include (from Greek authors), the *Alexander Romance*, Apollonios of Rhodes, Aristotle's *Athenian Constitution*, *Politics*, and philosophical works, Arrian, *Hippocratic Works* (small selection), Josephus (*Jewish War*), Pausanias (with extensive topographical and archaeological notes by P. Levi), Polybios (extensive selection, introduced by Walbank), Plutarch (selections of lives including *The Age of Alexander*, which contains *Agesilaos*, *Demosthenes*, *Phokion*, *Alexander*, *Demetrios*, and *Pyrrhos*; Talbert's selection in *Plutarch on Sparta* includes *Agis*, *Kleomenes*, and other works), Theokritos, the *Greek Anthology* (selection), Xenophon (including *Oikonomikos* or *The Estate Manager*), and many others. An older volume containing Menander and Theophrastos's *Characters* can still be found in libraries. Latin authors include Apuleius, Caesar, Cicero (various works), Curtius Rufus, Livy (esp. *Rome and the East*), Pliny the Elder (limited selection only), and Tacitus.

The Loeb Classical Library (not normally listed in the Bibliography; Cambridge, MA: Harvard UP) includes most of the major classical works. Greek Loebs not covered in Penguin translations include Aeneas Tacticus, Appian, Aristotle (many works), Athenaeus, Cassius Dio, Diodoros, Diogenes Laërtios, Galen *On the Natural Faculties*, Herodas (new edition by Cunningham), Hippocrates (many works),

Isokrates, Josephus, Kallimachos, Lykophron, Manethon, Menander, Plutarch (*Lives* and *Moralia*), Polybios (complete), Ptolemy's *Tetrabiblos*, Strabo, and Theophrastos (*Characters* and botanical works); among Latin authors Cato on agriculture, Celsus, Columella, Nepos, Pliny the Elder, Varro on agriculture, and Vitruvius. Particularly good is Brunt's revised edition of Arrian, entitled *History of Alexander and Indica*. Mathematical texts (including some on engineering and astronomy) are made available by Thomas, *Greek Mathematical Works*, i–ii.

Some translations are listed in the next section.

(b) Discussions

Methodological guides to evidence include (on general issues) Davies, 'Documents and "documents" '; Hornblower, 'Sources and their uses'; Walbank, 'Sources for the period'; (on historians) Hornblower (ed.), *Greek Historiography*; (on coins) Crawford, 'Numismatics'; Howgego, *Ancient History from Coins*; (on epigraphy) Millar, 'Epigraphy'; Woodhead, *Study of Greek Inscriptions*; (on papyri) Bagnall, *Reading Papyri*; Turner, *Greek Papyri*.

Tracy's detailed works *Athenian Democracy in Transition* and *Attic Letter-cutters* have significantly advanced the study of the Athenian inscriptions. Welles, *RC*, includes discussion of epigraphic styles and a table of letter-forms (not always included in reprints).

On coinage, see also Carradice and Price, *Coinage in the Greek World*; Davis and Kraay, *The Hellenistic Kingdoms*; Fleischer, 'Hellenistic royal iconography on coins'; Grunauer-von Hoerschelmann, *Die Münzprägung der Lakedaimonier*; Guillaume, *Graeco-Bactrian and Indian Coins from Afghanistan*; Mørkholm, *Early Hellenistic Coinage*; Parise, 'Le emissioni monetarie'; Warren, 'The autonomous bronze coinage of Sicyon' (and other papers).

Easterling and Knox (eds), *Cambridge History of Classical Literature* (*CHCL*), contains introductory essays on most authors, though the new *Oxford Classical Dictionary* (*OCD*³) is more up to date. On historical sources, see also (on Alexander legends) Stoneman, *The Greek Alexander Romance* and *Legends of Alexander the Great*; Schwarz (ed.), *Miriam's Tambourine*; (on Appian) Brodersen, *Appians Abriss der Seleukidengeschichte* and *Appians Antioche*; (on Berossos) Burstein, *The Babyloniaca of Berossus*; Kuhrt, 'Berossus' Babyloniaka'; (on Hekataios) Murray, 'Hecataeus of Abdera and pharaonic kingship'; Stern and Murray, 'Hecataeus of Abdera and Theophrastus'; (on Justin/Trogus) the first modern English translation of Justin's epitome of Pompeius Trogus (Yardley, introduced by Develin); the translation and commentary by Watson and Miller covers books 7–12 on Macedonia before and under Alexander, that by Yardley and Heckel books 11–12 on Alexander; (on Livy) Briscoe's *Commentary* on books 31–3 and 34–7; Walsh's five volumes and translations covering books 36–40; (on Pausanias) Arafat, *Pausanias' Greece*; Reverdin and Grange (eds), *Pausanias historien*, including papers by Alcock, Ameling, and Lafond; Habicht, *Pausanias' Guide to Classical Greece* (*Pausanias und seine Beschreibung Griechenlands*); (on Polybios) Derow, 'Historical explanation' and 'Polybius (205?–125? BC)'; Eckstein, *Moral Vision in the Histories of Polybius* and 'Physis and nomos'; Walbank's *Historical Commentary* above all, also his *Polybius*, 'Polybius and Rome's eastern policy', and introduction to the Penguin Classics edition; (on Strabo) Baladié, *Le Péloponnèse de Strabon*; Clarke, 'In search of the author'; (on Timaios) Momigliano, 'Athens in the third century BC'.

Recent studies of non-historiographical authors include (on Apollonios of Rhodes) Campbell, *Echoes and Imitations of Early Epic in Apollonius Rhodius* and *A Commentary on Apollonius Rhodius, Argonautica III 1–471*; Clauss, *The Best of the*

Argonauts; Green, *The Argonautika* (trans., comm.) and '"These fragments have I shored against my ruins"'; Hunter, *Apollonius of Rhodes, Argonautica, Book III* and *The Argonautica of Apollonius: Literary Studies*; (on Herodas) Cunningham, *Herodas: Mimiambi*; (on Kallimachos) Bulloch, 'The future of a hellenistic illusion' and *Callimachus: The Fifth Hymn*; Hopkinson, *Callimachus: Hymn to Demeter*; Lehnus, *Bibliografia callimachea*; (on Lykophron) Fusillo *et al.*, *Licofrone, Alessandra*; (on Moschos) Campbell, *Moschus of Syracuse: Europa*; (on Posidonius) the new edition of the fragments by Edelstein and Kidd (vol. i), Kidd (vol. ii. 1–2); (on Ptolemy) Toomer, *Ptolemy's Almagest*, trans. and notes; (on Theokritos) Burton, *Theocritus's Urban Mimes*; Levi, 'People in a landscape', with Halperin, 'Response'; (on Theophrastos) Fortenbaugh *et al.* (eds), *Theophrastus of Eresus: On his Life and Work*; Fortenbaugh and Sharples (eds), *Theophrastean Studies on Natural Science*; Fraser, 'The world of Theophrastus'; Scarborough, 'The pharmacology of sacred plants, herbs, and roots'; Sharples, *Theophrastus of Eresus: Sources ... on Biology*; Ussher, *The Characters of Theophrastus*; (on Vitruvius) Gros *et al.*, *Vitruvio* (trans., comm.); M. H. Morgan (trans.)

A standard collection of poetry, in Greek with English commentary, is Hopkinson, *Hellenistic Anthology*.

(c) Archaeology

On archaeology, there is no general handbook or survey, but see Ling's *Plates* for an excellent selection of photographs and commentaries. Rostovtzeff, *SEHHW*, makes continual references to the results of archaeology as known in his day and includes a wide range of photographs of artefacts (both representational and functional) and coins. Green, *Alexander to Actium*, is lavishly illustrated though the pictures are not made relevant to the text. For representative ceramic groups see Edwards, *Corinthian Hellenistic Pottery*; Hausmann, *Hellenistische Keramik* (on Olympia); Rotroff, *Hellenistic Pottery* (two volumes). Many studies of local pottery groups (mainly in modern Greeek) are published in the four *Hellenistic Pottery Conference* volumes. Many other reports on Corinth and the Athenian Agora are contained in *Hesperia* and in the two series of relevant volumes published by the American School of Classical Studies at Athens. Other site reports are cited in the notes, particularly to Chapters 3–4, 6, and 8.

On field survey, refer first to works cited in the notes to Chapters 1 and 3, then to Alcock *et al.*, 'Intensive survey, agricultural practice and the classical landscape of Greece' and Alcock, 'Surveying the peripheries of the hellenistic world'; Bintliff and Snodgrass, 'Mediterranean survey and the city' and 'Off-site pottery distributions'; Macready and Thompson, *Archaeological Field Survey*; Moody *et al.* 'Surveying poleis'. Alcock's *Graecia Capta* develops ideas which appeared in earlier papers, such as 'Archaeology and imperialism' and 'Roman imperialism in the Greek landscape'.

Many surveys of particular areas are cited in the notes to Chapter 1. Others not mentioned there include (for Greece north of the Isthmus) Lohmann, 'Atene (Ἀτήνη), eine attische Landgemeinde klassischer Zeit', 'Landleben im klassischen Attika', and *Atene* (his conclusions about Attic settlement patterns are not, to my mind, convincing); Munn and Zimmermann Munn, 'Studies on the Attic–Boiotian frontier'; Bintliff, 'The Boeotia Survey, central Greece' and 'The Roman countryside in central Greece'; Keller, 'Archaeological survey in southern Euboea, Greece'; Fossey, *The Ancient Topography of Opountian Lokris*; (for the Peloponnese) Alcock, 'Urban survey and the polis of Phlius'; Davis *et al.* and Zangger *et al.*, 'The Pylos Regional Archaeological Project'; Lloyd *et al.*, 'The Megalopolis survey in Arcadia';

411

McDonald *et al.*, *The Minnesota Messenia Expedition*; papers in Nielsen and Roy, *Defining Arkadia*; Roy *et al.*, 'Tribe and polis in the chora at Megalopolis' and 'Megalopolis under the Roman empire'; Van Andel *et al.*, *Beyond the Acropolis*; Wright *et al.*, 'The Nemea Valley Archaeological Project'; (for Asia) Marchese, *The Lower Maeander Flood Plain*; Bartl and Hauser, *Continuity and Change in Northern Mesopotamia from the Hellenistic to the Early Islamic Period*.

In addition to regional archaeological-historical studies cited in the notes (e.g. works by Buck, Figueira, Reger, Shipley, and Sherwin-White), see Jost, 'Sanctuaries and civic space in Arkadia'; Tomlinson, *Argos and the Argolid*; Ragone, 'Il santuario di Apollo Grynios'. On ancient attitudes to landscape and the environment, see papers in Shipley and Salmon (eds), *Human Landscapes in Classical Antiquity*.

(d) Art

Among recent studies of sculpture, the works of Pollitt, Robertson, Ridgway, Smith, and A. Stewart listed in the Bibliography (some also cited in the notes) offer a good foundation and include many references to further studies. On Greek art in western Asia, see the various works of Colledge. Brief, though specialized, treatments of regional styles in sculpture are to be found in Horn, *Hellenistische Bildwerke auf Samos*; Palagia and Coulson, *Regional Schools in Hellenistic Sculpture* (see especially Fullerton on the chronology of Attic styles, Jockey on Delos, Marszal on Pergamon, and Mattusch on Rhodes, the last two arguing against the existence of local 'schools').

On art generally, in addition to works cited in the notes (notably to Chapter 3), see Reeder (ed.), *Hellenistic Art in the Walters Art Gallery*; (on royal portraits) Brown, *Royal Portraits*; Fleischer, *Studien zur seleukidischen Kunst*, i; (on particular places) *Alexandria and Alexandrianism*; Connelly, *Votive Sculpture of Hellenistic Cyprus*; Fehr, 'Society, consanguinity and the fertility of women', on the Pergamon altar; Hannestad and Potts, 'Temple architecture in the Seleucid kingdom'; Houby-Nielsen, '"Burial language"' and 'Revival of archaic funerary practices'; Palagia, 'Classical encounters'; (on architecture) Lauter, *Architektur des Hellenismus*; Macready and Thompson (eds), *Roman Architecture in the Greek World*; Nielsen, 'From periphery to centre: Italic palaces'; Walker, 'Roman nymphaea'; (on particular genres) Parlasca, *Syrische Grabreliefs*; Plantzos, 'Hellenistic cameos'; Rice, 'The glorious dead: commemoration of the fallen and portrayal of victory'; D. B. Thompson, *Ptolemaic Oinochoai and Portraits in Faience*.

On cities and their monuments, see also section 3 (a) below.

2 ALEXANDER AND HIS SUCCESSORS TO 276 BC

(a) Philip and Alexander

On Alexander, Arrian is better than any modern writer as a place to start. On Philip and Alexander, in addition to works cited under 'General' (above), see the many works by Bosworth and Hammond listed in the Bibliography; also Hornblower, *Greek World*; Adams and Borza (eds), *Philip II, Alexander the Great and the Macedonian Heritage*. Short introductions to Alexander include Briant, *Alexander the Great* (*Alexandre le Grand, Alexander den Store*); Hamilton, *Alexander the Great*; Rice, *Alexander the Great*; Stoneman, *Alexander the Great*. Refer next to works cited in the notes to Chapter 2.

More specialized studies include (on Philip) Hammond and Griffith, *History of Macedonia*, ii; Cawkwell, *Philip of Macedon*; Ellis, *Philip II*; (on Alexander) Briant, 'Conquête territoriale et stratégie idéologique'; Hammond and Walbank, *History of Macedonia*, iii, authoritative; Carlsen *et al.*, *Alexander the Great: Reality and Myth*. On specific aspects see Austin, 'Alexander and the Macedonian invasion of Asia'; Cawkwell, 'The deification of Alexander the Great'; Lane Fox, 'Text and image'; Worthington, 'The Harpalus affair'. For Alexander's aims see also Hornblower, 'Epilogue'.

(b) The Successors

Primary sources include Diodoros and Plutarch's lives of *Eumenes*, *Demetrios*, and *Pyrrhos*.

For narrative, begin with Will, *Histoire politique* or his chapters in *CAH*² vii. 1; or with Rostovtzeff, *SEHHW* i. 1–43. Refer next to works cited in the notes to Chapter 2, both on 323–281 generally and on figures such as Eumenes, Cassander, and Lysimachos.

For more specialized studies see (generally) Billows, *Kings and Colonists*; G. M. Cohen, 'The Diadochoi and the new monarchies'; (on Antigonos I) Billows, *Antigonos the One-eyed and the Creation of the Hellenistic State*, with Derow's critical review; Briant, *Antigone le Borgne*; (on Antipater) Baynham, 'Antipater'; (on Lysimachos) Franco, 'Lisimaco e Atene' and *Il regno di Lisimaco*; Hatzopoulos, *Une donation du roi Lysimaque*; Landucci Gattinoni, *Lisimaco di Tracia*; (on Seleukos) Grainger, *Seleukos Nikator*; Mehl, *Seleukos Nikator und sein Reich*, i. On Macedonia see also section 4 below.

3 KINGS AND CITIES

(a) Cities

Aristotle's *Politics* (or 'Civics') is important but is not necessarily to be taken as a description of the actual state of the Greek *polis* in the late fourth century. Austin, Burstein, and Bagnall and Derow collect a wide range of documents, which are probably the best starting-point; modern works tend to be specialized. Refer next to works cited in the notes to Chapter 3.

For weightier reading, Davies's chapter in *CAH*² vii. 1 is a key essay, while Gauthier's 'Les cités hellénistiques' in *CPC Acts 1* (as distinct from his similarly titled 1984 essay, though that is relevant) is a marvellously sympathetic sketch encapsulating much recent rethinking. Generally, the volumes of the Copenhagen Polis Centre (*CPC Acts* and *CPC Papers*), though focused pre-300 BC, are fundamental to debates about the *polis* (see Bibliography under M. H. Hansen, T. H. Nielsen, and Whitehead). Note also Gruen, 'The polis in the Hellenistic world'.

Gauthier's *Les Cités grecques et leurs bienfaiteurs* is partly a response to Veyne, *Le Pain et le cirque* (*Bread and Circuses*). In addition to his paper in *Acts 1*, Gauthier surveys *polis* institutions in 'Les cités hellénistiques: épigraphie et histoire des institutions et des régimes politiques' and 'Quorum et participation civique'.

See also Hansen, *Demography and Democracy*; Murray and Price (eds), *The Greek City: From Homer to Alexander*; Raaflaub, 'City-state, territory, and empire'.

Ehrenberg, *Greek State*², is still useful but exaggerates the change from classical to hellenistic. Rostovtzeff, *SEHHW* i. 189–247, surveys the cities of Greece and the islands in the third century. A. H. M. Jones, *The Greek City: From Alexander to Justinian*, usefully crosses the Greek–Roman chronological divide and contains a wealth of detail, though now somewhat outdated.

On federalism, see Larsen, *Greek Federal States* and *Representative Government*; Rhodes, *Greek City States*; Walbank, 'Were there Greek federal states?'.

On socio-economic change, important papers include Fuks, 'Patterns and types of social-economic revolution in Greece'; and still Tarn, 'The social question in the third century'. Also important are McKechnie, *Outsiders*; Ogden, *Greek Bastardy*.

On changes under the influence of Roman power, see also Geagan, 'The Athenian elite'. In addition to works cited in the notes (particularly in Chapter 3), on city foundations see G. M. Cohen, 'Colonization and population transfer'; Tscherikower, *Die hellenistischen Städtegründungen*.

On cities other than Athens and Sparta (for which see section 4), see also Bilde (ed.), *Rhodos i hellenistisk tid* (which I have not seen); Figueira, *Excursions in Epichoric History*, including 'Notes on hellenistic Aigina'; Lanzillotta, *Paro dall'età arcaica all'età ellenistica*. On the Cyclades, see Nigdelis, Πολίτευμα και κοινωνία των πόλεων των Κυκλάδων; Reger, 'Athens and Tenos' and 'The political history of the Kyklades: 260–200 BC'. On the Aitolians, I have not yet seen Scholten, *The Politics of Plunder*.

On civic monuments, besides specialized works cited in the notes (esp. to Chapter 3), see Lawrence, *Greek Architecture*; Travlos, *Pictorial Dictionary*; Wycherley, *Stones of Athens*. Details of the Pergamon excavations are in the 'Altertümer von Pergamon' volumes of the Deutsches Archäologisches Institut (Berlin: de Gruyter; not listed in Bibliography).

On town planning, see Di Vita, 'Town planning in the Greek colonies of Sicily'; Hoepfner (ed.), *Geschichte des Wohnens*, i; Hoepfner and Schwandner, *Haus und Stadt* (especially ch. 9, pp. 235–56, on Alexandria, and sections on other hellenistic towns); Owens, *The City*; Winter, 'Building and townplanning', brief; Wycherley, *How the Greeks Built Cities*.

On foreign judges, a fundamental study is L. Robert, 'Les juges étrangers'. On education and sport, see Moretti, 'La scuola' and 'Lo sport'.

On the western Greeks, besides works cited under 'General' (above), see Carter, 'Sicily and Magna Graecia', with good illustrations; Marcone, 'La Sicilia fra ellenismo e romanizzazione'.

(b) Economies

Again, the best primary sources are translated documents in the sourcebooks. Refer next to works cited in the notes to Chapter 3, particularly the sections on *asylia*, piracy, and *euergesia*; also Chapter 2 on demographic change. Also consult the Indexes.

Fundamental works include Davies, 'Cultural, social, and economic features'; Rostovtzeff, *SEHHW* (though he tends to see development in proto-capitalist terms; see esp. ii. 1026–301 for a general economic survey); and chapters in *CAH*[2] vii. 1 (see above or in Bibliography).

On the ancient economy generally, see Finley, *Ancient Economy*[2] (with responses such as D. J. Mattingly, 'Beyond belief?' and papers in Garnsey *et al*., *Trade in the Ancient Economy* and Parkins and Smith (eds), *Trade, Traders and the Ancient City*. Davies develops his views interestingly in 'Finance, administration, and *Realpolitik*' and 'Ancient economies: models and muddles'.

On the agricultural economy, see Burford, 'Greek agriculture in the classical period'; Osborne, 'Building and residence on the land'; D. J. Thompson, 'Agriculture'; White, *Greek and Roman Farming*.

See also Moretti *et al.*, *La società ellenistica*, iv. 2, containing chapters on finance, food supply, and banking by Moretti, Bogaert, and Parise, listed in the Bibliography; Bilde, *Centre and Periphery*, with papers by Alcock, Buraselis, Cunliffe, Engberg-Pedersen, Gabrielsen, Guldager Bilde, Hannestad, Invernizzi, Kaul, I. Nielsen, Randsborg, Shipley, and Skydsgaard; Foraboschi, 'Archeologia della cultura economica'; Petropoulou, *Beiträge zur Wirtschafts- und Gesellschaftsgeschichte Kretas*.

(c) Gender and the family

Menander's comedies (some fragmentary) are a key source, and Plutarch's *Demetrios* contains a version of the story of Stratonike. Other sources are cited in the text.

On the roles and identities of women, the works of Pomeroy listed in the Bibliography give a wide introduction. The classic study of Macurdy, *Hellenistic Queens*, is worth consulting. Refer next to works cited in the notes (including notes to Chapters 4 and 8), and consult the Indexes.

For other specific studies, see (on the construction of masculinity) Foxhall and Salmon (eds), *Thinking Men* and *When Men Were Men*, the former including Heap, 'Understanding the men in Menander'; (on the construction of the female) Dean-Jones, 'The cultural construct of the female body in classical Greek science'; Henry, 'The edible woman: Athenaeus's concept of the pornographic'; (on women's roles) Archer, 'The role of Jewish women in ... Palestine' and *Her Price is Beyond Rubies*; Pomeroy, *Women in Hellenistic Egypt* and 'Women in Roman Egypt'; (on the family) see also Pomeroy, 'Infanticide in hellenistic Greece', *Families in Classical and Hellenistic Greece* and 'Family values: the uses of the past'; Salmenkivi, 'Family life in the comedies of Menander'; (on poetic images) Alan Cameron, 'Two mistresses of Ptolemy Philadelphus'.

On royal women, besides Macurdy and works cited in the notes, see (on Ptolemaic women) Becher, *Das Bild der Kleopatra in der griechischen und lateinischen Literatur*; Burstein, 'Arsinoe II Philadelphus: a revisionist view'; Hauben, 'Arsinoé et la politique extérieure de l'Égypte'; Hughes-Hallett, *Cleopatra*; D. B. Thompson, 'More Ptolemaic queens'; (on other dynasties) Carney, 'Olympias and the image of the virago' and 'Olympias, Adea Eurydice, and the end of the Argead dynasty'; H. Müller, 'Königin Stratonike, Tochter des Königs Ariarathes'; Wehrli, 'Phila, fille d'Antipater'.

(d) Kingship

For sources, see Chapter 3. Good starting-points are Préaux, *Monde hellénistique*; Walbank, 'Monarchies'. Refer next to works cited in the notes.

For additional specialized work, Bilde, *Kingship*, is an important collection of essays; see esp. Gruen, 'Hellenistic kingship: puzzles, problems, and possibilities'; Murray, 'Hellenistic royal symposia'.

For other aspects see (on the king's role as warrior) Austin, 'Hellenistic kings, war, and the economy'; Gehrke, 'Der siegreiche König'; Gundlach and Weber (eds), *Legitimation und Funktion des Herrschers*; (on ceremonial of other periods including Mesopotamia earlier) Cannadine and Price (eds), *Rituals of Royalty*; (on dynastic alliances) Seibert, *Historische Beiträge zu den dynastischen Verbindungen*; (on cultural roles) R. R. R. Smith, 'Kings and philosophers'; von Hesberg, 'Temporäre Bilder oder die Grenzen der Kunst'; (on titles) Muccioli, 'Considerazioni generali sull'epiteto *Φιλάδελφος*'; (on Friends) the works of Herman listed in the Bibliography, and others cited in the notes.

See also sections 1 (d) and 2 above.

4 MACEDONIA AND GREECE

For primary sources, see the text. In addition to works cited under 'General' (above) and under Chapter 2 (a), see, above all, Hammond and Walbank, *History of Macedonia*, iii; Hammond, *Macedonian State*; and the excellent studies by Hatzopoulos listed in the Bibliography. Errington, *History of Macedonia* (*Geschichte Makedoniens*) is authoritative but limited to political history. On the history of Athens, Habicht, *Athens from Alexander to Antony* is accessible though detailed. Refer next to works cited in the Notes (also Notes to Chapter 2 and 10).

For additional specialized work, see (on Macedonian imperialism in Greece, Briscoe, 'The Antigonids and the Greek states, 276–196 BC'; (on archaeology, illustrated) Tomlinson, 'Macedonia, Greece and the Cyclades'; (on Antigonos Gonatas) Cioccolo, 'Enigmi dell' *ἦθος*'; (on Athens) the many works of Habicht listed in the Bibliography; the classic work of W. S. Ferguson, *Hellenistic Athens*, still valuable; Hoff, 'Laceratae Athenae'; Lambert, *The Phratries of Athens*; papers in Frösén, *Early Hellenistic Athens*, especially Lönnqvist on the Athenian money market, and Hakkarainen on private wealth; H. Mattingly, 'Athens between Rome and the kings'; Mikalson, *Sacred and Civil Calendar*; Reger, 'Athens and Tenos'; (on Sparta) Badian, 'Agis III: revisions and reflections'; David, *Sparta between Empire and Revolution*; Forrest, *History of Sparta*; Oliva, *Sparta and her Social Problems*; Shimron, *Late Sparta*; papers in Cavanagh and Walker, *Sparta in Laconia* (especially Cartledge on the city and its territory; Mee and Cavanagh on recent fieldwork; Raftopoulou on recent work in the town, which was not planned before the Roman period; and Karafotias on Nabis and Crete).

On Macedonia under the Successors, see also section 2 above. On federalism, see 3 (a) above. The conference volumes *Ancient Macedonia 1* to *5* contain many valuable studies.

5 RELIGION AND PHILOSOPHY

(a) Religion

On ancient religion generally see Beard and North (eds), *Pagan Priests*; Easterling and Muir (eds), *Greek Religion and Society*; Bruit Zaidman and Schmitt Pantel, *Religion in the Ancient Greek City*. Refer next to works cited in the notes to Chapters 3 and 5.

For more specialized studies, see (on hellenistic religion generally) Mikalson, *Religion in Hellenistic Athens*; Pakkanen, *Interpreting Early Hellenistic Religion*; Z. Stewart, 'La religione'; (on *polis* religion) Alcock, 'Tomb cult and the post-classical polis' and 'The heroic past in a hellenistic present'; Jost, 'Sanctuaries and civic space in Arkadia'; Leiwo, 'Religion, or other reasons?'; Schmitt Pantel, 'Public feasts'; (on magic) Faraone and Obbink (eds), *Magika Hiera*; Gordon, 'Quaedam veritatis umbrae'; D. B. Martin, 'Hellenistic superstition'; (on ruler-cult) Price, *Rituals and Power*; Préaux, *Monde hellénistique*; Walbank, 'Monarchies'; (on Asklepios) Aleshire, *The Athenian Asklepieion*; ead. and Matthaiou, 'Νέο θραῦσμα τῆς IG II^2 1534' or 'A new fragment of *IG* II^2 1534A and B'; (on other aspects) Sfameni Gasparro, 'Daimon and tuchê'; Teixidor, *The Pagan God*; van Straten, 'Images of gods and men'; (on non-Greek religions) Hjerrild, 'The survival and modification of Zoroastrianism in Seleucid times'; Waldmann, *Der kommagenische Mazdaismus*.

(b) Philosophy

Diogenes Laërtios is a late but crucial source of anecdotes and doctrines, and devotes a striking amount of space to the hellenistic thinkers. For other primary sources, see Chapter 5.

The works of Long, listed in the Bibliography, provide good introductions; also Long and Sedley, *The Hellenistic Philosophers* (translations in vol. i); Sharples, *Stoics, Epicureans and Sceptics*. Refer next to works cited in the Notes.

More detailed treatments include Baldry, *The Unity of Mankind in Greek Thought*, somewhat outdated; Bracht Branham and Goulet-Cazé, *The Cynics*; Dillon and Long, *The Question of 'Eclecticism': Studies in Later Greek Philosophy*; Korhonen, 'Self-concept and public image'; R. R. R. Smith, 'Kings and philosophers'; (on Stoicism) Garnsey, 'The middle Stoics and slavery'; Schofield, *The Stoic Idea of the City*.

More technical studies include Annas, *Hellenistic Philosophy of Mind*; Annas and Barnes, *The Modes of Scepticism*; Bodei Giglioni, 'Una leggenda sulle origini dell'ellenismo: Alessandro e i cinici'; Engberg-Pedersen, *The Stoic Theory of Oikeiosis*; Gill, 'Panaetius on the virtue of being yourself', with Annas, 'Response'; Inwood, *Ethics and Human Action in Early Stoicism*; Inwood and Gerson, *Hellenistic Philosophy: Introductory Readings*.

6 PTOLEMAIC EGYPT

The history of Ptolemaic Egypt inevitably tends to be studied in different publications from the rest of the Greek world after Alexander, and sometimes seems daunting. There could be few better introductions, however, than simply to read through the documents (mainly papyri) translated by Austin, Burstein, or Bagnall and Derow. See also Bagnall, *Reading Papyri*; Turner, *Greek Papyri*.

General introductions are found in Bowman, *Egypt after the Pharaohs*, and James, *Introduction to Ancient Egypt*. Turner's chapter in *CAH²* vii. 1 is accessible though general. N. Lewis's *Greeks in Ptolemaic Egypt* is highly readable and foregrounds specific documents (translated). Kuhrt, *Ancient Near East*, gives background.

Fundamental studies are those of Bouché-Leclercq, *Histoire des Lagides*; Préaux, *Monde hellénistique* and *L'Économie royale*; and Rostovtzeff, *SEHHW* i. 255–422, but their views are now in need of revision. The series of studies by D. J. Thompson (earlier D. J. Crawford), however, embodies a new perspective based on the study of papyri (for the papyrological work itself, see the many publications of Clarysse, Pestman, and others listed in the Bibliography). For the archaeology and history see D. J. Thompson, 'The Ptolemaic kingdom' (with illustrations).

For more details of narrative history, see Will, *Histoire politique*, and the chapters by Will and Heinen, in *CAH²* vii. 1. Thompson's chronological chapter on the later Ptolemies in *CAH²* ix (a mainly Roman volume) should not be overlooked. McGing, 'Revolt', is a key paper with wider relevance than its title may suggest. On Alexandria, Fraser's monumental study is crucial though somewhat conservative in methodology. Bagnall, *Administration*, remains the starting-point for the overseas possessions. Refer next to works cited in the Notes.

See also the methodological essay of Bagnall, 'Decolonizing Ptolemaic Egypt'; Herz, 'Die frühen Ptolemaier bis 180 v.Chr.'. A fundamental work of reference is

Prosopographia Ptolemaica (see Bibliography, under Clarysse; Mooren and Swinnen; Peremans); also Peremans and van 't Dack, *Prosopographica*.

The works of A. E. Samuel (e.g. 'The Ptolemies and the ideology of kingship'; *From Athens to Alexandria*; *The Shifting Sands of History*) are important, if sometimes controversial. See also (on chronology) Samuel, *Ptolemaic Chronology*; Clarysse, 'A royal visit to Memphis and the end of the second Syrian war'; (on ethnic identity) Ambaglio, 'Tensioni etniche e sociali nella chora tolemaica'; Delia, ' "All army boots and uniforms?"; Goudriaan, *Ethnicity in Ptolemaic Egypt* and 'Ethnical strategies in Graeco-Roman Egypt'; (on foreign relations) Beyer-Rotthoff, *Untersuchungen zur Aussenpolitik Ptolemaios' III*; Buraselis, 'Ambivalent roles of centre and periphery'; Hauben, *Callicrates of Samos* and 'Arsinoé et la politique extérieure de l'Égypte'; (on the organization of the kingdom) Lavigne, *De epistates van het dorp*; Mooren, *Hiérarchie de cour*; Peremans, 'Les Lagides, les élites indigènes et la monarchie bicéphale'; (on revolts) Clarysse, 'Notes de prosopographie thébaine, 7'; Pestman, 'Harmachis et Anchmachis' and 'Haronnophris et Chaonnophris'; Vandorpe, 'The chronology of the reigns of Hurgonaphor and Chaonnophris'; (on literacy) Thompson, 'Language and literacy in early hellenistic Egypt'; (on the economy) Gara, 'Limiti strutturali dell'economia monetaria nell'Egitto tardo-tolemaico'; an interesting sidelight on production is offered by Chouliara-Raïos, *L'Abeille et le miel en Égypte d'après les papyrus grecs*; (on cults) Perpillou-Thomas, *Fêtes d'Égypte ptolémaïque et romaine*; D. J. Crawford, 'Ptolemy, Ptah and Apis in hellenistic Memphis'; (on Zenon and his work) Clarysse, 'Philadelphia and the Memphites in the Zenon archive'; Orrieux, *Les Papyrus de Zénon* and *Zénon de Caunos*.

7 LITERATURE AND SOCIAL IDENTITY

See first the works listed under 'General' and in section 1 (a–b) above. Refer next to works cited in the Notes to Chapters 1 and 7.

For further discussions see (on the social context) Engberg-Pedersen, 'The relationship between intellectual and political centres'; Thomas, *Literacy and Orality*; (on literary aspects) Gelzer, 'Transformations' and Parsons, 'Identities in diversity', with Henrichs, 'Response' to both; Handley, 'Comedy'; Holzberg, *The Ancient Novel: An Introduction*; Hutchinson, *Hellenistic Poetry*; (on scholarship) Pfeiffer, *History of Classical Scholarship: From the Beginnings to the End of the Hellenistic Age*; (on reception) Hornblower, 'The fourth-century and hellenistic reception of Thucydides'; (on courtly context) Weber, *Dichtung und höfische Gesellschaft* and 'Herrscher, Hof, und Dichter'.

I have not yet seen Gutzwiller, *Poetic Garlands: Hellenistic Epigrams in Context*. Canfora, *The Vanished Library* (*La biblioteca scomparsa*; *La Véritable Histoire de la bibliothèque d'Alexandrie*) is not to be relied on.

8 THE SELEUKID EMPIRE AND PERGAMON

(a) General

Appian, *Syrian Wars* and other works, gives a partial narrative based on wars. A modern narrative is given by Will, *Histoire politique*, and in chapters of *CAH*² vii. 1 and viii noted under 'General' (pp. 407–9 above). The most radical treatment of Seleukid institutions is by Sherwin-White and Kuhrt, *Samarkhand to Sardis*. On the Attalids, the principal works in English are E. V. Hansen, *Attalids*, and Allen,

Attalid Kingdom, both readable. Good illustrations in Colledge, 'The Seleucid kingdom', and Sherwin-White, 'Asia Minor'. Kuhrt, *Ancient Near East*, and Hornblower, 'Persia', give background down to 330 BC. Refer next to works cited in the notes to Chapter 7.

For more detail see Bickerman, 'The Seleucid period', and other chapters in Yarshater (ed.), *The Cambridge History of Iran*, iii. Bikerman (*sic*), *Institutions des Séleucides*, and Rostovtzeff, *SEHHW* i. 422–551 (Seleukid administration), 553–66 (Pergamon), and 566–602 (rest of Asia Minor), remain important and cover an impressive range of detail. Bevan, *House of Seleucus*, is sympathetic and rigorous, if more dated; similarly Bouché-Leclercq, *Histoire des Séleucides*.

For more specialized work see (on the Achaemenid legacy) Briant, 'Des Achéménides aux rois hellénistiques', *L'Asie centrale*, and 'The Seleucid kingdom, the Achaemenid empire and the history of the Near East in the first millennium BC'; Wolski, 'Les Séleucides et l'héritage d'Alexandre le Grand en Iran'; (on land and economy) Briant, 'Villages et communautés villageoises', 'Colonisation hellénistique et populations indigènes' and 'Colonisation hellénistique et populations indigènes, II', and 'Remarques sur "laoi" et esclaves ruraux'; (on temples) Isager, 'Kings and gods in the Seleucid empire'; Baroni, 'I terreni e i privilegi del tempio di Zeus a Baitokaike'; Virgilio, 'I kátochoi del tempio di Zeus a Baitokaike' and 'Strutture templari e potere politico'; (on Asia Minor) Hannestad, ' "This contributes in no small way to one's reputation": the Bithynian kings and Greek culture'; (on the Attalids) Hopp, *Untersuchungen zur Geschichte der letzten Attaliden*; Virgilio, 'Strabone e la storia di Pergamo e degli Attalidi'; (on the Levant) Grainger, *Hellenistic Phoenicia*; Roueché and Sherwin-White, 'Some aspects of the Seleucid empire: the Greek inscriptions from Failaka in the Arabian gulf'; Salles, 'The Arab-Persian gulf under the Seleucids'; (on Mesopotamia) Invernizzi, 'Seleucia on the Tigris'; Kuhrt, 'The Seleucid kings and Babylonia'; van der Spek, 'The Babylonian city'; (on Baktria) Rostovtzeff, *SEHHW* i. 542–51; Tarn, *Greeks in Bactria and India*[3]; Holt, *Alexander the Great and Bactria* and *Thundering Zeus* (the latter not yet seen by me); Rapin, 'Greeks in Afghanistan: Aï Khanoum'; (on India) Woodcock, 'The Indian Greeks' and *The Greeks in India*.

(b) Hellenization

On general issues see Cartledge, *The Greeks*; Cunliffe, *Greeks, Romans and Barbarians*; Hornblower, 'Asia Minor' and 'Hellenism, hellenization'; Momigliano, *Alien Wisdom*; Østergård, 'What is national and ethnic identity?'; Randsborg, 'Greek peripheries and barbarian centres'. Refer next to works cited in the notes to Chapter 8 (also Chapters 2, 6, and 7) and consult the Indexes.

For more specialized work see S. Said (ed.), Ἑλληνισμός; (on Gauls/Celts) Hannestad, 'Greeks and Celts'; Kaul, 'The Gundestrup cauldron'; Nachtergael, *Les Galates en Grèce*; (on western Asia) Eddy, *The King is Dead*; Wiesehöfer, ' "Kings of kings" and "philhellên": kingship in Arsacid Iran; the works of Colledge on art; (on Jewish culture) Borgen, 'Philo and the Jews in Alexandria'; Holladay, 'Jewish responses to hellenistic culture in early Ptolemaic Egypt'; Kasher, 'The civic status of Jews in Ptolemaic Egypt'; Otzen, 'Crisis and religious reaction: Jewish apocalypticism'; (on other relationships) Burstein, 'The hellenistic fringe: the case of Meroë', with Holt, 'Response'; Podemann Sørensen, 'Native reactions to foreign rule and culture in religious literature'; Skydsgaard, 'The Greeks in southern Russia'; Funck, *Hellenismus*, which came to my notice after this book went to press, includes discussions of Seleukid relations with various regional cultures: Funck on the Seleukids' image outside their empire; Funck and Gehrke on acculturation; Hengel on

Jerusalem; Huyse on Greek culture in Iran; Košelenko et al. on Margiane; Olbrycht on the steppe nomads; Pičikian on new work in Baktria; Szelényi-Graziotto on the cult of Bablyon; Wiesehöfer on the early Seleukids and Iran.

See also section 6 (above).

(c) The Jews

Some of the hundreds of publications on the crisis of the 160s are listed in Chapter 8 n. 119. For primary sources, see the main text and consult the Indexes.

Good starting-points are Rajak, 'Jews', with further bibliography; Bickerman, *Jews in the Greek Age*; Davies and Finkelstein, *Cambridge History of Judaism*, ii; Tcherikover, *Hellenistic Civilization and the Jews*. Refer next to works cited in the Notes to Chapter 8.

For more detail, see (general) Schürer, *History*[2]; (on sources) Bar-Kochva, *Pseudo-Hecataeus 'On the Jews'*; Millar, 'Hellenistic history in a near eastern perspective: the book of Daniel'; Troiani, 'Per un'interpretazione della storia ... nelle "Antichità Giudaiche" di Giuseppe'; (on the *Letter of Aristeas*) Virgilio (ed.), *Studi ellenistici*, 1, with the papers by Foraboschi, Gara, Harari, Murray (in English), and Troiani (I have not yet seen Feldman, *Josephus's Interpretation of the Bible*); (on the 160s) Bunge, '"Theos Epiphanes"' and '"Antiochos-Helios"'; (on the aftermath) Rajak, 'Hasmonean kingship and the invention of tradition'. See also sections 3 (c), 8 (b) (above).

(I have not seen Bilde, *Jødedommen og hellenismen*; S. D. Cohen, *The Beginnings of Jewishness*; Gruen, *Heritage and Hellenism*.)

9 UNDERSTANDING THE COSMOS: GREEK 'SCIENCE' AFTER ARISTOTLE

A feature of scholarship on science is that, on technical matters at least, the older bibliography is often still reliable. Chapter 9, however, seeks to give a new emphasis, interpreting science against the background of society and wider culture.

For primary sources, see Chapter 9, and section 1 above (particularly on Theophrastos). A convenient translation of fragmentary works is Thomas, *Greek Mathematical Works*; relevant Loeb volumes of individual authors are listed in section 1.

The best general starting-point is G. E. R. Lloyd, *Greek Science after Aristotle*; Neugebauer, *Exact Sciences*, is also good. Lloyd, 'Hellenistic science' and 'Medicine', are accessible but tend not to present primary evidence. More detailed introductions are in French, *Ancient Natural History*; Sarton, *History of Science*. Starting-points on other fields are Barton, *Ancient Astrology*; Toomer, 'Astronomy' and 'Mathematics'; Dilke, *Greek and Roman Maps*; Vallance, 'Medicine', with bibliography; Finley, 'Technical innovation and economic progress' and 'Technology in the Greco-Roman world', with Pleket, 'Technology and society'. Refer next to the works cited in the Notes to Chapter 9.

For more specialized work, see (generally) the other books by Lloyd listed in the Bibliography; Fraser, *Ptolemaic Alexandria*, on Alexandrian science; (on astronomy and astrology) Konstan, 'Conventional values of the hellenistic Greeks: the evidence from astrology'; Dicks, *Early Greek Astronomy to Aristotle*; Neugebauer, 'The early history of the astrolabe'; J. D. North, *The Fontana History of Astronomy and Cosmology*; Weinberg, 'The Antikythera shipwreck reconsidered'; (on geography) Brodersen, *Pomponius Mela*, text and German trans.; Peretti, *Il periplo di Scilace*; Romer,

Pomponius Mela's Description of the World, introduction and trans.; (on geology) Caley and Richards, *Theophrastus on Stones*; Eichholz, *Theophrastus: De Lapidibus*; (on mathematics) W. H. S. Jones and T. L. Heath, 'Hellenistic science and mathematics'; (on medicine) Dean-Jones, 'The cultural construct of the female body in classical Greece science'; Dobson, 'Erasistratus' and 'Herophilus of Alexandria'; Longrigg, *Greek Rational Medicine*; von Staden, *Herophilus*; (on technology) Oleson, *Greek and Roman Mechanical Water-lifting Devices*; White, '"The base mechanic arts"?', with Scarborough, 'Response'; (on time measurement) Field, 'Some Roman and Byzantine portable sundials and the London sundial-calendar'; Gibbs, *Greek and Roman Sundials*; M. T. Wright, 'Rational and irrational reconstruction: the London sun-dial and the early history of geared mechanisms'; R. M. Wright, *Cosmology in Antiquity*; (on warfare) Connolly, 'Hellenistic warfare', with illustrations; Garlan, *War in the Ancient World: A Social History*, also 'Warfare', referring to the fourth century; McNicoll, *Hellenistic Fortifications from the Aegean to the Euphrates*; Marsden, *Greek and Roman Artillery: Historical Developments* and *Technical Treatises*; Ober, 'Towards a typology of Greek artillery towers'; Winter, 'Philon of Byzantium'. Farrington, *Greek Science*, is now outdated.

10 ROME AND GREECE

On the Romans' wars, the principal sources are Livy and Polybios; see further Chapter 10. Some key studies of Roman imperialism are listed in Chapter 10 n. 1. For introductory narratives, see M. Crawford, *The Roman Republic*; Will, *Histoire politique*; on the nature of the Roman state in the third century, see Cornell, *Beginnings of Rome*. Refer next to works cited in the Notes.

For more specialized treatments, see Fuks, 'The Bellum Achaicum and its social aspect'; Grimal [*et al.*], *Hellenism and the Rise of Rome*; Harris (ed.), *The Imperialism of Mid-republican Rome*; Holleaux, *Études d'épigraphie et d'histoire grecques*, iv; Kallet-Marx, *Hegemony to Empire*; Orsi, *L'alleanza acheo-macedone*; Rostovtzeff, *SEHHW* ii. 603–1025; Walbank, 'Polybius and Rome's eastern policy'; also (on the romanization of Greece) various works of Alcock listed in the Bibliography, also those papers in Hoff and Rotroff (eds), *Romanization of Athens*, that are not cited in the notes: Geagan on the Athenian élite; Kroll on coinage; Lamberton on Plutarch; Rotroff on ceramic change; Spawforth on imperial cult; Walker on Augustan Athens; E. L. Will on amphora trade; (on Roman Athens) Willers, 'The redesigning of Athens under Hadrian'; (on general considerations about romanization in the East) Woolf, 'Becoming Roman, staying Greek'. On the Roman takeover of one region, see de Souza, 'Late hellenistic Crete'.

NOTES

1 APPROACHES AND SOURCES

1 For an exhaustive, and authoritative, deconstruction of the term and its uses see R. Bichler, *'Hellenismus': Geschichte und Problematik eines Epochenbegriffs* (Darmstadt, 1983).

2 J. G. Droysen, *Geschichte des Hellenismus*[2] (Gotha, 1877–8). For the invention of the term, and for the intellectual predecessors of Droysen (including Heyne, Niebuhr, Letronne, and Boeckh), see A. Momigliano, 'J. G. Droysen between Greeks and Jews', *History and Theory*, 9 (1970), 139–53; repr. in *Quinto contributo*, i. 109–26; in id., *Essays in Ancient and Modern Historiography* (Oxford, 1977), ch. 18 (pp. 307–23); and in A. D. Momigliano, *Studies on Modern Scholarship* (Berkeley, etc., 1994), ch. 10 (pp. 147–61).

3 Droysen's work was particularly influential in its French translation by A. Bouché-Leclercq *et al.*, entitled *Histoire de l'hellénisme* (Paris, 1883–5). Among scientific studies of particular institutions written in the succeeding generations and still cited today are E. R. Bevan's work on the Seleukids (*The House of Seleucus*, London, 1902) and Bouché-Leclercq's own histories of the Ptolemies and Seleukids (*Histoire des Lagides*, Paris, 1903–7; *Histoire des Séleucides (323–64 avant J.-C.)*, Paris, 1913–14).

4 J. Kaerst, *Geschichte des hellenistischen Zeitalters*, ii. 1: *Das Wesen des Hellenismus* (Leipzig and Berlin, 1909), follows Droysen in positing a 'hellenistische Gesamtkultur'. He also stresses the relevance of hellenistic history to the problems of his own day, and protests against dilettantism and the philological approach (pp. v–vii).

5 K. J. Beloch, *Griechische Geschichte*[2] (Strasbourg, Berlin and Leipzig, 1912–27), iv. 1–2. On Beloch, his preference for Greek over Roman culture, his sympathy for bourgeois capitalism, and his modernizing tendencies, see Momigliano, *Studies*, ch. 8 (pp. 97–120), esp. 110–11.

6 C. Schneider, *Kulturgeschichte des Hellenismus* (Munich, 1967–9), in an exhaustive synthesis of documents and artefacts (not illustrated), distinguishes (at ii. 963–88) four phases of 'hellenism': early (to 280), high (280–220), crisis and Roman invasion (to 133), and late (into the imperial period). Even his nuanced treatment seems over-schematic, and the notion that Greek culture conquered oriental and Roman culture ('Der Späthellenismus bedeutet den Sieg des Griechischen über den Orient und das Lateinertum im geistigen, künstlerischen, philosophischen, religiösen und allgemein menschlichen Bereich', ['Late hellenism signifies the victory of Greek over Orient and Latin, in the spiritual, artistic, philosophical, religious, and generally human sphere'], ii. 983) no

longer seems tenable. For a devastating critique of a more extreme view, see A. Kuhrt's review of H. Bengtson, *Die hellenistische Weltkultur* (Stuttgart, 1988), in *CR* 103 [n.s. 39] (1989), 286–8.

7 *Moralia*, 326 d–333 c.

8 On the construction of the 'Orient' by modern colonialism, see E. Said, *Orientalism* (London and New York, 1978).

9 A. H. M. Jones, *The Greek City: From Alexander to Justinian* (Oxford, 1940).

10 This is brought out in Schneider, *Kulturgeschichte*, i. 78–117.

11 e.g. W. W. Tarn, 'Alexander: the conquest of the far east', *CAH*[1] vi (1927), ch. 13 (pp. 387–437), esp. pp. 423–37; *Alexander the Great* (Cambridge, 1948); *The Greeks in Bactria and India* ([1]1938, [2]1951; [3]Chicago, 1985).

12 Rostovtzeff, *SEHHW*. See also A. Momigliano, 'M. I. Rostovtzeff', *Cambridge Journal*, 7 (1954), 334–46, repr. in A. Momigliano, *Studies in Historiography* (London, 1966), ch. 5 (pp. 91–104); Momigliano, *Studies*, ch. 3 (pp. 32–43). I do not mean to diminish the contribution of these historians; it is, of course, a purely rhetorical exercise to present their varied *œuvres* so reductively.

13 e.g. A. Momigliano, *Alien Wisdom: The Limits of Hellenization* (Cambridge, 1975); id., 'The fault of the Greeks', in Momigliano, *Essays*, ch. 2 (pp. 9–23); id., 'Greek culture and the Jews', in M. I. Finley (ed.), *The Legacy of Greece: A New Appraisal* (Oxford, 1981), ch. 11 (pp. 325–46). Tarn and Rostovtzeff's personalities were stamped on the first edition of the influential *Cambridge Ancient History*.

14 M. Hadas, *Hellenistic Culture: Fusion and Diffusion* (New York, 1959).

15 F. W. Walbank, *Aratos of Sicyon* (Cambridge, 1933); id., *Philip V of Macedon* (Cambridge, 1940); Walbank, *HW*.

16 See esp. C. Préaux, *L'Économie royale des Lagides* (Brussels, 1939); ead., *Le Monde hellénistique: la Grèce et l'Orient de la mort d'Alexandre à la conquête romaine de la Grèce (323–146 av. J.-C.)* (Paris, 1978).

17 J. Ferguson, *The Heritage of Hellenism* (London, 1973); id., *Utopias of the Classical World* (London, 1975). P. Green, *Alexander to Actium: The Hellenistic Age* (London, Berkeley, etc., 1990).

18 A meticulous approach to historical sources can be seen in the work of Edouard Will, albeit narrowly focused on the political narrative of the age (see *Histoire politique du monde hellénistique (323–30 av. J.-C.)*[2], Nancy, 1979–82; summarized in *CAH*[2] vii. 1, chs 2 and 4). A particularly important contribution has been made by C. Habicht in many works on Athenian political history (see Bibliography). Most chapters in *CAH*[2] vii. 1 (1984) and viii (1989) are fundamental to the study of the period, though varied in quality and approach; some, e.g. by J. K. Davies, P. S. Derow, and C. Habicht, are not without passion and engagement. Among those writing in English, D. J. Thompson has done most in recent years to rewrite the Ptolemaic kingdom. The largely excellent and rigorous 'Hellenistic Culture and Society' series from the University of California Press has made specialist studies more accessible. The translated sourcebooks of Bagnall and Derow, Burstein, and especially Austin are indispensable.

19 Where not explicitly cited, the up-to-date essays on particular sources in *OCD*[3] should be consulted.

20 See D. Whitehead, 'Site-classification and reliability in Stephanus of Byzantium', *CPC Papers 1* (1994), 99–124.

21 F. W. Walbank, 'Sources for the period', *CAH*[2] vii. 1 (1984), ch. 1 (pp. 1–22), at p. 22.

22 P. S. Derow, 'Polybius (1)', *OCD*[3] 1209–10, at 1210.

23 The title 'Philippic' is probably meant to denote a particular type of moralistic history, recalling the title of Theopompos's anti-Macedonian work in the fourth century BC, rather than referring to the Macedonian kingdoms; so R. Develin, in J. C. Yardley and R. Develin (eds), *Justin: Epitome of the Philippic History of Pompeius Trogus* (Atlanta, GA, 1994), 6.

24 I give the latinized names used by Justin, but have added regnal numbers.

25 See S. M. Burstein, *The Babyloniaca of Berossus* (Malibu, 1978), 1–12 ('Introduction'); A. Kuhrt, 'Berossus' *Babyloniaka* and Seleucid rule in Babylonia', in A. Kuhrt and S. Sherwin-White (eds), *Hellenism in the East: The Interaction of Greek and Non-Greek Civilizations from Syria to Central Asia after Alexander* (London, 1987), ch. 2 (pp. 32–56).

26 P. M. Fraser, *Ptolemaic Alexandria* (Oxford, 1972), i. 505–6.

27 W. G. Waddell, 'Introduction', in his *Manetho* (Loeb Classical Library; Cambridge, MA, and London, 1940), xv–xvii; R. Laqueur, 'Manethon (1)', *RE* xiv. 1 (1928), cols 1060–101; Fraser, *Ptolemaic Alexandria*, i. 505–11. Fragments of Manethon are here numbered as by Waddell.

28 Pre-Ptolemaic chronology, based on Manethon, is conveniently summarized by A. B. Lloyd, 'Egypt: pre-Ptolemaic', *OCD*[3] 510–11.

29 On ancient geographical authors see O. A. W. Dilke, *Greek and Roman Maps* (London, 1985), chs 4 (pp. 55–71), 5 (72–86).

30 See C. Nicolet, *L'Inventaire du monde: géographie et politique aux origines de l'empire romain* (Paris, 1988), trans. as *Space, Geography, and Politics in the Early Roman Empire* (Ann Arbor, MI, 1991). K. Clarke, 'In search of the author of Strabo's *Geography*', *Journal of Roman Studies*, 87 (1997), 92–110, seeks to rehabilitate Strabo as a literary artist.

31 For Pausanias's treatment of the rulers of Roman Greece, see K. W. Arafat, *Pausanias' Greece: Ancient Artists and Roman Rulers* (Cambridge, 1996). See also C. Habicht, *Pausanias' Guide to Classical Greece* (Berkeley, CA, 1985).

32 Frontinus, 3. 2. 11; App. *Syr.* 65; Trog. *Prol.* 26; Welles, *RC* 14 and p. 75; Will, i[2], 234–5; F. W. Walbank, 'Macedonia and Greece', *CAH*[2] vii. 1 (1984), ch. 7 (pp. 221–56), at p. 237 and n. 27; G. Shipley, *A History of Samos 800–188 BC* (Oxford, 1987), 186–7, with additional references in the last two works.

33 For a clear introduction to epigraphy, see F. Millar, 'Epigraphy', in M. Crawford (ed.), *Sources for Ancient History* (Cambridge, 1983), ch. 2 (pp. 80–136), esp. on this period 83–91 *passim*, 113–17 *passim*. See also A. G. Woodhead, *The Study of Greek Inscriptions*[2] (Cambridge, 1981; repr. London, 1992).

34 *IG* xi. 2. 161 *a*.

35 On the character of Greek civic decrees of all periods, see P. J. Rhodes with D. M. Lewis, *The Decrees of the Greek States* (Oxford, 1997).

36 P. M. Fraser, *Rhodian Funerary Monuments* (Oxford, 1977); V. Gabrielsen, *The Naval Aristocracy of Hellenistic Rhodes* (Aarhus, 1997), esp. ch. 5 (pp. 112–36).

37 e.g. Shipley, *Samos*, ch. 13.

38 Royal letters are found in the famous collection by C. Bradford Welles (*RC*).

39 For the range of historical issues illuminated by coins, and for an overview of hellenistic coinage, see C. Howgego, *Ancient History from Coins* (London, 1995), esp. on this period pp. 9–10, 40–2, 48–56, 64–7, and 98–100. More informative on basic concepts and tools of coin studies, but saying little specifically about this period, is M. Crawford, 'Numismatics', in Crawford (ed.), *Sources for Ancient History*, ch. 4 (pp. 185–233).

40 *I. Cret.* iv. 222–5, no. 162; R. Bogaert, *Epigraphica*, iii: *Texts on Bankers, Banking and Credit in the Greek World* (Leiden, 1976), no. 22.

41 M. J. Price, *The Coinage in the Name of Alexander the Great and Philip Arrhidaeus: A British Museum Catalogue* (London, 1991).

42 G. Le Rider, 'Éphèse et Arados au IIe siècle avant notre ère', *Quaderni ticinesi*, 20 (1991), 193–212, at 195.

43 Préaux, i. 109.

44 On Attalid coinage see G. Le Rider, 'La politique monétaire du royaume de Pergame après 188', *Journal des savants* (1989), 163–90.

45 *Sel. Pap.* ii. 409.

46 Howgego, *Ancient History from Coins*, 55.

47 O. Mørkholm, 'The monetary system in the Seleucid empire after 187 BC', in W. Heckel and R. Sullivan (eds), *Ancient Coins of the Graeco-Roman World: The Nickle Numismatic Papers* (Waterloo, Ont., 1984), 93–113.

48 I refer to forthcoming studies by A. Meadows (British Museum), presented at the 'Hellenistic Economies' conference in Liverpool, June 1998.

49 R. Ling, 'Hellenistic civilization', *CAH*² vii. 1, *Plates*, 110–15 and figs 137–43 (Delos); Petracos, *Amphiareion* (Athens, 1995), 55–9.

50 J. J. Pollitt, *Art in the Hellenistic Age* (Cambridge, 1986), ch. 6; A. Stewart, *Greek Sculpture: An Exploration* (New Haven, CT, and London, 1990), i, chs 17–19.

51 A more representative selection of artefacts is illustrated in Ling, 'Hellenistic civilization', under the following headings: industry and trade (pp. 91–108, figs 119–36), houses and life (pp. 108–32, figs 136–74), sport and education (pp. 132–45, figs 175–89), theatre (pp. 145–63, figs 190–209), religion (pp. 163–76, figs 210–30), death and burial (pp. 177–96, figs 231–54), and philosophy and science (pp. 196–206, figs 255–68). Unfortunately the volume contains no index.

52 See e.g. R. Horn, *Hellenistische Bildwerke auf Samos* (Bonn, 1972), 65–8; A. Stewart, *Attika: Studies in Athenian Sculpture of the Hellenistic Age* (London, 1979); P. Zanker, 'The hellenistic grave stelai from Smyrna: identity and self-image in the polis', in Bulloch, *Images* (1993), 212–30; L. Hannestad, 'Death on Delos: conventions in an international context', in Bilde, *Values* (1997), 285–302 and pls 15–31.

53 e.g. H. A. Thompson, 'Two centuries of hellenistic pottery', *Hesp.* 3 (1934), 310–476; F. F. Jones, 'The pottery', in H. Goldman (ed.), *The Hellenistic and Roman Periods: Excavations at Gözlü Küle* (Tarsus, 1; Princeton, NJ, 1950); G. R. Edwards, *Corinthian Hellenistic Pottery* (Corinth, 7. 3; Princeton, NJ, 1975); S. I. Rotroff, *Hellenistic Pottery: Athenian and Imported Moldmade Bowls* (Athenian Agora, 22; Princeton, NJ, 1982).

54 See A. W. Johnston and V. R. Grace, 'Amphorae and amphora stamps, Greek', *OCD*³ 76–7; Y. Garlan, 'Koukos: données nouvelles pour une nouvelle interprétation des timbres amphoriques thasiens', in *Thasiaca* (BCH suppl. 5; 1979), 213–68; V. R. Grace, 'The Middle Stoa dated by amphora stamps', *Hesp.* 54 (1985), 1–54; J.-Y. Empereur and Y. Garlan, 'Bulletin archéologique: amphores et timbres amphoriques (1980–1986)', *REG* 108 (1987), 56–109; iid., 'Bulletin archéologique: amphores et timbres amphoriques (1987–1991)', *REG* 105 (1992), 176–220. See also the lucid methodological discussion of Rhodian finds in Gabrielsen, *Naval Aristocracy*, 64–71.

55 On field survey in general see D. R. Keller and D. W. Rupp (eds), *Archaeological Survey in the Mediterranean Area* (1983); A. M. Snodgrass, *An Archaeology of Greece: The Present State and Future Scope of a Discipline* (Berkeley, etc., 1987), 99–131; id., 'Survey archaeology and the rural landscape of the Greek city', in O. Murray and S. Price (eds), *The Greek City: From Homer to Alexander* (Oxford, 1990), ch. 5

(pp. 113–36); G. Barker and J. Lloyd (eds), *Roman Landscapes: Archaeological Survey in the Mediterranean Region* (London, 1991).

56 S. E. Alcock, 'Minding the gap in hellenistic and Roman Greece', in S. E. Alcock and R. Osborne (eds), *Placing the Gods: Sanctuaries and Sacred Space in Ancient Greece*, ch. 11 (Oxford, 1994) (pp. 247–61).

57 M. H. Jameson, C. N. Runnels, and T. H. van Andel, *A Greek Countryside: The Southern Argolid from Prehistory to the Present Day* (Stanford, CA, 1994), 383–4.

58 L. S. Bommeljé and P. K. Doorn (eds), *Strouza Region Project: An Historical-topographical Fieldwork (1981–1984). 1984: Third Interim Report* (Utrecht, 1985), table 1; L. S. Bommeljé *et al.*, *Aetolia and the Aetolians: Towards the Interdisciplinary Study of a Greek Region* (Utrecht, 1987), 30 and list of sites at 68–72.

59 R. Dalongeville *et al.*, *Paysages d'Achaïe*, i: *Le Bassin du Peiros et la plaine occidentale* (Athens, 1992), 68–9.

60 C. Mee and H. Forbes (eds), *A Rough and Rocky Place: The Landscape and Settlement History of the Methana Peninsula, Greece* (Liverpool, 1997), 69–75.

61 C. Müller, *Geographi Graeci minores* (Paris, 1861), i. 97–110; F. Pfister, *Die Reisebilder des Herakleides: Einleitung, Text, Übersetzung und Kommentar* (Vienna, 1951), text at pp. 72–95. The author's identity is uncertain; from a reference in another ancient work it has been inferred that he was called Herakleides Kretikos (ibid. 17–19). See also Walbank, *HCP* iii. 72 (on Polyb. 20. 6. 1).

62 Walbank, *HCP* iii. 72–4.

63 J. L. Bintliff and A. M. Snodgrass, 'The Cambridge/Bradford Boeotian expedition: the first four years', *Journal of Field Archaeology*, 12 (1985), 123–61, at 139, 145, 147.

64 On the population of Athens, see M. H. Hansen, *Demography and Democracy: The Number of Athenian Citizens in the Fourth Century BC* (Herning, 1985). For alleged depopulation, see H. Lauter, *Attische Landgemeinden in klassischer Zeit* (Marburg, 1993), 129, 142; H. Lohmann, 'Agriculture and country life in classical Attica', in B. Wells (ed.), *Agriculture in Ancient Greece* (Stockholm, 1992), 29–57, at pp. 30, 38; both followed by R. Parker, *Athenian Religion: A History* (Oxford, 1996), 264–5. For a more rigorous assessment, arguing for only a slight reduction, see G. J. Oliver, 'The Athenian state under threat: politics and food supply, 307 to 229 BC' (unpublished Oxford D.Phil. thesis, 1995), 10–29. On the probably stable population of Greece in general, J. K. Davies, 'Cultural, social and economic features of the hellenistic world', *CAH*² vii. 1 (1984), ch. 8 (pp. 257–320), at pp. 291–2.

65 J. F. Cherry *et al.*, *Landscape Archaeology as Long-term History: Northern Keos in the Cycladic Islands from Earliest Settlement until Modern Times* (Los Angeles, CA, 1991), 343–4, fig. 17.7.

66 C. Renfrew and M. Wagstaff (eds), *An Island Polity: The Archaeology of Exploitation in Melos* (Cambridge, etc., 1982), 252–3.

67 Raw data in G. Shipley, 'Site catalogue of the survey', in W. Cavanagh, J. Crouwel, R. W. V. Catling, and G. Shipley, *Continuity and Change in a Greek Rural Landscape: The Laconia Survey*, ii: *Archaeological Data* (London, 1996), 315–438; G. Shipley, 'The survey area in the hellenistic and Roman periods', forthcoming in volume i.

68 S. E. Alcock, 'Breaking up the hellenistic world: survey and society', in I. Morris (ed.), *Classical Greece: Ancient Histories and Modern Archaeologies* (Cambridge, 1994), ch. 9 (pp. 171–90).

2 ALEXANDER AND HIS SUCCESSORS TO 276 BC

1 For the tribute system of the Persian empire, see S. Hornblower, 'Persia', *CAH*[2] vi (1994), ch. 3 (pp. 45–96), at pp. 59–62; for its perpetuation by Alexander in western Asia Minor, A. B. Bosworth, 'Alexander the Great part 2: Greece and the conquered territories', *CAH*[2] vi, ch. 17 (pp. 846–75), at pp. 868–70.

2 e.g. A. W. Gomme, 'The end of the Greek city-state', in A. W. Gomme, *Essays in Greek History and Literature* (Oxford, 1937), ch. 11 (pp. 204–48).

3 On the definition of the *polis*, and the so-called 'end of the *polis*', see M. H. Hansen, 'Introduction: the *polis* as a citizen-state', *CPC Acts 1* (1993), 7–29, at pp. 20–2 (quotation, p. 21); more fully in *CPC Acts 5* (1998); P. J. Rhodes, 'Athenian democracy after 403 BC', *Classical Journal*, 75 (1980), 305–23; W. G. Runciman, 'Doomed to extinction: the polis as an evolutionary dead-end', in O. Murray and S. Price (eds), *The Greek City* (Oxford, 1990), ch. 14 (pp. 347–67). C. Mossé, *Athens in Decline 404–86 BC* (London, 1973), takes a pessimistic view; such views are convincingly rebutted by P. Gauthier, 'Les cités hellénistiques', *CPC Acts 1* (1993), 211–31. See also E. S. Gruen, 'The polis in the hellenistic world', in R. M. Rosen and J. Farrell (eds), *Nomodeiktes: Greek Studies in Honor of Martin Ostwald* (Ann Arbor, MI, 1993), 339–54.

4 See P. J. Rhodes with D. M. Lewis, *The Decrees of the Greek States* (Oxford, 1997), esp. part 3, ch. 5, 'Democracy and freedom' (pp. 528–49), on the broad continuity of democratic forms until at least the second century BC.

5 Habicht, *Athens*, 2. See also D. M. Lewis, 'Democratic institutions and their diffusion', Πρακτικά τοῦ Η΄ Διεθνοῦς Συνεδρίου Ἑλληνικῆς καὶ Λατινικῆς Ἐπιγραφικῆς [Proceedings of the 8th International Congress of Greek and Latin Epigraphy] (Athens, 1984), i. 55–61, repr. in id., *Selected Papers in Greek and Near Eastern History* (Cambridge, 1997), ch. 8 (pp. 51–9). Continuity of participation in Athens is also stressed by G. J. Oliver, 'The Athenian state under threat: politics and food supply, 307 to 229 BC' (unpublished D.Phil. thesis, Oxford, 1995).

6 Gauthier, 'Les cités hellénistiques', 213–14.

7 J. K. Davies, 'Cultural, social and economic features of the hellenistic world', *CAH*[2] vii. 1 (1984), ch. 8 (pp. 257–320), at pp. 270–85.

8 Respectively, *IG* xii, suppl. 348; *I. Délos*, 509; *IG* ii[2] 1013.

9 G. Klaffenbach, *Die Astynomeninschrift von Pergamon* (Berlin, 1954); *SEG* xiii. 21.

10 On Alexander's reign, in addition to works cited in Further Reading, see N. G. L. Hammond, in N. G. L. Hammond and F. W. Walbank, *A History of Macedonia*, iii: *336–167 BC* (Oxford, 1988), chs 1–4 (pp. 3–94).

11 *Lives of the Ten Orators* = *Moralia*, 832 b–852 e. On Harpalos see W. Heckel, *The Marshals of Alexander's Empire* (London and New York, 1992), 213–21.

12 Habicht, *Athens*, 13.

13 For the 'Alexander Romance' see ch. 7, pp. 251–2. Medieval Jewish folk-tales about Alexander are to be found in H. Schwarz (ed.), *Miriam's Tambourine: Jewish Folktales from around the World* (Oxford, 1988), 118–34 (I owe this reference to Martyn Richards).

14 The validity of the Last Plans is accepted by A. B. Bosworth, *From Arrian to Alexander: Studies in Historical Interpretation* (Oxford, 1988), as also by N. G. L. Hammond, e.g. reviewing Bosworth in *CR* 103 [n.s. 39] (1989), 21–3.

15 Cf. Préaux, i. 136; H. S. Lund, *Lysimachus: A Study in Early Hellenistic Kingship* (London and New York, 1992), 52.

16 Among many detailed accounts of 323–301 BC, see E. Will, 'The succession to Alexander', *CAH*[2] vii. 1 (1984), ch. 2 (pp. 23–61); N. G. L. Hammond, in Hammond and Walbank, *Macedonia*, iii, chs 5–8 (pp. 95–196)

17 Details in Will, 'Succession', 26–8. For details of the careers of Alexander's lieutenants see Heckel, *Marshals*, esp. 50–6 (Antigonos), 107–33 (Krateros),
134–63 (Perdikkas), 222–7 (Ptolemy), 253–7 (Seleukos), 267–75 (Lysimachos,
with Lund, *Lysimachus*, 4).

18 The phrase is Walbank's, *HW* 46–7.

19 See Walbank, *HW* 52–3.

20 Cf. Lund, *Lysimachus*, 51–2, for reasons why we should suppose *all* the Diadochoi in
fact aspired to rule the whole empire. For the view that Antigonos sought the
kingship of all Macedonians see N. G. L. Hammond, 'The Macedonian imprint
on the hellenistic world', in Green, *HHC* 12–23, at p. 15; but E. N. Borza,
'Response' (ibid. 23–35), at p. 25, denies it, with reason.

21 Both trans. A. Stewart, *Greek Sculpture: An Exploration* (New Haven, CT, and
London, 1990), i. 298–9, nos T 142–3.

22 *Staatsv.* iii. 446.

23 As E. Will seems to do in 'The formation of the hellenistic kingdoms', *CAH*²
vii. 1 (1984), ch. 4 (pp. 101–17). For other details of 301–276 BC, see F. W.
Walbank, in Hammond and Walbank, *Macedonia*, iii, chs 9–11 (pp. 199–258).

24 The meaning of his surname is uncertain, possibly a soldiers' nickname meaning
'knock-kneed': W. W. Tarn, *Antigonos Gonatas* (Oxford, 1913; reprinted 1969),
15 n. 1; F. W. Walbank, in Hammond and Walbank, *Macedonia*, iii. 316 n. 3.

25 *Staatsv.* iii. 429.

26 J. Hornblower, *Hieronymus of Cardia* (Oxford, 1981), 106, 154 n. 210, 197,
203–40.

27 P. Briant, 'D'Alexandre le Grand aux diadoques: le cas d'Eumène de Kardia',
REA 74 (1972), 32–73; 75 (1973), 43–81 (reprinted in Briant, *RTP* 13–93);
esp. *REA* 75: 79–80 (*RTP* 92–3); quotation at *REA* 75: 79 (*RTP* 91): 'ni ses
origines grecques, ni sa loyauté envers les rois, ne constituent une explication
satisfaisante de la carrière du Kardien'.

28 Lund, *Lysimachus*, 27–9. On the campaigns of Philip, Alexander, and the early
Successors in Thrace, and on cultural change in Odrysian Thrace in the fourth
and third centuries, see Z. H. Archibald, *The Odrysian Kingdom of Thrace: Orpheus
Unmasked* (Oxford, 1998), 304–16.

29 *IG* ii² 657. See Lund, *Lysimachus*, 85–7, 101–2, 181, and index s.v. Athens;
Oliver, 'Athenian state under threat', 235–8.

30 G. Rogers, *The Sacred Identity of Ephesos: Foundation Myths of a Roman City*
(London and New York, 1991), 99.

31 Ibid. 89.

32 On these points see Lund, *Lysimachus*, 139–42, 165–82.

33 Ibid. 37–9, 147–52; quotation, p. 152.

34 Ibid. 198.

35 Ibid. 199–200; the evidence for city revolts before Koroupedion is thin, ibid.
200–1.

36 F. W. Walbank, 'Macedonia and Greece', *CAH*² vii. 1 (1984), ch. 7 (pp. 221–56), at
p. 221. On the episode as a whole see Lund, *Lysimachus*, 186–95.

37 On these kingdoms see H. Heinen, 'The Syrian–Egyptian wars and the new
kingdoms of Asia Minor', *CAH*² vii. 1 (1984), ch. 11 (pp. 412–45), at pp.
425–6; Préaux, i. 184 and n. 2.

38 The negative view is forcefully put by K. Meister, 'Agathocles', *CAH*² vii. 1
(1984), ch. 10 (pp. 384–411), esp. pp. 409–11; id., 'Agathocles (1)', *OCD*³ 37.
For a more positive view of Agathokles' achievements, see e.g. C. Mossé, *La
Tyrannie dans la Grèce antique* (Paris, ¹1969), part 3, ch. 3 (pp. 167–77).

39 As Meister, 'Agathocles', 405, remarks of his subject.

40 On the Celts in third-century Anatolia see S. Mitchell, *Anatolia: Land, Men, and Gods in Asia Minor*, i: *The Celts in Anatolia and the Impact of Roman Rule* (Oxford, 1993), ch. 2 (pp. 13–26); R. E. Allen, *The Attalid Kingdom: A Constitutional History* (Oxford, 1983), esp. ch. 5 (pp. 136–44).

41 N. G. L. Hammond, *The Macedonian State: Origins, Institutions, and History* (Oxford, 1989), 298–302.

42 The consensus of the sources that makes it 150,000 is unlikely to be reliable (see esp. Paus. 10. 19–23).

43 Mitchell, *Anatolia*, i. 14–15.

44 *Staatsv.* iii. 469.

45 M. Wörrle, 'Antiochos I., Achaios der Ältere und die Galater: eine neue Inschrift in Denizli', *Chiron*, 5 (1975), 59–87; *Bull. ép.* 1976, 667.

46 Cf. Allen, *Attalid Kingdom*, 138: 'The aims of the Galatians seem from the beginning to have been settlement and security.'

47 On these episodes see Mitchell, *Anatolia*, i. 22–3; also Heinen, 'Syrian–Egyptian wars', 423–5.

48 Hammond, *Macedonian State*, 301; he rather perversely blames the Macedonians for having the leaders they did.

49 Habicht, *Athens*, 132.

50 Préaux, i. 137: 'ceux qui la font [i.e. history] savent-ils où mène leur action?'

51 For the career of Leosthenes see S. V. Tracy, *Athenian Democracy in Transition: Attic Letter-cutters of 340 to 290 BC* (Berkeley, etc., 1995), 24–6, 27.

52 R. Sallares, *The Ecology of the Ancient Greek World* (London, 1991).

53 G. L. Cawkwell, 'Isocrates', *OCD³* 769–71, argues that it is false to suppose that Isokrates' urgings were the main reason for Philip's invasion of Persia.

54 G. Shipley, *A History of Samos 800–188 BC* (Oxford, 1987), ch. 10. See C. Habicht, 'Athens, Samos, and Alexander the Great', *Proceedings of the American Philosophical Society*, 140.3 (1996), 397–405; Habicht, *Athens*, 19, 30–4 passim, 41–2. K. Hallof and C. Habicht, 'Buleuten und Beamte der athenischen Kleruchie in Samos', *Ath. Mitt.* 110 (1995), 273–304, publish a Samian inscription of *c.*350 BC listing members of the council (*boulê*) of the Athenian cleruchy; it is now clear that the cleruchy contained a large percentage of the whole Athenian citizen body, which partly explains why the Athenians saw it as important.

55 See Préaux, i. 312–15, on the varied origins of mercenaries.

56 e.g. ibid. i. 296–7.

57 Figures from Walbank, *HW* 31, 44; G. T. Griffith, *The Mercenaries of the Hellenistic World* (Cambridge, 1935), 20–3.

58 See Préaux, ii. 404–6, on emigration to new cities via the army; i. 298–303, on the possible effects of casualties in war. On Plut. *Ages.* see D. R. Shipley, *A Commentary on Plutarch's Life of Agesilaos: Response to Sources in the Presentation of Character* (Oxford, 1997). See also P. A. Cartledge, *Agesilaos and the Crisis of Sparta* (London, 1987), ch. 15 (pp. 314–30), esp. pp. 325–30.

59 On military service and social advancement cf. Préaux, i. 305–6.

60 *Staatsv.* iii. 481.

3 KINGS AND CITIES

1 Cf. remarks of I. Nielsen, *Hellenistic Palaces: Tradition and Renewal* (Aarhus, 1994), 209.

2 Préaux, i. 234: 'assurer la mémoire du passé'.

3 H. Thesleff, *An Introduction to the Pythagorean Writings of the Hellenistic Period* (Åbo, 1961), 99–101, prefers a late third-century date. For the Greek text of Diotogenes, see id., *The Pythagorean Texts of the Hellenistic Period* (Åbo, 1965), 71–7; for the pseudo-Ekphantean treatise, ibid. 78–84. O. Murray, 'Kingship', *OCD*³ 807, does not accept a hellenistic date as proven; D. O'Meara, 'Diotogenes', *OCD*³ 485, leaves the date open between the third century BC and second century AD.

4 A. W. Erskine, *The Hellenistic Stoa: Political Thought and Action* (London, 1990).

5 For examples of divine attributes in royal coin portraits see Préaux, i. 252–3.

6 N. Kyparissis and W. Peek, 'Attische Urkunden', *Ath. Mitt.* 66 (1941), 218–39, at pp. 221–7 no. 3; A. Wilhelm, 'Beschluss zum Ehren des Demetrios ὁ μέγας', *ÖJh* 35 (1943), 157–63; on the appellation, W. S. Ferguson, 'Demetrius Poliorcetes and the Hellenic league', *Hesp.* 17 (1948), 112–36, at p. 116 n. 7.

7 See L. Koenen, 'The Ptolemaic king as a religious figure', in Bulloch, *Images* (1993), 25–115, at pp. 61–6. See also his discussion (pp. 48–50) of the trilingual Rosetta Stone (Austin 227), in which the cult titles appear in Greek and Egyptian forms. On royal epithets see also Préaux, i. 250–1, cf. 211–12.

8 Its origin is uncertain: R. R. R. Smith, *Hellenistic Sculpture: A Handbook* (London, 1991), 20.

9 Préaux, i. 227–9.

10 For Macedonian kings' rituals see R. M. Errington, *A History of Macedonia* (Berkeley, Los Angeles, and Oxford, 1990), 219.

11 Koenen, 'The Ptolemaic king as a religious figure', 71.

12 E. E. Rice, *The Grand Procession of Ptolemy Philadelphus* (Oxford, 1983).

13 Préaux, i. 229: 'en matière de culture, les rois sont conservateurs: ils assument la promotion des valeurs de la cité classique'.

14 The fundamental study of Alexander's image and its legacy is now A. Stewart, *Faces of Power: Alexander's Image and Hellenistic Politics* (Berkeley, etc., 1993).

15 Smith, *Hellenistic Sculpture*, 23 and no. 12.

16 Ibid. 21.

17 This is a particular habit of P. Green, *Alexander to Actium: The Hellenistic Age* (Berkeley, London, etc., 1990), though also of other authors.

18 Smith, *Hellenistic Sculpture*, nos 265–6.

19 Préaux, i. 285, cites coins of three kings of Pontos.

20 E. Carney, ' "What's in a name?" The emergence of a title for royal women in the hellenistic period', in S. B. Pomeroy (ed.), *Women's History and Ancient History* (Chapel Hill, NC, and London, 1991), 154–72.

21 S. B. Pomeroy, 'Hellenistic women', in her *Goddesses, Whores, Wives, and Slaves: Women in Classical Antiquity* (New York, 1975), ch. 7 (pp. 120–48), at p. 122.

22 See also S. Sherwin-White and A. Kuhrt, *From Samarkhand to Sardis: A New Approach to the Seleucid Empire* (London, 1993), 24, 25, 130. For the exceptional prominence of Stratonike in Seleukid documents, A. Kuhrt and S. M. Sherwin-White, 'Aspects of Seleucid royal ideology: the cylinder of Antiochus I from Borsippa', *JHS* 111 (1991), 71–86, at 83–5.

23 As forcefully argued by K. Brodersen, 'Der liebeskranke Königssohn und die seleukidische Herrschaftsauffassung', *Athenaeum*, 63 (1985), 459–69.

24 The date of June 268 rather than 270 is proposed by E. Grzybek, *Du calendrier macédonien au calendrier ptolémaïque: problèmes de chronologie hellénistique* (Basle, 1990); see review by F. W. Walbank, *CR* 108 [n.s. 42] (1992), 371–2. See also Chapter 5, n. 15 on p. 441 below.

25 Pomeroy, 'Hellenistic women', 124.

26 *Staatsv.* iii. 428.

27 M. H. Hansen, 'The "autonomous" city-state: ancient fact or modern fiction?', *CPC Papers* 2 (1995), 21–43. For a different view, see e.g. J. K. Davies, 'On the non-usability of the concept of "sovereignty" in an ancient Greek context', in L. A. Foresti *et al.* (eds 1994), *Federazioni e federalismo nell'Europa antica* (Milan, 1994), 51–65, at 61–2 (arguing that by the late fifth century *autonomia* was regarded as insufficient without *eleutheria*, freedom). See also Chapter 4, n. 95 on p. 440 below.

28 Préaux, ii. 410, 'un état passif'.

29 Cf. *SEG* xv. 717.

30 Austin, *Hellenistic World*, p. 70. See also S. L. Ager, *Interstate Arbitrations in the Greek World, 337–90 BC* (Berkeley, etc., 1996), 61–4 no. 13.

31 On the effects of kings' war-making on towns, see Préaux, ii. 425–32.

32 G. Shipley, *A History of Samos 800–188 BC* (Oxford, 1987), 192–4.

33 Préaux, ii. 409–10, 417–21, 425–7.

34 On royal taxes see ibid. ii. 438–41.

35 K. Bringmann, 'The king as benefactor: some remarks on ideal kingship in the age of hellenism', in Bulloch, *Images*, 7–24; F. W. Walbank, 'Response' (ibid. 116–24), at p. 117; G. Herman, 'The "friends" of the early hellenistic rulers: servants or officials?', *Talanta*, 12–13 (1980–1), 103–49; id., *Ritualised Friendship and the Greek City* (Cambridge, 1987), 153–5, cf. 38, 44, 162–3; id., 'The court society of the hellenistic age', in Cartledge, *Constructs*, 199–224; S. Le Bohec, 'L'entourage royal à la cour des Antigonides', in E. Lévy (ed.), *Le Système palatial en Orient, en Grèce et à Rome* (Strasbourg, 1987), 315–26.

36 I. Kralli, 'Athens and her leading citizens in the early hellenistic period (338 BC–261 BC): the evidence of the decrees awarding the highest honours', forthcoming in *Αρχαιογνωσία*, 10 (1997–8), 132–61.

37 *IGLS* iii. 2. 992 and 1183, respectively.

38 See Préaux, i. 218.

39 Welles, *RC*, ad loc., comments that the term 'does not mean that all were connections of the royal family' (p. 250).

40 All literary texts and documents relevant to arbitration at state level are collected by Ager, *Interstate Arbitrations*, 37–509; see also her introduction (pp. 3–33).

41 Civic subdivisions of the Samian citizen body.

42 Cf. Shipley, *Samos*, 300.

43 S. L. Ager, 'Hellenistic Crete and κοινοδίκιον', *JHS* 114 (1994), 1–18, argues that *koinodikion* was a concept or type of arbitration court rather than a specific institution; cf. Ager, *Interstate Arbitrations*, 178–81 no. 67 (*CIG* 2256, *SGDI* 5040, etc.; Hierapytna and Priansos, early second century), 297–8 no. 110 (Polyb. 22. 15; Gortyn and Knossos, 184 BC).

44 See also Ager, *Interstate Arbitrations*, 446–50 no. 159.

45 The case is discussed by Shipley, *Samos*, 181–2; Ager, *Interstate Arbitrations*, 89–93 no. 26; cf. 196–210 no. 74 (Rhodian arbitration, c.197–190 BC) and p. 22.

46 *IG* iv^2 1. 71.

47 Habicht, *Athens*, 3.

48 K. J. Rigsby, *Asylia: Territorial Inviolability in the Hellenistic World* (Berkeley, 1996), 55–9 no. 1. First complete edition: J. Bousquet, 'Inscriptions de Delphes', *BCH* 82 (1958), 61–91, at pp. 74–7.

49 Rigsby, *Asylia*, 102–5 no. 7, with pp. 95–102.

50 P. Herrmann, 'Antiochos III und Teos', *Anadolu*, 9 (1965), 29–159, at 34–6; Rigsby, *Asylia*, 281–2 (no number).

51 *RDGE* 34; Rigsby, *Asylia*, 314–16 no. 153.
52 Ibid. 580–5.
53 *Staatsv.* iii. 482; *I. Cret.* i. 60–1, no. 6.
54 *IG* xii. 7. 386.
55 *IG* ii^2 844. 1.
56 *I. Cret.* iii. 31–6, no. 31 *a*; *Staatsv.* iii. 551.
57 See P. de Souza, 'Piracy', *OCD*^{3} 1184–5; id., 'Greek piracy', in A. Powell (ed.), *The Greek World* (London and New York, 1995), 179–98 (bibliography, p. 198); id., *Piracy in the Graeco-Roman World* (Cambridge, 2000); J. K. Davies, 'Cultural, social and economic features of the hellenistic world', *CAH*^{2} vii. 1 (1984), ch. 8 (pp. 257–320), at pp. 285–90; P. Brulé, *La Piraterie crétoise hellénistique* (Paris, 1978); H. A. Ormerod, *Piracy in the Ancient World: An Essay in Mediterranean History* (Liverpool and London, 1924), esp. chs 4 ('The eastern Mediterranean', pp. 108–50) and 6 ('The pirates of Cilicia', pp. 190–247).
58 See generally Rigsby, *Asylia*, 13–25.
59 *Staatsv.* iii. 545. On interactions between cities in the hellenistic period see e.g. A. Giovannini, 'Greek cities and Greek commonwealth', in Bulloch, *Images*, 265–86; A. Dihle, 'Response', ibid. 287–95.
60 *Staatsv.* iii. 554; *I. Cret.* iii. 78–81, no. 1.
61 P. Gauthier, *Les Cités grecques et leurs bienfaiteurs* (Athens, 1985), 74–5; R. van Bremen, 'Women and wealth', in A. Cameron and A. Kuhrt (eds), *Images of Women in Antiquity* (London and Canberra, 1983), ch. 14 (pp. 223–42); ead., *The Limits of Participation: Women and Civic Life in the Greek East in the Hellenistic and Roman Periods* (Amsterdam, 1996).
62 Préaux, i. 208.
63 F. Millar, *The Roman Near East: 31 BC–AD 337* (Cambridge, MA, and London, 1993), ch. 7 (pp. 236–63), esp. 242.
64 On new towns in the east see G. M. Cohen, *The Seleucid Colonies: Studies in Founding, Administration and Organization* (Wiesbaden, 1978); for the west see id., *The Hellenistic Settlements in Europe, the Islands, and Asia Minor* (Berkeley, etc., 1995). On the relatively small number of Alexander's new towns, and on the purposes for which they were founded, see P. M. Fraser, *Cities of Alexander the Great* (Oxford, 1996).
65 Shipley, *Samos*, 203–4.
66 *IG* vii. 4263.
67 See e.g. Préaux, ii. 443–4.
68 See e.g. Bringmann, 'The king as benefactor', 14–15.
69 On the relationship of Pergamon to the kings see R. E. Allen, *The Attalid Kingdom: A Constitutional History* (Oxford, 1983), ch. 7 (pp. 159–77).
70 Bringmann, 'The king as benefactor'; Walbank, 'Response', 120.
71 G. Pugliese-Caratelli, 'Supplemento epigrafico di Iasos', *Annuario della Scuola Archeologica di Atene*, 45–6 (1967–8), 437–86, at 445–53, no. 2; *Bull. ép.* 1971, 621; *SEG* xxvi. 1226.
72 F. Sokolowski, *Lois sacrées des cités grecques* (Paris, 1969), no. 80.
73 Préaux, i. 206: 'une authentique piété, une générosité désintéressé ne sont pas nécessairement exclues'. Cf. also Walbank, 'Response', 120, stressing that royal benefactions extend far beyond Greek *poleis*. For Ptolemaic *philanthrôpia* as reflecting pharaonic tradition too, see A. E. Samuel, 'The Ptolemies and the ideology of kingship', in Green, *HHC* 168–92; D. Delia, 'Response' (ibid. 192–204), at p. 201.
74 Préaux, ii. 437.
75 Davies, 'Cultural, social and economic features', 270–85.

76 *Bull. ép.* 1978, 274; M. B. Hatzopoulos, *Macedonian Institutions under the Kings* (Athens, 1996), ii, no. 60.

77 For the date see S. B. Aleshire, *Asklepios at Athens: Epigraphic and Prosopographic Essays on the Athenian Healing Cults* (Amsterdam, 1991), 13–32.

78 *Quaestiones conviviales*, or *Table Talk*; *Moralia*, 612 c–748 d.

79 On Odós Kyrrhístou: S. G. Miller, 'Architecture as evidence for the identity of the early polis', *CPC Acts 2* (1995), 201–44, at 202–9. Some, however, link it with Ptolemy VI in the mid-second century: R. E. Wycherley, *The Stones of Athens* (Princeton, NJ, 1978), 232 and n. 42, and J. Travlos, *Pictorial Dictionary of Ancient Athens* (Athens, 1971), 578–9, revising Travlos, 233–4.

80 Wycherley, *Stones of Athens*, 77.

81 Ibid. 82.

82 H. J. Kienast, 'Untersuchungen am Turm der Winde', *Archäologischer Anzeiger*, 1993, 271–5; id., 'The Tower of the Winds in Athens: hellenistic or Roman?', in M. C. Hoff and S. I. Rotroff (eds), *The Romanization of Athens* (Oxford, 1997), 53–65.

83 S. D. Lambert, *Rationes Centesimarum: Sales of Public Land in Lykourgan Athens* (Amsterdam, 1997), esp. 280–91.

84 On Greek town-planning in general, see R. E. Wycherley, *How the Greeks Built Cities* ([1]London, 1949; [2]London and New York, 1962), ch. 1 (pp. 15–35 in both editions), with other chapters for particular building types; R. Martin, *L'Urbanisme dans la Grèce antique* (Paris, [1]1956, [2]1974).

85 Wycherley, *Cities*, 25–7; E. J. Owens, *The City in the Greek and Roman World* (London and New York, 1991), 65–6.

86 A. Peschlow-Bindokat, 'Herakleia am Latmos: vorläufiger Bericht über die Arbeiten in den Jahren 1974 und 1975', *Archäologischer Anzeiger*, 1977, 90–104, esp. 91 Abb. 1; Owens, *City*, 85.

87 Owens, *City*, 86–7.

88 Ibid., esp. ch. 7 (pp. 121–48); earlier Roman and Italian towns, however, show flexibility (pp. 106–20).

89 Ibid. 75–6.

90 S. C. Bakhuizen (ed.), *A Greek City of the Fourth Century* BC: *By the Gorítsa Team* (Rome, 1992), esp. 213–26, 313–16; Owens, *City*, 78–9.

91 Owens, *City*, 79–80; P. Marzolff, 'Zur Stadtanlage des Demetrias', in V. Milojčić and D. Theocharis, *Demetrias*, i (Bonn, 1976), 5–16.

92 H. R. Reinders, *New Halos: A Hellenistic town in Thessalía, Greece* (Utrecht, 1988), esp. ch. 7 (pp. 180–202), emphasizing the atypicality of the town; *Archaeological Reports*, 40 (1993–4), 47. Old Halos was destroyed by the Macedonian general Parmenion in 346 BC.

93 Owens, *The City*, 88–9; E. V. Hansen, *The Attalids of Pergamon*[2] (Ithaca, NY, 1971), 245–84 *passim*.

94 The fundamental study is Nielsen, *Palaces* (quotation, p. 11). The subject has been delineated further by the twenty-eight papers in W. Hoepfner and G. Brands (eds), *Basileia: die Paläste der hellenistischen Könige* (Mainz am Rhein, 1996).

95 H. Lauter, 'Les éléments de la regia hellénistique', in Lévy (ed.), *Système palatial*, 345–55; P. Marzolff, 'Intervention sur les rapports de S. Le Bohec et H. Lauter (21/06/1995)', ibid. 357–8.

96 Nielsen, *Palaces*, esp. 'Conclusion' (pp. 209–17) and 'Catalogue of palaces' (pp. 240–305); ead., 'Oriental models for hellenistic palaces?', in Hoepfner and Brands (eds), *Basileia*, 209–12.

97 Owens, *City*, 77–8, 80–4. For a review of the excavation of Doura-Europos and the problems of understanding its hellenistic phases, see F. Millar, 'Dura-Europos under Parthian rule', in J. Wiesehöfer (ed.), *Das Partherreich und seine Zeugnisse/The Arsacid Empire: Sources and Documentation* (Stuttgart, 1998), 473–92, esp. 473–5.

98 Cf. J. K. Davies, 'Economy, hellenistic', *OCD*³ 504.

99 *Euergesia* is preferred by P. Gauthier, *Les Cités grecques et leurs bienfaiteurs* (Athens, 1985), the primary work on this topic.

100 Habicht, *Athens*, 55–6.

101 *IG* xii. 5. 129.

102 Cf. Habicht, *Athens*, 26–7. The inscription is reedited by A. Laronde, *Cyrène et la Libye hellénistique: Libykai historiai de l'époque républicaine au principat d'Auguste* (Paris, 1987), 30–4.

103 L. Foxhall and H. A. Forbes, '*Sitometreia*: the role of grain as a food in classical antiquity', *Chiron*, 12 (1982), 41–90.

104 On the Samian corn law see Shipley, *Samos*, 218–21; L. Migeotte, 'Distributions de grain à Samos à la période hellénistique: le "pain gratuit" pour tous?', in M. Geerard, with J. Desmet, and R. vander Plaetse (eds), *Opes Atticae* (= *Sacris erudiri*, 31 (1989–90); Steenbrugge and The Hague, 1990), 297–308 (*SEG* xl. 735); D. J. Gargola, 'Grain distributions and the revenue of the temple of Hera on Samos', *Phoenix*, 46 (1992), 12–28 (*SEG* xlii. 776), with additional references on p. 12.

105 *I. Cret.* i. 62, no. 7.

106 C. Habicht, 'Samische Volksbeschlüsse der hellenistischen Zeit', *Ath. Mitt.* 72 (1957), 152–274, at 233–41 no. 64.

107 L. Cohn-Haft, *The Public Physicians of Ancient Greece* (Northampton, MA, 1956).

108 Gauthier, *Bienfaiteurs*, 69–70.

109 Kralli, 'Athens and her leading citizens'.

110 On these changes, see Gauthier, *Bienfaiteurs*, 72–3; id., 'Les cités hellénistiques', 215–17.

111 See also C. Mossé, 'Women in the Spartan revolutions of the third century BC', in S. B. Pomeroy (ed.), *Women's History and Ancient History* (Chapel Hill, NC, and London, 1991), 138–53.

112 The translation of the first words is adapted from D. R. Shipley, *A Commentary on Plutarch's Life of Agesilaos: Response to Sources in the Presentation of Character* (Oxford, 1997), 32.

113 J. Roy, 'The masculinity of the hellenistic king', in L. Foxhall and J. Salmon (eds), *When Men Were Men: Masculinity, Power and Identity in Classical Antiquity* (London and New York, 1998), 111–35, at 123–6.

114 *Sel. Pap.* iii. 120; *Anth. Pal.* 7. 710, 712. Erinna's date is disputed (archaic or fourth century), and the authenticity of her fragments in doubt; see e.g. C. Carey, 'Erinna', *OCD*³ 556. For other women poets see Lefkowitz and Fant, pp. 8–10.

115 *P. Oxy.* 2082; *IG* ix. 2. 526; ii² 2313–14. Compare the earlier dedication at Olympia by Kyniska, sister of king Agesilaos in the early fourth century (Plut. *Ages.* 20. 1; D. R. Shipley, *Commentary*, 246, 247).

116 Not 'made love to', as in Lefkowitz and Fant. The verb συγγίγνομαι normally has a non-sexual sense, cf. LSJ s.v.

117 Pomeroy, 'Hellenistic women', 146–7; see. however, R. Hawley, 'The problem of women philosophers in ancient Greece', in L. J. Archer *et al.* (eds), *Women in Ancient Societies: An Illusion of the Night* (Basingstoke and London, 1994), 70–87,

stressing that these women are treated in the sources as women first and philosophers only second.

118 A similar point is made by S. G. Cole, 'Could Greek women read and write?', in H. P. Foley, *Reflections of Women in Antiquity* (London, etc., 1981), 219–45, e.g. at pp. 233, 238.

119 W. Peek, *Griechische Versinschriften*, i: *Grabepigramme* (Berlin, 1995), no. 1881; Sardis, vii. 1. 111.

120 Phila: *I. Priene*, 208. Restrictions: Pomeroy, 'Hellenistic women', 131. Benefactions: van Bremen, 'Women and wealth', esp. 223; ead., *Limits of Participation*, ch. 2.

121 Van Bremen, 'Women and wealth', 230–1.

122 J. D. Mikalson, *Religion in Hellenistic Athens* (Berkeley and London, 1998), 309–11, accepts only this, somewhat subtle, form of increased individualism.

123 S. Houby-Nielsen, 'Grave gifts, women, and conventional values in hellenistic Athens', in Bilde, *Values* (1997), 220–62 (and pls 8–13), esp. 243–7.

124 L. Hannestad, 'Death on Delos: conventions in an international context', ibid. 285–302 (and pls 15–31), at pp. 291–5. Diversity of other sculpture on Delos: A. Stewart, *Greek Sculpture: An Exploration* (New Haven, CT, and London, 1990), i. 226.

125 *Erotikos* = *Moralia*, 748 e–771 e. See H. Moxnes, 'Conventional values in the hellenistic world: masculinity', in Bilde, *Values*, 263–84.

126 W. G. Runciman, 'Doomed to extinction: the polis as an evolutionary dead-end', in O. Murray and S. Price (eds), *The Greek City: From Homer to Alexander* (Oxford, 1990), ch. 14 (pp. 347–67).

4 MACEDONIA AND GREECE

1 On the geography of Macedonia, see the excellent summaries by N. G. L. Hammond, *History of Macedonia*, i: *Historical Geography and Prehistory* (Oxford, 1972), chs 1 (pp. 3–18) and 6 (pp. 205–11); in more detail, chs 2–5 (pp. 19–204), including ch. 4 (pp. 142–76) on the central plain (with map 14, pp. 140–1). On the extent of Macedonian territory see R. M. Errington, *A History of Macedonia* (Berkeley, Los Angeles, and London, 1990), ch. 1 (pp. 1–34); on the formation of the territory and the evolution of its political structures, see the excellent survey of M. B. Hatzopoulos, *Macedonian Institutions under the Kings* (Athens, 1996), i. 463–86.

2 Hammond, *Macedonia*, i. 205–6, 209; 'un-Greek', 210–11.

3 On the Arrian passage and its effect on scholarship about Macedonia, see the remarks of Hatzopoulos, *Institutions*, i. 49–50; on the civic tradition, ibid. 51–125, cf. 464.

4 N. G. L. Hammond, in N. G. L. Hammond and G. T. Griffith, *A History of Macedonia*, ii: *550–336 BC* (Oxford, 1979), p. 659. The reclamation took at most twenty years (356–336). Hammond speculates that Philip did the same in the coastal plain of the Thermaic gulf.

5 S. Hornblower, *The Greek World 479–323 BC* (London and New York, ²1991), 74–5; N. G. L. Hammond, *The Macedonian State: Origins, Institutions, and History* (Oxford, 1989), 14 (though not un-Greek in their language: see below).

6 Hammond, *Macedonian State*, 19; W. W. Tarn, *Antigonos Gonatas* (Oxford, 1913; reprinted 1969), 175–85.

7 Hammond, *Macedonian State*, 13–15, seems conclusive. Errington, *Macedonia*, 3, rightly observes that in the end 'The question of the actual racial origins of the ancient Macedonians ... is ... historically an unprofitable question'. In an

overview O. Masson, 'Macedonian language', *OCD*[3] 905–6, argues for the view that Macedonian was a dialect of north-western Greek, not a non-Greek language related to Illyrian or Thraco-Phrygian. See also M. Oppermann, 'Macedonia, cults', *OCD*[3] 905.

8   See A. Laks and G. W. Most (eds), *Studies on the Derveni Papyrus* (Oxford, 1997), esp. the editors' provisional translation (pp. 9–22) and M. S. Funghi's general discussion (ch. 1, pp. 25–37), esp. 26 (date).

9   Hatzopoulos, *Institutions*, i. 51–125, cf. 208–9. Peripheral areas: ibid. 207–8. Federal character: ibid. 495.

10 Errington, *Macedonia*, 5 and n. 6, posits an informal structure, but see Hatzopoulos, *Institutions*, 323–59, esp. 346–50; N. G. L. Hammond, in Hammond and Griffith, *Macedonia*, ii. 158–60; G. T. Griffith, ibid. 383–4, 397–400; Hammond, *Macedonian State*, 53–8.

11 Ibid. 230.

12 Ibid. 231; R. Herzog and G. Klaffenbach, *Asylieurkunden aus Kos* (Berlin, 1952), nos 6–7; Hatzopoulos, *Institutions*, ii, nos 36, 41, 47, 58; S. M. Sherwin-White, *Ancient Cos: An Historical Study from the Dorian Settlement to the Imperial Period* (Göttingen, 1978), 93 and n. 58, 96 and n. 68. At pp. 231–2 Errington collects examples of kings intervening in city finances.

13 A. Giovannini, 'Le statut des cités de Macédoine sous les Antigonides', *Ancient Macedonia 2* (1977), 465–72; Hatzopoulos, *Institutions*, 365–9.

14 On these economic aspects see Errington, *Macedonia*, 7, 222–3; cf. Hammond, *Macedonian State*, 179, on 'the almost complete concentration of the State's wealth in the hands of the king'.

15 The association with Philip II is still disputed, but see M. Andronicos, *Vergina: The Royal Tombs and the Ancient City* (Athens, 1984), 218–35; N. G. L. Hammond, 'The royal tombs at Vergina: evolution and identities', *BSA* 86 (1991), 69–82. Errington, *Macedonia*, 132 and n. 5, thinks the grand tomb could belong to Philip Arrhidaios and Eurydike; similarly E. N. Borza, *In the Shadow of Olympus: The Emergence of Macedon* (Princeton, NJ, 1990), 256–66.

16 Hatzopoulos, *Institutions*, i. 268; G. T. Griffith, in Hammond and Griffith, *Macedonia*, ii. 421–4.

17 Hatzopoulos, *Institutions*, 261–322.

18 For details of the *pezhetairoi*, see G. T. Griffith, in Hammond and Griffith, *Macedonia*, ii. 414–21, 705–13.

19 For a brief overview of Archelaos's achievements, see Hatzopoulos, *Institutions*, i. 469–71; N. G. L. Hammond, in Hammond and Griffith, *Macedonia*, ii. 137–41, with 141–50.

20 On these aspects see Hammond, *Macedonian State*, 154–60.

21 Errington, *Macedonia*, 101.

22 Ibid. 106.

23 *IG* ii[2] 447–8.

24 For outlines of the Lamian war, see E. Will, 'The succession to Alexander', *CAH*[2] vii. 1 (1984), ch. 2 (pp. 23–61), at pp. 31–3; Habicht, *Athens*, 36–42; S. V. Tracy, *Athenian Democracy in Transition: Attic Letter-cutters of 340 to 290 BC* (Berkeley, etc., 1995), 23–9 (dates at pp. 23, 29 n. 35).

25 e.g. Tarn, *Antigonos Gonatas*, 167: 'anarchy' and 'no effective government' – not the same thing! – under Sosthenes and other leaders, 279–276 BC. F. W. Walbank, 'Macedonia and Greece', *CAH*[2] vii. 1 (1984), ch. 7 (pp. 221–56), at 224: Macedonia 'devastated' by the Gauls and 'torn apart' by the wars of the Successors. Hammond, *Macedonian State*, 302: Macedonia 'shattered' in 278 BC

after the Gallic invasions; 311, 'The economy of the Greek mainland was also weakened by the years of war'. Errington, *Macedonia*, 164: the army 'worn out by the dynastic troubles' *before* the Gauls' invasion.

26 Errington, *Macedonia*, 148.

27 Before Berenike, Ptolemy married Antipater's daughter Eurydike (not to be confused with Eurydike, wife of Philip Arrhidaios).

28 M. B. Hatzopoulos, 'Succession and regency in classical Macedonia', in *Ancient Macedonia 4* (1986), 279–92; id., *Institutions*, i. 276–9, agreeing with N. G. L. Hammond, in N. G. L. Hammond and F. W. Walbank, *A History of Macedonia*, iii: *336–167 BC* (Oxford, 1988), 3, 99, etc. (cf. Errington's review in *CR* 103 [n.s. 39] (1989), 288–90). For the contrary view, see R. M. Errington, 'The nature of the Macedonian state under the monarchy', *Chiron*, 8 (1977), 77–133; Errington, *Macedonia*, 7.

29 On events involving Cassander see Errington, *Macedonia*, 130–47, esp. 133–6. Demetrios I: ibid. 150–4.

30 Habicht, *Athens*, 42; 13 n. 11.

31 Demetrios's career is reassessed by Tracy, *Athenian Democracy*, 36–51 (quotation, p. 48). See also Habicht, *Athens*, 51–2, 53–66.

32 Habicht, *Athens*, 68–9. Tribal heroes: T. L. Shear, jun. 'The monument of the eponymous heroes in the Athenian agora', *Hesp.* 39 (1970), 145–222, at 171–6, 196–8.

33 Habicht, *Athens*, 70.

34 The date of the battle is not precisely known, but Antigonos's title appears in Athens *c*. April 305: ibid. 76 n. 31.

35 Ibid. 77–80.

36 Probably in spring 300. On Lachares and his fall see ibid. 82–7.

37 Ibid. 84.

38 Ibid. 90–1.

39 On the period 319–307 BC see Errington, *Macedonia*, 124–5, 126, 136–7; on 306–288 BC, ibid. 147, 149, 151–2. For Athens in those periods, see Habicht, *Athens*, 47–66 and 67–97, respectively.

40 See also T. L. Shear, jun., *Kallias of Sphettos and the Revolt of Athens in 286 BC* (Hesp. suppl. 17; 1978); C. Habicht, *Untersuchungen zur politischen Geschichte Athens im 3. Jahrhundert v.Chr.* (Munich, 1979), 45–67; other important references in Habicht, *Athens*, 95 n. 99.

41 Habicht, *Athens*, 96–7, 124–5, 174. Attic forts: ibid. 129–30. Generals: ibid. 137.

42 Will, i² 99–100, 106. Lemnos: Habicht, *Athens*, 130.

43 Will, i² 107–9.

44 For varying assessments see Tarn, *Antigonos Gonatas*; more soberly, F. W. Walbank, in Hammond and Walbank, *Macedonia*, iii, chs 12–14 (pp. 259–316); J. J. Gabbert, *Antigonus II Gonatas: A Political Biography* (London and New York, 1997).

45 Habicht, *Athens*, 135.

46 Ibid. 127–9. See also Habicht, *Untersuchungen*, 68–86.

47 Hammond, *Macedonian State*, 306–8; cf. Errington, *Macedonia*, 166–7.

48 On the chronology, see J. J. Gabbert, 'The anarchic dating of the Chremonidean war', *Classical Journal*, 82 (1987), 230–5; Gabbert, *Antigonus*, 77 and n. 43 (to p. 46), prefers the later date, and late summer 263 for the surrender of Athens.

49 Aims: Habicht, *Athens*, 147, cf. 144; id., *Untersuchungen*, 108–12. Egypt: Habicht, *Athens*, 142–3.

50 *IG* ii² 687; *Staatsv.* iii. 476.

51 R. Étienne and M. Piérart, 'Un décret du koinon des Hellènes à Platées en l'honneur de Glaucon, fils d'Étéoclès, d'Athènes', *BCH* 99 (1975), 51–75.

52 H. Heinen, *Untersuchungen zur hellenistischen Geschichte des 3. Jahrhunderts v.Chr.: zur Geschichte der Zeit des Ptolemaios Keraunos und zum chremonideischen Krieg* (Wiesbaden, 1972), 95–213 (on the war generally), at pp. 152–4; other references in Austin.

53 *IG* ii² 665. Koróni: Habicht, *Athens*, 145, referring to E. Vanderpool, J. R. McCredie, and A. Steinberg, 'Koroni, a Ptolemaic camp on the east coast of Attica', *Hesp.* 31 (1962), 26–61; iid., 'Koroni: the date of the camp and the pottery', *Hesp.* 33 (1964), 69–75; and later works. On the war generally, see Habicht, *Athens*, 142–9. Chronology: Heinen, *Untersuchungen*, 139–40, 180–9, 199–202, 213. (I owe this reference to Dr I. Kralli.)

54 Epeiros: Hammond, *Macedonian State*, 310–11. Athens' position at this time is summarized by C. Habicht, *Studien zur Geschichte Athens in hellenistischer Zeit* (Göttingen, 1982), 13–20; Habicht, *Athens*, 150–61; A. Erskine, *The Hellenistic Stoa: Political Thought and Action* (London, 1990), 80–5. Demetrios as ruler is proposed by Habicht, *Studien*, 17–20; cf. Habicht, *Athens*, 151–4. For other detailed problems in the history of Athens after the war, see Habicht, *Studien*, 20–63.

55 Plutarch, *On Praising Oneself Inoffensively* (*Moralia*, 539 a–547 f), 545 b; id., *Sayings of Kings and Emperors* (*Moralia*, 172 a–208 a), 183 c. See K. Buraselis, *Das hellenistische Makedonien und die Ägäis: Forschungen zur Politik des Kassandros und der drei ersten Antigoniden im ägäischen Meer und im Westkleinasien* (Munich, 1982), 119–51 (255/4 BC); Will, i² 224–6; F. W. Walbank, in Hammond and Walbank, *Macedonia*, iii, appendix 4 (pp. 587–600); id., 'Macedonia and Greece', 239–40 (the last two with references to earlier discussions), accepting spring 261. Habicht, *Athens*, 146–7, is cautious: 'either at the end of the Chremonidean war or in the next decade (255)'. Gabbert (*Antigonus*, 53) calls the battle of Kos 'the *coda* for the Chremonidean War'.

56 Will, i² 237–8; Buraselis (246/5 BC), and Walbank's appendix, cited in previous note; Walbank, 'Macedonia and Greece', 248–9 (with references to earlier discussions), not excluding Antigonos Doson's reign (*c*.229–222 BC).

57 Hammond, *Macedonian State*, 311–12, 313; Habicht, *Athens*, 162–3.

58 Errington, *Macedonia*, 163 n. 4 (on p. 286).

59 Hammond, *Macedonian State*, 313–15.

60 Errington (*Macedonia*, 166 n. 18 on p. 287) denies that Bion of Borysthenes visited the court, though it is known that they met; and adds the tragedian Alexandros of Aitolia, the epic poet Antagoras of Rhodes, and two pupils of Zeno, Persaios – see below – and Philonides (Diog. Laërt. 7. 6–9).

61 Hammond, *Macedonian State*, 314–15.

62 See e.g. Walbank, 'Macedonia and Greece', 255–6.

63 *IG* ii² 448.

64 Habicht, *Athens*, 58, with p. 66 for reduced franchise.

65 I. Kralli, 'Athens and her leading citizens in the early hellenistic period (338 BC–261 BC): the evidence of the decrees awarding the highest honours', forthcoming in Αρχαιογνωσία, 10 (1997–8).

66 On the *Characters* as evoking the everyday atmosphere of Athens see Habicht, *Athens*, 122–3; on Menander and the role of New Comedy, ibid. 99–103.

67 C. Mossé, *Athens in Decline 404–86 BC* (London and Boston, 1973), 114–15 (cf. 117: 'the growing importance of the love interest in the New Comedy is to be explained less by a change in sexual mores or the emancipation of women than by the withdrawal of the bourgeois [*sic*] class from any real political activity').

68 See e.g. G. Shipley, *A History of Samos 800–188 BC* (Oxford, 1987), 210–15, 306–13.

69 J. K. Davies, *Democracy and Classical Greece*[2] (London, 1993), 228–9.

70 Habicht, *Athens*, 16–17 (330s); 233–4, 237, cf. 158, 193 (restriction); 234–7, cf. 167–8 (ephebic service); 289–90, 344, cf. 110–11, 262 (late second-century reforms), 335–6 (first century). Details in C. Pélékidis, *Histoire de l'éphébie attique: des origines à 31 avant Jésus-Christ* (Athens and Paris, 1962).

71 P. Gauthier, 'Les cités hellénistiques', *CPC Acts 1* (1993), 211–31, esp. 217–21.

72 C. Vial, *Délos indépendante* (Athens, 1984), 191–6.

73 Cf. R. Sallares, *The Ecology of the Ancient Greek World* (London, 1991); and comments at p. 55 above.

74 *Staatsv.* iii. 446.

75 *I. Cret.* iii. 89–91, no. 8.

76 *I. Cret.* ii. 84–8, no. 1.

77 On Greek leagues see generally Walbank, *HW* ch. 8; id., 'Were there Greek federal states?', *Scripta classica Israelica*, 3 (1976–7), 27–51 (= ch. 2 (pp. 20–37) of his *Selected Papers: Studies in Greek and Roman History and Historiography*; Cambridge, 1985). The key works remain J. A. O. Larsen, *Representative Government in Greek and Roman History* (Berkeley and Los Angeles, 1955), chs 4–5 (pp. 66–105); id., *Greek Federal States: Their Institutions and History* (Oxford, 1968), part II, ch. 1, §§2–4 (pp. 180–240). See also F. W. Walbank, 'Macedonia and Greece'; id., 'Macedonia and the Greek leagues', ibid. ch. 12; Préaux, ii. 466–73. On the classical leagues, see P. J. Rhodes, *The Greek City States: A Source Book* (London and Sydney, 1986), 172–220; id., 'The polis and the alternatives', *CAH*[2] vi (1994), ch. 11 (pp. 565–91), esp. pp. 579–89; more generally id., 'The Greek poleis: demes, cities and leagues', in *CPC Acts 1* (1993), 161–82, esp. 168–9, 175–7.

78 On the non-technical meaning of *koinon*, see A. Giovannini, *Untersuchungen über die Natur und die Anfänge der bundesstaatlichen Sympolitie in Griechenland* (Göttingen, 1971), 16–20; cf. Hatzopoulos, *Institutions*, 321, on the Macedonian use of the term.

79 C. J. Buck, *A History of Boeotia* (Edmonton, 1979); id., *Boiotia and the Boiotian League, 432–371 BC* (Edmonton, 1994); Larsen, *Federal States*, 175–80.

80 Ibid. 180–95.

81 H. Engelmann and R. Merkelbach, *Die Inschriften von Erythrai und Klazomenai*, ii (Bonn, 1973), no. 504.

82 Larsen, *Federal States*, 195–215. For the league's earlier history, see ibid. 78–80.

83 Walbank, *HW* 154.

84 For the early history of the Achaean league, see Larsen, *Federal States*, 80–9; for its hellenistic institutions, ibid. 215–40.

85 Walbank, *HW* 157.

86 Head[2] 416–18; Larsen, *Federal States*, 234; see Walbank, *HW* 155, for the date. On the coins see J. A. W. Warren, 'Towards a resolution of the Achaian league silver coinage controversy: some observations on methodology', in M. Price *et al.* (eds), *Essays in Honour of Robert Carson and Kenneth Jenkins* (London, 1993), 87–99; ead., 'The Achaian league, Sparta, Lucullus: some late hellenistic coinages', in *Charaktir* (Athens, 1996), 297–308. Warren supports the recent down-dating of the final Achaean league coins from just before 146 to the late second or early first century, but does not comment on the earlier issues, for which Head's dating appears to stand.

87 Walbank, *HW* 156. Walbank, *HCP* iii. 404–14, concludes that both council and primary assembly met quarterly down to 146, though from about the end of the third century important issues were discussed at a joint meeting or *synklêtos*.
88 On the events that follow see e.g. Walbank, 'Macedonia and Greece', 243–52.
89 On Aratos see also F. W. Walbank, *Aratos of Sicyon* (Cambridge, 1933).
90 On these aspects see Préaux, ii. 463–6.
91 Epeirotai: Larsen, *Federal States*, 273–81. Thessalians: ibid. 281–94. Phokians: ibid. 40–8, 300–2. Akarnanians: ibid. 89–95, 264–73.
92 Thessalians: ibid. 295. Lykians: ibid. 240–63. Macedonian republics: ibid. 295–300, noting that they are often mistakenly omitted from discussions of federal states; on the relationships between cities, villages, and sympolities, see Hatzopoulos, *Institutions*, i. 51–125.
93 S. L. Ager, *Interstate Arbitrations in the Greek World, 337–90 BC* (Berkeley, etc., 1996), 254–5 no. 92, cf. pp. 22–6.
94 *IG* v. 2. 344, *Staatsv.* iii. 499.
95 On *autonomia* as distinct from 'autonomy' in the English sense see M. H. Hansen, 'The "autonomous" city-state: ancient fact or modern fiction?', *CPC Papers 2* (1995), 21–43; A. G. Keen, 'Were the Boiotian poleis autonomoi?', *CPC Papers 3* (1996), 113–25; M. H. Hansen, 'Were the Boiotian poleis deprived of their autonomia during the first and second Boiotian federations? A reply', ibid. 127–36; G. Shipley, '"The other Lakedaimonians": the dependent perioikic poleis of Laconia and Messenia', *CPC Acts 4* (1997), 189–281, at pp. 210–11 and nn. 66, 71. See also Chapter 3 n. 27 on p. 431 above.
96 For this view of the Perioikoi see Shipley, '"The other Lakedaimonians"'.
97 S. Hodkinson, 'Land tenure and inheritance in classical Sparta', *CQ* 80 [n.s. 36]: 378–406; id., 'Warfare, wealth, and the crisis of Spartiate society', in J. Rich and G. Shipley (eds), *War and Society in the Greek World* (Leicester–Nottingham Studies in Ancient Society, 4; London and New York, 1993), 146–76.
98 Hammond, *Macedonian State*, 204. For these and the events mentioned below see P. Cartledge and A. Spawforth, *Hellenistic and Roman Sparta: A Tale of Two Cities* (London and New York, 1989), 22–3, 30–2, 34, 37, 40–1.
99 The king's name is Areus (Ἀρεύς), not Areios as sometimes implied in modern works.
100 Head² 434.
101 N. Mitchison, *The Corn King and the Spring Queen* (London, 1931; repr. with new introduction by the author, Edinburgh, 1990).
102 Probably a synonym for Mt. Parnon to the east of Sparta, rather than the town and district of Malea in north-western Laconia.
103 See Walbank, *HCP* i. 272–87; id., in Hammond and Walbank, *Macedonia*, iii. 354–62.
104 Perioikoi: Shipley, '"The other Lakedaimonians"'. Helots: Cartledge and Spawforth, *Hellenistic and Roman Sparta*, 56, 70 (quotation, p. 39). Kleomenes' action was not unprecedented: see Xen. *Hell.* 6. 5. 28–9 (the same number of helots recruited in the crisis of 370 BC). On the absence of genuinely revolutionary programmes in antiquity, see M. I. Finley, 'Revolution in antiquity', in R. Porter and M. Teich (eds), *Revolution in History* (Cambridge, 1986), 47–60.
105 Cartledge and Spawforth, *Sparta*, 69, 70. On Sparta after 222, see ibid. ch. 5 (pp. 59–79).
106 Habicht, *Athens*, 164–5, cf. 159.
107 Ibid. 165–6, 175–6.
108 Ibid. 174–5. On detailed problems in the history of Athens in the 220s, see also Habicht, *Studien*, 79–117.

109 Ibid. 127–42.

110 Habicht, *Athens*, 4, 175–6.

111 Discussed by Habicht, *Athens*, 175–6; Will, i² 368.

112 Habicht, *Athens*, 178, 182–3; Habicht, *Studien*, 105–12; C. Habicht, 'Athens and the Ptolemies', *Classical Antiquity*, 11 (1992), 68–90 (repr. in id., *Athen in hellenistischer Zeit* (Munich, 1994), 140–63).

113 Habicht, *Athens*, 185–6.

114 Ibid. 197–8.

115 Ibid. 198–201, 212–13, 220.

116 For details see F. W. Walbank, in Hammond and Walbank, *Macedonia*, iii, ch. 15 (pp. 317–36).

117 Ibid. ch. 16 (pp. 337–64).

118 For Philip's reign, see N. G. L. Hammond, in Hammond and Walbank, *Macedonia*, iii, chs 17–22 (pp. 367–487).

119 For Perseus's reign, see ibid. chs 23–6 (pp. 488–569); Perseus is sympathetically sketched by P. S. Derow, 'Perseus (2)', *OCD*³ 1143–4.

120 See Errington, *Macedonia*, 224–7, on these topics. On Philip see also F. W. Walbank, *Philip V of Macedon* (Cambridge, 1940).

121 *IG* xi. 4. 1102.

122 Hammond, *Macedonian State*, 325.

5 RELIGION AND PHILOSOPHY

1 I have not been able to take full account of the major new study by J. D. Mikalson, *Religion in Hellenistic Athens* (Berkeley and London, 1998). For important comments on hellenistic religion, see esp. his 'Conclusion' (pp. 288–323).

2 For convenience I sometimes use 'god' and 'gods' to cover both male and female deities – on the analogy of 'author' and 'actor', which have become gender-unspecific.

3 Cf. e.g. Tarn and Griffith, 336–60; Walbank, *HW* 209–10.

4 This point is well made by M. Beard and M. Crawford, *Rome in the Late Republic: Problems and Interpretations* (London, 1985), ch. 3.

5 S. R. F. Price, *Rituals and Power: The Roman Imperial Cult in Asia Minor* (Cambridge, 1984).

6 Préaux, i. 251–3. On ruler-cult in general, the fundamental study is C. Habicht, *Gottmenschentum und griechische Städte*² (Munich, 1970).

7 L. Robert, *Hellenica*, vii (Paris, 1949), 5–22.

8 See Sherwin-White and Kuhrt, *Samarkhand*, 202–5. (NB p. 204 for the date of 193, not 204.) Another copy found at Kermanshah (Iran): ibid. 204.

9 *IGLS* iii. 2. 1184.

10 As argued by Préaux, i. 238–41, 257.

11 Several non-Greek documents are quoted at Sherwin-White and Kuhrt, *Samarkhand*, 202–3, including the foundation inscription by Anu-uballit-Nikarchos, governor of Uruk under Seleukos II in 244/3 (see also J. D. Grainger, *A Seleukid Prosopography and Gazetteer* (Leiden, etc., 1997), pp. 522–3, Nikarchos son of Anu-iksur (with false cross-reference to his entry Anu-uballit (19)). On double names see S. M. Sherwin-White, 'Aristeas Ardibelteios: some aspects of the use of double names in Seleucid Babylonia', *ZPE* 50 (1983a), 209–21, on an inscription on a clay jar lid reading Ἀριστέας ᾧ ἄλλο ὄνομα Ἀρδιβηλτειος Sherwin-White identifies him as a Babylonian 'who probably operated in a Greek context', no doubt an educated professional such as interpreter, agent, or administrator (p. 221).

12 See Austin's n. 1 ad loc.

13 F. W. Walbank, 'Monarchies and monarchic ideas', *CAH*[2] vii. 1 (1984), ch. 3 (pp. 62–100), at p. 96.

14 Walbank, *HW* 213.

15 *ap.* Walbank, *HW* 213; cf. F. W. Walbank, *CR* 108 [n.s. 42] (1992), 371–2, reviewing Grzybek's study of Ptolemaic chronology (see Chapter 3 n. 24 on p. 430 above), confirming that Arsinoë was deified in her lifetime (also noted by Walbank, *HW*, 1992 reprint, p. 214).

16 For the hieroglyphic documents and the history of the cult, see J. Quaegebeur, 'Documents concerning a cult of Arsinoe Philadelphos at Memphis', *Journal of Near Eastern Studies*, 30 (1971), 239–70; the priesthood lasted until at least 76 (p. 270).

17 J. Quaegebeur, 'The Egyptian clergy and the cult of the Ptolemaic dynasty', *Ancient Society*, 20 (1989), 93–116; cf. R. S. Bagnall, *Reading Papyri, Writing Ancient History* (London and New York, 1995), 54.

18 Habicht, *Athens*, 92–3.

19 Interestingly, at 19. 90 Diodoros tells a similar story: Seleukos I in 312 stiffens the resolve of his ageing army by saying that Alexander has prophesied kingship for him in the future.

20 e.g. Walbank, 'Monarchies', 87.

21 Préaux, i. 248–50.

22 Ibid. i. 262–4; cf. ii. 643.

23 U. Wilcken, *Urkunden der Ptolemäerzeit*, ii (Berlin and Leipzig, 1957), 56; M. Launey, *Recherches sur les armées hellénistiques*, ii (Paris, 1950), 1026–31.

24 With P. Foucart, 'Inscriptions de Béotie', *BCH* 9 (1885), 403–33, at p. 405, no. 16.

25 Habicht, *Athens*, 103–4, 277–8, 303.

26 R. E. Wycherley, *The Stones of Athens* (Princeton, NJ, 1978), 181–2.

27 S. M. Sherwin-White, *Ancient Cos: An Historical Study from the Dorian Settlement to the Imperial Period* (Göttingen, 1978), 341–4, 349–52.

28 E. J. Edelstein and L. Edelstein, *Asclepius: A Collection and Interpretation of the Testimonies* (Baltimore, MD, 1945), i. 221–38 no. 423; *IG* iv[2] 1. 121–2.

29 J. K. Davies, 'Cultural, social and economic features of the hellenistic world', *CAH*[2] vii. 1 (1984), ch. 8 (pp. 257–320), at p. 316 and n. 372.

30 We need not go as far as Tarn, who dismisses the medical aspect of the cult, along with that of Serapis, as the 'half-world' of medical practice, rationalizing its popularity with the observation that 'doubtless some patients really were healed by suggestion' (Tarn and Griffith, 307).

31 R. Ling, in *CAH*[2] vii. 1, *Plates*, no. 230 and commentary; cf. Davies, 'Cultural, social and economic features', 317.

32 I owe this formulation to Fergus Millar.

33 Préaux, ii. 639–40.

34 Extended discussion in P. M. Fraser, *Ptolemaic Alexandria* (Oxford, 1972), i. 246–76; for sources and bibliography see ibid. ii. 397–432 (nn. 443–716), *passim*.

35 Préaux, ii. 649–51; E. G. Turner, 'A commander-in-chief's order from Saqqâra', *JEA* 60 (1974), 239–42. This, the earliest Greek papyrus and only known public notice on papyrus, is probably an order from Alexander's commander Peukestas himself.

36 See L. Robert, *Hellenica: receuil d'épigraphie, de numismatique et d'antiquités grecques*, xi–xii (Paris, 1960), 85–91.

37 Préaux, ii. 653–4; Ling, *CAH*[2] vii. 1, *Plates*, nos 221–2.

38 Préaux, ii. 655–60, esp. 656, 658, 659.
39 L. H. Martin, *Hellenistic Religions* (New York and Oxford, 1987), 81–2; see now P. Bilde, 'Atargatis/Dea Syria: hellenization of her cult in the hellenistic–Roman period?' in Bilde, *Religion* (1990), 151–87.
40 P. Bruneau, *Recherches sur les cultes de Délos à l'époque hellénistique et à l'époque impériale* (Paris, 1970), 457–66.
41 *IG* xi. 4. 1299, *SEG* xxiv. 1158. See H. Engelmann, *The Delian Aretalogy of Sarapis* (Leiden, 1975), 7–9.
42 Bruneau, *Recherches*, 459.
43 Ibid. 466–73.
44 G. Siebert, 'Sur l'histoire du sanctuaire des dieux syriens à Délos', *BCH* 92 (1968), 359–74; Bruneau, *Recherches*, 466–7.
45 Gods of Askalon: Bruneau, *Recherches*, 474. Kybele: ibid. 431–5. Zeus Dusares: ibid. 244, cf. 476. Chauan: ibid. 449, cf. 478. 'Other oriental sanctuaries': ibid. 474–80. Synagogue, Jews: ibid. 480–93.
46 Préaux, ii. 646–9.
47 R. M. Errington, *A History of Macedonia* (Berkeley, Los Angeles, and London, 1990), 226 and 228–9, overemphasizes the 'ecstatic' element and infers that there was a Macedonian tendency to mysticism and irrationality (!). On the cult of the Kabeiroi at Thebes, see Paus. 9. 25. 5–7.
48 As does Martin, *Hellenistic Religions*, 84.
49 Préaux, ii. 640–1.
50 Préaux, i. 250: 'un monde toujours en fête'.
51 L. Moretti, *Iscrizione agonistiche greche* (Rome, 1953), no. 41.
52 *IG* v. 2. 118.
53 For details see e.g. Habicht, *Athens*, 333–4.
54 Ἐφ. ἀρχ. 1886, 57, no. 18. Cf. nn. 56–7 below.
55 Petracos, *Amphiareion*, 36–47.
56 'The same storm fell upon the colossi of Eumenes and Attalos at Athens, which had been inscribed as Antony's, and overturned them, alone out of many' (Plutarch); 'and their images, which the Athenians had placed on the Acropolis and which had the likeness of the gods, were thrown down into the theatre by bolts of lightning' (Cassius Dio, 50. 15. 2); Habicht, *Athens*, 364. C. B. R. Pelling, in his *Plutarch: Life of Antony* (Cambridge, 1988), 265–6, suggests that only the inscriptions, not the statues, may have been changed, and that Dio's story is a confused version of Plut. *Ant.* 60. 4, 'at Athens the Dionysos from the Gigantomachy was displaced by winds and borne down into the theatre'; apparently this was one of the figures donated by Attalos I (cf. Paus. 1. 25. 2). Cf. W. B. Dinsmoor, 'The monument of Agrippa at Athens' (conference abstract), *American Journal of Archaeology*, 24 (1920), 83; *IG* ii² 4122; J. Travlos, *Pictorial Dictionary of Ancient Athens* (Athens, 1971), 483, 493 fig. 622; P. Graindor, *Athènes sous Auguste* (Cairo, 1927), 48–9. The two rededications, at least, of the monument are not in doubt.
57 Note also *IG* ii² 4123, another inscribed base from the same area, which omits 'thrice consul' and may therefore be evidence of an earlier visit by Agrippa to Athens.
58 Travlos, *Pictorial Dictionary*, 365.
59 R. Parker, *Athenian Religion: A History* (Oxford, 1996), 264–5, who possibly overstates the evidence for large-scale depopulation.
60 P. Green, *Alexander to Actium: The Hellenistic Age* (London, 1990), 400.
61 Walbank, *HW* 219–20 (quotation, 220); cf. id., introduction to Penguin Classics translation, 27–30.

62 Martin, *Hellenistic Religions*, 84.

63 *SGDI* ii. 2143 and 1854.

64 *IG* ii^2 2499.

65 Cf. Préaux, ii. 642.

66 Mikalson, *Religion in Hellenistic Athens*, ch. 2 (pp. 46–74), esp. pp. 68–74, rebuts the view that Athens by the end of the fourth century had undergone any significant shift towards religious scepticism.

67 Habicht, *Athens*, 73–4.

68 Biographical data and bibliographies: *CHCL* 835–56.

69 A. A. Long, *Hellenistic Philosophy: Stoics, Epicureans, Sceptics* (London, 1974), 622. On the chronology of Pyrrhon and the early Sceptics see F. D. Caizzi, 'Pirroniani ed Accademici nel III secolo a. C.', in O. Reverdin and B. Grange (eds), *Aspects de la philosophie hellénistique* (Vandoeuvres, Geneva, 1986), 147–78.

70 The site of the Lykeion building has allegedly been excavated in east-central Athens, though the identification is disputed. See E. Ligouri, *Archaeological Reports*, 43 (1996–7), 8–10.

71 Long, *Hellenistic Philosophy*, 622, quoting Kahn.

72 Ibid. 624–5.

73 Ibid. 99.

74 On these points see ibid. 15, 626; D. Clay, 'Individual and community in the first generation of the Epicurean school', in Συζήτησις [*Syzetesis*]: *studi sull'epicureismo greco e romano offerti a Marcello Gigante* (Naples, 1983), 255–79; A. A. Long, 'Hellenistic ethics and philosophical power', in Green, *HHC* 138–56 (with 'Response' by P. Woodruff, 157–62); F. D. Caizzi, 'The porch and the garden: early hellenistic images of the philosophical life', in Bulloch, *Images* (1993), 303–29.

75 Walbank, *HW* 180.

76 J. Blomqvist, 'Alexandrian science: the case of Eratosthenes', in Bilde, *Ethnicity* (1992), 53–75, at pp. 58–9, suggests that the scientist Eratosthenes, and many other hellenistic philosophers, were men of humble origin. His arguments are unconvincing, however.

77 On the social context and implications of Epicureanism, see A. Long, 'Pleasure and social utility: the virtues of being Epicurean', in Reverdin and Grange, *Aspects*, 283–316.

78 A. Erskine, *The Hellenistic Stoa: Political Thought and Action* (London, 1990), 9–15.

79 My translation tries to convey the intricate, allusive language of the original with its long, invented compound words. A prose version may be found at Walbank, *HW* 168.

80 J. L. López Cruces, *Les Méliambes de Cercidas de Mégalopolis: politique et tradition littéraire* (Amsterdam, 1995).

81 *On the Education of Children* = *Moralia*, 1 a–14 c. See J. U. Powell, *Collectanea Alexandrina: reliquiae minores poetarum Graecorum aetatis Ptolemaicae 323–146* AC *epicorum, elegiacorum, lyricorum, ethicorum* (Oxford, 1925), p. 238, Sotades, fr. 1.

82 As do Tarn and Griffith, 327: 'at the Rhodian docks he drew the sailors in crowds' goes beyond the evidence.

83 I follow Erskine, *Hellenistic Stoa*, ch. 1.

84 Ibid. 33.

85 Ibid. ch. 4, arguing against the idea that Zeno and Antigonos II Gonatas were closely linked.

86 On these points see ibid. 98–9, 205–10 (quotation, 210).

87 Listed among extant towns on Athos by Pliny, *HN* 4. 10. 37 (*nunc sunt Uranopolis, Palaeohorium, Thyssus, Cleonae, Apollonia*).

88 J. Ferguson, *The Heritage of Hellenism* (London, 1973), 59–63; id., *Utopias of the Classical World* (London, 1975), 108–10; W. R. Connor, 'Historical writings in the fourth century BC and in the hellenistic period', *CHCL* ch. 13.4 (pp. 458–71), at p. 463.

89 M. Grant, *From Alexander to Cleopatra: The Hellenistic World* (London, 1982), 256.

90 L. Robert and J. Robert, *Claros*, i: *Décrets hellénistiques* (Paris, 1989), 11–62 ('Décret pour Polémaios'), at p. 13: col. ii, lines 31–51 (esp. 37), with commentary at pp. 36–8. The honorand, Polemaios, is thanked by the Kolophonians for his diplomatic efforts with the Romans, which put a stop to raids on the city's territory 'at Slavestown'. The editors link this to the revolt of Aristonikos. (I am grateful to Fergus Millar for this reference.)

91 Cf. R. M. Errington, 'Aristonicus (1)', *OCD*^{3} 163; C. Habicht, 'The Seleucids and their rivals', *CAH*^{2} viii, ch. 10 (pp. 324–87), at pp. 378–80.

92 J. Ferguson, *Utopias of the Classical World* (London, 1975).

93 Tarn and Griffith, 327.

94 Ibid. 327; A. A. Long, 'Post-Aristotelian philosophy', *CHCL* ch. 19 (pp. 622–41), at p. 625; M. Grant, *The Hellenistic Greeks: From Alexander to Cleopatra* (the quotation is the title of his ch. 4).

95 Habicht, *Athens*, 105–11; quotation, 106. Philosophers' embassy: ibid. 266.

6 PTOLEMAIC EGYPT

1 For descriptions of Egypt see T. G. H. James, *An Introduction to Ancient Egypt* (London, 1979), ch. 1 (pp. 17–36); A. K. Bowman, *Egypt after the Pharaohs: 332 BC–AD 642: From Alexander to the Arab Conquest* (London, 1986; Oxford, 1990), ch. 1 (pp. 11–20); A. Kuhrt, *The Ancient Near East c.3000–330 BC* (London and New York, 1995), i. 118–22.

2 James, *Introduction to Ancient Egypt*, 20.

3 D. J. Thompson, *Memphis under the Ptolemies* (Princeton, NJ, 1988), 32–5.

4 Oases: James, *Introduction to Ancient Egypt*, 20. Myos Hormos: Strabo, 17. 1. 45. 815; Ptol. 4. 5. 8 Müller; H. Kees, 'Myos Hormos', *RE* xvi (1935), 1081–3. Leukos Limen: Ptol. l.c.; H. Kees, '*Λευκὸς λιμήν*', *RE* xii (1925), 2290.

5 See also Pliny, *HN* 6. 26. 103; 6. 33. 168 (who says Berenike was named after Philadelphos's mother); Steph. Byz. s.v. *Βερενίκη*; K. Sethe, 'Berenike 5', *RE* iii (1899), 280–1.

6 Mineral resources are enumerated by Bowman, *Egypt*, 15.

7 *PSI* 488; *Sel. Pap.* ii. 346.

8 For a summary of hellenistic kings' involvement with drainage, land reclamation, and water management, particularly in Egypt, see D. J. Thompson, 'Agriculture', *CAH*^{2} vii. 1, ch. 9 *c* (pp. 363–70), esp. 365, 366, 369; ead., chapters in A. K. Bowman and E. Rogan (eds), *Agriculture in Egypt from Pharaonic to Modern Times* (Oxford, 1999), 123–8.

9 R. S. Bagnall, *The Administration of the Ptolemaic Possessions outside Egypt* (Leiden, 1976), 224–9.

10 R. S. Bagnall, 'Ptolemaic correspondence in P. Tebt. 8', *JEA* 61 (1975), 168–80, at 168–9; *P. Tebt.* 8; W. *Chrest.* 2.

11 *C. Ord. Ptol.* 33; *IG* xii. 3. 327.

12 On ethnic groups see Thompson, *Memphis*, ch. 3 (pp. 82–105). On the character of Egyptian towns see ibid. 6–9.

13 Justice: E. G. Turner, 'Ptolemaic Egypt', *CAH*² vii. 1 (1984), ch. 5 (pp. 118–74), at p. 131. Slavery: I. Bieżuńska-Małowist, *L'Esclavage dans l'Égypte gréco-romaine*, i (Wrocław, etc., 1974), e.g. pp. 134–41 ('Conclusion'). She suggests (pp. 140–1) that P. M. Fraser's implied estimate of 400,000 slaves in Alexandria (*Ptolemaic Alexandria* (Oxford, 1972), i. 90–1 and n. 358 at ii. 171–2) is excessive. *Anachoresis*: Préaux, ii. 482.

14 Central control: Turner, 'Ptolemaic Egypt', 130; on Egyptian unification see Kuhrt, *Ancient Near East*, i. 125–34. Foreign rulers: cf. Turner, 'Ptolemaic Egypt', 167.

15 On temple land at Kerkeosiris and elsewhere, see D. J. Crawford, *Kerkeosiris: An Egyptian Village in the Ptolemaic Period* (Cambridge, 1971), 86–102.

16 On temples and their income, see Thompson, *Memphis*, 75–8 and ch. 4 (pp. 106–54). The diet of temple employees is studied by D. J. Thompson, 'Food for Ptolemaic temple workers', in J. Wilkins *et al.* (eds), *Food in Antiquity* (Exeter, 1995), 316–25.

17 On the character of papyrus evidence, and the methodological problems it raises, see R. S. Bagnall, *Reading Papyri, Writing Ancient History* (London, 1995), esp. ch. 1 (pp. 9–16). On Demotic see J. Ray, 'Literacy and language in Egypt in the late and Persian periods', in A. K. Bowman and G. Woolf (eds), *Literacy and Power in the Ancient World* (Cambridge, 1994), ch. 4 (pp. 51–66), esp. 59–60; Bagnall, *Reading Papyri*, 18–19.

18 Bagnall, *Reading Papyri*, 11.

19 Ibid. 12.

20 Cf. ibid. 69–70; D. J. Thompson, 'Literacy and power in Ptolemaic Egypt', in Bowman and Woolf (eds), *Literacy and Power*, ch. 5 (pp. 67–83), at p. 71.

21 On the term 'archive', which reasonably continues to be current, see Bagnall, *Reading Papyri*, 40 and n. 13.

22 Turner, 'Ptolemaic Egypt', 119; Bagnall, *Reading Papyri*, 20.

23 Thompson, 'Literacy and power', 80–3. Bagnall, *Reading Papyri*, 33–5, examines a paradigmatic papyrus text for Greek attitudes to Demotic (*c.* second century BC), discussing the study by R. Rémondon, 'Problèmes de bilinguisme dans l'Égypte lagide (U.P.Z. I, 148)', *Chronique d'Égypte*, 39 (1964), 126–46.

24 For recent work see e.g. *Alessandria e il mondo ellenistico-romano* (Rome, 1995), which contains many short papers on a wide range of subjects to do with the culture, archaeology and art of the city.

25 For the Ptolemies and their dates see T. C. Skeat, *The Reigns of the Ptolemies* (Munich, 1969); G. Hölbl, *Geschichte des Ptolemäerreiches: Politik, Ideologie und religiöse Kultur von Alexander dem Grossen bis zur römischen Eroberung* (Darmstadt, 1994). For Ptolemy I see the sympathetic sketch by W. M. Ellis, *Ptolemy of Egypt* (London and New York, 1994), who tends to emphasize personal and psychological explanations.

26 The speech is preserved among Demosthenes' works but is probably not by him. See C. Carey and R. A. Reid (eds), *Demosthenes: Selected Private Speeches* (Cambridge, 1985), 201–4, 211–12.

27 Turner, 'Ptolemaic Egypt', 123.

28 Memphis: Thompson, *Memphis*, 4. Alexandria: Fraser, *Ptolemaic Alexandria*, i. 14–17.

29 Préaux, i. 135; Will i² 94, 96. R. S. Bagnall, *AJP* 101 (1980), 244–7 (reviewing T. L. Shear, jun., *Kallias of Sphettos and the Revolt of Athens in 286 BC*; Hesp. suppl. 17; 1978), at 246, argues for the earlier date. I owe the last reference to G. J. Oliver, 'The Athenian state under threat: politics and food supply, 307 to 229 BC' (unpublished Oxford D.Phil. thesis, 1995), 239–41 (citation at 239 n. 104).

30 M. Holleaux, 'Décret de Naxos', in id., *Études d'épigraphie et d'histoire grecques*, iii (Paris, 1942), 27–37.

31 Samos: G. Shipley, *A History of Samos 800–188 BC* (Oxford, 1987), 182. For the Syrian (or Syrian–Egyptian) wars, see H. Heinen, 'The Syrian–Egyptian wars and the new kingdoms of Asia Minor', *CAH²* vii. 1 (1984), ch. 11 (pp. 412–45).

32 Will, i² 224–6, 231–3.

33 J.-P. Rey-Coquais, 'Inscription grecque découverte à Ras Ibn Hani: stèle de mercenaires lagides sur la côte syrienne', *Syria*, 55 (1978), 313–25.

34 Wars: Préaux, i. 141–2; Will, i² 234–44 (1st Syrian war), 248–61 (2nd); Heinen, 'Syrian–Egyptian wars', 418–19 (2nd), 420–1 (3rd). Revolts: B. C. McGing, 'Revolt Egyptian style: internal opposition to Ptolemaic rule', *Archiv für Papyrusforschung*, 43 (1997), 273–314, at 274–7.

35 On the fourth Syrian war see Heinen, 'Syrian–Egyptian wars', 433–40.

36 τὸ προσταττόμενον, misleadingly translated 'an imposed system' by Turner, 'Ptolemaic Egypt', 166; but McGing, 'Revolt', 278, reads τὸ πραττόμενον, 'what was being done'.

37 Préaux, i. 151.

38 On these and other revolts see McGing, 'Revolt', esp. 278–83 on Rhaphia and its aftermath.

39 W. Huss, *Untersuchungen zur Aussenpolitik Ptolemaios' IV* (Munich, 1976).

40 *I. Cret.* iii. 83–5, no. 4.

41 *IG* xii. 8. 156.

42 Miletos: Austin 270, *RC* 14. Termessos: Austin 271, *OGIS* 55, *TAM* ii. 1. Soloi: Austin 272, *RC* 30. Cyprus: Polyb. 27. 13, Austin 273. See Bagnall, *Administration*, ch. 2 (pp. 11–24) on Syria and Phoenicia, ch. 3 (pp. 25–37) on Kyrene, ch. 4 (pp. 38–79) on Cyprus, ch. 5 (pp. 80–116) on Samos and Asia Minor, ch. 6 *a* (pp. 117–23) on Crete, and chs 6 *b*–7 (pp. 123–75) on the rest of the Aegean. See also Bowman, *Egypt*, 28 fig. 2.

43 On this and other issues see Heinen, 'Syrian–Egyptian wars', 442–5.

44 'In the mid-fourth century the strategic importance of Cyprus for the defence of Egypt was demonstrated by Euagoras' tenacious defence of the island against the Persians. During Alexander's march through Syria a fleet based on Cyprus had covered his western flank' (Turner, 'Ptolemaic Egypt', 134).

45 Commodities: Walbank, *HW* 102–3. Cyprus: Bagnall, *Administration*, 73.

46 McGing, 'Revolt', 285–9.

47 Heinen, 'Syrian–Egyptian wars', 440–2, brings out the importance of Koile-Syria to the Ptolemies.

48 On the lives and political fortunes of the Ptolemaic Kleopatras (and others), see J. Whitehorne, *Cleopatras* (London, 1994), chs 7–15 (pp. 80–196).

49 McGing, 'Revolt', 285–9.

50 For that debate see C. Habicht, 'The Seleucids and their rivals', *CAH²* viii (1989), ch. 10 (pp. 324–87), at 344 and n. 69.

51 J. D. Ray, *The Archive of Ḥor* (London, 1976), 14–20, no. 2ʳ, at pp. 18–19 (extract). The second text is ibid. 20–9, no. 3. The texts are discussed, and their implications summarized, by Walbank, *HCP* iii. 404.

52 Bagnall, *Administration*, 122. The garrison had been withdrawn sometime after 195.

53 On Kleopatra II see Whitehorne, *Cleopatras*, chs 8–10 (pp. 89–131).

54 On the revolt or revolts of these years see McGing, 'Revolt', 289–95; N. Lewis, *Greeks in Ptolemaic Egypt: Case Studies in the Social History of the Hellenistic World* (Oxford, 1986), 87.

55 *SEG* ix. 7.

56 On these and succeeding events, see the lucid synthesis by D. J. Thompson, 'Egypt, 146–31 BC', *CAH²* ix (1994), ch. 8 *c* (pp. 310–26); on Kleopatra III and her offspring, see Whitehorne, *Cleopatras*, ch. 11 (pp. 132–48).

57 B. Kramer, and H. Heinen (1997), 'Der κτίστης Boethos und die Einrichtung einer neuen Stadt', *Archiv für Papyrusforschung*, 43: 315–63; McGing, 'Revolt', 295–6; Thompson, 'Egypt', 313.

58 Turner, 'Ptolemaic Egypt', 160.

59 Ibid.

60 Thompson, 'Egypt', following E. Badian, 'The testament of Ptolemy Alexander', *Rheinisches Museum*, 110 (1967), 178–92.

61 The identifications of some of these royal personages vary. I follow Thompson, 'Egypt', with family tree at *CAH²* ix. 778–9 (rather than that at vii. 1. 488–9). Kleopatra IV, not mentioned in my text, was sister and wife of Soter II and married Antiochos IV.

62 Whitehorne, *Cleopatras*, 175, assumes they were married, but there is no direct evidence for it.

63 McGing, 'Revolt', 285–99, with references to earlier bibliography.

64 Thompson, 'Egypt', 319.

65 Kleopatra V Tryphaina I, not named in my text, was Ptolemy XII's wife and possibly sister.

66 On her death see Whitehorne, *Cleopatras*, ch. 15 (pp. 186–96).

67 Ptolemaïs Hermiou: Ptol. 4. 5. 66; W. Helck, 'Ptolemais 4', *RE* xxiii. 2 (1959), 1868–9. Ptolemaïs Theron: H. Treidler, 'Ptolemais 8', *RE* xxiii. 2 (1959), 1870–83. Arsinoë in Cilicia: C. P. Jones and C. Habicht, 'A hellenistic inscription from Arsinoe in Cilicia', *Phoenix*, 43 (1989), 317–46.

68 For an exhaustive account of Alexandrian topography see Fraser, *Ptolemaic Alexandria*, ch. 1 (vol. i, pp. 1–37); A. Bernand, *Alexandrie la grande* (Paris, 1966), is fuller but inevitably largely based on ancient sources. New work is presented by J.-Y. Empereur, *Alexandria Rediscovered* (London, 1998; not yet seen by me). For plans see Bernand, pp. 376–7 [unnumbered]; more schematically, Austin, p. 389. The *Alexandrie* series of excavation reports, published in Warsaw, deals mainly with late Roman material, but note Z. Kiss, *Alexandrie*, iv: *Sculptures des fouilles polonaises à Kôm el-Dikka 1960–1982* (Warsaw, 1988), including hellenistic fragments.

69 R. A. Tomlinson, 'The town plan of hellenistic Alexandria', in *Alessandria*, 236–40.

70 Fraser's estimate (*Ptolemaic Alexandria*, i. 90–1 and n. 358 at ii. 171–2) of 1 million, on the ground that Rome in the first century BC numbered *c.*900,000, seems excessive. (Josephus in the first century AD states that the population of Egypt outside Alexandria is 7.5 million.) See also Rostovtzeff, *SEHHW* iii. 1137–40.

71 On the ethnic make-up of Alexandria see Fraser, *Ptolemaic Alexandria*, i. 38–92. On institutions see Turner, 'Ptolemaic Egypt', 145 and n. 71. On the relationship between the city and the Ptolemaic kings see Fraser, *Ptolemaic Alexandria*, ch. 3 (vol i, pp. 93–131), esp. 94–8.

72 W. Huss, 'Memphis und Alexandreia in hellenistischer Zeit', in *Alessandria*, 75–82.

73 W. Clarysse, 'Greeks and Egyptians in the Ptolemaic army and administration', *Aegyptus*, 65 (1985), 57–66, building on P. W. Pestman, 'L'agoranomie: un avant-poste de l'administration grecque enlevé par les égyptiens?', in H. Maehler and V. M. Strocka (eds), *Das ptolemäische Ägypten (Akten des interna-*

tionalen Symposions, 27–29 Sept. 1976 in Berlin) (Mainz am Rhein, 1978), 203–10.

74 On cleruchs in Egypt in general see Crawford, *Kerkeosiris*, 53–8; in Kerkeosiris, ibid. 58–85. See also Lewis, *Greeks*, 21.

75 L. Koenen, *Eine agonistische Inschrift aus Ägypten und frühptolemaische Königsfeste* (Meisenheim am Glan, 1977).

76 Leasing: Lewis, *Greeks*, 32. Family of Dionysios: ibid. ch. 8, esp. p. 130. Original texts in E. Boswinkel and P. W. Pestman (eds), *Les Archives privées de Dionysios, fils de Kephalas* (Leiden, 1982).

77 Ibid. *Archives privées de Dionysios*, 164–71, no. 11.

78 Part also trans. at Lewis, *Greeks*, 21 n. 14 (on p. 162), but he omits the phrase 'a Persian of the *epigonê*'. See also ibid. 35, ch. 7 (pp. 104–24), and pp. 125 and 126–7. For a possible meaning of 'Persian' in other contexts, see D. J. Thompson, 'The infrastructure of splendour: census and taxes in Ptolemaic Egypt', in Cartledge, *Constructs*, 242–57, at 247–8 and n. 35; ead., 'Literacy and power', 75; ead., 'Literacy and the administration in early Ptolemaic Egypt', in J. H. Johnson (ed.), *Life in a Multi-cultural Society: Egypt from Cambyses to Constantine and Beyond* (Chicago, 1992), 323–6. It may in those contexts denote a Greek whose family was in Egypt during the Persian period (before Alexander). 'Persian of the *epigonê*', however, has a much more uncertain meaning; cf. P. W. Pestman, reviewing J. F. Oates, 'The status designation: Πέρσης, τῆς ἐπιγονῆς' (*Yale Classical Studies*, 18 (1963), 1–129), in *Aegyptus*, 43 (1963), 405–7.

79 Salaries: Turner, in 'Ptolemaic Egypt', 140. Kleon's career is the subject of Lewis, *Greeks*, ch. 2.

80 A good, illustrated introduction to the Zenon archive is W. Clarysse and K. Vandorpe, *Zénon: un homme d'affaires grec à l'ombre des pyramides* (Louvain, 1995). More detailed reference may be made via P. W. Pestman, *A Guide to the Zenon Archive*, i–ii (Leiden, 1981).

81 Turner, 'Ptolemaic Egypt', 155.

82 Presumably, since he had earlier been left in Syria, the writer had since moved elsewhere in the performance of his duties.

83 Thompson, *Memphis*, ch. 7 (pp. 212–65), discusses the nature of permanent 'detention' (*katochê*) – whose nature (whether voluntary or penal) is much debated – of inmates as servants of the god, and reconstructs the life and history of the temple from the Sarapieion archive (mid-second century) and other sources such as ostraka.

84 U. Wilcken, *Urkunden der Ptolemäerzeit (ältere Funde)*, i: *Papyri aus Unterägypten* (Berlin and Leipzig, 1927), no. 8. See also Lewis, *Greeks*, 85–6.

85 See McGing, 'Revolt', 291, for this translation rather than 'despite the fact that I am a Greek' (Lewis, *Greeks*, 85).

86 B. Kramer, *Das Vertragsregister von Theogonis (P. Vindob. G 40618)* (Vienna, 1991), with review by D. W. Rathbone, *CR* 107 [n.s. 43] (1993), 400–1.

87 Advancement: Lewis, *Greeks*, 28. Promotion of hellenism: Thompson, 'Literacy and power', esp. 75, 79, 82; or ead., 'Conquest and literacy: the case of Ptolemaic Egypt', in D. Keller-Cohen (ed.), *Literacy: Interdisciplinary Conversations* (Cresskill, NJ, 1994), 71–89.

88 W. Clarysse, 'Greeks in Ptolemaic Thebes', in S. P. Vleeming (ed.), *Hundred-gated Thebes: Acts of a Colloquium on Thebes and the Theban Area in the Graeco-Roman Period* (Leiden, 1995), 1–19.

89 Turner, 'Ptolemaic Egypt', 126.

90 Petosiris: M. Lichtheim, *Ancient Egyptian Literature: A Book of Readings*, iii: *The Late Period* (Berkeley, etc., 1980), 44–54, at p. 48; for his tomb see G. Lefebvre,

Le Tombeau de Petosiris, i–iii (Cairo, 1923–4). Wennofer: Lichtheim, *Literature*, 54–8, at 55, from col. 3. Anonymous quotation: J. Quaegebeur, 'The genealogy of the Memphite high priest family in the hellenistic period', in D. J. Crawford *et al.*, *Studies on Ptolemaic Memphis* (Studia hellenistica, 24; Louvain, 1980), 43–82, at 78. Tathot: ibid. 78–9.

91 Turner, 'Ptolemaic Egypt', 126–7.

92 'Born in this land': Lewis, *Greeks*, 106. On the meaning of 'Hellenes', see Thompson, 'Literacy and power', 75; ead., 'Literacy and the administration'; ead., 'Hellenistic Hellenes: the case of Ptolemaic Egypt', forthcoming in I. Malkin and K. Raaflaub (eds), *Ancient Perceptions of Greek Ethnicity* (Cambridge, MA, and London, 2000); C. A. La'da, 'Ethnicity, occupation and tax-status in Ptolemaic Egypt', in *Acta Demotica: Acts of the 5th International Conference for Demotists* (Pisa, 1994), 183–9. On the problem of identifying ethnicity from names, see esp. Clarysse, 'Greeks and Egyptians'.

93 *P. Tebt.* 9, 10 (*Sel. Pap.* ii. 339), and 11.

94 Peteharsemtheus: Lewis, *Greeks*, 139–41.

95 Ibid. ch. 6, esp. p. 97.

96 Turner, 'Ptolemaic Egypt', 157–8.

97 On Préaux's view of the 'étanchéité' of the two groups, see p. 323. For this change from an earlier orthodoxy, see Bagnall, *Reading Papyri*, 50.

98 Turner, 'Ptolemaic Egypt', 167, estimates 'seven million Egyptians and 100,000 immigrants'.

99 Ibid. 147, 149.

100 Ibid. 147; D. J. Crawford, 'The good official of Ptolemaic Egypt', in Maehler and Strocka (eds), *Das ptolemäische Ägypten*, 195–202.

101 *W. Chrest.* 411; *Sel. Pap.* ii. 414.

102 Translated by Crawford, 'The good official', 200.

103 See J. Bingen, *Le Papyrus Revenue Laws: tradition grecque et adaptation hellénistique* (Opladen, 1978).

104 J. Bingen, *Papyrus Revenue Laws* (Göttingen, 1952). See now W. Clarysse and K. Vandorpe, 'The Ptolemaic apomoira', in H. Melaerts (ed.) *Le Culte du souverain dans l'Égypte ptolémaïque au IIIe siècle avant notre ère* (Louvain, 1998), 5–42.

105 *Sel. Pap.* ii. 203.

106 Estimates: Turner, 'Ptolemaic Egypt', 149. Quotation: Austin, p. 427. See also P. Vidal-Naquet, *Le Bordereau d'ensemencement dans l'Égypte ptolémaïque* (Brussels, 1967); Crawford, *Kerkeosiris*, 25–6.

107 On individuals in the Zenon archive, see Pestman, *Guide to the Zenon Archive*; the entry on Damis is at vol. i, p. 310.

108 *P. Hib.* 110; *W. Chrest.* 435; *Sel. Pap.* ii. 397.

109 For Apollonios see Thompson, *Memphis*, 245–52, esp. 248.

110 Lewis, *Greeks*, 79.

111 Quotation from Turner, 'Ptolemaic Egypt', 152. Luxury imports: ibid. 139; Walbank, *HW* 103.

112 I refer to an unpublished paper by A. Meadows (British Museum).

113 *P. Hib.* 98; *W. Chrest.* 441; *Sel. Pap.* ii. 365.

114 Turner, 'Ptolemaic Egypt', 131, 132.

115 Thompson, 'Infrastructure', 256–7 (collection), 245 (multiplicity of taxes). For the constellation of taxes see e.g. C. Préaux, *L'Économie royale des Lagides* (Brussels, 1939; repr., New York, 1979), 379–405 ('Impôts frappant les personnes').

116 Turner, 'Ptolemaic Egypt', 158–61; Walbank, *HW* 122.

117 Though there are 1,080 persons, the writer adds 60 *naubia* to the total without explanation (Austin, p. 424) – perhaps in order to make the final calculation a round number.

118 Heinen, 'Syrian–Egyptian wars', 420 and n. 19; Turner, 'Ptolemaic Egypt', 158. Cash shortages, reduced rations: ibid. 159 and nn.

119 Thompson, 'Infrastructure', 245–9 and table 1 (p. 246). On exemptions, see also ead., 'Literacy and power', 76.

120 See e.g. A. B. Lloyd, 'Saites', *OCD*³ 1346–7 (on the 26th dynasty, 664–525 BC); id., 'Egypt, 404–332 BC', *CAH*² vi (1994), ch. 8 *e* (pp. 337–60).

121 Crawford, *Kerkeosiris*, 117–21, 139. For the possible impact of social and political troubles upon the agricultural system under the later Ptolemies, see Thompson, 'Egypt', 322–4.

122 *UPZ* i. 113 and *P. Tebt.* 786, respectively.

123 Thompson, 'Egypt', 323, referring to *C. Ord. Ptol.* 73 + *PSI* 1098. 28–9 (shortage, 50 BC); *BGU* 1842 (drought, 50/49); Pliny, *HN* 5. 58 (low flood, 48 BC); and D. J. Thompson, 'Nile grain transport under the Ptolemies', in P. Garnsey, K. Hopkins, and C. R. Whittaker (eds), *Trade in the Ancient Economy* (London, 1983), 64–75.

124 Thompson, 'Egypt', 319, 320, 322.

125 McGing, 'Revolt', 296–9.

126 Bowman, *Egypt*, 31. Different versions are preserved; that translated by Burstein is published by L. Koenen, 'Die Prophezeiungen des "Töpfers"', *ZPE* 2 (1968), 178–209. Others are *P. Rainer* 19.813 and *P. Oxy.* 2332. A 'frame story' is preserved in *P. Graf* 29787.

7 LITERATURE AND SOCIAL IDENTITY

1 A. K. Bowman, *Egypt after the Pharaohs, 332 BC–AD 642: From Alexander to the Arab Conquest* (London, 1986; Oxford, 1990), 192, 205, 225.

2 A. W. Bulloch, 'Hellenistic poetry', *CHCL* ch. 18 (pp. 541–621), at pp. 544–9.

3 See e.g. R. Williams, *Culture* (London, 1981), 10–14.

4 See e.g. T. Eagleton, *Literary Theory* (Oxford, 1983), ch. 1, esp. p. 16.

5 Despite the picture painted by Blomqvist: see Chapter 5 n. 76 (on p. 444 above).

6 Préaux, i. 319.

7 Bulloch, *CHCL* 570–86.

8 Ibid. 610–11.

9 Cf. R. Wells (ed. and trans.), *Theocritus: The Idylls* (London, 1988), 9–52 ('Introduction'), at 23–5.

10 Bulloch, *CHCL* 571–2.

11 On Ptolemaic patronage of the Mouseion and Library, and on their organization, see P. M. Fraser, *Ptolemaic Alexandria* (Oxford, 1972), ch. 6 (vol. i, pp. 305–35).

12 For the possible involvement of Demetrios of Phaleron in the fate of Aristotle's works, see S. V. Tracy, *Athenian Democracy in Transition: Attic Letter-cutters of 340 to 290 BC* (Berkeley, etc., 1995), 50–1.

13 Tonal accents had been recognized by Plato and others, but a written system was not invented till now. On their significance, see W. S. Allen, *Vox Graeca: The Pronunciation of Classical Greek* (Cambridge, ³1987), ch. 6 (pp. 116–39), at pp. 116–30. The change to a stress accent came in the late Roman period, as did the majority of changes in the pronunciation of vowels and consonants.

14 Quoted from E. A. Barber, 'Alexandrian literature', *CAH*¹ vii (1928), ch. 8 (pp. 249–83), at p. 252.

15 The evidence for silent reading is reviewed by A. K. Gavrilov, 'Reading techniques in classical antiquity', *CQ* 91 [n.s. 47] (1997), 54–73; M. F. Burnyeat, 'Postscript on silent reading', ibid. 74–6.

16 Préaux, i. 234, cf. 236. She even describes hellenistic philology as a rational technique with a mystical intention (i. 238).

17 Cf. e.g. M. Beard and J. Henderson, *Classics: A Very Short Introduction* (Oxford and New York, 1995), 1–6; K. Walsh, *The Representation of the Past: Museums and Heritage in the Postmodern World* (London and New York, 1992).

18 I am grateful to Lin Foxhall for this observation.

19 *Lives of the Ten Orators = Moralia*, 832 b–852 e. R. Thomas, *Oral Tradition and Written Record in Classical Athens* (Cambridge, 1989), 48–9; who, however, points out that the actors did not then learn their lines from written copies, but had the play read out to them by the secretary of the *polis*. On oral aspects of fourth-century culture, see ibid. ch. 2 (pp. 95–154), ch. 4 (pp. 195–237), pp. 251–7, etc.; ead., 'Orality', OCD^3 1072.

20 Tarn and Griffith, 272.

21 Préaux, e.g. ii. 675.

22 Ibid., ii. 675–6.

23 Bulloch, *CHCL* 549–70, with bibliography. Fraser, *Ptolemaic Alexandria*, ch. 11 (vol. i, pp. 717–93), is an important study, though beginners may find it hard.

24 Bulloch, *CHCL* 552–3.

25 Ibid. 600.

26 Ibid. 603.

27 Ibid. 604–5; Habicht, *Athens*, 120.

28 See the sketch by Habicht, *Athens*, 119–20, 121.

29 H. Lloyd-Jones and P. Parsons, *Supplementum hellenisticum* (Berlin and New York, 1983).

30 S. West, *Ptolemaic Papyri of Homer* (Cologne, 1967).

31 A. H. R. E. Paap, *De Herodoti reliquiis in papyris et membranis Aegyptiis servatis* (Papyrologica Lugduno-Batava, 4; Leiden, 1948), collects 21 papyri of Hdt. dating mainly from the first and second centuries AD (some from the third and fourth) and mainly (12) found at Oxyrhynchos. Nearly half are from book 1 (9 papyri), followed by books 5 (4), 2 (3), 7 (2), 8 (2), and 3 (1). None comes from books 4, 6, or 9.

32 Bulloch, *CHCL* 548–9.

33 Ibid.

34 See P. M. Fraser's extended discussion, 'Lycophron (2)', OCD^3 895–7; S. West, 'Lycophron italicised', *JHS* 104 (1984), 127–51.

35 Bulloch, *CHCL* 548.

36 These are preserved at *Anth. Pal.* 15. 21–2, 24, 26–7; Greek texts at A. S. F. Gow, *Bucolici Graeci* (Oxford, 1952), pp. 172–83, together with the later *Altar* attributed to one Besantinos, the initial letters of whose lines apparently spell out a dedication to the emperor Hadrian (*Anth. Pal.* 15. 25).

37 D. R. Shipley, *A Commentary on Plutarch's Life of Agesilaos: Response to Sources in the Presentation of Character* (Oxford, 1997), 264.

38 Cf. Alan Cameron, 'Asclepiades' girl friends', in H. P. Foley (ed.), *Reflections of Women in Antiquity* (New York, etc., 1981), 275–302, at p. 296.

39 I. C. Cunningham, *Herodas: Mimiambi* (Oxford, 1971).

40 As Tarn assumed: Tarn and Griffith, 278–9.

41 Bulloch, *CHCL* 612.

42 I follow the order of sections as given by Stoneman, retaining earlier numeration. Parts of the verse passages are also in J. Rusten *et al.* (eds and trans.),

Theophrastus: Characters, Herodas, Mimes, Cercidas and the Choliambic Poets (Loeb Classical Library; Cambridge, MA, and London, ²1993), 503–47.

43 R. Stoneman (trans. and ed. 1991), *The Greek Alexander Romance* (London, 1991), 1–27 ('Introduction'), at pp. 9–10.

44 See Bowman, *Egypt*, 31, 163–4. Oracle of the Potter: J. Johnson, 'The Demotic Chronicle as an historical source', *Enchoria*, 4 (1974), 1–19. Story-cycles: M. Lichtheim, *Ancient Egyptian Literature; A Book of Readings*, iii: *The Late Period* (Berkeley, etc., 1980), 125ff. Instruction Texts: ibid. 159ff. Roman adaptation: S. West, 'The Greek version of the legend of Tefnut', *JEA* 55 (1969), 161–83.

45 On epigrams see Bulloch, *CHCL* 615–21; Fraser, *Ptolemaic Alexandria*, i. 553–617, surveys the entire range.

46 Bulloch, *CHCL* 616–17.

47 On *symposia* see O. Murray (ed.), *Sympotica: A Symposium on the Symposion* (Oxford, 1990).

48 See Cameron, 'Asclepiades' girl friends', for the epigrams of Asklepiades as manipulating stereotypes of *hetairai* (courtesans and prostitutes) rather than documenting reality.

49 See A. S. F. Gow and D. L. Page, *The Greek Anthology: Hellenistic Epigrams* (Cambridge, 1965), ii. 191–2, on Callimachus, no. xxxiv. Cory's version:

They gave me bitter news to hear and bitter tears to shed.
I wept, as I remember'd, how often you and I
Had tired the sun with talking and sent him down the sky.
And now that thou art lying, my dear old Carian guest,
A handful of grey ashes, long, long ago at rest,
Still are thy pleasant voices, thy nightingales, awake,
For Death, he taketh all away, but them he cannot take.
Source: William (W. J.) Cory, *Ionica* (London, 1858), 7;
quoted from T. F. Higham and C. M. Bowra (eds),
The Oxford Book of Greek Verse in Translation
(Oxford, 1938), no. 513, and from Bulloch,
CHCL 618.

50 Cf. e.g. Préaux, i. 674–9, one of the more reasoned statements of such views.

51 The humour of this phrase is discussed by L. Koenen, 'The Ptolemaic king as a religious figure', in Bulloch, *Images* (1993), 25–115, at pp. 84–9.

52 Bulloch, *CHCL* 586–98; Fraser, *Ptolemaic Alexandria*, i. 624–40 (with a particular focus on the language and subject-matter of Apollonios, and influences upon him).

53 Bulloch, *CHCL* 581.

54 Cf. F. T. Griffiths, 'Home before lunch: the emancipated woman in Theocritus', in Foley (ed.), *Reflections*, 247–73, esp. 270: 'Theocritus and his contemporaries are at least paying women the compliment of new sorts of attention, even if that attention yields little of direct documentary value.'

55 Conveniently translated as Archilochus, no. 4, in M. L. West, *Greek Lyric Poetry: The Poems and Fragments of the Greek Iambic, Elegiac, and Melic Poets (excluding Pindar and Bacchylides) down to 450 BC* (Oxford and New York, 1993), 3–4.

56 H. N. Parker, 'Love's body anatomized: the ancient erotic handbooks and the rhetoric of sexuality', in A. Richlin (ed.), *Pornography and Representation in Greece and Rome* (New York and Oxford, 1992), 90–111.

57 Ibid. 98.

58 Préaux, ii. 676.

59 M. Hadas, *Hellenistic Culture: Fusion and Diffusion* (New York, 1959, reprinted 1972), e.g. ch. 2 (pp. 11–19).

60 R. Lane Fox, 'Hellenistic culture and literature', in J. Boardman, J. Griffin, and O. Murray (eds), *The Oxford History of the Classical World* (Oxford and New York, 1986), ch. 14 (pp. 338–64), at p. 343; = iid. (eds), *The Oxford History of the Classical World*, i: *Greece and the Hellenistic World* (Oxford and New York, 1988), ch. 14 (pp. 332–58), at p. 337.

61 R. Alston, 'Conquest by text: Juvenal and Plutarch on Egypt', in J. Webster and N. Cooper (eds), *Roman Imperialism: Post-colonial Perspectives (Proceedings of a Symposium held at Leicester University in November 1994)* (Leicester, 1996), 99–109; quotation, p. 105 (italics original).

62 See O. Murray, 'Hecataeus of Abdera and pharaonic kingship', *JEA* 56 (1970), 141–71; id., 'Herodotus and hellenistic culture', *CQ* 66 [n.s. 22] (1972), 200–13; M. Stern and O. Murray, 'Hecataeus of Abdera and Theophrastus on Jews and Egyptians', *JEA* 59 (1973), 159–68.

63 Murray, 'Hecataeus of Abdera', 166.

64 Cf. Murray, 'Herodotus and hellenistic culture', 212–13.

65 As emphasized by F. Millar, 'The background to the Maccabean revolution: reflections on Martin Hengel's "Judaism and Hellenism" ', *Journal of Jewish Studies*, 29 (1978), 1–21, at p. 8.

66 D. M. Lewis, 'The first Greek Jew', *Journal of Semitic Studies*, 2 (1957), 264–6; repr. in id., *Selected Papers in Greek and Near Eastern History* (Cambridge, 1997), ch. 37 (pp. 380–2).

67 Koenen, 'The Ptolemaic king as a religious figure', e.g. 81–4, 113–15.

68 There is a Loeb translation. See also Fraser, *Ptolemaic Alexandria*, i. 505–11.

69 Fragments translated by S. M. Burstein, *The Babyloniaca of Berossus* (Malibu, CA, 1978). See also A. Kuhrt, 'Berossus' *Babyloniaka* and Seleucid rule in Babylonia', in Kuhrt and Sherwin-White, *Hellenism*, ch. 2 (pp. 32–56).

70 Much in the way that, in Dickens's *Great Expectations*, as Edward Said points out, 'Pip … is revived … and … takes on a new career … as a hardworking trader in the East'. E. Said, *Culture and Imperialism* (London, 1993), xvii.

71 H. S. Lund, *Lysimachus: A Study in Early Hellenistic Kingship* (London and New York, 1992), 15–17, correcting G. Shipley, *A History of Samos 800–188 BC* (Oxford, 1987), 180–1.

72 R. B. Kebric, *In the Shadow of Macedon: Duris of Samos* (Historia Einzelschriften, 29; 1977), 81. On Douris see also A. Mastrocinque, 'Demetrios tragodoumenos: propaganda e letteratura al tempo di Demetrio Poliorcete', *Athenaeum*, 57 (1979), 260–76, arguing that Douris is largely responsible for the hostile construction of Demetrios I as a tragic king; P. Pédech, *Trois historiens méconnus: Théopompe, Duris, Phylarque* (Paris, 1989), 257–389.

73 Comparison with Douris: W. R. Connor, 'Historical writings in the fourth century BC and in the hellenistic period', *CHCL* ch. 13.4 (pp. 458–71), at p. 467. See also F. W. Walbank, 'Polemic in Polybius', *JRS* 52 (1962), 1–12, at pp. 6–9 (= his *Selected Papers: Studies in Greek and Roman History and Historiography* (Cambridge, 1985), 262–79, at pp. 270–8); Habicht, *Athens*, 117–19.

74 Habicht, *Athens*, 116–17 (quotation, 117). See also F. Jacoby, *Atthis* (Oxford, 1949); P. E. Harding, *Androtion and the Atthis* (Oxford, 1994).

75 On Phylarchos see Pédech, *Trois historiens méconnus*, 393–493.

76 Préaux, i. 95–6.

77 J. Hornblower, *Hieronymus of Cardia* (Oxford, 1981), 5.

78 Ibid. 235–6.

79 Préaux, i. 96.

80 Ibid. i. 215–16, 221.

81 I have drawn upon A. Lesky, *A History of Greek Literature* (London, 1966), 764–71, who ranges more widely than Connor, 'Historical writings', 466–71.

82 A. J. Sachs and D. J. Wiseman, 'A Babylonian king list of the hellenistic period', *Iraq*, 16 (1954), 202–11 and 212 pl. 53; other references in Austin.

83 S. Smith, *Babylonian Historical Texts* (London, 1924), 150–9.

84 A. K. Grayson, *Assyrian and Babylonian Chronicles* (Locust Valley, NY, 1975), no. 10; S. Sherwin-White, 'Seleucid Babylonia: a case study for the installation and development of Greek rule', in Kuhrt and Sherwin-White, *Hellenism*, ch. 1 (pp. 1–31), at pp. 10–15; Sherwin-White and Kuhrt, *Samarkhand*, 8–9, 137.

85 On Jewish-Alexandrian literature generally, see Fraser, *Ptolemaic Alexandria*, i. 687–716.

86 Translated extracts and commentary in J. R. Bartlett, *Jews in the Hellenistic World: Josephus, Aristeas, the Sibylline Oracles, Eupolemus* (Cambridge, 1985), 11–34.

87 See E. J. Bickerman, *The Jews in the Greek Age* (Cambridge, MA, and London, 1988), esp. chs 9 (pp. 51–65, 'Aramaic literature'), 13 (pp. 101–6, 'The Greek Torah'), and 22 (pp. 201–36, 'New literature'); T. Rajak, 'Jewish-Greek literature', OCD^3 795–6. On Jewish apocalypticism see E. S. Gruen, 'Fact and fiction: Jewish legends in a hellenistic context', in Cartledge, *Constructs*, 72–88.

88 See Schürer² iii. 1 (1986), 180–5, on I Macc., which covers 175–135/4 BC, was written in the early first century BC in Hebrew or Aramaic, and survives in a Greek translation; 531–7, on II Macc., a précis of a work by Jason of Cyrene dealing with 175–161 BC; 537–42, on III Macc., 'a romantic fiction' (p. 537) about Ptolemy IV visiting Jerusalem after Rhaphia.

89 See Fraser, *Ptolemaic Alexandria*, i. 495–519, for the particular characteristics of historiography produced in Alexandria.

90 F. W. Walbank, 'Sources for the period', CAH^2 vii. 1 (1984), ch. 1 (pp. 1–22), at p. 4.

91 Préaux, i. 322–3.

92 Barber, 'Alexandrian literature', 255.

93 Préaux, i. 88–9.

94 Ibid. i. 216.

95 Ibid. i. 88: 'l'abrégé tue l'original'.

96 Ibid. i. 216.

97 Cf. W. V. Harris, 'Literacy and epigraphy', *ZPE* 52 (1983), 87–111; id., *Ancient Literacy* (Cambridge, MA, 1989).

98 Typically during disasters: e.g. Hdt. 6. 27 (most of the 120 children in a school on Chios die in an earthquake); Paus. 6. 9. 6 (sixty killed at Astypalaia when a man who went mad pulls over a column); Thuc. 7. 29 (a very large number massacred in their school at Mykalessos in Boiotia).

99 D. J. Thompson, 'Literacy and power in Ptolemaic Egypt', in A. K. Bowman and G. Woolf (eds), *Literacy and Power in the Ancient World* (Cambridge, 1994), ch. 5 (pp. 67–83), at p. 76.

100 Sherwin-White and Kuhrt, *Samarkhand*, 179; P. Bernard, 'Campagne de fouilles 1976–1977 à Aï Khanoum (Afghanistan)', *CRAI* 1978, 421–63, at pp. 456–60, illustrated at p. 457 fig. 20.

101 L. Robert, 'De Delphes à l'Oxus: inscriptions nouvelles de la Bactriane', *CRAI* 1968, 416–57, at pp. 422, 424.

8 THE SELEUKID KINGDOM AND PERGAMON

1   On royal correspondence: Welles, *Royal Correspondence in the Hellenistic Period* (New Haven, etc., 1934); non-Greek sources generally: Sherwin-White and Kuhrt, *Samarkhand*, 3–4. Cuneiform: A. J. Sachs and H. Hunger, *Astronomical Diaries and Related Texts from Babylonia*, i: *Diaries from 652 BC to 252 BC* (Vienna, 1988); J. Oelsner, *Materialien zur babylonischen Gesellschaft und Kultur in hellenistischer Zeit* (Budapest, 1986).

2   R. McC. Adams, *Land behind Baghdad: A History of Settlement on the Diyala Plains* (Chicago and London, 1965); id., *Heartland of Cities: Surveys of Ancient Settlement and Land Use in the Central Floodplain of the Euphrates* (Chicago, 1981); id. and H. J. Nissen, *The Uruk Countryside: The Natural Setting of Urban Societies* (Chicago and London, 1972). The state of hellenistic archaeology in Asia is summarized by S. E. Alcock, 'Breaking up the hellenistic world: survey and society', in I. Morris (ed.), *Classical Greece: Ancient Histories and Modern Archaeologies* (Cambridge, 1994), 171–90, at pp. 181–7.

3   See preliminary reports by J. J. Coulton, all entitled 'Balboura survey', in *Anatolian Studies*, 36 (1986), 7–8; 37 (1987), 11–13; 38 (1988a), 14–17; 39 (1989), 12–13; 41 (1991a), 17–19; 42 (1992a), 6–8; id., 'Balboura and district research project', ibid. 43 (1993a), 4–6; 'Balboura and district research project 1993', ibid. 44 (1994), 8–10; more fully, 'Balboura survey 1987', *Araştırma sonuçları toplantısı*, 6 (1988b), 225–31; 'Balboura survey 1988, 1990', ibid. 9 (1991b), 47–57; 'Balboura survey 1991', ibid. 10 (1992b), 459–72; and 'Balboura survey 1992', ibid. 11 (1993b), 429–36. Hellenistic material is mentioned by P. Catling and P. Roberts, 'Balboura survey pottery study', *Anatolian Studies*, 41 (1991), 19; T. J. Smith, with N. P. Milner, 'Votive reliefs from Balboura and its environs', ibid. 47 (1997), 3–39.

4   See O. Bopearachchi, *Monnaies gréco-bactriennes et indo-grecques: catalogue raisonné* (Paris, 1991); earlier reconstructions, e.g. those by A. K. Narain, *The Indo-Greeks* (Oxford, 1957; 3rd impression, 1980); id., 'The Greeks of Bactria and India', *CAH²* viii (1989), ch. 11 (pp. 388–421), have been revised perforce, thanks to newly discovered coin types.

5   M. Cary, *The Geographic Background of Greek and Roman History* (Oxford, 1949), 151.

6   General landscape: A. Kuhrt, *The Ancient Near East c.3000–330 BC* (London and New York, 1995), i. 6–7.

7   On the geography of Anatolia see also S. Mitchell, *Anatolia: Land, Men, and Gods in Asia Minor*, i: *The Celts in Anatolia and the Impact of Roman Rule* (Oxford, 1993), 5–9.

8   Cary, *Geographical Background*, 153.

9   Locations of cities: ibid. 154–5. The areas in which Seleukid control was less than total are indicated by D. Musti, 'Syria and the east', *CAH²* vii. 1 (1984), ch. 6 (pp. 175–220), at pp. 183–4.

10   Cary, *Geographical Background*, 159, 161.

11   Mesopotamian landscape: Kuhrt, *Ancient Near East*, i. 19, 21 (with map on p. 20).

12   Cary, *Geographical Background*, 178–9.

13   Rostovtzeff, *SEHHW* i. 78–9; Cary, *Geographical Background*, 183 n. 1.

14   See G. M. Cohen, *The Seleucid Colonies: Studies in Founding, Administration and Organization* (Wiesbaden, 1978), 88.

15   Location of core: Sherwin-White and Kuhrt, *Samarkhand*, 1. Babylonian ceremonies: ibid. 140.

16 On the cedars of Lebanon and other timber resources of the region, see R. Meiggs, *Trees and Timber in the Ancient Mediterranean World* (Oxford, 1982), ch. 3 (pp. 49–87), esp. 49–55, 83–7. The Diodoros passage is quoted and discussed by Meiggs, ibid. 133–4.

17 Cary, *Geographical Background*, 167.

18 Ibid. 168 (resources), 171 (routes). A more southerly link was by the desert route from Damascus or Emesa via Palmyra to Doura-Europos (ibid. 172), but there is no evidence of trade through Palmyra in the hellenistic period.

19 Sherwin-White and Kuhrt, *Samarkhand*, 34, 35; Walbank, *HW* 103.

20 J. D. Grainger, *The Cities of Seleukid Syria* (Oxford, 1990), 38–9; destruction of Antigoneia, ibid. 47.

21 Cary, *Geographical Background*, 169.

22 Sherwin-White and Kuhrt, *Samarkhand*, 17–18.

23 On the geography of Iran as a whole, and of the lands around, see the excellent survey by R. N. Frye, *The History of Ancient Iran* (Munich, 1984), ch. 1 (pp. 1–20). Inner Iran is defined by Sherwin-White and Kuhrt, *Samarkhand*, 18.

24 History: Sherwin-White and Kuhrt, *Samarkhand*, 14, 190. Landscapes: Cary, *Geographical Background*, 154.

25 Cappadocia: ibid. 154, 155 n. 1. Pontos: ibid. 156–7, 158.

26 On the Armenian landscape see Kuhrt, *Ancient Near East*, ii. 552–4, and map on p. 549. Alexander: Sherwin-White and Kuhrt, *Samarkhand*, 191. Mines: Rostovtzeff, *SEHHW* ii. 1175. Horses: Sherwin-White and Kuhrt, *Samarkhand*, 15–16. Mountains: ibid. 17. Winters: Cary, *Geographical Background*, 174–6.

27 Cary, *Geographical Background*, 176. The two are interestingly paired on Cary's map, p. 175; cf. above, Figure 8.4.

28 Sherwin-White and Kuhrt, *Samarkhand*, 192–4.

29 Ibid. 9, 18, 77–8; Cary, *Geographical Background*, 191.

30 Greater Media: Rostovtzeff, *SEHHW* i. 461; 77. Media Paraitakene: Sherwin-White and Kuhrt, *Samarkhand*, 81. Landscape in general: Cary, *Geographical Background*, 189–94 *passim*.

31 Rostovtzeff, *SEHHW* i. 480.

32 Sherwin-White and Kuhrt, *Samarkhand*, 74, 77–9, in contrast to earlier accounts.

33 Ibid. 17; P. Briant, *État et pasteurs au Moyen-Orient ancien* (Cambridge and Paris, 1982), ch. 2.

34 Outer Iran is defined and described by Sherwin-White and Kuhrt, *Samarkhand*, 79–90.

35 Cary, *Geographical Background*, 191; Sherwin-White and Kuhrt, *Samarkhand*, 82.

36 I have not yet seen J. W. Drijvers, 'Strabo on Parthia and the Parthians', in J. Wiesehöfer (ed.), *Das Partherreich und seine Zeugnisse/The Arsacid Empire: Sources and Documentation* (Stuttgart, 1998), 279–94.

37 Cary, *Geographical Background*, 196–7; cf. Frye, *History of Ancient Iran*, 19–20. Fertility: Rostovtzeff, *SEHHW* i. 461.

38 Details: Sherwin-White and Kuhrt, *Samarkhand*, 82–4.

39 Quotations from Rostovtzeff, *SEHHW* i. 545 and 78, respectively.

40 Sogdiane: Sherwin-White and Kuhrt, *Samarkhand*, 103, 105–7. Alexandria Eschate–Antiocheia may be Khodzend (Leninabad) in Tadjikistan, ibid. 106.

41 Cary, *Geographical Background*, 191; Sherwin-White and Kuhrt, *Samarkhand*, 80–1.

42 Western Arachosia: Cary, *Geographical Background*, 196. Karmania: ibid. 191.

43 Sherwin-White and Kuhrt, *Samarkhand*, 72–3, 110.

44 W. W. Tarn, *The Greeks in Bactria and India* (³Chicago, 1985), 103.

45 Wealth: Rostovtzeff, *SEHHW* i. 543, 545. Cf. Sherwin-White and Kuhrt, *Samarkhand*, 113, 63 (little evidence as to whether the kings exploited its gold and other metal resources). Agriculture: Cary, *Geographical Background*, 198–9; 197. Villages: Sherwin-White and Kuhrt, *Samarkhand*, 112.

46 Cary, *Geographical Background*, 199–200.

47 Sherwin-White and Kuhrt, *Samarkhand*, 107; 108; 19. Tarn, *Greeks in Bactria and India*, appendix 14 (pp. 488–90).

48 Rostovtzeff, *SEHHW* i. 78.

49 Cary, *Geographical Background*, 194.

50 Pushkalavati probably = modern Charsad(d)a: Tarn, *Greeks in Bactria and India*, 135 ('Pushkalāvatī'); Frye, *History of Ancient Iran*, 185.

51 Sherwin-White and Kuhrt, *Samarkhand*, 98, 100.

52 D. Schlumberger, L. Robert, A. Dupont-Sommer, and E. Benveniste, 'Une bilingue gréco-araméenne d'Asoka', *Journal asiatique*, 246 (1958), 1–48; N. A. Nikam and R. McKeon, *The Edicts of Aśoka* (Chicago, 1959); further references in Burstein ad loc.

53 Sherwin-White and Kuhrt, *Samarkhand*, 65.

54 Cf. ibid. 95–7, contrasting his work with those of (e.g.) Berossos and Hekataios as a 'legitimation of … non-conquest' (p. 97). The Greek sources on India are usefully collected and translated by U. P. Arora, *Greeks on India: Skylax to Aristoteles* (Bareilly, India, 1996), 111–54.

55 *Precepts of Statecraft* = *Moralia*, 798 a–825 f. Demetrios II: Narain, 'Greeks of Bactria and India', 399–401, with estimated dates on p. 420. Menander: ibid. 406–12.

56 Ibid. 413–15.

57 R. N. Frye, *The History of Ancient Iran* (Munich, 1984), 20.

58 Sherwin-White and Kuhrt, *Samarkhand*, 10.

59 Ibid. 9, cf. also 93.

60 Ibid. 14–15.

61 Ibid. 21–2 (quotation, 22). The source is a fragment of a Babylonian chronicle from 282 and 281 BC: A. K. Grayson, *Assyrian and Babylonian Chronicles* (Locust Valley, NY, 1975), no. 12, obv. 3–5, rev. 1–2; cf. S. M. Sherwin-White, 'Babylonian chronicle fragments as a source for Seleucid history', *Journal of Near Eastern Studies*, 42 (1983b), 265–70, at pp. 267–8.

62 Sherwin-White and Kuhrt, *Samarkhand*, 23–4, *contra* Will² i. 88.

63 Cf. Sherwin-White and Kuhrt, *Samarkhand*, 29.

64 Ibid. 29–30.

65 On the landscape of Syria see Grainger, *Cities*, 7–11; F. Millar, *The Roman Near East: 31 BC–AD 337* (Cambridge, MA, and London, 1993), 236–42; on Apameia's Greek origins, ibid. 256–63 *passim*.

66 Apameia, in fact, was an existing settlement with a Macedonian name, Pella: Grainger, *Cities*, 39.

67 Sherwin-White and Kuhrt, *Samarkhand*, 37.

68 Musti, 'Syria and the east', 212.

69 Ibid. 213.

70 As suggested by Frye, *History of Ancient Iran*, 188, with a review of alternative scenarios including that of Tarn, *Greeks in Bactria and India*, 222–3.

71 Sherwin-White and Kuhrt, *Samarkhand*, 197. For Antiochos's *anabasis*, see also R. M. Errington, 'Rome against Philip and Antiochus', *CAH*² viii (1989), ch. 8 (pp. 244–89), at pp. 248–50.

72 On the stereotyping of pastoralists, see A. J. S. Spawforth, 'Nomads', *OCD*³ 1047.

73 Sherwin-White and Kuhrt, *Samarkhand*, 198–9.

74 Ibid. 210–15.

75 Sherwin-White and Kuhrt, *Samarkhand*, 221–2; Gruen, *HW* 646–7; C. Habicht, 'The Seleucids and their rivals', *CAH* viii² (1989), ch. 10 (pp. 324–87), at pp. 338–41, cf. 355.

76 Habicht, 'Seleucids', 344–5; Gruen, *HW* 658–60.

77 Cf. Ath. 10. 439. On the procession see also Sherwin-White and Kuhrt, *Samarkhand*, 220–1.

78 Antiochos's reign is favourably assessed by Habicht, 'Seleucids', 341–53; details of the expedition, with many source references, ibid. 350–2.

79 On the satrapal system generally see Sherwin-White and Kuhrt, *Samarkhand*, 42–8.

80 Aramaic, etc.: ibid. 50. Borrowing of Greek script to render non-Greek languages: ibid. 160.

81 Ezida temple: ibid. 36–7; Kuhrt and Sherwin-White, *Hellenism*, 28; J. B. Pritchard (ed.), *Ancient Near Eastern Texts relating to the Old Testament* (Princeton, 1969), 317.

82 Sherwin-White and Kuhrt, *Samarkhand*, 38.

83 Ibid. 55 (cf. 43–4, 198); Cohen, *Seleucid Colonies*, 5–9 (dated 212–205/4 BC).

84 G. Shipley, 'Distance, development, decline? World-systems analysis and the "hellenistic" world', in Bilde, *Centre and Periphery* (1993), 271–84.

85 The Loeb translation is unreliable; that of §3 at Sherwin-White and Kuhrt, *Samarkhand*, 67, incomplete. Details of the passage are interpreted variously: see e.g. Rostovtzeff, *SEHHW* i. 440–6; Sherwin-White and Kuhrt (above). Rostovtzeff, i. 471, points out that the *cheirônaxion* is mentioned only in Egyptian documents, though this need not prove its absence in the Seleukid empire.

86 *RDGE* 2. See also Sherwin-White and Kuhrt, *Samarkhand*, 65.

87 *IGLS* vii. 4028 c.

88 So Austin, p. 292 n. 4.

89 *IGLS* vii. 4028 d; see Millar, *Roman Near East*, 271–2, cf. 266.

90 J. K. Davies, 'Cultural, social and economic features of the hellenistic world', *CAH²* vii. 1 (1984), ch. 8 (pp. 257–320), at p. 297.

91 On the fiscal system see Rostovtzeff, *SEHHW* i. 469–72. E. R. Bevan, *The House of Seleucus* (London, 1902; reprinted 1966), still contains useful material. More recently, see Sherwin-White and Kuhrt, *Samarkhand*. As Rostovtzeff says (i. 472), 'Of the total amount of their revenues no idea can be formed. The Seleukids were certainly as rich as the Ptolemies.'

92 References gathered by P. Briant, 'Forces productives, dépendance rurale et idéologies religieuses dans l'empire achéménide', in *RTP* 431–73, at 451 n. 109.

93 Sherwin-White and Kuhrt, *Samarkhand*, 70.

94 Ibid. 55.

95 See ibid. 69–70 for objections to the simplistic marxist category of 'Asiatic mode of production', and to the idea that the Greeks fundamentally altered the economy of Asia by introducing chattel slavery.

96 W. H. Buckler and D. M. Robinson, *Sardis*, vii: *Greek and Latin Inscriptions* (Leiden, 1932), part 1, pp. 1–7, no. 1; R. Bogaert, *Epigraphica*, iii: *Texts on Bankers, Banking and Credit in the Greek World* (Leiden, 1976), no. 36.

97 L. Robert and J. Robert, *La Carie: histoire et géographie historique*, ii: *Le Plateau de Tabai et ses environs* (Paris, 1954), 285–302, no. 166.

98 But see Sherwin-White and Kuhrt, *Samarkhand*, 59–61, for the non-validity of 'temple state' as a formal category.

99 Cf. ibid. 68.

100 Ibid. 202–9 and 28.

101 Ibid. 129–32.

102 R. R. R. Smith, *Hellenistic Royal Portraits* (Oxford, 1988), 81–2; though in *Hellenistic Sculpture: A Handbook* (London, 1991), e.g. at pp. 23–4, he accepts some identifications.

103 *Moralia*, 326 d–333 c.

104 P. M. Fraser, *Cities of Alexander the Great* (Oxford, 1996).

105 Sherwin-White and Kuhrt, *Samarkhand*, 20–1.

106 Briant suggests that he turned them from villagers running a mixed arable and pastoral economy into peasants supplying the cities (*État et pasteurs,* 94–6); but this model appears to presuppose a 'consumer city' model, after the style of M. I. Finley, *The Ancient Economy* (London, ^{1}1973, ^{2}1985), based on the fundamental opposition of town and country, which does not seem appropriate. For criticisms of certain applications of the model, see D. J. Mattingly, 'Beyond belief? Drawing a line beneath the consumer city', in H. M. Parkins (ed.), *Roman Urbanism: Beyond the Consumer City* (London and New York, 1997), 210–18; H. Parkins, 'The "consumer city" domesticated? The Roman city in élite economic strategies', ibid. 83–111, esp. 84–6.

107 Uruk: Sherwin-White and Kuhrt, *Samarkhand*, 149–55. Babylon: ibid. 155–8.

108 Sardis: ibid. 171, 180–3. Sousa: ibid. 179.

109 C. B. Welles, J. O. Fink, and J. F. Gilliam, *The Excavations at Dura-Europos: Final Report*, v. 1: *The Parchments and Papyri* (New Haven, CT, 1959), 76–9, no. *12.

110 Préaux, ii. 403–8, makes useful distinctions between different kinds of city foundations.

111 Cohen, *Seleucid Colonies*, 72–86, and summary at 87–9.

112 Sherwin-White and Kuhrt, *Samarkhand*, 23.

113 Ibid. 20–1.

114 Ibid. 103–5, 108–9.

115 Ibid. 177 fig. 11, 178–9; 111; C. Rapin, *Fouilles d'Aï Khanoum*, viii: *La Trésorerie du palais hellénistique d'Aï Khanoum: l'apogée et la chute du royaume grec de Bactriane* (Paris, 1992), and other volumes in the series: P. Bernard (ed.), i: *Campagnes 1965, 1966, 1967, 1968: rapport préliminaire* (1973); O. Guillaume, ii: *Les Propylées de la rue principale* (1983); H.-P. Francfort, iii: *Le Sanctuaire du temple à redans, 2: Les Trouvailles* (1984); P. Bernard, iv: *Les Monnaies hors trésors: questions d'histoire gréco-bactrienne* (1985); P. Leriche, v: *Les Remparts et les monuments associés* (1986); S. Veuve, vi: *Le Gymnase: architecture, céramique, sculpture* (1987); O. Guillaume and A. Rougeulle, vii: *Les Petits Objets* (1987). See also the overview by P. Bernard, 'Aï Khanum on the Oxus: a hellenistic city in central Asia', *Proceedings of the British Academy*, 53 (1967), 71–95.

116 Governors: Sherwin-White and Kuhrt, *Samarkhand*, 50. Institutions: ibid. 162. Magnesia: ibid. 162–3.

117 *I. Didyma* 479; Sherwin-White and Kuhrt, *Samarkhand*, 26 (part), cf. 25.

118 Ibid. 26–7.

119 The following is a selection of recent writings, ordered approximately by date: E. J. Bickerman, *From Ezra to the Last of the Maccabees: Foundations of Post-biblical Judaism* (New York, 1962); E. Bickerman, *The God of the Maccabees: Studies on the Meaning and Origin of the Maccabean Revolt* (Leiden, 1979; trans. of 1937 German edition); id., *The Jews in the Greek Age* (Cambridge, MA, and

London, 1988); Schürer[2] i (1973), ch. 5 (pp. 164–73), also chs 4 (pp. 137–63) and 6 (pp. 174–88); A. Momigliano, *Alien Wisdom: The Limits of Hellenization* (Cambridge, etc., 1975), ch. 5 (pp. 97–122); M. Hengel, *Judaism and Hellenism: Studies in their Encounter in Palestine during the Early Hellenistic Period* (London, 1974), i. 277–309, with criticisms by F. Millar, 'The background to the Maccabean revolution: reflections on Martin Hengel's "Judaism and Hellenism"', *Journal of Jewish Studies*, 29 (1978), 1–21; K. Bringmann, 'Die Verfolgung der jüdischen Religion durch Antiochos IV.: ein Konflikt zwischen Judentum und Hellenismus?', *Antike und Abendland*, 26 (1980), 176–90; id., *Hellenistische Reform und Religionsverfolgung in Judäa: eine Untersuchung zur jüdisch-hellenistischen Geschichte (175–163 v.Chr.)* (Göttingen, 1983);O. Mørkholm, 'Antiochus IV', in W. D. Davies and L. Finkelstein (eds), *The Cambridge History of Judaism*, ii: *The Hellenistic Age* (Cambridge, 1989), ch. 8 (pp. 278–91); J. A. Goldstein, 'The Hasmonean revolt and the Hasmonean dynasty', ibid. ch. 9 (pp. 292–351; the last two have extensive bibliographies); Habicht, 'Seleucids', 346–50; B. Bar-Kochva, *Judas Maccabaeus: The Jewish Struggle against the Seleucids* (Cambridge, 1989); N. Hyldahl, 'The Maccabean rebellion and the question of "hellenization"', in Bilde, *Religion*, 188–203; S. D. Cohen, 'Religion, ethnicity and "hellenism" in the emergence of Jewish identity in Maccabean Palestine', ibid. 204–23; Sherwin-White and Kuhrt, *Samarkhand*, 226–9; E. S. Gruen, 'Hellenism and persecution: Antiochus IV and the Jews', in Green, *HHC* 238–64 (with 'Response' of M. G. Morgan, 264–9); T. Rajak, 'Maccabees', *OCD*[3] 904.

120 Date of Daniel: Millar, 'Background', 9; Habicht, 'Seleucids', 346 n. 77. The sources (other than Maccabees) are printed and translated by M. Stern, *Greek and Latin Authors on Jews and Judaism* (Jerusalem, 1974–80); see especially i. 185–7, Diodorus Siculus no. 64 (= Diod. 40. 2), and indexes (in vol. iii) s.v. 'Hasmonaeans'. Note also the German trans. and commentary by C. Habicht, *2. Makkabäerbuch* (Gütersloh, 1979a).

121 Millar, 'Background', is a clear and consistent reconstruction, which I follow here; yet the debate continues.

122 On the disputed issue of whether a new *polis* was envisaged, see Millar, 'Background', 10 and n. 29.

123 Hyldahl, 'Maccabean rebellion', 193.

124 Millar, 'Background', 5–6, 9, 12.

125 Ibid. 10–11, 17, 20.

126 Hyldahl, 'Maccabean rebellion', 194–7, 199, dates the ban on Jewish religion to autumn 168 (with Bringmann, *Hellenistische Reform*, 15–28).

127 Cf. Habicht, 'The Seleucids and their rivals', 352.

128 The phrase is a stock one in English, but its content is uncertain. It also appears at Dan. 11: 31: 'the abominable thing that causes desolation', in the NEB version.

129 Cf. Austin's n. 10 ad loc.

130 Also quoted by Sherwin-White and Kuhrt, *Samarkhand*, 227.

131 Cf. Habicht, 'Seleucids', 370; summary of history in T. Rajak, 'Hasmoneans', *OCD*[3] 668–9.

132 Its cultural legacy can be seen in the festival of Hanukkah, commemorating the rededication of the Temple, and oddly in the word 'macabre', deriving from a legendary martyrdom during the persecution (Rajak, 'Maccabees').

133 On Philetairos, see R. E. Allen, *The Attalid Kingdom: A Constitutional History* (Oxford, 1983), ch. 2 (pp. 9–26), at pp. 9–20; on Eumenes I, ibid. 20–6. See also E. V. Hansen, *The Attalids of Pergamon*[2] (Ithaca, NY, 1971), ch. 2 (pp. 14–25).

134 On Attalos's assumption of the title of king, see Allen, *Attalid Kingdom*, appendix 2 (pp. 195–9). On his first twenty-five years, see ibid. ch. 3 (pp. 27–75), at pp. 27–65; Hansen, *Attalids*², ch. 3 (pp. 26–69), at pp. 26–45.

135 The cultural significance of the sculptures is concisely brought out by H. Heinen, 'The Syrian–Egyptian wars and the new kingdoms of Asia Minor', *CAH*² vii. 1 (1984), ch. 11 (pp. 412–45), at p. 424. For the sculptures, and for Attalos's other monuments in Pergamon and elsewhere, see H.-J. Schalles, *Untersuchungen zur Kulturpolitik der pergamenischen Herrscher im dritten Jahrhundert vor Christus* (Tübingen, 1985), 51–126 and pls 3–6; A. Stewart, *Greek Sculpture: An Exploration* (New Haven, CT, and London, 1990), i. 205–8; ii, pls 667–75.

136 *Staatsv.* iii. 481.

137 On Attalos's last eighteen years, see Allen, *Attalid Kingdom*, 65–75 (and, on the Byzantine appeal, p. 37 and n. 32); Hansen, *Attalids*², 46–69.

138 Allen, *Attalid Kingdom*, 38–58.

139 Habicht, *Athens*, 197–8.

140 The Small Dedication is placed in the mid-second century by some art historians, however, and linked to Eumenes II's defeat of the Gauls (168–166). See Stewart, *Greek Sculpture*, i. 210; for Roman copies of statues probably from this group, ibid. ii, pls 685–91.

141 Allen, *Attalid Kingdom*, 75–9.

142 L. Jonnes and M. Ricl, 'A new royal inscription from Phrygia Paroreios: Eumenes II grants Tyriaion the status of a polis', *Epigraphica Anatolica*, 29 (1997), 1–30.

143 C. Howgego, *Ancient History from Coins* (London and New York, 1995), 54–6; Habicht, 'Seleucids', 331–2; Allen, *Attalid Kingdom*, 78, 109–14.

144 On Pergamon between 188 and 158, see Habicht, 'Seleucids', 324–34; Hansen, *Attalids*², 97–129.

145 Habicht, 'Seleucids', 334–8.

146 On Rhodes after 164 see Habicht, 'Seleucids', 380–1.

147 Ibid. 359–61.

148 On the Attalids between 158 and 133, see ibid. 373–80; on this point, ibid. 373–4.

149 So Allen, *Attalid Kingdom*, 83–5, who suggests (at 84 n. 40) that a precedent may be found in the will of Nikomedes I of Bithynia (*c*.255), who named the Romans, the kings of Macedonia and Egypt, and the cities of Herakleia, Kios, and Byzantion as guardians for his children by his second wife in order to protect the succession (Memnon, *FGH* 434 fr. 14) – unavailingly, as it turned out.

150 *IGRR* iv. 301; *RDGE* 11.

151 E. S. G. Robinson, 'Cistophori in the name of king Eumenes', *Numismatic Chronicle* (6th series), 14 (1954), 1–8. On the revolt, see Habicht, 'Seleucids', 378–80.

152 F. Sokolowski, *Lois sacrées de l'Asie Mineure* (Paris, 1955), no. 15.

153 On these events see Habicht, 'Seleucids', 353–6.

154 Demetrios's reign: ibid. 356–62.

155 Contrary to earlier opinion: Sherwin-White and Kuhrt, *Samarkhand*, 84–90, 223.

156 On these events see Habicht, 'Seleucids', 362–5, with further source references.

157 Details at ibid. 365–9, with many additional ancient references. The ancient evidence includes coin issues; fragments of Diodoros, Livy, and other sources; and the Jewish sources I–II Macc. and Jos. *AJ*. The chronology is disputed.

158 T. Rajak, 'The Jews under Hasmonean rule', *CAH*² ix, ch. 8 *b* (pp. 274–309), examines the period between the Maccabaean revolt and the Pompeian settlement.

159 E. Meyer, *Ursprung und Anfänge des Christentums*, ii (Stuttgart, 1921), 272, quoted with approval by Habicht, 'Seleucids', 372.

160 The confusing events are lucidly expounded by Will ii² 445–7 (with a helpful family tree).

161 As argued by Sherwin-White and Kuhrt, *Samarkhand*, 225–6; M. Colledge, 'Greek and non-Greek interaction in the art and architecture of the hellenistic east', in Kuhrt and Sherwin-White, *Hellenism*, ch. 6 (pp. 134–62), at pp. 158–9.

162 Sherwin-White and Kuhrt, *Samarkhand*, 73, 121–5, 137–40.

163 Rostovtzeff, *SEHHW* i. 472–6.

164 C. Habicht, 'Die herrschende Gesellschaft in den hellenistischen Monarchien', *Vierteljahrschrift für Soziologie und Wirtschaftsgeschichte*, 45 (1958), 1–16.

165 S. Sherwin-White, 'Seleucid Babylonia: a case study for the installation and development of Greek rule', in Kuhrt and Sherwin-White, *Hellenism*, ch. 1 (pp. 1–31), at p. 6; restated at Sherwin-White and Kuhrt, *Samarkhand*, 122.

166 Sherwin-White and Kuhrt, *Samarkhand*, 121. However, the authors may be wrong to describe Habicht's sample as worthless because 'random geographically and chronologically' (p. 122); if it were truly random it would be a perfect statistical basis for calculation. The point is that it is biased towards certain areas, places, and arguably social groups.

167 Sherwin-White, 'Seleucid Babylonia', 6 = Sherwin-White and Kuhrt, *Samarkhand*, 122.

168 M. Wörrle, 'Antiochos I., Achaios der Ältere und die Galater: eine neue Inschrift in Denizli', *Chiron*, 5 (1975), 59–87; *Bull. ép.* 1976, 667.

169 Sherwin-White, 'Seleucid Babylonia', 6–7, with Sherwin-White and Kuhrt, *Samarkhand*, 122.

170 Préaux, e.g. ii. 550–2, 554–6. 'Étanchéité': ibid. i. 102, 106; ii. 551, 554, etc. She also points to the 'imperméabilité quasi totale' of the Greek language, as attested epigraphically, to the influence of native languages (i. 99).

171 Aï Khanum: above, p. 305. Failaka: Sherwin-White and Kuhrt, *Samarkhand*, 176.

172 Sherwin-White and Kuhrt, *Samarkhand*, 137.

173 Walbank, *HW* 122.

174 H. Kreissig, *Wirtschaft und Gesellschaft im Seleukidenreich: die Eigentums- und die Abhängigkeitsverhältnisse* (Berlin, 1978), 124–5.

175 Sherwin-White and Kuhrt, *Samarkhand*, 64.

176 Ibid. 72.

177 Ibid. 218.

9 UNDERSTANDING THE COSMOS: GREEK 'SCIENCE' AFTER ARISTOTLE

1 Cf. G. E. R. Lloyd, *Greek Science after Aristotle* (London, 1973), xiii; cf. p. 7, 'science is a modern, not an ancient, category'.

2 For these and other, less frequent senses see *Concise Oxford Dictionary* (9th edn; Oxford, 1995), s.v. 'science'. *Epistêmê* is the nearest Greek term, but is more akin to 'knowledge'. The wider sense survives more actively in e.g. French *science*, German *Wissenschaft*. Lloyd, *Greek Science after Aristotle*, xiii, notes the range of terms used to describe ancient scientific investigations: *peri physeôs historia*

(inquiry concerning nature), *philosophia* (love of wisdom), *theôria* (speculation), and *epistêmê* (knowledge).

3 Several are worth citing here. In date order: Lloyd, *Greek Science after Aristotle*; 'Introduction', in G. E. R. Lloyd (ed.), J. Chadwick and W. N. Mann (trans.), *Hippocratic Writings* (Harmondsworth, 1978), 9–60; *Magic, Reason and Experience: Studies in the Origin and Development of Greek Science* (Cambridge, etc., 1979); *Science, Folklore and Ideology: Studies in the Life Sciences in Ancient Greece* (Cambridge, 1983); 'Hellenistic science', *CAH²* vii. 1 (1984), ch. 9 *a* (pp. 321–52); *The Revolutions of Wisdom: Studies in the Claims and Practice of Ancient Greek Science* (Berkeley, etc., 1987); *Adversaries and Authorities: Investigations into Ancient Greek and Chinese Science* (Cambridge, 1996). An earlier authoritative study is O. Neugebauer, *The Exact Sciences in Antiquity* (Providence, RI, ²1957); for a more compendious and florid account, see G. Sarton, *A History of Science* (London and Cambridge, MA, 1953–9).

4 Tarn and Griffith, 305.

5 Cf. e.g. ibid. 307, 'Zoology and botany did little more than make a start'; ibid. 308, 'Too much must not be made of Hellenistic science, exciting as it is, since … chemistry … never got started and physics died with Strato'! Nuclear science, of course, never got started either.

6 For a discussion of the difficulties of categorizing ancient science without imposing modern ideas, and an emphasis on the scientific discourse as a species of rhetoric, see T. S. Barton, *Power and Knowledge: Astrology, Physiognomics, and Medicine under the Roman Empire* (Ann Arbor, MI, 1994), esp. 'Introduction' (pp. 1–26).

7 Cf. Préaux, ii. 631, on 'la polymathie des savants'.

8 See *GMW* ii. 261.

9 New collection of fragments: W. W. Fortenbaugh, P. M. Huby, R. W. Sharples, and D. Gutas (eds and trans.), *Theophrastus of Eresus: Sources for his Life, Writings, Thought, and Influence* (Leiden, 1992), i–ii. On Theophrastos generally, see R. French, *Ancient Natural History: Histories of Nature* (London and New York, 1994), ch. 3 (pp. 83–113).

10 Examples in Préaux, i. 216–17, 219–21.

11 *Contra* Blomqvist: see 444 n. 76.

12 Cf. Lloyd, *Greek Science after Aristotle*, 3–6; id., 'Hellenistic science', 333.

13 Lloyd, 'Hellenistic science', 322. On the organization of the Mouseion see also P. M. Fraser, *Ptolemaic Alexandria* (Oxford, 1972), i. 312–19; for an exhaustive examination of Alexandrian science, see ibid. 336–446.

14 Lloyd, *Greek Science after Aristotle*, 5.

15 This and related texts are discussed by Lloyd, ibid. 91.

16 The phrase *hydraulicas machinas* at 9. 8. 4 (quoted above) is translated 'hydraulic machines' in the Loeb edition, but as 'water-organs' in the reliable translation by M. H. Morgan, *Vitruvius: The Ten Books on Architecture* (Cambridge, MA., London, and Oxford, 1914; reprinted, New York, 1960 and often).

17 On Heron and his works, see J. G. Landels, *Engineering in the Ancient World* (Berkeley and Los Angeles, 1978), 198–208.

18 *CAH²* vii. 1, *Plates*, no. 260. On the *kochlias*, see Landels, *Engineering*, 59–63.

19 See R. J. Forbes, 'Power', in his *Studies in Ancient Technology*, ii² (Leiden, 1965), 78–125, at pp. 86–90; Landels, *Engineering*, 19–25; K. D. White, *Greek and Roman Technology* (London, 1984), 55; Ö. Wikander, 'Water-power and technical progress in classical antiquity', in *Ancient Technology: Finnish Institute at Athens, Symposium held 30.3–4.4.1987* (Helsinki, 1990), 68–84, emphasizing that water-mills were invented in the east Mediterranean as early as the first century BC, though the real take-off was in about the second century AD.

20 D. J. Thompson, 'Agriculture', *CAH*² vii. 1 (1984), ch. 9 *c* (pp. 363–70), at p. 369 and n. 97.

21 In translating ἀνάλημμα as 'diagram' rather than 'sundial', I follow Morgan's trans. (in *Vitruvius: The Ten Books on Architecture*) of 9. 1. 1 ('the figure of the analemma'), and P. Gros (ed.), A. Corso, and E. Romano (trans.), *Vitruvio: de architectura* (Turin, 1997), ii. 1257 n. 66. See now LSJ Suppl.² s.v. ἀνάλημμα, III: '*projection* on a plane of circles and points on the celestial sphere ... used for the construction of a sun-dial' (italics original).

22 A. Corso, 'Vitruvius and Attic monuments', *BSA* 92 (1997), 373–400, at pp. 373–7, believes that V. did see the tower. For a detailed description in the light of recent re-examination (still in progress), and arguments for a hellenistic (rather than mid-first-century BC) date, see H. J. Kienast, 'Untersuchungen am Turm der Winde', *Archäologischer Anzeiger*, 1993, 271–5; id., 'The Tower of the Winds at Athens: hellenistic or Roman?', in M. C. Hoff and S. I. Rotroff (eds), *The Romanization of Athens* (Oxford, 1997), 53–65.

23 J. M. Camp, *The Athenian Agora: Excavations in the Heart of Classical Athens* (London, 1986), 157–9 and figs 130–1; also *Athenian Agora*⁴ (Athens, 1990), 181 no. 69; 182 figs 122–3.

24 V. Ch. Petrakos, Ὁ Ὠρωπὸς καὶ τὸ ἱερὸν τοῦ Ἀμφιαράου (Athens, 1968), 70; 113–16 and figs 29–32; or Petracos, *Amphiareion*, 55; 58 fig. 45.

25 T. D. Boyd, 'The arch and the vault in Greek architecture', *American Journal of Archaeology*, 82 (1978), 83–100; cf. brief remarks of F. Winter, 'Building and townplanning', *CAH*² vii. 1 (1984), ch. 9 *d* (pp. 371–83), at p. 373. Nemea: *CAH*² vii. 1, *Plates*, no. 71. Stoa of Eumenes: ibid. no. 85. Delos cistern: ibid. no. 141.

26 R. Ginouvès, *L'Établissement thermal de Gortys d'Arcadie* (Paris, 1959); cf. Winter, 'Building and townplanning', 381 n. 159.

27 P. Cartledge and A. Spawforth, *Hellenistic and Roman Sparta: A Tale of Two Cities* (London and New York, 1989), 26–7 and 237 n. 26 (temporary wall), 71 and 246 n. 20 (permanent wall), 76 and 247 n. 28 (retained after political settlement of 195/4), 78 and 248 n. 31 (demolished 188), 82 and 249 n. 6 (senate recommends restoration, winter 184/3), 84 and 249–50 n. 10 (restored in or after 179), and 217 no. 9 (archaeological evidence from this phase).

28 See now the translation and commentary by D. Whitehead, *Aineias the Tactician: How to Survive under Siege* (Oxford, 1990).

29 See Walbank, *HCP* ad loc. For Diades, see A. B. Bosworth, *A Historical Commentary on Arrian's History of Alexander*, i: *Commentary on Books I–III* (Oxford, 1980), 241 (on 2. 20. 6); W. W. Tarn, *Hellenistic Naval and Military Developments* (Cambridge, 1930), 111.

30 Text and trans.: E. W. Marsden, *Greek and Roman Artillery: Technical Treatises* (Oxford, 1971), 66–77; commentary, 78–103. At p. 78 Marsden favours a date early in the reign of Attalos I.

31 Philon's *Belopoiika* is translated in Marsden, *Technical Treatises*, 105–55 (commentary, 156–84). On catapults see Landels, *Engineering*, ch. 5 (pp. 99–132), esp. pp. 120–31 on Philon.

32 Marsden, *Technical Treatises*, 135–45.

33 Cf. Préaux, i. 329–31.

34 Garlan, 'War and siegecraft', 359.

35 Layouts: ibid. 359–60. Eleutherai: J. Ober, *Fortress Attica: Defense of the Athenian Land Frontier 404–322 BC* (Leiden, 1985), 160–3; details of gates in E. G. Stikas, Ἀνασκαφὴ Ἐλευθερῶν (Πανάκτου)', *PAE* 1938, 41–9.

36 Ober, *Fortress Attica*, 168–9.
37 On gigantism see Préaux, i. 329–30.
38 On the possible significance of these names see Tarn, *Hellenistic Naval and Military Developments*, 132–41.
39 Garlan, 'War and siegecraft', 361–2; quotation, 361.
40 See Fortenbaugh *et al.*, *Theophrastus*.
41 A convenient list is to be found in M. C. Nussbaum, 'Aristotle', *OCD*[3] 165–9, §9 (p. 166).
42 R. W. Sharples, 'Theophrastus', *OCD*[3] 1504–5.
43 P. M. Fraser, 'The world of Theophrastus', in S. Hornblower (ed.), *Greek Historiography* (Oxford, 1994), ch. 6 (pp. 167–91).
44 Lloyd, *Greek Science after Aristotle*, 12–13.
45 Lloyd, *Magic, Reason and Experience*, esp. ch. 1 (pp. 10–58).
46 See generally Fortenbaugh *et al.*, *Theophrastus*, vol. ii.
47 Fraser, 'World of Theophrastus', 172.
48 G. Shipley, *A History of Samos 800–188 BC* (Oxford, 1987), 82–3.
49 Thompson, 'Agriculture', 366.
50 C. Préaux, *Les Grecs en Égypte d'après les archives de Zénon* (Brussels, 1947), 26–7 ('Les arbres fruitiers'), with many additional references.
51 Préaux, i. 379–80; ead., *L'Économie royale des Lagides* (Brussels, 1939), 170–1; cf. Thompson, 'Agriculture', 364–6.
52 Préaux, ii. 476, 477, with additional modern references.
53 Cf. F. Millar, 'The problem of hellenistic Syria', in Kuhrt and Sherwin-White, *Hellenism*, ch. 5 (pp. 110–33), at p. 120.
54 Celsus, 5. 19. 11; Pliny, *HN* 32. 8. 27. 87, and indexes of authors to books 28, 31; Galen, 12. 250–1, 13. 162, 13. 409–16 Kühn.
55 Galen, 12. 252, 14. 2 Kühn. See E. V. Hansen, *The Attalids of Pergamon* (Ithaca, NY, [2]1971), 144–5.
56 Préaux, ii. 477; Rostovtzeff, *SEHHW* ii. 1162–70, who cites many other examples; Sherwin-White and Kuhrt, *Samarkhand*, 70.
57 For a detailed account of Alexandrian medicine see Fraser, *Ptolemaic Alexandria*, i, ch. 7. i (pp. 338–76). More generally, see Lloyd, 'Hellenistic science', 347–52; on the classical background, id., 'Medicine', *CAH*[2] vi (1994), ch. 12 *b* (pp. 634–46).
58 On Praxagoras, see Fraser, *Ptolemaic Alexandria*, i. 345–6; J. T. Vallance, 'Praxagoras', *OCD*[3] 1241–2. Fragment 10 of Praxagoras, on the thorax, is quoted in Greek by Fraser, *Ptolemaic Alexandria*, ii. 502 n. 41, and trans. by F. Steckerl, *The Fragments of Praxagoras of Cos and his School* (Leiden, 1958), p. 49.
59 There was no agreement in antiquity as to how many humours there were, or which were most important. J. T. Vallance, 'Humours', *OCD*[3] 733.
60 H. von Staden, *Herophilus: The Art of Medicine in Early Alexandria. Edition, Translation and Essays* (Cambridge and New York, 1989); id., 'Herophilus', *OCD*[3] 699.
61 id., 'Erasistratus', *OCD*[3] 552–3; texts in I. Garofalo (ed.), *Erasistrati fragmenta* (Pisa, 1988).
62 Cf. Préaux, ii. 447; Austin ad loc.
63 Translation modified from that of Fraser, *Ptolemaic Alexandria*, i. 348.
64 Lloyd, 'Hellenistic science', 348. Lloyd, *Greek Science after Aristotle*, 75–7, inclines to accept Celsus's statement.
65 Fraser, *Ptolemaic Alexandria*, ii. 512–13 n. 97 (to i. 352), quoting Ps.-Ruf. *Anat.* 71–4 (pp. 184–5 Ruelle), and Galen (8. 212 Kühn), judges it uncertain (despite the Rufus extract) whether Erasistratos and Herophilos distinguished motor and

sensory nerves. Galen (8. 605) also attacked Herophilos for claiming that the nerves are the actual motive power of the body (Fraser, *Ptolemaic Alexandria*, ii. 513 n. 98).

66 In his lost work Περὶ σφυγμῶν, in which he reacted against his master Praxagoras of Kos. Galen's accounts of Herophilos's work on the pulse (8. 723–4, 869, 871 Kühn) are quoted in Greek by Fraser, *Ptolemaic Alexandria*, ii. 515 n. 104, 517 n. 110, 525 n. 147.

67 For ancient sources on the cult, see E. J. Edelstein and L. Edelstein, *Asclepius: A Collection and Interpretation of the Testimonies* (Baltimore, MD, 1945).

68 Cf. S. M. Sherwin-White, *Ancient Cos: An Historical Study from the Dorian Settlement to the Imperial Period* (Göttingen, 1978), 97–106, also ch. 7. Philadelphos: ibid. 83–4.

69 The oath is translated by Chadwick and Mann in Lloyd, *Hippocratic Writings*, 67; and by W. H. S. Jones, *Hippocrates*, i. 299–301 (Cambridge, MA, 1923). For brief discussions, see Lloyd's introduction, 19–20; J. T. Vallance, 'Medicine', *OCD*[3] 945–9, at 946.

70 Translated by J. Chadwick and W. N. Mann, *The Medical Works of Hippocrates* (Oxford, 1950); reprinted in Lloyd (ed.), *Hippocratic Writings*, 148–69. Also translated by Jones, *Hippocrates*, i. 65–137.

71 See G. J. Toomer, 'Astronomical instruments', *OCD*[3] 195–6; and especially his excellent general essay, 'Astronomy', ibid. 196–8.

72 Lloyd, *Greek Science after Aristotle*, 67–9 and figs 10–11; id., 'Hellenistic science', 344 fig. 5; F. Hultsch, 'Dioptra', *RE* v. 1 (1903), 1073–9, with A. G. Drachmann, *RE* suppl. vi (1935), 1287–90. Passages from Heron's *Dioptra* (ch. 23, on measuring a piece of ground of irregular area; ch. 37, on the forces transmitted by toothed wheels) are translated in *GMW* ii. 485–97.

73 The device is illustrated by Lloyd, 'Hellenistic science', 345 fig. 6; see also O. Neugebauer, *The Exact Sciences in Antiquity*[2] (New York, 1957; repr. 1962), 185, 219.

74 Translation in G. J. Toomer, *Ptolemy's Almagest* (London, 1984; repr. Princeton, NJ, 1998), 321. See Lloyd, 'Hellenistic science', 321, 344; G. J. Toomer, 'Hipparchus', *OCD*[3] 708; id., 'Timocharis', *OCD*[3] 1528.

75 For the Augustan age, the relation between geography and imperialist culture is well explored by C. Nicolet, *L'Inventaire du monde: géographie et politique aux origines de l'empire romain* (Paris, 1988), now translated as *Space, Geography, and Politics in the Early Roman Empire* (Ann Arbor, MI, 1991).

76 See T. Heath, *Aristarchus of Samos: The Ancient Copernicus* (Oxford, 1913).

77 Lloyd, *Greek Science after Aristotle*, 57.

78 *Platonic Questions* = *Moralia*, 999 c–1011 e. Lloyd, 'Hellenistic science', 321; id., *Greek Science after Aristotle*, 55. Seleukos: Fraser, *Ptolemaic Alexandria*, i. 398, ii. 576 nn. 169–70.

79 *On the Face on the Moon* = *Moralia*, 920 a–945 d.

80 Préaux, ii. 624.

81 As J. L. E. Dreyer suggested in his classic work, *A History of the Planetary Systems from Thales to Kepler* (Cambridge, 1906); reprinted as *A History of Astronomy from Thales to Kepler* (New York, 1958 and often).

82 Lloyd, *Greek Science after Aristotle*, 61–7, explains the model in detail; quotation, p. 67.

83 Préaux, ii. 635–6; Lloyd, 'Hellenistic science', 346–7.

84 T. Barton, *Ancient Astrology* (London and New York, 1994), ch. 1 (pp. 1–31), esp. 15–16, 30–1. D. Pingree, 'Legacies in astronomy and celestial omens', in S.

Dalley (ed.), *The Legacy of Mesopotamia* (Oxford, 1998), 125–37, at 134, agrees that horoscopic astrology was probably invented in Egypt *c.*100 BC 'on the basis of Aristotelian physics, hellenistic planetary theory and ... elements of Mesopotamian astral science'.

85 The full form of this alternative title is *Mathematike tetrabiblos syntaxis*, i.e. *Mathematical* (significant name!) *Systematic Treatise in Four Books*. On the two procedures see Lloyd, *Greek Science after Aristotle*, 130.

86 Préaux, ii. 627; C. Préaux, *La Lune dans la pensée grecque* (Brussels, 1973).

87 Discovery of the tides in the Atlantic and Persian gulf in the time of Alexander: Préaux, ii. 623, cf. 627.

88 See e.g. E. Hussey, *The Presocratics* (London, 1972), 4 (Babylonians), 65–7 (Pythagoreans), 119–20 (fifth-century advances), 152 (Eudemos); G. S. Kirk, J. E. Raven, and M. Schofield, *The Presocratic Philosophers: A Critical History with a Selection of Texts*[2] (Cambridge, 1983); G. J. Toomer, 'Mathematics', *OCD*[3] 936–7.

89 Tarn and Griffith, 299.

90 *GMW* ii. 280 n.

91 A myriad, *myrias* in Greek, is 10,000 or 10^4. The nth order $= 10^{8n}$. The nth period $= 10^8$ to the power $(8 \times 10^8) \times 10^{8n}$. The precise details matter less than the way of thinking about numbers which they embody.

92 Lloyd, *Greek Science after Aristotle*, 47.

93 Lloyd, 'Hellenistic science', 335–6.

94 D. J. de S. Price, *Gears from the Greeks: The Antikythera Mechanism, a Calendar Computer from ca. 80 BC* (Transactions of the American Philosophical Society, n.s. 64.7; Philadelphia, PA, 1974; also New York, 1975). A good account of its operation is given by J. V. Field, 'European astronomy in the first millennium: the archaeological record', in C. Walker (ed.), *Astronomy before the Telescope* (London, 1996), 110–22, at pp. 114–18. See also *CAH*[2] vii. 1, Plates, no. 261; N. Yalouris, 'The shipwreck of Antikythera: new evidence of its date after supplementary investigation', in J.-P. Descoeudres (ed.), Εὐμουσία: *Ceramic and Iconographic Studies in Honour of Alexander Cambitoglou* (Sydney, 1990), 135–6.

95 See Nicolet, *L'Inventaire du monde* or *Space, Geography, and Politics*. For details of Alexandrian geographical writing, see Fraser, *Ptolemaic Alexandria*, i. 520–53. On the political and philosophical context of ancient geography, see French, *Ancient Natural History*, ch. 3 (pp. 114–48).

96 Lloyd, 'Hellenistic science', 333; id., *Greek Science after Aristotle*, 49. For details of Eratosthenes' work, and for his sources, see Fraser, *Ptolemaic Alexandria*, i. 525–39.

97 *GMW* ii. 271–3. Kleomedes' date is uncertain, possibly *c.* AD 360: G. J. Toomer, 'Cleomedes', *OCD*[3] 345; O. Neugebauer, *A History of Ancient Mathematical Astronomy* (Berlin and New York, 1975), ii. 652–7, 959–65. His work was largely based on that of Poseidonios. Toomer, however, says Kleomedes' account of Eratosthenes' measurement 'appears to be largely fictitious'; no doubt his exposition was formulated in his own terms.

98 See e.g. T. C. Young, 'The consolidation of the empire and its limits of growth under Darius and Xerxes', *CAH*[2] iv (1988), ch. 2 (pp. 53–111), at pp. 98–9; A. D. H. Bivar, 'The Indus lands', ibid. ch. 3 *d* (pp. 194–210), at p. 201.

99 Cf. J. O. Thomson, *History of Ancient Geography* (Cambridge, 1948), 71.

100 See the excellent edition by L. Casson, *The Periplus Maris Erythraei* (Princeton, NJ, 1989); also O. A. W. Dilke, *Greek and Roman Maps* (London, 1985), 138–40.

101 Dilke, *Maps*, 138–40. Trans. and commentary by S. M. Burstein, *Agatharchides of Cnidus: On the Erythraean Sea* (London, 1989). For an overview of Agatharchides' work, see Fraser, *Ptolemaic Alexandria*, i. 539–50.

102 Discussed in detail by Walbank, *HW* 204–6; Dilke, *Maps*, 136.

103 Walbank, *HW* 197.

104 On the existence, but also the limitations, of empirical approaches in Greek technology, see Landels, *Engineering*, ch. 8 (pp. 186–98).

105 Préaux, ii. 623–8 *passim*.

106 Préaux, *La Lune*, 255–6, quoting the end of Pappos, book 1; the passage is translated by Heath, *Aristarchus*, 341–2.

107 Préaux, ii. 622–36.

108 T. S. Kuhn, *The Structure of Scientific Revolutions*[2] (Chicago, 1970), e.g. chs 6–8 (pp. 43–75) and 'Postscript' (pp. 143–72); he defines 'paradigm' on pp. 8–9 (cf. 145).

109 Lloyd, *Greek Science after Aristotle*, 178.

110 Lloyd, *Magic, Reason, and Experience*, esp. ch. 4. In *Adversaries and Authorities*, too, Lloyd observes that whereas Chinese science reflects the absence of the political confrontation characteristic of Greek society, with its notion of 'the radical revisability of basic assumptions', Greek science developed 'without a deep sense of political cohesion such as is exemplified in China … and without the guiding idea that what counted was not the ability to give an account, let alone to win an argument, but the ideal of the sage as the living embodiment of wisdom' (p. 227).

111 Préaux, i. 390.

112 Cf. P. J. Rhodes with D. M. Lewis, *The Decrees of the Greek States* (Oxford, 1997), v, reacting against De Ste. Croix's view of ' "the destruction of Greek democracy" after the classical period'.

113 Lloyd, *Greek Science after Aristotle*, 77.

114 Lloyd, 'Hellenistic science', 337.

115 Préaux, ii. 633; quotation at 631, 'Le type humain idéal n'est pas le «chercheur», mais *l'orateur* efficace dans les conseils du roi' (emphasis original). I am grateful to Céline Marquaille and Paul Tipper for advice on how best to translate the second clause.

116 Rightly emphasized by Lloyd, *Revolutions of Wisdom*, e.g. 335–6; he refers to 'a new kind of wisdom' at (e.g.) pp. 49, 214; on p. 335 to 'a wisdom with a difference'.

10 ROME AND GREECE

1 A full treatment would engage with such fundamental studies of the past generation as those of E. Badian, *Foreign Clientelae (264–70 BC)* (Oxford, 1958), who examines the role of Roman–Greek relationships of amicitia (friendship), analogous to the patron–client nexus of Roman society. W. V. Harris, *War and Imperialism in Republican Rome 327–70 BC* (Oxford, [1]1979, [2]1984), paints a more sinister picture of systematic aggression resulting from the social dynamics of the aristocracy (see also id., 'Rome and Carthage', *CAH*[2] viii (1989), ch. 5 (pp. 107–62), esp. pp. 152–6). E. S. Gruen, *The Hellenistic World and the Coming of Rome* (Berkeley, etc., 1984; henceforth 'Gruen, *HW*') and other works (see Bibliography), takes a view more akin to older studies which saw Rome as essentially reactive, and emphasizes the Greek tradition of *philia* (friendship) that lay behind these connections; for comments on his arguments see J. Briscoe, *CR* 100 [n.s. 36] (1986), 91–6; cf. id., *Commentary on Livy: Books XXXIV–XXXVII*

(Oxford, 1981); id., 'Rome and the class struggle in the Greek states 200–146 BC', *Past and Present*, 36 (1967), 3–20, repr. in M. I. Finley (ed.), *Studies in Ancient Society* (London, 1974), ch. 3 (pp. 53–73). J.-L. Ferrary, similarly, examines the operation of patronage after 146 in 'The hellenistic world and Roman patronage', in Cartledge, *Constructs*, 105–19, building on his *Philhellénisme et impérialisme: aspects idéologiques de la conquête romaine du monde hellénistique, de la seconde guerre de Macédoine à la guerre contre Mithridate* (Rome, 1988), 117–32, which is reviewed by J. Briscoe, *CR* 104 [n.s. 40] (1990), 373–7; for other reviews see n. 9 below. R. M. Errington, 'Rome and Greece to 205 BC', *CAH*² viii (1989), ch. 4 (pp. 81–106), and 'Rome against Philip and Antiochus', ibid. ch. 8 (pp. 244–89), prefers to allow an interpretation to emerge from events: while pragmatic considerations were uppermost on all sides, the Romans by the early second century were lulled by success into pursuing their interests in defiance of the sensibilities of others.

2 Particularly for the later phases of conquest, my chapter reflects intermittent discussions over many years with the late W. G. Forrest and with P. S. Derow, though the opinions expressed are not theirs in all respects. Derow has presented his views with elegance and clarity in 'Rome, the fall of Macedon and the sack of Corinth', *CAH*² viii (1989), ch. 9 (pp. 290–323); 'Polybius, Rome, and the east', *JRS* 69 (1979), 1–15; and in other articles cited below.

3 Harris, *War and Imperialism*.

4 On the development of Roman power in Italy, see T. J. Cornell, *The Beginnings of Rome: Italy and Rome from the Bronze Age to the Punic Wars (c.1000–264 BC)* (London and New York, 1995), ch. 14 (pp. 345–68); id., 'The conquest of Italy', *CAH*² vii. 2 (1989), ch. 8 (pp. 351–419). On the nature of the Roman state in the third century, see id., *Beginnings*, ch. 15 (pp. 369–98), at pp. 369–80.

5 Earlier contacts between Rome and the Greeks are summarized by Errington, 'Rome and Greece', 81–5; Walbank, *HW* 227–9; Cornell, *Beginnings*, 394–8 (cf. 145–6, arguing for conscious imitation of the archaic Greek tyrants by the contemporary kings of Rome; 261–4, influence of Greek cults and democracy on fourth-century Rome). On the Roman adoption of Greek culture down to the sack of Corinth, see E. Rawson, 'Roman tradition and the Greek world', *CAH*² viii (1989), ch. 12 (pp. 422–76).

6 Cornell, *Beginnings*, 397, cites Q. Publilius Philo (praetor in 336 BC), P. Sempronius Sophus (cos. 304), and Q. Marcius Philippus (cos. 281).

7 Rawson, 'Roman tradition', 425–6; A. Momigliano, 'Fabius Pictor and the origins of national history', in id., *The Classical Foundations of Modern Historiography* (Berkeley, etc., 1990), ch. 4 (pp. 80–108).

8 On the stages by which Greek culture was translated, then adapted, see M. Beard and M. Crawford, *Rome in the Late Republic: Problems and Interpretations* (London, 1985), ch. 2 (pp. 12–24).

9 See e.g. P. S. Derow, 'Philhellenism', *OCD*³ 1159–60, with many further references including Ferrary, *Philhellénisme*, with reviews by E. S. Gruen, *Classical Philology*, 85 (1990), 324–9, and P. S. Derow, *JRS* 80 (1990), 197–200; A. Erskine, 'The Romans as common benefactors', *Historia*, 43 (1994), 70–87.

10 See e.g. A. Momigliano, *Alien Wisdom: The Limits of Hellenization* (Cambridge, etc., 1975), esp. ch. 1 (pp. 1–21).

11 P. R. Franke, 'Pyrrhus', *CAH*² vii. 2 (1989), ch. 10 (pp. 456–85); Cornell, *Beginnings*, 363–4.

12 Paxos, etc.: details in F. W. Walbank, 'Macedonia and the Greek leagues', *CAH*² vii. 1 (1984), ch. 12 (pp. 446–81), at pp. 452–3.

13 First Illyrian war: Gruen, *HW* 359–68; Errington, 'Rome and Greece', 86–90.

14 See discussion at Errington, 'Rome and Greece', 85–8, with K.-E. Petzold, 'Rom und Illyrien: ein Beitrag zur römischen Aussenpolitik im 3. Jahrhundert', *Historia*, 20 (1971), 199–223; P. S. Derow, 'Kleemporos', *Phoenix*, 27 (1973), 118–34; Gruen, *HW* 360–2.

15 Errington, 'Rome and Greece', 97; Gruen, *HW* 375–6. Details of second Illyrian war: Errington, 'Rome and Greece', 91–4; Gruen, *HW* 370–3.

16 Walbank, 'Macedonia and the Greek leagues', 474–81; Errington, 'Rome and Greece', 99–101; Gruen, *HW* 17–21, 377–8. Details of first Macedonian war: Errington, 'Rome and Greece', 94–106.

17 *IG* ix. 1^2 241; *Staatsv.* iii. 536.

18 Discussed by A. D. Rizakis, *Achaïe*, i: *Sources textuelles et histoire régionale* (Athens and Paris, 1995), 126–7 no. 167.

19 Errington, 'Rome and Greece', 103; Gruen, *HW* 379–80.

20 Habicht, *Athens*, 195–6; C. Habicht, *Studien zur Geschichte Athens in hellenistischer Zeit* (Göttingen, 1982), 138–42 (with references to earlier literature); *contra*, E. S. Gruen, *Studies in Greek Culture and Roman Policy* (Leiden, etc., 1990), 27–33, 150.

21 Details of second Macedonian war: Errington, 'Rome against Philip and Antiochus', 261–74; Gruen, *HW* 382–98.

22 Errington, 'Rome against Philip and Antiochus', 252–3; Gruen, *HW* 532–4.

23 Alleged pact: Walbank, *HCP* ii. 471–3; Will, ii^2 114–24; G. Shipley, *A History of Samos 800–188 BC* (Oxford, 1987), 192; Errington, 'Rome against Philip and Antiochus', 254; Gruen, *HW* 387–8. Events surrounding the capture of Samos: Shipley, *Samos*, 191–4.

24 Habicht, *Athens*, 197–8.

25 Also M. Holleaux, *Études d'épigraphie et d'histoire grecques*, v (Paris, 1957), 141–55; P. Frisch, *Die Inschriften von Lampsakos* (Bonn, 1978), no. 4.

26 Errington, 'Rome against Philip and Antiochus', 271, 274–6.

27 Ibid. 278–9; Gruen, *HW* 626–9.

28 See n. 1. A negative view is forcefully argued, with reference to the period after 188, by Derow, 'Rome, the fall of Macedon ...', and by C. Habicht, 'The Seleucids and their rivals', CAH^2 viii (1989), ch. 10 (pp. 324–87), especially §5, 'Epilogue: Roman policy in the east, 189–129 BC' (pp. 382–7).

29 Errington, 'Rome against Philip and Antiochos', 263, 268.

30 Ibid. 283.

31 *RDGE* 35.

32 On the origins, course, and aftermath of Rome's war against Antiochos, see Errington, 'Rome against Philip and Antiochus', 274–89; cf. Gruen, *HW* 632–44, also 547–50.

33 M. Holleaux, 'Inscription trouvée à Brousse', in his *Études d'épigraphie et d'histoire grecques*, ii: *Études sur la monarchie attalide* (Paris, 1938), 73–125; *SEG* ii. 663.

34 On these events, see Derow, 'Rome, the fall of Macedon ...', 290–5.

35 M. B. Hatzopoulos, *Macedonian Institutions under the Kings* (Athens, 1996), ii, no. 12.

36 Derow, 'Rome, the fall of Macedon . . .', 301; cf. Gruen, *HW* 497–502.

37 On these events see Derow, 'Rome, the fall of Macedon ...', 302–5; Gruen, *HW* 404–5.

38 On the Lykian–Rhodian dispute, see Habicht, 'Seleucids', 335–6.

39 *RDGE* 40.

40 e.g. Derow, 'Rome, the fall of Macedon...', 310–11.

41 J. A. O. Larsen, *Greek Federal States: Their Institutions and History* (Oxford, 1968), 295–300.

42 V. Gabrielsen, 'Rhodes and Rome after the third Macedonian war', in Bilde, *Centre and Periphery* (1993), 132–61, esp. 145–51; *contra*, Gruen, *HW* 311–12. On Rhodes, see also R. M. Berthold, *Rhodes in the Hellenistic Age* (Ithaca, NY, and London, 1984); on the economy of Delos down to this time, see the ground-breaking study of G. Reger, *Regionalism and Change in the Economy of Independent Delos, 314–167 BC* (Berkeley, etc., 1994).

43 Habicht, *Athens*, 220–6, 280–2.

44 M. Thompson, *The New Style Silver Coinage of Athens* (New York, 1961); M. J. Price, 'Southern Greece', in A. M. Burnett and M. H. Crawford (eds), *The Coinage of the Roman World in the Late Republic* (Oxford, 1987), 95–103; C. Howgego, *Ancient History from Coins* (London and New York, 1995), 57; Habicht, *Athens*, 242–5 (with additional references), 291–2.

45 Habicht, *Athens*, 243.

46 Inferred, on the basis of career data for Athenian letter-cutters, by S. V. Tracy, *Attic Letter-cutters of 229 to 86 BC* (Berkeley, etc., 1990), 223–6.

47 Habicht, *Athens*, 247 (relatives), 249 (autonomy), 257–9 (Italians), 259–61 (associations of non-Greeks), 262 (ephebes), 287 (late second-century pros-perity), 295 and 349–50 (statues); and generally ch. 10 (pp. 246–63) on Delian society under Athenian rule.

48 *I. Délos*, 1510, *RDGE* 5. Delians: Habicht, *Athens*, 248–9, 255–6.

49 *IG* vii. 411. See Habicht, *Athens*, 264–7, 271.

50 Or perhaps 'were in a state of snivelling weakness'; literally, 'had runny noses'.

51 Walbank, *HCP* iii. 706.

52 Habicht, *Athens*, 271–4, 279. Eretria: D. Knoepfler, 'L. Mummius Achaicus et les cités du golfe euboïque: à propos d'une nouvelle inscription d'Erétrie', *Museum Helveticum*, 48 (1991), 252–80, at 279.

53 Austin, p. 193 n. 12, inclines to see the whole documents as merely 'a market-policing operation', but see Habicht, *Athens*, 291 and n. 51.

54 On Mithradates, see B. C. McGing, *The Foreign Policy of Mithridates VI Eupator King of Pontus* (Leiden, 1986); J. G. F. Hind, 'Mithridates', *CAH*² ix (1994), ch. 5 (pp. 129–64); Habicht, *Athens*, ch. 13 (pp. 297–314). Still useful: M. Rostovtzeff and H. A. Ormerod, 'Pontus and its neighbours: the first Mithridatic war', *CAH*¹ ix (1932), ch. 5 (pp. 211–60); H. A. Ormerod and M. Cary, 'Rome and the east', *CAH*¹ ix, ch. 8 (pp. 350–96).

55 Hind, 'Mithridates', 133–6; Habicht, *Athens*, 297–8.

56 On the early part of Mithradates' reign see Hind, 'Mithridates', 137–42.

57 On these events, see ibid. 142–9 (quotation, p. 148).

58 Y. Béquignon, 'Études thessaliennes', *BCH* 59 (1935), 36–73, at pp. 64–70 no. 3; Habicht, *Athens*, 286.

59 Athenion: Habicht, *Athens*, 300–2; id., 'Zur Geschichte Athens in der Zeit Mithridates VI.', *Chiron*, 6 (1976), 127–42. *Nouveaux riches*: Habicht, *Athens*, 287–8; J. Day, *An Economic History of Athens under Roman Domination* (New York, 1942), 100; E. Candiloro, 'Politica e cultura in Atene da Pidna alla guerra mitridatica', *Studi classici e orientali*, 14 (1965), 134–76, at p. 143.

60 See K. Bringmann, 'Poseidonios and Athenion: a study in hellenistic historio-graphy', in Cartledge, *Constructs*, ch. 7 (pp. 145–58).

61 Habicht, *Athens*, 305 n. 20, accepts the orthodoxy that they were different, as does Bringmann, 'Poseidonios and Athenion'. See also G. R. Bugh, 'Athenion and Aristion of Athens', *Phoenix*, 46: 108–23 (arguing that Athenion has been 'absorbed' into Aristion, and citing alternative views at p. 111 n. 8).

62 H. A. Thompson, 'The American excavations in the Athenian Agora, eleventh report: buildings on the west side of the Agora', *Hesp.* 6 (1937), 1–226, at

218–22 ('East slope of Kolonos Agoraios'), specifically p. 221; T. L. Shear, jun., 'The monument of the eponymous heroes in the Athenian agora', *Hesp.* 39 (1970), 145–222, at 201; H. A. Thompson and R. E. Wycherley, *The Agora of Athens: The History, Shape and Uses of an Ancient City Center* (The Athenian Agora, 14; Princeton, NJ, 1971), 23; W. Hoepfner, *Das Pompeion und seine Nachfolgebauten* (Berlin, 1976), 122, 129, 139.

63 Habicht, *Athens*, 310; at pp. 308–9 he dissociates the Antikythera wreck, and that of Mahdia off Tunisia, from these events (see also above, ch. 9 n. 94, on p. 468).

64 S. V. Tracy, *Athenian Democracy in Transition: Attic Letter-cutters of 340 to 290 BC* (Berkeley, etc., 1995), 50–1.

65 Habicht, *Athens*, 311–13, 315–18.

66 Cf. A. N. Sherwin-White, 'Lucullus, Pompey and the east', *CAH*[2] ix (1994), ch. 8 *a* (pp. 229–73), at pp. 246–8. On the events of 88–84 see Hind, 'Mithridates', 149–63.

67 Sherwin-White, 'Lucullus', 232–3.

68 On the events of the third Mithradatic war see Sherwin-White, 'Lucullus', 233–48; on Pompey in the east, the end of Mithradates, and Pompey's reorganization of Asia, ibid. 248–70.

69 Sherwin-White, 'Lucullus', 260; on the rise of Parthian power in the late second and first century, ibid. 262–5.

70 For a recent description of the site and its monuments, see D. H. Sanders (ed.), *Nemrud Daği: The Hierothesion of Antiochus I of Commagene* (Winona Lake, IN, 1996); main inscription at i. 207–17; ii. 114–31 figs 211–29.

71 Sherwin-White, 'Lucullus', 270.

72 Habicht, *Athens*, 339–40.

73 Ibid. 341.

74 Ibid. 319, 320 (Caesar), 350–2 (Pompey), 357–8 (Brutus), 359–60, 365 (Antony). Politics: ibid. 322–7, 355.

75 Ibid. 364, 367.

76 Ibid. 334. On Cicero and earlier Italians in Athens, see C. Habicht, 'Roman citizens in Athens (228–31 BC)', in M. C. Hoff and S. I. Rotroff (eds), *The Romanization of Athens* (Oxford, 1997), 9–17; Habicht, *Athens*, 342–50.

77 Habicht, *Athens*, 331–2. At pp. 336–7 he discusses the Tower of Winds, which may date from this time (above, ch. 9 n. 22, on p. 465).

78 On the Roman Agora and surrounding area, see Wycherley, *Stones of Athens*, 83–9; M. Hoff, in S. Walker and A. Cameron (eds), *The Greek Renaissance in the Roman Empire* (London, 1989), 1–8. The Tower of the Winds is now dissociated from the first-century Roman Agora: H. J. Kienast, 'The Tower of the Winds in Athens: hellenistic or Roman?', in Hoff and Rotroff (eds), *Romanization*, 53–65.

79 S. E. Alcock, *Graecia Capta: The Landscapes of Roman Greece* (Cambridge, 1993).

80 e.g. G. Finlay, *Greece under the Romans* (London and New York, n.d.); G. Grote, *A History of Greece*, xii (London and New York, n.d.).

81 Alcock, *Graecia Capta*, p. 70 and ch. 3.

82 On the ideology of Roman restructuring of space in the empire, see C. Nicolet, *L'Inventaire du monde: géographie et politique aux origines de l'empire romain* (Paris, 1988), trans. as *Space, Geography, and Politics in the Early Roman Empire* (Ann Arbor, MI, 1991). Relocations of temples: R. Parker, *Athenian Religion: A History* (Oxford, 1996), 264–5; J. M. Camp, *The Athenian Agora: Excavations in the Heart of Classical Athens* (London, 1986), 184–7; *Athenian Agora*[4] (Athens, 1990), 114–15.

83 Corinth was not completely dead after 146. On activity between its destruction and its refoundation, see I. B. Romano, 'A hellenistic deposit from Corinth: evidence for interim period activity (146–44 BC)', *Hesp.* 63 (1994), 57–104.

84 A. J. Spawforth and S. Walker, 'The world of the Panhellenion, I: Athens and Eleusis', *JRS* 75 (1985), 78–104; iid., 'The world of the Panhellenion, II: three Dorian cities', *JRS* 76 (1986), 88–105.

85 On Hadrian's building programme at Athens, and the significance of Hadrian's Arch, see A. Adams, 'The Arch of Hadrian at Athens', in Walker and Cameron, *Greek Renaissance*, 10–16, who denies the existence of a 'Hadrianic quarter'. On Hadrian and Eleusis, see K. Clinton, 'Hadrian's contribution to the renaissance of Eleusis', ibid. 56–68; id., 'Eleusis and the Romans: late Republic to Marcus Aurelius', in Hoff and Rotroff, *Romanization*, 161–81.

86 See J. Tobin, *Herodes Attikos and the City of Athens: Patronage and Conflict under the Antonines* (Amsterdam, 1997); K. W. Arafat, *Pausanias' Greece: Ancient Artists and Roman Rulers* (Cambridge, 1996), ch. 6 (pp. 191–201); earlier studies include P. Graindor, *Un milliardaire antique: Hérode Atticus et sa famille* (Cairo, 1930); W. Ameling, *Herodes Atticus* (Hildesheim, etc., 1983).

BIBLIOGRAPHY

Names beginning Mc- are indexed as Mac-. Superscript figures (^{1}, ^{2}, etc.) indicate edition numbers. Note that *ä*, *ö*, *ü* are treated as *ae*, *oe,* and *ue* for alphabetization purposes.

Acta Demotica (1994), *Acta Demotica: Acts of the 5th International Conference for Demotists*. Pisa: Giardini.

Adams, A. (1989), 'The Arch of Hadrian at Athens', in Walker and Cameron (eds) (1989), 10–16.

Adams, R. McC. (1965), *Land behind Baghdad: A History of Settlement on the Diyala Plains*. Chicago and London: Univ. of Chicago Press.

—— (1981), *Heartland of Cities: Surveys of Ancient Settlement and Land Use in the Central Floodplain of the Euphrates*. Chicago: Univ. of Chicago Press.

—— and Nissen, H. J. (1972), *The Uruk Countryside: The Natural Setting of Urban Societies*. Chicago and London: Univ. of Chicago Press.

Adams, W. L., and Borza, E. N. (eds) (1982), *Philip II, Alexander the Great and the Macedonian Heritage*. Washington, DC: Univ. Press of America.

Ager, S. L. (1994), 'Hellenistic Crete and κοινοδίκιον', *JHS* 114: 1–18.

—— (1996), *Interstate Arbitrations in the Greek World, 337–90 BC* (Hellenistic Culture and Society, 18). Berkeley, Los Angeles, London: Univ. of California Press.

Alcock, S. E. (1989a), 'Archaeology and imperialism: Roman expansion and the Greek city', *Journal of Mediterranean Archaeology*, 2: 87–135.

—— (1989b), 'Roman imperialism in the Greek landscape', *Journal of Roman Archaeology*, 2: 5–34.

—— (1991a), 'Tomb cult and the post-classical polis', *American Journal of Archaeology*, 95: 447–67.

—— (1991b), 'Urban survey and the polis of Phlius', *Hesp.* 60: 421–63.

—— (1993a), *Graecia Capta: The Landscapes of Roman Greece*. Cambridge: CUP.

—— (1993b), 'Surveying the peripheries of the hellenistic world', in Bilde *et al.* (eds) (1993), 162–75.

—— (1994a), 'Breaking up the hellenistic world: survey and society', in Morris (ed.) (1994), ch. 9 (pp. 171–90).

—— (1994b), 'Minding the gap in hellenistic and Roman Greece', in Alcock and Osborne (eds) (1994), ch. 11 (pp. 247–61).

—— (1996), 'Landscapes of memory and the authority of Pausanias', in Reverdin and Grange (eds) (1996), ch. 7 (pp. 241–67; 'Discussion', 268–76).

—— (ed.) (1997a), *The Early Roman Empire in the East* (Oxbow Monographs, 95). Oxford: Oxbow Books.

—— (1997b), 'The heroic past in a hellenistic present', in Cartledge *et al.* (eds) (1997), 20–34.

—— (1997c), 'The problem of romanization, the power of Athens', in Hoff and Rotroff (eds) (1997), 1–7.

——, Cherry, J. F., and Davis, J. L. (1994), 'Intensive survey, agricultural practice and the classical landscape of Greece', in Morris (ed.) (1994), 137–70.

—— and Osborne, R. (eds) (1994), *Placing the Gods: Sanctuaries and Sacred Space in Ancient Greece*. Oxford: Clarendon.

Aleshire, S. B. (1989), *The Athenian Asklepieion: The People, their Dedications, and the Inventories*. Amsterdam: Gieben.

—— (1991), *Asklepios at Athens: Epigraphic and Prosopographic Essays on the Athenian Healing Cults*. Amsterdam: Gieben.

—— and Matthaiou, A. P. (1990–1), 'Νέο θραῦσμα τῆς IG II² 1534', *Horos*, 8–9: 45–51; repr. in Aleshire 1991: 5–12 ('A new fragment of *IG* II² 1534A and B').

Alessandria (1995), *Alessandria e il mondo ellenistico-romano: I* [i.e. primo] *centenario del Museo Greco-Romano (Alessandria, 23–27 novembre 1992). Atti del II Congresso Internazionale Italo-Egiziano*. Rome: 'L'Erma' di Bretschneider.

Alexandria and Alexandrianism (1996), *Alexandria and Alexandrianism: Papers Delivered at a Symposium Organized by the J. Paul Getty Museum and the Getty Center for the History of Art and the Humanities and Held at the Museum (April 22–25, 1993)*. Malibu, CA: J. Paul Getty Museum.

Allen, R. E. (1983), *The Attalid Kingdom: A Constitutional History*. Oxford: Clarendon.

Allen, W. S. (¹1968, ³1987), *Vox Graeca: The Pronunciation of Classical Greek*. Cambridge: CUP.

Alston, R. (1996), 'Conquest by text: Juvenal and Plutarch on Egypt', in Webster and Cooper (eds) (1996), 99–109.

Ambaglio, D. (1987), 'Tensioni etniche e sociali nella chora tolemaica', in Virgilio (ed.) (1987c), 129–62.

Ameling, W. (1983), *Herodes Atticus*, i: *Biographie*; ii: *Inschriftenkatalog* (Subsidia epigraphica, 11). Hildesheim, Zurich, New York: Olm.

—— (1996), 'Pausanias und der hellenistische Geschichte', in Reverdin and Grange (eds) (1996), ch. 4 (pp. 117–60; 'Discussion', 161–6).

Ancient Macedonia 1 (1970), Ἀρχαία Μακεδονία· ἀνακοινώσεις κατὰ τὸ πρῶτον διεθνές συμπόσιο ἐν Θεσσαλονίκη, 26–29 Αὐγούστου 1968/*Ancient Macedonia: Papers Read at the 1st International Symposium held in Thessaloniki, 26–29 August 1968* (ed. V. Laourdas and Ch. Makaronas) (Etaireia Makedonikon Spoudon, Idryma Meleton Chersonisou tou Aimou/Institute for Balkan Studies, 122). Thessaloniki: EMS, IMCA/IBS.

—— *2* (1977), Αρχαία Μακεδονία, 2: ανακοινώσεις κατά το δεύτερο διεθνές συμπόσιο (Θεσσαλονίκη, 19–24 Αυγούστου 1973/*Ancient Macedonia, 2: Papers*

Read at the 2nd International Symposium held in Thessaloniki, 19–24 August, 1973 (IMCA/IBS 155). Thessaloniki: IMCA/IBS.

—— 3 (1983), Αρχαία Μακεδονία, 3: ανακοινώσεις κατά το τρίτο διεθνές συμπόσιο (Θεσσαλονίκη, 21–25 Σεπτεμβρίου 1977)/*Ancient Macedonia, 3: Papers Read at the 3rd International Symposium held in Thessaloniki, September 21–25, 1977* (IMCA/IBS 193). Thessaloniki: IMCA/IBS.

—— 4 (1986), Αρχαία Μακεδονία, 4: ανακοινώσεις κατά το τέταρτο διεθνές συμπόσιο (Θεσσαλονίκη, 21–25 Σεπτεμβρίου 1983)/*Ancient Macedonia, 4: Papers Read at the 4th International Symposium held in Thessaloniki, September 21–25, 1983* (IMCA/IBS 204). Thessaloniki: IMCA/IBS.

—— 5 (1993), Αρχαία Μακεδονία, 5: ανακοινώσεις κατά το πέμπτο διεθνές συμπόσιο (Θεσσαλονίκη, 10–15 Οκτωβρίου 1989)/*Ancient Macedonia, 5: Papers Read at the 5th International Symposium held in Thessaloniki, October 10–15, 1989)*, i–iii. IMCA/IBS 240. Thessaloniki: IMCA/IBS.

Andronicos, M. (1984), *Vergina: The Royal Tombs and the Ancient City*. Athens: Ekdotiki Athinon.

Annas, J. (1992), *Hellenistic Philosophy of Mind* (Hellenistic Culture and Society, 8). Berkeley, Los Angeles, London: Univ. of California Press.

—— (1993), 'Response' [to Caizzi and Gill], in Bulloch *et al.* (eds) (1993), 354–68.

—— and Barnes, J. (1985), *The Modes of Scepticism* (Ancient Texts and Modern Interpretations. Cambridge: CUP.

Arafat, K. W. (1996), *Pausanias' Greece: Ancient Artists and Roman Rulers*. Cambridge: CUP.

Archer, L. J. (1983), 'The role of Jewish women in the religion, ritual and cult of Graeco-Roman Palestine', in Cameron and Kuhrt (eds) (1983), ch. 17 (pp. 273–87).

—— (1990), *Her Price is Beyond Rubies: The Jewish Woman in Graeco-Roman Palestine* (*Journal for the Study of the Old Testament*, suppl. 60). Sheffield: JSOT Press/Sheffield Academic Press.

——, Fischler, S., and Wyke, M. (eds) (1994), *Women in Ancient Societies: An Illusion of the Night*. Basingstoke and London: Macmillan.

Archibald, Z. H. (1998), *The Odrysian Kingdom of Thrace: Orpheus Unmasked* (Oxford Monographs on Classical Archaeology). Oxford: Clarendon.

Arora, U. P. (1996), *Greeks on India: Skylax to Aristoteles*. Bareilly, India: ISGARS (Indian Society for Greek and Roman Studies).

Ashton, R., and Hurter, S., with G. Le Rider and R. Bland (eds) (1998), *Studies in Greek Numismatics in Memory of Martin Jessop Price*. London: Spink.

Aspekter af hellenismen (1990) (Hellenismestudier, 2). Aarhus: Aarhus Universitetsforlag.

Astin, A. E., Walbank, F. W., Frederiksen, M. W., and Ogilvie, R. M. (eds) (1989), *The Cambridge Ancient History*[2], viii: *Rome and the Mediterranean to 133 BC*. Cambridge: CUP.

Athenian Agora (1990), *The Athenian Agora: A Guide to the Excavation and Museum*[4]. Athens: American School of Classical Studies at Athens.

Austin, M. (1993), 'Alexander and the Macedonian invasion of Asia: aspects of the historiography of war and empire in antiquity', in Rich and Shipley (eds) (1993), ch. 10 (pp. 197–223).

——, Harries, J., and Smith, C. (eds) (1998), *Modus Operandi: Essays in Honour of Geoffrey Rickman* (BICS supp. 71). London: ICS, School of Advanced Study, Univ. of London.

Austin, M. M. (1981), *The Hellenistic World from Alexander to the Roman Conquest: A Selection of Ancient Sources in Translation*. Cambridge: CUP.

—— (1986), 'Hellenistic kings, war, and the economy', *CQ* 80 [n.s. 36], 450–66.

—— (1992), review of Green, *Alexander to Actium*, in *CR* 106 [n.s. 42]: 105–6.

—— (1994), 'Society and economy', *CAH*² vi, ch. 10 (pp. 528–64).

Badian, E. (1958), *Foreign Clientelae (264–70 BC)*. Oxford: Clarendon.

—— (1967), 'The testament of Ptolemy Alexander', *Rheinisches Museum*, 110: 178–92.

—— (1994), 'Agis III: revisions and reflections', in Worthington (ed.) (1994a), 258–92.

Bagnall, R. S. (1975), 'Ptolemaic correspondence in P. Tebt. 8', *JEA* 61: 168–80.

—— (1976), *The Administration of the Ptolemaic Possessions Outside Egypt* (Columbia Studies in the Classical Tradition, 4). Leiden: Brill.

—— (1980), review of Shear 1978, in *AJP* 101: 244–7.

—— (1995), *Reading Papyri, Writing Ancient History* (Approaching the Ancient World). London and New York: Routledge.

—— (1997), 'Decolonizing Ptolemaic Egypt', in Cartledge *et al.* (eds) (1997), 225–41.

—— and Derow, P. (1981), *Greek Historical Documents: The Hellenistic Period* (SBL [Society for Biblical Literature] Sources for Biblical Study, 16). Chico, CA: Scholars Press.

Bakhuizen, S. C. (ed.) (1992), *A Greek City of the Fourth Century BC: By the Gorítsa Team* (Bibliotheca archaeologica, 10). Rome: 'L'Erma' di Bretschneider.

Baladié, R. (1980), *Le Péloponnèse de Strabon: étude de géographie historique* (Collection d'études anciennes publiée sous le patronage de l'Association Guillaume Budé). Paris: Les Belles Lettres.

Baldry, H. C. (1965), *The Unity of Mankind in Greek Thought*. Cambridge: CUP.

Barber, E. A. (1928), 'Alexandrian literature', *CAH*¹ vii, ch. 8 (pp. 249–83).

Barker, G., and Lloyd, J. (eds) (1991), *Roman Landscapes: Archaeological Survey in the Mediterranean Region* (Archaeological Monographs of the British School at Rome, 2). London: British School at Rome.

Bar-Kochva, B. (1989), *Judas Maccabaeus: The Jewish Struggle against the Seleucids*. Cambridge: CUP.

—— (1996), *Pseudo-Hecataeus 'On the Jews': Legitimizing the Jewish Diaspora* (Hellenistic Culture and Society, 21). Berkeley, Los Angeles, London: Univ. of California Press.

Baroni, A. (1984), 'I terreni e i privilegi del tempio di Zeus a Baitokaike (IGLS VII, 4028)', in Virgilio (ed.) (1984b), 135–67.

Barron, J. P. (1966), *The Silver Coins of Samos*. London: Univ. of London/Athlone.

Bartl, K., and Hauser, S. R. (1996), *Continuity and Change in Northern Mesopotamia from the Hellenistic to the Early Islamic Period* (Berliner Beiträge zum vorderen Orient, 17), Berlin: Reimer.

Bartlett, J. R. (1985), *Jews in the Hellenistic World: Josephus, Aristeas, the Sibylline Oracles, Eupolemus* (Cambridge Commentaries on Writings of the Jewish and Christian World, 200 BC to AD 200). Cambridge: CUP.

478

Barton, T. (1994), *Ancient Astrology* (Sciences of Antiquity). London and New York: Routledge.

Barton, T. S. (1994), *Power and Knowledge: Astrology, Physiognomics, and Medicine under the Roman Empire* (The Body in Theory: Histories of Cultural Materialism). Ann Arbor, MI: Univ. of Michigan Press.

Baynham, E. J. (1994), 'Antipater: manager of kings', in Worthington (ed.) (1994), 331–56.

Beard, M., and Crawford, M. (1985), *Rome in the Late Republic: Problems and Interpretations*. London: Duckworth.

—— and Henderson, J. (1995), *Classics: A Very Short Introduction*. Oxford and New York: OUP.

—— and North, J. (eds) (1990), *Pagan Priests: Religion and Power in the Ancient World*. London: Duckworth.

Becher, I. (1966), *Das Bild der Kleopatra in der griechischen und lateinischen Literatur* (Deutsche Akademie der Wissenschaften zu Berlin, Schriften der Sektion für Altertumswissenschaft, 51). Berlin: Akademie-Verlag.

Beloch, K. J. (1912–27), *Griechische Geschichte*[2]. Strasbourg: Trübner/Berlin and Leipzig: de Gruyter.

Bengtson, H. (1988), *Die hellenistische Weltkultur*. Stuttgart: Steiner.

Béquignon, Y. (1935), 'Études thessaliennes', *BCH* 59: 36–73.

Bernand, A. (1966), *Alexandrie la grande* (Collections signes des temps). Paris: Arthaud.

Bernard, P. (1967), 'Aï Khanum on the Oxus: a hellenistic city in central Asia', *Proceedings of the British Academy*, 53: 71–95.

—— (ed.) (1973), *Fouilles d'Aï Khanoum*, i: *Campagnes 1965, 1966, 1967, 1968. Rapport préliminaire* (Mémoires de la Délégation Archéologique Française en Afghanistan, 21; Paris: Klinksieck).

—— (1978), 'Campagne de fouilles 1976–1977 à Aï Khanoum (Afghanistan), *CRAI* 421–63.

—— (1985), *Fouilles d'Aï Khanoum*, iv: *Les Monnaies hors trésors: questions d'histoire gréco-bactrienne* (Mémoires de la Délégation Archéologique Française en Afghanistan, 28; Paris: de Boccard).

Berthold, R. M. (1984), *Rhodes in the Hellenistic Age*. Ithaca, NY and London: Cornell UP.

Bevan, E. R. (1902), *The House of Seleucus*, i–ii. London: Arnold (repr. London: Routledge & Kegan Paul, 1966).

Beyer-Rotthoff, B. (1993), *Untersuchungen zur Aussenpolitik Ptolemaios' III* (Habelts Dissertationsdrücke, Alte Geschichte, 37). Bonn: Habelt.

Bichler, R. (1983), *'Hellenismus': Geschichte und Problematik eines Epochenbegriffs* (Impulse der Forschung, 41). Darmstadt: Wissenschaftliche Buchgesellschaft.

Bickerman, E. (1979), *The God of the Maccabees: Studies on the Meaning and Origin of the Maccabean Revolt*. Trans. H. R. Moering. Leiden: Brill.

—— (1983), 'The Seleucid period', in Yarshater (ed.) (1983), ch. 1 (pp. 3–20).

Bickerman, E. J. (1937), *Der Gott der Makkabäer: Untersuchungen über Sinn und Ursprung der makkabäischen Erhebung*. Berlin: Schocken.

—— (1962), *From Ezra to the Last of the Maccabees: Foundations of Post-biblical Judaism*. New York: Schocken.

—— (1988), *The Jews in the Greek Age*. Cambridge, MA, and London: Harvard UP.

479

Bieżuńska-Małowist, I. (1974), *L'Esclavage dans l'Égypte gréco-romaine*, i: *Période gréco-ptolémaïque* (Archiwum filologiczne, 30). Wrocław, Warsaw, Cracow, and Gdansk: Polska Akademia Nauk, Komitet Nauk o Kulturze Antycznej/Zakład Narodowy Imienia Ossolińskich Wydawnictwo Polskiej Akademii Nauk.

Bikerman, E. (1938), *Institutions des Séleucides* (Haut-commissariat de la République Française en Syrie et au Liban, Service des Antiquités, Bibliothèque archéologique et historique, 26). Paris: Librairie Orientaliste Paul Geuthner.

Bilde, P. (1990), 'Atargatis/Dea Syria: hellenization of her cult in the hellenistic–Roman period?', in Bilde *et al.* (eds) (1990), 151–87.

—— (ed.) (1991), *Rhodos i hellenistisk tid* (Hellenismestudier, 5). Aarhus: Aarhus Universitetsforlag.

—— (ed.) (1995), *Jødedommen og hellenismen* (Hellenismestudier, 9). Aarhus: Aarhus Universitetsforlag.

—— Engberg-Pedersen, T., Hannestad, L., and Zahle, J. (eds) (1990), *Religion and Religious Practice in the Seleucid Kingdom* (Studies in Hellenistic Civilization, 1). Aarhus: Aarhus UP.

——, ——, —— and —— (eds) (1992), *Ethnicity in Hellenistic Egypt* (Studies in Hellenistic Civilization, 3). Aarhus: Aarhus UP.

——, ——, —— and —— (eds) (1996a), *Aspects of Hellenistic Kingship* (Studies in Hellenistic Civilization, 7). Aarhus: Aarhus UP.

——, ——, —— and —— (eds) (1997), *Conventional Values of the Hellenistic Greeks* (Studies in Hellenistic Civilization, 8). Aarhus: Aarhus UP.

——, ——, ——, —— and Randsborg, K. (eds [1]1993; [2]1996b), *Centre and Periphery in the Hellenistic World* (Studies in Hellenistic Civilization, 4). Aarhus: Aarhus UP.

Billows, R. A. (1990), *Antigonos the One-eyed and the Creation of the Hellenistic State* (Hellenistic Culture and Society, 4). Berkeley, Los Angeles, London: Univ. of California Press.

—— (1995), *Kings and Colonists: Aspects of Macedonian Imperialism* (Columbia Studies in the Classical Tradition, 22). Leiden, New York, and Cologne: Brill.

Bingen, J. (1952), *Papyrus Revenue Laws* (SB, Beiheft i). Göttingen: Hubert.

—— (1978), *Le Papyrus Revenue Laws: tradition grecque et adaptation hellénistique* (Vorträge der Rheinisch-Westfälischen Akademie der Wissenschaften, G.321). Opladen: Westdeutscher Verlag.

Bintliff, J. L. (1985), 'The Boeotia Survey, central Greece', in Macready and Thompson (eds) (1985), 196–216.

—— (1991), 'The Roman countryside in central Greece: observations and theories from the Boeotia Survey (1978–87)', in Barker and Lloyd (eds) (1991), 122–32.

—— and Snodgrass, A. M. (1985), 'The Cambridge/Bradford Boeotian expedition: the first four years', *Journal of Field Archaeology*, 12: 123–61.

—— and —— (1988a), 'Mediterranean survey and the city', *Antiquity*, 62: 57–71.

—— and —— (1988b), 'Off-site pottery distributions: a regional and inter-regional perspective', *Current Anthropology*, 29: 506–12.

Bivar, A. D. H. (1988), 'The Indus lands', *CAH*[2] iv, ch. 3 *d* (pp. 194–210).

Blomqvist, J. (1992), 'Alexandrian science: the case of Eratosthenes', in Bilde *et al.* (eds) (1992), 53–75.

Boardman, J., Griffin, J., and Murray, O. (eds) (1986), *The Oxford History of the Classical World*. Oxford and New York: OUP.

——, —— and —— (eds) (1988a), *The Oxford History of the Classical World*, i: *Greece and the Hellenistic World*. Oxford and New York: OUP.

——, Hammond, N. G. L., Lewis, D. M., and Ostwald, M. (eds) (1988b), *The Cambridge Ancient History*², iv: *Persia, Greece and the Western Mediterranean c.525 to 479 BC*. Cambridge: CUP.

Bodei Giglioni, G. (1984), 'Una leggenda sulle origini dell'ellenismo: Alessandro e i cinici', in Virgilio (ed.) (1984b), 51–73.

Bogaert, R. (1976), *Epigraphica*, iii: *Texts on Bankers, Banking and Credit in the Greek World* (Textus minores, 47). Leiden: Brill.

—— (1977), 'Il commercio internazionale e le banche', in Moretti *et al.* (eds) (1977), ch. 5.5 (pp. 375–99).

Bommeljé, L. S., and Doorn, P. K. (eds) (1985), *Strouza Region Project: An Historical-topographical Fieldwork (1981–1984). 1984: Third Interim Report*. Utrecht: Strouza Region Project.

——, ——, Deylius, M., Vroom, J., Bommeljé, Y., Fagel, R., and van Wijngaarden, H. (1987), *Aetolia and the Aetolians: Towards the Interdisciplinary Study of a Greek Region*. Utrecht: Parnassus.

Bopearachchi, O. (1991), *Monnaies gréco-bactriennes et indo-grecques: catalogue raisonné*. Paris: Bibliothèque Nationale.

Borgen, P. (1992), 'Philo and the Jews in Alexandria', in Bilde *et al.* (eds) (1992), 122–38.

Borza, E. N. (1990), *In the Shadow of Olympus: The Emergence of Macedon*. Princeton, NJ: Princeton UP.

—— (1993), 'Response' [to Hammond], in Green (ed.) (1993), 23–35.

Boswinkel, E., and Pestman, P. W. (eds) (1982), *Les Archives privées de Dionysios, fils de Kephalas: textes grecs et démotiques. Texte* (Papyrologica Lugduno-Batava, 22 A). Leiden: Brill.

Bosworth, A. B. (1980a), 'Alexander and the Iranians', *JHS* 100: 1–21.

—— (1980b), *A Historical Commentary on Arrian's History of Alexander*, i: *Commentary on Books I–III*. Oxford: Clarendon.

—— (1988a), *Conquest and Empire: The Reign of Alexander the Great*. Cambridge: CUP.

—— (1988b), *From Arrian to Alexander: Studies in Historical Interpretation*. Oxford: Clarendon.

—— (1994a), 'Alexander the Great part 1: the events of the reign', *CAH*² vi, ch. 16 (pp. 791–845).

—— (1994b), 'Alexander the Great part 2: Greece and the conquered territories', *CAH*² vi, ch. 17 (pp. 846–75).

—— (1996), *Alexander and the East: The Tragedy of Triumph*. Oxford: Clarendon.

Bouché-Leclercq, A. (1903–7), *Histoire des Lagides*. Paris: Leroux.

—— (1913–14), *Histoire des Séleucides (323–64 avant J.-C.)*. Paris: Leroux; repr. Brussels: Culture et civilisation, 1963.

—— *et al.* (1883–5), *Histoire de l'hellénisme*. Paris.

Bousquet, J. (1958), 'Inscriptions de Delphes', *BCH* 82: 61–91.

Bowman, A. K. ([1]1986, [2]1990), *Egypt after the Pharaohs, 332 BC–AD 642: From Alexander to the Arab Conquest*. [1]London: British Museum Publications; [2]Oxford: OUP.

—— and Rogan, E. (1999), *Agriculture in Egypt: From Pharaonic to Modern Times* (Proceedings of the British Academy, 96). Oxford: OUP for British Academy.

—— and Woolf, G. (eds) (1994), *Literacy and Power in the Ancient World*. Cambridge: CUP.

Boyd, T. D. (1978), 'The arch and the vault in Greek architecture', *American Journal of Archaeology*, 82: 83–100.

Bracht Branham, R., and Goulet-Cazé, M.-O. (eds) (1996), *The Cynics: The Cynic Movement in Antiquity and its Legacy* (Hellenistic Culture and Society, 23). Berkeley, CA: Univ. of California Press.

Briant, P. (1972, 1973a), 'D'Alexandre le Grand aux diadoques: le cas d'Eumène de Kardia', *REA* 74 (1972), 32–73; *REA* 75 (1973), 43–81; repr. in Briant, *RTP* 13–54, 55–93.

—— (1973b), *Antigone le Borgne: les débuts de sa carrière et les problèmes de l'assembleé macédonienne* (Centre de Recherche d'Histoire Ancienne, 10/Annales littéraires de l'Université de Besançon, 152). Paris: Les Belles Lettres.

—— (1973c), 'Remarques sur "laoi" et esclaves ruraux en Asie Mineure hellénistique', *Actes du colloque 1971 sur l'esclavage* (Paris), 93–133; repr. in Briant, *RTP* 95–135 (title incorrect in Contents of *RTP*).

—— (1974), *Alexandre le Grand* ([1]Document archeologia, 5; Dijon: Archeologia; [2–4]1977, 1987, 1994, Que sais-je? 622; Paris: Presses Universitaires de France).

—— (1975), 'Villages et communautés villageoises d'Asie achéménide et hellénistique', *Journal of the Economic and Social History of the Orient*, 18: 165–88; repr. in Briant, *RTP* 137–60.

—— (1978), 'Colonisation hellénistique et populations indigènes: la phase d'installation', *Klio*, 60: 57–92; repr. in Briant, *RTP* 227–62.

—— (1979), 'Des Achéménides aux rois hellénistiques: continuités et ruptures (bilan et propositions)', *Annali della Scuola Normale Superiore di Pisa, classe di lettere e filologia*, 1375–414; repr. in Briant, *RTP* 291–330.

—— (1980a), 'Conquête territoriale et stratégie idéologique: Alexandre le Grand et l'idéologie monarchique achéménide', in *Actes du colloque international sur l'idéologie monarchique dans l'antiquité (Cracovie-Mogilany du 23 au 26 octobre 1977)* (Zeszyty naukowe Uniwersytetu Jagiellonskiego, prace historyczne, 536, zesz. 63; Warsaw and Cracow: Nakl. Uniwersytetu Jagiellonskiego; Panstwowe Wydawn. Nauk), 37–83; repr. in Briant, *RTP* 357–403.

—— (1980b), 'Forces productives, dépendance rurale et idéologies religieuses dans l'empire achéménide', in *RTP* 431–73.

—— (1982a), 'Colonisation hellénistique et populations indigènes, II: renforts grecques dans les cités hellénistiques d'Orient', *Klio*, 64: 83–98; repr. in Briant, *RTP* 263–79 (title incorrect in Contents of *RTP*).

—— (1982b), *État et pasteurs au Moyen-Orient ancien* (Production pastorale et société). Cambridge: CUP; Paris: Éditions de la Maison des Sciences de l'Homme.

—— (1982c), *Rois, tributs et paysans: études sur les formations tributaires du Moyen-Orient ancien* (Centre de Recherches d'Histoire Ancienne, 43/Annales littéraires de l'Université de Besançon, 269). Paris: Les Belles Lettres.

—— (1984), *L'Asie centrale et les royaumes proche-orientaux du premier millénaire (c. VIIIe–IVe siècles avant notre ère)* (Mémoires, 42). Paris: Éditions Recherches sur les Civilisations.

—— (1990), 'The Seleucid kingdom, the Achaemenid empire and the history of the Near East in the first millennium BC', in Bilde *et al*. (eds) (1990), 40–65.

—— (1991), *Alexander den Store* (Hellenismestudier, 6). [Aarhus]: Aarhus Universitetsforlag.

—— (1996), *Alexander the Great*. London: Thames & Hudson.

Bringmann, K. (1980), 'Die Verfolgung der jüdischen Religion durch Antiochos IV.: ein Konflikt zwischen Judentum und Hellenismus?', *Antike und Abendland*, 26: 176–90.

—— (1983), *Hellenistische Reform und Religionsverfolgung in Judäa: eine Untersuchung zur jüdisch-hellenistischen Geschichte (175–163 v.Chr.)* (Abhandlungen der Akademie der Wissenschaften in Göttingen, philol.-hist. Kl., 3. Folge, 132). Göttingen: Vandenhoeck & Ruprecht.

—— (1993), 'The king as benefactor: some remarks on ideal kingship in the age of hellenism', in Bulloch *et al*. (eds) (1993), 7–24.

—— (1997), 'Poseidonios and Athenion: a study in hellenistic historiography', in Cartledge *et al*. (eds) (1997), 145–58.

Briscoe, J. (1967), 'Rome and the class struggle in the Greek states 200–146 BC', *Past and Present*, 36: 3–20; repr. in Finley (ed.) (1974), ch. 3 (pp. 53–73).

—— (1973), *A Commentary on Livy: Books XXXI–XXXIII*. Oxford: Clarendon.

—— (1978), 'The Antigonids and the Greek states, 276–196 BC', in Garnsey and Whittaker (eds) (1978), pp. 145–57.

—— (1981), *A Commentary on Livy: Books XXXIV–XXXVII*. Oxford: Clarendon.

—— (1986), review of Gruen 1984, in *CR* 100 [n.s. 36]: 91–6.

—— (1990), review of Ferrary 1986, in *CR* 104 [n.s. 40]: 373–7.

Brodersen, K. (1985), 'Der liebeskranke Königssohn und die seleukidische Herrschaftsauffassung', *Athenaeum*, 63: 459–69.

—— (1989), *Appians Abriss der Seleukidengeschichte (Syriake 45, 232–70, 369): Text und Kommentar* (Münchener Universitätschriften: Münchener Arbeiten zur alten Geschichte, 1). Munich: Editio Maris.

—— (1991), *Appians Antioche (Syriake, 1,1–44,232): Text und Kommentar* (Münchener Universitätschriften: Münchener Arbeiten zur alten Geschichte, 3). Munich: Editio Maris.

—— (1994), *Pomponius Mela: Kreuzfahrt durch die alte Welt*. Darmstadt: Wissenschaftliche Buchgesellschaft.

Brown, B. R. (1995), *Royal Portraits in Sculpture and Coins: Pyrrhos and the Successors of Alexander the Great* (Hermeneutics of Art, 5). New York: Peter Lang.

Bruit Zaidman, L., and Schmitt Pantel, P. (1992), *Religion in the Ancient Greek City*. Trans. P. Cartledge. Cambridge: CUP.

Brulé, P. (1978), *La Piraterie crétoise hellénistique* (Centre de Recherches d'Histoire Ancienne, 27/Annales littéraires de l'Université de Besançon, 223). Paris: Les Belles Lettres.

Bruneau, P. (1970), *Recherches sur les cultes de Délos à l'époque hellénistique et à l'époque impériale* (Bibliothèque des Écoles Françaises d'Athènes et de Rome, 217). Paris: de Boccard.

Brunt, P. A. (trans. 1976–83), *Arrian*, i–ii (Loeb Classical Library). Cambridge, MA, and London: Harvard UP.

Buck, C. J. (1979), *A History of Boeotia*. Edmonton: Univ. of Alberta Press.

—— (1994), *Boiotia and the Boiotian League, 432–371 BC*. Edmonton: Univ. of Alberta Press.

Buckler, W. H., and Robinson, D. M. (1932), *Sardis*, vii: *Greek and Latin Inscriptions*, 1. Leiden: Brill.

Bugh, G. R. (1992), 'Athenion and Aristion of Athens', *Phoenix*, 46: 108–23.

Bulloch, A. W. (1984), 'The future of a hellenistic illusion: some observations on Callimachus and religion', *Museum Helveticum*, 41: 209–30.

—— (1985a), *Callimachus: The Fifth Hymn* (Cambridge Classical Texts and Commentaries, 26). Cambridge: CUP.

—— (1985b), 'Hellenistic poetry', *CHCL* ch. 18 (pp. 541–621).

——, Gruen, E. S., Long, A. A., and Stewart, A. (eds) (1993), *Images and Ideologies: Self-definition in the Hellenistic World* (Hellenistic Culture and Society, 12). Berkeley, Los Angeles, London: Univ. of California Press.

Bunge, J. G. (1974), ' "Theos Epiphanes": zu den ersten fünf Regierungsjahren Antiochos' IV Epiphanes', *Historia*, 23: 57–85.

—— (1975), ' "Antiochos-Helios": Methoden und Ergebnisse der Reichspolitik Antiochos' IV Epiphanes von Syrien im Spiegel seiner Münzen', *Historia*, 24: 164–88.

Buraselis, K. (1982), *Das hellenistische Makedonien und die Ägäis: Forschungen zur Politik des Kassandros und der drei ersten Antigoniden im ägäischen Meer und im West-kleinasien* (Münchener Beiträge zur Papyrusforschung und antiken Rechtsge-schichte, 73). Munich: Beck.

—— (1993), 'Ambivalent roles of centre and periphery: remarks on the relation of the cities of Greece with the Ptolemies until the end of Philometor's age', in Bilde *et al.* (eds) (1993), 251–70.

Burford, A. (1994), 'Greek agriculture in the classical period', *CAH*² vi, ch. 12 *d* (pp. 661–77).

Burnett, A. M., and Crawford, M. H. (eds) (1987), *The Coinage of the Roman World in the Late Republic* (BAR international series, 326). Oxford: British Archaeological Reports.

Burnyeat, M. F. (1997), 'Postscript on silent reading', *CQ* 91 [n.s. 47]: 74–6.

Burstein, S. M. (1978), *The Babyloniaca of Berossus* (Sources and Monographs on the Ancient Near East: Sources from the Ancient Near East, 1. 5). Malibu, CA: Undena.

—— (1982), 'Arsinoe II Philadelphus: a revisionist view', in Adams and Borza (eds) (1982), 197–212.

—— (1985), *The Hellenistic Age: From the Battle of Ipsos to the Death of Kleopatra VII* (Translated Documents of Greece and Rome, 3). Cambridge: CUP.

—— (1989), *Agatharchides of Cnidus: On the Erythraean Sea* (Hakluyt Society Second Series, 172). London: Hakluyt Society.

—— (1993), 'The hellenistic fringe: the case of Meroë', in Green (ed.) (1993), 38–54.

Burton, J. B. (1995), *Theocritus's Urban Mimes: Mobility, Gender, and Patronage* (Hellenistic Culture and Society, 19). Berkeley, Los Angeles, London: Univ. of California Press.

Bury, J. B., Barber, E. A., Bevan, E., and Tarn, W. W. (eds) (1923), *The Hellenistic Age*. Cambridge: CUP.

——, Cook, S. A., and Adcock, F. E. (eds) (1927), *The Cambridge Ancient History*[1], vi: *Macedon 401–301 BC*. Cambridge: CUP.

Caizzi, F. D. (1986), 'Pirroniani ed Accademici nel III secolo a. C.' in Reverdin and Grange (eds) (1986), 147–78 ('Discussion', 179–83).

—— (1993), 'The porch and the garden: early hellenistic images of the philosophical life', in Bulloch *et al.* (eds) (1993), 303–29.

Caley, E. R., and Richards, J. F. C. (1956), *Theophrastus on Stones*. Columbus, OH: The Ohio State Univ.

Cameron, Alan (1981), 'Asclepiades' girl friends', in Foley (ed.) (1981), 275–302.

—— (1990), 'Two mistresses of Ptolemy Philadelphus', *Greek, Roman and Byzantine Studies,* 31: 287–311.

Cameron, Averil, and Kuhrt, A. (eds [1]1983, [2]1993), *Images of Women in Antiquity*. London and Canberra: Croom Helm.

Camp, J. M. (1986), *The Athenian Agora: Excavations in the Heart of Classical Athens*. London: Thames & Hudson.

Campanile, M. D. (1994), *I sacerdoti del koinon d'Asia (I sec. a.C.–III sec. d.C.): contributo allo studio della romanizzazione delle elites provinciali nell'Oriente greco* (Studi ellenistici, 7/Biblioteca di studi antichi, 74). Pisa: Giardini.

Campbell, M. (1981), *Echoes and Imitations of Early Epic in Apollonius Rhodius* (Mnemosyne, supp. 72). Leiden: Brill.

—— (1991), *Moschus of Syracuse: Europa* (Altertumswissenschaftliche Texte und Studien, 0175-8411, Bd. 19). Hildesheim, Zürich, and New York: Olms–Weidemann.

—— (1994), *A Commentary on Apollonius Rhodius, Argonautica III 1–471* (Mnemosyne, supp. 141). Leiden, New York, Cologne: Brill.

Candiloro, E. (1965), 'Politica e cultura in Atene da Pidna alla guerra mitridatica', *Studi classici e orientali*, 14: 134–76.

Canfora, L. (1986), *La biblioteca scomparsa*. Palermo: Sellerio.

—— (1988), *La Véritable Histoire de la bibliothèque d'Alexandrie*. Trans. J.-P. Manganaro and D. Dubroca. Paris: Desjonquères.

—— (1989), *The Vanished Library*. London: Hutchinson Radius. (Trans.) (Also published as *The Vanished Library: A Wonder of the Ancient World*; London: Vintage, 1991; and as Hellenistic Culture and Society, 7; Berkeley, Los Angeles, London: Univ. of California Press, 1989.)

Cannadine, D., and Price, S. (eds) (1987), *Rituals of Royalty: Power and Ceremonial in Traditional Societies*. Cambridge: CUP.

Carey, C. (1996), 'Erinna', *OCD*[3] 556.

—— and Reid, R. A. (eds) (1985), *Demosthenes: Selected Private Speeches* (Cambridge Greek and Latin Classics). Cambridge: CUP.

Carlier, P. (ed.) (1996), *Le IVe siècle av. J.-C.: approches historiographiques* (Études anciennes, 15). Nancy: ADRA (Association pour la Diffusion de la Recherche sur l'Antiquité)/Paris: de Boccard.

Carlsen, J., Due, B., Steen Due, O., and Poulsen, B. (eds) (1993), *Alexander the Great: Reality and Myth* (Analecta Romana Instituti Danici, supp. 20). Rome: 'L'Erma' di Bretschneider.

Carney, E. (1991), ' "What's in a name?" The emergence of a title for royal women in the hellenistic period', in Pomeroy (ed.) (1991), 154–72.

Carney, E. D. (1993), 'Olympias and the image of the virago', *Phoenix*, 47: 29–55.

—— (1994), 'Olympias, Adea Eurydice, and the end of the Argead dynasty', in Worthington (ed.) (1994), 357–80.

Carradice, I., and Price, M. J. (1988), *Coinage in the Greek World*. London: Seaby.

Carter, J. C. (1984), 'Sicily and Magna Graecia', in Ling (ed.) (1984b), ch. 6 (pp. 71–80).

Cartledge, P. (1987), *Agesilaos and the Crisis of Sparta*. London: Duckworth.

—— (1993), *The Greeks: A Portrait of Self and Others* (Opus). Oxford: OUP.

—— (1998), 'City and chora in Sparta: archaic to hellenistic', in Cavanagh and Walker (eds) (1998), 39–47.

——, Garnsey, P., and Gruen, E. (eds) (1997), *Hellenistic Constructs: Essays in Culture, History and Historiography* (Hellenistic Culture and Society, 26). Berkeley, Los Angeles, London: Univ. of California Press.

—— and Spawforth, A. (1989), *Hellenistic and Roman Sparta: A Tale of Two Cities* (States and Cities of Ancient Greece). London and New York: Routledge.

Cary, M. (1949), *The Geographic Background of Greek and Roman History*. Oxford: Clarendon.

Casson, L. (1989), *The Periplus Maris Erythraei: Text with Introduction, Translation, and Commentary*. Princeton, NJ: Princeton UP.

Catling, P., and Roberts, P. (1991), 'Balboura survey pottery study', *Anatolian Studies*, 41: 19.

Cavanagh, W., Crouwel, J., Catling, R. W. V., and Shipley, G. (1996), *Continuity and Change in a Greek Rural Landscape: The Laconia Survey*, ii: *Archaeological Data* (Annual of the British School at Athens, supp. vol. 27). London: British School at Athens.

——, ——, —— and —— (forthcoming), *Continuity and Change in a Greek Rural Landscape: The Laconia Survey*, i: *Results and Interpretation* (Annual of the British School at Athens, supp. vol. 26). London: British School at Athens.

Cavanagh, W. G., and Curtis, M., with J. N. Coldstream and A. W. Johnston (eds) (1998), *Post-Minoan Crete: Proceedings of the 1st Colloquium on Post-Minoan Crete held by the British School at Athens and the Institute of Archaeology, University College London (10–11 November 1995)* (British School at Athens Studies, 2). London: British School at Athens.

—— and Walker, S. E. C. (eds) (1998), *Sparta in Laconia: Proceedings of the 19th British Museum Classical Colloquium held with the British School at Athens and King's and University Colleges, London (6–8 December, 1995)* (British School at Athens Studies, 4). London: British School at Athens.

Cawkwell, G. (1978), *Philip of Macedon*. London: Faber & Faber.

Cawkwell, G. L. (1994), 'The deification of Alexander the Great: a note', in Worthington (ed.) (1994), 293–306.

—— (1996) 'Isocrates', *OCD*[3] 769–71.

Chadwick, J., and Mann, W. N. (trans. 1950), *The Medical Works of Hippocrates*. Oxford: Blackwell. [See also G. E. R. Lloyd 1978a.]

Charaktir (1996). Χαρακτήρ· αφιέρωμα στη Μάντω Οικονομίδου. Athens: Ypourgeio Politismou, TAPA.

Cherry, J. F., Davis, J. L., and Mantzourani, E. (1991), *Landscape Archaeology as Long-term History: Northern Keos in the Cycladic Islands from Earliest Settlement until*

Modern Times (Monumenta Archaeologica, 16). Los Angeles, CA: Univ. of California Institute of Archaeology.

Chouliara-Raïos, H. (1989), *L'Abeille et le miel en Égypte d'après les papyrus grecs* (Ἐπιστημονική ἐπετηρίδα Φιλοσοφικῆς Σχολῆς ʾΔωδώνηʾ, 30). Ioannina: Univ. of Ioannina.

Cioccolo, S. (1990), 'Enigmi dell'ἦθος: Antigono II Gonata in Plutarco e altrove', in Virgilio (ed.) (1990), 135–90.

Clarke, K. (1997), 'In search of the author of Strabo's Geography', *JRS* 87: 92–110.

Clarysse, W. (1978), 'Notes de prosopographie thébaine, 7: Hurgonaphor et Chaonnophris, les derniers pharaons indigènes', *Chronique d'Égypte*, 53: 243–53.

—— (1980a), 'A royal visit to Memphis and the end of the second Syrian war', in D. J. Crawford *et al.* (1980), 83–90.

—— (1980b), 'Philadelphia and the Memphites in the Zenon archive', in D. J. Crawford *et al.* (1980), 91–122.

—— (1981), *Prosopographia Ptolemaica, ix: Addenda et corrigenda au volume iii (1956)* (Studia hellenistica, 25). Louvain: [W. Peremans].

—— (1985), 'Greeks and Egyptians in the Ptolemaic army and administration', *Aegyptus*, 65: 57–66.

—— (1995), 'Greeks in Ptolemaic Thebes', in Vleeming (ed.) (1995), 1–19.

—— and Vandorpe, K. (1995), *Zénon: un homme d'affaires grec à l'ombre des pyramides* (Ancorae: steunpunten voor studie en onderwijs, 14). Louvain: Faculteit Letteren van de K. U. Leuven/Presses Universitaires de Louvain.

—— and —— (1998), 'The Ptolemaic apomoira', in Melaerts (ed.) (1998), 5–42.

Clauss, J. J. (1993), *The Best of the Argonauts: The Redefinition of the Epic Hero in Book One of Apollonius' Argonautica* (Hellenistic Culture and Society, 10). Berkeley, Los Angeles, London: Univ. of California Press.

Clay, D. (1983), 'Individual and community in the first generation of the Epicurean school', in *Syzetesis*, 255–79.

Clinton, K. (1989), 'Hadrian's contribution to the renaissance of Eleusis', in Walker and Cameron (eds) (1989), 56–68.

—— (1997), 'Eleusis and the Romans: late Republic to Marcus Aurelius', in Hoff and Rotroff (eds) (1997), 161–81.

Cohen, G. M. (1974), 'The Diadochoi and the new monarchies', *Athenaeum*, 52: 177–9.

—— (1978), *The Seleucid Colonies: Studies in Founding, Administration and Organization* (Historia Einzelschriften, 30). Wiesbaden: Steiner.

—— (1983), 'Colonization and population transfer in the hellenistic world', in van 't Dack *et al.* (eds) (1983), 63–74.

—— (1995), *The Hellenistic Settlements in Europe, the Islands, and Asia Minor* (Hellenistic Culture and Society, 17). Berkeley, Los Angeles, London: Univ. of California Press.

Cohen, S. D. (1990), 'Religion, ethnicity and "hellenism" in the emergence of Jewish identity in Maccabean Palestine', in Bilde *et al.* (eds) (1990), 204–23.

—— (1998), *The Beginnings of Jewishness: Boundaries, Varieties, Uncertainties* (Hellenistic Culture and Society, 31). Berkeley, Los Angeles, London: Univ. of California Press.

Cohn-Haft, L. (1956), *The Public Physicians of Ancient Greece* (Smith College Studies in History, 42). Northampton, MA: Department of History, Smith College.

Cole, S. G. (1981), 'Could Greek women read and write?', in Foley (ed.) (1981), 219–45.

Colledge, M. (1986), *The Parthian Period*, (Iconography of Religions, 14: Iran, fasc. 3). Leiden: Brill.

—— (1987), 'Greek and non-Greek interaction in the art and architecture of the hellenistic east', in Kuhrt and Sherwin-White (eds) (1987), ch. 6 (pp. 134–62).

Colledge, M. A. R. (1984a), 'The Greek kingdoms in Bactria and India', in Ling (ed.) (1984b), ch. 3 (pp. 25–32).

—— (1984b), 'The Seleucid kingdom', in Ling (ed.) (1984b), ch. 2 (pp. 17–24).

—— (1990), 'Some observations on Greek art in western Asia after Alexander's conquest', in Descoeudres (ed.) (1990b), 323–8.

Connelly, J. B. (1988), *Votive Sculpture of Hellenistic Cyprus*. Nicosia: Department of Antiquities/New York: New York UP.

Connolly, P. (1984), 'Hellenistic warfare', in Ling (ed.) (1984b), ch. 7 (pp. 81–90).

Connor, W. R. (1985), 'Historical writings in the fourth century BC and in the hellenistic period', *CHCL* ch. 13. 4 (pp. 458–71).

Cook, S. A., Adcock, F. E., and Charlesworth, M. P. (eds) (1928), *The Cambridge Ancient History*[1], vii: *The Hellenistic Monarchies and the Rise of Rome*. Cambridge: CUP.

——, —— and —— (eds) (1930), *The Cambridge Ancient History*[1], viii: *Rome and the Mediterranean 218–133 BC*. Cambridge: CUP.

Cornell, T. J. (1989), 'The conquest of Italy', *CAH*[2] vii. 2, ch. 8 (pp. 351–419).

—— (1995), *The Beginnings of Rome: Italy and Rome from the Bronze Age to the Punic Wars (c.1000–264 BC)* (Routledge History of the Ancient World). London and New York: Routledge.

Corso, A. (1997), 'Vitruvius and Attic monuments', *BSA* 92: 373–400.

Cory, W. J. (1858), *Ionica*. London: Smith, Elder & Co.

Coulton, J. J. (1986), 'Balboura survey', *Anatolian Studies*, 36: 7–8.

—— (1987), 'Balboura survey', *Anatolian Studies*, 37: 11–13.

—— (1988a), 'Balboura survey', *Anatolian Studies*, 38: 14–17.

—— (1988b), 'Balboura survey 1987', *Araştırma sonuçları toplantısı*, 6: 225–31.

—— (1989), 'Balboura survey', *Anatolian Studies*, 39: 12–13.

—— (1991a), 'Balboura survey', *Anatolian Studies*, 41: 17–19.

—— (1991b), 'Balboura survey 1988, 1990', *Araştırma sonuçları toplantısı*, 9: 47–57.

—— (1992a), 'Balboura survey', *Anatolian Studies*, 42: 6–8.

—— (1992b), 'Balboura survey 1991', *Araştırma sonuçları toplantısı*, 10: 459–72.

—— (1993a), 'Balboura and district research project', *Anatolian Studies*, 43: 4–6.

—— (1993b), 'Balboura survey 1992', *Araştırma sonuçları toplantısı*, 11: 429–36.

—— (1994), 'Balboura and district research project 1993', *Anatolian Studies*, 44: 8–10.

Crawford, D. J. (1971), *Kerkeosiris: An Egyptian Village in the Ptolemaic Period* (Cambridge Classical Studies). Cambridge: CUP.

—— (1978), 'The good official of Ptolemaic Egypt', in Maehler and Strocka (eds) (1978), 195–202.

—— (1980), 'Ptolemy, Ptah and Apis in hellenistic Memphis', in D. J. Crawford *et al.* (eds) (1980), 1–42.

——, Quaegebeur, J., and Clarysse, W. (1980), *Studies on Ptolemaic Memphis* (Studia hellenistica, 24). Louvain: [W. Peremans].

Crawford, M. ([1]1978, [2]1992), *The Roman Republic* (Fontana History of the Ancient World). [1]Hassocks: Harvester Press/[London]: Collins; [2][London]: HarperCollins.

—— (1983a), 'Numismatics', in M. Crawford (ed.) (1983b), ch. 4 (pp. 185–233).

—— (ed.) (1983b), *Sources for Ancient History* (The Sources of History: Studies in the Use of Historical Evidence). Cambridge: CUP.

Crook, J. A., Lintott, A., and Rawson, E. (eds) (1994), *The Cambridge Ancient History*[2], ix: *The Last Age of the Roman Republic, 146–43 BC*. Cambridge: CUP.

Cunliffe, B. (1988), *Greeks, Romans and Barbarians: Spheres of Interaction*. London: Batsford.

—— (1993), 'Core–periphery relationships: Iberia and the Mediterranean', in Bilde *et al.* (eds) (1993), 53–85.

Cunningham, I. C. (1971), *Herodas: Mimiambi*. Oxford: Clarendon.

—— (1987), *Herodas: Mimiambi, cum appendice fragmentorum mimorum papyraceorum* (Bibliotheca Teubneriana). Leipzig: Teubner.

Dalley, S. ([ed.]) 1998), *The Legacy of Mesopotamia*. Oxford: OUP.

Dalongeville, R., Lakakis, M., and Rizakis, A. D. (1992), *Paysages d'Achaïe*, i: *Le Bassin du Peiros et la plaine occidentale* (Μελετήματα, 15). Athens: Ethnikon Idryma Erevnon, Kentron Ellinikis kai Romaïkis Archaiotitos/Paris: de Boccard.

David, E. (1981), *Sparta between Empire and Revolution* (Monographs in Classical Studies). Salem, NH: Ayer.

Davies, J. K. (1984), 'Cultural, social and economic features of the hellenistic world', *CAH*[2] vii. 1, ch. 8 (pp. 257–320).

—— (1993), *Democracy and Classical Greece*[2] (Fontana History of the Ancient World). London: HarperCollins.

—— (1994), 'On the non-usability of the concept of "sovereignty" in an ancient Greek context', in Foresti *et al.* (eds) (1994), 51–65.

—— (1996a), 'Economy, hellenistic', *OCD*[3] 504.

—— (1996b), 'Documents and "documents" in fourth-century historiography', in Carlier (ed.) (1996), 29–39.

—— (1998a), 'Finance, administration, and *Realpolitik*: the case of fourth-century Delphi', in Austin *et al.* (eds) (1998), 1–14.

—— (1998b), 'Ancient economies: models and muddles', in Parkins and Smith (eds) (1998), 225–56.

Davies, W. D., and Finkelstein, L. (eds) (1989), *The Cambridge History of Judaism*, ii: *The Hellenistic Age*. Cambridge: CUP.

Davis, J. L., Alcock, S. E., Bennet, J., Lolos, Y. G., and Shelmerdine, C. W. (1997), 'The Pylos Regional Archaeological Project, part I: overview and the archaeological survey', *Hesp.* 66: 391–494.

Davis, N. and Kraay, C. M. (1973), *The Hellenistic Kingdoms: Portrait Coins and History*. London: Thames & Hudson.

Day, J. (1942), *An Economic History of Athens under Roman Domination*. New York: Columbia UP (repr., New York: Arno, 1973).

Dean-Jones, L. (1991), 'The cultural construct of the female body in classical Greek science', in Pomeroy (ed.) (1991), 111–37.

Delia, D. (1993), 'Response' [to Samuel], in Green (ed.) (1993), 192–204.

—— (1996), ' "All army boots and uniforms?" Ethnicity in Ptolemaic Egypt', in *Alexandria and Alexandrianism*, 41–53.

Del Monte, G. F. (ed.) (1997), *Testi dalla Babilonia ellenistica*, i: *Testi cronografici* (Studi ellenistici, 9). Pisa, etc.: Istituti Editoriali e Poligrafici Internazionali.

Derow, P. (1994), 'Historical explanation: Polybius and his predecessors', in Hornblower (ed.) (1994c), ch. 2 (pp. 73–90).

Derow, P. S. (1973), 'Kleemporos', *Phoenix*, 27: 118–34.

—— (1979), 'Polybius, Rome, and the east', *JRS* 69: 1–15.

—— (1982), 'Polybius (205?–125? BC)', in Luce (ed.) (1982), i. 525–39.

—— (1989), 'Rome, the fall of Macedon and the sack of Corinth', *CAH*² viii, ch. 9 (pp. 290–323).

—— (1990), review of Ferrary, *Philhellénisme*, in *JRS* 80: 197–200.

—— (1993), review of Billows, *Antigonos*, in *CR* 107 [n.s. 43]: 326–32.

—— (1996a), 'Perseus (2), *OCD*³ 1143–4.

—— (1996b), 'Philhellenism', *OCD*³ 1159–60.

—— (1996c), 'Polybius (1)', *OCD*³ 1209–10.

Descoeudres, J.-P. (ed.) (1990a), Εὐμουσία: *Ceramic and Iconographic Studies in Honour of Alexander Cambitoglou* (Mediterranean Archaeology, supp. 1). Sydney: Meditarch.

—— (ed.) (1990b), *Greek Colonists and Native Populations: Proceedings of the 1st Australian Congress of Classical Archaeology Held in Honour of Emeritus Professor A. D. Trendall (Sydney, 9–14 July 1985)*. Canberra: Humanities Research Centre/ Oxford: Clarendon.

de Souza, P. (1995), 'Greek piracy', in A. Powell (ed.) (1995), 179–98.

—— (1996), 'Piracy', *OCD*³ 1184–5.

—— (1998), 'Late hellenistic Crete and the Roman conquest', in Cavanagh and Curtis (eds) (1998), 112–16.

—— (2000), *Piracy in the Graeco-Roman World*. Cambridge: CUP.

Dicks, D. R. (1970), *Early Greek Astronomy to Aristotle*. London: Thames & Hudson.

Dihle, A. (1993), 'Response' [to van Straten and Giovannini], in Bulloch *et al.* (eds) (1993), 287–95.

Dilke, O. A. W. (1985), *Greek and Roman Maps*. London: Thames & Hudson (repr. Baltimore and London: Johns Hopkins UP, 1998).

Dillon, J. M., and Long, A. A. (eds) (1988), *The Question of 'Eclecticism': Studies in Later Greek Philosophy* (Hellenistic Culture and Society, 3); Berkeley, Los Angeles, London: Univ. of California Press.

Dindorf, L. A. (ed.) (1831), *Ioannis Malalae chronographia* (Corpus scriptorum historiae byzantinae). Bonn: Weber.

Dindorf, W. (ed.) (1829), *Georgius Syncellus et Nicephorus* (Corpus scriptorum historiae byzantinae). Bonn: Weber.

Dinsmoor, W. B. (1920), 'The monument of Agrippa at Athens', *American Journal of Archaeology*, 24: 83.

Dittenberger, W. (¹1883, ²1898–1901), *Sylloge inscriptionum Graecarum*. Leipzig: Hirzel. (¹i, ²iii vols.)

—— (1903–5), *Orientis Graecae inscriptiones selectae*, i–ii. Leipzig: Hirzel.

—— [rev. Hiller von Gaertringen, F., Kirchner, J., Pomtow, J., and Ziebarth, E.] (1915–24), *Sylloge inscriptionum Graecarum*³, i–iv. Leipzig: Hirzel.

—— and Purgold, K. (1896), *Die Inschriften von Olympia* (Olympia, v). Berlin: Asher.

Di Vita, A. (1990), 'Town planning in the Greek colonies of Sicily from the time of their foundations to the Punic wars', in Descoeudres (ed.) (1990b), 343–63.

Dobson, J. F. (1925), 'Herophilus of Alexandria', *Proceedings of the Royal Society of Medicine*, 18: 19–32.

—— (1926–7), 'Erasistratus', *Proceedings of the Royal Society of Medicine*, 20: 825–32.

Drachmann, A. G. (1935), 'Dioptra', *RE* suppl. vi. 1287–90.

Dreyer, J. L. E. (1906), *A History of the Planetary Systems from Thales to Kepler*. Cambridge: CUP (repr. as *A History of Astronomy from Thales to Kepler*; New York: Dover, 1958 and later).

Drijvers, J. W. (1998), 'Strabo on Parthia and the Parthians', in Wiesehöfer (ed.) (1998), 279–94.

Droysen, J. G. (1877–8), *Geschichte des Hellenismus*[2], i: *Geschichte Alexanders des grossen*; ii: *Geschichte der Diadochen*; iii: *Geschichte der Epigonen*. Gotha: Perthes.

—— (1883–5), *Histoire de l'hellénisme*, i: *Histoire d'Alexandre le Grand*; ii: *Histoire des successeurs d'Alexandre (Diadoques)*; iii: *Histoire des successeurs d'Alexandre (Epigones)* (Histoire grecque, 6–8). Trans. A. Bouché-Leclercq with E. Legrand, P. P. Huschard, and A. M. Chuquet. Paris: Leroux.

Dürrbach, F. (1921–3), *Choix d'inscriptions de Délos*, i. Paris: Leroux.

Eagleton, T. (1983), *Literary Theory*. Oxford: Blackwell.

Easterling, P. E., and Knox, B. M. W. (eds) (1985), *The Cambridge History of Classical Literature*, i: *Greek Literature*. Cambridge: CUP.

—— and Muir, J. V. (eds) (1985), *Greek Religion and Society*. Cambridge: CUP.

Eckstein, A. M. (1995), *Moral Vision in the Histories of Polybius* (Hellenistic Culture and Society, 16). Berkeley, Los Angeles, London: Univ. of California Press.

—— (1997), 'Physis and nomos: Polybius, the Romans, and Cato the Elder', in Cartledge *et al.* (eds) (1997), 175–98.

Eddy, S. K. (1961), *The King is Dead: Studies in the Near Eastern Resistance to Hellenism 334–31 BC*. Lincoln, NB: Univ. of Nebraska Press.

Edelstein, E. J., and Edelstein, L. (1945), *Asclepius: A Collection and Interpretation of the Testimonies*, i–ii (Publications of the Institute of the History of Medicine, The Johns Hopkins University, 2nd series: Texts and Documents, 2. 1–2). Baltimore, MD: Johns Hopkins UP.

Edelstein, L., and Kidd, I. G. ([1]1972, [2]1989), *Posidonius*, i: *The Fragments* (Cambridge Classical Texts and Commentaries, 13). Cambridge, New York, etc.: CUP.

Edgar, C. C. (ed.) (1925–31), *Zenon Papyri*, i–iv (Catalogue général des antiquités égyptiennes du Musée du Caire, 79, 82, 85, 90). Cairo: Institut Français d'Archéologie Orientale.

Edwards, G. R. (1975), *Corinthian Hellenistic Pottery* (Corinth, 7. 3). Princeton, NJ: American School of Classical Studies at Athens.

Ehrenberg, V. ([1]1960, [2]1969), *The Greek State*. [1]Oxford: Blackwell; [2]London: Methuen.

Eichholz, D. E. (1965), *Theophrastus: De Lapidibus*. Oxford: Clarendon.

Ellis, J. R. (1976), *Philip II and Macedonian Imperialism* (Aspects of Greek and Roman Life). London: Thames & Hudson.

—— (1994a), 'Macedon and north-west Greece', *CAH*[2] vi, ch. 14 (pp. 723–59).

—— (1994b), 'Macedonian hegemony created', *CAH*[2] vi, ch. 15 (pp. 760–90).

Ellis, W. M. (1994), *Ptolemy of Egypt*. London and New York: Routledge.

Empereur, J.-Y. (1998), *Alexandria Rediscovered*. London: British Museum.

—— and Garlan, Y. (1987), 'Bulletin archéologique: amphores et timbres amphoriques (1980–1986)', *REG* 108: 56–109.

—— and —— (1992), 'Bulletin archéologique: amphores et timbres amphoriques (1987–1991)', *REG* 105: 176–220.

Engberg-Pedersen, T. (ed.) (1989), *Pejlinger af hellenismen* ['Directions in Hellenism'] (Hellenismestudier, 1). Aarhus: Aarhus Universitetsforlag.

—— (1990), *The Stoic Theory of Oikeiosis* (Studies in Hellenistic Civilization, 2). Aarhus: Aarhus UP.

—— (ed.) (1992), *Fra Alexander til apokalypser* ['From Alexander to Apocalypses'] (Hellenismestudier, 7). Aarhus: Aarhus Universitetsforlag.

—— (1993), 'The relationship between intellectual and political centres in the hellenistic world', in Bilde *et al.* (eds) (1993), 285–315.

—— (ed.) (1995), *Sproget i hellenismen* ['Language in the Hellenistic Age'] (Hellenismestudier, 10). [Aarhus]: Aarhus Universitetsforlag.

Engelmann, H. (1975), *The Delian Aretalogy of Sarapis*. Leiden: Brill.

—— and Merkelbach, R. (1973), *Die Inschriften von Erythrai und Klazomenai*, ii (Inschriften Griechischer Städte aus Kleinasien, 2). Bonn: Kommission für die Archäologische Erforschung Kleinasiens bei der Österreichisches Akademie der Wissenschaften/Institut für Altertumskunde der Universität Köln.

Errington, R. M. (1977), 'The nature of the Macedonian state under the monarchy', *Chiron*, 8: 77–133.

—— (1986), *Geschichte Makedoniens: von den Anfängen bis zum Untergang des Königreiches*. Munich: Beck.

—— (1989a), 'Rome against Philip and Antiochus', *CAH*[2] viii, ch. 8 (pp. 244–89).

—— (1989b), 'Rome and Greece to 205 BC', *CAH*[2] viii, ch. 4 (pp. 81–106).

—— (1989c), review of Hammond and Walbank, *History of Macedonia*, iii, in *CR* 103 [n.s. 39]: 288–90.

—— (1990), *A History of Macedonia* (Hellenistic Culture and Society, 5). Berkeley, Los Angeles, Oxford: Univ. of California Press. (Trans., by C. Errington, of Errington 1986; repr. in paperback 1993.)

—— (1996), 'Aristonicus (1)', *OCD*[3] 163.

Erskine, A. (1990), *The Hellenistic Stoa: Political Thought and Action*. London: Duckworth.

—— (1994), 'The Romans as common benefactors', *Historia*, 43: 70–87.

Étienne, R., and Piérart, M. (1975), 'Un décret du koinon des Hellènes à Platées en l'honneur de Glaucon, fils d'Étéoclès, d'Athènes', *BCH* 99: 51–75.

Faraone, C. A., and Obbink, D. (eds) (1991), *Magika Hiera: Ancient Greek Magic and Religion*. New York and Oxford: OUP.

Farrington, B. (1961), *Greek Science*[2] (Pelican Books). Harmondsworth: Penguin.

Fehr, B. (1997), 'Society, consanguinity and the fertility of women: the community of deities on the great frieze of the Pergamum altar as a paradigm of cross-cultural ideas', in Bilde *et al.* (eds) (1997), 48–66 and pls 1–7.

Feldman, L. H. (1998), *Josephus's Interpretation of the Bible* (Hellenistic Culture and Society, 27). Berkeley, CA: Univ. of California Press.

Ferguson, J. (1973), *The Heritage of Hellenism* (Library of European Civilization). London: Thames & Hudson.

—— (1975), *Utopias of the Classical World* (Aspects of Greek and Roman Life). London: Thames & Hudson.

Ferguson, W. S. (1911), *Hellenistic Athens: An Historical Essay*. London: Macmillan.

—— (1928), 'The leading ideas of the new period', *CAH*[1] vii, ch. 1 (pp. 1–40).

—— (1948), 'Demetrius Poliorcetes and the Hellenic league', *Hesp.* 17: 112–36.

Ferrary, J.-L. (1988), *Philhellénisme et impérialisme: aspects idéologiques de la conquête romaine du monde hellénistique, de la seconde guerre de Macédoine à la guerre contre Mithridate* (Bibliothèque des Écoles Françaises d'Athènes et de Rome, 271). Rome: École Française de Rome.

—— (1997), 'The hellenistic world and Roman patronage', in Cartledge *et al.* (eds) (1997), 105–19.

Field, J. V. (1990), 'Some Roman and Byzantine portable sundials and the London sundial-calendar', *History of Technology*, 12: 103–35.

—— (1996), 'European astronomy in the first millennium: the archaeological record', in C. Walker (ed.) (1996), 110–22.

Figueira, T. J. (1993a), *Excursions in Epichoric History: Aiginetan Essays* (Greek Studies: Interdisciplinary Approaches). Lanham, MD: Rowman & Littlefield.

—— (1993b), 'Notes on hellenistic Aigina', in Figueira 1993*a*, ch. 14 (pp. 377–98).

Finlay, G. (n.d.), *Greece under the Romans* (Everyman's Library). London: Dent/New York: Dutton.

Finley, M. I. (1965), 'Technical innovation and economic progress in the ancient world', *Economic History Review* (2nd series), 18: 29–45; repr. in Finley (1981), ch. 11 (pp. 176–95).

—— ([1]1973a, [2]1985), *The Ancient Economy*. [1]London: Chatto & Windus; [2]London: Hogarth Press.

—— (1973b), 'Technology in the Greco-Roman world: a general report', *Talanta*, 5: 6–47.

—— (ed.) (1974), *Studies in Ancient Society* (Past and Present). London: Routledge & Kegan Paul.

—— (1975a), *The Use and Abuse of History*. London: Chatto & Windus.

—— (1975b), 'The historical tradition: the *Contributi* of Arnaldo Momigliano', in Finley (1975a), ch. 4 (pp. 75–86).

—— (ed.) (1981), *The Legacy of Greece: A New Appraisal*. Oxford: Clarendon.

—— (1986), 'Revolution in antiquity', in Porter and Teich (eds) (1986), 47–60.

Fleischer, R. (1991), *Studien zur seleukidischen Kunst*, i: *Herrscherbildnisse*. Mainz am Rhein: DAI/von Zabern.

—— (1996), 'Hellenistic royal iconography on coins', in Bilde *et al.* (eds) (1981), 28–40.

Foley, H. P. (ed.) (1981), *Reflections of Women in Antiquity*. New York, London, and Paris: Gordon Breach.

Foraboschi, D. (1984), 'Archeologia della cultura economica: ricerche economiche ellenistiche', in Virgilio (ed.) (1984b), 75–105.

—— (1987), 'L'ideologia della ricchezza in Aristea', in Virgilio (ed.) (1987c), 63–74.

Forbes, R. J. (^{1}1955–64, ^{2}1964–72), *Studies in Ancient Technology*, i–ix. Leiden: Brill.

Foresti, L. A., Barzanò, A., Bearzot, C., Prandi, L., and Zecchini, G. (eds) (1994), *Federazioni e federalismo nell'Europa antica (Bergamo, 21–25 settembre 1992): alle radici della casa comune europea* (Vita e pensiero). Milan: Università Cattolica del Sacro Cuore, Centro Culturale Nicolò Rezzara.

Forrest, W. G. (^{1}1968, ^{2}1980), *A History of Sparta 950–192 BC*. ^{1}London: Hutchinson; ^{2}London: Duckworth.

—— (1987) 'A Samian proxeny decree', *Horos*, 5: 91–3.

Fortenbaugh, W. W., with Huby, P. M., and Long, A. A. (eds) (1985), *Theophrastus of Eresus: On his Life and Work* (Rutgers Univ. Studies in Classical Humanities, 2). New Brunswick, NJ, and Oxford: Transaction Books.

——, Huby, P. M., Sharples, R. W., and Gutas, D. (eds and trans. 1992), *Theophrastus of Eresus: Sources for his Life, Writings, Thought and Influence*, i: *Life, Writings, Various Reports, Logic, Physics, Metaphysics, Theology, Mathematics*; ii: *Psychology, Human Physiology, Living Creatures, Botany, Ethics, Religion, Politics, Rhetoric and Poetics, Music, Miscellanea* (Philosophia antiqua, 54.1–2). Leiden: Brill.

—— and Sharples, R. W. (eds) (1988), *Theophrastean Studies on Natural Science, Physics and Metaphysics, Ethics, Religion and Rhetoric* (Rutgers Univ. Studies in Classical Humanities, 3). New Brunswick and Oxford: Transaction Books.

Fossey, J. M. (ed.) (1989), *Boiotia Antiqua*, i: *Papers on Recent Work in Boiotian History and Archaeology* (Monographies en archéologie et histoire classiques de l'Université McGill/McGill University Monographs in Classical Archaeology and History, 7). Amsterdam: Gieben.

—— (1990), *The Ancient Topography of Opountian Lokris*. Amsterdam: Gieben.

Foucart, P. (1885), 'Inscriptions de Béotie', *BCH* 9: 403–33.

Foxhall, L., and Forbes, H. A. (1982), '*Sitometreia*: the role of grain as a food in classical antiquity', *Chiron*, 12: 41–90.

—— and Salmon, J. (eds) (1998a), *Thinking Men: Masculinity and its Self-representation in the Classical Tradition* (Leicester–Nottingham Studies in Ancient Society, 7). London and New York: Routledge.

—— and —— (eds) (1998b), *When Men were Men: Masculinity, Power and Identity in Classical Antiquity* (Leicester–Nottingham Studies in Ancient Society, 8). London and New York: Routledge.

Francfort, H.-P. (1984), *Fouilles d'Aï Khanoum*, iii: *Le Sanctuaire du temple à redans*, 2. *Les Trouvailles* (Mémoires de la Délégation Archéologique Française en Afghanistan, 27; Paris: de Boccard).

Franco, C. (1990), 'Lisimaco e Atene', in Virgilio (ed.) (1990), 113–34.

—— (1993), *Il regno di Lisimaco: strutture amministrative e rapporti con le città* (Studi ellenistici, 6/Biblioteca di studi antichi, 71). Pisa: Giardini.

Franke, P. R. (1989), 'Pyrrhus', *CAH*^{2} vii. 2, ch. 10 (pp. 456–85).

Fraser, P. M. (1972), *Ptolemaic Alexandria*, i–iii. Oxford: Clarendon.

—— (1977), *Rhodian Funerary Monuments*. Oxford: Clarendon.

—— (1994), 'The world of Theophrastus', in Hornblower (ed.) (1994c), ch. 6 (pp. 167–91).

—— (1996a), *Cities of Alexander the Great*. Oxford: Clarendon.

—— (1996b), 'Lycophron (2)', *OCD*^{3} 895–7.

Fra Xenophon til Augustus (1990) (Hellenismestudier, 3). Aarhus: Aarhus Universitetsforlag.

494

French, R. (1994), *Ancient Natural History: Histories of Nature* (Sciences of Antiquity). London and New York: Routledge.

Frisch, P. (1978), *Die Inschriften von Lampsakos*. Bonn: Habelt.

Frösén, J. (ed.) (1997), *Early Hellenistic Athens: Symptoms of a Change* (Papers and Monographs of the Finnish Institute at Athens, 6). Helsinki: Suomen Ateenan-instituutin säätiö/Foundation of the Finnish Institute at Athens.

Frye, R. N. (1984), *The History of Ancient Iran* (Handbuch der Altertumswissenschaft, iii. 7; Munich: Beck).

Fuks, A. (1970), 'The Bellum Achaicum and its social aspect', *JRS* 80: 78–89.

—— (1974), 'Patterns and types of social-economic revolution in Greece from the fourth to the second century BC', *Ancient Society*, 5: 51–81.

Fullerton, M. D. (1998), 'Atticism, classicism, and the origins of neo-Attic sculpture', in Palagia and Coulson (eds) (1998), 93–9.

Funck, B. (ed.) (1996a), *Hellenismus: Beiträge zur Erforschung von Akkulturation und politischer Ordnung in den Staaten des hellenistischen Zeitalters (Akten des internationalen Hellenismus-Kolloquiums 9.–14. März 1994 in Berlin)*. Tübingen: Mohr.

—— (1996b), ' "König Perserfreund": die Seleukiden in der Sicht ihrer Nachbarn (Beobachtungen zu einigen ptolemäischen Zeugnissen des 4. und 3. Jh.s v. Chr.)', in Funck (ed.) (1996a), 195–215.

—— and Gehrke, H.-J. (1996), 'Akkulturation und politische Ordnung im Hellenismus', in Funck (ed.) (1996a), 1–10.

Funghi, M. S. (1997), 'The Derveni papyrus', in Laks and Most (eds) (1997b), ch. 1 (pp. 25–37).

Fusillo, M., Hurst, A., and Paduano, G. (eds) (1991), *Licofrone, Alessandra* (Biblioteca letteraria, 10). Milan: Guerini.

Gabbert. J. J. (1987) 'The anarchic dating of the Chremonidean War', *Classical Journal*, 82: 230–5.

—— (1997), *Antigonus II Gonatas: A Political Biography*. London and New York: Routledge.

Gabrielsen, V. (1993), 'Rhodes and Rome after the third Macedonian war', in Bilde *et al.* (eds) (1993), 132–61.

—— (1997), *The Naval Aristocracy of Hellenistic Rhodes* (Studies in Hellenistic Civilization, 6). Aarhus: Aarhus UP.

Gara, A. (1984), 'Limiti strutturali dell'economia monetaria nell'Egitto tardo-tolemaico', in Virgilio (ed.) (1984b), 107–34.

—— (1987), 'Schiavi e soldati nella Lettera di Aristea', in Virgilio (ed.) (1987c), 75–89.

Gargola, D. J. (1992), 'Grain distributions and the revenue of the temple of Hera on Samos', *Phoenix*, 46: 12–28.

Garlan, Y. (1975), *War in the Ancient World: A Social History*. London: Chatto & Windus.

—— (1979), 'Koukos: données nouvelles pour une nouvelle interprétation des timbres amphoriques thasiens', *Thasiaca*, 213–68.

—— (1984), 'War and siegecraft', *CAH*² vii. 1, ch. 9 *b* (pp. 353–62).

—— (1994), 'Warfare', *CAH*² vi, ch. 12 *e* (pp. 678–92).

Garnsey, P. (1997), 'The middle Stoics and slavery', in Cartledge *et al.* (eds) (1997), 159–74.

——, Hopkins, K., and Whittaker, C. R. (eds) (1983), *Trade in the Ancient Economy*. London: Chatto & Windus.

Garnsey, P. D. A., and Whittaker, C. R. (eds) (1978), *Imperialism in the Ancient World*. Cambridge: CUP.

Garofalo, I. (ed.) (1988), *Erasistrati fragmenta* (Biblioteca di studi antichi, 62). Pisa: Giardini.

Gauthier, P. (1984), 'Les cités hellénistiques: épigraphie et histoire des institutions et des régimes politiques', Πρακτικά τοῦ Η΄ Διεθνοῦς Συνεδρίου Ἑλληνικῆς καὶ Λατινικῆς Ἐπιγραφικῆς (Ἀθῆνα, 3–9 Ὀκτωβρίου 1982) [Proceedings of the 8th International Congress of Greek and Latin Epigraphy (Athens, 3–9 Oct. 1982)], i. 82–107. Athens: Ypourgeio Politismou kai Epistimon.

—— (1985), *Les Cités grecques et leurs bienfaiteurs* (BCH suppl. 12). Athens: École Française d'Athènes.

—— (1990), 'Quorum et participation civique dans les démocraties grecques', in Nicolet (ed.) (1990), 73–99.

—— (1993), 'Les cités hellénistiques', *CPC Acts 1*, 211–31.

Gavrilov, A. K. (1997), 'Reading techniques in classical antiquity', *CQ* 91 [n.s. 47]: 54–73.

Geagan, D. J. (1997), 'The Athenian elite: romanization, resistance, and the exercise of power', in Hoff and Rotroff (eds) (1997), 19–32.

Geerard, M., with Desmet, J., and vander Plaetse, R. (eds) (1989–90), *Opes Atticae: miscellanea philologica et historica Raymondo Bogaert et Hermanno van Looy oblata* (= *Sacris erudiri: jaarboek voor godsdienstwetenschapen*, 31 [publ. 1990]). Steenbrugge: Sint-Pietersabdij/The Hague: Nijhoff.

Gehrke, H. J. (1982), 'Der siegreiche König: Überlegungen zur hellenistischen Monarchie', *Archiv für Kulturgeschichte*, 64: 247–77.

Gelzer, T. (1993), 'Transformations', in Bulloch *et al.* (eds), 130–51.

Gibbs, S. L. (1976), *Greek and Roman Sundials*. New Haven, CT, and London: Yale UP.

Gill, C. (1993), 'Panaetius on the virtue of being yourself', in Bulloch *et al.* (eds) (1993), 330–53.

Ginouvès, R. (1959), *L'Établissement thermal de Gortys d'Arcadie* (École Française d'Athènes, études péloponnésiennes, 2). Paris: Librairie Philosophique J. Vrin.

Giovannini, A. (1971), *Untersuchungen über die Natur und die Anfänge der bundesstaatlichen Sympolitie in Griechenland* (Hypomnemata, 33). Göttingen: Vandenhoeck & Ruprecht.

—— (1977), 'Le statut des cités de Macédoine sous les Antigonides', *Ancient Macedonia 2*, 465–72.

—— (1993), 'Greek cities and Greek commonwealth', in Bulloch *et al.* (eds) (1993), 265–86.

Glare, P. G. W., with Thompson, A. A. (1996), *Greek–English Lexicon: Revised Supplement*. Oxford: Clarendon.

Goldman, H. (ed.) (1950), *The Hellenistic and Roman Periods* (Excavations at Gözlü Küle, Tarsus, 1). Princeton, NJ: Princeton UP/Oxford: OUP.

Goldstein, J. A. (1989), 'The Hasmonean revolt and the Hasmonean dynasty', in W. D. Davies and Finkelstein (eds) (1989), 292–351.

Gomme, A. W. (1937a), *Essays in Greek History and Literature*. Oxford: Blackwell.

—— (1937b), 'The end of the Greek city-state', in Gomme (1937a), ch. 11 (pp. 204–48).

Goodman, M. (1997), *The Roman World 44 BC–AD 180* (Routledge History of the Ancient World). London and New York: Routledge.

Gordon, R. (1997), 'Quaedam veritatis umbrae: hellenistic magic and astrology', in Bilde *et al.* (eds) (1997), 128–58.

Goudriaan, K. (1988), *Ethnicity in Ptolemaic Egypt* (Dutch Monographs on Ancient History and Archaeology, 5). Amsterdam: Gieben.

—— (1992), 'Ethnical strategies in Graeco-Roman Egypt', in Bilde *et al.* (eds) (1992), 74–99.

Gow, A. S. F. (1952), *Bucolici Graeci* (Oxford Classical Texts). Oxford: Clarendon.

—— and Page, D. L. (1965), *The Greek Anthology: Hellenistic Epigrams*, i–ii. Cambridge: CUP.

Grace, V. R. (1985), 'The Middle Stoa dated by amphora stamps', *Hesp.* 54: 1–54.

Graindor, P. (1927), *Athènes sous Auguste* (Université Égyptienne, Recueil des travaux publiés par la Faculté des Lettres, 1). Cairo: Misr.

—— (1930), *Un milliardaire antique: Hérode Atticus et sa famille* (Université Égyptienne, Recueil des travaux publiés par la Faculté des Lettres, 5). Cairo: Misr.

Grainger, J. D. (1990a), *The Cities of Seleukid Syria*. Oxford: Clarendon.

—— (1990b), *Seleukos Nikator: Constructing a Hellenistic Kingdom*. London and New York: Routledge.

—— (1991), *Hellenistic Phoenicia*. Oxford: Clarendon.

—— (1997), *A Seleukid Prosopography and Gazetteer* (Mnemosyne, suppl. 172). Leiden, New York, Cologne: Brill.

Grant, M. (1982), *From Alexander to Cleopatra: The Hellenistic World*. London: Weidenfeld & Nicolson. [1st edn of Grant 1990.]

—— (1990), *The Hellenistic Greeks: From Alexander to Cleopatra*. London: Weidenfeld & Nicolson. [2nd edn of Grant 1982.]

Grayson, A. K. (1975), *Assyrian and Babylonian Chronicles* (Texts from Cuneiform Sources, 5). Locust Valley, NY: Augustin.

Green, P. (1990), *Alexander to Actium: The Hellenistic Age* (London: Thames & Hudson); first published as *Alexander to Actium: The Historical Evolution of the Hellenistic Age* (Hellenistic Culture and Society, 1; Berkeley, Los Angeles: Univ. of California Press; 1990, repr. 1993).

—— (ed.) (1993), *Hellenistic History and Culture* (Hellenistic Culture and Society, 9). Berkeley, Los Angeles, Oxford: Univ. of California Press.

—— (1997a), *The Argonautika, by Apollonios Rhodios, Translated, with Introduction, Commentary, and Glossary* (Hellenistic Culture and Society, 25). Berkeley, CA: Univ. of California Press.

—— (1997b), ' "These fragments have I shored against my ruins": Apollonios Rhodios and the social revalidation of myth for a new age', in Cartledge *et al.* (eds) (1997), 35–71.

Grenfell. B. P., Hunt, A. S., *et al.* (eds) (1896–), *Oxyrhynchus Papyri*. London: Egypt Exploration Fund, etc.

——, ——, *et al.* (eds) (1902–), *The Tebtunis Papyri*. Oxford: OUP, etc.

——, ——, Turner, E. G., and Lenger, M. T. (eds) (1906–56), *The Hibeh Papyri*. London: Egypt Exploration Fund, etc.

—— and Mahaffy, J. P. (1896), *Revenue Laws of Ptolemy Philadelphus*. Oxford: Clarendon.

Griffith, G. T. (1935), *The Mercenaries of the Hellenistic World*. Cambridge: CUP.

Griffiths, F. T. (1981), 'Home before lunch: the emancipated woman in Theocritus', in Foley (ed.) (1981), 247–73.

Grimal, P. (1968), *Hellenism and the Rise of Rome* (Weidenfeld & Nicolson Universal History, 6). London: Weidenfeld & Nicolson; trans. of 1965 German edn, Frankfurt am Main and Hamburg: Fischer. (Sections by H. Bengtson, W. Caskel, P. Derchain, M. Meuleau, M. Smith.)

Gros, P. (ed.), A. Corso and E. Romano (trans. 1997), *Vitruvio: de architectura*. Turin: Einaudi, 2 vols.

Grote, G. (n.d.), *A History of Greece* (Everyman's Library), xii. London: Dent/New York: Dutton.

Gruen, E. S. (1984), *The Hellenistic World and the Coming of Rome*. Berkeley, Los Angeles, London: Univ. of California Press.

—— (1990a), *Studies in Greek Culture and Roman Policy* (Cincinnati Classical Studies, n.s. 7). Leiden, New York, Copenhagen, Cologne: Brill.

—— (1990b), review of Ferrary, *Philhellénisme*, in *Classical Philology*, 85: 324–9.

—— (1993a), 'Hellenism and persecution: Antiochus IV and the Jews', in Green (ed.) (1993), 238–64.

—— (1993b). 'The polis in the hellenistic world', in Rosen and Farrell (eds) (1993), 339–54.

—— (1996), 'Hellenistic kingship: puzzles, problems, and possibilities', in Bilde *et al.* (eds) (1996a), 116–25.

—— (1997), 'Fact and fiction: Jewish legends in a hellenistic context', in Cartledge *et al.* (eds) (1997), 72–88.

—— (1998), *Heritage and Hellenism: The Reinvention of Jewish Tradition* (Hellenistic Culture and Society, 30). Berkeley and London: Univ. of California Press.

Grunauer-von Hoerschelmann, S. (1978), *Die Münzprägung der Lakedaimonier* (Antike Münzen and Geschnittene Steine, 7). Berlin: DAI/de Gruyter.

Grzybek, E. (1990), *Du calendrier macédonien au calendrier ptolémaïque: problèmes de chronologie hellénistique* (Schweizerische Beiträge zur Altertumswissenschaft, 20). Basle: Reinhardt.

Guillaume, O. (1983), *Fouilles d'Aï Khanoum*, ii: *Les Propylées de la rue principale* (Mémoires de la Délégation Archéologique Française en Afghanistan, 26; Paris: de Boccard).

—— (1991), *Graeco-Bactrian and Indian Coins from Afghanistan* (trans. O. Bopearachchi; French Studies in South Asian Culture and Society, 5). Delhi, Oxford, New York: OUP.

—— and Rougeulle, A. (1987), *Fouilles d'Aï Khanoum*, vii: *Les Petits Objets* (Mémoires de la Délégation Archéologique Française en Afghanistan, 31; Paris: de Boccard).

Guldager Bilde, P. (1993), 'Mouldmade bowls, centres and peripheries in the hellenistic world', in Bilde *et al.* (eds) (1993), 192–209.

Gundlach, R., and Weber, H. (eds) (1992), *Legitimation und Funktion des Herrschers: vom ägyptischen Pharao zum neuzeitlichen Diktator* (Schriften der Mainzer Philosophischen Fakultätsgesellschaft, 13). Stuttgart: Steiner.

Gutzwiller, K. J. (1998), *Poetic Garlands: Hellenistic Epigrams in Context* (Hellenistic Culture and Society, 28). Berkeley and London: Univ. of California Press.

Habicht, C. (^{1}1956, ^{2}1970), *Gottmenschentum und griechische Städte* (Zetemata, 14). Munich: Beck.

—— (1957), 'Samische Volksbeschlüsse der hellenistischen Zeit', *Ath. Mitt.* 72: 152–274.

—— (1958), 'Die herrschende Gesellschaft in den hellenistischen Monarchien', *Vierteljahrschrift für Soziologie und Wirtschaftsgeschichte*, 45: 1–16.

—— (1976), 'Zur Geschichte Athens in der Zeit Mithridates VI.', *Chiron*, 6: 127–42.

—— (1979a), *2. Makkabäerbuch* (Jüdische Schriften aus hellenistisch-römischer Zeit, i: Historische und legendarische Erzahlungen, 3). Gütersloh: Mohn.

—— (1979b), *Untersuchungen zur politischen Geschichte Athens im 3. Jahrhundert v.Chr.* (Vestigia, 30). Munich: Beck.

—— (1982), *Studien zur Geschichte Athens in hellenistischer Zeit* (Hypomnemata, 73). Göttingen: Vandenhoeck & Ruprecht.

—— (1985a), *Pausanias' Guide to Classical Greece* (Sather Classical Lectures, 50). Berkeley, CA: Univ. of California Press.

—— (1985b), *Pausanias und seine Beschreibung Griechenlands* (trans. of Habicht 1985a). Munich: Beck.

—— (1988), *Hellenistic Athens and Her Philosophers* (David Magie Lecture). Princeton, NJ: Princeton Univ. Program in the History, Archaeology, and Religions of the Ancient World; repr. in Habicht (1994), 231–47.

—— (1989a), 'Athen und die Seleukiden', *Chiron*, 19: 7–26; repr. in Habicht (1994), 164–82.

—— (1989b), 'The Seleucids and their rivals', *CAH*^{2} viii, ch. 10 (pp. 324–87).

—— (1990), 'Athens and the Attalids in the second century BC', *Hesp.* 59: 561–77; repr. in Habicht (1994), 183–201.

—— (1992), 'Athens and the Ptolemies', *Classical Antiquity*, 11: 68–90; repr. in Habicht (1994), 140–63.

—— (1994), *Athen in hellenistischer Zeit: gesammelte Aufsätze*. Munich: Beck.

—— (1995), *Athen: die Geschichte der Stadt in hellenistischer Zeit*. Munich: Beck.

—— (1996), 'Athens, Samos, and Alexander the Great', *Proceedings of the American Philosophical Society*, 140.3: 397–405.

—— (1997a), *Athens from Alexander to Antony*. Cambridge, MA, and London: Harvard UP.

—— (1997b), 'Roman citizens in Athens (228–31 BC)', in Hoff and Rotroff (eds) (1997), 9–17.

Hadas, M. (1959), *Hellenistic Culture: Fusion and Diffusion*. New York: Columbia UP (repr. New York: Norton, 1972).

Hakkarainen, M. (1997), 'Private wealth in the Athenian public sphere during the late classical and the early hellenistic period', in Frösén (ed.) (1997), 1–32.

Hallof, K., and Habicht, C. (1995), 'Buleuten und Beamte der athenischen Kleruchie in Samos', *Ath. Mitt.* 110: 273–304.

Halperin, D. M. (1993), 'Response' [to Levi], in Green (ed.) (1993), 127–32.

Hamilton, J. R. (1973), *Alexander the Great* (Hutchinson University Library). London: Hutchinson.

Hammond, N. G. L. (1972), *A History of Macedonia*, i: *Historical Geography and Prehistory*. Oxford: Clarendon (repr., New York: Arno, 1981).

—— (1983), *Three Historians of Alexander*. Cambridge: CUP.

—— (1989a), *The Macedonian State: Origins, Institutions, and History*. Oxford: Clarendon.

—— (1989b), review of Bosworth, *From Arrian to Alexander*, in *CR* 103 [n.s. 39]: 21–3.

—— (1991), 'The royal tombs at Vergina: evolution and identities', *BSA* 86: 69–82.

—— (1993a), 'The Macedonian imprint on the hellenistic world', in Green (ed.) (1993), 12–23.

—— (1993b), *Sources for Alexander the Great: An Analysis of Plutarch's Life and Arrian's Anabasis Alexandrou*. Cambridge: CUP.

—— (1994a), 'Illyrians and north-west Greeks', *CAH*² vi, ch. 9 *d* (pp. 422–43).

—— (1994b), *Philip of Macedon*. London: Duckworth.

—— (1997), *The Genius of Alexander the Great*. London: Duckworth.

—— and Griffith, G. T. (1979), *A History of Macedonia*, ii: *550–336 BC*. Oxford: Clarendon.

—— and Walbank, F. W. (1988), *A History of Macedonia*, iii: *336–167 BC*. Oxford: Clarendon.

Handley, E. W. (1985), 'Comedy', *CHCL* ch. 12 (pp. 355–425; esp. pp. 414–25, 'Menander and the new comedy').

Hannestad, L. (1993), 'Greeks and Celts: the creation of a myth', in Bilde *et al.* (eds) (1993), 15–38.

—— (1996), ' "This contributes in no small way to one's reputation": the Bithynian kings and Greek culture', in Bilde *et al.* (eds) (1996a), 67–98.

—— (1997), 'Death on Delos: conventions in an international context', in Bilde *et al.* (eds) (1997), 285–302 and pls 15–31.

—— and Potts, D. (1990), 'Temple architecture in the Seleucid kingdom', in Bilde *et al.* (eds), 91–124.

Hansen, E. V. (¹1947, ²1971), *The Attalids of Pergamon* (Cornell Studies in Classical Philology, ¹29, ²36). Ithaca, NY: Cornell UP.

Hansen, M. H. (1985), *Demography and Democracy: The Number of Athenian Citizens in the Fourth Century BC*. Herning: Systime.

—— (ed.) (1993a), *The Ancient Greek City-state (Symposium on the Occasion of the 250th Anniversary of the Royal Danish Academy of Sciences and Letters, July 1–4 1992)* (Royal Danish Academy of Sciences and Letters, Historisk-filosofiske Meddelelser, 67; retrospectively, and on dust-jacket, entitled Acts of the Copenhagen Polis Centre, 1). Copenhagen: Munksgaard.

—— (1993b), 'Introduction: the polis as a citizen-state', *CPC Acts 1*, 7–29.

—— (1995a), 'The "autonomous" city-state: ancient fact or modern fiction?', *CPC Papers 2*, 21–43.

—— (1995b), 'Kome: a study in how the Greeks designated and classified settlements which were not poleis', *CPC Papers 2*, 45–81.

—— (ed.) (1995c), *Sources for the Ancient Greek City-state (Symposium August, 24–27 1994)* (Acts of the Copenhagen Polis Centre, 2; Royal Danish Academy of Sciences and Letters, Historisk-filosofiske Meddelelser, 72). Copenhagen: Munksgaard.

—— (ed.) (1996a), *Introduction to an Inventory of Poleis (Symposium August, 23–26 1995)* (Acts of the Copenhagen Polis Centre, 3; Royal Danish Academy of Sciences and Letters, Historisk-filosofiske Meddelelser, 74). Copenhagen: Munksgaard.

—— (1996b), 'Were the Boiotian poleis deprived of their autonomia during the first and second Boiotian federations? A reply', *CPC Papers 3*, 127–36.

—— (ed.) (1997), *The Polis as an Urban Centre and as a Political Community (Symposium, August, 29–31 1996)* (Acts of the Copenhagen Polis Centre, 4/Royal Danish Academy of Sciences and Letters, Historisk-filosofiske Meddelelser, 75). Copenhagen: Munksgaard.

—— (1998), *Polis and City-state: An Ancient Concept and its Modern Equivalent* (Acts of the Copenhagen Polis Centre, 5/Royal Danish Academy of Sciences and Letters, Historisk-filosofiske Meddelelser, 76). Copenhagen: Munksgaard.

—— and Raaflaub, K. (eds) (1995), *Studies in the Ancient Greek Polis* (Papers from the Copenhagen Polis Centre, 2/Historia Einzelschriften, 95). Wiesbaden: Steiner.

—— and —— (eds) (1996), *More Studies in the Ancient Greek Polis* (Papers from the Copenhagen Polis Centre, 3/Historia Einzelschriften, 108). Wiesbaden: Steiner.

Harari, M. (1987), 'Un punto di vista archeologico sulla Lettera di Aristea', in Virgilio (ed.) (1987c), 91–106.

Harding, P. (1985), *From the End of the Peloponnesian War to the Battle of Ipsus* (Translated Documents of Greece and Rome, 2). Cambridge: CUP.

Harding, P. E. (1994), *Androtion and the Atthis: Fragments Translated with Introduction and Commentary* (Clarendon Ancient History Series). Oxford: Clarendon.

Harris, W. V. ([1]1979, [2]1984), *War and Imperialism in Republican Rome 327–70 BC*. Oxford: Clarendon.

—— (1983), 'Literacy and epigraphy', *ZPE* 52: 87–111.

—— (ed.) (1984), *The Imperialism of Mid-republican Rome*. Rome: American Academy in Rome.

—— (1989a), *Ancient Literacy*. Cambridge, MA, and London: Harvard UP.

—— (1989b), 'Rome and Carthage', *CAH²* viii, ch. 5 (pp. 107–62).

Hatzopoulos, M. B. (1986), 'Succession and regency in classical Macedonia', in *Ancient Macedonia 4*, 279–92.

—— (1988), *Une donation du roi Lysimaque* (Μελετήματα, 5). Athens: Fondation Nationale de la Recherche Scientifique, Centre de Recherches de l'Antiquité Grecque et Romaine/Paris: de Boccard.

—— (1994), *Cultes et rites de passage en Macédoine* (Μελετήματα, 19). Athens: Fondation Nationale de la Recherche Scientifique, Centre de Recherches de l'Antiquité Grecque et Romaine/Paris: de Boccard.

—— (1996), *Macedonian Institutions under the Kings* (Μελετήματα, 22), i: *A Historical and Epigraphic Study*; ii: *Epigraphic Appendix*. Athens: Fondation Nationale de la Recherche Scientifique, Centre de Recherches de l'Antiquité Grecque et Romaine/Paris: de Boccard.

Hauben, H. (1970), *Callicrates of Samos: A Contribution to the Study of the Ptolemaic Admiralty* (Studia hellenistica, 18). Louvain: [W. Peremans].

—— (1983), 'Arsinoé et la politique extérieure de l'Égypte', in van 't Dack *et al.* (eds) (1983), 99–127.

Hausmann, U. (1996), *Hellenistische Keramik* (Olympische Forschungen, 27). Berlin: DAI/de Gruyter.

Hawley, R. (1994), 'The problem of women philosophers in ancient Greece', in Archer *et al.* (eds), 70–87.

Head, B. V., with Hill, G. F., Macdonald, G., and Wroth, W. (1911), *Historia Numorum: A Manual of Greek Numismatics*[2]. Oxford: Clarendon.

Heap, A. (1998), 'Understanding the men in Menander', in Foxhall and Salmon (eds) (1998a), ch. 9 (pp. 115–29).

Heath, T. (1913), *Aristarchus of Samos: The Ancient Copernicus. A History of Greek Astronomy to Aristarchus together with Aristarchus's Treatise on the Sizes and Distances of the Sun and Moon: A New Greek Text with Translation and Notes.* Oxford: Clarendon.

Heckel, W. (1992), *The Marshals of Alexander's Empire.* London and New York: Routledge.

—— and Sullivan, R. (eds) (1984), *Ancient Coins of the Graeco-Roman World: The Nickle Numismatic Papers.* Waterloo, Ont.: Calgary Institute for the Humanities/Wilfrid Laurier UP.

Heinen, H. (1972), *Untersuchungen zur hellenistischen Geschichte des 3. Jahrhunderts v.Chr.: zur Geschichte der Zeit des Ptolemaios Keraunos und zum chremonideischen Krieg* (Historia Einzelschriften, 20). Wiesbaden: Steiner.

—— (1984), 'The Syrian–Egyptian wars and the new kingdoms of Asia Minor', *CAH*[2] vii. 1, ch. 11 (pp. 412–45).

—— (1997), 'Der κτίστης Boethos und die Einrichtung einer neuen Stadt: Teil II', *Archiv für Papyrusforschung*, 43: 340–63. [For part I see Kramer.]

Helck, W. (1959), 'Ptolemais 4', *RE* xxiii. 2. 1868–9.

1st Hellenistic Pottery Conference (1989), *Α΄ Συνάντηση για την Ελληνιστική Κεραμεική (Δεκέμβρης 1986).* Ioannina: Panepistimio Ioanninon, Tomeas Archaiologias.

2nd Hellenistic Pottery Conference (1990), *Β΄ Επιστημονική Συνάντηση για την Ελληνιστική Κεραμική· χρονολογικά προβλήματα της ελληνιστικής κεραμεικής. Πρακτικά (Ρόδος 22–25 Μαρτίου 1989).* Athens: ΚΒ΄ Ephoreia Proïstorikon kai Klasikon Archaiotiton, Rodos.

3rd Hellenistic Pottery Conference (1994), *Γ΄ Επιστημονική Συνάντηση γιὰ τὴν Ελληνιστικὴ Κεραμική· χρονολογημένα σύνολα – ἐργαστήρια (24–27 Σεπτεμβρίου 1991, Θεσσαλονίκη),* i–ii (Bibliothiki tis en Athinais Archaiologikis Etaireias, 137). Athens: Archaiologiki Etaireia.

4th Hellenistic Pottery Conference (1997), *Δ΄ Επιστημονική Συνάντηση για την Ελληνιστικὴ Κεραμική· χρονολογικά προβλήματα – κλειστά σύνολα – εργαστήρια (Μυτιλήνη, Μάρτιος 1994).* Athens: Ypourgeio Politismou/Κ΄ Ephoreia Proïstorikon kai Klasikon Archaiotiton.

Hengel, M. (1974), *Judaism and Hellenism: Studies in their Encounter in Palestine during the Early Hellenistic Period,* i–ii. London: SCM Press.

—— (1976), *Juden, Griechen und Barbaren: Aspekte der Hellenisierung des Judentums in vorchristlicher Zeit* (Stuttgarter Bibelstudien, 76). Stuttgart: Verlag Katholisches Bibelwerk.

—— (1980), *Jews, Greeks and Barbarians: Aspects of the Hellenization of Judaism in the Pre-Christian Period.* Trans., by J. Bowden, of Hengel 1976. London: SCM Press.

—— (1996), 'Jerusalem als jüdische *und* hellenistische Stadt', in Funck (ed.) (1996a), 269–306.

Henrichs, A. (1993) 'Response' [to Gelzer and Parsons], in Bulloch *et al.* (eds) (1993), 171–95.

Henry, M. M. (1992), 'The edible woman: Athenaeus's concept of the pornographic', in Richlin (ed.) (1992), 250–68.

Herman, G. (1980–1), 'The "friends" of the early hellenistic rulers: servants or officials?', *Talanta*, 12–13: 103–49.

—— (1987), *Ritualised Friendship and the Greek City*. Cambridge: CUP.

—— (1997), 'The court society of the hellenistic age', in Cartledge *et al.* (eds) (1997), 199–224.

Herrmann, P. (1965), 'Antiochos III und Teos', *Anadolu*, 9: 29–159.

Herz, P. (1992), 'Die frühen Ptolemaier bis 180 v.Chr.', in Gundlach and Weber (eds) (1992), 51–97.

Herzog, R., and Klaffenbach, G. (1952), *Asylieurkunden aus Kos* (Abhandlungen der Deutschen Akademie der Wissenschaften zu Berlin, Klasse für Sprachen, Literatur und Kunst, Jahrgang 1952. 1). Berlin: Akademie-Verlag.

Higham, T. F., and Bowra, C. M. (eds) (1938), *The Oxford Book of Greek Verse in Translation*. Oxford: Clarendon.

Hiller von Gaertringen, F. (1906), *Inschriften von Priene*. Berlin: Königliche Museen/Reimer.

Hind, J. G. F. (1994), 'Mithridates', *CAH*² ix, ch. 5 (pp. 129–64).

Hjerrild, B. (1990), 'The survival and modification of Zoroastrianism in Seleucid times', in Bilde *et al.* (eds) (1990), 140–50.

Hodkinson, S. (1986), 'Land tenure and inheritance in classical Sparta', *CQ* 80 [n.s. 36]: 378–406.

—— (1993), 'Warfare, wealth, and the crisis of Spartiate society', in Rich and Shipley (eds) (1993), 146–76.

Hölbl, G. (1994), *Geschichte des Ptolemäerreiches: Politik, Ideologie und religiöse Kultur von Alexander dem Grossen bis zur römischen Eroberung*. Darmstadt: Wissenschaftliche Buchgesellschaft.

Hoepfner, W. (1976), *Das Pompeion und seine Nachfolgebauten* (Kerameikos, 10). Berlin: de Gruyter.

—— (ed.) (1999), *Geschichte des Wohnens*, i: *5000 v. Chr.–500 n. Chr.: Vorgeschichte–Frühgeschichte–Antike*. Ludwigsburg: Wüstenrot Stiftung Deutscher Eigenheimverein e. V./Stuttgart: Deutsche Verlags-Anstalt.

—— and Brands, G. (eds) (1996), *Basileia: die Paläste der hellenistischen Könige (Internationales Symposion in Berlin vom 16. 12. 1992 bis 20. 12. 1992)* (Schriften des Seminars für klassische Archäologie der Freien Universität Berlin). Mainz am Rhein: von Zabern.

—— and Schwandner, E.-L. (1994), *Haus und Stadt im klassischen Griechenland*² (Wohnen in der klassischen Polis, 1). Muniche: DAI Architekturreferat/Seminar für klassische Archäologie der Freien Universität Berlin/Deutscher Kunstverlag.

Hoff, M. (1989), 'The early history of the Roman agora at Athens', in Walker and Cameron (eds) (1989), 1–8.

Hoff, M. C. (1997), 'Laceratae Athenae: Sulla's siege of Athens in 87/6 BC and its aftermath', in Hoff and Rotroff (eds) (1997), 33–51.

—— and Rotroff, S. I. (eds) (1997), *The Romanization of Athens: Proceedings of an International Conference held at Lincoln, Nebraska (April 1996)* (Oxbow Monographs, 94). Oxford: Oxbow.

Holladay, C. R. (1992), 'Jewish responses to hellenistic culture in early Ptolemaic Egypt', in Bilde *et al.* (eds) (1992), 139–63.

Holleaux, M. (1928), 'The Romans in Illyria', *CAH*[1] vii, ch. 26 (pp. 822–57).

—— (1930a), 'Rome and Antiochus', *CAH*[1] viii, ch. 7 (pp. 199–240).

—— (1930b), 'Rome and Macedon: Philip against the Romans', *CAH*[1] viii, ch. 5 (pp. 116–37).

—— (1930c), 'Rome and Macedon: the Romans against Philip', *CAH*[1] viii, ch. 6 (pp. 138–98).

—— (1938a), *Études d'épigraphie et d'histoire grecques*, ii: *Études sur la monarchie attalide*. Paris, 1938. Paris: de Boccard.

—— (1938b), 'Inscription trouvée à Brousse', in Holleaux (1938a), 73–125.

—— (1942a), *Études d'épigraphie et d'histoire grecques*, iii: *Lagides et Séleucides*. Paris: de Boccard.

—— (1942b), 'Décret de Naxos', in Holleaux (1942a), 27–37.

—— (1952), *Études d'épigraphie et d'histoire grecques*, iv: *Rome, la Macédoine et l'Orient grec. Première partie*. Paris: Libraire d'Amérique et d'Orient.

—— (1957), *Études d'épigraphie et d'histoire grecques*, v. Paris: Librairie d'Amérique et d'Orient, Adrien-Maisonneuve.

Holt, F. (1993), 'Response' [to Burstein], in Green (ed.) (1993), 54–64.

Holt, F. L. (1988), *Alexander the Great and Bactria: The Formation of a Greek Frontier in Central Asia* (Mnemosyne supp. 104). Leiden, New York, Copenhagen, and Cologne: Brill.

—— (1999), *Thundering Zeus: The Making of Hellenistic Bactria* (Hellenistic Culture and Society, 32). Berkeley, CA: Univ. of California Press.

Holzberg, N. (1995), *The Ancient Novel: An Introduction*. London and New York: Routledge.

Hopkinson, N. (1984), *Callimachus: Hymn to Demeter* (Cambridge Classical Texts and Commentaries, 27). Cambridge: CUP.

—— (ed.) (1988), *A Hellenistic Anthology*. Cambridge: CUP.

Hopp, J. (1977), *Untersuchungen zur Geschichte der letzten Attaliden* (Vestigia, 25). Munich: Beck.

Horn, R. (1972), *Hellenistische Bildwerke auf Samos* (Samos, 12). Bonn: DAI/Habelt.

Hornblower, J. (1981), *Hieronymus of Cardia* (Oxford Classical and Philological Monographs). Oxford: Clarendon.

Hornblower, S. ([1]1983, [2]1991), *The Greek World 479–323 BC* (Routledge History of the Ancient World). London and New York: Routledge.

—— (1994a), 'Asia Minor', *CAH*[2] vi, ch. 8 *a* (pp. 209–33).

—— (1994b), 'Epilogue', *CAH*[2] vi, ch. 18 (pp. 876–81).

—— (ed.) (1994c), *Greek Historiography*. Oxford: Clarendon.

—— (1994d), 'Persia', *CAH*[2] vi, ch. 3 (pp. 45–96).

—— (1994e), 'Sources and their uses', *CAH*[2] vi, ch. 1 (pp. 1–23).

—— (1995), 'The fourth-century and hellenistic reception of Thucydides', *JHS* 115: 47–68.

—— (1996), 'Hellenism, hellenization', *OCD*[3] 677–9.

—— and Spawforth, A. (eds) (1996), *The Oxford Classical Dictionary*³. Oxford and New York: OUP.

Houby-Nielsen, S. (1997), 'Grave gifts, women, and conventional values in hellenistic Athens', in Bilde *et al.* (eds) (1997), 220–62 and pls 8–13.

—— (1998), 'Revival of archaic funerary practices in the hellenistic and Roman Kerameikos', *Proceedings of the Danish Institute at Athens*, 2: 129–46.

Houby-Nielsen, S. H. (1995), '"Burial language" in archaic and classical Kerameikos', *Proceedings of the Danish Institute at Athens*, 1: 131–91.

Howgego, C. (1995), *Ancient History from Coins* (Approaching the Ancient World). London and New York: Routledge.

Hughes-Hallett, L. (1990), *Cleopatra: Histories, Dreams and Distortions*. London: Bloomsbury (repr., London: Vintage, 1991).

Hultsch, F. (1903), 'Dioptra', *RE* v. 1. 1073–9.

Hunter, R. (1989), *Apollonius of Rhodes, Argonautica, Book III* (Cambridge Greek and Latin Classics). Cambridge: CUP.

—— (1993), *The Argonautica of Apollonius: Literary Studies*. Cambridge: CUP.

Huss, W. (1976), *Untersuchungen zur Aussenpolitik Ptolemaios' IV* (Münchener Beiträge zur Papyrusforschung und antiken Rechtsgeschichte, 69). Munich: Beck.

—— (1995), 'Memphis und Alexandreia in hellenistischer Zeit', in *Alessandria*, 75–82.

Hussey, E. (1972), *The Presocratics*. London: Duckworth.

Hutchinson, G. O. (1988), *Hellenistic Poetry*. Oxford: Clarendon.

Huyse, P. (1996), 'Die Rolle des Griechischen im "hellenistischen" Iran', in Funck (ed.) (1996a), 57–76.

Hyldahl, N. (1990), 'The Maccabean rebellion and the question of "hellenization"', in Bilde *et al.* (eds) (1990), 188–203.

Inscriptiones Graecae (1873–). Berlin: de Gruyter, etc.

Invernizzi, A. (1993), 'Seleucia on the Tigris: centre and periphery in Seleucid Asia', in Bilde *et al.* (eds) (1993), 230–50.

Inwood, B. (1985), *Ethics and Human Action in Early Stoicism*. Oxford: Clarendon.

—— and Gerson, L. P. (1988), *Hellenistic Philosophy: Introductory Readings*. Indianapolis and Cambridge: Hackett.

Isager, S. (1990), 'Kings and gods in the Seleucid empire: a question of landed property in Asia Minor', in Bilde *et al.* (eds) (1990), 79–90.

Jacoby, F. (1923–58), *Die Fragmente der griechiscshen Historiker*. Berlin: Weidmann, etc.)

—— (1949), *Atthis*. Oxford: Clarendon Press.

Jalabert, L., Mouterde, P., and Rey-Coquais, J.-P. (eds) (1929), *Inscriptions grecques et latines de la Syrie*. Paris: Geuthner.

James, T. G. H. (1979), *An Introduction to Ancient Egypt*. London: British Museum Publications.

Jameson, M. H., Runnels, C. N., and van Andel, T. H. (1994), *A Greek Countryside: The Southern Argolid from Prehistory to the Present Day*. Stanford, CA: Stanford UP.

Jockey, P. (1998), 'Neither school nor koine: the local workshops of Delos and their unfinished sculpture', in Palagia and Coulson (eds) (1998), 177–84.

Johnson, J. (1974), 'The Demotic Chronicle as an historical source', *Enchoria*, 4: 1–19.

Johnson, J. H. (ed.) (1992), *Life in a Multi-cultural Society: Egypt from Cambyses to Constantine and Beyond* (Studies in Ancient Oriental Civilization, 51). Chicago, IL: Oriental Institute of the Univ. of Chicago.

Johnston, A. W., and Grace, V. R. (1996), 'Amphorae and amphora stamps, Greek', *OCD*³ 76–7.

Jones, A. H. M. (1940), *The Greek City: From Alexander to Justinian*. Oxford: Clarendon.

Jones, C. P., and Habicht, C. (1989), 'A hellenistic inscription from Arsinoe in Cilicia', *Phoenix*, 43: 317–46.

Jones, F. F. (1950), 'The pottery', in Goldman (ed.) (1950), 149–296.

Jones, W.H.S. (trans.), (1923) *Hippocrates*, i (Loeb Classical Library). London: Heinemann/ Cambridge, MA: Harvard UP.

—— and Heath, T. L. (1928), 'Hellenistic science and mathematics', *CAH*¹ vii, ch. 9 (pp. 284–311).

Jonnes, L., and Ricl, M. (1997), 'A new royal inscription from Phrygia Paroreios: Eumenes II grants Tyriaion the status of a polis', *Epigraphica Anatolica*, 29: 1–30.

Jost, M. (1994), 'Sanctuaries and civic space in Arkadia', in Alcock and Osborne (eds) (1994), 217–30.

Kaerst, J. (1909), *Geschichte des hellenistischen Zeitalters*, ii. 1: *Das Wesen des Hellenismus*. Leipzig and Berlin: Teubner.

Kallet-Marx, R. (1995), *Hegemony to Empire: the Development of the Roman Imperium in the East from 148 to 62 BC* (Hellenistic Culture and Society, 15). Berkeley, Los Angeles, London: Univ. of California Press.

Karafotias, A. (1998), 'Crete in search of a new protector: Nabis of Sparta and his relations with the island', in Cavanagh and Curtis (eds) (1998), 105–11.

Kasher, A. (1992), 'The civic status of Jews in Ptolemaic Egypt', in Bilde *et al.* (eds) (1992), 100–21.

Kaul, F. (1993), 'The Gundestrup cauldron and the periphery of the hellenistic world', in Bilde *et al.* (eds) (1993), 39–52.

Kebric, R. B. (1977), *In the Shadow of Macedon: Duris of Samos* (Historia Einzelschriften, 29). Wiesbaden: Steiner.

Keen, A. G. (1996), 'Were the Boiotian poleis autonomoi?', *CPC Papers 3*, 113–25.

Kees, H. (1925), 'Λευκὸς λιμήν', *RE* xii. 2290.

—— (1935), 'Myos Hormos', *RE* xvi. 1081–3.

Keller, D. R. (1985), 'Archaeological survey in southern Euboea, Greece', Ph.D. thesis, Indiana Univ.

—— and Rupp, D. W. (eds) (1983), *Archaeological Survey in the Mediterranean Area* (BAR International Series, 155). Oxford: British Archaeological Reports.

Keller-Cohen, D. (ed.) (1994), *Literacy: Interdisciplinary Conversations* (Written Language Series). Cresskill, NJ: Hampton Press.

Kidd, I. G. (1988), *Posidonius*, ii: *The Commentary*, 1: *Testimonia and Fragments 1–149*; 2: *Fragments 150–293* (Cambridge Classical Texts and Commentaries, 14 *a*). Cambridge, New York, etc.: CUP.

Kienast, H. J. (1993), 'Untersuchungen am Turm der Winde', *Archäologischer Anzeiger*, 271–5.

—— (1997), 'The Tower of the Winds in Athens: hellenistic or Roman?', in Hoff and Rotroff (eds) (1997), 53–65.

Kirk, G. S., Raven, J. E., [and [2]Schofield, M.] ([1]1957, [2]1983), *The Presocratic Philosophers: A Critical History with a Selection of Texts*. Cambridge: CUP.

Kiss, Z. (1988), *Alexandrie*, iv: *Sculptures des fouilles polonaises à Kôm el-Dikka 1960–1982*. Warsaw: Centre d'Archéologie Méditerranéenne de l'Académie Polonaise des Sciences/Centre Polonais d'Archéologie Méditerranéenne de l'Université de Varsovie au Caïre/PWN: Państwowe Wydawnictwo Naukowe (Éditions Scientifiques de Pologne).

Klaffenbach, G. (1954), *Die Astynomeninschrift von Pergamon* (Abhandlungen der Deutschen Akademie der Wissenschaften zu Berlin, Klasse für Sprachen, Literatur und Kunst, Jahrgang 1953 Nr. 6). Berlin: Akademie-Verlag.

Knoepfler, D. (1991), 'L. Mummius Achaicus et les cités du golfe euboïque: à propos d'une nouvelle inscription d'Erétrie', *Museum Helveticum*, 48: 252–80.

Kock, T. (1880–8), *Comicorum Atticorum Fragmenta*. Leipzig: Teubner.

Koenen, L. (1968), 'Die Prophezeiungen des "Töpfers"', *ZPE* 2: 178–209.

—— (1977), *Eine agonistische Inschrift aus Ägypten und frühptolemaische Königsfeste* (Beiträge zur klassischen Philologie, 56). Meisenheim am Glan: Hain.

—— (1993), 'The Ptolemaic king as a religious figure', in Bulloch *et al.* (eds) (1993), 25–115.

Konstan, D. (1997), 'Conventional values of the hellenistic Greeks: the evidence from astrology', in Bilde *et al.* (eds) (1997), 159–76.

Korhonen, T. (1997), 'Self-concept and public image of philosophers and philosophical schools at the beginning of the hellenistic age', in Frösén (ed.) (1997), 33–101.

Košelenko, G., Bader, A., and Gaibov, W. (1996), 'Die Margiana in hellenistischer Zeit', in Funck (ed.) (1996a), 121–45.

Kralli, I. (1997–8), 'Athens and her leading citizens in the early hellenistic period (338 BC–261 BC): the evidence of the decrees awarding the highest honours', in *Αρχαιογνωσία*, 10: 132–61.

Kramer, B. (1991), *Das Vertragsregister von Theogonis (P. Vindob. G 40618)* (Corpus Papyrorum Raineri, xviii: Griechische Texte, 13). Vienna: Hollinek/Österreichische Nationalbibliothek.

—— (1997), 'Der κτίστης Boethos und die Einrichtung einer neuen Stadt: Teil I (P.UB Trier S 135-3 und S 135-1)', *Archiv für Papyrusforschung*, 43: 315–39. [For part II see Heinen.]

Kreissig, H. (1978), *Wirtschaft und Gesellschaft im Seleukidenreich: die Eigentums- und die Abhängigkeitsverhältnisse* (Akademie der Wissenschaften der DDR, Zentralinstitut für Alte Geschichte und Archäologie, Schriften zur Geschichte und Kultur der Antike, 16; Berlin: Akademie-Verlag).

Kroll, J. H. (1997), 'Coinage as an index of romanization', in Hoff and Rotroff (eds) (1997), 135–50.

Kühn, K. G. (ed.) (1821), *Claudii Galeni opera omnia*. Leipzig: Knobloch.

Kuhn, T. S. ([1]1962, [2]1970), *The Structure of Scientific Revolutions*. Chicago: Univ. of Chicago Press (repr. (Masterpieces of Science series), New York: New American Library, 1986).

Kuhrt, A. (1987), 'Berossus' *Babyloniaka* and Seleucid rule in Babylonia', in Kuhrt and Sherwin-White (1987), ch. 2 (pp. 32–56).

—— (1989), review of Bengtson 1988, in *CR* 103 [n.s. 39]: 286–8.

—— (1995), *The Ancient Near East c.3000–330 BC*, i–ii (Routledge History of the Ancient World). London and New York: Routledge.

—— (1996), 'The Seleucid kings and Babylonia: new perspectives on the Seleucid realm in the east', in Bilde *et al.* (eds) (1996a), 41–54.

—— and Sherwin-White, S. (eds) (1987), *Hellenism in the East: The Interaction of Greek and Non-Greek Civilizations from Syria to Central Asia after Alexander*. London: Duckworth; also published as *Hellenistic Culture and Society*, 2; Berkeley, Los Angeles, London: Univ. of California Press.

—— and —— (1991), 'Aspects of Seleucid royal ideology: the cylinder of Antiochus I from Borsippa', *JHS* 111: 71–86.

Kyparissis, N., and Peek, W. (1941), 'Attische Urkunden', *Ath. Mitt.* 66: 218–39.

La'da, C. A. (1994), 'Ethnicity, occupation and tax-status in Ptolemaic Egypt', *Acta Demotica*, 183–9.

Lafond, Y. (1996), 'Pausanias et l'histoire du Péloponnèse depuis la conquête romaine', in Reverdin and Grange (eds) (1996), ch. 5 (pp. 167–98; 'Discussion', 199–205).

Laks, A., and Most, G. W. (1997a), 'A provisional translation of the Derveni papyrus', in Laks and Most (eds) (1997b), 9–22.

—— and —— (eds) (1997b), *Studies on the Derveni Papyrus*. Oxford: Clarendon.

Lambert, S. D. ([1]1993, [2]1998), *The Phratries of Athens*. Ann Arbor, MI: Univ. of Michigan Press.

—— (1997), *Rationes Centesimarum: Sales of Public Land in Lykourgan Athens* (Ἀρχαία Ἑλλάς: Monographs on Ancient Greek History and Archaeology, 3). Amsterdam: Gieben.

Lamberton, P. (1997), 'Plutarch and the romanizations of Athens', in Hoff and Rotroff (eds) (1997), 151–60.

Landels, J. G. (1978), *Engineering in the Ancient World*. Berkeley and Los Angeles: Univ. of California Press.

Landucci Gattinoni, F. (1992), *Lisimaco di Tracia: un sovrano nella prospettiva del primo ellenismo* (Edizioni universitarie Jaca, storia, 90). Milan: Jaca.

Lane Fox, R. (1986), 'Hellenistic culture and literature', in Boardman *et al.* (eds) (1986), ch. 14 (pp. 338–64); repr. in Boardman *et al.* (eds) (1988a), ch. 14 (pp. 332–58).

Lane Fox, R. J. (1997), 'Text and image: Alexander the Great, coins and elephants', *BICS* 41: 87–108.

Lanzillotta, E. (1987), *Paro dall'età arcaica all'età ellenistica* (Università degli Studi di Macerata, Pubblicazioni della Facoltà di Lettere e Filosofia, 40). Rome: Bretschneider.

Laqueur, R. (1928), 'Manethon (1)', *RE* xiv. 1, 1060–101.

Laronde, A. (1987), *Cyrène et la Libye hellénistique: Libykai historiai de l'époque républicaine au principat d'Auguste* (Études d'antiquités africaines). Paris: Éditions du Centre de la Recherche Scientifique.

Larsen, J. A. O. (1955), *Representative Government in Greek and Roman History* (Sather Classical Lectures, 28). Berkeley and Los Angeles: Univ. of California Press.

—— (1968), *Greek Federal States: Their Institutions and History*. Oxford: Clarendon.

Launey, M. (1949–50), *Recherches sur les armées hellénistiques*, i–ii (Bibliothèque des Écoles Françaises d'Athènes et de Rome, 169–70). Paris: Boccard (repr. with revisions, 1987).

Lauter, H. (1986), *Die Architektur des Hellenismus*. Darmstadt: Wissenschaftliche Buchgesellschaft.

—— (1987), 'Les éléments de la regia hellénistique', in Lévy (ed.) (1987), 345–55.

—— (1993), *Attische Landgemeinden in klassischer Zeit* (Attische Forschungen, 4/Marburger Winckelmannsprogramm 1991). Marburg/Lahn: Philipps-Universität.

Lavigne, E. (1945), *De epistates van het dorp in ptolemaeisch Egypte* (Studia hellenistica, 3). Louvain: [W. Peremans].

Lawrence, A. W., rev. R. A. Tomlinson (1996), *Greek Archtiecture*[6] (Pelican History of Art). London: Penguin.

Le Bohec, S. (1987), 'L'entourage royal à la cour des Antigonides', in Lévy (ed.) (1987), 315–26.

Lefebvre, G. (1923–4), *Le Tombeau de Petosiris*, i–iii. Cairo: Imprimerie de l'Institut Français d'Archéologie Orientale.

Lefkowitz, M. R., and Fant, M. B. (1982), *Women's Life in Greece and Rome*. London: Duckworth.

Lehnus, L. (1989), *Bibliografia callimachea 1489–1988* (Pubblicazioni dell'Istituto di Filologia Classica et Medievale dell'Università di Genova). Genoa: Università di Genova, Facoltà di Lettere.

Leiwo, M. (1997), 'Religion, or other reasons? Private associations in Athens', in Frösén (ed.), 103–17.

Leriche, P. (1986), *Fouilles d'Aï Khanoum*, v: *Les Remparts et les monuments associés* (Mémoires de la Délégation Archéologique Française en Afghanistan, 29; Paris: de Boccard).

Le Rider, G. (1989), 'La politique monétaire du royaume de Pergame après 188', *Journal des savants*, 163–90.

—— (1991), 'Éphèse et Arados au IIe siècle avant notre ère', *Quaderni ticinesi*, 20: 193–212.

Lesky, A. (1966), *A History of Greek Literature*. Trans., by J. Willis and C. de Heer, of *Geschichte der griechischen Literatur* (Bern: Franke, [1]1957–8, [2]1963). London: Methuen.

Levi, P. (1993), 'People in a landscape: Theokritos', in Green (ed.) (1993), 111–27.

Lévy, E. (ed.) (1987), *Le Système palatial en Orient, en Grèce et à Rome: actes du colloque de Strasbourg (19–22 juin 1985)* (Université des Sciences Humaines de Strasbourg, Travaux du Centre de Recherche sur le Proche-Orient et la Grèce Antiques, 9). Strasbourg: Brill.

Lewis, D. M. (1957), 'The first Greek Jew', *Journal of Semitic Studies*, 2: 264–6; repr. in Lewis (1997), ch. 37 (pp. 380–2).

—— (1984), 'Democratic institutions and their diffusion', Πρακτικὰ τοῦ Η΄ Διεθνοῦς Συνεδρίου Ἑλληνικῆς καὶ Λατινικῆς Ἐπιγραφικῆς (Ἀθῆνα, 3–9 Ὀκτωβρίου 1982) [Proceedings of the 8th International Congress of Greek and Latin Epigraphy (Athens, 3–9 Oct. 1982)], i. 55–61; repr. in Lewis (1997), ch. 8 (pp. 51–9). Athens: Ypourgeio Politismou kai Epistimon.

——, ed. Rhodes, P. J. (1997), *Selected Papers in Greek and Near Eastern History*. Cambridge: CUP.

——, Boardman, J., Hornblower, S., and Ostwald, M. (eds) (1994), *The Cambridge Ancient History*[2], vi: *The Fourth Century BC*. Cambridge: CUP.

Lewis, N. (1986), *Greeks in Ptolemaic Egypt: Case Studies in the Social History of the Hellenistic World*. Oxford: Clarendon.

Lichtheim, M. (1980), *Ancient Egyptian Literature; A Book of Readings*, iii: *The Late Period*. Berkeley, Los Angeles, London: Univ. of California Press.

Liddell, H. G., and Scott, R. (1940), *Greek–English Lexicon*[9]. Rev. by H. S. Jones with R. McKenzie. Oxford: Clarendon Press.

Ligouri, E. (1996–7), 'The Odos Rigillis site', *Archaeological Reports*, 43: 8–10.

Ling, R. (1984a), 'Hellenistic civilization', in Ling (ed.) (1984b), ch. 8 (pp. 91–206).

—— (ed.) (1984b), *The Cambridge Ancient History* [2nd edn]: *Plates to Volume vii Part 1. The Hellenistic World to the Coming of the Romans*. Cambridge: CUP.

Lloyd, A. B. (1994), 'Egypt, 404–332 BC', *CAH*[2] vi, ch. 8 *e* (pp. 337–60).

—— (1996a), 'Egypt: pre-Ptolemaic', *OCD*[3] 510–11.

—— (1996b) 'Saites', *OCA*[3] 1346–7.

Lloyd, G. E. R. (1973), *Greek Science after Aristotle* (Ancient Culture and Society). London: Chatto & Windus (repr., New York: Norton, n.d.).

—— (ed.) (1978a), *Hippocratic Writings* (Penguin Classics). [Expanded reissue of Chadwick and Mann 1950.] Harmondsworth: Penguin.

—— (1978b), 'Introduction', in Lloyd (ed.) (1978a), 9–60.

—— (1979), *Magic, Reason and Experience: Studies in the Origin and Development of Greek Science*. Cambridge, etc.: CUP.

—— (1983), *Science, Folklore and Ideology: Studies in the Life Sciences in Ancient Greece*. Cambridge: CUP.

—— (1984), 'Hellenistic science', *CAH*[2] vii. 1, ch. 9 *a* (pp. 321–52).

—— (1987), *The Revolutions of Wisdom: Studies in the Claims and Practice of Ancient Greek Science* (Sather Classical Lectures, 52). Berkeley, Los Angeles, and London: Univ. of California Press.

—— (1994), 'Medicine', *CAH*[2] vi, ch. 12 *b* (pp. 634–46).

—— (1996), *Adversaries and Authorities: Investigations into Ancient Greek and Chinese Science* (Ideas in Context). Cambridge: CUP.

Lloyd, J. A., Owens, E. J., and Roy, J. (1985), 'The Megalopolis survey in Arcadia: problems of strategy and tactics', in Macready and Thompson (eds), 217–24.

Lloyd-Jones, H., and Parsons, P. (1983), *Supplementum hellenisticum* (Texte und Kommentare, 11). Berlin and New York: de Gruyter.

Lönnqvist, K. (1997), 'Studies on the hellenistic coinage of Athens: the impact of Macedonia on the Athenian money market in the 3rd century BC', in Frösén (ed.) (1997), 119–45.

Lohmann, H. (1983), 'Atene (Ἀτήνη), eine attische Landgemeinde klassischer Zeit', *Hellenika: Jahrbuch für die Freunde Griechenlands* (Vereinigung der Deutsch-griechischen Gesellschaften e.V.), 98–117.

—— (1985), 'Landleben im klassischen Attika: Ergebnisse und Probleme einer archäologischen Landesaufnahme des Demos Atene', *Ruhr-Universität Bochum, Jahrbuch 1985* (Bochum: Gesellschaft der Freunde der Ruhr-Universität Bochum e. V.), 71–96.

—— (1992), 'Agriculture and country life in classical Attica', in B. Wells (ed.) (1992), 29–57.

—— (1993), *Atene: Forschungen zu Siedlungs- und Wirtschaftsstruktur des klassischen Attika*, i–ii (paginated consecutively). Cologne, etc.: Böhlau.

Long, A. (1986), 'Pleasure and social utility: the virtues of being Epicurean', in Reverdin and Grange (eds) (1986), 283–316 ('Discussion', 317–24).

Long, A. A. (1974), *Hellenistic Philosophy: Stoics, Epicureans, Sceptics* (Classical Life and Letters). London: Duckworth.

—— (1985a), 'Aristotle', *CHCL* ch. 17 (pp. 527–40).

—— (1985b), 'Post-Aristotelian philosophy', *CHCL* ch. 19 (pp. 622–41).

—— (1993), 'Hellenistic ethics and philosophical power', in Green (ed.) (1993), 138–56.

—— and Sedley, D. N. (1987), *The Hellenistic Philosophers*, i: *Translations of the Principal Sources with Philosophical Commentary*; ii: *Greek and Latin Texts with Notes and Bibliography*. Cambridge: CUP.

Longrigg, J. (1993), *Greek Rational Medicine: Philosophy and Medicine from Alcmaeon to the Alexandrians*. London and New York: Routledge.

López Cruces, J. L. (1995), *Les Méliambes de Cercidas de Mégalopolis: politique et tradition littéraire* (Classical and Byzantine Monographs, 32). Amsterdam: Hakkert.

Luce, T. J. (ed.) (1982), *Ancient Writers: Greece and Rome*, i: *Homer to Caesar*; ii: *Lucretius to Ammianus Marcellinus*. New York: Scribner.

Lund, H. S. (1992), *Lysimachus: A Study in Early Hellenistic Kingship*. London and New York: Routledge.

McDonald, W. A., and Rapp, G. R., jun. (eds) (1972), *The Minnesota Messenia Expedition: Reconstructing a Bronze Age Regional Environment*. Minneapolis: Univ. of Minnesota Press.

McGing, B. C. (1986), *The Foreign Policy of Mithridates VI Eupator King of Pontus* (Mnemosyne, supp. 89). Leiden: Brill.

—— (1997), 'Revolt Egyptian style: internal opposition to Ptolemaic rule', *Archiv für Papyrusforschung*, 43: 273–314.

McKechnie, P. (1989), *Outsiders in the Greek Cities in the Fourth Century BC*. London and New York: Routledge.

McNicoll, A., rev. Milner, N. P. (1997), *Hellenistic Fortifications from the Aegean to the Euphrates* (Oxbow Monographs on Classical Archaeology). Oxford: Oxbow.

Macready, S., and Thompson, F. H. (eds) (1985), *Archaeological Field Survey in Britain and Abroad* (Society of Antiquaries Occasional Papers, 6). London: Society of Antiquaries.

—— and —— (eds) (1987), *Roman Architecture in the Greek World* (Society of Antiquaries Occasional Papers, 10). London: Society of Antiquaries.

McShane, R. B. (1964), *The Foreign Policy of the Attalids of Pergamum* (Illinois Studies in the Social Sciences, 53). Urbana, IL: Univ. of Illinois Press.

Macurdy, G. (1932), *Hellenistic Queens: A Study of Woman-power in Macedonia, Seleucid Syria and Ptolemaic Egypt* (Johns Hopkins Univ. Studies in Archaeology, 14). Baltimore, MD: Johns Hopkins UP.

Maehler, H., and Strocka, V. M. (eds) (1978), *Das ptolemäische Ägypten (Akten des internationalen Symposions, 27–29 Sept. 1976 in Berlin)*. Mainz am Rhein: DAI/von Zabern.

Maier, F. G. (1994), 'Cyprus and Phoenicia', *CAH²* vi, ch. 8 *d* (pp. 297–336).

Malkin, I., and Raaflaub, K. (eds) (2000), *Ancient Perceptions of Greek Ethnicity*. Cambridge, MA, and London: Harvard UP.

Marchese, R. T. (1986), *The Lower Maeander Flood Plain: A Regional Settlement Study*, i–ii (BAR International Series, 292). Oxford: BAR.

Marcone, A. (1987), 'La Sicilia fra ellenismo e romanizzazione: III–I secolo a.C.', in Virgilio (ed.) (1987c), 163–79.

Marsden, E. W. (1969), *Greek and Roman Artillery: Historical Development*. Oxford: Clarendon.

—— (1971), *Greek and Roman Artillery: Technical Treatises*. Oxford: Clarendon.

Marszal, J. R. (1998), 'Tradition and innovation in early Pergamene sculpture', in Palagia and Coulson (eds) (1998), 117–27.

Martin, D. B. (1997), 'Hellenistic superstition: the problems of defining a vice', in Bilde *et al.* (eds) (1997), 110–27.

Martin, L. H. (1987), *Hellenistic Religions*. New York and Oxford: OUP.

Martin, R. (^{1}1956, ^{2}1974), *L'Urbanisme dans la Grèce antique*. Paris: Picard.

Marzolff, P. (1976), 'Zur Stadtanlage des Demetrias', in Milojčić and Theocharis, 5–16.

—— (1987), 'Intervention sur les rapports de S. Le Bohec et H. Lauter (21/06/1995)', in Lévy (ed.) (1987), 357–8.

Masson, O. (1996), 'Macedonian language', *OCD*^{3} 905–6.

Mastrocinque, A. (1979), 'Demetrios tragodoumenos: propaganda e letteratura al tempo di Demetrio Poliorcete', *Athenaeum*, 57: 260–76.

Mattingly, D. J. (1997), 'Beyond belief? Drawing a line beneath the consumer city', in Parkins (ed.), 210–18.

Mattingly, H. (1997), 'Athens between Rome and the kings: 229/8 to 129 BC', in Cartledge *et al.* (eds) (1997), 120–44.

Mattusch, C. C. (1998), 'Rhodian sculpture: a school, a style, or many workshops?', in Palagia and Coulson (eds) (1998), 149–56.

Mee, C., and Forbes, H. (eds) (1997), *A Rough and Rocky Place: The Landscape and Settlement History of the Methana Peninsula, Greece (Results of the Methana Survey Project Sponsored by the British School at Athens and the University of Liverpool)*. Liverpool: Liverpool UP.

Mee, C. B., and Cavanagh, W. G. (1998), 'Diversity in a Greek landscape: the Laconia Survey and Rural Sites Project', in Cavanagh and Walker (eds) (1998), 141–8.

Mehl, A. (1986), *Seleukos Nikator und sein Reich*, i: *Seleukos' Leben und die Entwicklung seiner Machtposition* (Studia hellenistica, 28). Louvain: Studia Hellenistica.

Meiggs, R. (1982), *Trees and Timber in the Ancient Mediterranean World*. Oxford: Clarendon.

—— and Lewis, D. M. (1969), *A Selection of Greek Historical Inscriptions to the End of the Fifth Century BC*. Oxford: Clarendon.

Meister, K. (1984), 'Agathocles', *CAH*^{2} vii. 1, ch. 10 (pp. 384–411).

Melaerts, H. (ed.) (1998), *Le Culte du souverain dans l'Égypte ptolémaïque au IIIe siècle avant notre ère (actes du colloque international 10 mai 1995)* (Studia hellenistica, 34). Louvain: Studia hellenistica/Peeters.

Meyer, E. (1921), *Ursprung und Anfänge des Christentums*, ii. Stuttgart and Berlin: Cotta.

Migeotte, L. (1989–90), 'Distributions de grain à Samos à la période hellénistique: le "pain gratuit" pour tous?', in Geerard *et al.* (eds), 297–308.

Mikalson, J. D. (1975), *The Sacred and Civil Calendar of the Athenian Year*. Princeton, NJ: Princeton UP.

—— (1998), *Religion in Hellenistic Athens* (Hellenistic Culture and Society, 29). Berkeley and London: Univ. of California Press.

Millar, F. (1978), 'The background to the Maccabean revolution: reflections on Martin Hengel's "Judaism and Hellenism" ', *Journal of Jewish Studies*, 29: 1–21.

—— (1983), 'Epigraphy', in M. Crawford (ed.) (1983), ch. 2 (pp. 80–136).

—— (1987), 'The problem of hellenistic Syria', in Kuhrt and Sherwin-White 1987), ch. 5 (pp. 110–33).

—— (1993), *The Roman Near East: 31 BC–AD 337*. Cambridge, MA, and London: Harvard UP.

—— (1997), 'Hellenistic history in a near eastern perspective: the book of Daniel', in Cartledge *et al.* (eds) (1997), 89–104.

—— (1998), 'Dura-Europos under Parthian rule', in Wiesehöfer (ed.) (1998), 473–92.

Miller, S. G. (1995), 'Architecture as evidence for the identity of the early polis', *CPC Acts 2*, 201–44.

Milojčić, V., and Theocharis, D., (1976), *Demetrias: die deutschen archäologischen Forschungen in Thessalien*, i (Beiträge zur ur- und frühgeschichtlichen Archäologie des Mittelmeer-kulturraumes, 12). Bonn: Habelt.

Mitchell, S. (1993), *Anatolia: Land, Men, and Gods in Asia Minor*, i: *The Celts in Anatolia and the Impact of Roman Rule*. Oxford: Clarendon.

Mitchison, N. (1931), *The Corn King and the Spring Queen*. London: Cape (repr. with new introduction by author; Edinburgh: Canongate Classics, 1990).

Molho, A., Raaflaub, K., and Emlen, J. (eds) (1991), *City States in Classical Antiquity and Medieval Italy*. Stuttgart: Steiner.

Momigliano, A. (1954), 'M. I. Rostovtzeff', *Cambridge Journal*, 7: 334–46; repr. in *Primo contributo*, 341–54; Momigliano 1966b, ch. 5 (pp. 91–104); Momigliano 1994, ch. 3 (pp. 32–43).

—— (1955), *Contributo alla storia degli studi classici* (Storia e letteratura, 47). Rome: Edizioni di storia e di letteratura.

—— (1959), 'Atene nel III secolo a. C. e la scoperta di Roma nelle storie di Timeo di Tauromenio', *Rivista storica italiana*, 71: 529–56; repr. in *Terzo contributo*, i. 23–53.

—— (1960), 'Linee per una valutazione di Fabio Pictore', *Rendiconti Accademia dei Lincei, classe di scienze morali, storiche e filologiche*, series 8, vol. 15.7–12, pp. 310–20; repr. in *Terzo contributo*, i. 55–68.

—— (1966a), 'Giulio Beloch', *Dizionario biografico degli Italiani*, 8 (1966), 32–45; repr. in *Terzo contributo*, i. 239–65.

—— (1966b), *Studies in Historiography*. London: Weidenfeld & Nicolson.

—— (1966c), *Terzo contributo alla storia degli studi classici e del mondo antico*, i–ii [consecutively paginated] (Storia e letteratura, 108–9). Rome: Edizioni di storia e di letteratura.

—— (1970), 'J. G. Droysen between Greeks and Jews', *History and Theory*, 9: 139–53; repr. in *Quinto contributo*, i. 109–26; Momigliano 1977*a*, ch. 18 (pp. 307–23); Momigliano 1994, ch. 10 (pp. 147–61).

—— (1975a), *Alien Wisdom: The Limits of Hellenization*. Cambridge, etc.: CUP.

—— (1975b), *Quinto contributo alla storia degli studi classici e del mondo antico* (Storia e letteratura, 135), i–ii. Rome: Edizioni di storia e di letteratura.

—— (1977a), *Essays in Ancient and Modern Historiography*. Oxford: Blackwell.

—— (1977b), 'Athens in the third century BC and the discovery of Rome in the histories of Timaeus of Tauromenium', in Momigliano (1977a), ch. 4 (pp. 37–66).

—— (1977c), 'The fault of the Greeks', in Momigliano (1977a), ch. 2 (pp. 9–23).

—— (1981), 'Greek culture and the Jews', in Finley (ed.) (1981), ch. 11 (pp. 325–46).

—— (1990a), *The Classical Foundations of Modern Historiography* (Sather Classical Lectures, 54). Berkeley, Los Angeles, Oxford: California UP.

—— (1990b), 'Fabius Pictor and the origins of national history', in Momigliano (1990a), ch. 4 (pp. 80–108).

Momigliano, A. D. (1994a), *Studies on Modern Scholarship*, ed. G. W. Bowersock and T. J. Cornell. Berkeley, Los Angeles, and London: Univ. of California Press.

—— trans. T. J. Cornell (1994b), 'Julius Beloch', in Momigliano (1994a), ch. 8 (pp. 97–120).

Moody, J., Nixon, L., Price, S., and Rackham, O. (1998), 'Surveying poleis and larger sites in Sphakia', in Cavanagh and Curtis (eds) (1998), 87–95.

Mooren, L. (1977), *La Hiérarchie de cour ptolémaïque: contribution à l'étude des institutions et des classes dirigeantes à l'époque hellénistique* (Studia hellenistica, 23). Louvain: Studia Hellenistica.

—— and Swinnen, W. (1975), *Prosopographia Ptolemaica*, viii: *Addenda et corrigenda aux volumes i (1950) et ii (1952)* (Studia hellenistica, 21). Louvain: Studia Hellenistica.

Moretti, L. (1953), *Iscrizione agonistiche greche* (Studi pubblicati dall'Instituto Italiano per la Storia Antica, 12). Rome: Signorelli.

—— (1967–76), *Iscrizione storiche ellenistiche*, i–ii (Biblioteca di studi superiori: storia antica ed epigrafia, 53; 62). Florence: Nuova Italia.

—— (1977a), 'Finanze della polis', in Moretti *et al.* (eds) (1977), ch. 5.3 (pp. 337–53).

—— (1977b), 'Il problema del grano e del denaro', in Moretti *et al.* (eds) (1977), ch. 5.4 (pp. 354–74).

—— (1977c), 'La scuola, il ginnasio, l'efebia', in Moretti *et al.* (eds) (1977), ch. 6.4 (pp. 469–90).

—— (1977d), 'L'economia ellenistica', in Moretti *et al.* (eds) (1977), ch. 5.1 (pp. 319–25).

—— (1977e), 'Lo sport', in Moretti *et al.* (eds) (1977), ch. 6.5 (pp. 491–9).

——, Bogaert, R., Parise, F. N., Bianchini, M., and Stewart, Z. (eds) (1977), *La società ellenistica*, iv. 2: *Economia, diritto, religione* (Storia e civiltà dei Greci, 8). Milan: Bompiani.

Morgan, M. G. (1993), 'Response' [to Gruen], in Green (ed.) (1993), 264–9.

Morgan, M. H. (trans. 1914), *Vitruvius: The Ten Books on Architecture*. Cambridge, MA: Harvard UP/London: Milford/Oxford: OUP (repr. New York: Dover Paperbacks, 1960.)

Mørkholm, O. (1984), 'The monetary system in the Seleucid empire after 187 BC', in Heckel and Sullivan (eds) (1984), 93–113.

—— (1989), 'Antiochus IV', in W. D. Davies and Finkelstein (eds), 278–91.

——, ed. P. Grierson, U. Westermark (1991), *Early Hellenistic Coinage from the Accession of Alexander to the Peace of Apamea (226–188 BC)*. Cambridge: CUP.

Morris, I. (ed.) (1994), *Classical Greece: Ancient Histories and Modern Archaeologies* (New Directions in Archaeology). Cambridge: CUP.

Mossé, C. ([1]1969, [2]1989), *La Tyrannie dans la Grèce antique* ([1]Collection Hier, [2]Collection Dito). Paris: Presses Universitaires de France.

—— (1973), *Athens in Decline 404–86 BC* (trans. J. Stewart). London and Boston: Routledge & Kegan Paul.

—— (1991), 'Women in the Spartan revolutions of the third century BC' (trans. S. B. Pomeroy), in Pomeroy (ed.) (1991), 138–53.

Moxnes, H. (1997), 'Conventional values in the hellenistic world: masculinity', in Bilde *et al.* (eds) (1997), 263–84.

Muccioli, F. (1994), 'Considerazioni generali sull'epiteto *Φιλάδελφος* nelle dinastie ellenistiche e sulla sua applicazione nelle titolatura degli ultimi Seleucidi', *Historia*, 43: 402–22.

Müller, C. (1861), *Geographi Graeci minores*, i–ii. Paris: Firmin-Didot.

Müller, H. (1991), 'Königin Stratonike, Tochter des Königs Ariarathes', *Chiron*, 21: 393–424.

Munn, M. H., and Zimmermann Munn, M. L. (1989), 'Studies on the Attic–Boiotian frontier: the Stanford Skoúrta plain project, 1985', in Fossey (ed.) (1989), 73–127.

Murray, O. (1970), 'Hecataeus of Abdera and pharaonic kingship', *JEA* 56: 141–71.

—— (1972), 'Herodotus and hellenistic culture', *CQ* 66 [n.s. 22], 200–13.

—— (1987), 'The Letter of Aristeas', in Virgilio (ed.) (1987c), 15–29.

—— (ed.) (1990), *Sympotica: A Symposium on the Symposion*. Oxford: Clarendon.

—— (1996a), 'Hellenistic royal symposia', in Bilde *et al.* (eds), 15–27.

—— (1996b), 'Kingship', *OCD*[3] 807.

—— and Price, S. (eds) (1990), *The Greek City: From Homer to Alexander*. Oxford: Clarendon.

Musti, D. (1984), 'Syria and the east', *CAH*[2] vii. 1, ch. 6 (pp. 175–220).

Nachtergael, G. (1977), *Les Galates en Grèce et les Sôtéria de Delphes: recherches d'histoire et d'épigraphie hellénistiques* (Mémoires de la Classe des Lettres, collection in 8°, 2e ser., 63.1). Brussels: Palais des Académies.

Narain, A. K. (1957), *The Indo-Greeks*. Oxford: Clarendon (repr. 1967; repr. Delhi: OUP, 1980).

—— (1989), 'The Greeks of Bactria and India', *CAH*[2] viii, ch. 11 (pp. 388–421).

Neugebauer, O. (1949), 'The early history of the astrolabe', *Isis*, 40: 240–56.

—— ([1]1952, [2]1957), *The Exact Sciences in Antiquity*. [1]Princeton, NJ: Princeton UP; [2]Providence, RI: Brown UP; repr. New York: Harper 1962; New York: Dover, 1969).

—— (1975), *A History of Ancient Mathematical Astronomy*, i–iii (Studies in the History of Mathematics and Physical Sciences, 1). Berlin, Heidelberg, New York: Springer.

Nicolet, C. (1988), *L'Inventaire du monde: géographie et politique aux origines de l'empire romain*. Paris: Fayard.

—— (ed.) (1990), *Du pouvoir dans l'antiquité: mots et réalités* (Hautes études du monde gréco-romain, 16; Cahiers du Centre Gustave Glotz, 5.1). Geneva: Droz.

—— (1991), *Space, Geography, and Politics in the Early Roman Empire* (Jerome Lectures, 19). (Trans. of Nicolet 1988.) Ann Arbor, MI: Univ. of Michigan Press.

Nielsen, I. (1993), 'From periphery to centre: Italic palaces', in Bilde *et al.* (eds) (1993), 210–29.

—— (1994), *Hellenistic Palaces: Tradition and Renewal* (Studies in Hellenistic Civilization, 5). Aarhus: Aarhus UP.

—— (1996), 'Oriental models for hellenistic palaces?', in Hoepfner and Brands (eds) (1996), 209–12.

Nielsen, T. H. (ed.) (1997), *Yet More Studies in the Ancient Greek Polis* (Papers from the Copenhagen Polis Centre, 4/Historia Einzelschriften, 117). Wiesbaden: Steiner.

—— and Roy, J. (eds) (1999), *Defining Ancient Arkadia (Symposium, April 1–4, 1998)* (Royal Danish Academy of Sciences and Letters, Historisk-filosofiske Meddelelser, 78; Acts of the Copenhagen Polis Centre, 6). Copenhagen: Munksgaard.

Nigdelis, P. M. (1990), *Πολίτευμα και κοινωνία των πόλεων των Κυκλάδων κατά την ελληνιστική και αυτοκρατορική εποχή.* Thessaloniki: Aristoteleio Panepistimio.

Nikam, N. A., and McKeon, R. (1959), *The Edicts of Aśoka*. Chicago: Univ. of Chicago Press.

North, J. D. (1994), *The Fontana History of Astronomy and Cosmology* (Fontana History of Science). London: HarperCollins.

Nussbaum, M. C. (1996), 'Aristotle', *OCD*[3] 165–9.

Oates, J. F. (1963), 'The status designation: *Πέρσης, τῆς ἐπιγονῆς*', *Yale Classical Studies*, 18: 1–130.

——, Bagnall, R. S., Willis, W. H., and Worp, K. A. (1992), *Checklist of Editions of Greek and Latin Papyri*[4] (Bulletin of the American Society of Papyrologists, supp. 7). Atlanta, GA: Scholars Press.

Ober, J. (1985), *Fortress Attica: Defense of the Athenian Land Frontier 404–322 BC*. Leiden: Brill.

—— (1992), 'Towards a typology of Greek artillery towers: the first and second generations (*c.* 375–275 BC)', in van der Maele and Fossey (eds) (1992), ch. 8 (pp.147–69).

Oelsner, J. (1986), *Materialien zur babylonischen Gesellschaft und Kultur in hellenistischer Zeit* (Assyriologia, 7; Az Eötvös Loránd Tudományegyetem Okori Történeti Tanszékeinek kiadványai, 40). Budapest: Eötvös Univ.

Ogden, D. (1996), *Greek Bastardy in the Classical and Hellenistic Periods*. Oxford: Clarendon.

Olbrycht, M. J. (1996), 'Die Beziehungen der Steppennomaden Mittelasiens zu den hellenistischen Staaten (bis zum Ende des 3. Jahrhunderts vor Chr.)', in Funck (ed.) (1996a), 147–69.

Oleson, J. P. (1984), *Greek and Roman Mechanical Water-lifting Devices: The History of a Technology* (Phoenix, supp. 16). Dordrecht: Reidel.

Oliva, P. (1971), *Sparta and her Social Problems*. Prague: Academie/Amsterdam, Hakkert. [Trans. by I. Urwin-Lewitová of *Sparta a její sociální problémy*.]

Oliver, G. J. (1995), 'The Athenian state under threat: politics and food supply, 307 to 229 BC', unpublished Oxford D.Phil. thesis.

O'Meara, D. (1996), 'Diotogenes', *OCD*[3] 485.

Oppermann, M. (1996), 'Macedonia, cults', *OCD*[3] 905.

Ormerod, H. A. (1924), *Piracy in the Ancient World: An Essay in Mediterranean History*. Liverpool: UP of Liverpool/London: Hodder & Stoughton.

—— and Cary, M. (1932), 'Rome and the east', *CAH*[1] ix, ch. 8 (pp. 350–96).

Orrieux, C. (1983), *Les Papyrus de Zénon: l'horizon d'un grec en Égypte au III* siècle avant *J.C.* Paris: Macula.

—— (1985), *Zénon de Caunos, parépidèmos, et le destin grec* (Annales littéraires de l'Université de Besançon, 320). Paris: Les Belles Lettres.

Orsi, D. P. (1991), *L'alleanza acheo-macedone: studio su Polibio* (Documenti e studi, 9; Collana del Dipartimento di Scienze dell'antichità dell'Università di Bari, sezione storica). Bari: Edipuglia.

Osborne, R. G. (1985), 'Building and residence on the land in classical and hellenistic Greece: the contribution of epigraphy', *BSA* 80: 119–28.

Østergård, U. (1991), *Akropolis–Persepolis tur/retur: hellenismeforskningen mellem orientalisme, hellenisme, imperialisme og afkolonisering* (Hellenismestudier, 4). Aarhus: Aarhus Universitetsforlag.

—— (1992), 'What is national and ethnic identity?', in Bilde *et al.* (eds) (1992), 16–38.

Ostwald, M., and Lynch, J. P. (1994), 'The growth of schools and the advance of knowledge,' *CAH*[2] vi, ch. 12 *a* (pp. 592–633).

Otzen, B. (1990), 'Crisis and religious reaction: Jewish apocalypticism', in Bilde *et al.* (eds) (1990), 224–36.

Owens, E. J. (1991), *The City in the Greek and Roman World*. London and New York: Routledge.

Paap, A. H. R. E. (1948), *De Herodoti reliquiis in papyris et membranis Aegyptiis servatis* (Papyrologica Lugduno-Batava, 4). Leiden: Brill.

Pakkanen, P. (1996), *Interpreting Early Hellenistic Religion* (Papers and Monographs of the Finnish Institute at Athens, 3). Helsinki: Suomen Ateenan-instituutin säätiö/Foundation of the Finnish Institute at Athens.

Palagia, O. (1997), 'Classical encounters: Attic sculpture after Sulla', in Hoff and Rotroff (eds) (1997), 81–95.

—— and Coulsen, W. (eds) (1998), *Regional Schools in Hellenistic Sculpture (Proceedings of an International Conference held at the American School of Classical Studies at Athens, March 15–17, 1996)* (Oxbow Monographs, 90). Oxford: Oxbow.

Parise, N. F. (1977), 'Le emissioni monetarie', in Moretti *et al.* (eds) (1977), ch. 5.6 (pp. 400–19).

Parker, H. N. (1992), 'Love's body anatomized: the ancient erotic handbooks and the rhetoric of sexuality', in Richlin (ed.) (1992), 90–111.

Parker, R. (1996), *Athenian Religion: A History*. Oxford: Clarendon.

Parkins, H. (1997), 'The "consumer city" domesticated? The Roman city in élite economic strategies', in H. M. Parkins (ed.) (1997), 83–111.

—— and Smith, C. (eds) (1998), *Trade, Traders and the Ancient City*. London and New York: Routledge.

Parkins, H. M. (ed.) (1997), *Roman Urbanism: Beyond the Consumer City*. London and New York: Routledge.

—— and Shipley, G. (1998), 'Greek kings and Roman emperors', in Sparkes (ed.) (1998), 76–95.

Parlasca, K. (1982), *Syrische Grabreliefs hellenistischer und römischer Zeit: Fundgruppen und Probleme* (Trierer Winckelmannsprogramm, 3). Mainz: von Zabern.

Parsons, P. (1993), 'Identities in diversity', in Bulloch *et al.* (eds) (1993), 152–70.

Pédech, P. (1989), *Trois historiens méconnus: Théopompe, Duris, Phylarque* (Collection d'études anciennes publiée sous le patronage de l'Association Guillaume Budé, 119). Paris: Les Belles Lettres.

Peek, W. (ed.) (1955), *Griechische Versinschriften*, i: *Grabepigramme*. Berlin: Akademie-Verlag.

Pélékidis, C. (1962), *Histoire de l'éphébie attique: des origines à 31 avant Jésus-Christ* (Travaux et mémoires, 13). Athens: École Française d'Athènes/Paris: de Boccard.

Pelling, C. B. R. (1988), *Plutarch: Life of Antony* (Cambridge Greek and Latin Classics). Cambridge: CUP.

Peremans, W. (1987), 'Les Lagides, les élites indigènes et la monarchie bicéphale', in Lévy (ed.) (1987), 328–44.

—— and van 't Dack, E. (1950), *Prosopographia Ptolemaica*, i: *L'Administration civile et financière, n°s 1–1824* (Studia hellenistica, 6). Louvain: [W. Peremans].

—— and —— (1952), *Prosopographia Ptolemaica*, ii: *L'Armée de terre et la police, n°s 1825–4983* (Studia hellenistica, 8). Louvain: [W. Peremans].

—— and —— (1953), *Prosopographica* (Studia hellenistica, 9). Louvain: [W. Peremans].

—— and —— (1959), *Prosopographia Ptolemaica*, iv: *L'Agriculture et l'élevage, n°s 8041–12459* (Studia hellenistica, 12). Louvain: [W. Peremans] (repr. 1977).

—— and —— (1963), *Prosopographia Ptolemaica*, v: *Le Commerce et l'industrie, le transport sur terre et la flotte, la domesticité, n°s 12460–14478* (Studia hellenistica, 13). Louvain: [W. Peremans] (repr. 1977).

——, ——, de Meulenaire, H., and IJsewijn, J. (1956), *Prosopographia Ptolemaica*, iii: *Le Clergé, le notariat, les tribunaux, n°s 4984–8040* (Studia hellenistica, 11). Louvain: [W. Peremans].

——, ——, Mooren, L. and Swinnen, W. (1968), *Prosopographia Ptolemaica*, vi: *La Cour, les relations internationales et les possessions extérieures, la vie culturelle, n°s 14479–17250* (Studia hellenistica, 17). Louvain: [W. Peremans].

Peretti, A. (1979), *Il periplo di Scilace: studio sul primo portolano del Mediterraneo* (Biblioteca di studi antichi, 23). Pisa: Giardini.

Perpillou-Thomas, F. (1993), *Fêtes d'Égypte ptolémaïque et romaine d'après la documentation papyrologique grecque* (Studia hellenistica, 31). Louvain: Universitas Catholica Lovaniensis.

Peschlow-Bindokat, A. (1977), 'Herakleia am Latmos: vorläufiger Bericht über die Arbeiten in den Jahren 1974 und 1975', *Archäologischer Anzeiger*, 90–104.

Pestman, P. W. (1963), review of Oates (1963), in *Aegyptus*, 43: 405–7.

—— (1965), 'Harmachis et Anchmachis, deux rois indigènes du temps des Ptolémées', *Chronique d'Égypte*, 40: 157–70.

—— (1978), 'L'agoranomie: un avant-poste de l'administration grecque enlevé par les égyptiens?', in Maehler and Strocka (eds) (1978), 203–10.

—— (1981), *A Guide to the Zenon Archive*, i: *Lists and Surveys*; ii: *Indexes and Maps* (Papyrologica Lugduno-Batava, 21 A–B). [Volumes consecutively paginated.] Leiden: Brill.

—— (1995), 'Haronnophris et Chaonnophris: two indigenous pharaohs in Ptolemaic Egypt (205–186 BC), in Vleeming (ed.) (1995), 101–37.

Petracos, B. [Petrakos, V. Ch.] (1995), *The Amphiareion of Oropos* (Greece: Monuments and Museums). [Trans., with same pagination, of Petrakos 1992.] Athens: Clio.

Petrakos, V. Ch. (1968), ʽΟ Ὠρωπὸς καὶ τὸ ἱερὸν τοῦ Ἀμφιαράου (Βιβλιοθήκη τῆς ἐν Ἀθήναις Ἀρχαιολογικῆς Ἑταιρείας, 63). Athens: [Archaiologiki Etaireia].

—— (1992), Τὸ Ἀμφιάρειο τοῦ Ὠρωποῦ. Athens: Kleio.

Petropoulou, A. (1985), *Beiträge zur Wirtschafts- und Gesellschaftsgeschichte Kretas in hellenistischer Zeit* (Europäische Hochschulschriften, 3. 240). Frankfurt am Main, Bern, New York, Nancy: Peter Lang.

Petzold, K.-E. (1971), 'Rom und Illyrien: ein Beitrag zur römischen Aussenpolitik im 3. Jahrhundert', *Historia*, 20: 199–223.

Pfeiffer, R. (1949), *Callimaschus*, 2 vols. Oxford: Clarendon.

—— (1968), *History of Classical Scholarship: From the Beginnings to the End of the Hellenistic Age*. Oxford: Clarendon.

Pfister, F. (1951), *Die Reisebilder des Herakleides: Einleitung, Text, Übersetzung und Kommentar mit einer Übersicht über die Geschichte der griechischen Volkskunde* (Österreichische Akademie der Wissenschaften, phil.-hist. Klasse, 227.2). Vienna: Rohrer.

Picard, G. C. (1994), 'Carthage from the battle at Himera to Agathocles' invasion', 480–308 BC', *CAH*[2] vi, ch. 9 *a* (pp. 361–80).

Pičikian, I. (1996), 'Neue Entdeckungen in Baktrien und die hellenistische Kultur', in Funck (ed.) (1996a), 77–89.

Pingree, D. (1998), 'Legacies in astronomy and celestial omens', in Dalley (ed.) (1998), 125–37.

Plantzos, D. (1997), 'Hellenistic cameos: problems of classification and chronology', *BICS* 41: 115–31 and 6 pp. of plates.

Pleket, H. W. (1967), 'Technology and society in the Graeco-Roman world', *Acta historiae Neerlandica*, 2: 1–25.

Podemann Sørensen, J. (1992), 'Native reactions to foreign rule and culture in religious literature', in Bilde *et al.* (eds) (1992), 164–81.

Pollitt, J. J. ([1]1965, [2]1990), *The Art of Ancient Greece: Sources and Documents*. Cambridge: CUP.

—— (1974), *The Ancient View of Greek Art: Criticism, History and Terminology*. New Haven, CT, and London: Yale UP.

—— (1986), *Art in the Hellenistic Age*. Cambridge: CUP.

—— (1993), 'Response' [to Robertson], in Green (ed.) (1993), 90–103.

—— (1994), 'Greek art: classical to hellenistic', *CAH*[2] vi, ch. 12 *c* (pp. 647–60).

Pomeroy, S. B. (1975a), *Goddesses, Whores, Wives, and Slaves: Women in Classical Antiquity*. New York: Schocken.

—— (1975b), 'Hellenistic women', in Pomeroy (1975a), ch. 7 (pp. 120–48).

—— (1981), 'Women in Roman Egypt: a preliminary study based on papyri', in Foley (ed.) (1981), 303–22.

—— (1983), 'Infanticide in hellenistic Greece', in Cameron and Kuhrt (eds) (1983), ch. 13 (pp. 207–22).

—— ([1]1984, [2]1990), *Women in Hellenistic Egypt: From Alexander to Cleopatra.* [1]New York: Schocken; [2]Detroit: Wayne State UP.

—— (ed.) (1991), *Women's History and Ancient History.* Chapel Hill, NC, and London: Univ. of North Carolina Press.

—— (1997a), *Families in Classical and Hellenistic Greece: Representations and Realities.* Oxford: Clarendon.

—— (1997b), 'Family values: the uses of the past', in Bilde *et al.* (eds) (1997), 204–19.

Poole, R. S. (1883), *The Ptolemies, Kings of Egypt* (Catalogue of the Greek Coins in the British Museum, xxiv). London: Trustees of the British Museum.

Porter, R., and Teich, M. (eds) (1986), *Revolution in History.* Cambridge: CUP.

Potter, D. (1991), review of Green, *Alexander to Actium*, in *Bryn Mawr Classical Review* at http://ccat.sas.upenn.edu/bmcr/1991/02.06.09.html.

Powell, A. (ed.) (1995), *The Greek World.* London and New York: Routledge.

Powell, J. U. (1925), *Collectanea Alexandrina: reliquiae minores poetarum Graecorum aetatis Ptolemaicae 323–146 AC epicorum, elegiacorum, lyricorum, ethicorum.* Oxford: Clarendon.

Préaux, C. (1939), *L'Économie royale des Lagides.* Brussels: Fondation Égyptologique Reine Élisabeth (repr. (Ancient Economic History series), New York: Arno, 1979).

—— (1947), *Les Grecs en Égypte d'après les archives de Zénon* (Collection Lebègue, 7th series, 78). Brussels: Office de Publicité.

—— (1973), *La Lune dans la pensée grecque* (Académie Royale de Belgique, Mémoires de la Classe des Lettres, Collection in 8°, 2me série, vol. 61.4). Brussels: Palais des Académies.

—— (1978), *Le Monde hellénistique: la Grèce et l'Orient de la mort d'Alexandre à la conquête romaine de la Grèce (323–146 av. J.-C.)*, i–ii [paginated consecutively] (Nouvelle Clio, 6; 6 *bis*). Paris: Presses Universitaires de France.

Price, D. J. de S. (1974), *Gears from the Greeks: The Antikythera Mechanism, a Calendar Computer from ca. 80 BC* (Transactions of the American Philosophical Society, n.s. 64.7). Philadelphia, PA: American Philosophical Society.

—— (1975), *Gears from the Greeks: the Antikythera Mechanism, a Calendar Computer from ca. 80 BC.* New York: Science History Publications.

Price, M., Burnett, A., and Bland, R. (eds) (1993), *Essays in Honour of Robert Carson and Kenneth Jenkins.* London: Spink.

Price, M. J. (1987), 'Southern Greece', in Burnett and Crawford (eds) (1987), 95–103.

—— (1991), *The Coinage in the Name of Alexander the Great and Philip Arrhidaeus: A British Museum Catalogue*, i–ii. London: British Museum/Zurich: Swiss Numismatic Society.

Price, S. R. F. (1984), *Rituals and Power: The Roman Imperial Cult in Asia Minor.* Cambridge: CUP.

Pritchard, J. B. (1969), *Ancient Near Eastern Texts relating to the Old Testament.* Princeton, NJ: Princeton UP.

Pugliese-Caratelli, G. (1967–8), 'Supplemento epigrafico di Iasos', *Annuario della Scuola Archeologica in Atene*, 45–6: 437–86.

Purcell, N. (1994), 'South Italy in the fourth century BC', *CAH*[2] vi, ch. 9 *b* (pp. 381–403).

Quaegebeur, J. (1971), 'Documents concerning a cult of Arsinoe Philadelphos at Memphis', *Journal of Near Eastern Studies*, 30: 239–70.
—— (1980), 'The genealogy of the Memphite high priest family in the hellenistic period', in D. J. Crawford *et al.* (1980) 43–82.
—— (1989), 'The Egyptian clergy and the cult of the Ptolemaic dynasty', *Ancient Society*, 20: 93–116.
Raaflaub, K. A. (1991), 'City-state, territory, and empire in classical antiquity', in Molho *et al.* (eds) (1991), 565–88.
Radt, W. (1998), *Pergamon: Geschichte und Bauten. Funde und Enforschung einer antiken Metropole*. Köln: Dumont.
Raftopoulou, S. (1998), 'New finds from Sparta', in Cavanagh and Walker (eds) (1998), 125–40.
Ragone, G. (1990), 'Il santuario di Apollo Grynios in Eolide: testimonianze anti-quarie, fonti antiche, elementi per la ricerca topografica', in Virgilio (ed.) (1990), 9–112.
Rajak, T. (1994), 'The Jews under Hasmonean rule', *CAH*² ix, ch. 8 *b* (pp. 274–309).
—— (1996a), 'Hasmonean kingship and the invention of tradition', in Bilde *et al.* (eds) (1996a), 99–115.
—— (1996b), 'Hasmoneans', *OCD*³ 668–9.
—— (1996c), 'Jewish-Greek literature', *OCD*³ 795–6.
—— (1996d), 'Jews', *OCD*³ 796–8.
—— (1996e), 'Maccabees', *OCD*³ 904.
Randsborg, K. (1993), 'Greek peripheries and barbarian centres: economic realities and cultural responses', in Bilde *et al.* (eds) (1993), 86–123.
Rapin, C. (1990), 'Greeks in Afghanistan: Aï Khanoum', in Descoeudres (1990b), 329–42.
—— (1992), *Fouilles d'Aï Khanoum*, viii: *La Trésorerie du palais hellénistique d'Aï Khanoum: l'apogée et la chute du royaume grec de Bactriane* (Mémoires de la Déléga-tion Archéologique Française en Afghanistan, 33; Paris: de Boccard).
Rathbone, D. W. (1993), review of Kramer 1991, in *CR* 107 [n.s. 43]: 400–1.
Rawson, E. (1989), 'Roman tradition and the Greek world', *CAH*² viii, ch. 12 (pp. 422–76).
Ray, J. (1994), 'Literacy and language in Egypt in the late and Persian periods', in Bowman and Woolf (eds), ch. 4 (pp. 51–66).
Ray, J. D. (1976), *The Archive of Ḥor* (Excavations at North Saqqâra, Documentary Series, 1). London: Egypt Exploration Society.
Reeder, E. D. (ed.) (1988), *Hellenistic Art in the Walters Art Gallery*. Baltimore, MD: Walters Art Gallery/Princeton: Princeton UP.
Reger, G. (1992), 'Athens and Tenos in the early hellenistic age', *CQ* 86 [n.s. 42]: 365–83.
—— (1994a), 'The political history of the Kyklades: 260–200 BC', *Historia*, 43: 32–69.
—— (1994b), *Regionalism and Change in the Economy of Independent Delos, 314–167 BC* (Hellenistic Culture and Society, 14). Berkeley, CA: Univ. of California Press.
Rehm, A. (1941), *Didyma*, ii: *Die Inschriften*. Berlin: Mann.
Reinders, H. R. (1988), *New Halos: A Hellenistic Town in Thessalía, Greece*. Utrecht: HES Publishers.

Reinhold, M. (1946), 'Historian of the classic world: a critique of Rostovtzeff', *Science and Society*, 10: 361–91.

Rémondon, R. (1964), 'Problèmes de bilinguisme dans l'Égypte lagide (U.P.Z. I, 148)', *Chronique d'Égypte*, 39: 126–46.

Renault, M. (1981), *Funeral Games*. London: John Murray.

Renfrew, C., and Wagstaff, M. (eds) (1982), *An Island Polity: The Archaeology of Exploitation in Melos*. Cambridge, London, New York, New Rochelle, Melbourne, and Sydney: CUP.

Reverdin, O., and Grange, B. (eds) (1986), *Aspects de la philosophie hellénistique* (Entretiens sur l'antiquité classique, 32). Vandoeuvres, Geneva: Fondation Hardt.

—— and —— (eds) (1996), *Pausanias historien* (Entretiens sur l'antiquité classique, 41). Vandoeuvres, Geneva: Fondation Hardt.

Rey-Coquais, J.-P. (1970) *Inscriptions grecques et latines de la Syrie*, vii: *Arados et régions voisines (nᵒˢ 4001–4061)* (Institut Français d'Archéologie de Beyrouth, bibliothèque archéologique et historique, 89). Paris.

—— (1978), 'Inscription grecque découverte à Ras Ibn Hani: stèle de mercenaires lagides sur la côte syrienne', *Syria*, 55: 313–25.

Rhodes, P. J. (1980), 'Athenian democracy after 403 BC', *Classical Journal*, 75: 305–23.

—— (1986), *The Greek City States: A Source Book*. London and Sydney: Croom Helm.

—— (1993), 'The Greek poleis: demes, cities and leagues', in *CPC Acts 1*, 161–82.

—— (1994), 'The polis and the alternatives', *CAH²* vi, ch. 11 (pp. 565–91).

——, with Lewis, D. M. (1997), *The Decrees of the Greek States*. Oxford: Clarendon.

Rice, E. (1993), 'The glorious dead: commemoration of the fallen and portrayal of victory in the late classical and hellenistic world', in Rich and Shipley (eds) (1993), ch. 11 (pp. 224–57).

Rice, E. E. (1983), *The Grand Procession of Ptolemy Philadelphus*. Oxford: Clarendon.

—— (1997), *Alexander the Great* (Pocket Biographies). Stroud: Sutton.

Rich, J., and Shipley, G. (eds) (1993), *War and Society in the Greek World* (Leicester–Nottingham Studies in Ancient Society, 4). London and New York: Routledge.

Richlin, A. (ed.) (1992), *Pornography and Representation in Greece and Rome*. New York and Oxford: OUP.

Ridgway, B. S. (1988), 'The study of hellenistic art', in Reeder (ed.) (1988), 27–34.

—— (1993), 'Response' [to Smith and Zanker], in Bulloch *et al.* (eds) (1993), 231–41.

Rigsby, K. J. (1996), *Asylia: Territorial Inviolability in the Hellenistic World* (Hellenistic Culture and Society, 22). Berkeley, Los Angeles, London: Univ. of California Press.

Rizakis, A. D. (1995), *Achaïe*, i: *Sources textuelles et histoire régionale* (Μελετήματα, 20). Athens: Ethnikon Idryma Erevnon, Kentron Ellinikis kai Romaïkis Archaiotitos/Paris: de Boccard.

Robert, L. (1949), *Hellenica: recueil d'épigraphie, de numismatique et d'antiquités grecques*, vii (Librairie d'Amérique et d'Orient). Paris: Adrien-Maisonneuve.

—— (1960), *Hellenica: recueil d'épigraphie, de numismatique et d'antiquités grecques*, volume xi–xii (Librairie d'Amérique et d'Orient). Paris: Adrien-Maisonneuve.

—— (1968), 'De Delphes à l'Oxus: inscriptions nouvelles de la Bactriane', *CRAI*, 416–57.

—— (1969–90), *Opera minora selecta*, i–vii. Amsterdam: Hakkert.

—— (1973), 'Les juges étrangers dans la cité grecque', in von Caemmerer (ed.) (1973), 765–82; repr. in Robert 1969–90, v. 137–54.

—— and Robert, J. (1954), *La Carie: histoire et géographie historique*, ii: *Le Plateau de Tabai et ses environs*. Paris: Librairie de'Amérique et d'Orient/Adrien-Maison-neuve.

—— and —— (1989), *Claros*, i: *Décrets hellénistiques*. Paris: Éditions Recherches sur les Civilisations.

Robertson, M. (1993), 'What is "hellenistic" about hellenistic art?', in Green (ed.) (1993), 67–90.

Robinson, E. S. G. (1954), 'Cistophori in the name of king Eumenes', *Numismatic Chronicle* (6th series), 14: 1–8.

Rogers, G. MacL. (1991), *The Sacred Identity of Ephesos: Foundation Myths of a Roman City*. London and New York: Routledge.

Romano, I. B. (1994), 'A hellenistic deposit from Corinth: evidence for interim period activity (146–44 BC)', *Hesp*. 63: 57–104.

Romer, F. E. (1998), *Pomponius Mela's Description of the World*. Ann Arbor, MI: Michigan UP.

Rosen, R. M., and Farrell, J. (eds 1993), *Nomodeiktes: Greek Studies in Honor of Martin Ostwald*. Ann Arbor, MI: Univ. of Michigan Press.

Rostovtzeff, M. (1928a), 'Ptolemaic Egypt', *CAH*[1] vii, ch. 4 (pp. 109–54).

—— (1928b), 'Syria and the east', *CAH*[1] vii, ch. 5 (pp. 155–96).

—— (1930a), 'The Bosporan kingdom', *CAH*[1] viii, ch. 18 (pp. 561–89).

—— (1930b), 'Pergamum', *CAH*[1] viii, ch. 19 (pp. 590–618).

—— (1930c), 'Rhodes, Delos and hellenistic commerce', *CAH*[1] viii, ch. 20 (pp. 619–67).

—— (1941), *The Social and Economic History of the Hellenistic World*, i–iii (paginated consecutively). Oxford: Clarendon.

—— and Ormerod, H. A. (1932), 'Pontus and its neighbours: the first Mithridatic war', *CAH*[1] ix, ch. 5 (pp. 211–60; 211–38 by Rostovtzeff, 238–60 by Ormerod).

Rotroff, S. I. (1982), *Hellenistic Pottery: Athenian and Imported Moldmade Bowls* (The Athenian Agora, 22). Princeton, NJ: American School of Classical Studies at Athens.

—— (1997a), 'From Greek to Roman in Athenian ceramics', in Hoff and Rotroff (eds) (1997b), 97–116.

—— (1997b), *Hellenistic Pottery: Athenian and Imported Wheelmade Table Ware and Related Material* (The Athenian Agora, 29.1–2). Princeton, NJ: American School of Classical Studies at Athens.

Roueché, C., and Sherwin-White, S. M. (1985), 'Some aspects of the Seleucid empire: the Greek inscriptions from Failaka in the Arabian gulf', *Chiron*, 15: 1–39.

Roy, J. (1998), 'The masculinity of the hellenistic king', in Foxhall and Salmon (eds) (1998b), ch. 5 (pp. 111–35).

——, Owens, E. J., and Lloyd, J. A. (1988), 'Tribe and polis in the chora at Mega-lopolis', *PAE* 179–82.

——, —— and —— (1989), 'Megalopolis under the Roman empire', in Walker and Cameron (eds) (1989), 146–50.

Ruelle, C.-E. (ed.) (1879), *Oeuvres de Rufus d'Éphèse* (Collection des médecins grecs et Latins). Paris: Imprimerie Nationale.

Runciman, W. G. (1990), 'Doomed to extinction: the polis as an evolutionary dead-end', in Murray and Price (eds) (1990), ch. 14 (pp. 347–67).

Rusten, J., Cunningham, I. C., and Knox, A. D. (eds and trans.) (1993), *Theophrastus: Characters, Herodas: Mimes, Cercidas and the Choliambic Poets* (Loeb Classical Library). Cambridge, MA, and London: Harvard UP.

Sachs, A. J., and Hunger, H. (1988, 1989), *Astronomical Diaries and Related Texts from Babylonia*, i: *Diaries from 652 BC to 262 BC*; ii: *Diaries from 261 BC to 165 BC* (Österreichische Akademie der Wissenschaften, Phil.-hist. Kl., Denkschr. 195; 210). Vienna: Akademie der Wissenschaften.

—— and Wiseman, D. J. (1954), 'A Babylonian king list of the hellenistic period', *Iraq*, 16: 202–11, 212 pl. 53.

Said, E. (1978), *Orientalism*. London: Routledge and Kegan Paul/New York: Random House (repr. London and Harmondsworth: Penguin, 1985).

—— (1993), *Culture and Imperialism*. London: Vintage.

Said, S. (ed.) (1991), Ἑλληνισμός: *quelques jalons pour une histoire de l'identité grecque. Actes du colloque de Strasbourg (25–27 octobre 1989)*. Leiden, New York, Copenhagen, Cologne: Brill.

Sallares, R. (1991), *The Ecology of the Ancient Greek World*. London: Duckworth.

Salles, J.-F. (1987), 'The Arab-Persian gulf under the Seleucids', in Kuhrt and Sherwin-White (eds) (1987), ch. 4 (pp. 75–109).

Salmenkivi, E. (1997), 'Family life in the comedies of Menander', in Frösén (ed.) (1997), 183–94.

Samuel, A. E. (1962), *Ptolemaic Chronology* (Münchener Beiträge zur Papyrusforschung und antiken Rechtsgeschichte, 43). Munich: Beck.

—— (1983), *From Athens to Alexandria: Hellenism and Social Goals in Ptolemaic Egypt* (Studia hellenistica, 26). Louvain: [W. Peremans].

—— (1989), *The Shifting Sands of History: Interpretations of Ptolemaic Egypt* (Publications of the Association of Ancient Historians, 2). Lanham, New York, London.

—— (1993), 'The Ptolemies and the ideology of kingship', in Green (ed.) (1993), 168–92.

Sanders, D. H. (ed.) (1996), *Nemrud Dağı: The Hierothesion of Antiochus I of Commagene*, i: *Text*; ii: *Illustrations*. Winona Lake, IN: Eisenbrauns.

Sarton, G. (1953), *A History of Science*, [i]: *Ancient Science through the Golden Age of Greece*. London: Cumberlege/OUP.

—— (1959), *A History of Science*, [ii]: *Hellenistic Science and Culture in the Last Three Centuries BC*. Cambridge, MA: Harvard UP/London: OUP.

Scarborough, J. (1991), 'The pharmacology of sacred plants, herbs, and roots', in Faraone and Obbink (eds) (1991), ch. 5 (pp. 138–74).

—— (1993), 'Response' [to White], in Green (ed.) (1993), 220–33.

Schalles, H.-J. (1985), *Untersuchungen zur Kulturpolitik der pergamenischen Herrscher im dritten Jahrhundert vor Christus* (Istanbuler Forschungen, 36). Tübingen: Wasmuth.

Schlumberger, D., Robert, L., Dupont-Sommer, A., and Benveniste, E. (1958), 'Une bilingue gréco-araméenne d'Asoka', *Journal asiatique*, 246: 1–48.

Schmitt, H. H. (ed.) (1969), *Die Staatsverträge des Altertums*, iii: *Die Verträge der griechisch-römischen Welt von 338 bis 200 v. Chr.* [nos 401–586]. Munich: DAI/Beck.

Schmitt Pantel, P. (1997), 'Public feasts in the hellenistic Greek city: forms and meanings', in Bilde *et al.* (eds) (1997), 29–47.

Schneider, C. (1967–9), *Kulturgeschichte des Hellenismus*, i–ii [separately paginated]. Munich: Beck.

Schofield, M. (1991), *The Stoic Idea of the City*. Cambridge: CUP.

Scholten, J. B. (1997), *The Politics of Plunder: Aitolians and their Koinon in the Early Hellenistic Era, 279–217 BC* (Hellenistic Culture and Society, 24). Berkeley, Los Angeles, London: Univ. of California Press.

Schürer, E. (1973, 1979, 1986–7), *The History of the Jewish People in the Age of Jesus Christ (175 BC–AD 135)*, i (rev. and ed. G. Vermes and F. Millar); ii (rev. and ed. G. Vermes, F. Millar, and M. Black); iii. 1–2 (rev. and ed. G. Vermes, F. Millar, and M. Goodman). Edinburgh: T. &. T. Clark.

Schwarz, H. (ed.) (1986, repr. 1988), *Miriam's Tambourine: Jewish Folktales from around the World*. Oxford: OUP.

Seibert, J. (1967), *Historische Beiträge zu den dynastischen Verbindungen in hellenistischer Zeit* (Historia Einzelschriften, 10). Wiesbaden: Steiner.

Sethe, K. (1899), 'Berenike 5', *RE* iii. 280–1.

Sfameni Gasparro, G. (1997), 'Daimon and tuchê in the hellenistic religious experience', in Bilde *et al.* (eds) (1997), 67–109.

Sharples, R. W. (1995), *Theophrastus of Eresus: Sources for his Life, Writings, Thought and Influence. Commentary*, v: *Sources on Biology (Human Physiology, Living Creatures, Botany: Texts 328–435)* (Philosophia antiqua, 64). Leiden, New York, Cologne: Brill.

—— (1996), *Stoics, Epicureans and Sceptics: An Introduction to Hellenistic Philosophy*. London and New York: Routledge.

—— (1996), 'Theophrastus', *OCD*³ 1504–5.

Shear, T. L., jun. (1970), 'The monument of the eponymous heroes in the Athenian agora', *Hesp.* 39: 145–222.

—— (1978), *Kallias of Sphettos and the Revolt of Athens in 286 BC* (Hesp. suppl. 17).

Sherk, R. K. (1969), *Roman Documents from the Greek East: Senatus Consulta and Epistulae to the Age of Augustus*. Baltimore, MD: Johns Hopkins UP.

—— (1984), *Rome and the Greek East to the Death of Augustus* (Translated Documents of Greece and Rome, 4). Cambridge: CUP.

—— (1988), *The Roman Empire: Augustus to Hadrian* (Translated Documents of Greece and Rome, 6). Cambridge: CUP.

Sherwin-White, A. N. (1994), 'Lucullus, Pompey and the east', *CAH*² ix, ch. 8 *a* (pp. 229–73).

Sherwin-White, S. (1987), 'Seleucid Babylonia: a case study for the installation and development of Greek rule', in Kuhrt and Sherwin-White (eds) (1987), ch. 1 (pp. 1–31).

—— and Kuhrt, A. (1993), *From Samarkhand to Sardis: A New Approach to the Seleucid Empire*. London: Duckworth; also published as Hellenistic Culture and Society, 13, Berkeley, Los Angeles, London: Univ. of California Press, 1993.

Sherwin-White, S. M. (1978), *Ancient Cos: An Historical Study from the Dorian Settlement to the Imperial Period* (Hypomnemata, 51). Göttingen: Vandenhoeck & Ruprecht.

—— (1983a), 'Aristeas Ardibelteios: some aspects of the use of double names in Seleucid Babylonia', *ZPE* 50: 209–21.

—— (1983b), 'Babylonian chronicle fragments as a source for Seleucid history', *Journal of Near Eastern Studies,* 42: 265–70.

—— (1984), 'Asia Minor', in Ling (ed.) (1984), ch. 4 (pp. 33–52).

Shimron, B. (1972), *Late Sparta: The Spartan Revolution 243–146 BC* (Arethusa Monographs, 3). New York: Department of Classics, State Univ. of New York at Buffalo.

Shipley, D. R. (1997), *A Commentary on Plutarch's Life of Agesilaos: Response to Sources in the Presentation of Character*. Oxford: Clarendon.

Shipley, G. (1987), *A History of Samos 800–188 BC*. Oxford: Clarendon.

—— (1991), review of Green (1990), *The Higher: The Times Higher Education Supplement* (22 March), p. 20.

—— (1993), 'Distance, development, decline? World-systems analysis and the "hellenistic" world', in Bilde *et al.* (eds) (1993), 271–84.

—— (1996), 'Site catalogue of the survey', in Cavanagh *et al* (1996). ii. 315–438.

—— (1997), ' "The other Lakedaimonians": the dependent perioikic poleis of Laconia and Messenia', *CPC Acts 4*, 189–281.

—— (forthcoming), 'The survey area in the hellenistic and Roman periods', in Cavanagh *et al*. i.

—— and Salmon, J. (eds) (1996), *Human Landscapes in Classical Antiquity: Environment and Culture* (Leicester–Nottingham Studies in Ancient Society, 6).

Siebert, G. (1968), 'Sur l'histoire du sanctuaire des dieux syriens à Délos', *BCH* 92: 359–74.

Skeat, T. C. (²1969), *The Reigns of the Ptolemies* (Münchener Beiträge zur Papyrusforschung und antiken Rechtsgeschichte, 39). Munich: Beck.

—— (1974), *Greek Papyri in the British Museum (Now in the British Library)*, vii: *The Zenon Archive*. London: BM Publications for British Library Board.

Skydsgaard, J. E. (1993), 'The Greeks in southern Russia: a tale of two cities', in Bilde *et al*. (eds) (1993), 124–31.

Smith, R. R. R. (1988), *Hellenistic Royal Portraits* (Oxford Monographs on Classical Archaeology). Oxford: Clarendon.

—— (1991), *Hellenistic Sculpture: A Handbook* (World of Art). London: Thames & Hudson.

—— (1993), 'Kings and philosophers', in Bulloch *et al*. (eds) (1993), 202–11.

Smith, S. (1924), *Babylonian Historical Texts*. London: Methuen.

Smith, T. J., with Milner, N. P. (1997), 'Votive reliefs from Balboura and its environs', *Anatolian Studies*, 47: 3–39.

Snodgrass, A. (1990), 'Survey archaeology and the rural landscape of the Greek city', in Murray and Price (eds) (1990), ch. 5 (pp. 113–36).

Snodgrass, A. M. (1987), *An Archaeology of Greece: The Present State and Future Scope of a Discipline* (Sather Classical Lectures, 53). Berkeley, Los Angeles, and Oxford: Univ. of California Press.

Sokolowski, F. (1955), *Lois sacrées de l'Asie Mineure* (Travaux et mémoires, 9). Athens: École Française d'Athènes/Paris: de Boccard.

—— (1969), *Lois sacrées des cités grecques* (Travaux et mémoires 18). Athens: École Française d'Athènes/ Paris: de Boccard.

Sparkes, B. A. (ed.) (1998), *Greek Civilization: An Introduction*. Oxford: Blackwell.

Spawforth, A. J., and Walker, S. (1985), 'The world of the Panhellenion, I: Athens and Eleusis', *JRS* 75: 78–104.

—— and —— (1986), 'The world of the Panhellenion, II: three Dorian cities', *JRS* 76: 88–105.

Spawforth, A. J. S. (1996), 'Nomads', *OCD*³ 1047.

—— (1997), 'The early reception of the imperial cult in Athens: problems and ambiguities', in Hoff and Rotroff (eds) (1997), 183–201.

Steckerl, F. (1958), *The Fragments of Praxagoras of Cos and his School: Collected, Edited and Translated* (Philosophia antiqua, 8). Leiden: Brill.

Stern, M. (1974, 1980a, 1980b), *Greek and Latin Authors on Jews and Judaism*, i: *From Herodotus to Plutarch*; ii: *From Tacitus to Simplicius*; iii: *Appendixes and Indexes* (Fontes ad res Judaicas spectantes). Jerusalem: Israel Academy of Sciences and Humanities, Section of Humanities.

—— and Murray, O. (1973), 'Hecataeus of Abdera and Theophrastus on Jews and Egyptians', *JEA* 59: 159–68.

Stewart, A. (1979), *Attika: Studies in Athenian Sculpture of the Hellenistic Age* (Supplementary Papers, 14). London: Society for the Promotion of Hellenic Studies.

—— (1988), 'Hellenistic art and the coming of Rome', in Reeder (ed.) (1988), 35–44.

—— (1990), *Greek Sculpture: An Exploration*, i: *Text*; ii: *Plates*. New Haven, CT, and London: Yale UP.

—— (1993), *Faces of Power: Alexander's Image and Hellenistic Politics* (Hellenistic Culture and Society, 11). Berkeley, Los Angeles, London: Univ. of California Press.

Stewart, Z. (1977), 'La religione', in Moretti *et al.* (eds), (1977), ch. 7 (pp. 503–616).

Stikas, E. G. (1938), Ἀνασκαφὴ Ἐλευθερῶν (Πανάκτου)', *PAE* 41–9.

Stolper, M. W. (1994), 'Mesopotamia, 482–330 BC', *CAH*² vi, ch. 8 *b* (pp. 234–60).

Stoneman, R. (trans. and ed. 1991), *The Greek Alexander Romance* (Penguin Classics). London: Penguin.

—— (trans. and ed. 1994), *Legends of Alexander the Great* (Everyman). London: Dent.

—— (1997), *Alexander the Great* (Lancaster Pamphlets). London and New York: Routledge.

Stucky, R. A., Jucker, I., and Gelzer, T. (eds) (1980), *Eikones: Studien zum griechischen und römischen Bildnis Hans Jucker zum 60. Geburtstag gewidmet* (Antike Kunst, Beiheft 12). Bern: Francke.

Syzetesis. (1983) Συζήτησις: *studi sull'epicureismo greco e romano offerti a Marcello Gigante* (Biblioteca della parola del passato, 16). Naples: Macchiaroli.

Szelényi-Graziotto, K. (1996), 'Der Kult in Babylon in seleukidischer Zeit: Tradition oder Wandel?', in Funck (ed.) (1996a), 171–94.

Talbert, R. J. A. (ed. 1985), *Atlas of Classical History*. London and New York: Routledge.

Tarn, W. W. (1913), *Antigonos Gonatas*. Oxford: Clarendon (repr. 1969).

—— (1923), 'The social question in the third century', in Bury *et al.* (1923), 108–40.

—— (1927a), 'Alexander: the conquest of Persia', *CAH*[1] vi, ch. 12 (pp. 352–86).

—— (1927b), 'Alexander: the conquest of the far east', *CAH*[1] vi, ch. 13 (pp. 387–437).

—— (1927c), 'Greece: 335 to 321 BC', *CAH*[1] vi, ch. 14 (pp. 438–60).

—— (1927d), 'The heritage of Alexander', *CAH*[1] vi, ch. 15 (pp. 461–504).

—— (1928a), 'The Greek leagues and Macedonia', *CAH*[1] vii, ch. 23 (pp. 732–68).

—— (1928b), 'Macedonia and Greece', *CAH*[1] vii, ch. 6 (pp. 197–223).

—— (1928c), 'The new hellenistic kingdoms', *CAH*[1] vii, ch. 3 (pp. 75–108).

—— (1928d), 'The struggle of Egypt against Macedonia', *CAH*[1] vii, ch. 22.

—— (1930), *Hellenistic Naval and Military Developments*. Cambridge: CUP.

—— (1932), 'Parthia', *CAH*[1] ix, ch. 14 (pp. 574–613).

—— ([1]1938, [2]1951, [3]1985), *The Greeks in Bactria and India*. [1, 2]Cambridge: CUP; [3]ed. F. L. Holt, Chicago: Ares.

—— (1948), *Alexander the Great*. Cambridge: CUP.

—— and Griffith, G. T. ([3]1952), *Hellenistic Civilisation*. London: Arnold.

Tcherikover, V. (1959), *Hellenistic Civilization and the Jews*. Trans. S. Applebaum. Philadelphia, PA: Jewish Publication Society of America/Jerusalem: Magnes Press, Hebrew Univ.

Teixidor, J. (1977), *The Pagan God: Popular Religion in the Greco-Roman Near East*. Princeton: Princeton UP.

—— (1990), 'Interpretations and misinterpretations of the east in hellenistic times', in Bilde *et al.* (eds) (1990), 66–78.

Thasiaca (1979). *Thasiaca* (BCH suppl. 5). Athens: École Française d'Athènes/Paris: de Boccard.

Thesleff, H. (1961), *An Introduction to the Pythagorean Writings of the Hellenistic Period* (Acta Academiae Aboensis, humaniora, 24.3). Åbo: Åbo Akademi.

—— (1965), *The Pythagorean Texts of the Hellenistic Period* (Acta Academiae Aboensis, series A, humaniora, 30.1). Åbo: Åbo Akademi.

Thomas, I. (trans. 1939a), *Greek Mathematical Works*, i: *From Thales to Euclid* (Loeb Classical Library). London: Heinemann/Cambridge, MA: Harvard UP.

—— (trans. 1939b) *Greek Mathematical Works* ii: *From Aristarchus to Pappus* (Loeb Classical Library). London: Heinemann/Cambridge, MA: Harvard UP.

Thomas, R. (1989), *Oral Tradition and Written Record in Classical Athens* (Cambridge Studies in Oral and Literate Culture, 18). Cambridge: CUP.

—— (1992), *Literacy and Orality in the Ancient World* (Key Themes in Ancient History). Cambridge: CUP.

—— (1996), 'Orality', *OCD*[3] 1072.

Thompson, D. B. (1973), *Ptolemaic Oinochoai and Portraits in Faience: Aspects of the Ruler-cult* (Oxford Monographs on Classical Archaeology). Oxford: Clarendon.

—— (1980), 'More Ptolemaic queens', in Stucky *et al.* (eds) (1980), 181–4.

Thompson, D. F. (ed.) (1995), *The Concise Oxford Dictionary of Current English*[9]. Oxford: Clarendon.

Thompson, D. J. (1983), 'Nile grain transport under the Ptolemies', in Garnsey *et al.* (1983) (eds), 64–75 (nn. at 190–2).

—— (1984a), 'Agriculture', *CAH*² vii. 1, ch. 9 *c* (pp. 363–70).

—— (1984b), 'The Ptolemaic kingdom', in Ling (ed.) (1984), ch. 1 (pp. 3–16).

—— (1988), *Memphis under the Ptolemies*. Princeton, NJ: Princeton UP.

—— (1992a), 'Language and literacy in early hellenistic Egypt', in Bilde *et al.* (eds) (1992), 39–52.

—— (1992b), 'Literacy and the administration in early Ptolemaic Egypt', in J. H. Johnson (ed.) (1992), 323–6.

—— (1994a), 'Conquest and literacy: the case of Ptolemaic Egypt', in Keller-Cohen (ed.) (1994), 71–89.

—— (1994b), 'Egypt, 146–31 BC', *CAH*² ix, ch. 8 *c* (pp. 310–26).

—— (1994c), 'Literacy and power in Ptolemaic Egypt', in Bowman and Woolf (eds) (1994), ch. 5 (pp. 67–83).

—— (1995), 'Food for Ptolemaic temple workers', in Wilkins *et al.* (eds) (1997), 316–25.

—— (1997), 'The infrastructure of splendour: census and taxes in Ptolemaic Egypt', in Cartledge *et al.* (eds) (1997), 242–57.

—— (1999a), 'Irrigation and drainage in the early Ptolemaic Fayum', in Bowman and Rogan (eds) (1999), 107–22.

—— (1999b), 'New and old in the Ptolemaic Fayum', in Bowman and Rogan (eds) (1999), 123–8.

—— (2000), 'Hellenistic Hellenes: the case of Ptolemaic Egypt', in Malkin and Raaflaub (eds).

Thompson, H. A. (1934), 'Two centuries of hellenistic pottery', *Hesp.* 3: 310–476.

—— (1937), 'The American excavations in the Athenian Agora, eleventh report: buildings on the west side of the Agora', *Hesp.* 6: 1–226 (at pp. 218–22, 'East slope of Kolonos Agoraios').

—— and Wycherley, R. E. (1971), *The Agora of Athens: The History, Shape and Uses of an Ancient City Center* (The Athenian Agora, 14; Princeton, NJ: American School of Classical Studies at Athens).

Thompson, M. (1961), *The New Style Silver Coinage of Athens*, i: *Text*; ii: *Plates* (Numismatic Studies, 10). New York: American Numismatic Society.

Thomson, J. O. (1948), *History of Ancient Geography*. Cambridge: CUP.

Tobin, J. (1997), *Herodes Attikos and the City of Athens: Patronage and Conflict under the Antonines* (Ἀρχαία Ἑλλάς, 4). Amsterdam: Gieben.

Tod, M. N. (1948), *A Selection of Greek Historical Inscriptions*, ii: *From 403 to 323 BC*. Oxford: Clarendon.

Tomlinson, R. A. (1972), *Argos and the Argolid: From the End of the Bronze Age to the Roman Occupation* (States and Cities of Ancient Greece). London: Routledge & Kegan Paul.

—— (1984), 'Macedonia, Greece and the Cyclades', in Ling (ed.) (1984), ch. 5 (pp. 53–70).

—— (1995), 'The town plan of hellenistic Alexandria', in *Alessandria*, 236–40.

Toomer, G. J. (1984), *Ptolemy's Almagest* (Duckworth Classical, Medieval, and Renaissance Editions). London: Duckworth (repr. Princeton, NJ: Princeton UP, 1998).

—— (1996a), 'Astronomical instruments', *OCD*³ 195–6.

—— (1996b), 'Astronomy', *OCD*³ 196–8.

—— (1996c), 'Cleomedes', *OCD*³ 345.

—— (1996d), 'Hipparchus', *OCD*³ 708.

—— (1996e), 'Mathematics', *OCD*³ 936–7.

—— (1996f), 'Timocharis', *OCD*³ 1528.

Tortzen, C. G. (1993), *Den hellenistiske skole* (Hellenismestudier, 8). Aarhus: Aarhus Universitetsforlag.

Tracy, S. V. (1990), *Attic Letter-cutters of 229 to 86 BC* (Hellenistic Culture and Society, 6). Berkeley, Los Angeles, London: Univ. of California Press.

—— (1995), *Athenian Democracy in Transition: Attic Letter-cutters of 340 to 290 BC* (Hellenistic Culture and Society, 20). Berkeley, Los Angeles, London: Univ. of California Press.

Travlos, J. (1971a), *Bildlexikon zur Topographie des antiken Athen*. Tübingen: Wasmuth.

—— (1971b), *Pictorial Dictionary of Ancient Athens*. Athens: DAI.

Treidler, H. (1959), 'Ptolemais 8', *RE* xxiii. 2. 1870–83.

Troiani, L. (1984), 'Per un'interpretazione della storia ellenistica e romana contenuta nelle "Antichità Giudaiche" di Giuseppe (libri XII–XX)', in Virgilio (ed.) (1984b), 39–50.

—— (1987), 'Il libro di Aristea ed il Giudaismo ellenistico: premesse per un'interpretazione', in Virgilio (ed.) (1987c), 31–61.

Tscherikower, V. (1927), *Die hellenistischen Städtegründungen von Alexander dem Grossen bis auf die Römerzeit* (Philologus, suppl. 19.1). Leipzig: Dieterich.

Turner, E. G. (¹1968, ²1980), *Greek Papyri: An Introduction*. Oxford: Clarendon.

—— (1974), 'A commander-in-chief's order from Saqqâra', *JEA* 60: 239–42.

—— (1984), 'Ptolemaic Egypt', *CAH*² vii. 1, ch. 5 (pp. 118–74).

Ussher, R. G. (1993), *The Characters of Theophrastus: Introduction, Commentary and Index*. London: Bristol Classical Press.

Vallance, J. T. (1996a), 'Humours', *OCD*³ 733.

—— (1996b), 'Medicine', *OCD*³ 945–9.

—— (1996c), 'Praxagoras', *OCD*³ 1241–2.

Van Andel, T. H., and Runnels, C. N. (1987), *Beyond the Acropolis: A Rural Greek Past*. Stanford, CA: Stanford UP.

van Bremen, R. (1983), 'Women and wealth', in Cameron and Kuhrt (eds) (1983), ch. 14 (pp. 223–42).

—— (1996), *The Limits of Participation: Women and Civic Life in the Greek East in the Hellenistic and Roman Periods* (Dutch Monographs on Ancient History and Archaeology). Amsterdam: Gieben.

van de Maele, S., and Fossey, J. M. (eds) (1992), *Fortificationes Antiquae (including the Papers of a Conference held at Ottawa University/incluant les communications lues à un colloque tenu à l'Université d'Ottawa October/octobre 1988)* (Monographies en archéologie et histoire classiques de l'Université McGill/McGill University Monographs in Classical Archaeology and History, 12). Amsterdam: Gieben.

Vanderpool, E., McCredie, J. R., and Steinberg, A. (1962), 'Koroni, a Ptolemaic camp on the east coast of Attica', *Hesp.* 31: 26–61.

——, —— and —— (1964), 'Koroni: the date of the camp and the pottery', *Hesp.* 33: 69–75.

van der Spek, R. J. (1987), 'The Babylonian city', in Kuhrt and Sherwin-White (eds) (1987), ch. 3 (pp. 57–74).

Vandorpe, K. (1986), 'The chronology of the reigns of Hurgonaphor and Chaonnophris', *Chronique d'Égypte*, 61: 294–307.

van Straten, F. (1993), 'Images of gods and men in a changing society: self-identity in hellenistic religion', in Bulloch *et al.* (eds) (1993), 248–64.

van't Dack. E., van Dessel, P., and van Gucht, W. (eds) (1983) *Egypt and the Hellenistic World: Proceedings of the International Colloquium (Leuven, 24–26 May 1982)* (Studia hellenistica, 27). Leuven: Studia hellenistica/Librairie Orientaliste.

Veuve, S. (1987), *Fouilles d'Aï Khanoum*, vi: *Le Gymnase: architecture, céramique, sculpture* (Mémoires de la Délégation Archéologique Française en Afghanistan, 30). Paris: de Boccard.

Veyne, P. (1976), *Le Pain et le cirque*. Paris: Éditions du Seuil.

——— (1990), *Bread and Circuses: Historical Sociology and Political Pluralism*, introduced by O. Murray, trans. B. Pearce. London: Penguin.

Vial, C. (1984), *Délos indépendante* (BCH suppl. 10). Athens: École Française d'Athènes.

Vidal-Naquet, P. (1967), *Le Bordereau d'ensemencement dans l'Égypte ptolémaïque* (Papyrologica Bruxellensia, 5). Brussels: Fondation Égyptologique Reine Elisabeth.

Virgilio, B. (1984a), 'Strabone e la storia di Pergamo e degli Attalidi', in Virgilio (ed.) (1984b), 21–37.

——— (ed.) (1984b), *Studi ellenistici*, 1 (Biblioteca di studi antichi, 48). Pisa: Giardini.

——— (1987a), 'I kátochoi del tempio di Zeus a Baitokaike', in Virgilio (ed.) (1987c), 193–8 (= *Parola del passato*, 40 (1985), 218–22).

——— (1987b), 'Strutture templari e potere politico in Asia Minore', in Virgilio (ed.) (1987c), 199–207 (= *Athenaeum*, 65 (1987), 227–31).

——— (ed.) (1987c), *Studi ellenistici*, 2 (Biblioteca di studi antichi, 54). Pisa: Giardini.

——— (ed.) (1990), *Studi ellenistici*, 3 (Biblioteca di studi antichi, 64). Pisa: Giardini.

——— (1993), *Gli Attalidi di Pergamo: fama, eredità, memoria* (Studi ellenistici, 5/Biblioteca di studi antichi, 70). Pisa: Giardini.

——— (ed.) (1994), *Aspetti e problemi dell'ellenismo (atti del convegno di studi Pisa 6–7 novembre 1992)* (Studi ellenistici, 4/Biblioteca di studi antichi, 73). Pisa: Giardini.

——— (ed.) (1996), *Studi ellenistici*, 8 (Biblioteca di studi antichi, 78). Pisa, Rome: Instituti Editoriali e Poligrafici Internazionali.

Vleeming, S. P. (ed.) (1995), *Hundred-gated Thebes: Acts of a Colloquium on Thebes and the Theban Area in the Graeco-Roman Period* (Papyrologica Lugduno-Batava, 27). Leiden: Brill.

von Caemmerer, E. (ed.) (1973), *Jarbuch des deutschen Archäologischen Instituts*, *Xenion: Festschrift für Pan. J. Zepos anlässlich seines 65. Geburtstages am 1. Dezember 1973*, i–iii. Athens, Freiburg/Br., and Cologne: Katsikalis.

von Hesberg, H. (1989), 'Temporäre Bilder oder die Grenzen der Kunst: zur Legitimation frühhellenistischer Königsherrschaft im Fest', *Jahrbuch des Deutschen Archäologischen Instituts*, 104: 61–82.

von Staden, H. (1989), *Herophilus: The Art of Medicine in Early Alexandria. Edition, Translation and Essays*. Cambridge and New York: CUP.

——— (1996a), 'Erasistratus', *OCD*³ 552–3.

—— (1996b), 'Herophilus', *OCD*³ 699.

Waddell, W. G. (1940), *Manetho* (Loeb Classical Library). Cambridge, MA: Harvard UP; London: Heinemann.

Walbank, F. W. (1933), *Aratos of Sicyon* (Thirlwall Prize Essay). Cambridge: CUP.

—— (1940), *Philip V of Macedon*. Cambridge: CUP.

—— (1957–79), *A Historical Commentary on Polybius*. 3 vols. Oxford: Clarendon.

—— (1962), 'Polemic in Polybius', *JRS* 52: 1–12; repr. in Walbank (1985), ch. 17 (pp. 262–79).

—— (1963/1985), 'Polybius and Rome's eastern policy', *JRS* 53: 1–13; repr. in Walbank (1985), ch. 10 (pp. 138–56).

—— (1972), *Polybius* (Sather Classical Lectures, 42). Berkeley, Los Angeles, London: Univ. of California Press (repr. 1990).

—— (1976–7/1985), 'Were there Greek federal states?', *Scripta classica Israelica*, 3: 27–51; repr. in Walbank (1985), ch. 2 (pp. 20–37).

—— (1979), introduction to Polybius, *Rise of the Roman Empire*. Harmondsworth: Penguin.

—— (1981, rev. 1986, 1992), *The Hellenistic World* (Fontana History of the Ancient World). London: HarperCollins.

—— (1984a), 'Macedonia and Greece', *CAH*² vii. 1, ch. 7 (pp. 221–56).

—— (1984b), 'Macedonia and the Greek leagues', *CAH*² vii. 1, ch. 12 (pp. 446–81).

—— (1984c), 'Monarchies and monarchic ideas', *CAH*² vii. 1, ch. 3 (pp. 62–100).

—— (1984d), 'Sources for the period', *CAH*² vii. 1, ch. 1 (pp. 1–22).

—— (1985), *Selected Papers: Studies in Greek and Roman History and Historiography*. Cambridge: CUP.

—— (1992), review of Grzybek 1990, *CR* 108 [n.s. 42]: 371–2.

—— (1993), 'Response' [to Bringmann and Koenen], in Bulloch *et al*. (eds) (1993), 116–24.

——, Astin, A. E., Frederiksen, M. W., and Ogilvie, R. M. (eds) (1984), *The Cambridge Ancient History*², vii. 1: *The Hellenistic World*. Cambridge: CUP.

——, ——, ——, —— and Drummond, A. (eds) (1989), *The Cambridge Ancient History*², vii. 2: *The Rise of Rome to 220 BC*. Cambridge: CUP.

Waldmann, H. (1991), *Der kommagenische Mazdaismus* (DAI, Istanbuler Mitteilungen, 37). Tübingen: Wachsmuth.

Walker, C. (ed.) (1996), *Astronomy before the Telescope*. London: British Museum Press.

Walker, S. (1987), 'Roman nymphaea in the Greek world', in Macready and Thompson (eds) (1987), 60–71.

—— (1997), 'Athens under Augustus', in Hoff and Rotroff (eds) (1997), 67–80.

—— and Cameron, Averil (eds) (1989), *The Greek Renaissance in the Roman Empire* (Bulletin of the Institute of Classical Studies, supp. 55).

Wallace, R. W., and Harris, E. M. (eds) (1996), *Transitions to Empire: Essays in Greco-Roman History, 360–146 BC, in Honor of E. Badian* (Oklahoma Series in Classical Culture, 21). Norman, OK: Univ. of Oklahoma Press.

Walsh, K. (1992), *The Representation of the Past: Museums and Heritage in the Post-modern World*. London and New York: Routledge.

Walsh, P. G. (1990), *Livy: Book XXXVI (191 BC). Edited with an Introduction, Translation, and Commentary*. Warminster: Aris & Phillips.

—— (1992), *Livy: Book XXXVII (191–189 BC)*. *Edited with an Introduction, Translation, and Commentary.* Warminster: Aris & Phillips.

—— (1993), *Livy: Book XXXVIII (189–187 BC)*. *Edited with an Introduction, Translation, and Commentary.* Warminster: Aris & Phillips.

—— (1994), *Livy: Book XXXIX (187–183 BC)*. *Edited with an Introduction, Translation, and Commentary.* Warminster: Aris & Phillips.

—— (1996), *Livy: Book XL (182–179 BC)*. *Edited with an Introduction, Translation, and Commentary.* Warminster: Aris & Phillips.

Warren, J. A. W. (1983–5), 'The autonomous bronze coinage of Sicyon: part 1', *Numismatic Chronicle*, 143: 23–56; 'part 2', 144: 1–24; 'part 3', 145: 45–66.

—— (1993), 'Towards a resolution of the Achaian league silver coinage controversy: some observations on methodology', in M. Price *et al.* (eds) (1993), 87–99.

—— (1996), 'The Achaian league, Sparta, Lucullus: some late hellenistic coinages', in *Charaktir*, 297–308.

—— (1998), 'Updating (and downdating) the autonomous bronze coinage of Sikyon', in Ashton and Hurter *et al.* (eds) (1998), 347–61, pls 74–5.

—— (1999a), 'The Achaian league silver coinage controversy resolved: a summary', forthcoming in *Numismatic Chronicle*, 159.

—— (1999b), 'More on the "new landscape" in the late hellenistic coinage of the Peloponnese', forthcoming in *Mélanges de numismatique grecque en l'honneur de Georges Le Rider*.

Watson, J. S. (trans.), Miller, M. C. J. (ed.) (1992), *M. Junianus Justinus: Epitoma Historiarum Philippicarum, Books VII–XII. Excerpta de Historia Macedonia.* Chicago: Ares.

Weber, G. (1993a), *Dichtung und höfische Gesellschaft: die Rezeption von Zeitgeschichte am Hof der ersten drei Ptolemäer* (Hermes Einzelschriften, 62).

—— (1993b), 'Herrscher, Hof, und Dichter: Aspekte der Legitimierung und Repräsentation hellenistischer Könige am Beispiel der ersten drei Antigoniden', *Historia*, 44: 283–316.

Webster, J., and Cooper, N. J. (eds) (1996), *Roman Imperialism: Post-colonial Perspectives (Proceedings of a Symposium held at Leicester University in November 1994)* (Leicester Archaeology Monographs, 3; Leicester: University of Leicester, School of Archaeological Studies).

Wehrli, C. (1964), 'Phila, fille d'Antipater et épouse de Démétrius, roi des Macédoniens', *Historia*, 13: 140–6.

Weinberg, G. D. (1965), 'The Antikythera shipwreck reconsidered', *Transactions of the American Philosophical Society*, n.s. 55.3.

Welles, C. B. (1934), *Royal Correspondence in the Hellenistic Period: A Study in Greek Epigraphy.* New Haven, CT: Yale UP/London: Humphrey Milford, OUP/Prague: Kondakov Institute (repr. Chicago: Ares, 1974).

——, Fink, J. O., and Gilliam, J. F. (1959), *The Excavations at Dura-Europos: Final Report*, v. 1: *The Parchments and Papyri.* New Haven, CT: Yale UP.

Wells, B. (ed.) (1992), *Agriculture in Ancient Greece (Proceedings of the 7th International Symposium at the Swedish Institute at Athens, 16–17 May 1990)* (Skrifter utgivna av Svenska Institutet in Athen/Acta Instituti Atheniensis Regni Sueciae, series in 4°, 42). Stockholm: Swedish Institute at Athens/Åström.

Wells, R. (ed. and trans. 1988), *Theocritus: The Idylls* (Penguin Classics). London: Penguin.

West, M. L. (1993), *Greek Lyric Poetry: The Poems and Fragments of the Greek Iambic, Elegiac, and Melic Poets (excluding Pindar and Bacchylides) down to 450 BC* (The World's Classics). Oxford and New York: OUP.

West, S. (1967), *Ptolemaic Papyri of Homer* (Papyrologica Coloniensia, 3). Cologne: Westdeutscher Verlag.

—— (1969), 'The Greek version of the legend of Tefnut', *JEA* 55: 161–83.

—— (1984), 'Lycophron italicised', *JHS* 104: 127–51.

Westermann, W. L., and Hasenoerl, E. S. (eds) (1934), *Zenon Papyri: Business Papyri of the Third Century BC Dealing with Palestine and Egypt,* i (= *P. Col.* iii). New York: Columbia UP.

——, Keyes, C. W., and Liebesny, H. (eds) (1940), *Zenon Papyri: Business Papyri of the Third Century BC Dealing with Palestine and Egypt,* ii (= *P. Col.* iv). New York: Columbia UP.

Westlake, H. D. (1994), 'Dion and Timoleon', *CAH*² vi, ch. 13 (pp. 693–722).

White, K. D. (1970), *Greek and Roman Farming* (Aspects of Greek and Roman Life). London: Thames & Hudson.

—— (1984), *Greek and Roman Technology*. London: Thames & Hudson.

—— (1993), ' "The base mechanic arts"? Some thoughts on the contribution of science (pure and applied) to the culture of the hellenistic age', in Green (ed.) (1993), 211–20.

Whitehead, D. (1990), *Aineias the Tactician: How to Survive under Siege* (Clarendon Ancient History Series). Oxford: Clarendon.

—— (1994a), 'Site-classification and reliability in Stephanus of Byzantium', *CPC Papers 1*, 99–124.

—— (ed.) (1994b), *From Political Architecture to Stephanus Byzantius: Sources for the Ancient Greek Polis* (Papers from the Copenhagen Polis Centre, 1/Historia Einzelschriften, 87). Wiesbaden: Steiner.

Whitehorne, J. (1994), *Cleopatras*. London and New York: Routledge.

Wiesehöfer, J. (1996a), ' "Kings of kings" and "philhellên": kingship in Arsacid Iran', in Bilde *et al.* (eds) (1996a), 55–66.

—— (1996b) 'Discordia et defectio – dynamis kai pithanourgia: die frühen Seleukiden und Iran', in Funck (ed.) (1996a), 29–56.

—— (ed.) (1998), *Das Partherreich und seine Zeugnisse/The Arsacid Empire: Sources and Documentation. Beiträge des internationalen Colloquiums, Eutin (27–30. Juni 1996).* Stuttgart: Steiner.

Wikander, Ö. (1990), 'Water-power and technical progress in classical antiquity', in *Ancient Technology: Finnish Institute at Athens, Symposium held 30.3–4.4.1987* (Helsinki: Tekniikan museon julkaisuja [Museum of Technology]), 68–84.

Wilcken, U. (1912), *Grundzüge und Chrestomathie der Papyruskunde,* i. 2: *Chrestomathie*. Leipzig und Berlin: Teubner.

—— (1927–57), *Urkunden der Ptolemäerzeit (ältere Funde),* i (1927): *Papyri aus Unterägypten*; ii: *Papyri aus Oberägypten*. Berlin and Leipzig: de Gruyter.

Wilhelm, A. (1943), 'Beschluss zum Ehren des Demetrios ὁ μέγας', *ÖJh* 35: 157–63.

Wilkins, J., Harvey, D., and Dobson, M. (eds) (1995), *Food in Antiquity*. Exeter: Univ. of Exeter Press.

Will, E. ([1]1966, [2]1979–82), *Histoire politique du monde hellénistique (323–30 av. J.-C.)*, i–ii (Annales de l'est, mémoires 30; 32). Nancy: Université de Nancy II.

—— (1984a), 'The formation of the hellenistic kingdoms', *CAH*[2] vii. 1, ch. 4 (pp. 101–17).

—— (1984b), 'The succession to Alexander', *CAH*[2] vii. 1, ch. 2 (pp. 23–61).

Will, E. L. (1997), 'Shipping amphoras as indicators of economic romanization in Athens', in Hoff and Rotroff (eds) (1997), 117–33.

Willers, D. (1989), 'The redesigning of Athens under Hadrian (summary)', in Walker and Cameron (eds) (1989), 9.

Williams, R. (1981), *Culture* (Fontana New Sociology). London: Collins.

Winter, F. E. (1984), 'Building and townplanning', *CAH*[2] vii. 1, ch. 9 *d* (pp. 371–83).

—— (1992), 'Philon of Byzantium and the hellenistic fortifications of Rhodos', in van der Maele and Fossey (eds) (1992), ch. 10 (pp. 185–209).

Wissowa, G. *et al*. (eds) (1893–1981) *Paulys Real-Encyklopädie der klassischen Altertumswissenschaft*. Stuttgart: Metzler, etc.

Wörrle, M. (1975), 'Antiochos I., Achaios der Ältere und die Galater: eine neue Inschrift in Denizli', *Chiron*, 5: 59–87.

Wolski, J. (1984), 'Les Séleucides et l'héritage d'Alexandre le Grand en Iran', in Virgilio (ed.) (1984b), 9–20.

Woodcock, G. (1962), 'The Indian Greeks', *History Today*, 12: 558–76.

—— (1966), *The Greeks in India*. London: Faber & Faber.

Woodhead, A. G. ([1]1959, [2]1981), *The Study of Greek Inscriptions*[2]. [1, 2]Cambridge: CUP ([2]repr. London: Bristol Classical Press, 1992).

Woodruff, P. (1993), 'Response' [to Long], in Green (ed.) (1993), 157–62.

Woolf, G. (1994), 'Becoming Roman, staying Greek: culture, identity and the civilizing process in the Roman east', *Proceedings of the Cambridge Philological Society*, 220 [n.s. 40]: 116–43.

Worthington, I. (ed.) (1994a), *Ventures into Greek History*. Oxford: Clarendon.

—— (1994b), 'The Harpalus affair and the Greek response to the Macedonian hegemony', in Worthington (ed.) (1994a), 307–30.

Wright, J. C., Cherry, J. F., Davis, J. L., Mantzourani, E., Sutton, S. B., and Sutton, R. F., jun. (1990), 'The Nemea Valley Archaeological Project: a preliminary report', *Hesp*. 59: 579–659.

Wright, M. T. (1990), 'Rational and irrational reconstruction: the London sun-dial and the early history of geared mechanisms', *History of Technology*, 12: 65–102.

Wright, R. M. (1995), *Cosmology in Antiquity* (Sciences of Antiquity). London and New York: Routledge.

Wycherley, R. E. ([1]1949, [2]1962), *How the Greeks Built Cities*. [1, 2]London: Macmillan; [2]New York: Norton.

—— (1978), *The Stones of Athens*. Princeton, NJ: Princeton UP.

Yalouris, N. (1990), 'The shipwreck of Antikythera: new evidence of its date after supplementary investigation', in Descoeudres (1990a), 135–6.

Yardley, J. C. (trans.), and Develin, R. (ed.) (1994), *Justin: Epitome of the Philippic History of Pompeius Trogus* (American Philological Association Classical Resources, 3). Atlanta, GA: Scholars Press.

—— and Heckel, W. (1997), *Justin: Epitome of the Philippic History of Pompeius Trogus*, i: *Books 11–12: Alexander the Great* (Clarendon Ancient History Series). Oxford: Clarendon.

Yarshater, E. (ed.) (1983), *The Cambridge History of Iran*, iii: *The Seleucid, Parthian and Sasanian Periods* (2 vols, pp. consecutively numbered). Cambridge: CUP.

Young, T. C. (1988), 'The consolidation of the empire and its limits of growth under Darius and Xerxes', *CAH*^{2} iv, ch. 2 (pp. 53–111).

Zahle, J., Bilde, P., Engberg-Pedersen, T., and Hannestad, L. (eds) (1995), *Ideal og Virkelighed: mennesket i kunsten fra Alexander den Store til dronning Kleopatra* (Hellenismestudier, 11). [Copenhagen]: Statens Museum for Kunst/Aarhus Universitetsforlag.

Zangger, E., Timpson, M. E., Yazvenko, S. B., Kuhnke, F., and Knauss, J. (1997), 'The Pylos Regional Archaeological Project, part II: landscape evolution and site preservation', *Hesp.* 66: 549–641.

Zanker, P. (1993), 'The hellenistic grave stelai from Smyrna: identity and self-image in the polis', in Bulloch *et al.* (eds) (1993), 212–30.

INDEX OF SOURCES

For general references to authors, see the General Index. The citation of a translation does not necessarily imply that this is the version quoted. Abbreviations follow *OCD*³ with a few obvious exceptions.

An asterisk (*) indicates a quotation, however brief.

Aelian, *VH* (2. 20), 128*
Agatharchides (ap. Diod. 1. 41. 4–8), 362*
Ager, *Interstate Arbitrations*: (no. 13) 75 n. 30; (26) 80* n. 45; (67) 80 n. 43; (74) 80 n. 45; (92) 140 n. 93; (110) 80 n. 43; (159) 80 n. 44
Alexander Romance, (1. 4–11, 14; 2. 13–14, 32–3, 38–40; 3. 31), 251
Alexis (fr. 204 Kock), 345
Anadolu (9 (1965), 34–6), 81 n. 50
Anth. Pal.: (5. 199) 254*; (7. 710, 712) 103 n. 114; (9. 418) 332; (12. 135) 253*; (15. 21–2, 24–7) 248 n. 36
Antipater of Thessalonike (*Anth. Pal.* 9. 418), 332
Apollonios of Rhodes (3. 744–60), 255–6*
Appian: *B Civ.* (1), 318; *Ill.* (2. 7–8), 371; *Mac.* (fr. 4), 375
    Mith.: (15. 50–58. 240) 389; (21. 80) 389*; (22. 85–23. 91) 389; (26. 103–27. 105, 28. 109, 30. 118–38. 150) 390; (30. 121) 391; (38. 148–50) 391*; (41. 157) 391; (56. 227–58. 240, 61. 251) 392; (63. 261–3) 393*; (63. 261) 392; (64. 265–66. 281, 68. 289–113. 555, 83. 370–4) 394; (83. 376) 395; (92. 416–93. 427) 393; (92. 417) 393*; (94. 428–111. 539) 395; (115. 561–2) 396

Syr.: (38) 314; (47) 320 *bis*; (52–63) 304; (54) 43; (55) 61*; (57) 305*; (57–8) 61*; (58) 277*, 302*; (59–61) 71; (63) 312; (65) 65, 424 n. 32; (67) 321; (68–9) 322
Apuleius, *Met.* (8. 24–30), 168
Archilochos (fr. 196a W), 257
Archimedes, *Sand-reckoner*: (1) 352*; (1. 11) 351
Aristotle: *Cael.* (2. 13), 353; [*Oec.*] (2. 1. 2–4, 1345 a–b) 296–7*; (2. 2. 33. 1352 a–b) 201; *Pol.* (2. 6. 1265 b-1266 a) 102; (2. 8. 1267 b-1269 a) 89; (4. 1292 b 15) 35; (7. 11. 1330 b) 89; (9. 7. 1327 b 23–1328 a 33) 349*
Arrian: *Anab.* (1. 1. 2) 264; (1. 16. 5) 113*; (1. 17) 35; (1. 17) 48; (1. 9. 9–10) 36; (3. 1) 214*; (3. 6. 4–7, 18. 10–12) 37; (4. 7. 5) 39; (4. 10–12) 159; (4. 19. 5–6) 38; (5. 26. 1–2) 39; (5. 27. 5) 57; (5. 28–9. 1) 37; (6. 27. 3–5) 38; (7. 1. 1–4) 39; (7. 4. 4, 4. 4–8) 38; (7. 9) 109*; (7. 21. 6–7) 277*; (7. 26. 3) 40
    Indikê (40. 8) 303; *Ta meta Al.* (*FGH* 156): 7; (fr. 9. 34–8) 42
ASAA 45–6 (1967–8), 445–53 no. 2: 85 n. 71
Asklepiades, *Anth. Pal.*: (5. 207) 254*; (12. 135) 253*
Athenaeus: 1 (4) 240; (3 a–b) 391; (22

d) 241*; **4** (184 b–c) 366; **5** (193 d)
62; (194) 293*; (201 b–c) 345; (b–f)
68*; (203 d–e) 430; (203 e–204 d)
340*; (208 f) 332*; **6** (253 b–c) 160;
(d–f) 160–1*; (272 c) 128; **7** (302 e)
5*; **8** (335) 258; **10** (439 a) 62; (457
d–e) 258; **12** (521 b–e) 264; (536 e)
263–4*; (539 b–540 a) 264; (540
d–e) 344; **13** (590 a) 345; **14** (614
f–615 a) 48; (621 a) 185*; (d–e) 249;
(654 c) 345

Ath. Mitt.: (66 (1941), 221–7, no. 3) 65
n. 6; (72 (1957), 233–41 no. 64)
101* n. 106

Aulus Gellius (7. 17. 3), 235

Austin: (1) 265; (2) 36; (3 *a*) 113; (4)
35, 48; (5) 35; (7 *a*) 214*; (7 *b*)
214*; (9) 37; (11) 159; (12) 37;
(13–14) 38; (15) 109*; (16) 38, 54,
134; (17–18) 39; (19) 1, 302–3*;
(20) 174*; (21) 51*, 265*, 348; (22
a, 24) 7; (23) 122, 134; (24) 42; (25)
43; (26) 115, 128*; (27 a) 132; (28)
57; (29) 73–4*; (30) 43, 119; (31)
74*; (32) 156*; (33) 46; (34) 85,
160; (35) 160–1*; (36) 43, 63*; (37)
63*; (38) 187–8*; (39) 163; (40) 74;
(41) 122*; (42) 44, 132*, 138; (43)
48; (44) 123–4*; (45) 47, 264; (46)
61*, 302*, 304, 305*; (47 *b*) 67;
(48) 52–3*; (49) 126*; (50) 82, 126
(51) 126; (52) 134–6*; (53)
136–7*, 268; (54) 140; (55 *a*) 142;
(55 *b*) 144*; (56 *a*) 146; (56 *b*) 145;
(57) 145; (58) 149; (59) 372*; (60)
84*; (61) 372; (62 *a*) 373; (62 *b*)
373*; (63) 147; (64) 374 *bis*; (65–6)
375; (67) 341; (68) 375, 375* *bis*;
(69–70) 377; (71) 378; (72) 377;
(73–4) 378; (75) 380, 381; (76–7)
380; (78) 297; (79–80) 382; (81) 30;
(82) 385; (83) 29–30*, 148; (84–5)
30; (86) 81; (87) 82*; (88–9) 82;
(90) 132*; (91) 132; (92) 89; (93)
85; (94) 106; (95) 82; (96) 106;
(97–8) 99
(100–1) 84; (102–3) 85; (104) 21;
(105) 21; (106) 26; (107) 382;
(108–9) 36; (110) 99; (111) 36,
385–6*; (112) 100; (113) 99,
159–60*; (114–16) 100; (117) 126;
(118–20) 87; (121–2) 171; (123)

163; (124) 100–1*; (125) 101*;
(126) 164*; (127–30) 175; (131)
169; (132–3) 82–3; (135) 78–9*;
(136) 80; (137) 384; (138) 265;
(138) 271; (139) 65*, 287*, 301*;
(140) 53; (142) 53, 323; (143) 134;
(144) 290; (145) 282; (146) 290;
(147) 76; (148–9) 204; (150) 51,
291
(151) 81; (152) 208; (153–4) 376;
(155) 376*; (156) 85; (157) 81;
(158) 158; (159–61) 377; (162) 292;
(163 *a–b*) 62; (164) 292; (165) 209*;
(166) 260–1*; (167) 296*, 298*,
299*, 307; (168) 308*, 309, 309*,
310*; (169) 321; (171) 168, 393;
(172) 311; (174) 288*, 304; (175–6)
77; (177) 158; (178) 297–8*; (179)
303; (180) 299–300*; (181) 300;
(182) 77–8*; (183) 75–6*; (184)
306; (185) 300; (186) 301*; (187)
300; (188) 277; (189) 295*; (190)
57; (191) 283*; (192) 269; (193–4)
312; (195) 314; (195 *a*) 85*; (196)
58, 313; (197) 312; (198) 314, 375;
(199) 61, 314
(200–1) 377; (202) 301*; (203)
317; (204) 73; (205) 317; (206) 86*;
(207) 61; (208) 317*; (209) 374;
(210 *a–b*) 318; (211) 319*; (212)
189, 310; (213) 319; (214) 319;
(215) 102; (216) 36; (217) 61, 202,
238; (218) 139*, 159, 202; (219)
68*, 340, 345; (220–1) 203; (222)
166, 203; (223) 205–6*, 290; (224)
57, 204; (225 *a*) 204*; (225 *b*) 204;
(226) 207; (227) 166, 204; (228)
210; (229) 209–10*; (230) 210;
(231) 211*; (232) 215, 215*, 241*;
(233) 214; (234) 217; (235) 225* *bis*;
(236) 226; (237) 228*; (238) 26;
(239) 166; (240) 226–7*; (241)
226*, 265; (242) 195; (244) 217;
(245) 220*; (246) 196; (247) 227;
(248) 229; (249–50) 230
(251) 230–1*; (252) 217; (253)
226, 231; (254) 225; (255) 270;
(256) 224*; (257) 221*; (258–9)
232; (260) 223; (261) 165; (262)
265; (263) 194; (264) 347*; (265–6)
195; (267) 205; (268) 202; (269)
205; (270–3) 205 & n. 42; (274–5)

203; (276) 67; (277) 194*; (278–9) 214

Bagnall and Derow, *see* BD
BCH: (9 (1885), 405 no. 16) 163* n. 24; (82 (1958), 74–7) 80 n. 48; (92 (1968), 359–74) 169*; (99 (1975), 51–75) 126 n. 51
BD: (2) 35; (3) 100; (6) 74*, 156*; (7) 74; (8) 44, 132*, 138; (9) 84; (12) 48, 80*; (13) 48; (16) 65*, 287*, 301*; (17) 52–3*; (18) 299–300*; (19) 126*; (20) 134; (21) 205 (& n. 42); (22) 75–6*; (23) 58; (25) 300; (26–7) 203; (28) 80–1*; (29) 77–8*; (30) 140; (31) 84*; (32) 373*; (33) 376*; (38) 377; (40) 297
   (41) 317; (42) 317*; (43) 210; (45) 211*; (63) 100; (64) 99, 159–60*; (65) 87; (67) 85*; (68) 223; (71) 227; (84) 26; (85) 224*; (87) 81, 226, 231; (93) 229; (95) 225* *bis*, 226; (103–4) 230; (114) 220*; (115) 221*; (127) 87; (128) 306; (131) 158*; (132) 77; (136) 166, 203; (137) 166, 204
Berossos (1. 1. 5), 11*
BGU (no. 1842), 232 n. 123
Biton, *Constructions* (pp. 66–77 Marsden), 336 & n. 30
Bogaert, *Epigraphica* (iii, no. 36), 300 n. 96
Boswinkel–Pestman, *Archives privées de Dionysios* (164–71, no. 11), 218* & n. 77
Bruneau, *Recherches*: (459) 169* n. 42; (466–7) 169* n. 44
Bull. Ép.: (1971, 621) 86 n. 71; (1976, 667) 323 n. 168; (1978, 274) 87 n. 76
Burstein: (2) 306; (5) 122; (7) 160–1*; (11) 48; (12) 48, 80*; (15) 65*, 287*, 301*; (16, 19) 53; (21) 299–300*; (23) 75–6*; (24) 300; (29) 296*, 299*; (30) 87; (32) 57; (33) 81; (35) 296, 298*, 299*, 307; (36) 85; (38) 292; (42) 310; (43) 311*; (44) 311; (45) 104*; (46) 265; (46 c) 37*; (48) 396*; (49) 270; (50) 285*; (51 c (a)) 283*; (55) 123–4*; (56) 126*; (65) 84*; (66) 378; (68) 99; (72) 152; (75) 383; (80) 80; (85)

312; (88) 317; (89) 86*; (91) 319*; (92) 139*, 159, 202; (94) 225; (95) 205 (& n. 42); (98–9) 203; (100) 205 (& n. 42); (101) 224*; (102) 169; (103) 166, 204; (104) 210; (105) 366; (106) 233

Callimachus, *see* Kallimachos
Cassius Dio: (bks 36–7) 395; (50. 15. 2) 172 & n. 56*
Catullus (63), 168
Celsus, *De medicina, prooem.* (23–4, 26), 347–8*
Cercidas (fr. 2), 184*
Chiron (5 (1975), 59–87), 53 n. 45, 323 n. 168
Choix: (31) 269; (48) 100; (50) 100; (55) 152*; (75) 163
Chrysippos (ap. Ath. 8. 335), 258
Cicero: *Att.* (6. 1. 25, 6. 6. 2) 398; *Fam.* (4. 5) 398; *Fin.* (5. 1) 398; *Rep.* (1. 14. 21–2) 331; *Verr.* (2. 1. 44–5, 2. 4. 71) 398
CIG (2256), 80 n. 43
Columella, *RR* (1. 8), 344
C. Ord. Ptol.: (21–2) 203; (33) 195 n. 11; (73) 232 n. 123
CRAI: (1968, 422, 424) 270 n. 101; (1978, 456–60) 269 n. 100
Curtius: 10. 1. 17–18: 39

Daniel: (11: 31) 310 n. 128*; (11: 39) 310
Demetrios of Phaleron (*FGH* 228) (fr. 39), 174*
Demochares (*FGH* 75) (fr. 2), 160
Demosthenes, *Against Phormion* (§6), 131; [*Or.* 56] (§7) 201
Dio Chrysostom, *Or.* 34 (21–3), 278
Diodorus Siculus: 1 (21. 7) 196; (25) 165, 168; (31. 6–8) 215*; (34) 332; (41. 4–8) 362*; (73. 2–3, 6, 7) 196; 2 (35–42) 261; (55–60) 188; (57. 1, 2. 58. 1) 188–9*; 3 (12. 1–3) 194; (36–7) 214; (38) 264; 5 (37) 332; 6 (1. 4, 6) 187–8*; 16 (31 and 34) 114*; 17 251; (14) 36; (16) 115; (52. 6) 215; (70–2) 37; (99. 5–6) 284; (109) 54; (111) 55
   18 (4. 4) 39; (7. 1–2) 284*; (7. 5–9) 284; (8) 38, 54, 134; (14) 201;

(16. 3, 22. 1) 46; (29–19. 44, *passim*)
46; (37. 5) 42; (39. 5–7, 48–50) 42;
(55) 73*; (55–7) 120; (56) 73*;
(60–1) 46; (61) 162*; (61. 2) 46*;
(68) 120

    19 (5–31. 17, *passim*) 51; (9) 132;
(9. 4) 51; (11. 3–7) 118–19*; (11. 8)
119; (27) 57; (44) 46; (51. 4–5)
119*; (52) 119; (58. 2–5) 278; (61)
73–4*; (68. 5–7) 46; (90) 162 n. 19;
(92) 286; (98) 278; (100) 286; (105)
43, 119

    20 (1) 268*; (37) 121; (40) 132*;
(45–6) 121; (48. 2–3, 6–7) 338; (53.
2–3) 43; (54. 1) 51*; (73) 57; (91.
2–6) 338–9*; (95. 1–2) 340; (95. 5,
96. 4, 7, 99. 1) 340; (100) 163; (102)
112*; (111) 51

    31 (frs 15 a, 17 b) 210; (16) 62;
(19. 6–8) 320; (19. 8) 240; (27a, 32)
320; **32** (9d, 10. 1) 321; 321; **33** (4)
321; **34/35** (5. 1) 310; **40** (2) 307 n.
120; (3) 260–1*

Diogenes Laërtios: (2. 113–20) 185; (4.
46, 54) 240; (4. 53) 185*; (5. 37)
344; (5. 42–50) 328; (5. 75–85) 179;
(6. 22–80) 184; (6. 96–8) 103*; (7.
6) 240; (7. 32–3) 186*; (7. 129)
186*; (8. 86–91) 351; (9. 103) 180*;
(10. 121–35) 182; (10. 125) 182*;
(10. 131–2) 182*

Douris (*FGH* 76) (fr. 13), 160–1*

Edelstein–Edelstein, *Asclepius*, i (221–38
no. 423), 164* n. 28

Engelmann–Merkelbach, *Inschr. v.
Erythrai u. Klazomenai*, ii (504), 134
n. 81

Ἐφ.ἀρχ. (1886, 57 no. 18), 171* n. 54

Epigraphica Anatolica (29 (1997), 3–4),
315–16*, cf. 309

Euclid, *Elements*: (1) 356*; (12. 2) 357*

Eusebios, *Praep. Evang.* (14. 18. 758
c–d), 180*

FGH: (160) 203; (275 *a*) 122; (63 fr. 2)
187–8*

Frontinus (3. 2. 11), 424 n. 32

Galen: (8. 212, 8. 605 Kühn): 348 n.
65; (8. 723–4, 869, 871) 348 n. 66;
(12. 252, 14. 2) 345 n. 55; *On Habits*
(1) 364*

GMW: (i. 3–5) 352*; (437–9) 356*;
(459–61) 357*; (ii. 20) 337; (21)
332*; (35) 332*; (261) 327* n. 8;
(271–3) 361* n. 97; (485–97) 351 n.
72; (489–97) 359; (615) 330*;
(617–19) 331*

Gow–Page, *Greek Anthology*: Asclepiades
(vii) 254*; Callimachus (xxxiv) 254*
n. 49

Grayson, *Assyrian and Babylonian
Chronicles*: (no. 10) 265 n. 84; (12)
287* n. 61

Harding: (1) 265; (1 *a*) 51*; (54) 134;
(116) 100; (120) 37; (123) 115; (123
a) 128*; (126) 347*; (132) 74*;
(138) 44, 132*

Hatzopoulos, *Macedonian Institutions*, ii:
(no. 12) 378 n. 35; (36, 41, 47, 58)
112 n. 12; (60) 87 n. 76

Hedylos (*Anth. Pal.* 5. 199), 254*

Hekataios of Abdera (*FGH* 264) (fr. 6),
260–1*

Herakleides Kretikos (Müller, *GGM* i.
97–110): (1. 1–2) 148; (1. 8–9, 12)
29–30*

Herodas, *Mimes*: (2–4) 249; (6. 12–19)
249–50*; (6. 74–84) 250*; (8) 250

Herodotos: (1. 66. 1) 158; (2. 154) 217;
(2. 61) 168; (2. 67) 269 n. 98; (3.
89–95) 294; (4. 42) 361; (5. 20)
111*; (5. 52) 297; (5. 58) 239; (6.
119) 281; (9. 121) 272

Heron, *Dioptra*: (3) 351; (23) 351 n. 72;
(37) 351 n. 72, 359; *Pneumatika*
(proem, 16. 23–4) 332

Herophilos: (ap. Galen 8. 723–4, 869,
871 Kühn) 348 n. 66; (π. σφυγμῶν)
348 n. 66

Herzog–Klaffenbach, *Asylieurkunden*
(nos 6–7), 112 n. 12

Hippokrates: (i. 299–301 Loeb) 349* n.
69; *Airs, Waters, Places* (16 and 23),
349 & n. 70

Holleaux, *Études*: (ii. 73–125) 377 n.
33; (iii. 27–37) 202 n. 30; (v.
141–55) 376* n. 25

Horos (5 (1987), 91–3), *Fig. 1.2*

Hypereides, *Epitaphios* (6. 21), 159*

I. Cret.: (i. 60–1 no. 6) 82 n. 53; (i. 62, no. 7) 101* n. 105; (ii. 84–8, no. 1) 132 n. 76; (iii. 4. 18) *Fig. 1.3*; (iii. 31–6 no. 31 *a*) 82 n. 56; (iii. 83–5, no. 4) 205 n. 40; (iii. 89–91, no. 8) 132* n. 75; (iv. 222–5, no. 162) 21 n. 40

I. Délos: (509) 36 n. 8; (1510) 383 n. 48; (1719, 2308–9, 2311, 2315, 2318, 2320–1) 169

I. Didyma (479), 306 n. 117

IG: (ii² 447–8) 116 n. 23; (448) 128* n. 63; (657) 48 n. 29; (665) 126 n. 53; (687) 126* n. 50; (844. 1) 82 n. 55; (1013) 36 n. 8, 385–6*; (1685) 87; (2313–14) 103 n. 115; (2499) 175 n. 64; (3426–7) 398; (4122) 172 & n. 56; (4123) 172 n. 57
　(iv² 1. 71) 80 n. 46, (121–2) 164* n. 28; (v. 2. 118) 171 n. 52, (344) 140 n. 94; (vii. 411) 384 n. 49, (4263) 84 n. 66; (ix. 1² 241), 373* n. 17; (ix. 2. 517) 84*, (526) 103 n. 115; (xi. 2. 161 *a*), 21 n. 34; (xi. 4. 1064) 140, (1102) 152* n. 121, (1299) 169 n. 41; (xii. 3. 327) 195 n. 11, (443) 163; (xii. 5. 129), 99 n. 101; (xii. 7. 386), 82* n. 54; (xii. 8. 156), 205 n. 41; (xii, suppl. 348), 36 n. 8

IGLS: (iii. 2. 992) 77 n. 37; (iii. 2. 1183) 77 n. 37; (iii. 2. 1184) 158 n. 9; (vii. 4028 c) 298* n. 87; (vii. 4028 d) 298* n. 89

IGRR (iv. 301), 319 n. 150

I. Lampsakos (4), 376* n. 25

I. Olympia (52), 80

I. Priene: (37) 265; (208) 105 n. 120

Iraq (16 (1954), 202–11), 265 n. 82

ISE: (7) 65, *Fig. 1.1*; (28) 149; (ii. 114) 378; (ii. 130) 85; (ii. 131) 99; (ii. 199) 85; (ii. 74) 80

Isokrates (*Letters*, 2–3) 55; (9, *To Archidamos*) 55; (*Paneg.*) 55, (167–8) 55–6*, (96, 120–1) 56; (*Philip*) 55; (*To Philip 1, 2*) 55

JEA (60 (1974), 239–42), 166 & n. 35, *Fig. 5.1*

Jerome, *On Daniel* (ad 8. 14–15, 11. 31), 310

Johannes Tzetzes: (*Book of Histories*, ii. 130) 332*; (*Chil.* 2. 118–27) 337

Josephus: *AJ* 12 (140–1 307; (142–4) 298*; (148–53) 296*; (148–53) 299*; (151) 298; (175) 67; (258–63) 310; 13 (109–16) 320; 14 (29–79, 91) 396; *BJ* 1 (34) 310; (127–57, 170) 396

Journal asiatique (246 (1958), 1–48), 285* n. 52

Justin: (9. 2) 115*; (15. 2. 10–12) 43; (24. 1) 125; (24. 6) 53; (27. 3. 1) 9; (36. 1. 10) 311, 321*; (36. 4. 3) 345; (37. 2) 387–8*; (39–40) 322

Kallimachos: *Aitia* (fr. 110. 47–56) 244*; *Anth. Pal.* (7. 80) 254*; (fr. 28 Pfeiffer): 255*; *Hymn* 1 (*To Zeus*) (15–33) 244–5*

Kallixeinos (ap. Ath. 5. 201 b–c), 345

Kerkidas (fr. 2), 184*

Klearchos of Soloi (ap. Ath. 10. 457 d–e), 258

Kleomedes, *On the Circular Motion of the Heavenly Bodies* (1. 10. 52), 361*

Kock, *CAF*: (ii. 372) 345; (ii. 490) 345

Ktesikles (*FGH* 245) (fr. 1), 128

Laronde, *Cyrène* (30–4), 100 n. 102

Lefkowitz and Fant: (nos 9–10) 103; (43) 103*; (45–7) 103; (48) 104*; (49) 104*

Libanius, *Oration* 11 (101), 304*

Lichtheim, *Ancient Egyptian Literature*, iii: (55) 222*; (48) 222*

Lindian Chronicle (*FGH* 532): 265; (ch. 38) 37*

Livy: **26** (24. 7–15) 373; **27** (30. 4–6) 150; 29 (12. 11–16) 374; (12. 14) 374; **31** (2) 375; (14. 7–10) 150; (16. 2) 150; (24. 4–25. 2) 150; (44. 2–9) 150, 375; (45. 7) 314; **32** (1–7) 381–2; (22. 10) 373*; **33** (38) 376; **34** (57–9) 376; **35** (33. 8) 377*; 37 (2) 378; (40–4) 377; **38** (16. 14) 313; (34) 378; **39** (23. 5) 378; (24. 1–4) 378; (25–9) 378; (35–7) 378; (37. 19) 378*; **41** (19. 4) 380; (20) 62; (23–4) 379; (25) 380; **42** (5. 3) 315*; (6. 7) 292; (11–13) 380; (15–17) 380; (29) 380; (30. 1–7)

381; (39–42) 380; (47) 380; (47. 9) 380*; (51) 380; (58–61) 380; (62) 380; (63. 11–12) 382; **43** (4. 8–13) 381; **44** (29. 3–30) 381; **44** (43. 1) 109

Lykophron, *Alexandra* (648–58), 247–8*

I Maccabees: (1) 310; (1: 10–14) 308*; (1: 20–36) 309; (1: 41) 309*; (1: 44–50) 309*; (1: 54) 310*; (10: 1) 320; (10: 15–20) 311; (10: 29–30) 298–9*; (11: 1–13) 320; (12: 1–23) 266–7*; (14: 16–23) 267; (14: 40) 321; (15: 1–9) 311

II Maccabees: (2: 21) 308; (3: 4–40) 292; (4: 7–14) 308*; (4: 13) 308*; (4: 26–5: 27) 309; (5: 5) 309; (5: 9) 267; (6) 310; (6: 1–2) 310; (8: 22–32) 311; (11: 22–6) 311*; (11: 27–33) 311; (11: 34–8) 320

Malalas (pp. 206–7 Dindorf), 310

Manethon: (fr. 54) 12; (fr. 75 a–c) 12*

Marmor Parium, see *Parian Marble*

Memnon (*FGH* 434) (fr. 11), 53

Memnon of Herakleia (*FGH* 336), 394

Menander: *Perikeiromene* (239–43) 258*; *Sikyonian* (3–15) 81

Menekles of Barka (*FGH* 270) (fr. 9), 366

ML (no. 12), 344

Moretti, *Iscrizioni agonistiche greche*, no. 41: 171 n. 51

Moretti, *ISE*, see *ISE*

Mus. Helv. (48 (1991), 252–80), 385 n. 52

Nepos, *De regibus* (3. 1–4), 14*

Nicander, *Theriaka* (345–53), 248

Nikam–McKeon (*Edicts of Aśoka*), 285* n. 52

OGIS: (5) 74*; (6) 156*; (13) 48, 80*; (39) 340*; (43) 202; (46) 84; (48) 214; (54) 203; (55) 205 & n. 42; (56) 166, 203; (59) 195; (86) 214; (90) 166, 204; (165) 206; (213) 306; (219) 65*, 287*, 301*; (221) 299–300*; (222) 134; (223) 75–6*; (224) 158*; (225) 300; (227) 301*; (228) 80–1*; (229) 77–8*; (231)

306; (233) 57; (244) 77; (245) 158; (248) 292; (266) 58, 313; (267) 314; (267 i) 85*; (273–9) 312; (308) 73; (311) 163*; (315 c vi) 317*; (326) 163; (329) 374; (331 ii–iv) 318; (332) 157*; (338) 319*; (339) 102; (367) 163*; (383) 396*; (435) 319; (483) 36; (748) 312; (751, 763) 317

Orosius: (5. 9. 5) 382; (6. 15. 31–2) 235

P. Amherst (ii. 30), 221

Pappos, *Collection*: (8, preface, 2), 331*; (8. 1–2) 330*; (8. 11. 19) 332*

Parian Marble (*FGH* 239): 265; (B 12) 51*; (B 19) 348

Pausanias: **1** (3. 5–4. 6) 54; (6. 1) 268; (6. 3) 201; (8. 6) 163; (9–10) 47; (9. 8) 264; (10. 3–4) 50*; (20. 5) 390; (25) 122, 134; (25. 2) 172 n. 56 (25. 4) 443 n. 56; **2** (8. 6) 87; (18. 6) 149; **4** (6) 269; **6** (9. 6) 269 n. 98; **7** (8. 6, 9. 1, 9. 5) 378; (11. 1–3) 383; (11. 4–7. 12. 9, 13. 2–8, 14. 1–15. 1, 14. 5–6, 15. 4–6) 384; (16. 1, 4) 385; (16. 8) 318, 385 bis; (16. 9) 385*; (16. 10) 385; **9** (7. 5) 391; **10** (19. 4–23. 7) 54; (21. 5–6) 391

P. Col. (54), 217

P. Col. Zen. (66), 220*

PCZ: (59012) 228*; (59021) 26; (59033) 344; (59034) 166; (59155, 59195, 59430) 344; (59541) 196; (59782a) 332; (59816) 226*; (59849, 59851) 332

Peek, *Griechische Versinschriften*, i (no. 1881), 104* n. 119

P. Enteuxeis: (no. 8) 270; (119–21, no. 48) 218–19*

Petracos, *Amphiareion*: (no. 19) 171*; (20) 171*

P. Graf (29787), 233 n. 126

P. Gr. Rein. (18), 218*

P. Hib.: (81) 217; (98) 229 n. 113; (110) 227 n. 108; (199) 160*

Philemon (fr. 47 Kock), 345

Philochoros (*FGH* 328) (fr. 163), 37

Philon: *Belopoiika* (50. 14–26) 336*, (67. 28–72. 23) 336; *On the Seven Wonders of the World* (4), 44

Philostratos, *Lives of the Sophists* (2. 5. 4), 172

Phylarchos (*FGH* 81) (fr. 40) 263–4*;

(41) 264
Pindar, *Ol.* (12), 173
Plato, *Rep.* (1. 327 a 1–3), 165
P. L. Bat. (22, no. 11), 218*
Pliny the Elder, *HN*: (2. 162) 360; (4.
10. 37) 188 n. 87; (5. 9) 363; (5. 58)
232 n. 123; (6. 26. 103, 33. 168)
194 n. 5; (6. 49) 284; (8. 191) 281;
(11. 75) 277; (13. 13. 53) 361; (13.
17) 239; (13. 73) 277; (indexes to
bks 14–15, 18), 344; (18. 97) 332;
(25. 6. 28. 64, 8. 55. 99) 345; (34.
41) 44; (36. 45) 391
P. Lond. (no. 1948) 345*; (1954)
226–7*
Plutarch *Aem.* (28. 6), 240; *Ages.* (21. 8),
249; *Agis* (5) 142; (8) 144*; (13)
144; (20) 102*; *Alex.* (10. 6–11) 36;
(15) 113; (26) 214*; (64) 67; *Ant.*
(58) 235; (60. 4, 6) 172 & n. 56*,
382; *Arat.* (4. 3, 9. 3–4, 11. 2) 137;
(17. 2) 138; (34) 149; (39. 8) 145;
Cato the Elder (9), 383
  Demetr. (10) 85, 121, 160; (12)
123; (12. 4) 161; (18) 63*; (18. 1)
43 *bis*; (20) 345*; (24) 122; (25. 4–6)
48; (26) 122; (26. 3) 161; (27)
130–1; (29) 44; (30. 4) 122; (33–4,
34) 123; (38) 71; (41–2) 120; (43)
123; (49. 7–8) 123
  Education of Children (11 a), 185*;
Erotikos, 106 & n. 125; *Eum.* (2) 264;
(5. 3, 7. 1) 58; (11) 67*; (12. 2) 58;
(13) 162*; *Face on the Moon* (923 a),
353; *Fortune or Courage of Alexander*, i
(328 c–f), 1, 302–3*; *Isis and Osiris*
(28), 165
  Kleom. (1) 102–3*, 144; (2) 144;
(11) 145; (13) 146; (16–17, 20) 145;
(23) 147; (38) 146; (39) 146*; (39.
1) 102*; *Lives of the Ten Orators* (841
f) 243 & n. 19; (846 a–b) 37; *Luc.*
(2–4) 389; (7–35, 11–12, 19) 394;
(20) 395; (23) 394; *Marc.* (14. 4)
330*; (14. 7–9) 332; (15. 1–17. 3)
336; (17. 4) 330*
  Pelopidas (2), 127; *Platonic
Questions* (1006 c), 353*; *Pompey*,
395; (27. 3) 398; *Praising Oneself
Inoffensively* (545 b), 127; *Precepts of
Statecraft* (821 d–f), 285 & n. 55;

Publicola (15. 4), 391; *Pyrrh.* (14) 67;
(21) 265
  Quaestiones conviviales (9. 1. 1, 736
d), 87; *Sayings of Kings and Emperors*
(183 c), 127; *Sull.* (11–14) 389;
(13–14) 390; (24) 389; (24–5) 392;
Ti. Gracch., 318
P. Mich. Zen. (84), 165
Polyainos (4. 2. 12), 115*
Polybios: **1** (1. 5) 369*; (3. 3) 16–17*;
(7–9) 52; (22. 3) 336; **2** (2–12) 371;
(37–8) 136–7*; (40) 268; (46, 47,
48–50, 49) 145; (54) 146, 138;
(56–63) 263; (63–71) 268; (65) 138;
(65–9) 146; (70) 146 *bis*, 174*; (71)
290; **3** (19) 372; **4** (9) 138; (25–6)
149; (38, 46. 5–47. 6) 106; (48) 290;
(48. 1–3, 48. 11) 314; (73. 5–74. 2)
30; **5** (34) 205–6*, 290; (39) 146*;
(41) 76; (43. 1) 387*; (63) 204;
(63–5) 57; (65, 67) 204; (77–8) 314;
(79) 204; (80–6) 268; (87) 204;
(88–90) 85; (101) 77; (103–6) 372*;
(106. 6–8) 149*; (107) 204*; (107.
4) 314; **7** (9) 372; (14. 6) 77
  10 (15) 373*; (45–6) 334; **11** (34)
51; (34. 1–10) 291; **12** 262–3; (11)
263; **13** (6) 147; **14** (12) 204; **15**
(20) 207; (21–3) 374; (24) 75*; (25.
3–18) 207; (26–36) 208; (33. 6–10)
208*; (34–5) 77; **16** (1) 374–5;
(2–10) 374; (25–6) 314, 375; (27. 1)
150; (27. 2–3) 375; (28) 61*; (30–1)
375; **18** (11. 5) 113*; (16) 156;
(19–27) 375; (28–32) 341; (33) 264;
(41) 61, 313; (41. 7–8) 313; (44. 2)
375*; (44–5, 46. 1) 375; (46. 5)
375*; (47) 375; (49–51) 376; **20** (6.
1) 30 n. 61; (6. 1–6) 30; (9–10) 377
  21 (17. 6) 314; (22–3, 32, 43, 46)
377; **22** (4. 5) 378; (5) 377; (6) 378;
(8. 10) 374; (10) 378; (15) 80 n. 43;
(18. 10) 378; **23** (4) 378; (9. 8–10)
378; (17. 3) 378; (17. 4) 378–9*; **24**
9. 5) 379*; (10. 4–5) 379*; (10. 8)
379*; **25** (2. 12–13) 316; (3. 1)
380*; (4. 5–7) 379–80*; (4. 8) 380;
26 (1 a–2) 62; **27** (8) 380; (9. 1)
381*; (13) 205 n. 42; **29** (19. 5) 382;
(21) 174*; (22) 317; (27) 292; **30**
(1–3) 317; (2) 67*; (3. 7–9) 317;
(10. 1–9) 382; (19. 12) 317; (20. 7)

382; (25–6) 293*; (28, 30. 6) 317;
(31, 31. 9–12) 382
    31 (2) 320; (2. 7) 320; (3, 5) 320;
(6. 6) 317; (10) 209–10*; (18) 320;
32 (7) 383; (8) 61; (10) 320; (11.
5–7) 384; (13) 383; **34** (5–7) 363;
(5. 3) 363*; (5. 7) 363*; **35** (6) 383;
36 (17. 5–10) 30; **38** (12. 4–5) 384*;
(14. 3) 384; **39** (2) 385; (7) 321
Poseidonios (*FGH* 87): (fr. 28) 326; (35)
382; (36) 390; (fr. 49 E–K) 326
P. Oxy.: (2082) 103 n. 115; (2332) 233
n. 126; (3777) *Fig. 6.2*
P. Rainer (19.813), 233 n. 126
Praxagoras (fr. 10), 346 n. 58
P. Rev.: (col. 24) 225*; (33) 226; (37)
225*
Pritchard, *Ancient Near Eastern Texts*
(317), 295* n. 81
Proclus, *Outline of the Astronomical
Hypotheses* (4), 351
Procopius, *On Buildings* (4. 3. 27), 109
Ps.-Callisthenes (1. 4–3. 31 *passim*), 251
PSI: (1098) 232 n. 123; (488) 195 n. 7
Ps.-Lykophron, *Alexandra* (648–58),
247–8*
Ps.-Rufus, *Anat.* (71–4, pp. 184–5
Ruelle), 348 n. 65
P. Tebt.: (5) 211*; (8) 195 n. 10; (9–11)
223 n. 93; (758) 225; (786) 232 n. 122
Ptolemy: *Alm.* (5. 1, 12, 14) 351; (7. 1)
351; *Geog.* (4. 5. 66) 214 n. 67;
Syntaxis (4. 2. 270–1) 364; *Tetr.* (1.
2. 4) 354–5*, 355; (1. 2. 5) 355; (2.
2. 55–8) 350*

Ray, *Archive of Ḥor*: (14–20, no. 2r) 209*
& n. 51, *Fig. 6.3*; (20–9, no. 3) 209
n. 51
RC: (1) 74*; (3–4) 74; (7) 48, 80*; (9)
77*; (13) 299–300*; (14) 205 & n.
42, 424 n. 32; (15) 75–6*; (18–20)
300; (22) 301*; (23) 85*, 314; (30)
205 & n. 42; (31) 306; (36) 158*;
(37) 158*; (44–5) 77; (52, 54) 317;
(61) 77*, 317*; (66–7) 318; (70)
297–8*
RDGE: (2) 297 n. 86; (5) 383 n. 48;
(11) 319 n. 150; (34) 81 n. 51; (35)
377; (40) 380 n. 39; (43) 221
Rigsby, *Asylia*: (55–9 no. 1) 80 n. 48;
(102–5 no. 7) 80–1* n. 49; (pp.

281–2) 81 n. 50; (314–16 no. 153)
81 n. 51
Rizakis, *Achaïe* i (126–7 no. 167) 373*
n. 18
Robert, *Hellenica*: (vii. 5–22) 158 n. 7;
(xi–xii. 85–91) 166*
Robert–Robert: *La Carie*, ii (285–302 no.
166) 300 n. 97; *Claros*, i (13) 189 n. 90

Sanders, *Nemrud Dağı*, i (207–17), 396
n. 70
Sappho (fr. 31), 255
Sardis, vii. 1: (1) 300 n. 96; (111) 104*
n. 119
SEG: (i. 363) 21, 78–9*, (366) 99,
159–60*; (ii. 663) 377 n. 33; (vii.
17) *Fig. 1.4*; (ix. 1) 347*, (2) 100, (7)
210 n. 55; (xii. 373–4) 112; (xiii. 21)
36 n. 9; (xv. 293) 261, (717) 74 n.
29; (xvi. 452) 169*; (xviii. 240) 80;
(xx. 325) 166*; (xxiii. 491) 140;
(xxiv. 154) 126, (1158) 169 n. 41;
(xxv. 149) *Fig. 1.1*; (xxvi. 1226) 86
n. 71; (xl. 735, xlii. 776) 100 n. 104
Sel. Pap.: ii (no. 409) 26 n. 45, (203)
226 n. 105, (339) 223 n. 93, (346)
195 n. 7, (365) 229 n. 113, (397)
227 n. 108, (414) 225 n. 101; (iii.
120) 103 n. 114
Seneca: *Tranq.* (9. 5) 235; *Med.* (375) 327*
Sextus, *Math.* (7. 183), 181*
SGDI: (1854) 175 n. 63; (2143) 175 n.
63; (5040) 80 n. 43
Shear, *Kallias of Sphettos*, 124*
Sherk: (8) 81; (14) 377; (19) 380; (21) 297;
(28) 383; (29) 317*; (39) 319*; (40)
319; (44) 319; (50) 221; (55) 376*
Smith, *Babylonian Historical Texts*
(150–9), 265 n. 83
Sokolowski: *Lois sacrées de l'Asie Mineure*
(no. 15) 319 n. 155; *Lois sacrées des
cités grecques* (no. 80) 86* n. 72
Sotades (fr. 1 Powell), 185* n. 81
Staatsv. iii: (428) 74* n. 26; (429) 46 n.
25; (446) 44 n. 22, 132* n. 74; (469)
53 n. 44; (476) 126* n. 50; (481) 58 n.
60, 313 n. 136; (482) 82 n. 53; (499)
140 n. 94; (507) 149; (536) 373*
n. 17; (545) 83 n. 59; (551) 82 n. 56
Steph. Byz. s.v. Βερενίκη, 194 n. 5
Stobaeus, *Florilegium*: (1. 6. 1) 173*; (1.
6. 16) 173*

Strabo: **1** (4. 2 (63)) 363*; (4. 6 (65)) 326; **2** (1. 2–9 (67–70), 1. 14 (73)) 284; (1. 17 (74), 1. 35–6 (87–8)) 361; (3. 4–5 (98–102)) 361–2*; (3. 6 (102)) 326; (4. 1 (104)) 363*; (4. 1–5 (104–7)) 363; (4. 2 (104)) 363*; **3** (2. 7 (145)) 6*; **7** (fr. 34) 114; **9** (2. 30 (411)) 382; (2. 40 (415)) 36*; **11** (7. 3 (509)) 284, 361; (9. 2–3 (515), 10. 2 (516)) 282; (11. 1 (516)) 283*; (13. 7 (525)) 281; (14. 4 (528)) 279, 280*; **12** (1. 4 (534)) 387; (2. 1 (535), 2. 10 (540), 3. 15 (547)) 279; (3. 30 (556)) 332; (3. 40 (562)) 279; (8. 16 (578)) 393*

    13 (1. 54 (608–9)) 240, (609) 391; (4. 1–2 (623–4)) 312; **14** (1. 38 (646)) 189, 310; (2. 5 (652–3)) 89; (5. 2 (668–9)) 168, 393; **15** (2. 10 (724), 2. 14 (726–7)) 283; (3. 11 (731)) 345*; **16** (1. 5 (738)) 277; (1. 9–11 (740–1)) 276; (1. 14 (742)) 277*; (2. 3 (749)) 279*; (2. 4 (749)) 304; (2. 4–6 (749–50)) 288*; (2. 8–10 (751–2)) 288*; (2. 10 (752)) 278*; (2. 14 (754)) 290; (4. 7 (770)) 214; **17** (1. 6–10 (791–5)) 215; (1. 8 (793)) 215*, (794) 241*; (1. 13 (798)) 232; (1. 17 (801)) 166*; (1. 44–5 (815)) 194*

Studia hellenistica, 24 (78, 78–9), 222*

Suda: s.v. Aristophanes of Byzantion, 237; *basileia*, 63*; Eratosthenes, 327*

*Syll.*² (p. 467), 77*

*Syll.*³ (272) 85; (283) 35; (317) 115, 128*; (322) 85; (344) 74; (354) 100; (364) 84; (374) 48; (380) 165; (385) 126; (390) 139*, 159, 202; (398) 52–3*; (434–5) 126*; (443) 134–6*; (463) 205; (471) 80; (490) 140; (495) 99; (521) 82*; (525) 21; (526) 132*; (527) 132; (528) 100–1*; (530) 26; (535) 82; (543) 84*; (544) 84; (575) 152*; (577–8) 87; (581) 82; (591) 376*; (601) 81; (602) 205; (613 a, 618) 377; (643) 380; (646) 297; (647) 82–3; (663) 169; (664) 383; (672) 86*; (675) 384; (683) 80; (684) 221; (694) 319; (729) 382; (975) 36; (976) 100; (1003, 1024) 175; (1080) 171; (1097) 175; (1168) 164*

Synkellos (p. 531 Dindorf), 310

Syria (55 (1978), 313–25), 203 n. 33

Tacitus, *Ann.* (3. 60–3) 81, (4. 14. 1–2) 81, (4. 43. 1–6) 80; *Hist.* (4. 83–4) 165, (5. 8. 4) 310*

TAM ii. (1), 205 n. 42

Tertullian, *De anima* (10. 4), 348*

Theokritos: (1) 238; (2. 23–37) 256–7*; (6–7, 11) 238; (14) 261; (15) 72, 165, 219–20*, 238, 239*, 260; (17) 61, 202*, 238*

Theophrastos: *Char.* (23) 57–8; *Caus. Pl.* (bks 1–7) 343, (4. 13. 3) 343–4*, (5. 14. 5) 111; *Hist. Pl.* (1. 1. 1) 341–2*, (bks 2–9) 342, (2. 7. 1) 342*, (3. 17. 3) 342–3*, (8. 11. 4) 344, (9. 9. 3) 343*, (9. 8. 6) 343; *On Stones* (53, 58–9) 364

Theopompos (*FGH* 115), fr. 31: 152

Thucydides: (2. 99) 109; (2. 99) 112*; (2. 100) 114; (7. 29) 269 n. 98

Timaios (*FGH* 566) (T 9 b–c) 263; (frs 59–61, 139) 263

Timon (ap. Ath. 1. 22 d), 241*

Tod: (91, 111) 109; (192) 35; (196) 100; (205) 265

Trogus, *Prol.*: (26) 289, 424 n. 32; (27) 9*, 127

Tzetzes, *see* Johannes Tzetzes

UPZ (i. 7) 221*; (8) 221*; (14) 227*; (113) 232 n. 122; (ii. 157) 230–1*

Varro, *RR*, 344; (1. 1. 8) 344

Vitruvius: **3** (2. 8) 87; **5** (9. 1) 398; **6** (1. 11) 350*; **9** (pref. 10) 358*; (8. 2) 328; (8. 2–5) 328, 332; (8. 4) 330–1* & n. 16; (8. 6–7) 332–3* & n. 21; **10** (4–5) 332; (6) 332; (7–8) 331; (7. 1–8. 6) 328; (10–16) 337; (16. 3–4) 336; (16. 3–8) 339

W. Chrest. (2) 195 no. 10; (411) 225 n. 101; (435) 227 n. 108; (441) 229 n. 113

Welles, *see also* 'RC'

Welles *et al.*, *Dura-Europus*, v. 1 (76–9, no. *12), 303 n. 109

Xenophon, *Oec.* (2. 5–6), 98–9*

ZPE (2 (1968), 178–209), 233 n. 126

GENERAL INDEX

'Hl' = hellenistic; 'bro.' = brother of; 'f.' = father of; 's.' = son of; 'w.' = wife of. For ancient authors and their works, see also the Index to Sources. Page numbers in *italics* refer to Figures.

Abdera, enslaved by Hortensius, 381
Abydos, besieged by Philip V, 375
Academy (Athenian) 177 *bis*. 180, 182
accents, Greek, 240
Achaea (*see also* Achaia), survey data, 29
Achaean league, 136–8; and Antigonos II, 127; and Athens, 149, 384; and Mithridates, 390; and Sparta, 145, 148, 378 *bis*, 379, 384; and Rome, 378, 383, 384–5
Achaeans: deported to Italy, 381, 383; wars of, 371, 373
Achaia (*see also* Achaea) (Roman province), 397
Achaios (Seleukid official), 323
Achaios (Seleukid pretender), 290, 313
Acrocorinth, 113
acrostics, 248
Admetos, 218
Adonis, cult of, 165, 219
Aemilius Paullus, L., 381
Aeneas Tacticus, 335
Africa, circumnavigated, 361–2
Agatharchides (geographer), 199, 362
Agathokles of Istria, 98
Agathokles of Samos, 77, 204, 207–8
Agathokles of Syracuse (tyrant), 49–50, 51–2, 262 *bis*
Agathokles s. Agathokles (of Syracuse), 52

Agelaos of Naupaktos, 372
Agesistrata of Sparta, 102
Agiatis of Sparta, 102–3, 144
Agis III of Sparta, 142
Agis IV of Sparta, 144
'agnosticism', in Hl period, 155–6
Agora (Athenian), altered, 87–8
agoranomoi, 98, 199
agriculture: in Egypt, 194–5, 224, 225, 226–7, 230–1, 232; in Seleukid empire, 272–86 *passim*; intensification of, 31; writers on, 344
Agrippa, honoured in Attica, 171–2 & n. 57
Aigai (Vergína), 128
Aigina, 150, 314, 374
Aigosthena, 338, *339*
Ai Khanum, 83, 92, 305, *306*, 323; texts from, 269
Aineias Taktikos, 335
Aiolis, 275
air, in arteries, 348
Aitolia: loses independence, 377; survey data, 29
Aitolian league, 134–6; and Antiochos III, 371; and Antiochos IV, 139; and Attalos I, 314; and Chios, 134–6; and Macedonia, 128; attacks Sparta, 377; campaigns in S. Greece, 138, 144; estranged from Rome, 376–7; expands, 125; in 1st Macedonian war, 373, 374; leaders executed, 381; treaty with Rome, 373; war of 229 BC, 371
Aitolians: as enemies of Athens, 161; as pirates (?), 82; independent, 106
Akarnanian league, 140, 150, 371

Akkadian, 295
Alep (Beroia), hellenized, 303
Alexander, *see also* Alexandros
Alexander I (Ptolemy X), 211–12
Alexander II (Ptolemy XI), 212
Alexander II of Molossia, 127
Alexander III of Macedonia (the Great):
    after-life, 251–2; and Diogenes, 184;
    and Zeus, 69; as civilizer, 302–3; as
    model for later kings, 38, 116;
    buried at Alexandria, 201; coinage,
    21; divine honours, 159; empire
    unstable, 39; invasion of Persia,
    36–8, 39, 115; plans to divert
    Euphrates, 276–7; use of artillery,
    335; visual image, 38, 69, *70*
Alexander IV of Macedonia, 41, 43, 119
Alexander V (s. Cassander), 44
Alexander Balas, 311, 320
Alexander histories, 6–7, 251
Alexander Romance, 251–2
'Alexanders' (coins), 21, 22, 27
Alexandria, 92, 214–15; in Theokritos,
    219–20; Ptolemy II's procession, 68;
    scientists at, 329
Alexandria Eschate, 282, 283
Alexandros (s. Cassander), 116–17
Alexandros (s. Krateros, nephew of
    Antigonos II), governor of Corinth,
    127, 137
Alexandros of Aitolia, at Pella, 240
Alexarchos (bro. Cassander), 188
Alinda, layout, 90
Ambrosia, patient at Epidauros, 164
Ammon, oracle of, 162
Ammonios, works by, 242
Amorgos, and pirates, 82
Amphiareion (Oropos), 171, 333
amphiktyony, Delphic, 133, 377, 382
Amphipolis, 111, 112
amphoras, as evidence, 28
Amu Darya (Oxus), R., 283
anabasis, of Antiochos III, 290
anachorêsis, 195, 207
anagrams, 248
Anaia (*see also* Anaiitai), 80
Anaiitai (*see also* Anaia), 100
anaischyntographoi, 258
anastolê, 70
Anatolia, *see* Asia Minor
anatomical investigation, 347 *bis*, 348
Andriskos, rebel in Macedonia, 384

Andronicus, Livius, 370
Andronikos of Kyrrhestos, 333, *334*
Andros, battle of, 127
Antagoras of Rhodes, at Pella, 240
Antigoneia (Syria), refounded, 304
Antigonids (*see also* Antigonos I, II, II):
    earlier, *404*; later, 151; patrons of
    literature, 239–40; strategic aims,
    152
Antigonis (Athenian tribe), 121, 150
Antigonos I Monophthalmos, 44; and
    Athens, 85, 121, 148, 160; and
    Greek freedom, 73–4; and Lebedos,
    Teos, 74–5; and Skepsis, 156; at
    Triparadeisos, 42; becomes king,
    122, 160
Antigonos II Gonatas, 45, **124–5**,
    126–8; and Athens, 128–9; and Pan,
    65; and S. Greeks, 124, 125, 127;
    cultural interests, 152; executes
    Philochoros, 263; patron of
    literature, 239–40
Antigonos III Doson, **151**; and Achaean
    league, 145 *bis*, 146; Greek alliance,
    138
Antigonos of Karystos, 239
Antikythera Mechanism, 359, *360*
Antikythera shipwreck, 473 n. 63
Antioch, *see* Antiocheia (*five entries*)
Antiocheia (Alexandria Eschate), 282
Antiocheia (Jerusalem), 303
Antiocheia-in-Margiane, 283
Antiocheia-in-Skythia, 283
Antiocheia-on-Orontes, 96, 288, 304
Antiochos I of Kommagene, 396
Antiochos I Soter (Seleukid), **287–8**,
    289; and Attalids, 312; and
    Baitokaike (?), 297–8; and Didyma,
    306; and Ezida temple, 295; and
    Ionians, 134; and Miletos, 306; and
    Stratonike, 71; city foundations, 282,
    283, 305; coins, 24–6; defeats Gauls,
    53; war v. Hierax, 290
Antiochos II Theos, **289**; and Baitokaike
    (?), 297–8; and Laodike, 300; in 2nd
    Syrian war, 203; sacks Sardis, 303
Antiochos III Megas, **290–1**; and
    Aitolian league, 371; and
    Aristodikides, 299–300; and Attalos
    I, 314; and Jews, 296, 299, 307; and
    ruler-cult, 158; invades Greece, 377;
    pact with Philip V (?), 208, 375; war

v. Romans, 291, 377; western campaigns, 376
Antiochos IV Epiphanes, **292–3**; and Aitolian league, 139; and Athens, 87, 382; and Atargatis, 168; and Eumenes II, 317; and Jerusalem, 303; and Jews, 307–8, 309–10, 311; invades Egypt, 208–9
Antiochos V Eupator, 311, 320
Antiochos VI, 321
Antiochos VII Sidetes, 311, 321
Antiochos VIII Grypos, 322
Antiochos IX Kyzikenos, 322
Antiochos X Eusebes, 322
Antiochos XI, 322
Antiochos XII Dionysos, 322
Antiochos XIII Asiatikos Philadelphos, 322, 325, 394, 396
Antiochos Hierax, 290, 313
Antiochos of Askalon, 180
Antiochos Philadelphos, *see* Antiochos XIII
Antiochos Philopappos (of Kommagene), 399
Antipater (regent of Macedonia), 42, 115, 128
Antipater I (II) (s. Cassander), 44, 116
Antipatros, *see* Antipater *(two entries)*
antiquities, taken by Romans, 385, 391
Antonius, M. (1), campaign v. pirates, 390
Antonius, M. (2), *see* Mark Antony
Antony, *see* Mark Antony
Anu-uballit-Nikarchos, 441 n. 11
Apame (mother of Antiochos I), 307
Apameia, 96, 288; peace of, 291, 377
Apellikon (Peripatetic, Athenian leader), 390
Apion (Ptolemy), 212
apoklêtoi, Aitolian, 134
Apollo: patron of Seleukids, 65; syncretized, 396
Apollodoros of Athens, 246
Apollonios (bro. of Ptolemaios), 227
Apollonios (*dioiketes*), 219, 226 *bis*, 227, 228; promotes agriculture, 344, 345
Apollonios of Perge, 354
Apollonios of Rhodes, 240, 243; poem, 255–6
Apollonis (w. Attalos I), 72
apomoira, 226
Appian, as historical source, 10

Appius Claudius Pulcher, 171, 398
Apuleius, 166
Aquillius, M'., 389
Arabia, 272, 277, 279, 344, 396
Arabian deities, 169
Arabic sources, 19, 252, 328
Arabs (*see also* Iamboulos): in Egypt, 220 (?); in Seleukid empire, 279, 291, 322
Arachosia, 283
Aramaic, 295
Aratos of Sikyon, 137–8, 267–8
Aratos of Soloi, 128, 245
archaeological evidence (*see also* building *types*): for Hl period, 27–31; for Roman Greece, 398; for sack of Athens, 391; for social relations, 105–6; for Sparta, 148
Archagathos of Syracuse, 52
Archelaos, king of Macedonia, 114
Archelaos (Mithradates' general), 390, 391, 392
arches, 333–4
Archimedean screw, 332
Archimedes: and practicality, 330; applied maths, 358–9; death, 365; machines, 330; mathematical works, 357–8; military inventions, 337–8; planetarium, 331; pulleys, 332
'archive' of Hor, 209
archives, 81, 88, 221, 242–3, 264; of papyri, 197, 219
archivists, royal, 9, 264
area, calculation of, 357
Areia, 282, 283
Ares, temple of, at Athens, 398
Areus I of Sparta, 125, 142 & n., 266
Argolid (southern), survey data, 29
Argos: and Sparta, 145, 148, 383; mentioned, 125, 127
Ariarathes, satrap of Cappadocia, 46
Ariarathes III of Cappadocia, 51
Ariarathes V of Cappadocia, 240, 318
Ariobarzanes II of Cappadocia, 130, 398
Aristarchos of Samos, 352–3
Aristarchos of Samothrace, 240, 241
Aristeas, Letter of, 265
Aristion (Epicurean, statesman), 190, 390
Aristoboulos (Alexander historian), 6
Aristoboulos of Alexandria, 266
Aristodikides of Assos, 299–300

Aristokrates (Thracian), 218
Aristonikos (Attalid pretender), 319
Aristophanes of Byzantion, 237, 240, 241–2
Aristotle, 18, 177–9, 349; library, 240, 391
Aristyllos (astronomer), 351
Arkadian federation (4th c.), 134
Arkesilaos (Academic), 179, 180
Armenia, 279–81, 305
armies, Macedonian, 47, 56–8; and kings, 40, 115
Arrian, as historical source, 6–7
Arsakes V (Mithradates I) of Parthia, 320
Arsinoë I, 405
Arsinoë II, 49, 50, 72, 185, 239; cult, 160, 226
Arsinoë III, 207
Arsinoite nome, 194
art, of Hl period, 27–8
art works, taken by Romans, 385, 391
Artabarzanes of Atropatene, 281
arteries, function of, 348
artillery, 335, 336
artists of Dionysos, 163
Asandros (satrap), 323
Asia, Roman province, 319, 389
Asia Minor: geography and economy, 272–5, 279–81; and Mithradates, 389; problems of control, 275; Roman treatment of, 392, 394–6
Asklepiades of Samos, 253, 254
Asklepieion, of Athens, 87, 122, 164
Asklepieion, of Kos, 346, 348
Asklepios, cult of, 163–5, 170, 348
Aśoka, 284–6
assemblies, Macedonian, 114
Assos, layout, 90
Astarte, cult of, at Delos, 169
astrolabes, 351
astrology, 354–5
astronomy, 350–4; in poetry, 245, 246
Aswan (Syene), 192, 194, 361
asylia, 80–1, 82–3
ataraxia, 182
Atargatis, 168, 169
atheism, 155–6
Athena, Itonia (at Koroneia), 80
Athenaeus (author), 5–6, 15, 263–4
Athenaios, see Athenaeus

Athenion (philosopher, statesman), 190, 390
Athens (see also Demetrios of Phaleron; democracy, Athenian; see also under coinage; Demetrios I; Eumenes II; garrisons): and Aitolians, 82, 161; and Antigonos I, 85; and Attalids, 150, 314, 316, 318, 382, 443 n. 56; and Cassander, 122, 128; and Crete, 82; and Cyrene, 100; and Delos, 382, 383 bis, 390 bis, 392; and Demetrios II, 148; and Lysimachos, 48; and Mithradates, 390, 398; and Oropos, 384; and Ptolemies, 125, 149 bis, 150, 382; and Samos, 56; and Seleukids, 345, 382; as ally of Rome, 150–1, 382, 385, 397; described by Herakleides, 148; doesn't use dikasts, 80; given territory by Rome, 382, 385; in 1st Mithridatic war, 390–1; in 239–192 BC, 148–51; in 2nd Macedonian war, 375; in peace of Phoinike, 374; liberation of 229 BC, 149; monuments, 87–9, 122, 382, 398; other foreign benefactors, 398; philosophy at, 176–8; political change, 128–30; Roman monuments, 399; sacked by Sulla, 391; trade, 385–6; under Successors, 120–4
Atropatene, 281
Atropates of Atropatene, 281
Attalid dynasty, 312–19, 402; and artists of Dionysos, 163; and Dionysos, 64–5; coinage, 26; land administration, 300–1; patrons of literature, 239
Attalis (Athenian tribe), 150, 375
Attalists, of Teos, 163
Attalos (bro. of Eumenes II), Friends of, 77
Attalos (f. Philetairos), 312
Attalos I, 312–15; and Athens, 150, 443 n. 56; and Gauls, 53–4; and Rome, 375; and Sikyon, 156; benefactions in Greece, 314; defends Piraeus, 375; first Attalid king, 312; in 2nd Macedonian war, 375; patron of historian, 265; praised, 61–2
Attalos II, 317–18; and Athens, 382; and Eumenes II, 317; benefactions in Greek cities, 318, 382; stoa of, 87

Attalos III, 156–7, **318**; cultural
    interests, 318, 344, 345
Attica, archaeology of, 30–1
Atticus, Herodes, 399
Atticus, T. Pomponius, 398
Attis, cult of, at Delos, 169
audiences (*see also* readerships), for
    mime, 250–1
Augustus (Octavian), and Greece, 397
Auletes (Ptolemy XII), 212–13, 232
autonomia, 74, 140 *bis* & n. 95, 381
Axios, R., 109

Babylon: continuity at, 303; king-lists,
    265
Babylonia: and Seleukos I, 42, 286;
    viticulture, 344–5
Babylonians: and astrology, 354; and
    astronomy, 351
Bacchon the nesiarch, 139
Bagadates (official at Amyzon), 323
Baitokaike, sanctuary at, 297–8
Baktria, 283; history, 16, 51, 283–4,
    285–6, *402–3*
balance of power (?), 206
Banabelos (Seleukid official), 323
banquets, royal, 67
'barbarians', attitudes to, 259–60
Basileia (festival), 217
basilikê chôra, 299
basilissa, 71
basilistai, 163
battles, in historical narratives, 268
benefaction, see *euergesia*
benefactors, Roman, 171, 398
Berenike (port), 194
Berenike II (d. of Ptolemy I), 71, 203,
    244, 289
Berenike III (Kleopatra), 212
Berenike IV, *198*, 213
Beroia (Alep), 87, 96, 303
Berossos, 11, 261, 270
Berrhoia, see Beroia
Bindusara, 284
biography, 12–14, 262–3
biology, 341–4
Bion (poet), 238
Bion of Borysthenes (Cynic), 185, 240,
    438 n. 60
birds, imported to Egypt, 345
Bithynia, 51, 275, 396
blood, 346, 348

Blossius of Cumae, 189
Boiotia, 29–30; *asylia* in, 80
Boiotian confederacy, 133
Boiotians: and Rome, 378; and
    Mithradates, 390
Borsippa, temple at, 295
Bosporos, 393, 396
botany, 341–4
Boulagoras of Samos, 98–100, 159–60
boundary disputes, 80
Brennos, 53, 118
Britain, 363
Bronzes, Piraeus, 391
Brouch(e)ion (at Alexandria), 239
Brutus, in Athens, 397
bucolic poetry (*see also* pastoral), 238
Buddhism, 284, 285
bureaucracy: in Egypt, 227; Seleukid,
    295
Byzantion, 106, 374

Cabiri, cult of, 170
Caesar (Ptolemy XV), 213
Caesar, Julius, 213, 397, 398
Caesarion (Ptolemy XV), 213, 397
Callisthenes, see Kallisthenes
camel-driver, complains to Zenon, 220
Canopus, see Canopus decree; Kanobos
Canopus decree, 166, 203, 206
capitals, Persian, 272, 281
Cappadocia, 51, 279, 387; and
    Mithradates, 388–9; in Roman
    empire, 396
Cassander, 43, 44, **119–20**, 187; and
    Athens, 122, 128; and Olympias,
    119; as ruler of Greeks, 120; takes
    Macedonia, 116
Cassius Dio, as historical source, 10–11
cataloguing (*see also* classification), in
    science, 352
catapults, 336
Cato the Elder, 370–1
Celsus (medical writer), 19
Celts, see Gauls
centre–periphery theory, 295–6
cereals, Theophrastos on, 343–4
ceremonies, of kingship, 67–8
Chaironeia, battle of (86 BC), 392
Chalkis, 113; taken by Cassander, 122
Chandragupta, 283, 284, 287
Chaonians, 139
Chaonnophris, 208

Chares of Mytilene, 251
China, science in, 469 n. 110
Chinese, invade Seleukid empire, 285
Chios, 134–6, 374, 392
chôra, of Egypt, 216–17
Chremonidean war, 125–7
Chremonides, 126
Chronicle of the Diadochoi, 265
chronological research, 246, 263
Chrysippos (Stoic), 187, 258
Cicero, 180, 398
Cilicia, *see* Kilikia
circulation of coinages, 26–7
cistophoric coinage, 27, 316–17
cities (see also *poleis*): and kings, 48,
    59–60, 68, 70–1, 106; and Friends,
    76, 77; freedom of, 73; in Asia
    Minor, 275; in Egypt, 199, 214; in
    Levant, 275, 278; in rest of Seleukid
    empire, 277, 281, 282
citizens, Greek, attitude to Rome, 379,
    381, 384
citizenship: at Larisa, 84; at Athens,
    129; changes in, 83, 101–2, 104–5,
    131, 259, 365–6; in Euemeros, 188
city foundations, 83–4; by Alexander,
    303; by Lysimachos, 48; Seleukid,
    288, 303, 304–5
city-states, see *poleis*
civic ruler-cult, 157
civilization, by conquest, 302–3
civil wars, Roman, 213, 397
class conflict, 132–3, 147, 379, 381
classicism, in literature, 269
classification (*see also* cataloguing): in
    astronomy, 352; in science, 241, 242,
    246, 341–2, 349
Claudius Ptolemaeus, *see* Ptolemy
Claudius Pulcher, App., 171, 398
Cleopatra, *see* Kleopatra
cleruchs, in Egypt, 217
clocks, 331, 332–3
Clodius, 212, 397
cogwheels, 359
coinage: cistophoric, 27, 316; as
    historical source, 21–7; in Egypt,
    228, 229; in trade, 26–7; of Achaean
    league, 137; of Areus I, 142; of
    Athens, 382–3, 386; of Eumenes I,
    312; of Philetairos, 312; portraits on,
    69–70; Seleukid, 301; symbolic
    significance, 21–6

coins, *see* coinage
collecting, as cultural activity, 242
colonies, Seleukid, 304
Colossus of Rhodes, 44
Coma Berenices, 244, 352
comedy, *see* Menander
Commagene (Kommagene), 279, 322,
    396
conic sections, 357
constellations (*see also* Coma Berenices),
    351
contests, at festivals, 171
continents, 361
core–periphery theory, 295–6
Corinth (*see also* Acrocorinth; league of
    Corinth): Achaean congress at, 384;
    captured, 121, 122, 127, 137, 138
    bis; dispute with Epidauros, 80;
    razed, 385; refounded, 399
Cornelii Scipiones, 377
Cornelius Sulla, *see* Sulla
corn law, Samian, 100, 101
cosmology: in Dervéni papyrus, 111; in
    poetry, 246; pre-Hl, 350–1
Cossutius (architect), 87
courts, 76–7; Macedonian, 127–8, 152
craftsmen of Dionysos, 163
Crete (*see also particular places;* pirates):
    and Athens and Rhodes, 82;
    arbitration in, 80; *stasis* in cities, 132
Crimea, 388, 395, 396
'crowns', as tribute, 195
cultic landscapes, 29
cults, *see* religion; ruler-cult; *and
    particular deities*
culture (*see also* culture contact; culture,
    Greek; *gymnasia*; material cultures):
    Greek: and non-Greek, 1–5 *passim*;
    and *polis*, 87, 366; and science,
    365–7; constructed by literature,
    236–7, 241–3, 252, 270; Epicurus
    on, 183; in Egypt, 207, 217, 219–23
    passim; in Macedonia, 111, 127;
    innovation in, 246; Romans and,
    370–1, 398–9
culture contact (*see also* hellenization),
    Greek–non-Greek, 259–60, 270; in
    Egypt, 219–23 *passim*; in Syria, 83
curse tablets, 165
Curtius (Q. Curtius Rufus), 7
Cybele (Kybele), 168, 169
cyclamen, 343

Cynicism, 183–5; and Stoicism, 186
Cyprus: and Ptolemies, 205, 206;
    bequeathed to Rome, 212
Cyrene: bequeathed to Rome, 212;
    doctors in, 347; grain donated by,
    100

Dalmatia, Roman war in, 383
Damascus, layout, 96
Daniel (book of), 307
Daphnai (Daphne), 278, 288; procession
    at, 292–3
Dardanos, conference of, 392
data, in Hl science, 355, 364; and
    theory, 351
debt problems, 84, 132–3, 145, 390
debt records, destroyed, 221
decrees, as historical source, 21
defence technology, 335, 336 bis, 337
deification (see also divine honours; ruler-
    cult; tychê; Rhômê), 156–7, 159, 226
Delos: and Athens, 382, 383, 390 bis,
    392; Antigonid sitônês in, 100;
    gender roles in, 105–6; Macedonians
    in, 152; made tax-free port, 382;
    non-Greek cults, 168–70; tax
    remitted, 397; wealth, 130
Delphi (see also Delphic amphiktyony):
    and Aitolians, 134; and Eumenes II,
    86; attacked by Gauls, 52;
    mentioned, 80, 81; Romans at, 370
Delphic amphiktyony, 133, 377, 382
demes, Attic, 30, 172
Demetrias (Athenian tribe), 121, 150
Demetrias (city), 92, 113, 377
Demetrios I of Baktria, 283
Demetrios I Poliorketes, 44, 66, 120,
    122, 160; as besieger, 44, 123; as
    ruler of Macedonia, 44, 117, 120;
    coins, 24–6; concessions to
    Athenians, 124; final captivity, 44;
    honoured at Athens, 121–3 passim,
    148, 160; hymn to, 160–1; invades
    Lakonike, 142; 'liberates' Athens,
    121, 122, 123; offends Athenians,
    122, 130–1; Plutarch's view, 62–3
Demetrios I Soter (Seleukid), 320
Demetrios II Nikator (Seleukid), 320,
    321 ter, 322
Demetrios II of Baktria, 285
Demetrios II of Macedonia, 151; and

Athens, 148; and Delos, 100;
    mentioned, 149
Demetrios III (Seleukid), 322
Demetrios of Phaleron: and Alexandria
    library, 239; and Menander, 258; as
    philosopher, 174, 179, 190; as ruler
    of Athens, 98, 104, 120–1, 128
Demetrios of Pharos, 77, 372
Demetrios s. Demetrios (landowner in
    Syria), 298
Demetrios s. Demetrios, of Phaleron,
    127
Demochares of Athens, 76, 265
democracy: abolished in Achaean
    league, 385; Athenian (curtailed),
    120, 122, 123, 127, 128–9, 391–2,
    397, (restored), 121; in 4th c., 34,
    35; in Hl period, 35–6, 130; in
    Macedonia, 112
Demodamas of Miletos, 284, 285,
    306–7
demography: of Egypt, 215 & n. 70; of
    Greece, 29, 30–1, 54–7
Demosthenes, honoured posthumously,
    129
Demotic (language), 197 bis; sources,
    199, 252
Demotic Chronicle, 252
Dervéni papyrus, 111
detention, in Egyptian temples, 449 n.
    83
diadem, as royal symbol, 66–7
Diades (engineer), 335
Diadochoi, see Successors
Diaios (Achaean), 384 bis, 384
diatribai (Cynic), 185
didactic poetry, 245–6, 258
Didyma, and Antiochos I, 306
Dikaiarchos (philosopher), 360 bis, 361
dikastai, 78–9, 80
Dio (Cassius Dio), as source, 10–11
Diodoros of Sicily (historian), 8–9; on
    Egypt, 199
Diodoros s. Dioskourides (doctor), 101
Diodotos (I) of Baktria, 283, 284
Diodotos Tryphon Autokrator, 321, 393
Diogeneion (gymnasium at Athens), 87
Diogenes (general), 87, 149
Diogenes Laërtios, as source, 177
Diogenes of Sinope (Cynic), 184
Diognetos (architect), 336
dioikêtês, 195, 217, 225, 227, 345

Dionysios of Syracuse, 335
Dionysios Petosarapis, 210
Dionysios s. Kephalas, 217–18
Dionysos (*see also* Ptolemy XII): cult, 170; patron of Attalids, 64–5
dioptra, 334, 351
Dioscorides (author), 19
Diotogenes, on kingship, 63
dissection, 347 *bis*, 348
divine honours (*see also* deification; ruler-cult), 156–7
Diÿllos of Athens (historian), 265
doctors: public, 100–1, 347; status of, 347
Dogmatists (in medicine), 347
dogs, downtrodden, 157
Dolopia, seized by Perseus, 380
domestic archaeology, 27–8
Doulon Polis, 189
Doura-Europos, 96, 303
Douris of Samos, 75, 161, 262
drainage projects, 111, 195 & n.
drama (*see also* Menander; mimes), evidence for, 18
Drangiane, 283, 285
dress, of kings, 66–7
Dryton of Ptolemaïs, 223
Dusares, syncretized with Zeus, 169
Dymê, 26, 373

earth: measurement of, 352, 360; as sphere, 326–7, 350–1
earthquakes, 85, 101
eccentric circles (in astronomy), 353
economics, of urbanization, 96
economy: of Greece, 36, 56, 130–3; of *poleis*, 86, 101; of Ptolemaic Egypt, 207, 224–30; of Seleukid empire, 262–86 *passim*, 296–301, 323–4
Egypt (*see also* Ptolemies): administrative structure, 216–17; and Rome, 209–13 *passim*, 232; ethnic groups, 195, 213–14, 219–23; land and resources, 192–5; literary representations, 260; population, 215 & n. 70; pre-Hl, 195, 196, 233; Ptolemaic rule assessed, 196, 230–2; sources, 196–201
Ekphantos, on kingship, 63
Elaia, 312, 319
elephants, 214, 361

Eleusinian mysteries, 122, 160, 398
Eleusis, 124, 171
Eleutherai, fortifications, 337–8
élites, Greek (*see also* Greeks, non-élite): and Antiochos III, 377; and astrology, 355; and entertainment, 330–1; and geography, 362, 363; and historiography, 267; and labour, 330; and literature, 236–7, 251, 269, 270; and Mithradates, 389; and non-Greek lands, 352; and philosophy, 189, 190; and religion, 176; and Rome, 379, 381, 389, 399; and science, 328, 329, 331–2, 365–6, 367; changing role, 191, 366; economic position, 132–3
emigration (*see also* mercenary service), from Greece, 55, 56–8, 132, 261
Empiricists (in medicine), 347
'empty throne' (Eumenes' ruse), 162
engineering, 330–41
entertainment, science as, 330–1
Epeiros, 34, 371, 381
Epeirote league, 139
ephêbeia, Athenian, 126, 130
Ephesos, 84, 100, 48
epic poetry, 255–6; historical, 269
Epicureanism, 182–3
Epicurus, 177, 182
epicycles, 353
Epidauros, 80, 164–5
epigonê, 217, 218, 219 & n. 78
epigrams, 253–5
epigraphy, evidence of, 20–1
Epimachos (engineer), 336
Epiphanes, *see* Ptolemy V
Epirote league, 139
Epirus, 34, 371, 381
epistatai (governors), 75
epithets, of kings, 65–6
equinoxes, precession of, 351
Erasistratos, 346 *bis*, 347, 348, 364
Eratosthenes, 240, 246, 360–1 & n. 97, 444 n. 76
Erinna, 103 & n.
Eriza, edict of Antiochos III from, 158
Erythrai, exempted from tribute, 75
étanchéité, 323
ethics, in philosophies, 179, 190
Ethiopic sources, 252
ethnê: classification of, 349–50; in Macedonia, 112

ethnic groups: in Ptolemaic Egypt, 195, 213–23; in Seleukid empire, 295–6, 323; representations of, 260–1
ethnicity, Macedonian, 111
ethnos, 133–4
Euboian league, 137, 138
Euclid, 356–7
Eudoxos of Knidos, 351, 354, 356
Eudoxos of Kyzikos, 361–2
Euemeros of Messene, 187–8
euergesia: between city and king, 77–8; by citizens, 96–102, 131; by kings, 77, 83–6, 87–9, 300; by women, 104
Euergetes I, *see* Ptolemy III
Euergetes II, *see* Ptolemy VIII
Euergetis (city), 210–11
euergetism, see *euergesia*
Euhemeros, *see* Euemeros
Eukleides (Euclid), 356–7
Eumenes I of Pergamon, 85, 312
Eumenes II of Pergamon, **315–17**; and Antiochos IV, 317; and Athens, 87, 172 & n., 334, 382; and Delphi, 86; and land tenure, 300–1; and Rome, 315, 316; and Seleukos IV, 292; and Tyriaion, 315–16; denounces Perseus, 380; gains by peace of Apameia, 377; praised, 62; subject of poems, 269
Eumenes III, *see* Aristonikos
Eumenes of Kardia, 46; archive of, 264; as host, 67; ingenuity, 46, 47, 162; significance, 47
Eupator, *see* Ptolemy VII
Eupatoristai, of Delos, 163
Euphrates, R., 275–7
Euphron of Sikyon, 128
Eurydike (w. Philip III), 43, 71, 118–19
Eurykleides (Athenian leader), 149, 150
Euthydemos of Baktria, 51, 291
Euxenia of Megalopolis, 104
evidence for Hl period, *see* sources
exhaustion, method of, 357
exiles, from Greek *poleis*, 38, 54–5, 56
Exiles Decree, 38, 54, 134
experimentation (*see also* innovation), 336, 363–4
explanation: in botany, 342, 343; nature of, 364
exploration, 359–60, 361–2
Ezida, temple at, 295

Fabius Pictor, Q., 370
Failaka (Ikaros), 305, 323
Faiyum, 194, 197
family, royal, 72, 73
federalism, 133, 138
federal states, 112, 133–40, 381, 385
festivals: Basileia, 217; continuity in, 171; funding of, 67, 85, 99, 101; in Attica, 148 *bis*; isopythian, 305; mentioned, 79, 81, 85 *bis*; new, 87, 123, 159, 217, 316, 319; of Adonis, 219; of *ethnê*, 138; of *poleis*, 68, 112, 122 *bis*, 148, 156, 157, 175; panhellenic, 112, 126, 175, 316; prevalence of, 171; Ptolemaieia, 124, 139, 159; women at, 103, 219–20
'Fetters of Greece', 113, 125
field survey, 28–9, 30–1
Flamininus, L. Quinctius, 376
Flamininus, T. Quinctius, 375
Foot Companions, 114
fortifications, 337–8
fortune, see *tychê*
fourth century, general character, 33–5
fragmentary sources, 5–6
freedom of the Greeks, 73–4, 375
Friends, of kings, 76–7
frontier disputes, 80

Galatia, 53, 388, 396
Galatians, *see* Gauls
Galen (medical writer), 19
Galilee, vines in, 345
games (*see also* Olympic games), at festivals, 171
Gandara, 284
gardens, 281, 299; of Epicurus, 183
Garland of Meleager, 253
garlic, 343
garrisons, Macedonian, 75; at Athens, 123, 127; in Attica, 120, 127; at Piraeus, 120, 124
Gauls: and Antigonos II, 125; and Attalids, 313, 316, 317 *bis*; and Rome, 317; as 'other', 54; in Asia Minor, 53; in Greece, 52–3; in Macedonia, 118; in Thrace, 54
Gedrosia, 284
gender relations, 102–6
genres, in Greek literature, 237
geographical sources, 14–15, 29–30
geography, 359–63

geometry, 356–7
Glaukon (bro. Chremonides), 126
gods, in Epicureanism, 182; in
  Euemeros, 188; in Stoicism, 185;
  new, 155; Olympian, 154, 175–6
Gonatas, see Antigonos II
Gorítsa (Orminion?), 91
Gortyn (Crete), 205
Gortys (Arkadia), 334
governors, of cities, 75
Graeco-Baktrian kings, 285
grain shortages, 98, 100, 232
grain supply, of cities, 98, 100
grave-goods, as evidence, 105
gravestones, as evidence, 21
gravity, specific, 358–9
Great Mother (Kybele), 168
Greece, under Roman rule, 397–9
Greek culture, see culture, Greek
'Greek freedom', 73–4
Greek identity (see also hellenization),
  1–2; of Macedonians, 111
Greek language, in Seleukid empire,
  295, 325
Greekness, construction of (see also
  culture, Greek), 236–7, 242,
  259–60, 270
Greeks: in Egypt, 213–14, 215,
  217–19, 220, 221, 222, 223; in
  Italy, 370; in Seleukid empire, 323;
  non-élite, and Rome, 379, 381, 384
Greek world, characterized, 2, 33
gymnasia: and hellenism, 87, 270; at
  Tyriaion, 315–16; of Ptolemy III
  (Athens), 87; cultural role, 304,
  308–9
gynaikonomoi, 104

Hadrian, and Greece, 399
Hagne Thea, cult of, at Delos, 169
hairstyle, of Alexander, 70
Haliakmon, R., 109
Haliartos, given to Athens, 382
Halikarnassos, 78, 79, 84
Halos, 91
Hannibal, 316; and Philip V, 151, 372
happiness, as goal of philosophy, 180,
  182, 185
Haronnophris, 207
Harpalos, deserts Alexander, 37
Harsiesis, 210
healing cults, 348

heart, investigated, 346
heating system, 334
hêdonê (Epicurean pleasure), 182
Hedyle of Samos, 253
Hedylos of Samos, 253–4
Hekataios of Abdera, 199, 260
helepolis, 338–40
heliocentric hypothesis, 352–3
Heliodoros, 292
Helios, cult of, at Delos, 169
Hellênes, status term in Egypt, 223
Hellenic leagues: of Antigonos and
  Demetrios, 44, 132, 138; of
  Antigonos III, 149; of Philip II, 35,
  133
hellênismos, 308
'hellenistic', as term, 1, 2
hellenistic period (see also sources):
  ancient treatments, 7–11, 16–17;
  continuity from classical, 39, 190;
  defined, 3; general issues, 3–5, 31–2,
  literary sources, 5–20; modern
  treatments, 1, 3–5, 16
hellenization: by Alexander, 302–3; in
  Asia Minor, pre-Hl, 274–5; in
  Egypt, 221–3, 270; in Judaea, 309,
  310; in Kommagene, 322; in Near
  East, 1, 270; in Seleukid empire,
  304; in town-planning, 96; in
  Jerusalem, 308–9, 310; in Rome,
  370–1
hellênokopein, 380
helots (of Lakonike), 141, 147 bis
Herakleia Pontica, 392, 394
Herakleia under Latmos, 90, 377
'Herakleides of Crete', 29–30, 148
Herakleitos, subject of epigram, 254
Hermaios (Graeco-Baktrian king), 286
Hermias, 290
Herodas, 164, 249–51
Herodes Atticus, 399
Herodotos, popular in Egypt, 247
heroes, in Greek religion, 154
heroization, of men, 158
Heron of Alexandria, 331–2, 357, 359;
  school of, 330
Herophilos (doctor), 346 bis, 347, 348
Hierapolis (Syria), 168
Hierapytna (Crete), 83
Hierax (Antiochos), 290, 313
Hieron II of Syracuse, 52; as writer, 344
Hieron of Laodikeia, 392–3

Hieronymos of Kardia (historian), 9, 46–7, 74, 264; in Macedonia, 128, 240
Hippalos (explorer), 362
Hipparchia (philosopher), 103–4
Hipparchos (astronomer), 351–2, 354, 361, 364
Hippocratic oath, 349
Hippodamian planning, 90, 303
Hippokrates (?), on nations, 349
Histiaia, honours importer, 100
historians, local (*see also next two entries*), 265
historiography, ancient (*see also preceding and following entries*): about Hl period, 7–11, 15–17; early Roman, 370–1; in Hl period, 7–11, 262–9; non-Greek, 11–12; of Alexander, 6–7, 251–2; in verse, 269; local, 265
historiography, modern (*see also preceding two entries*), 1, 3–5
hoi polloi, attitude to Rome, 379, 381, 384
Homer, popular in Egypt, 247
homopoliteia, 83
homosexuality (*see also* lesbianism), in Stoicism, 186
honorific decrees: for benefactors, 98–101, 102; for citizens, 126 *bis*; for dikasts, 78–80; for doctors, 100–1
honours, (*see also* deification; divine honours; honorific decrees): for Alexander, 159; for Antigonids, 121, 122, 123 *bis*, 148, 156, 160–1; for Antiochos I, 306; for Attalids, 150, 156, 156–7, 382; for citizens, 150–60; for Demosthenes, 129; for naval architect, 340; for Polemaios, 445 n. 90; for Ptolemies, 159, 162, 171; for Romans, 171–2
Hor: ostrakon, *200*; prophecy, 209
Horologion of Andronikos, 88–9, 333, *334*
Hôros, cult of, 168
horses, bred in Syria, 278
Hortensius, enslaves Abdera, 381
humours (of body), 346 & n.
hunting, 214
hymns: of Kallimachos, 244–5; to Demetrios I, 160–1

Hypereides, on Alexander's honours, 159
hypokauston, 334
hypomnêmata, 264
hypomnêmatographos, 264
Hyrkania, 282

Iamboulos, utopia of, 188–9
Iasos, and Laodike, 85
Ikaros (Failaka), 305, 323
Ilion, 299–300, 301, 374
Illyrian wars: (1st) 371–2; (2nd) 372
Imbros, and Athens, 121, 122
imperialism, Roman, 368–9 & n. 1, 376, 378–9
imports: to Athens, 385; to Egypt, 228–9
India, Greeks and, 284, 305
individualism, 105, 255
Indo-Greek kings, 285
innovation: in literature, 246, 255; in technology, 340–1; in science, 363–4
inquiry, Erasistratos on, 364
inscriptions: as source, 20–1; from Egypt, 199; from Kandahar, 284
Instruction Texts (Egyptian), 252
instruments of measurement, 351
intensification, of agriculture, 31
intermarriage, Greek–Egyptian, 222
inter-referential writing, 242
inviolability, see *asylia*
Ioannes Philoponus (scientific writer), 19
Ionia, 275
Ionian *koinon*, 134, 317
Ipsos, battle of, 44
Iran, inner, 279, 281
irrigation: in Asia Minor, 276; in Egypt, 194–5, 230–1
Isis, cult of, 265, 166–8
Islanders' league, 138–9, 159, 202, 317
Isokrates, 55–6
Istria, 84–5, 98
Italians: in Greece, 383, 397; massacred in Asia Minor, 389
Italy: Agathokles' power-base in, 52; Greeks in, 370; invaded by Pyrrhos, 371; trade with Athens, 385–6
Itanos: oath of, 132; Ptolemaic base, 205, 209
Iulius Antiochos Philopappos, C., 399
Iulius Caesar, C., 213, 398

Iunianus Iustinus, M., 9–10
Iustinus (Justin), 9–10

Jason (high priest), 308; at Sparta, 267
Jaxartes (Syr Darya), R., 283
Jerusalem: and Antiochos IV, 303; captured by Pompey, 396
Jewish literature, 11, 265–6
Jewish–Greek literature, 266
Jews: and Antiochos III, 296, 299; and Ptolemies, 307; and Rome, 311; and Seleukids, 307–12, 321, 460–1 n. 119; and Spartans, 260–1, 266–7; Hekataios on, 260–1; in Egypt, 215, 217; in Greece, 170, 261
John Hyrkanos, 321, 398
Jonathan (high priest), 266–7
Jonathan Makkabaios, 311, 320, 321
Judaea, 311, 320, 396
Judas Makkabaios, 311
Julius Antiochos Philopappos, C., 399
Julius Caesar, 213, 398
Justin (epitomator), 9–10

Kabeira, battle near, 394
Kabeiroi, cult, 170
Kalchedon, 136
Kallias (architect), 336
Kallias of Sphettos, 123–4
Kallikrates (Achaean), 379, 383, 384
Kallimachos, 241, 243–5, 254, 255
Kallisthenes (see also *Alexander Romance*), 6, 159, 264
Kalymnos, and Kos, 83
Kandahar, inscriptions from, 285
Kanobos (*see also* Canopus decree), Serapeion at, 166
Kappadokia, *see* Cappadocia
Kardakes, village of, 301
Kardia, 46
Karia, 275, 375, 382
Karmania, 283
Karneades (Sceptic), 180–1, 190
Kassandreia, 114
Kassandros, *see* Cassander
Kassope, 90–1
katoikiai, 304
Kea, *see* Keos
Keos: Ptolemaic base, 205; survey data, 31
Kerkidas (Cynic), 184

Kilikia: Leia, 278; Pedias, 278; as Roman province, 394, 396
king (*see also* kings; kingship), adopted as title, 43, 286
king-lists, Babylonian, 265
king of Macedonians: how chosen, 40, 118; content of title, 52
kings (*see also* deification; divine honours; ruler-cult; kingship; Successors; women, royal; *see also under* cities): divine patrons, 64–5, 69; dress, 66–7; other than Successors, 51–2; virtues, 61–4; visual representation, 69–71
kingship (*see also* king; kings; monarchy): ceremonial aspects, 67–8; exemplified by Kleomenes, 146; expressed in coins, 21–6; in classical Greece, 59; literary representations, 60–4; religious aspects, 64–6; Seleukid, 301–2
Kios, 136, 374
Kleanthes (Stoic), 187, 353
Klearchos of Soloi, 258, 269
Kleio, patient at Epidauros, 164
Kleitarchos, 6, 251
Kleomedes (astronomer), 361 n. 97
Kleomenes III of Sparta, 144–6, 189, 203
Kleomenes of Naukratis, 201
Kleopatra I, 208
Kleopatra II, 209, 210 *bis*, 211, 212
Kleopatra III, 210, 211, 212
Kleopatra IV, 448 n. 61
Kleopatra V Tryphaina I, 448 n. 65
Kleopatra VI Tryphaina II, *198*, 213
Kleopatra VII, 72, 213, 397
Kleopatra Berenike III, 212
Kleopatra Thea (w. Demetrios II of Syria), 322
Knossos, 81, 100–1
kochlias, 332
Koile Syria: and Ptolemies, 202, 205, 206, 209, 210, 320; and Seleukids, 208, 287; resources, 206
koinodikion (Cretan), 80
koinon, 133, 138
koloitia (tree), 342–3
Kolophon, 48, 445 n. 90
komarchs, 216–17
Kommagene, 279, 322, 396
Konon of Samos (astronomer), 352

korax, 335–6
Koroneia, 80
Koróni (Attica), 126
Koroupedion, battle of, 45, 287
Kos: as medical centre, 346;
    Asklepieion, 82, 164; and *asylia*, 82,
    112; and Kalymnos, 83; battle of,
    127; doctor from, 100–1; Ptolemaic
    possession, 205
Krannon: battle of, 116; public
    subscription at, 85
Krateros (half-bro. of Antigonos II), 128
Krateros (Successor), 40, 42
Krates of Mallos (philosopher), 103–4,
    239
Krates of Thebes (Cynic), 184 *bis*
Kratesikleia of Sparta, 102
Ktesibios, 328; inventions, 330–1,
    332–3, 336, 337
Kybele, cult of, 168, 169
Kynoskephalai, battle of, 375
Kyrene, *see* Cyrene

labour, *see* slave labour; unfree labour
Lachares, 122, 123, 128
Laconia (*see also* Lakonike), survey data,
    31
Laenas, C. Popillius, 209, 292
Lagidai, 201
Lagos, f. Ptolemy, 201
Lakonike (*see also* Laconia), 141, 142
Lamian war, 116, 120, 128
Lampsakos, and Romans, 376
land administration, Attalid, 300–1
land problems, 132–3, 145
landscape change, in Hl period, 28–31
landscapes, cultic, 29
land tenure, Seleukid, 297–8, 299–300
languages: of Egypt, 197, 199, 222; of
    Seleukid empire, 295, 325
Laodike (w. Antiochos II): 71, 289, 300;
    gifts to Iasos, 85
Laodikean war, 203, 231, 289
Laodikeia (Nihavend), 158, 281
Laodikeia-by-the-Sea, 96, 288, 393
Laodikeian war, 203, 231, 289–90
Larisa, and Philip V, 84
Last Plans, of Alexander, 39
Lathyros, *see* Ptolemy IX
latitude, 352, 361, 363
Laurion, 382
league of Corinth, *see* Hellenic leagues

leagues, 133–40 (*see also* Achaean,
    Aitolian, Akarnanian, Epeirote,
    Euboian, Hellenic, Ionian, Islanders,
    Lesbian, Magnesian, Phokian,
    Thessalian; *see also under* Lykia,
    Macedonia)
Lebanon, economy of, 278
Lebedos, 48, 75
legal systems, in Egypt, 199, 222
leitourgiai, abolished (?), 98
Lemnos, and Athens, 121, 122, 124,
    382
Leonidas, king of Sparta, 144 *bis*
Leontion (female philosopher), 104
Lesbian federation, 140
lesbianism, portrayed (?) in poetry, 254
Letter of Aristeas, 265
Leukos Limen, 194
Levant, geography and economy of,
    275–9
librarians, at Alexandria, 240
libraries: at Alexandria, 239, 240, 329
    (destroyed, 235); Greek, 240; Near
    Eastern, 242–3
Licinius Lucullus, L., 212, 394–5
life sciences, 341–50
Lindian Chronicle, 265
literary sources, 5–20
literature: defined, 236; general issues,
    235–7; popular, 250–2; survival,
    235; where written, 237–42
Livius Andronicus, 370
Livy, as source, 8, 368
local historians, 265
longitude, 352, 361, 363
Lucullus, 212, 394–5
Lyceum, 177, 179 & n. 70
Lydia, 275
Lykia, 275, 379, 382; league, 140
Lykophron, 247–8
Lykortas (f. Polybios), 379
Lykourgos, king of Sparta, 147
Lykourgos of Athens, 89, 243
Lysandra (w. Agathokles), 49
Lysias (regent), 311, 320
Lysimacheia, 136
Lysimachos, 15, 47–51; and
    Amphiareion, 171; as arbitrator, 80;
    coinage, 22–3; in Macedonia, 117;
    killed, 45; rules Thrace, 42, 45

Maccabees (books of), 266 *bis* & n. 88, 267, 307
Macedonia: economy, 109, 112–13; extent, 109; federalism in, 140; Greek attitude (mid-2nd-c.), 381; impact on Greece, 130–3; in 239–146 BC, 151; pre-Philip II, 109, 111; revolt of Andriskos, 384; rulers, *400*; ruler-cult absent (3rd-c.), 162; social structure, 111–12; under Philip II, 35, 115; under Rome, 381, 385; under Successors, 116–20; wars v. Rome, 151, 372–5, 380–1
Macedonian wars (of Rome), 151; (1st) 372–4; (2nd) 374–5; (3rd) 380–1
Macedonians of the *epigonê*, 217
Macedonians: and Persians, 38, 42; ethnic identity, 111, 242; in Egypt, 213–14, 215, 217, 221; in Seleukid empire, 323
Machanidas (Spartan ruler), 147
machines: for civic uses, 332–41; purposes, 330–2
Magas of Cyrene, 202, 288
Magi, and Seleukos I, 277, 302
Magnesia-by-Sipylos, battle of, 291, 377
Magnesia-on-Meander, 57, 306
Magnesian league, 140
Mahdia shipwreck, 473 n. 63
Makkabaios, Jonathan, 311, 320, 321
Makkabaios, Judas, 311
male values, 103
Manethon, 11–12, 261
Margiane, 282
Mark Antony, 172 & n., 213, 397
market, controlled in Egypt (?), 227
Marmor Parium, 265
Maroneia, Ptolemaic base, 205
marriage (*see also* intermarriage), changes in, 106
masculine values, 103
material cultures, of Hl world, 28
mathematics (*see also* astrology; astronomy): applied, 358–9; pure, 356–8
Mattathias, 311
Mauryan empire, 284, 287, 291
measurement, instruments of, 351
mechanics (*see also* machines), 359
Medeon (Phokis), 83
Media: Greater, 281; Paraitakene, 281

medicine, 19, 346–50
Megalopolis, 120, 137
Megarians, 80
Megasthenes, 285
Meleager (author), 253
Meleagros (satrap), 299
Melos, survey data, 31
Memphis, 194
men, and masculine values, 103
Menalkidas of Sparta, 384
Menander (comic poet), 129, 257–8
Menandros (Milinda) of Baktria, 285
Menches (scribe), 222–3
Menedemos of Eretria, 240
Menekrates of Xanthos, 265
Menelaos (high priest), 309 *bis*, 310
Menippos of Gadara, 185
Menodotos of Athens, 265
mercantilism, 229
mercenaries (*see also* emigration), 56–8, 131–2
Merv, 283
Mesopotamia, 275–8, 305
Messenians: and Achaean league, 378; in Rhianos, 269
metals, in engineering, 332
meteorology, in poetry, 245
Meter, sanctuary of, 312
Methana, 29, 205
method of exhaustion, 357
Metroön (Athens), 88
Middle Stoa (Athens), 87
Mikion (Athenian leader), 149, 150
Miletos, 78, 81, 87; and Seleukids, 301, 306
Milinda (Menandros), 285
military history, 268
military technology, 334–41
mills, 332
mimes, 249
mina (currency unit), revalued, 386
Mithradates I Arsakes V of Parthia, 285, 320
Mithradates I Ktistes of Pontos, 51, 387
Mithradates II of Parthia, 285 (?)
Mithradates II of Pontos, 51
Mithradates V of Pontos, 398
Mithradates VI Eupator of Pontos: and Athens, 390, 398; and pirates, 393; and ruler-cult, 163; early career, 387, 388; image, 387–8; wars v. Rome, 389–90, 392, 394–5

Mithradatic wars: (1st) 389–90, 392; (2nd) 394; (3rd) 394
Mnaseas, land of, 300
Molon, 76, 290
Molossians, 114, 127, 139
monarchy (*see also* kingship): in 4th c., 34; philosophy of, 63–4
monetization (*see also* coinage), 21; in Seleukid empire, 324
monopolies, in Egypt, 227
monuments, archaeology of, 27–8
moon: influence of, 355; measurement of, 364
mortar (building), 333
Moschos (poet), 238
Mother Goddess, sanctuary of, 312
Mother of Gods (Kybele), 168
Mouseion (Alexandria), 237, 239, 240–1, 329, 366
Mouseion hill (Athens), garrisoned, 123, 127
Mummius, sacks Corinth, 385
Murena, Licinius, 394
Mylasa, 81
Myndos, and Samos, 78, 79
Myonnesos, battle of, 377
Myos Hormos, 194
myriarouroi, 216

Nabis of Sparta, 147–8, 377; and walls of Sparta, 335
Nabû (god), 295
names, Greek: élite and other, 328; and non-Greek, in Egypt, 216–17, 222, 223; and non-Greek, in Seleukid empire, 323, 441 n. 11; in Rome, 370; of kings, 65–6; royal, in Kommagene, 322
nations, classified, 349–50
Naupaktos, peace of, 372
Neanthes of Kyzikos, 265
Neapolis (Naples), 82
Nemrud Daği, 396
Neos Dionysos, *see* Ptolemy XII
Nepos (biographer), 14
Nero, and Greece, 398
nerves, investigated, 346, 348
nesiarch, 202
Nesiotai, *see* Islanders
New Carthage, sack of, 373
New Halos, 91
New Style coinage (of Athens), 382–3

Nicander of Kolophon, 245, 248
nicknames, royal, 65–6
Nihavend (Laodikeia), 158, 281
Nikaia (w. Lysimachos), 49
Nikandros, *see* Nicander
Nikanor (ruler of Media), 286
Nikarchos (Anu-uballit), 441 n. 11
Nikokles, tyrant of Sikyon, 137 *bis*
Nikomedes I of Bithynia, 51, 53
Nikomedes II of Bithynia, 318
Nikomedes III of Bithynia, 388
Nikomedes IV of Bithynia, 394
Nile, R., 194–5, 362
nomads, threat to Seleukid empire (?), 291
nomarchs, 216
nomoi, in Egypt, 194, 216
Nova Carthago, 373
numbers, very large, 357–8
Nymphis of Herakleia (historian), 265
Nysa (Karia), 77

oases, of Egypt, 194
oaths: Hippocratic, 349; of Itanos, 132
observation, in science, 355
Octavian (Augustus), and Athens, 397
odours, Theophrastos on, 343
oikonomos, 217; duties, 224–5
Oinanthe, lynched, 207–8
Oiniadai (Akarnania), 134
Olbia, honours benefactor, 98
oliganthropy, Spartan, 141–2
Olympian religion, 175–6
Olympian Zeus: in Athens, 87, 310, 391, 399; in Jerusalem, 310; in Priene, 310
Olympias (m. of Alexander III), 43, 71, 114, 118–19
Olympic games, Romans at, 370
Olympichos of Samos, 265
Olympieion (Athens), 87, 310, 391, 399
Olympiodoros (Athenian archon), 123
Onesikritos of Astypalaia, 251
Onias (high priest), 267
Ophellas, governor of Cyrene, 131–2
Oracle of the Potter, 233
Orchomenos (Arkadia), 140
Orchomenos (Boiotia), battle of, 392
organs (musical), 331
organs (of body), 346
'oriental' cults, 165–70

Orminion (Gorítsa?), 91
Orontes, R., 278, 288
Orontes of Armenia, 281
Oropos (see also Amphiareion), 84, 384
ostraka, 199, 200
'other', representations of, 259–61
Ouliades of Samos, 265
Ouranopolis, 188
over-population, in Greece, 55, 132
Oxus (Amu Darya), R., 282, 283
Oxyrhynchos, 197

paideia, 183, 327
palaces, 91, 92, 96, 128
Palestine, 278
Pamphylia, 275
Pan, as Antigonid patron, 65
Panhellenion, 399
panhellenism, 36, 55
Paphlagonia, 275, 388
Pappos (scientist), 19, 331
papyri, 196–9, 200–1; Dervéni, 111;
    imprint of, at Ai Khanum, 269;
    literary, 247
papyrus, grown in Babylonia, 277
paradeisoi, 299
paradigms: in astronomy, 353; in
    medicine, 347; in science, 364–5
Paraitakene (Media), 281
parchment, 239
Parian Marble, 265
Paropamisadai, 283
Paros, 98
Parthia, 282, 283, 320; and Rome, 386,
    396, 397; and Seleukid empire, 324,
    325, 340; mentioned, 294, 285, 395;
    Seleukid cities in, 305; sources, 10;
    wars v. Seleukids, 290, 291, 293,
    310, 311, 321, 322
pastoral poetry (see also bucolic), 238
Patrokles (explorer), 284, 361
patronage, royal: motives, 345–6, 366;
    of agriculture, 344; of literature,
    237–43 passim; of medicine, 347,
    348–9; of military arts, 336, 340–1;
    Ptolemaic, 241, 242, 329 bis, 347,
    348–9
patrons, Roman, 171
pattern poems, 248
Paullus, L. Aemilius, 381
Pausanias, as source, 15
Paxos, battle of, 371

Pedieis (plainsmen) of Priene, 100
Pella (Macedonia), 114, 128
Pella (Syria), 278
Perdikkas, 40, 41, 42, 201, 284
Pergamon (see also Attalid dynasty): and
    Eumenes I, 85; and peace of
    Apameia, 377; citizenship, 319;
    honours Attalos III, 156–7; in 2nd
    Macedonian war, 374, 375; layout,
    92; ruler-cult absent in 3rd c., 162;
    territory, 314
Perioikoi (Lakedaimonian), 141, 145
Peripatos, 179
periploi, 362
Periplus maris Erythraei, 362
Persaios (philosopher), 240
Persepolis, 36–7
Perseus of Macedonia, 151, 380; library,
    240; war v. Rome, 378, 380–1
Persians, and Macedonians, 38, 42
Persians of the epigonê, 218, 219 & n. 78
'personal' concerns, in literature, 253,
    255, 256, 259
'personal' cults, 163–5
Peteharsemtheus, 223
Petosiris (priest), 222
Peukestas, 166, 167
pezhetairoi, 114
Philadelphos (city), 219
Philadelphos (name), see Ptolemy II
philanthrôpia, Ptolemaic, 432 n. 73
Phile of Priene, 104
Philetairos: and Gauls, 53; and
    stockbreeding, 345; career, 312;
    coins, 24–6; cult, 163; subject of
    poems, 269
Philetas of Kos, 235
philhellenism, Roman (see also
    hellenization), 371
Philip I (Seleukid), 322
Philip II of Macedonia, 35, 109–11,
    114–15, 290
Philip II (Seleukid), 322
Philip III Arrhidaios, 40–1, 118
Philip IV (s. Cassander), 44
Philip V of Macedonia, 151; and
    Hannibal, 372; and Larisa, 84; and
    Sparta, 147; attacks Athens, 150;
    criticized, 62; pact with Antiochos
    III (?), 208, 375; rebuilds army, 378;
    wars v. Romans, 374–5
Philippides of Kephale, 48, 76

Philippoi, 112, 114
Philitas of Kos, 235
philobasilistai, 163
Philochoros, 263
Philodemos (Epicurean), 177
philoi (Friends of kings), 48, 76–7
Philokles of Sidon, 78, 139
Philometor, *see* Ptolemy VI
Philon of Athens (Peripatetic, statesman), 390, 398
Philon of Byzantion (engineer), 336
Philopappos, 399
Philopator, *see* Ptolemy IV
Philopoimen, 148, 378
Philoponus, Ioannes, 19
philosophers: female, 103–4; practical achievements, 190
philosophy (*see also* cosmology), 18, 176–91; practical applications, 181, 188, 189–90
Phoenicia, 203, 278, 287
Phoinike, peace of, 374
Phokian league, 139
phoros (tribute), 75
Phraates, king of Parthia, 395
Phraates I of Pontos, 387
Phraates II of Pontos, 321
Phrygia, 275
Phylarchos, 143, 263–4
physics (*see also* engineering, machines), 330–1
Physkon, *see* Ptolemy VIII
pi, value of, 357
Pictor, Q. Fabius Pictor, 370
piracy, 81–2, 390, 393, 395
Piraeus: as 'Fetter', 113; in hostilities, 149, 314, 375, 390, 391; garrisoned, 120, 124
Piraeus Bronzes, 391
pirates, 82, 390, 393, 395
Piso, proconsul, 397
Pistos s. Leontomenes, 218–19
planetarium, 331
plants: in Theophrastos, 341–4; transplantations, 344–5, 346
Plato, 177, 351; and Stoicism, 186
Plotinus, 177
Plouton, sanctuary of, 77
Plutarch, 12–14; on Alexander, 302–3; on Kleomenes, 146
pneuma, 346
poetry (*see also* epic, epigrams, pastoral),

17–18, 235–6, 243–7; by women, 103; 'personal', 253, 254–5
poisons, 245, 345, 387–8
poleis (*see also* cities), 3, 35, 21, 190; and Greek culture, 87; and Rome, 368, 379, 380–1, 384, 399; and science, 332–4, 366 & n. 110; coinages, 26; economic changes, 86, 101, 131, 147; élites in, 131, 181, 191; evolution of, 106–7; historiography of, 265, 268; in Asia Minor, 275, 389, 392; in Egypt, 214; in federal states, 133, 134; in Macedonia, 112 *bis*; in Seleukid empire, 305–7; layouts, 86–96; military concerns, 334–5; political changes, 89, 101–2, 128–30, 147, 259, 366; pre-Hl, 33, 34, 59; religion in, 170–3, 175–6; status of, granted, 315
Polemaios, honoured at Kolophon, 445 n. 90
Polemon (Academic), 177, 185
Polemon of Ilion, 239
polis, see *poleis*
Polybios, 7–8; and Aratos, 267–8; at Rome, 383; on Achaean league, 136–7; on Attalos I, 314; on demography, 30; on historians, 262, 263; on Roman conquest, 368, 369; on Sparta, 143; on *tychê*, 174; reaches Atlantic, 363
Polyperchon, 43, 116, 120; and Greek freedom, 73
Pompeius Magnus, Cn., *see* Pompey
Pompeius Trogus, 9–10
Pompey, 395–6, 397, 398
Pomponius Atticus, T., 398
Pontos (*see also* Mithridatic wars), 51, 279, 316, 387
Popillius Laenas, C., 209, 252
population: in Egypt, 215 & n. 70; in Greece, 55, 132
Poremanres, cult of, 165
pornography, 258
portraits, of rulers, 24–6, 69–71, 301
Potter, Oracle of the, 233
pottery, Hl, 28
practice, and theory, 329
Praisos (Crete), 83
Praxagoras of Kos (doctor), 346
precession of equinoxes, 351
Priene, 80, 89–90, 318

priests, Egyptian, 195, 196, 223
'private' concerns, in literature, 249, 251, 257
processions, royal, 68, 292–3, 345
Proclus, 19
proofs, mathematical, 356–7
prosopographical studies, 21, 129
Protogenes of Olbia, 98
prôtos heuretês, 329
Prousias I of Bithynia, 316
Prousias II of Bithynia, 292, 317, 318, 380
provincia Asia, 319, 389
Prytanis of Karystos, 149
Psaon of Athens, 265
Pseudo-Kallisthenes, 251–2
Pseudo-Lykophron, 247–8
psychology, in poetry, 256
Ptolemaic dynasty, *see* Ptolemies
Ptolemaieia (festival), 124, 139, 159
Ptolemaios (detainee), 221
Ptolemaïs (Athenian tribe), 150
Ptolemaïs Hermiou (city), 214
Ptolemaïs of the Thebaid (city), 214
Ptolemaïs Theron (city), 214
Ptolemies (*see also* Egypt; patronage), 400–1, 405; ambitions, 206, 207; and Jews, 307; coinage, 25, 26–7; economic administration, 224–32; events of dynasty, 201–5, 207–13; general assessment, 230–4; overseas possessions, 195, 205–7; strategic aims, 205, 232
Ptolemy (Claudius Ptolemaeus), 19, 354 *bis*; on astrology, 354–5; on nations, 349–50
Ptolemy I Soter, 42 *bis*, **201–2**; and Greek states, 121, 124, 126, 138–9, 162; and Theophrastos, 344; as writer, 6, 264–5; coins, 24–6; deified, 159; founds library, 239
Ptolemy II Philadelphos, **202–3**; and agriculture, 344; and ruler-cult, 159, 160; and S. Greece, 126; and Seleukid empire, 287, 288 *bis*; criticized, 263–4; mentioned, 243, 340; praised, 238–9; procession, 68, 345; satirized, 185; virtues and achievements, 61
Ptolemy III Euergetes, **203–4**; and Achaean league, 138; and Athens, 149 *bis*, 150; and Kleomenes III,

146, 203; has Torah translated, 265; invades Asia Minor, 289–90
Ptolemy IV Philopator, **203–5**, 207–8; accession, 290; and Athens, 150; and Jews, 307; and Kleomenes III, 146; giant warships, 340; honoured at Amphiareion, 171; mentioned, 201
Ptolemy V Epiphanes, **207**; guardians, 77; mentioned, 204; seizes books (?), 239 *bis*
Ptolemy VI Philometor, **208–9**, 210, 320 *ter*
Ptolemy VII Eupator, 210
Ptolemy VIII Euergetes II Physkon, 209, 210, 211; writes autobiography, 265; imports birds, 345; expels scientists, 366
Ptolemy IX Soter II Lathyros, 211, 398
Ptolemy X Alexander I, 211–12
Ptolemy XI Alexander II, 212
Ptolemy XII Neos Dionysos Auletes, 212–13, 232
Ptolemy XIII, 213
Ptolemy XIV, 213
Ptolemy XV Caesar, 213
Ptolemy Apion, 212
Ptolemy Keraunos, 45, 124
Ptolemy of Termessos, 50
Ptolemy the Son, 16 & n.
public literature, about the 'private', 253, 259
publicani, 392
Pulcher, App. Claudius, 171, 398
pulleys, 332
pulse, investigated, 346
pumps, 333
Pushkalavati, 284
Pydna, battle of, 381
Pyrgoteles (naval architect), 340
Pyrrhon of Elis (Sceptic), 179
Pyrrhos of Epeiros: 117, 120, 123, 142, 371; autobiography, 265
Pytheas (explorer), 363
Pytheas (poet), 269

queens, 71, 72–3
Quinctius Flamininus, L., 376
Quinctius Flamininus, T., 375

races, classified, 349–50

racial prejudice: in Egypt, 219–21; in Seleukid empire, 323

readerships (*see also* audiences): in Asia, 269; in Egypt, 247, 248, 249, 251, 252, 256, 269

reading, methods of, 242

regionalism, in Seleukid empire, 293–4, 295–6

religion: classical, 153–5; Hl, characterized, 155–6, 175–6; Hl, particular aspects, 156–75; process of change, 170, 175–6, 190–1; rural, 29, 172–3; non-Greek, in Greece, 165–71

representation, of rulers, 60–4, 69–71

research, Erasistratos on, 364

'Revenue Laws' of Ptolemy II, 225–6

revolts: against Macedonia (*see also* Chremonidean war), 38, 123, 125, 142; in Baktria, 284; in Egypt, (in general) 233, (1st) 203, (2nd) 204, (3rd) 207, (4th) 208, (5th) 210, (6th) 210, (7th) 212; in Seleukid empire, 287

Rhamnous, 124, 126, 148, 149, 172

Rhaphia, battle of, 204, 233, 268

Rhianos, 269

Rhodes: after Apameia, 377; and Byzantion, 106; and Crete, 82; and dikasts, 80; and Islanders, 317; and Karia, 382; and Lykia, 382, 379–80; and Rome, 317; donations to, 85; economy, 382; honours Ptolemy I, 162; in 2nd Macedonian war, 374, 375; independence, 106; power, 208; praised, 89; sieges of, 44, 336, 338, 389–90; traders from, 100 *bis*

Rhômê (Roma), cult, 319

Rhoxane, 38, 41, 119

Roma (goddess), cult, at Pergamon, 319

Roman conquest: explanations, 369; sources, 368–9

Romans (*see also* Italians; Rome): as patrons, 171; in Lykophron, 248

Rome (*see also* imperialism; Romans; senate): and Jews, 311; and Andriskos, 384; and Antiochos IV, 292; and Antiochos V, 320; and Attalos I, 314 *bis*, 318; and Egypt, 209–13 *passim*, 232; and Eumenes II, 315, 317; and Greek culture, 398–9; and Mithradates VI, 388–90, 392,

393, 394–5; and piracy, 82, 393; and Seleukid empire, 325; and Seleukos IV, 292; as arbiter of Greece, 378–80, 381–2, 383–4; as ruler of Asia Minor, 395 *bis*, 396; as ruler of Greece, 385, 397–9; before 229 BC, 370; defeats Perseus, 380–1; defeats Philip V, 374, 375; hellenization, 370–1, 398–9; Polybios on, 368, 369; protects Athens (200 BC), 150; takes over Near East, 386; Timaios on, 263; treatment of Sparta, 148; treaty with Aitolians, 373; wars in Greek world, 371–7, 380–1, 384–5

Rosetta Stone, 166, 199, 204

Roxane, 38, 41, 119

royal economy (in 'Aristotle'), 296–7

royal family, 72, 73

royal ruler-cult, 157, 301

Rufus (medical writer), 19

Rufus, Q. Curtius, 7

ruler-cult, 156–63, 226; civic v. royal, 157; Seleukid, 301

rural landscapes, 29

Saka, 285

Salamis (Aegean), 149, 392

Salamis (Cyprus), battle of, 43, 121

Samos: and Athens, 56; and Philip V, 375; and Priene, 80; grain supply, 99–100; decrees, 78–80, 98–100, 101, 159–60; and Ptolemies, 205; layout, 84

Samothrace, Ptolemaic possession, 205

Sandrokottos (Chandragupta), 283, 284, 287

Sarapis, *see* Serapis

Sardis, 104, 300, 303

sarissa, 114

satire, by Cynic writers, 185

satraps, 293, 294 *bis*, 296–7

Scepticism, 179–81

scholarship, Hl, 241–2

schools (educational), 269 & n.

science, Hl: appraised, 326–7, 330–2, 365–7; civic application, 332–41; evidence for, 18, 327–8

scientists: defined, 327; expelled from Alexandria, 366; role, 328–9; social location, 366–7

Scipio brothers, 377

screws, 359; Archimedean, 332

scribes, 216
sculpture, 28, 69; in Delos, 105–6
Seleukeia-by-the-Sea (S.-in-Pieria), 158, 204, 288, 302, 303
Seleukeia-on-Eulaios, 281, 303
Seleukeia-on-Tigris, 96, 277, 302, 304
Seleukid empire: and Persian, 293–5, 299, 301, 324–5; and Rome, 325; appraised, 322–5; control of, 286, 321, 324; core, 277–8, 289, 296; economy, 262–86 *passim*, 296–301, 323–4; ethnic groups, 295–6; general issues, 271; history, 286–93, 320–2; land and resources, 271–86; political administration, 293–6; sources, 271–2
Seleukids, *401–2, 406*; ambitions, 325; and ruler-cult, 157–8; and viticulture, 344–5; city foundations, 96; coinage, 25, 27; events of dynasty, 286–93, 319–22
Seleukos I Nikator, 42, 45, **286–7**; ambitions, 287; and Apollo, 65; and Baktria, 284; and bull, 61; and elephants, 278; and Philetairos, 312; and tiger, 345; city foundations, 277, 304–5; coins, 24–6; in Macedonia, 117–18; virtues and achievements, 61, 302; visual image, 69
Seleukos II Kallinikos, 77–8, **289, 290**, 301
Seleukos III Soter Keraunos, 289, 290, 313
Seleukos IV Philopator, 158, **292**, 380, 382
Seleukos V, 322
Seleukos VI, 322
Seleukos of Seleukeia-on-Tigris (astronomer), 353
Seleukos s. Antiochos I, 289
Sellasia, battle of, 146, 268
senate, Roman: and *asylia*, 81; divided, 380; and Greek affairs, 378–80, 383–4; operation, 369
Septuagint, 265–6
Serap(i)eia: at Delos, 168–9; at Kanobos, 166
Serapis, cult of, in Macedonia, 152, 165–6, 168–9
settlement, Graeco-Macedonian, in Egypt, 217
settlement patterns, 29

Seuthopolis, layout, 96
sex, in literature, 249–50, 257, 258
sexes, relations between, 102–6
Sextus Empiricus, 180–1
ships, of war, 340
Sicily, Agathokles' empire in, 51–2
siege-engines, 338–40, 390
sieges, of Demetrios I, 44
siege techniques, 334–5, 336–7, 338–40, 390
signalling, 334
Sikyon, 121, 122, 137, 140, 156
silver production, in Attica, 382
Simmias of Rhodes, 248
Simon (high priest), 267, 321
Simplicius, 19
sitônai, 100
Skepsis, 74, 156, 240, 299, 391
Skerdilaidas, 372, 373
Skythians, 285, 305
slave labour, 96
Small Pergamene Dedication, 314
Smyrna, and Seleukos II, 77–8, 80–1, 102
social change, seen in literature, 259
social war (220–217 BC), 373
Sogdiane, 282
Soranus (medical writer), 19
Sosibios (guardian of Ptolemy V), 77, 204, 207
Sosibios (historian), 265
Sotades (satirist), 185
Soter, *see* Ptolemy I; Ptolemy IX
Sounion, 124, 173
sources: archaeological, 27–9, 30–1; literary, 5–20, 29–30; non-Greek, 11–12; non-historiographical, 17–20; non-literary, 20–31
Sousa, 38, 272, 281, 296, 303, 321
South Stoa 2 (Athens), 88
Sparta (*see also* Laconia; Lakonike): after Sellasia, 147–8; Agis and Kleomenes' reigns, 143–7; and Achaean league, 138, 378 *bis*, 379, 384; and Aitolians, 377; and Argos, 383; and Jews, 260–1, 266–7; and Rome, 378, 383; before Agis IV, 38, 141–3; supports Mithradates, 390; walls, 335 & n., 378; women of, 102–3, 141, 144, 146
specific gravity, 358–9
speculation, *see* theory

Sphairos of Borysthenes, 144, 187
Sporades, given to Athens, 385
star catalogues, 351
stasis, in *poleis*, 132–3
Stephanos of Byzantion, 6
Stilpon (philosopher), 185
Stiris (Phokis), 83
stoas, at Athens, 87–8; of Asklepieion, 87, 122, 164; of Attalos II, 87, 382; of Eumenes II, 87, 334, 382
Stoicism: and monarchy, 64; early, 185–7; later, 187; social context, 186–7
Strabo, 14–15, 19
stratêgoi: Achaean, 137, 139; Agathokles as, 51; Aitolian, 134; Athenian, 122, 124; in Cappadocia, 287; in Egypt, 209, 216, 218, 221; in Macedonian *poleis*, 112; in Pergamon, 314; in Thrace, 112
Straton (Peripatetic): 179, 332
Stratonike, 71, 168, 287, 302
subscriptions, public, 84–5
Successors of Alexander, 40–51, 52; and Athens, 120–4; and Macedonia, 116–20; armies, 57–8
Suda, 6
Sulla: captures Athens, 390–1; wages war on Mithradates, 389
sun: distance from earth, 364; influence of, 355; in utopianism, 188 *bis*, 189; understanding of, 352 *bis*
sundials, 331, 361
surnames, royal, 65–6
survey, *see* archaeological survey
surveying, Greek, 334, 360–1
Syene (Aswan), 192, 194, 361
sympoliteia, 82, 112
symposion, 67
sympotic poetry, 254
syncretism, 169, 170, 396
synedrion: Aitolian, 134; Macedonian, 11; of Friends, 76
Syr Darya (Jaxartes), R., 283
Syria (*see also* Koile Syria; Seleukid empire; Seleukids): geography, 278; and Ptolemies, 203, 205–6; and Rome, 325, 396; Seleukid cities, 288, 305
Syriac sources, 252, 328
Syrian Goddess, 168, 169
Syrian wars: (1st) 202, 288; (2nd) 203, 289; (3rd) 203, 231, 289–90; (4th) 204; (5th) 208, 307; (6th) 208, 292

Tanagra, 29–30
Tathot (Egyptian woman), 222
Tauros, Mt., 272
taxation (*see also* tribute): in Egypt, 196, 225–6, 228, 229, 231–2; in Macedonia, 113; in Macedonian territory, 131; in Seleukid empire, 297–9; remission, 211, 307
tax-farmers, Roman, 392, 396
Taxila, 284
technitai of Dionysos, 163
technology, *see* defence; engineering; innovation; military technology
Teles of Megara (Cynic), 185
Temple (Jerusalem), desecrated, 310
temples, Egyptian, 196
Teos, 75, 81, 87
Tetrapolis, Syrian, 288
Teuta, queen, 371
textual criticism, 240
Thasos, 75
Thebes (Boiotia), 30, 36, 133
Thebes (Egypt), social make-up, 222
Theoi Adelphoi, 160
Theokritos, 237, 256–7
Theophrastos, 18, 344, 391; works, 179, 328, 341–4
Theopompos, 152
theory, in science, 329, 351, 363–5
Thera, 195, 205
Thermon (Aitolia), 134, 374
Thermopylai, battle of (191 BC), 377
Thessalian league, 139; and Delphic amphiktyony, 377
Thessalonike (city), 114
Thessalonike (d. of Philip II), 44
Thoule (Thule), 363
tiger, sent to Athens, 345
Tigranes of Armenia, 322, 394, 395
Tigranocerta, battle of, 394
Tigris, R., 275–6
Timaios, 262
Timocharis (astronomer), 351
Timon of Phleious (Sceptic), 179, 240
tools, metal, 332
toparchs, 217
Torah, translated into Greek, 265
Toriaion, *see* Tyriaion

Tower of the Winds, 88–9, 333 & n. 22, 334
town-planning, 89–98, 303
trade: and coinage, 26–7; Athenian–Italian, 385–6; in Egypt, 228–9
tradition, defined, 246
Transjordania, 278–9
Transoxiana (Sogdiane), 282
treasury, Persian, size of, 36
trees, cultivated, 342
tribes (Athenian), 121, 150 ter, 375
tribute: in Seleukid empire, 294, 377; paid to kings, 75; paid to Macedonians, 130–1; paid to Ptolemies, 195; paid to Rome, 396
Triparadeisos, conference at, 42
Troad, 275
Trogus (Pompeius), 9–10
Tryphaina I (Kleopatra V), 448 n. 65
Tryphaina II (Kleopatra VI), 213
Tryphon, 321
Tullius Cicero, M., 180, 398
tychê, 173–5; of Eumenes of Kardia, 47; of Kleomenes III, 146
Tylis (Gaulish kingdom), 54
Tyre Declaration (Antigonos I), 73–4
Tyriaion, and Eumenes II, 315–16

unfree labour, 101
urban archaeology, 27
urban form, 86–96
urbanization, 31; in Seleukid empire, 303–5
Uruk, not hellenized, 303
utopian philosophies, 187–9

Vardar, R., 109
Varro, 344
vaults, 333–4
Vaxos (Crete), 136
Vergína (Aigai), 128
Verres, 398
victors, female, 103
vine: in Galilee, 345; in Babylonia, 344–5
virtues, royal, 61–4, 69–70
viticulture, see vine

Vitruvius, 19, 337, 350
vivisection, 347–8
volume, calculation of, 357

walls, city, 334–5; of Sparta, 378
warships, giant, 340
water-clocks, 331, 332–3
water-mills, 332
water-organs, 331
water-pumps, 333
Wennofer (Egyptian man), 222
wheat, see grain shortages; grain supply
wheels, toothed, 359
wills, of rulers, 210, 212, 318–19
women, 102–6; as citizens, 83; at festivals, 103, 219–20; Egyptian, 222; in Epicureanism, 183; in literature, 164, 219–20, 249–50, 254, 256–8; in Stoicism, 186; in utopias, 188–9; royal, 71, 72–3; Spartan, 141
'wonders' (scientific), 331, 332
works of art, taken by Romans, 385, 391

Xanthos, 379
Xenophilos of Lydia, 265
Xylopolis, 113

Yuëzhi, 285

Zagros, Mt., 272, 279, 281
Zela, battle of, 394
Zeno (Stoic), 128, 184, 185, 186, 240
Zenodotos of Ephesos, 240
Zenon (Ptolemaic official), 219
Zenon (Stoic), see Zeno
Zenon archive, 197, 219; mentioned, 226, 228, 332, 344, 345
Zeus: Alexander's patron, 69; Dusares, 169; Kallimachos's hymn to, 244–5; of Baitokaike, 297–8; Olympios, see Olympian Zeus; Oromasdes, 396; Xenios, 310
Zeuxis (Seleukid governor), 296
Ziailas of Bithynia, 51
Zipoites of Bithynia, 51